THE
ST. MARTIN'S
GUIDE
TO WRITING

Short Sixth Edition

THE ST. MARTIN'S GUIDE TO WRITING

Rise B. Axelrod

UNIVERSITY OF CALIFORNIA, RIVERSIDE

Charles R. Cooper

UNIVERSITY OF CALIFORNIA, SAN DIEGO

BEDFORD/ST. MARTIN'S

BOSTON ■ NEW YORK

For Bedford / St. Martin's

Developmental Editor: Diana M. Puglisi
Production Editor: Harold Chester
Senior Production Supervisor: Joe Ford
Marketing Manager: Brian Wheel
Editorial Assistants: Belinda Delpêche, Regan Park
Art Director: Lucy Krikorian
Text and Cover Design: Anna George
Copy Editor: Wendy Polhemus-Annibell
Photo Research: Joan Scafarello
Composition: Monotype Composition Company, Inc.
Printing and Binding: RR Donnelley & Sons Company

President: Charles H. Christensen
Editorial Director: Joan E. Feinberg
Editor in Chief: Nancy Perry
Marketing Director: Karen Melton
Director of Editing, Design, and Production: Marcia Cohen
Managing Editor: Erica T. Appel

Library of Congress Catalogue Numbers: 99-62153 (with Handbook)
99-62112 (without Handbook)

Manufactured in the United States of America.

6   5   4   3   2
f   e   d

For information, write: Bedford / St. Martin's, 75 Arlington Street, Boston, MA 02116
(617-399-4000)

ISBN: 0-312-20106-0 (with Handbook)
0-312-24059-7 (without Handbook)

Acknowledgments

Acknowledgments and copyrights appear at the back of the book on pages A1–A2, which constitute an extension of the copyright page.

Advisory Board

We owe an enormous debt to all the rhetoricians and composition specialists whose theory, research, and pedagogy have informed *The St. Martin's Guide to Writing*. We would be adding many pages if we were to name everyone to whom we are indebted.

The members of the Advisory Board for the sixth edition, a group of dedicated composition instructors from across the country, have provided us with extensive insights and suggestions for the chapters in Part One and have given us the benefit of their advice on new features, in many cases testing them in their own classrooms. *The St. Martin's Guide to Writing* has been greatly enhanced by their contributions.

Preface

When we first wrote *The St. Martin's Guide to Writing,* we tried to design a flexible composition textbook for instructors and a helpful guide for students. We took what we had learned from classical rhetoric as well as from contemporary composition theory and research and did our best to make it accessible to students. We wanted to write a book that would help students learn to write, not one that just talked about writing. The response from instructors and students has been overwhelmingly positive ever since the first publication of *The Guide* in 1985. That first edition immediately became the most widely adopted text of its kind in the nation, and the book has remained popular through five editions, with the number of copies sold actually increasing over the years. With such success, we might be tempted to approach the latest revision with caution, but instead we feel emboldened. In fact, our revisions to the Sixth Edition are the most thorough and wide-ranging we've ever undertaken, and they encompass both text and visual elements.

Although *The St. Martin's Guide to Writing* has changed over the years, our basic goals remain unchanged. From the beginning, we have tried to continue the classical tradition of teaching writing not only as a method of composing rhetorically effective prose but also as a powerful heuristic for thinking creatively and critically. To the best insights from that tradition, we have with each new edition added what we believed to be some promising developments in composition theory and research. In particular, we have tried to emphasize the idea that writing is both a social act and a way of knowing. We try to teach students that form emerges from context as well as content, that knowledge of writing comes not from analyzing genres alone but also from participating in a community of writers and readers.

Our principal aim is to demystify writing and authorize students as writers. To this end, we seek to teach students how to use the composing process as a means of seeing what they know as well as how they know it. We want students to learn to use writing to think critically and communicate effectively with others. Finally, we hope to inspire students with the desire to question their own certainties and provide them with the strategies for doing so.

■ AN OVERVIEW OF THE BOOK

As a rhetoric and reader, *The St. Martin's Guide* can serve as a comprehensive introduction to many types of discourse. It comprises several parts:

Part One, Writing Activities, presents nine different essay assignments, all reflecting actual writing situations that students may encounter both in and out of college, genres of writing that they should learn to read critically and to write intelligently. Among the types of essays included are autobiography, explanation, arguing a position, proposal, and literary interpretation.

You may choose among these chapters and teach them in any sequence you wish, though they are sequenced here to move students from writing based on personal experience and observation to writing calling for the analysis and synthesis of ideas and information derived from a variety of sources.

Each chapter follows the same organizational plan.

Chapter Organization for Part One

- Six brief **scenarios** identifying the genre covered in the chapter and suggesting the range of occasions when such writing is done—in other courses, in the community, and in the workplace

- A **collaborative activity** that gets students working with the genre taught in that chapter

- A set of four **readings** accompanied by a **critical apparatus** designed to help students explore connections to their culture and experience and to analyze writing strategies used in this genre

- A summary of the **purpose and audience** and the **basic features** of this genre

- A flexible **guide to writing,** tailored to the particular genre, that escorts students through the composing process, including a critical reading guide for peer review of drafts

- **Editing and proofreading guidelines** to help students check for several sentence-level problems likely to occur in that kind of writing

- A look at one **writer at work,** focusing on some aspect of the process of writing the student essay featured in that chapter

- A box exploring how writers work on **document design,** expanding on one of the scenarios presented at the beginning of the chapter

- A trio of **critical thinking activities** designed to help students reflect on and consolidate what they learned about writing and reading and consider the social dimensions of the genre taught in that chapter

Part Two, Critical Thinking Strategies, collects in two separate chapters practical heuristics for invention and reading. The catalog of invention strategies includes clustering, looping, dramatizing, and questioning, while the catalog of reading strategies includes annotating, summarizing, exploring the significance of figurative language, and evaluating the logic of an argument.

Part Three, Writing Strategies, looks at a wide range of writers' strategies: paragraphing and coherence, logic and reasoning, and the familiar methods of presenting information, such as narrating, defining, and classifying. Examples and exercises have been drawn from a wide range of contemporary nonfiction sources; in addition, many exercises deal with reading selections appearing in Part One. Because of the extensive cross-referencing between Parts One and Three, instructors will find it easier to teach writing strategies in the context of purpose and audience.

Part Four, Research Strategies, discusses field as well as library and Internet research and includes thorough, up-to-date guidelines for using and documenting sources, with detailed examples of the Modern Language Association (MLA) and American Psychological Association (APA) documentation styles. An annotated sample student research paper models ways students can integrate citations into their own work in accordance with the MLA documentation style.

Part Five, Writing for Assessment, covers essay examinations, showing students how to analyze different kinds of exam questions and offering strategies for writing answers. It also addresses portfolios, helping students select and assemble a representative sample of their writing.

Part Six, Writing and Speaking to Wider Audiences, helps students design written and online documents and prepare oral presentations. This new part of *The Guide* also includes chapters on collaborative learning and service learning, designed to help students work together on individual and joint writing projects and to support students' writing in the community.

Proven Features

Several proven features have made *The St. Martin's Guide to Writing* such an effective textbook: the practical guides to writing different genres, the systematic integration of reading and writing, activities to promote group discussion and inquiry, and activities that encourage students to reflect on what they have learned.

Practical Guides to Writing. We do not merely talk about the composing process; rather, we offer practical, flexible guides that escort students through the entire process, from invention through revision and self-evaluation. Thus, this book is more than just a rhetoric that students will refer to occasionally. It is a guidebook that will help them write. Commonsensical and easy to follow, these writing guides teach students to assess a rhetorical situation, identify the kinds of information they will need, ask probing questions and find answers, and organize their writing to achieve their purpose.

Systematic Integration of Reading and Writing. Because we see a close relationship between the ability to read critically and the ability to write intelligently, *The St. Martin's Guide* combines reading instruction with writing instruction. Each chapter in Part One introduces one genre, which students are led to consider both as readers and as writers. Each reading is accompanied by carefully focused critical apparatus. First is a response activity, Connecting to Culture and Experience, that relates a central theme of the reading to students' cultural knowledge and personal experience. Questions are designed to stimulate small-group discussion that helps students explore the essay's relevance to their lives as well as its broader social implications. The two sections following, Analyzing Writing Strategies and a brief Commentary, examine how each writer applies some of the basic features and strategies typical of the genre to the particular rhetorical situation. Taken together, these analytical activities and commentaries provide students with a comprehensive rhetorical introduction that prepares them to write an essay of their own in the genre. Finally, in Considering Topics for Your Own Essay, students are challenged to apply these insights to their own writing as they imagine their prospective readers, set goals, and write and revise their drafts.

Activities to Promote Group Discussion and Inquiry.   *The St. Martin's Guide* offers multiple opportunities for group work throughout each Part One chapter. At the start of each chapter is a collaborative activity that invites students to try out some of the thinking and planning they will be doing for the kind of writing covered in that chapter. The Connecting to Culture and Experience section that follows each reading is designed to provoke thoughtful responses about the social and political dimensions of the reading. The Guide to Writing contains another collaborative activity that gets students to discuss their work in progress with one another, along with a Critical Reading Guide, which guides students as they read and comment on each other's drafts. Finally, a discussion activity invites students to explore the social dimensions of the genre they have been learning to write. All of these materials include questions and prompts to guide students to work productively together.

Thinking Critically about What You Have Learned.   Each chapter in Part One concludes with three metacognitive activities to help students become aware of what they have learned about the process of writing, about the influences of reading on writing, and about the social and political dimensions of the genres they have learned to write. These activities are based on research showing that reflecting on what they have learned deepens students' understanding and improves their recall.

Changes in the Sixth Edition

We have tried in this new edition to continue our tradition of turning current theory and research into practical classroom activities—with a minimum of jargon. We have also incorporated guidelines for using the new electronic research and document design technologies that are increasingly available to students.

Enhanced Writing Assignment Chapters.   The chapters in Part One have been significantly revised.

- The chapters get off to an engaging start with photographs and other images chosen to evoke the genre and illuminate possible topics for student writing. The opening scenarios that have always been a feature of *The St. Martin's Guide* have been expanded and moved into the main text to highlight the important and diverse roles writing can play in college classes, the community, and the workplace.

- Thirty-five percent of the readings are new, and some of the readings now include elements such as photographs and charts that show students ways writers of the genre can make good use of visuals.

- The Commentaries following the readings are significantly abbreviated, each focusing on only one or two important features of the reading, thereby providing clearer models for student writing.

- The essential content of each chapter's central Guide to Writing has been retained, but these sections have been redesigned for easier reading and reference. A menu-style graphic overview, color-coded headings, and informative two-tiered running heads function as helpful navigational aids.

- Reflecting the inclusion of three new student essays, several Writer at Work sections present material new to *The Guide*.

Enhanced Writing Strategies Chapters.   The chapters in Part Three also have been substantially rewritten, with an array of new examples and exercises. We have incorporated a greater variety of models, including some that use visual elements to enhance the writing.

New Attention to Document Design.   Technology is making it increasingly easy for students to add visual images to documents produced via desktop publishing programs and to include audio and video elements on Web sites of their own creation. Responding to the concerns voiced by many instructors across the country, we have added to the sixth edition a new chapter on Designing Documents (Chapter 25), which not only provides practical guidelines for the effective and appropriate design of both print and online documents, but also includes a gallery of sample documents that students are likely to create. In addition we have added a new section, Designing Your Work, to eight of the Part One chapters, and we have added selected readings in Parts One and Three that demonstrate various ways of incorporating visual elements.

New Design and Format.   In keeping with the new emphasis on document design, *The St. Martin's Guide to Writing* itself has been redesigned. A wider trim size makes the text more visually appealing and gives students more room for making annotations. The color palette is used to make *The Guide*'s key sections and features easier to find and use (for instance, the pages in each Guide to Writing are bordered in green, and the accompanying readings are accented with a light tan background).

Up-to-Date Coverage of Electronic Research and Documentation.   Chapters 21 and 22 on Library and Internet Research and Using and Acknowledging Sources have been updated to reflect the latest MLA and APA guidelines. In addition, these chapters give students the skills and information they need for conducting research in today's electronic environment. New tables and diagrams, along with carefully revised text, will help students find the best online and traditional sources for their particular research subject, document these sources accurately, and successfully integrate source-based information into their own writing.

New Chapter on Oral Presentations.   We have added a chapter on Oral Presentations (Chapter 26) to help students present their writing in spoken form. The chapter includes many helpful hints on preparing and delivering presentations in academic and workplace settings.

New Chapter on Writing Collaboratively. *The St. Martin's Guide* has always supported collaborative learning through a variety of small group activities in the chapters in Part One (Writing Activities) and Part Three (Writing Strategies). We have added to the sixth edition a new chapter (Chapter 27) on working with others on individual and joint writing projects. This chapter helps students meet the challenges of working constructively with others.

New Chapter on Writing in the Community. In the previous edition we added to each Part One chapter a focus on writing in the community. To complement this emphasis, we have added to this edition a separate chapter, Writing in Your Community (Chapter 28), that suggests to students and instructors how the resources in *The St. Martin's Guide to Writing* can support service learning.

■ ADDITIONAL RESOURCES

Numerous resources accompany *The St. Martin's Guide to Writing*.

The Instructor's Resource Manual, by Rise B. Axelrod, Charles R. Cooper, and Lenora Penna Smith of the University of Houston, includes a catalog of helpful advice for new instructors (by Alison M. Warriner of Sacred Heart University), guidelines on common teaching practices such as assigning journals and setting up group activities, guidelines on responding to and evaluating student writing (by Charles Cooper), course plans, detailed chapter plans, an annotated bibliography in composition and rhetoric, and a selection of background readings. New to this edition are articles on community service writing, genres, and cohesion and coherence.

Sticks and Stones and other student essays, Fourth Edition, edited by Rise B. Axelrod, Charles R. Cooper, and Lawrence Barkley of Mount San Jacinto College–Menifee, is a collection of essays written by students across the nation using *The St. Martin's Guide*. The ten chapters in the book correspond to those in Part One of *The Guide*. The book includes forms for the submission of students' essays so that we may consider them for possible publication in future editions.

Writing Guide Software has been created specifically to complement the detailed, process-oriented support of *The St. Martin's Guide to Writing*. The new software presents nine interactive writing guides and supports them with detailed advice and instructions, student examples, grammar support, and more.

The St. Martin's Guide companion Web site <www.bedfordstmartins.com /theguide> provides additional information for students and instructors. Here instructors can access sample syllabi, ideas for integrating technology into the composition course, extensive up-to-date aids for online research and documentation, and more. Both students and instructors can link to a variety of useful resources.

TopLinks is a new database of topical links accessible through *The St. Martin's Guide to Writing* Web site. Students can search by topic or link to sites relevant to specific chapters in *The St. Martin's Guide*.

Exercise Central, available through *The St. Martin's Guide* Web site, offers a collection of grammar, punctuation, and word choice exercises with customized feedback so that students can work at their own speed. Exercise Central also offers instructors a reporting feature that allows them to monitor their students' progress.

Our content cartridge for WebCT makes it simple for instructors using this online learning architecture to build a course around *The St. Martin's Guide.* The content is drawn from the book and its ancillaries and includes activities, models, reference materials, and links to the interactive editing exercises in Exercise Central.

Who Are We? Readings in Identity and Community and Work and Career, prepared by Rise B. Axelrod and Charles R. Cooper, contains selections that expand on themes foregrounded in *The St. Martin's Guide to Writing.* Full of ideas for classroom discussion and writing, the readings offer students additional perspectives and thought-provoking analysis.

The St. Martin's Guide for Writing in the Disciplines: A Guide for Faculty, by Richard Bullock of Wright State University, is a handy reference for faculty, with ideas for using writing in courses across the curriculum. Among the topics covered are designing assignments that get students writing, using informal writing activities to help students to learn, assigning portfolios, and responding to student writing.

Additional Resources for Teaching with The St. Martin's Guide to Writing supports classroom instruction with over fifty transparency masters including lists of important features for each genre, critical reading guides, collaborative activities, and checklists, all adapted from the text, and more than fifty exercises designed to accompany the handbook section of *The Guide.* All the pages are perforated for easy removal and copying.

■ ACKNOWLEDGMENTS

We owe an enormous debt to all the rhetoricians and composition specialists whose theory, research, and pedagogy have informed *The St. Martin's Guide to Writing.* We would be adding many pages to an already long book if we were to name everyone to whom we are indebted; suffice it to say that we have been eclectic in our borrowing.

We must also acknowledge immeasurable lessons learned from all the writers, professional and student alike, whose work we analyzed and whose writing we used in this and earlier editions.

So many instructors and students have contributed ideas and criticism over the years. We want especially to thank the staff, instructors, and students in the Third College Writing Program at the University of California at San Diego, where from 1979 to 1991 we developed and revised *The Guide.* We are still benefiting from the astute insights of M. A. Syverson, Kate Gardner, Kristin Hawkinson, Michael Pemberton, Irv Peckham, Keith Grant-Davie, Evelyn Torres, Gesa Kirsch, James Degan, and other teaching assistants and lecturers from these years. Charles acknowledges the support of members of the English Department at Sacramento City College, where he tutors their students, and of Steven Tchudi, Susan Tchudi, and Katherine Boardman of the English Department, University of Nevada–Reno, who have invited him to teach summer-session writing courses for first-year students. Rise similarly acknowledges her colleagues and composition students at California State University, San Bernardino. She wants especially to thank the students in the graduate program, who have taught her so much about teaching at all levels, from elementary through community college, and the teaching assistants she supervises, who inspire her with their enthusiasm and commitment to helping students.

The members of the advisory board for the sixth edition, a group of dedicated composition instructors from across the country, have provided us with extensive insights and suggestions for the chapters in Part One and have given us the benefit of their advice on new features, in many cases testing them in their own classrooms. For all of their many contributions, we would like to thank Larry Barkley, Mt. San Jacinto College–Menifee; James L. Brown, Kansas City Kansas Community College; Sandy Cavanah, Hopkinsville Community College; Helen Deese, University of California–Riverside; Elizabeth M. Gardner, Millersville University; Judith G. Gardner, University of Texas–San Antonio; Gregory Glau, Arizona State University; Maurice Hunt, Baylor University; Michael Meeker, Winona State University; Michael A. Miller, Longview Community College; Donna M. Padgett, Georgia Southern University; Sharran S. Slinkard, Des Moines Area Community College; Lenora P. Smith, University of Houston; and Rosemary Winslow, Catholic University of America.

Many instructors across the nation have helped us improve the book. For responding to detailed questionnaires about the fifth edition, we thank Lisa Abney, Northwestern State University; Mary Adams, University of Oklahoma; Elizabeth Addison, Western Carolina University; Jim Addison, Western Carolina University; Helen Allen, UNC–Charlotte; Kathryn Amdahl, Harrisburg Area Community College; Patty Banks, Guilford Technical Community College; Charles Beall, San Diego Mesa College; Bob Brannan, Johnson County Community College; Paulette Brewington, UNC–Charlotte; Joanne Buck, Guilford Technical Community College; Vicky Campo, Arizona State University; Katherine Cipriano, Western Carolina University; John Clark, Bowling Green State University; Rocky Colavito, Northwestern State University; Glenda Lee Coppedge, Arkansas State University; Bonnie Crise, Guilford Technical Community College; Carmen Cucinotta, Triton College; Gerri Dobbins, Western Carolina University; David Dowling, University of Colorado–Colorado Springs; Pamela Doyle, Crowley County Community College; Sarah Duerden, Arizona State University; Jerry Erath, Northwestern State University; Marianne Falyk, Purdue University; Mary Grace Foret, Johnson County Community College; Dagmar Frerking, Purdue University; Kathy Gerend-Heinking, Miami University; Greg Glau, Arizona State University; Maureen Daly Goggin, Arizona State University; Catherine Goldberg, University of California–Riverside; Gretchen Golden, Arkansas State University; Barry Greer, Linn-Benton Community College; Launa Hall, Purdue University; Lynn Hamilton, Guilford Technical Community College; Mitzi Harris, Western Wyoming Community College; Mary Hegamyer, Harrisburg Area Community College; Marsha Holmes, Western Carolina University; George Horneker, Arkansas State University; Dorothy Howell, UNC–Charlotte; Renee Jarrett, East Carolina University; Karen Jobe, University of Oklahoma; Joan Johnson, Hagerstown Junior College; Katherine Kuck, John Carroll University; Bonnie Lenore Kyburz, Arizona State University; Bill Lamb, Johnson County Community College; Kathleen Lane, Cowley County Community College; Mark Lidmon,

Blue River Community College; Robyn Lyons, Columbus State Community College; David Mair, University of Oklahoma; Jennifer Martinez, University of Oklahoma; Marsha Maurer, Augusta State University; Julia McGregor, Inver Hills Community College; James McWard, Johnson County Community College; Carole Mehle, East Carolina University; Marie Nester, Harrisburg Area Community College; Jeanne Olson, Arizona State University; Ann Palazzo, Columbus State Community College; Clayann Gilliam Panetta, Mercyhurst College; Elizabeth Parker, Nashville State Technical Institute; John Pelot, Guilford Technical Community College; David Poston, UNC–Charlotte; Catherine Rahmes, Cincinnati State University; B. A. Ramick, Arizona State University; Shirley Rose, Purdue University; Jane Rosecrans, John Tyler Community College; Rhoda Royce, Anderson College; Lisa Ruffolo, Madison Area Technical College; Lois Sampson, Cowley County Community College; Victoria Sarkisian, Marist College; Carolyn Schneider, Guilford Technical Community College; Lisa Schneider, Columbus State Community College; Virginia Skinner-Linnenberg, North Central Michigan College; Becky Stamm, Columbus State Community College; Christy Stanlake, University of Oklahoma; Sharon Stover, Guilford Technical Community College; Linda Strahan, University of California–Riverside; Beverly Sweger, Harrisburg Area Community College; Kristen Taylor, Purdue University; Shelisa Theus, Northwestern State University; Amy Tylicki, Jackson State Community College; Matt VanBoening, Cowley County Community College; A. S. Weber, Penn State University; Joan West, Messiah College; Edd Williams, Riverside City College; Stephanie Burt Williams, UNC–Charlotte; and David Wolfe, Mountain View College.

For reviewing new readings, we thank Cathryn Amdahl, Harrisburg Area Community College; Larry Barkley, Mt. San Jacinto College–Menifee; James Brown, Kansas City Kansas Community College; Sandy Cavanah, Hopkinsville Community College; Helen Deese, University of California–Riverside; Elizabeth Gardner, Millersville University; Judith Gardner, University of Texas–San Antonio; Greg Glau, Arizona State University; Maurice Hunt, Baylor University; David Knapp, Front Range Community College; Alfred Lutz, Middle Tennessee State University; Mike Meeker, Winona State University; Michael Miller, Longview Community College; P. Andrew Miller, University of Cincinnati–Raymond Walters College; Donna Padgett, Georgia Southern University; Michele Peers, Northern Kentucky University; Sharran Slinkard, Des Moines Area Community College; Lee Smith, University of Houston; Phillip Smith, University of Nebraska–Omaha; and Rosemary Winslow, Catholic University of America.

For this new edition of *The St. Martin's Guide,* we also gratefully acknowledge the special contributions of a number of people, including Cathy Palmer, an English and comparative literature librarian and an instructional research librarian at the University of California–Irvine, who provided us with substantial assistance in updating the chapters on using and documenting sources. Nedra Reynolds of the University of Rhode Island prepared a helpful review of the portfolio chapter. Jim Frost of Boise State contributed to the chapters on oral presentations and document design. Craig Jacobsen of Arizona State University provided valuable insights and information for the service learning section, which was reviewed by Lenora P. Smith. Lee Smith also prepared the *Instructor's Resource Manual.* Grateful thanks are likewise due to Larry

Barkley of Mt. San Jacinto College–Menifee, our coeditor for *The Guide*'s ancillary collection of student essays, *Sticks and Stones,* and to Joanne Diaz, who helped with the huge task of pulling together the Writing Guide Software. Andrew Harnack and Eugene Kleppinger have graciously given us permission to adapt their guidelines for citing Internet sources, for which we thank them. Finally, we are especially grateful to the student authors for allowing us to reprint their work in *Sticks and Stones and other student essays* and in *The St. Martin's Guide,* and to Caryn Rosen's fifth-grade class in Little Neck, New York, for participating in field research.

We want to thank many people at Bedford/St. Martin's, especially Diana Puglisi, who ushered us through the editorial process with considerable skill and caring. Diana made many contributions to this edition, the most significant of which is probably the new emphasis on document design in the sections on Designing Your Work. Thank you for your patience and professionalism. We also are grateful to our production team of Harold Chester, Joe Ford, and Lucy Krikorian. Harold, thanks for your skillful juggling during the final stages of the process. We owe a special debt to Leah Edmunds for her masterful managing of the *Instructor's Resource Manual* and *Sticks and Stones and other student essays.* Leah also played a vital role in the development of the Writing Guide Software, as did Carla Samodulski; and without Denise Wydra's expertise and leadership the electronic supplements to *The St. Martin's Guide* would not have been possible. Our gratitude also goes to Sandy Schechter and Diane Kraut for their hard work clearing permissions, Belinda Delpêche for her invaluable assistance throughout the project, Joan Scafarello for her imaginative photo research, Wendy Polhemus-Annibell for her skillful copy-editing, Stephanie Hopkins for her painstaking help on the research chapters, and Jonna Perrillo for her creative contribution to the Designing Your Own Work sections. Kudos go to Anna George for her sensational new design for *The St. Martin's Guide to Writing.* We wish finally to express our appreciation to Nancy Perry for helping us to launch *The Guide* successfully so many years ago and continuing to stand by us, to Chuck Christensen and Joan Feinberg for their adroit leadership of Bedford/St. Martin's, and to marketing managers Karen Melton and Brian Wheel—along with their extraordinarily talented and hardworking sales staff—for their tireless efforts on behalf of *The Guide.*

Charles wishes to thank his wife, Mary Anne, for all the decades of support, affection, understanding, and good humor. It's been a great time, sweetheart, and it's not over yet. Rise wishes to thank her husband, Steven, for the loving care with which he so artfully cultivates their garden, and their son, Jeremiah, who blossoms more wondrously with each new year.

A Brief Contents

Contents

7 Proposing a Solution *293*

PART TWO   CRITICAL THINKING STRATEGIES

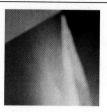

PART THREE WRITING STRATEGIES

PART FOUR   RESEARCH STRATEGIES

PART FIVE   WRITING FOR ASSESSMENT

PART SIX   WRITING AND SPEAKING TO
WIDER AUDIENCES

THE
ST. MARTIN'S
GUIDE
TO WRITING

Introduction

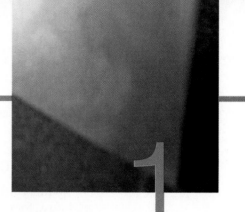

"Why should learning to write well be important to me? What is the connection between writing and thinking? How will reading help me learn to write better? How can I learn to write more effectively and efficiently?" These are some of the questions you may be asking as you begin this writing course. Read on—for *The St. Martin's Guide to Writing* offers some answers to these and other questions you may have.

■ WHY WRITING IS IMPORTANT

Writing has wide-ranging implications for the way we think and learn as well as for our chances of success, our personal development, and our relationships with other people.

Writing Influences the Ways We Think

First, the very act of writing encourages us to be creative as well as organized and logical in our thinking. When we write sentences, paragraphs, and whole essays, we generate ideas and connect these ideas in systematic ways. For example, by combining words into phrases and sentences with conjunctions such as *and, but,* and *because,* we can create complex, new ideas. By grouping related ideas into paragraphs, we develop their similarities and differences, and anchor our general ideas in specific facts and concrete examples.

By writing essays for different purposes and readers, we learn to develop our thinking in different ways. For example, writing about an important event in our lives develops our ability to select significant details and organize them into a meaningful narrative. Writing an explanation of a concept develops categorical thinking, as we connect new information to what we and our readers already know. Speculating about causes develops causal reasoning, proposing solutions develops problem-solving, and arguing positions develops logical thinking.

> Some of the things that happen to us in life seem to have no meaning, but when you write them down, you find the meanings for them. . . .
>
> —MAXINE HONG KINGSTON

1

> Those who are learning to compose and arrange their sentences with accuracy and order are learning, at the same time, to think with accuracy and order.
>
> — HUGH BLAIR

Writing Contributes to the Ways We Learn

Writing helps us learn by making us active, critical thinkers. When we take notes in class, for example, writing helps us identify and remember what is important. Writing in the margins as we read encourages us to question the reading's ideas and information in light of our experience and other reading. Writing in a journal frees us to explore our understanding and response to what we are learning.

Writing essays of various kinds helps us organize and present what we have learned and, in the process, to clarify and extend our own ideas. Writing an explanatory essay, for example, helps us better understand the concept or idea we are explaining. Researching a controversial issue helps us both learn from and question others' points of view.

> The mere process of writing is one of the most powerful tools we have for clarifying our own thinking. I am never as clear about any matter as when I have just finished writing about it.
>
> — JAMES VAN ALLEN

> Writing keeps me from believing everything I read.
>
> — GLORIA STEINEM

Writing Fosters Personal Development

In addition to influencing the ways we think and learn, writing can help us grow as individuals. We are led to reflect deeply on our personal experience, for example, when we write to understand the significance of a particular person in our life. Writing about a controversial issue can make us examine critically some of our most basic assumptions. Writing an evaluation requires that we think about what we value and how our values compare to those of others. Writing about stories invites us to reflect on how we understand ourselves and others. Perhaps most importantly, becoming an author confers authority on us; it gives us confidence to assert our own ideas and feelings.

> In a very real sense, the writer writes in order to teach himself, to understand himself, to satisfy himself. . . .
>
> — ALFRED KAZIN

> Writing has been for a long time my major tool for self-instruction and self-development.
>
> — TONI CADE BAMBARA

Writing Connects Us to Others

It is easier now than ever before to connect with others via email and the Internet. We can use writing to keep in touch with friends and family, take part in academic discussion, and participate actively in democratic debate and decision making. By writing about our experiences, ideas, and observations, we reach out to readers, offering them our own point of view and inviting them to share theirs in return. Writing an argument on a controversial issue, for example, we not only assert our position on the issue but also give readers an opportunity to assert theirs. Moreover, when you and others respond constructively to each other's writing, you can clarify your differences, reexamine your reasoning, and ultimately influence each other's opinions. Similarly, writing a proposal requires us to work collaboratively with others to invent new, creative ways of solving complex problems.

> Writing is the act of saying *I,* of imposing oneself upon other people, of saying *listen to me, see it my way, change your mind.*
>
> —JOAN DIDION

> I think writing is really a process of communication. . . . It's the sense of being in contact with people who are part of a particular audience that really makes a difference to me in writing.
>
> —SHERLEY ANNE WILLIAMS

Writing Promotes Success in College and at Work

As students, you are probably most aware of the many ways writing can contribute to your success in school. Students who learn to write for different readers and purposes do well in courses throughout the curriculum. No doubt you have been able to use writing to demonstrate your knowledge as well as to add to it. Eventually, you will need to use writing to advance your career by writing persuasive application letters for jobs or graduate school admission. Many businesses and professions expect people to write effective email messages, formal letters, and reports that present clear explanations, convincing evaluations, or constructive proposals.

> The aim of school is to produce citizens who are able to communicate with each other, to defend points of view, and to criticize. . . .
>
> —ALBERT SHANKER

> People think it's sort of funny that I went to graduate school as a biologist and then became a writer. . . . What I learned [in science] is how to formulate or identify a new question that hasn't been asked before and then to set about solving it, to do original research to find the way to an answer. And that's what I do when I write a book.
>
> —BARBARA KINGSOLVER

■ Exercise 1.1

Think of an occasion when writing helped you accomplish something important. For example, you may recall a time when writing helped you better understand a difficult subject you were studying, when you used writing to influence someone else, when writing helped you achieve a goal, when you expressed your feelings or worked through a problem by writing, or when you used writing for some other worthwhile purpose.

Write a page or so describing what happened on this particular occasion. Describe how you came to write and what you wrote about. Then explain how you used writing on this occasion and what you wanted your writing to accomplish. For example, did you use it to help you learn something, express yourself, or connect to others?

■ HOW WRITING IS LEARNED

Writing is important. But can it be learned? This question is crucial because writing traditionally has been veiled in mystery. Some people believe that writers are born, not made. They assume that people who are good at writing do not have to spend a lot of time learning to write; they just naturally know how to do so. Others may assume that if you have to spend time working on your writing—planning, rewriting, or editing—then you might as well give up and do something else. After all, "real" writers write perfectly the first time, every time, dashing off an essay with minimal effort. Their first draft is the last draft. They may need to spell-check their work, but nothing major needs to be clarified, developed, or corrected.

■ Exercise 1.2

List some of your assumptions about writers and writing. Then write a few sentences speculating about the sources of these assumptions—personal experience, teachers, textbooks, the media, and so forth.

Writers' testimonies, together with extensive research on how people write and learn to write, show that writing can—indeed must—be learned. Some writers may be more skilled than others. Some may find writing easier and more satisfying. But no one is born knowing how to write. Everyone must learn how to write.

> However great a [person's] natural talent may be, the art of writing cannot be learned all at once.
>
> —JEAN JACQUES ROUSSEAU

> Learning to write well takes time and much effort, but it can be done.
>
> —MARGARET MEAD

The St. Martin's Guide to Writing, now in its sixth edition, has helped many students learn how to become effective, confident writers. Using *The St. Martin's Guide,* you will read and write several different kinds of essays. From reading these essays, you will learn how other writers make their texts work for their particular readers. From writing the kinds of essays you are reading, you will learn to use your process of writing constructively to develop your thinking and compose texts that work effectively for your readers. To take full advantage of what you are learning by reading and writing, *The Guide* will also help you become self-reflective as a reader and writer. From thinking critically about your learning, you will be better able to remember and apply what you have learned, thereby earning a greater sense of confidence and control.

Reading

This section shows how reading texts that work well for their readers helps you learn to write texts for your own readers and how *The St. Martin's Guide* supports your learning from reading.

How Written Texts Work.   How a text works depends on what and who it is written for—its purpose and audience. A text's purpose and audience can be used to define the kind of writing it is, what we call its *genre*.

You may be familiar with genres as categories for literature (novel, poem, play) or film (science fiction, western, film noir, romance). College students read and write many different genres, such as lab reports in biology, ethnographies in anthropology, literary analysis or interpretation in English, research reviews in education. Academic disciplines rely on certain genres that have become established ways of making meaning and communicating among students and specialists in the field. The same is true of writing in business (some common genres include résumés and job-application letters, marketing reports, proposals, and personnel evaluations) and the professions (lawyers, for example, write briefs, appeals, closing arguments, and wills).

As these examples show, genres are shared by groups of people with common interests. Some genres are highly specialized and technical; to understand a biologist's lab report or a lawyer's brief, readers not only have to know the terminology but also have to be able to judge the reliability of the lab report's research methods or the credibility of the brief's arguments. Many genres, however, are widely shared and therefore do not require specialized knowledge. For example, because of our shared experience, we can all read and understand most news reports, opinion essays, autobiographies, profiles, and advertisements we encounter in general audience publications such as newspapers, magazines, and Web sites.

Genres develop in different communities to serve particular purposes. Biologists use the lab report to inform readers interested in biology about the results of their research and to enable other researchers to duplicate their experiments. Lawyers use briefs to convince judges that certain points of law apply to their case. Reporters write about news events to inform readers. Columnists write opinion essays to convince readers to adopt their views. Advertisers write ads to persuade readers to buy their clients' products.

A text's effectiveness—how well it achieves its purpose with its readers—depends on many factors, including how well it fulfills readers' expectations for the genre. Readers expect texts within a particular genre to have distinctive features, use specific strategies, and contain certain types of content. A remembered event essay, for example, has several basic features: a well-told story about the event, a vivid presentation of the people involved in the event and of the place where it occurred, and an indication of the event's significance. Writers of such essays use strategies of narration and description to help readers imagine what happened and understand the event's significance. Readers expect the content of autobiographical writing to be about events they consider important, such as events that have had some lasting impact—changing, challenging, or complicating the writer's sense of self or connection with others.

Although individual texts within the same genre vary (no two proposals, even those arguing for the same solution, will be identical), they nonetheless follow a general pattern using distinctive basic features, strategies, and special kinds of content to accomplish their purposes. This patterning allows for a certain amount of predictability, without which communication would be difficult, if not impossible. Language—whether spoken or written—is a system of social interaction. Everyone who speaks the same language learns to recognize certain patterns—how words should be ordered to make sentences comprehensible, how sentences can be related to one another to make coherent paragraphs, how examples can be used to explain new ideas, how arguments can be supported with quotations from authorities, and so forth. These language patterns, also called *conventions,* make communication possible.

To learn to write genres for particular groups of readers, we need to pay attention to how texts work for their readers. We have to understand also that writing in a genre does not mean that writing should be mechanical or formulaic. Each genre's basic features, strategies, and kinds of content represent broad frameworks within which writers are free to be creative. Most writers, in fact, find that working within a framework allows them to be more creative, not less so. Some even blur the boundaries between genres and invent new genres for new media such as Web sites. And as groups change, developing new interests and new ways of adding to their knowledge, genre conventions also change.

> You would learn very little in this world if you were not allowed to imitate. And to repeat your imitations until some solid grounding . . . was achieved and the slight but wonderful difference—that made *you* and no one else—could assert itself.
>
> —MARY OLIVER

How *The Guide* Helps You Write Texts That Work.   To learn the conventions of a particular genre, you need to read examples of that genre. At the same time, you should also practice writing in the genre.

> Read, read, read. . . . Just like a carpenter who works as an apprentice and studies the master. Read!
>
> —WILLIAM FAULKNER

Reading is crucial. As you read examples of a genre, you begin to recognize its predictable patterns as well as the possibilities for innovation. This knowledge is stored in your memory and used both when you read and when you write in that genre.

Experienced writers read and learn from positive examples as well as negative ones. Sometimes, they focus on a particular problem—how to write realistic-sounding dialogue or how to refute someone else's argument effectively, for example. They do not look for answers in a single example. Instead, they sample many texts to see how different writers work with a certain feature of the genre. This sampling is not slavish imitation, but education. Like artists and craftspeople, writers have always learned from others. *The St. Martin's Guide to Writing* presents a variety of examples in each genre accompanied by questions and commentary to help you see how writers use the conventional features and strategies of the genre to achieve their own purposes.

I practiced writing in every possible way that I could. I wrote a pastiche of other people. Just as a pianist runs his scales for ten years before he gives his concert: because when he gives that concert, he can't be thinking of his fingering or of his hands, he has to be thinking of his interpretation. He's thinking of what he's trying to communicate.

–Katherine Anne Porter

How *The Guide* Helps You Design Texts That Work.   Writers have long recognized that no matter how well organized, well reasoned, or compelling a piece of writing may be, how it looks on the page influences to some extent how it works for readers. Today, writers have many more options for designing their documents than ever before. Recent advances in computer technology, digital photography and scanning, and integrated word processing and graphics programs make it relatively easy for writers to heighten the visual impact of the page. For example, they can change type fonts and add colors, charts, diagrams, and photographs to written documents. To construct multimedia Web pages or CD-ROMs, writers can add sound, moving images, and hyperlinks.

Design is a funny word. Some people think design means how it looks. But of course, if you dig deeper, it's really how it works.

–Steve Jobs

These multiple possibilities, however, do not guarantee a more effective document. Writers need to learn to design effective texts by studying texts in their everyday lives that capture readers' attention and enhance understanding. As someone who has grown up watching television shows and videos, playing computer games, or looking at the photos, advertisements, cartoons, tables, and graphs in magazines, newspapers, and other sources, you are already a sophisticated visual consumer who has learned many of the conventions of document design for different genres and writing situations. This book will help you become aware of what you already know and help you make new discoveries about document design that you may be able to use in your own writing.

■ Exercise 1.3

Make two lists, one of the genres you have *read* recently, such as explanations of how to do something, stories, news reports, opinion pieces, and movie reviews; and the other of the genres you have *written* recently, both for college courses and for other purposes. Then write a few sentences speculating about how your reading influences your writing and the design of your texts.

Writing

This section shows how your writing process can become a more productive process of *thinking and writing* and how *The St. Martin's Guide* helps you develop a process to meet the demands of different writing situations.

How To Make Your Writing Process Work.   When you reflect on how you write, you probably think of the steps you take: First you read the writing assignment, next decide which points to cover, then begin writing the opening paragraph, and so forth. For familiar writing situations—when you know the subject well and feel confident writing in the genre for your particular readers—the process that works best may involve minimal planning and only one draft, followed by a little rewriting, spell-checking, and proofreading. But for most writing situations, you have to figure out what you can say about the subject to your particular readers and how to communicate effectively in the genre. In these situations, the writing process itself becomes a tool for discovery and not just a sequence of steps you take to produce a written text.

> I don't see writing as a communication of something already discovered, as "truths" already known. Rather, I see writing as a job of experiment. It's like any discovery job; you don't know what's going to happen until you try it.
>
> —William Stafford

To make writing a true process of discovery, you need to recognize that the process of writing is a process of thinking—not simply a sequence of steps. Using writing as a process of discovery means that you do not think and then write, but that the writing helps you think.

Few writers begin writing with a complete understanding of a subject. Most use writing as a way to learn about the subject, recording ideas and information they have collected, exploring connections and implications, letting the writing lead them to greater understanding. As they develop ideas and plan a draft, writers set goals for their writing: goals for the whole essay (to confront readers or inspire them, for example) and goals for particular passages (to make a sentence emphatic or include details in a paragraph).

> When I start a project, the first thing I do is write down, in longhand, everything I know about the subject, every thought I've ever had on it. This may be twelve or fourteen pages. Then I read it through, for quite a few days . . . then I try to find out what are the salient points that I must make. And then it begins to take shape.
>
> —Maya Angelou

While writing, most writers pause occasionally to reread what they have written. They often reread with their readers in mind to see whether they can make their writing more effective. Rereading sometimes leads to further invention—filling in a gap in the logic of an argument, for example—and frequently it leads to substantial rethinking and revising—cutting, reorganizing, rewriting.

> I think the writer ought to help the reader as much as he can without damaging what he wants to say; and I don't think it ever hurts the writer to sort of stand back now and then and look at his stuff as if he were reading it instead of writing it.
>
> —James Jones

> The writer must survey his work critically, coolly, as though he were a stranger to it. At the end of each revision, a manuscript may look . . . worked over, torn apart, pinned together, added to, deleted from, words changed and words changed back.
>
> —Eleanor Estes

Rereading your own writing with a critical eye is necessary, but many writers also share their ideas and writing with others, actively seeking constructive critical comments from friends and colleagues. Playwrights, poets, and novelists often join writers' workshops to get help from other writers. F. Scott Fitzgerald depended on his editor, Maxwell Perkins. When Perkins criticized the way Gatsby's character was being introduced in an early version of the novel, Fitzgerald made significant changes in chapters 3, 4, 5, 8, and 9 and completely rewrote chapters 6 and 7.

Writers also sometimes write collaboratively. Engineers, business executives, and research scientists usually write proposals and reports in teams. Graduate students and professors in many fields do research together and co-write conference papers and journal articles. This book is the product of extensive collaboration between the coauthors and numerous composition instructors, student writers, and editors over many years. Your instructor may ask you to try some of *The Guide*'s collaborative activities with other students in your class.

> [Ezra Pound] was a marvelous critic because he didn't try to turn you into an imitation of himself. He tried to see what you were trying to do.
>
> —T. S. ELIOT

> I like working collaboratively from time to time. I like fusing ideas into one vision. I like seeing that vision come to life with other people who know exactly what it took to get there.
>
> —AMY TAN

The continual shifting of attention—from setting goals to choosing words, from inventing new ideas to rereading to anticipate readers' likely objections, from adding supporting examples to reorganizing—characterizes the dynamic thinking that underlies the writing process. Although writing may seem to progress in a linear, step-by-step fashion, invention is a thought process that does not stop when drafting begins. It continues throughout drafting and revising. Most writers plan and revise their plans, draft and revise their drafts, write and read what they have written, and then write some more. This rereading and rethinking is what we mean when we describe the writing process as recursive rather than linear. Instead of progressing in a straight line from the first sentence to the last, from opening paragraph to conclusion, the experience of writing is more like taking a steep trail with frequent switchbacks; it appears that you are retracing old ground but you are really rising to new levels.

Seasoned writers depend on this recursiveness to lead them to new ideas and to develop their insights. Many writers claim that it is only by writing that they can figure out what they think.

> How do I know what I think until I see what I say?
>
> —E. M. FORSTER

> As a writer I would find out most clearly what I thought, and what I only thought I thought, when I saw it written down.
>
> —ANNA QUINDLEN

Even writers who plan in their head eventually have to work out their plans by writing them down. The advantage of writing down ideas is not only that writing makes a record you can review later, but also that the process of writing itself can help you articulate and develop your ideas.

> You have to work problems out for yourself on paper. Put the stuff down and read it —to see if it works.
>
> –JOYCE CARY

Inexperienced writers or those writing in a new genre or on a difficult subject especially benefit from writing outlines of where they are and where they hope to go so that they can then focus on how to get there. But outlines should not be written in stone; they must be flexible if the writer is to benefit from the recursiveness of the writing process.

> Somebody starting to write should have a solid foundation to build on. . . . When I first started to write I used to do two- or three-page outlines.
>
> –LILLIAN HELLMAN

> I began *[Invisible Man]* with a chart of the three-part division. It was a conceptual frame with most of the ideas and some of the incidents indicated.
>
> –RALPH ELLISON

> You are always going back and forth between the outline and the writing, bringing them closer together, or just throwing out the outline and making a new one.
>
> –ANNIE DILLARD

Sometimes, the hardest part of writing is getting down to work. Writers may procrastinate, but they learn to deal with procrastination. Many writers make writing a habit by setting a time to write and trying to stick to their schedule. Most importantly, they know that the only way to make progress on a writing project is to keep at it. They work at their writing, knowing it takes time and perseverance.

> I have to write every day because, the way I work, the writing generates the writing.
>
> –E. L. DOCTOROW

> It's a matter of piling a little piece here and a little piece there, fitting them together, going on to the next part, then going back and gradually shaping the whole piece into something. . . . You don't rely on inspiration—I don't anyway, and I don't think most writers do.
>
> –DAVE BARRY

Once immersed in invention—figuring out what they want to say about the subject, contemplating what readers already think about it, and so forth—most writers find that they continue inventing even when away from their desks. Once the process is underway, taking a walk or playing a game can be a productive part of the process rather than a means of procrastinating. Diverting a tired mind and body can help writers see connections or solve problems that had stymied them earlier.

> Often I write by not writing. I assign a task to my subconscious, then take a nap or go for a walk, do errands, and let my mind work on the problem.
>
> –DONALD MURRAY

Like most creative activities, writing is a form of problem-solving. As they work on a draft, most writers continually discover and try to solve writing problems—how to bring a scene to life, how to handle objections, whether to begin with this point or that. The more writers know about their subjects, genres, and readers, the better they can anticipate and solve problems as they write.

Experienced writers develop a repertoire of strategies for solving problems they are likely to encounter. These are the tools of the trade. *The St. Martin's Guide to Writing* will provide you with a full writer's toolbox and teach you how to select the right tool for the job.

How *The Guide* Helps You Develop a Writing Process That Works.   As a student learning to write, you need to develop a writing process that is flexible and yet systematic. It should be a process that neither oversimplifies nor overwhelms, one that helps you learn about a subject and write a successful essay. The Guides to Writing in Part One of this book are designed to meet this need. These guides, which you will find on the pages bordered in green, suggest what you need to think about for each different writing situation. The first few times you write in a new genre, you can rely on these guides. They provide a scaffolding to support your work until you become more familiar with each genre.

When engaging in any new and complex activity—driving, playing an instrument, skiing, or writing—we have to learn how to break down the activity into a series of manageable tasks. In learning to play tennis, for example, you can isolate lobbing from volleying or work on your backhand or serve. Similarly, in writing about an autobiographical event, you can work first on recalling what happened, imagining the scene, or reflecting on the event's significance. What is important is focusing on one aspect at a time. Dividing the process in this way enables you to tackle a complex writing project without oversimplifying it.

> You know when you think about writing a book, you think it is overwhelming. But, actually, you break it down into tiny little tasks any moron could do.
>
> —ANNIE DILLARD

■ Exercise 1.4

Write a page or so describing the process you followed the last time you wrote something that took time and effort. Do not choose something you wrote in class. Use the following questions to help you recall what you did, but feel free to write about any other aspects of your writing process that you remember.

- What initially led you to write? Who were you writing for and what was the purpose of your essay?

- What kinds of invention and planning did you do, if any, before you began writing the first draft?

- If you discussed your ideas and plans with someone, how did discussing them help you? If you had someone read your draft, how did getting a response help?

- If you rewrote, moved, added, or cut anything in your first draft, describe what you changed.

Thinking Critically

This section shows how thinking critically about your learning can help you make your writing more effective and how *The St. Martin's Guide* helps you think critically about your reading, your writing process, and the genres you are using.

How to Think Critically About Your Learning.   Thinking critically means becoming self-aware or what we call metacognitive, conscious of your own thinking and learning processes.

When writing, you will find that many of your decisions do not require conscious effort. You can rely on familiar strategies that usually produce effective writing for you in the genre. But there will nearly always be occasions as you write when you become aware of problems that require your full attention. Some problems may be fairly easy to remedy, such as an inappropriate word choice or a confusing sequence of events. Other problems may require considerable rethinking and writing, for example, if you discover that your readers' likely objections seriously undermine your argument.

After you have completed a final draft, reflecting on how you identified and tried to solve such problems can be a powerful aid to learning. Understanding the problem may enable you to anticipate similar problems in the future. It may also give you a firmer grip on the standards you need to apply when rereading your drafts. Most importantly, reflecting on a problem you solved should enhance your confidence as a writer, helping you realize that problems are not signs of bad writing, but that problem-solving signifies good writing.

> That's what a writer is: someone who sees problems a little more clearly than others.
> —Eugene Ionesco

To think critically about your learning, it also helps to reflect on what you have learned from reading texts in the genre you are writing. Much of our language and genre learning comes from modeling. As a young child, for example, we learn from hearing our parents and peers tell stories and from watching stories portrayed on television and in film. We learn ways of beginning and ending, strategies for building suspense, techniques for making time sequences clear, how to use dialogue to develop character, and so on. As an adult, we can reinforce and increase our repertoire of storytelling patterns by analyzing how stories that we admire work and by consciously trying out in our own writing the strategies we have seen work in those stories.

> I went back to the good nature books that I had read. And I analyzed them. I wrote outlines of whole books—outlines of chapters—so that I could see their structure. And I copied down their transitional sentences or their main sentences or their closing sentences or their lead sentences. I especially paid attention to how these writers made transitions between paragraphs and scenes.
> —Annie Dillard

Finally, contemplating what you have learned about writing different genres can help you examine what we call the social dimensions—how genres are used to make possible certain kinds of social actions and ways of knowing, while discouraging others. Concept explanations, for example, enable the efficient exchange of established knowledge, but they also discourage critical questioning about how certain kinds of knowledge, and not other kinds, get established as authoritative, and by whom. Similarly, writing about remembered events enables self-presentation and perhaps even self-knowledge, but it discourages critical questioning about the social construction of identity and the idea of a single true or essential self.

> You leave out a lot, and emphasize this and not that. Your actual experience is a complete flux . . . [and yet] you want the readers to say, this is true . . . to believe [they are] getting the *real* Robert Lowell.
>
> – ROBERT LOWELL

How *The Guide* Helps You Think Critically.   Thinking critically about your reading and writing experiences is not difficult. It simply requires that you shift focus from *what* you are reading and writing to *how* you are reading and writing.

The St. Martin's Guide to Writing helps you talk and write about the hows of reading and writing different genres by providing a shared vocabulary of specialized but not very technical words you can easily learn and many of which you already know. Words like *significance, narrating,* and *thesis,* for example, will help you identify the features and strategies of essays you are reading in different genres. Words like *invention, setting goals,* and *revising* will help you describe what you are doing as you write your own essays in these genres. Words like *established knowledge* and *essential self* will help you examine the social dimensions of genres you are reading and writing.

Each writing assignment chapter in Part One includes many opportunities for you to think critically about your understanding of the genre and to reflect on your writing process. A section entitled Thinking Critically about What You Have Learned concludes each chapter, giving you an opportunity to look back and reflect on these three aspects of your learning:

1. How writing worked for you as a creative problem-solving process.
2. How your reading of other essays in the genre helped you write your own essay.
3. How you understand the social dimensions of writing in the genre.

■ Exercise 1.5

Read the following quotes to see how writers use similes (writing is like _____) and metaphors (writing is _____) to describe the processes and products of writing.

Writing is like exploring . . . as an explorer makes maps of the country he has explored, so a writer's works are maps of the country he has explored.

– LAWRENCE OSGOOD

Writing is manual labor of the mind: a job, like laying pipe.

– JOHN GREGORY DUNNE

Write several similes or metaphors of your own that express aspects of your experience as a writer. Then write a page explaining and expanding on the ideas and feelings expressed in your similes and metaphors.

■ USING THIS BOOK

The St. Martin's Guide to Writing is divided into six major parts.

Part One presents writing assignments for nine important genres: autobiographical events, firsthand biography, profile, explanation, position paper, proposal, evaluation, causal analysis, and literary interpretation. Each of these writing assignment chapters provides readings that demonstrate how written texts of that genre work and a Guide to Writing that will escort you through a process to help you write an effective essay in the genre for your particular purpose and audience. Each chapter also includes a discussion of possible purposes and audiences for the genre, a summary of the genre's basic features and strategies, a narrative showing a Writer at Work on one of the readings in the chapter, and a section on designing documents in the genre. As we have mentioned, a section titled Thinking Critically about What You Have Learned concludes each of these chapters.

Parts Two through Five provide illustrations and practice using strategies for invention and critical reading, writing, and research. Also included are up-to-date guidelines for writing research papers, using a wide range of sources (library sources, the Internet, and your own field research), taking essay exams, and assembling a portfolio of your writing.

Part Six presents four brief chapters that will help you in writing and speaking for audiences beyond your first-year composition classroom, covering the diverse topics of service learning (writing in the community), collaboration learning (consulting and writing with others), print and electronic document design, and oral presentation.

■ Exercise 1.6

Preview each of the writing assignments in Part One (Chapters 2–10) of *The St. Martin's Guide*. Begin by reading the opening paragraphs of the chapter, which introduce the genre, and skimming the examples of Writing in Your Other Courses, Writing in the Community, and Writing in the Workplace. Then turn to the Guide to Writing in the chapter (easily identified by the green border around the pages), read the Writing Assignment, and skim the Invention activity immediately following the assignment to see examples of possible subjects for essays in the genre, including those listed under "Identity and Community" and "Work and Career." (As you will see, Chapter 10, Interpreting Stories, omits some of these sections.)

List the genres you would like to work on in this class. For each genre you list, write a few sentences explaining why you want to work on it.

The Part One Readings

Each Part One chapter includes readings, some written by professional writers and others by students who have used earlier editions of this book. All of the readings have been selected to reflect a wide range of topics and strategies. If you read these selections with a critical eye, you will see many different ways writers use a genre.

Each reading selection (except for those in Chapter 10) is accompanied by the following groups of questions, activities, and commentary to help you learn how essays in that genre work:

Connecting to Culture and Experience invites you to explore with other students an issue or question raised by the reading.

Analyzing Writing Strategies helps you examine closely the reading's basic features or writing strategies.

Commentary points out important features of the genre and strategies the writer uses in the essay.

Considering Topics for Your Own Essay suggests subjects related to the reading that you might write about in your own essay.

Most of the assignments in this book provide opportunities to explore your connections to the world. When you are choosing a topic to write about, you might consider suggestions listed under "Identity and Community" and "Work and Career" in the Guides to Writing. These topics enable you to explore your personal connections to the various communities of which you are a part, visit and learn more about places in your community, debate issues important to your community, examine your ideas and attitudes about work, and consider issues related to your future career.

The Part One Guides to Writing

Each Part One assignment chapter provides detailed suggestions for thinking about your subject and purpose as well as your readers and their expectations. These Guides to Writing will help you develop a truly recursive process of discovery that will enable you to write an effective essay in the genre for your particular purpose and audience.

To make the process manageable, the Guide to Writing is divided into sections: The Writing Assignment, Invention and Research, Planning and Drafting, a Critical Reading Guide, Revising, and Editing and Proofreading. The color-coded "menu" preceding the Writing Assignment shows you at a glance the sections and the headings under each section. But to understand how the activities in the Guide to Writing will help you do the kinds of thinking you need to do, you must look closely at the types of activities included in each section.

The Writing Assignment.   Each Guide to Writing begins with an assignment that defines the general purpose and basic features of the genre you have been studying in the chapter. The assignment does not tell you what subject to write about or who your readers will be. You will have to make these decisions, guided by the invention activities in the next section.

Invention and Research.   Every Guide to Writing includes invention activities and most also include suggestions for observational, library, or Internet research. The Invention and Research activities are designed to help you find a topic, discover what you already know about it, consider your purpose and audience, research the subject further to see what others have written about it, explore and develop your ideas, and compose a tentative thesis statement to guide your planning and drafting.

Remember that invention is not a part of the writing process you can skip. It is the basic, ongoing preoccupation of all writing. As writers, we cannot choose *whether* to invent; we can only decide *how*.

You can use the Invention activities before, during, and after you have written a first draft. However, the sequence of invention activities can be especially helpful before drafting because it focuses systematically on the basic genre features and writing strategies. The sequence reminds you of questions you need to think about as you collect, analyze, and synthesize ideas and information in light of your particular subject, purpose and readers. The entire sequence of invention activities takes only a couple of hours to complete. But it works best when spread over several days, giving yourself time to think. So, if at all possible, begin the invention process far enough ahead of the deadline to let your thinking develop fully. Here is some general advice to keep in mind as you do the invention activities:

Use Writing to Explore Your Ideas. You can use writing to gather your thoughts and see where they lead. The key to exploratory writing is to refrain from censoring yourself. Simply try writing for five to ten minutes. Explore your ideas freely, letting one idea lead to another. Later, you can reread what you have written and select the most promising ideas to develop.

Focus on One Issue at a Time. Explore your topic systematically by dividing it into its component parts and exploring them one at a time. For example, instead of trying to think of your whole argument, focus on one reason and the support you would give for it, or focus on how you might refute one objection to your argument.

■ Exercise 1.7

Preview the Invention section of one of the Guides to Writing. First choose an assignment chapter that interests you (Chapters 2–10). Then find the Invention (or Invention and Research) section and skim it from beginning to end. Notice the headings and subheadings, but also look closely at some of the activities to see what they ask you to do and think about.

Planning and Drafting. Each Guide to Writing includes suggestions for planning to get you started writing the first draft of your essay. These suggestions help you use the recursiveness of the writing process to continue making connections and developing your ideas. You set goals and try to implement them as you plan and write the draft. While drafting, you may make notes about new ideas or additional information you need to research, but you try to keep your focus on the ideas and information you have already discovered in order to work out their meanings.

The section is divided into four parts:

Seeing What You Have involves reviewing what you have discovered about your subject, purpose, and audience.

Setting Goals helps you think about your overall purpose as well as your goals for the various parts of your essay.

Outlining suggests some of the ways you might organize your essay.

Drafting launches you on the writing of your first draft.

As you begin your first draft, keep in mind the following practical points, many of which assist professional writers as they begin drafting:

Choose the Best Time and Place. You can write a draft anytime and anyplace. As you probably already know, people write under the most surprising or arduous conditions. Drafting is likely to go smoothly, however, if you choose a time and place ideally suited for sustained and thoughtful work. Many professional writers have a place where they can concentrate for a few hours without repeated interruptions. Writers often find one place where they write best, and they return there whenever they have to write. Try to find such a place for yourself.

Make Revision Easy. If possible, compose your draft on a word processor. If you do not have access to one and must write out or type your text, write on only one side of the page. Leave wide margins. Write on every other line or triple-space your typing. When you arrange your text on the page in these ways, you are looking ahead to when you will need to revise the draft, leaving yourself plenty of space to change, add, cut, and rearrange material later on.

Do the Easy Parts First. Divide your task into manageable portions and do the easy parts first. Just aim to complete a small part of the essay—one section or paragraph—at a time. Try not to agonize over difficult parts, such as the first paragraph or the right word. Start with the part you understand best.

Lower Your Expectations—for the Time Being. Be satisfied with less than perfect writing in a first draft, and do not be overly critical of what you are getting down on paper at this stage. Remember, you are working on a draft that you will revise later. For now, try things out. Follow digressions. Let your ideas flow. Later you can go back and cross out a sentence, rework a section, or make other changes. Now and then, of course, you will want to reread what you have written, but do not reread obsessively. Return to drafting new material as soon as possible. Avoid editing or proofreading during this stage.

Take Short Breaks—and Reward Yourself. Drafting can be hard work, and you may need to take a break to refresh yourself. But be careful not to wander off for too long or you may lose momentum. By setting small goals and rewarding yourself regularly, you will make it easier to complete the draft.

Critical Reading Guide.   Each Guide to Writing includes a Critical Reading Guide that will help you get a good critical reading of your draft as well as help you read others' drafts. Once you have finished drafting your essay, you will want to make every effort to have someone else read the draft and comment on how to improve it. Experienced writers often seek out such advice from critical readers to help them see their drafts as others do.

When you are asked to evaluate someone else's draft, you need to read it with a critical eye. You must be both positive and skeptical—positive in that you want to identify what is workable and promising in the draft, skeptical in that you need to question the writer's assumptions and decisions.

Here is some general advice on reading any draft critically:

Make a Written Record of Your Comments.   Although talking with the writer about your reading of the draft can be useful and even fun, you will be most helpful to the writer if you put your ideas down on paper. When you write down your comments and suggestions—either on the draft or on a separate sheet of paper—you leave a record that can be used later when the writer revises the material.

Read First for an Overall Impression.   On first reading, try not to be distracted by any errors in spelling, punctuation, or word choice. Look at the big issues: clear focus, compelling presentation, forcefulness of argument, novelty and quality of ideas. What seems particularly good? What problems do you see? Focus on the overall goal of the draft and how well it is met. Write just a few sentences expressing your initial reaction.

Read Again to Analyze the Draft.   For this second reading, focus on individual parts of the draft, bringing to bear what you know about the genre and the subject.

When you read the draft at this level, you must shift your attention from one aspect of the essay to another. Consider how well the opening paragraphs introduce the essay and prepare the reader for what follows. Pay attention to specific writing strategies, like narration or argument. Notice whether the parts seem logically sequenced. Look for detailing, examples, or other kinds of support.

As you analyze, you are evaluating as well as describing, but a critical reading involves more than criticism of the draft. A good critical reader helps a writer see how each part of an essay works and how all the parts work together. By describing what you see, you help the writer view the draft more objectively, a perspective that is necessary for thoughtful revising.

Offer Advice, but Do Not Rewrite.   As a critical reader, you may be tempted to rewrite the draft—to change a word here, correct an error there, add your ideas everywhere. Resist the impulse. Your role is to read carefully, to point out what you think is or is not working, to make suggestions and ask questions. Leave the revising to the writer.

In turn, the writer has a responsibility to listen to your comments but is under no obligation to do as you suggest. "Then why go to all the trouble?" you might ask. There are at least two good reasons. First, when you read someone else's draft critically, you learn more about writing—about the decisions writers make, about how a thoughtful reader reads, about the constraints of particular kinds of writing. Second, as a critical reader you embody for the writer the abstraction called "audience." By sharing your reactions with the writer, you complete the circuit of communication.

■ Exercise 1.8

Preview the Critical Reading Guide in the assignment chapter you chose for Exercise 1.7. Find the section and skim it. Then look closely at item 2 or 3 in the numbered list to get a sense of what you are being asked to think about when reading and responding to another writer's draft. If you have participated in draft workshops before, compare your previous experience as a reader to the experience you think you would have by following this Critical Reading Guide. Also compare the usefulness of the response you got in the past from readers of your draft to the kind of response you could expect from readers following this guide.

Revising.   Each Guide to Writing includes a Revising section to help you get an overview of your draft, chart a plan for revision, consider critical comments, and carry out the revisions.

Productive invention and smooth drafting rarely result in the essay a writer has imagined. Experienced writers are not surprised or disappointed, however, because they expect revision to be necessary. They know that revising will bring them closer to the essay they really want to write. When writers read their drafts thoughtfully and critically—and perhaps reflect on the advice of critical readers—they are able to see many opportunities for improvement. They may notice sentence-level problems such as misspelled words or garbled syntax, but more important, they discover ways to delete, move, rephrase, and add material in order to develop their ideas and say what they want to say more clearly.

Here is some general advice on revising:

Reconsider Your Purpose and Audience.   Remind yourself of what you are trying to accomplish in this essay. If someone has read and responded to your draft, you may now have a better understanding of your readers' likely interests and concerns. You may also have refined your purpose. Keep your purpose and audience in mind as you reread the essay and revise in stages. Do not try to do everything at once.

Look at Major Problems First.   Identify any major problems preventing the draft from achieving its purpose. Major problems might include a lack of awareness of your audience, inadequate development of key parts, missing or incomplete sections, or the need for further invention or research. Trying to solve these major problems will probably lead to some substantial rethinking and rewriting, so do not get diverted by sentence-level problems at this time.

Focus Next on Organization and Coherence.   Look at the introductory section of the essay to see how well it prepares readers for the parts that follow. It may help to make a paragraph-by-paragraph scratch outline to help you see at a glance what each paragraph does in the essay. If you have difficulty identifying the function of any paragraph, you may need to add an appropriate transition to clarify the paragraph's connection to the previous paragraphs or write a new topic sentence that better announces the subject of the paragraph. Or you may need to do some more extensive rewriting or reorganization.

Then Consider the Details.   As the saying goes, the devil is in the details. The details have to be selected for a specific purpose, such as to convey significance, support an argument, or provide a concrete example of an abstract idea. If any details seem unrelated to your larger purpose, you need to make the connections explicit. If your essay lacks details, you can review your invention notes or do some additional research to come up with the details you need.

Editing and Proofreading.   Once you have finished revising your essay, your next step is to edit and proofread it carefully. You want to make sure that every word, phrase, and sentence is clear and correct. Using language and punctuation correctly is an essential part of good writing. Errors will distract readers and lessen your credibility as a writer.

Be sure to save editing until the end—*after* you have planned and worked out a revision. Too much editing too early in the writing process can limit, or even block, invention and drafting.

Here are some other suggestions:

Keep a List of Your Common Errors.   Note the grammatical and spelling errors you discover in your own writing. You will probably start to recognize error patterns to check for as you edit your work.

Begin Proofreading with the Last Sentence.   To focus your attention on grammar and spelling, it may help to read backwards, beginning with the last sentence. When you read backwards, it is harder to pay attention to content and thus easier to recognize grammatical and spelling errors.

Exchange Drafts with Another Student.   Because it is usually easier to see errors in someone else's writing than in your own, consider trading essays with a classmate and proofreading one another's writing.

Thinking Critically about What You Have Learned.   Each chapter in Part One concludes with a set of activities to help you think about what you have learned studying the genre in that chapter. There are three different activities:

Reflecting on Your Writing asks you to consider how you solved problems writing that particular kind of essay.

Reviewing What You Learned from Reading helps you discover what specific influences your reading had on your writing.

Considering the Social Dimensions of the genre leads you to explore how thinking and writing in a particular genre reflect the social and cultural contexts in which thinking and writing occur.

Thinking and writing about what you have learned not only reinforces your learning by helping you remember what is important, but also helps you apply what you have learned to new situations. If you are compiling a portfolio of your coursework to hand in at the end of the term, these activities may help you decide what to include in your portfolio as well as help you write a reflective essay on the work you select for the portfolio. Finally, thinking critically about the social dimensions of genres may help you become a more perceptive cultural critic and constructive participant in conversations with others in school, at work, and in the larger community.

WRITING ACTIVITIES

Remembering Events

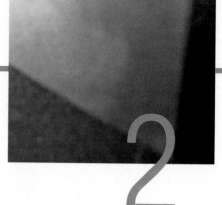

When you write about remembered events in your life, you write autobiography, a popular genre of writing. Autobiography is so popular because reading as well as writing it leads people to reflect deeply on their own lives. When you reflect on the meaning of experience, you examine the forces within yourself and within society that have shaped you into the person you have become.

When you write about a remembered event, your purpose is to present yourself to readers by telling a story that discloses something significant about your life. Autobiographical writers do not just pour out their memories and feelings. Instead, they shape those memories into a compelling story that conveys the meaning and importance of an experience—what can be called its autobiographical significance.

Writing about your life for others to read is not the same as writing for yourself. As a writer, you must remember that autobiography is public, not private. While it requires self-presentation, it does not require you to make unwanted self-disclosures. You choose the event to write about and decide how you will portray yourself.

As you work through this chapter, you will learn to tell a story that entertains readers and lets them know something important about how you came to be the person you are now. You also will learn to describe people and places vividly so that readers can see what makes them memorable for you. As you learn to write well about a remembered event, you will be practicing two of the most basic writing strategies —narration and description. These strategies can play a role in almost every kind of writing. As you will see in Chapters 4–10, narration and description can contribute to explanatory reports and persuasive arguments, in addition to playing an essential role in the remembered event assignment for this chapter.

You will encounter writing about a remembered event in many different contexts, as the following examples suggest.

Writing in Your Other Courses

- For an assignment in a psychology course, a student tests against her own experience an idea from the developmental psychologist Erik Erikson: "[Y]oung people . . . are sometimes preoccupied with what they appear to be in the eyes of others as compared with what they feel they are." The student recounted one event when she cared tremendously about what her peers thought about her.

Then she explained how her teammates' reactions influenced her feelings and sense of self.

- For a linguistics course, a student is asked to write about current research on men's and women's conversational styles. One researcher, Deborah Tannen, has reported that women and men have different expectations when they talk about problems. Women expect to spend a lot of time talking about the problem itself, especially about their feelings. Men, in contrast, typically want to cut short the analysis of the problem and the talk about feelings; they would rather discuss solutions to the problem. Applying Tannen's findings to her own experience, the student recounts a conversation about a family problem with her brother who is one year older. She reconstructs as much of the conversation as she can remember and explains which parts constitute feelings talk and which indicate problem-solving talk. She concludes that her conversation with her brother well illustrates Tannen's findings.

Writing in the Community

For more detail on the decisions these writers make about document design, see pp. 72–73.

- As part of a local history project in a small western ranching community, a college student volunteers to help an elderly rancher write about some of his early experiences. One experience seems especially dramatic and significant—a time in the winter of 1938 when a six-foot snowstorm isolated his family for nearly a month. The student tape-records the rancher talking about how he and his wife made preparations to survive and ensure the health of their infant sons and how he snowshoed eight miles to a logging train track, stopped the train, and gave the engineer a message to deliver to relatives in the nearest town explaining that they were going to be okay. On a second visit, the student and the rancher listen to the tape recording, and afterward talk about further details that might make the event more complete and dramatic for readers. The rancher then writes a draft of the remembered event and the student later helps him revise and edit the essay. The student copies an old snow-day photograph from the nearby town's newspaper files, and the rancher selects a photograph of his young family from a family photo album. The essay and photographs are published in a special supplement to the newspaper.

- To commemorate the retirement of the city's world-famous symphony orchestra conductor, a radio program director invites the conductor to talk about his early experiences with the orchestra. Aware of his tendency to ramble and digress in interviews, the conductor decides to write down a story about the first time he asked the orchestra members to play a never-before-performed modern composition noted for its lack of familiar tones, progressions, and rhythms. He describes how he tried to prepare the orchestra members for this experience and how they went about the hard, slow work of mastering the difficult music. The conductor expresses regret over posing this challenge so early in his experience of working with the orchestra members, but he proudly asserts that their great success with the music gave them the confidence to master any music they chose to play together. For the radio program, he alternates reading this remembered event aloud with playing brief recorded excerpts from the orchestra's polished performance.

Writing in the Workplace

- As part of an orientation manual for new employees, the founder of a highly successful computer software company describes the day she spent with the Silicon Valley venture capitalists who lent her the money to start the company. She describes how other venture capitalists had turned her down and how desperately anxious she was for this group to fund her company. The meeting had barely begun when she spilled her coffee across the top of the gleaming conference-room table. She describes some of the questions and her answers and traces her rising and falling hopes during the discussion. She left dejected and resigned to giving up the dream of founding her own company. The next morning a member of the group who had not asked any questions at the meeting phoned her to praise her proposal and announce that his group would fund her company. He invited her to a celebratory lunch with the group at the best restaurant in town, where she was careful not to spill her vodka martini served in a long-stemmed glass.

- In the highway department offices of a large upper-midwestern state, there have been sudden increases in violence and threats of violence. One worker has killed another, and several managers have been threatened. To keynote a statewide meeting of highway department managers seeking solutions to this problem, a manager writes a speech that includes a detailed description of an incident when he was confronted in his office by an employee unhappy about an overtime assignment. The employee came into the office without knocking and would not sit down. He talked loudly, waved his arms, and threatened to harm the manager and his family. He would not leave when asked to. The manager reflects on his fear and on his frustration about not knowing what to do when the employee finally left. The department's published procedures seemed not to apply to this case. He acknowledges his reluctance to report the incident to the state office because he did not want to appear to be ineffective and indecisive.

 The preceding scenarios suggest some occasions for writing about events in one's life. Think of an event in your life that you would feel comfortable describing to others in your class. The only requirements are that you remember the event well enough to tell the story and that the story lets your classmates learn something about you. Here are some guidelines to follow:

Practice Remembering an Event: A Collaborative Activity

Part 1. Consider several events and choose one you feel comfortable telling in this situation. Then, for two or three minutes, make notes about how you will tell your story.

Now, get together with two or three other students and take turns telling your stories. Be brief—each story should take only a few minutes.

Part 2. Take ten minutes or so to discuss what happened when you told about a remembered event:

- Tell each other how you chose your particular story. What did you think about when you were choosing an event? How did your purpose and audience—what you wanted your classmates to know and think about you—influence your choice?

- Review what each of you decided to include in your story. Did you plunge right into telling what happened, or did you first provide some background information? Did you decide to leave any of the action out of your story? If so, what did you leave out and why? Did you include a physical description of the scene? Did you describe any of the people, including yourself, or mention any specific dialogue? Did you tell your listeners how you felt at the time the event occurred or did you say how you feel now looking back on it?

- What was the easiest part of telling a story about a remembered event in your life? What was the most difficult part?

READINGS

The readings in this chapter illustrate the features of essays about remembered events and the strategies writers rely on to realize the features. No two essays in this genre are much alike, and yet they share defining features. The section Analyzing Writing Strategies and the Commentary following each reading touch on a few features best illustrated by that essay, capturing its special qualities and strengths. Together, the four essays cover many of the possibilities of the genre. Consequently, you will want to read as many of the essays as possible and, if time permits, complete the activities in Analyzing Writing Strategies and read the Commentaries. Following the readings is a section called Basic Features, which offers a concise description of the features of writing about remembered events and provides examples from all of the readings.

__Annie Dillard__ won the Pulitzer Prize for her very first book, Pilgrim at Tinker Creek *(1974). In that book, she describes herself as "no scientist," merely "a wanderer with a background in theology and a penchant for quirky facts." She has since written many other books, including collections of poetry, essays, and literary theory. Her most recent book,* For the Time Being *(1999), is a collection of essays. This selection comes from her autobiography,* An American Childhood *(1987).*

In "Handed My Own Life," we see the early stirrings of Dillard's lifelong enthusiasm for learning and fascination with nature. As you read her story, think about why she wrote it. What do you think she wants to tell readers about herself? What impression do you have of Annie Dillard from reading her story?

Handed My Own Life

Annie Dillard

1   After I read *The Field Book of Ponds and Streams* several times, I longed for a microscope. Everybody needed a microscope. Detectives used microscopes, both for the FBI and at Scotland Yard. Although usually I had to save my tiny allowance for things I wanted, that year for Christmas my parents gave me a microscope kit.

2   In a dark basement corner, on a white enamel table, I set up the microscope kit. I supplied a chair, a lamp, a batch of jars, a candle, and a pile of library books. The microscope kit supplied a blunt black three-speed microscope, a booklet, a scalpel, a dropper, an ingenious device for cutting thin segments of fragile tissue, a pile of clean slides and cover slips, and a dandy array of corked test tubes.

3   One of the test tubes contained "hay infusion." Hay infusion was a wee brown chip of grass blade. You added water to it, and after a week it became a jungle in a drop, full of one-celled animals. This did not work for me. All I saw in the microscope after a week was a wet chip of dried grass, much enlarged.

4   Another test tube contained "diatomaceous earth." This was, I believed, an actual pinch of the white cliffs of Dover. On my palm it was an airy, friable chalk. The booklet said it was composed of the siliceous bodies of diatoms—one-celled creatures that live in, as it were, small glass jewelry boxes with fitted lids. Diatoms, I read, come in a variety of transparent geometrical shapes. Broken and dead and dug out of geological deposits, they made chalk, and a fine abrasive used in silver polish and toothpaste. What I saw in the microscope must have been the fine abrasive—grit enlarged. It was years before I saw a recognizable, whole diatom. The kit's diatomaceous earth was a bust.

5   All that winter I played with the microscope. I prepared slides from things at hand, as the books suggested. I looked at the transparent membrane inside an onion's skin and saw the cells. I looked at a section of cork and saw the cells, and at scrapings from the inside of my cheek, ditto. I looked at my blood and saw not much; I looked at my urine and saw long iridescent crystals, for the drop had dried.

6   All this was very well, but I wanted to see the wildlife I had read about. I wanted especially to see the famous amoeba, who had eluded me. He was supposed to live in the hay infusion, but I hadn't found him there. He lived outside in warm ponds and streams, too, but I lived in Pittsburgh, and it had been a cold winter.

7   Finally, late that spring I saw an amoeba. The week before, I had gathered puddle water from Frick Park; it had been festering in a jar in the basement. This June night after dinner I figured I had waited long enough. In the basement at my microscope table I spread a scummy drop of Frick Park puddle water on a slide, peeked in, and lo, there was the famous amoeba. He was as blobby and grainy as his picture; I would have known him anywhere.

Before I had watched him at all, I ran upstairs. My parents were still at table, drinking coffee. They, too, could see the famous amoeba. I told them, bursting, that he was all set up, that they should hurry before his water dried. It was the chance of a lifetime. 8

Father had stretched out his long legs and was tilting back in his chair. Mother sat with her knees crossed, in blue slacks, smoking a Chesterfield. The dessert dishes were still on the table. My sisters were nowhere in evidence. It was a warm evening; the big dining-room windows gave onto blooming rhododendrons. 9

Mother regarded me warmly. She gave me to understand that she was glad I had found what I had been looking for, but that she and Father were happy to sit with their coffee, and would not be coming down. 10

She did not say, but I understood at once, that they had their pursuits (coffee?) and I had mine. She did not say, but I began to understand then, that you do what you do out of your private passion for the thing itself. 11

I had essentially been handed my own life. In subsequent years my parents would praise my drawings and poems, and supply me with books, art supplies, and sports equipment, and listen to my troubles and enthusiasms, and supervise my hours, and discuss and inform, but they would not get involved with my detective work, nor hear about my reading, nor inquire about my homework or term papers or exams, nor visit the salamanders I caught, nor listen to me play the piano, nor attend my field hockey games, nor fuss over my insect collection with me, or my poetry collection or stamp collection or rock collection. My days and nights were my own to plan and fill. 12

When I left the dining room that evening and started down the dark basement stairs, I had a life; I sat to my wonderful amoeba, and there he was, rolling his grains more slowly now, extending an arc of his edge for a foot and drawing himself along by that foot, and absorbing it again and rolling on. I gave him some more pond water. 13

I had hit pay dirt. For all I knew, there were paramecia, too, in that pond water, or daphniae, or stentors, or any of the many other creatures I had read about and never seen: volvox, the spherical algal colony; euglena with its one red eye; the elusive, glassy diatom; hydra, rotifers, water bears, worms. Anything was possible. The sky was the limit. 14

Connecting to Culture and Experience: Coming of Age

The story Dillard tells about her experience may be seen as a coming-of-age story. In many cultures around the world, a young person must undergo a rite of passage into adulthood, a coming-of-age experience that often attracts autobiographers. This experience usually tests the person's spiritual strength as well as physical prowess and know-how. The person must pass the test alone, without the help of friends or relatives. A coming-of-age story typically includes these rites-of-passage elements.

With other students in your class, find these elements in Dillard's essay. With these elements in mind, discuss why Dillard considers such an apparently trivial event important enough to write an essay about and pivotal enough to title "Handed My Own Life."

Analyzing Writing Strategies

1. At the beginning of this chapter, we make several assertions about remembered event essays. Consider which of these are true of Dillard's essay:
   - It tells an entertaining story.
   - It is vivid, letting readers see what makes the event as well as the people and places memorable for the writer.
   - It is purposeful, trying to give readers an understanding of why this particular event was significant in the writer's life.
   - It includes self-presentation but not unwanted self-disclosures.
   - It can lead readers to think in new ways about their own experiences or about how other people's lives differ from their own.

2. **Visual description**—naming objects and detailing their colors, shapes, sizes, and textures—is an important writing strategy in remembered event essays. To see how Dillard uses **naming** to present scenes and people, skim paragraphs 5–8, underlining the names of objects or people. These are nearly always nouns. To start, underline these names in the sentences of paragraph 5: *microscope, slides, books, membrane, skin, cells, cork, cells, scrapings, cheek, blood, urine, crystals,* and *drop.* To see how Dillard uses **detailing,** put brackets around all of the words and phrases that modify the nouns that name. Details help readers imagine more precisely and concretely the objects and people Dillard presents. To start, put brackets around these details in the sentences of paragraph 5: *transparent, onion's, from the inside of my cheek, long, iridescent, dried.*

   For more on describing strategies, see Chapter 15.

   Notice first how frequently naming and detailing occur in paragraphs 5–8. Notice also how many different kinds of objects and people are named. Then consider these questions: Does naming sometimes occur without any accompanying detailing? What do you think the naming contributes to this part of Dillard's essay? What do you think the detailing contributes?

   To learn more about naming and detailing, see Chapter 15, pp. 589–93.

Commentary: Organizing a Well-Told Story

"Handed My Own Life" is a well-told story. It provides a dramatic structure that arouses our curiosity, builds suspense, and completes the action.

From the very first sentence of Dillard's essay—"After I read *The Field Book of Ponds and Streams* several times, I longed for a microscope"—not only do we want to know what will happen, but we also want to know more about this girl who wants a microscope. We may not share her particular enthusiasm, but we can identify with her because we have all desired something as much as she "longed for" a microscope. Identification with the writer may get us to start reading, and our curiosity makes us want to continue reading. We wonder whether the girl will get the microscope and, if she does, what will happen.

In addition to arousing our curiosity, the search for the amoeba gives Dillard's story a simple structure, like that of a mystery.

For more on scratch outlining, see Chapter 12, p. 540.

We can see this simple narrative organization in the following paragraph-by-paragraph scratch outline:

1. Gives history of her desire to have a microscope and tells when she got one

2. Describes workplace and supplies

3. Tells of failed efforts to see one-celled animals in hay infusion

4. Tells of failed efforts to see diatoms—one-celled creatures—in diatomaceous earth

5. Summarizes what she saw or failed to see in microscope during the winter

6. Explains that what she wanted to see but failed repeatedly to find was the amoeba (the one-celled animal that lives in the hay infusion and elsewhere)

7. Announces that in late spring she saw the amoeba; tells what led up to her seeing the amoeba; describes the amoeba

8. Tells that as soon as she found the amoeba, she ran upstairs to tell her parents

9. Describes father and mother lounging after dinner

10. Summarizes what her mother said

11. Explains what she understood her mother to mean

12. Reflects on the significance of what she had learned from her mother by telling what happened in the years that followed this event

13. Returns to the time of the event to tell what she did that night—studied the amoeba and gave it pond water

14. Recalls looking forward to seeing many other creatures through the microscope

For more specific information on narrating events that take place over varying periods of time, see Chapter 14, pp. 573–79.

From the sample scratch outline, we can see that the story focuses on the evening when Dillard finally saw the elusive amoeba. This focus on a single brief incident is the hallmark of the remembered event essay. The entire essay, however, actually spans several months from before Christmas to late spring; but from these months Dillard includes only action and information that contribute to our understanding of why finding the amoeba was so significant. Her narrative follows a simple chronology, beginning some time before the amoeba sighting, pausing for the dramatic sighting of the amoeba and the significant interaction with her parents, and, at the conclusion, projecting into the future.

Considering Topics for Your Own Essay

List two or three occasions when you learned something important or made a significant discovery. Choose only occasions that, like Dillard's, focus on learning or discoveries that you can trace to one moment or brief time of unexpected insight.

Then choose one occasion that you would be interested in writing about for readers who do not know you. What would you want them to learn about you from reading your essay?

Tobias Wolff *is probably best known for his short stories and for a novel,* The Barracks Thief, *for which he won the 1985 PEN/Faulkner Award. Wolff has also written two autobiographical works,* In Pharaoh's Army *(1996) and* A Boy's Life *(1989), which was made into a movie in 1993 and from which "On Being a Real Westerner" comes. Reflecting on his writing process, Wolff has said that it is "part memory, part invention. I can no longer tell where one ends and the other begins. The very act of writing has transformed the original experience into another experience, more 'real' to me than what I started with."*

The story Wolff tells here is based on an actual experience that occurred when he was ten years old. He and his mother had just moved west from Florida to Salt Lake City, followed by Roy, his divorced mother's boyfriend. "Roy was handsome," Wolff writes, "in the conventional way that appeals to boys. He had a tattoo. He'd been to war and kept a silence about it that was full of heroic implication." As you read, notice how Wolff's storytelling skills help you imagine what happened.

On Being a Real Westerner
Tobias Wolff

Just after Easter Roy gave me the Winchester .22 rifle I'd learned to shoot with. It was a light, pump-action, beautifully balanced piece with a walnut stock black from all its oilings. Roy had carried it when he was a boy and it was still as good as new. Better than new. The action was silky from long use, and the wood of a quality no longer to be found. [1]

The gift did not come as a surprise. Roy was stingy, and slow to take a hint, but I'd put him under siege. I had my heart set on that rifle. A weapon was the first condition of self-sufficiency, and of being a real Westerner, and of all acceptable employment—trapping, riding herd, soldiering, law enforcement, and outlawry. I needed that rifle, for itself and for the way it completed me when I held it. [2]

My mother said I couldn't have it. Absolutely not. Roy took the rifle back but promised me he'd bring her around. He could not imagine anyone refusing him anything and treated the refusals he did encounter as perverse and insincere. Normally mute, he became at these times a relentless whiner. He would follow my mother from room to room, emitting one ceaseless note of complaint that was pitched perfectly to jelly her nerves and bring her to a state where she would agree to anything to make it stop. [3]

After a few days of this my mother caved in. She said I could have the rifle if, and only if, I promised never to take it out or even touch it except when she and Roy were with me. Okay, I said. Sure. Naturally. But even then she wasn't satisfied. She plain didn't like the fact of me owning a rifle. Roy said he had owned several rifles by the time he was my age, but this did not reassure her. She didn't think I could be trusted with it. Roy said now was the time to find out. [4]

For a week or so I kept my promises. But now that the weather had turned warm Roy was usually off somewhere and eventually, in the dead hours after school when I found myself alone in the apartment, I decided that there couldn't be any harm in taking the rifle out to clean it. Only to clean it, nothing more. I was sure it would be enough just to break it down, oil it, rub linseed into the stock, polish the octagonal barrel and then hold it up to the light to confirm the perfection of the bore. But it wasn't enough. From cleaning the rifle I went to marching around the apartment with it, and then to striking brave poses in front of the mirror. Roy had saved one of his army uniforms and I sometimes dressed up in this, together with martial-looking articles of hunting gear: fur trooper's hat, camouflage coat, boots that reached nearly to my knees.

The camouflage coat made me feel like a sniper, and before long I began to act like one. I set up a nest on the couch by the front window. I drew the shades to darken the apartment, and took up my position. Nudging the shade aside with the rifle barrel, I followed people in my sights as they walked or drove along the street. At first I made shooting sounds—kyoo! kyoo! Then I started cocking the hammer and letting it snap down.

Roy stored his ammunition in a metal box he kept hidden in the closet. As with everything else hidden in the apartment, I knew exactly where to find it. There was a layer of loose .22 rounds on the bottom of the box under shells of bigger caliber, dropped there by the handful the way men drop pennies on their dressers at night. I took some and put them in a hiding place of my own. With these I started loading up the rifle. Hammer cocked, a round in the chamber, finger resting lightly on the trigger, I drew a bead on whoever walked by—women pushing strollers, children, garbage collectors laughing and calling to each other, anyone—and as they passed under my window I sometimes had to bite my lip to keep from laughing in the ecstasy of my power over them, and at their absurd and innocent belief that they were safe.

But over time the innocence I laughed at began to irritate me. It was a peculiar kind of irritation. I saw it years later in men I served with, and felt it myself, when unarmed Vietnamese civilians talked back to us while we were herding them around. Power can be enjoyed only when it is recognized and feared. Fearlessness in those without power is maddening to those who have it.

One afternoon I pulled the trigger. I had been aiming at two old people, a man and a woman, who walked so slowly that by the time they turned the corner at the bottom of the hill my little store of self-control was exhausted. I had to shoot. I looked up and down the street. It was empty. Nothing moved but a pair of squirrels chasing each other back and forth on the telephone wires. I followed one in my sight. Finally it stopped for a moment and I fired. The squirrel dropped straight into the road. I pulled back into the shadows and waited for something to happen, sure that someone must have heard the shot or seen the squirrel fall. But the sound that was so loud to me probably seemed to our neighbors no more than the bang of a cupboard slammed shut. After a while I sneaked a glance into the street. The squirrel hadn't moved. It looked like a scarf someone had dropped.

When my mother got home from work I told her there was a dead squirrel in the street. Like me, she was an animal lover. She took a cellophane bag off a loaf of bread and we went outside and looked at the squirrel. "Poor little thing," she said. She stuck her hand in the wrapper and picked up the squirrel, then pulled the bag inside out away from her hand. We buried it behind our building under a cross made of popsicle sticks, and I blubbered the whole time.

I blubbered again in bed that night. At last I got out of bed and knelt down and did   11
an imitation of somebody praying, and then I did an imitation of somebody receiving divine reassurance and inspiration. I stopped crying. I smiled to myself and forced a feeling of warmth into my chest. Then I climbed back in bed and looked up at the ceiling with a blissful expression until I went to sleep.

For several days I stayed away from the apartment at times when I knew I'd be   12
alone there.

Though I avoided the apartment, I could not shake the idea that sooner or later I   13
would get the rifle out again. All my images of myself as I wished to be were images of myself armed. Because I did not know who I was, any image of myself, no matter how grotesque, had power over me. This much I understand now. But the man can give no help to the boy, not in this matter nor in those that follow. The boy moves always out of reach.

Connecting to Culture and Experience: Role Playing

Wolff shows us that he took great delight in playing the role of a soldier—looking at himself in the mirror dressed in camouflage and "striking brave poses." Another part of the attraction of playing soldier, he admits, is the sense of power he experienced. Still another part may have been that soldiers are generally considered heroes to many people in our culture and often serve as cultural role models, especially for young boys.

With other students in your class, discuss role playing and identity. Begin by telling one another one or two roles you liked to play when you were young. Then, discuss how you think you got the idea to play these particular roles and what attracted you to them. If you enjoyed dressing up and posing—either for yourself or for others—try to explain why doing so was pleasurable. How did your role playing make you feel—powerful, smart, talented, sophisticated, or some other feeling? Finally, discuss whether any of the roles you liked to play are typical role models in our society. What do you think children learn to value about themselves and about others when they play these particular roles?

Analyzing Writing Strategies

1. Writers convey the significance of autobiographical events by telling how they felt at the time the event occurred and by telling how they feel now as they look back on the event. Skim paragraphs 7, 8, and 13, noting where Wolff expresses his feelings and thoughts about the event. Try to distinguish between what he remembers thinking and feeling at the time and what he thinks and feels as he

looks back on the event. What impression do you get of the young Wolff? What does the adult Wolff seem to think about his younger self?

For more on specific narrative action, see Chapter 14, pp. 579–80.

2. Good stories show people in action—what we call **specific narrative action**—people moving or gesturing. Analyze paragraphs 7 and 9 by underlining the narrative actions and then putting brackets around the verb or verbal in each narrative action that specifically names the action. (A verbal is the *-ing* or *to* form of a verb: *laugh, laughing, to laugh*.) For example, here are the narrative actions (underlined) with their action verbs or verbals (in brackets) in paragraph 6: [set up] a nest, [drew] the shades, [took up] my position, [nudging] the shade aside, [followed] people, [walked] or [drove], [made shooting] sounds—kyoo! kyoo!, [started cocking] the hammer, [letting] it snap down.

Now that you have completed your analysis of paragraphs 7 and 9, how do you think specific narrative action contributes to autobiographical stories?

Commentary: Narrative Cueing in a Well-Told Story

This is a gripping story. One factor that makes it so dramatic is the subject: Putting a rifle in a child's hands immediately alerts readers to the possibility that something dreadful could happen. Thus the potential for suspense is great. But what makes the story so dramatic is Wolff's use of narrative strategies that move the action through time and help readers keep track of what happened.

If we look closely at Wolff's narration, we can see how two narrative strategies—**verb tense markers** and **temporal transitions**—create the impression of time passing. These strategies serve as cueing devices because, like road signs, they enable readers to follow the action. These cues indicate the order in which each action takes place as well as the duration of particular actions. Knowing the order is essential even when a narrative follows a simple chronology. But, as you will see, even a simple narrative like Wolff's interrupts the forward movement at certain points to present earlier or later actions.

For more on using verb tense markers as a narrating strategy, see Chapter 14, pp. 577–79.

Verb Tense Markers. Verb tenses signal when the action occurred—in the past, present, or future. Because remembered event essays tell about past events, most of the verbs are in the past tense. Looking at the verbs in Wolff's essay, we can find several different kinds of past tense signaled by the verb tense markers. In the first sentence of the essay, for example, Wolff shows an action that occurred at one point in the past (underlined) together with an action that was already completed (in brackets): "Just after Easter Roy gave me the Winchester .22 rifle [I'd learned to shoot] with." ("I'd learned" is a shortened form of "I had learned.") A second example shows an earlier action that was still going on (in brackets) when the more recent action occurred (underlined): "One afternoon I pulled the trigger. I [had been aiming] at two old people . . ." (paragraph 9).

Our final example is a little more complicated: "Roy took the rifle back but promised me [he'd bring] her around" (paragraph 3). This example presents three past actions. Whereas the first two actions (underlined) occurred at roughly the same time, the third (in brackets) predicts a future action that occurred after the first two actions were completed. (Here "he'd" is a short form of "he would," the past tense of "he will.")

You probably do not know the technical names for these tenses, nor do you need to know them. However, you do need to know what the different verb tenses mean and how to use them. In your remembered event essay, you will want to be sure that the verb tenses you use accurately indicate the time relations among various actions in your story.

Temporal Transitions.   In addition to using verb tense to show time, writers use transitions to move the narrative action forward in time and thereby keep readers oriented. Wolff uses many transitional words and phrases to locate an action at a particular point in time or to relate an action at one point in time to an action at another time. He uses four in the first paragraph alone: *just after, when, still,* and *no longer.* Time markers may appear at the beginning of a sentence or within a sentence. Notice how many paragraphs in Wolff's story include such a transition in the opening sentence: "Just after" (paragraph 1), "After a few days" (4), "For a week or so" (5), "before long" (6), "One afternoon" (9), "When" (10), "again" (11), and "For several days" (12). This extensive use of temporal transitions is not unusual in remembered event essays. You will want to use them liberally in your own essay to orient readers and propel your narrative through time.

For more on temporal relationships, see Chapter 13, pp. 568–69, and Chapter 14, pp. 576–77.

Considering Topics for Your Own Essay

In this selection, Wolff describes experiencing what he calls the "ecstasy of my power" to inflict harm on others (paragraph 7). Try to recall two or three incidents when you were in a position to exercise power over another person or when you were subject to someone else's power. You may have been in such relationships for long periods of time, but select only those relationships that can be well illustrated by one key incident that occurred within a day or two. Pick one such incident. Think about how you would present it, explaining what you did and how you felt.

Rick Bragg, a domestic correspondent for the New York Times, *lives in Atlanta, Georgia. Before coming to the* Times, *he reported for the* Los Angeles Times, St. Petersburg Times, *(as Miami bureau chief),* Birmingham News, *and* Anniston (Alabama) Star. *He has received the Pulitzer Prize for his* New York Times *feature writing as well as the American Society of Newspaper Editors' Distinguished Writing Award. From 1992 to 1993, Bragg was a Nieman Fellow at Harvard University. He has also taught writing at Harvard, Boston University, and the University of South Florida. This reading is from Bragg's autobiography of his small-town Alabama upbringing in a poor family,* All Over but the Shoutin' *(1997), a best-seller and a New York Times Notable Book of the Year.*

As you read, notice how the metaphor of the slingshot in the opening sentence anticipates what happens in the rest of the reading.

100 Miles per Hour, Upside Down and Sideways

Rick Bragg

Since I was a boy I have searched for ways to slingshot myself into the distance, faster and faster. When you turn the key on a car built for speed, when you hear that car rumble like an approaching storm and feel the steering wheel tremble in your hands from all that power barely under control, you feel like you can run away from anything, like you can turn your whole life into an insignificant speck in the rearview mirror.

In the summer of 1976, the summer before my senior year at Jacksonville High School, I had the mother of all slingshots. She was a 1969 General Motors convertible muscle car with a 350 V-8 and a Holley four-barreled carburetor as long as my arm. She got about six miles to the gallon, downhill, and when you started her up she sounded like Judgment Day. She was long and low and vicious, a mad dog cyclone with orange houndstooth interior and an eight-track tape player, and looked fast just sitting in the yard under a pine tree. I owned just one tape, that I remember, *The Eagles' Greatest Hits*.

I worked two summers in the hell and heat at minimum wage to earn enough money to buy her and still had to borrow money from my uncle Ed, who got her for just nineteen hundred dollars mainly because he paid in hundred-dollar bills. "You better be careful, boy," he told me. "That'un will kill you." I assured him that, Yes, Sir, I would creep around in it like an old woman.

I tell myself I loved that car because she was so pretty and so fast and because I loved to rumble between the rows of pines with the blond hair of some girl who had yet to discover she was better than me whipping in the breeze. But the truth is I loved her because she was my equalizer. She raised me up, at least in my own eyes, closer to where I wanted and needed to be. In high school, I was neither extremely popular nor one of the great number of want-to-bes. I was invited to parties with the popular kids, I had dates with pretty girls. But there was always a distance there, of my own making, usually.

That car, in a purely superficial way, closed it. People crowded around her at the Hardee's. I let only one person drive her, Patrice Curry, the prettiest girl in school, for exactly one mile.

That first weekend, I raced her across the long, wide parking lot of the TG&Y, an insane thing to do, seeing as how a police car could have cruised by at any minute. It was a test of nerves as well as speed, because you actually had to be slowing down, not speeding up, as you neared the finish line, because you just ran out of parking lot. I beat Lyn Johnson's Plymouth and had to slam on my brakes and swing her hard around, to keep from jumping the curb, the road and plowing into the parking lot of the Sonic Drive-In.

It would have lasted longer, this upraised standing, if I had pampered her. I guess I should have spent more time looking at her than racing her, but I had too much of the Bragg side of the family in me for that. I would roll her out on some lonely country road late at night, the top down, and blister down the blacktop until I knew the tires were about to lift off the ground. But they never did. She held the road, somehow, until I ran out of road or just lost my nerve. It was as if there was no limit to her, at how fast we could go, together.

It lasted two weeks from the day I bought her. 8

On Saturday night, late, I pulled up to the last red light in town on my way home. 9
Kyle Smith pulled up beside me in a loud-running Chevrolet, and raced his engine. I did not squall out when the light changed—she was not that kind of car—but let her rpm's build, build and build, like winding up a top.

I was passing a hundred miles per hour as I neared a long sweeping turn on High- 10
way 21 when I saw, coming toward me, the blue lights of the town's police. I cannot really remember what happened next. I just remember mashing the gas pedal down hard, halfway through that sweeping turn, and the sickening feeling as the car just seemed to lift and twist in the air, until I was doing a hundred miles per hour still, but upside down and sideways.

She landed across a ditch, on her top. If she had not hit the ditch in just the right 11
way, the police later said, it would have cut my head off. I did not have on my seat belt. We never did, then. Instead of flinging me out, though, the centrifugal force—I had taken science in ninth grade—somehow held me in.

Instead of lying broken and bleeding on the ground beside my car, or headless, I 12
just sat there, upside down. I always pulled the adjustable steering wheel down low, an inch or less above my thighs, and that held me in place, my head covered with mud and broken glass. The radio was still blaring—it was the Eagles' "The Long Run," I believe—and I tried to find the knob in the dark to turn it off. Funny. There I was in an upside-down car, smelling the gas as it ran out of the tank, listening to the tick, tick, tick of the hot engine, thinking: "I sure do hope that gas don't get nowhere near that hot manifold," but all I did about it was try to turn down the radio.

I knew the police had arrived because I could hear them talking. Finally, I felt a hand 13
on my collar. A state trooper dragged me out and dragged me up the side of the ditch and into the collective glare of the most headlights I had ever seen. There were police cars and ambulances and traffic backed up, it seemed, all the way to Piedmont.

"The Lord was riding with you, son," the trooper said. "You should be dead." 14

My momma stood off to one side, stunned. Finally the police let her through to look 15
me over, up and down. But except for the glass in my hair and a sore neck, I was fine. Thankfully, I was too old for her to go cut a hickory and stripe my legs with it, but I am sure it crossed her mind.

The trooper and the Jacksonville police had a private talk off to one side, trying to 16
decide whether or not to put me in prison for the rest of my life. Finally, they informed my momma that I had suffered enough, to take me home. As we drove away, I looked back over my shoulder as the wrecker dragged my car out of the ditch and, with the help of several strong men, flipped it back over, right-side up. It looked like a white sheet of paper someone had crumpled up and tossed in the ditch from a passing car.

"The Lord was riding with that boy," Carliss Slaughts, the wrecker operator, told my 17
uncle Ed. With so many people saying that, I thought the front page of the *Anniston Star* the next day would read: LORD RIDES WITH BOY, WRECKS ANYWAY.

> I was famous for a while. No one, no one, flips a convertible at a hundred miles per   18
> hour, without a seat belt on, and walks away, undamaged. People said I had a charmed
> life. My momma, like the trooper and Mr. Slaughts, just figured God was my copilot.
>
> The craftsmen at Slaughts' Body Shop put her back together, over four months. My   19
> uncle Ed loaned me the money to fix her, and took it out of my check. The body and
> fender man made her pretty again, but she was never the same. She was fast but not
> real fast, as if some little part of her was still broken deep inside. Finally, someone
> backed into her in the parking lot of the Piggly Wiggly, and I was so disgusted I sold her
> for fourteen hundred dollars to a preacher's son, who drove the speed limit.

Connecting to Culture and Experience: Social Status

Bragg worked hard and saved his money for two years when he was a teenager in high school in order to buy the convertible. Probably he had several motives for doing so; but after he started driving the car, he came to think of it as "my equalizer" that "closed" the distance between the most popular students and himself and gave him immediate "upraised standing."

With other students, discuss this concern with standing or status in high school. Was it a concern of yours personally? If not, speculate about the reasons. If so, what did you try to do, if anything, to raise your status? Why do you think you made this effort? How did other students you knew well respond to the concern about status? Does this concern with status seem to you to be realistic preparation for college and life after college, or does it strike you as a distortion of typical adult human relationships?

Analyzing Writing Strategies

For more on comparing strategies, including similes and metaphors, see Chapter 15, p. 593.

1. One important strategy used for describing people, places, and objects in autobiographical writing is **comparing**—using similes and metaphors to help readers imagine what happened. Similes are explicit comparisons. For example, in paragraph 1, Bragg writes, "you hear that car rumble like an approaching storm." As in this example, the word *like* or *as* introduces a simile. Metaphors are implied comparisons. For example, Bragg opens his essay by writing, "Since I was a boy I have searched for ways to slingshot myself into the distance, faster and faster." Here he implies a comparison between himself and a stone launched from a handheld slingshot; the stone speeds into space as Bragg hopes to speed into the future, to get to any place other than the place he is in now.

   There are several comparisons in paragraph 1 and one each in paragraphs 3, 7, 9, 13, and 16. Locate and underline the comparisons in these paragraphs. Which one is most vivid for you—that is, most helps you imagine the events Bragg describes? For you as one reader, what do the comparisons as a group add to this particular essay? They should not, of course, be merely decorative but highly substantive and functional. Comparisons are not a requirement of successful remembered event essays, but they can contribute to readers' experience.

2. To learn more about how Bragg tells his story, begin by marking off the three main parts of the essay: the context (paragraphs 1–8), the incident (paragraphs 9–16), and the conclusion (paragraphs 17–19). Notice how much time passes in each main section. How does the context prepare you for the incident, and does it do so adequately? What are the particular elements of the conclusion, and how do they help bring the story to a satisfactory close?

In the central incident (paragraphs 9–16), the defining element of a remembered event essay, Bragg narrates a compelling story. To understand more fully how Bragg organizes the incident, make a paragraph scratch outline of it. Does the order of events make sense? Are there further details you need to know in order to follow easily what happens? What does Bragg do to arouse your curiosity and build suspense?

For an example of a paragraph scratch outline, turn to the Commentary following Annie Dillard's essay on p. 29. For more information on scratch outlining, see Chapter 12, p. 540.

Commentary: Autobiographical Significance

Bragg's essay illustrates the two main ways writers convey the autobiographical significance of a remembered event: showing and telling. Bragg shows the event's significance through details and action. For example, he shows us how the car raised his status by describing its power and imposing appearance and the blond-haired girls he took for rides in it. He shows the importance of the car by recounting how terribly hard he worked to buy it and then to have it repaired after the wreck. He reveals perhaps his resigned acceptance that the car would not change his life by selling it decisively when it was dented in a parking lot. The least Bragg must do to succeed is to show consistently through details and action what the remembered event meant to him. This showing of significance, sometimes referred to as **creating a dominant impression,** gives readers a consistent impression throughout the essay of what the autobiographical significance might be.

For more on creating a dominant impression, see Chapter 15, p. 599.

Bragg also tells readers what he believes the autobiographical significance might be, and he does so in two ways: by telling his remembered thoughts and feelings from the time of the event as well as by giving his present perspective on the event.

Bragg's remembered thoughts and feelings frame his essay. In the first paragraph, he remembers thinking that owning a powerful car makes "you feel like you can run away from anything, like you can turn your whole life into an insignificant speck in the rearview mirror." In the final paragraphs, he remembers his temporary fame for surviving the accident and his disgust when someone damaged his car in a parking lot. These remembered thoughts and feelings reveal perhaps a change of values, from materialism to some yet-to-be-defined values, from Bragg's relying on a car for status to his parting with it readily for far less money than he had invested in it.

Bragg's present perspectives on this remembered event occur in paragraphs 4–7, between the time he bought the car and had the accident. From his perspective in his mid-thirties, as he was writing *All Over but the Shoutin',* Bragg writes, "I tell myself I loved that car because she was so pretty and so fast. . . . But the truth is I loved her because she was my equalizer." He now recognizes, "It would have lasted longer, this upraised standing, if I had pampered her. . . . [B]ut I had too much of the Bragg side of the family in me for that." He also acknowledges that racing in the parking lot was "an insane thing to do." Although Bragg devotes relatively little space in the essay to telling us what he believes the significance of the incident to be, he balances his remembered thoughts and feelings with his present perspectives.

Considering Topics for Your Own Essay

Bragg has focused on a particular incident that tells us something about himself both as an adolescent and as the man he would become by his mid-thirties. Think of incidents early in your life (before you were 11 or 12 years old) that are particularly revealing about you, both as a child and as a person of your present age. You might try to think of incidents that tested or challenged you, or incidents in which you behaved either typically or atypically in relation to the way you remember yourself to have been or think of yourself now. Perhaps you experienced a dreadful disappointment or an unexpected delight. Perhaps you were in danger or you accomplished something you now think you were unprepared for.

Jean Brandt wrote this essay as a first-year college student. In it she tells about a memorable event that occurred when she was thirteen. Reflecting on how she felt at the time, Brandt writes, "I was afraid, embarrassed, worried, mad." As you read, look for places where these tumultuous and contradictory remembered feelings are expressed.

Calling Home
Jean Brandt

As we all piled into the car, I knew it was going to be a fabulous day. My grandmother was visiting for the holidays; and she and I, along with my older brother and sister, Louis and Susan, were setting off for a day of last-minute Christmas shopping. On the way to the mall, we sang Christmas carols, chattered, and laughed. With Christmas only two days away, we were caught up with holiday spirit. I felt light-headed and full of joy. I loved shopping—especially at Christmas.

The shopping center was swarming with frantic last-minute shoppers like ourselves. We went first to the General Store, my favorite. It carried mostly knickknacks and other useless items which nobody needs but buys anyway. I was thirteen years old at the time, and things like buttons and calendars and posters would catch my fancy. This day was no different. The object of my desire was a 75-cent Snoopy button. Snoopy was the latest. If you owned anything with the Peanuts on it, you were "in." But since I was supposed to be shopping for gifts for other people and not myself, I couldn't decide what to do. I went in search of my sister for her opinion. I pushed my way through throngs of people to the back of the store where I found Susan. I asked her if she thought I should buy the button. She said it was cute and if I wanted it to go ahead and buy it.

When I got back to the Snoopy section, I took one look at the lines at the cashiers   3
and knew I didn't want to wait thirty minutes to buy an item worth less than one dollar.
I walked back to the basket where I found the button and was about to drop it when
suddenly, instead, I took a quick glance around, assured myself no one could see, and
slipped the button into the pocket of my sweatshirt. I hesitated for a moment, but once
the item was in my pocket, there was no turning back. I had never before stolen anything; but what was done was done. A few seconds later, my sister appeared and asked,
"So, did you decide to buy the button?"

"No, I guess not." I hoped my voice didn't quaver. As we headed for the entrance,   4
my heart began to race. I just had to get out of that store. Only a few more yards to go
and I'd be safe. As we crossed the threshold, I heaved a sigh of relief. I was home free.
I thought about how sly I had been and I felt proud of my accomplishment.

An unexpected tap on my shoulder startled me. I whirled around to find a middle-   5
aged man, dressed in street clothes, flashing some type of badge and politely asking me
to empty my pockets. Where did this man come from? How did he know? I was so sure
that no one had seen me! On the verge of panicking, I told myself that all I had to do was
give this man his button back, say I was sorry, and go on my way. After all, it was only
a 75-cent item.

Next thing I knew, he was talking about calling the police and having me arrested   6
and thrown in jail, as if he had just nabbed a professional thief instead of a terrified kid.
I couldn't believe what he was saying.

"Jean, what's going on?"   7

The sound of my sister's voice eased the pressure a bit. She always managed to   8
get me out of trouble. She would come through this time too.

"Excuse me. Are you a relative of this young girl?"   9

"Yes, I'm her sister. What's the problem?"   10

"Well, I just caught her shoplifting and I'm afraid I'll have to call the police."   11

"What did she take?"   12

"This button."   13

"A button? You are having a thirteen-year-old arrested for stealing a button?"   14

"I'm sorry, but she broke the law."   15

The man led us through the store and into an office, where we waited for the police   16
officers to arrive. Susan had found my grandmother and brother, who, still shocked,
didn't say a word. The thought of going to jail terrified me, not because of jail itself, but
because of the encounter with my parents afterward. Not more than ten minutes later,
two officers arrived and placed me under arrest. They said that I was to be taken to the
station alone. Then, they handcuffed me and led me out of the store. I felt alone and
scared. I had counted on my sister being with me, but now I had to muster up the
courage to face this ordeal all by myself.

As the officers led me through the mall, I sensed a hundred pairs of eyes staring at   17
me. My face flushed and I broke out in a sweat. Now everyone knew I was a criminal.
In their eyes I was a juvenile delinquent, and thank God the cops were getting me off the
streets. The worst part was thinking my grandmother might be having the same
thoughts. The humiliation at that moment was overwhelming. I felt like Hester Prynne
being put on public display for everyone to ridicule.

That short walk through the mall seemed to take hours. But once we reached the 18
squad car, time raced by. I was read my rights and questioned. We were at the police
station within minutes. Everything happened so fast I didn't have a chance to feel
remorse for my crime. Instead, I viewed what was happening to me as if it were a movie.
Being searched, although embarrassing, somehow seemed to be exciting. All the
movies and television programs I had seen were actually coming to life. This is what it
was really like. But why were criminals always portrayed as frightened and regretful? I
was having fun. I thought I had nothing to fear—until I was allowed my one phone call.
I was trembling as I dialed home. I didn't know what I was going to say to my parents,
especially my mother.

"Hi, Dad, this is Jean." 19

"We've been waiting for you to call." 20

"Did Susie tell you what happened?" 21

"Yeah, but we haven't told your mother. I think you should tell her what you did and 22
where you are."

"You mean she doesn't even know where I am?" 23

"No, I want you to explain it to her." 24

There was a pause as he called my mother to the phone. For the first time that 25
night, I was close to tears. I wished I had never stolen that stupid pin. I wanted to give
the phone to one of the officers because I was too ashamed to tell my mother the truth,
but I had no choice.

"Jean, where are you?" 26

"I'm, umm, in jail." 27

"Why? What for?" 28

"Shoplifting." 29

"Oh no, Jean. Why? Why did you do it?" 30

"I don't know. No reason. I just did it." 31

"I don't understand. What did you take? Why did you do it? You had plenty of money 32
with you."

"I know but I just did it. I can't explain why. Mom, I'm sorry." 33

"I'm afraid sorry isn't enough. I'm horribly disappointed in you." 34

Long after we got off the phone, while I sat in an empty jail cell, waiting for my 35
parents to pick me up, I could still distinctly hear the disappointment and hurt in my
mother's voice. I cried. The tears weren't for me but for her and the pain I had put her
through. I felt like a terrible human being. I would rather have stayed in jail than confront
my mom right then. I dreaded each passing minute that brought our encounter closer.
When the officer came to release me, I hesitated, actually not wanting to leave. We went
to the front desk, where I had to sign a form to retrieve my belongings. I saw my parents
a few yards away and my heart raced. A large knot formed in my stomach. I fought back
the tears.

Not a word was spoken as we walked to the car. Slowly, I sank into the back seat 36
anticipating the scolding. Expecting harsh tones, I was relieved to hear almost the opposite from my father.

"I'm not going to punish you and I'll tell you why. Although I think what you did was   37
wrong, I think what the police did was more wrong. There's no excuse for locking a
thirteen-year-old behind bars. That doesn't mean I condone what you did, but I think
you've been punished enough already."

As I looked from my father's eyes to my mother's, I knew this ordeal was over.   38
Although it would never be forgotten, the incident was not mentioned again.

Connecting to Culture and Experience: Shame

In paragraph 17, Brandt gives us a vivid portrait of how excruciating the feeling of
shame can be: "I sensed a hundred pairs of eyes staring at me. My face flushed and I
broke out in a sweat." Shame, as this description indicates, involves a desire for the
community's approval or a dread of its disapproval. (The words *shame* and *guilt* are
often used interchangeably, but they have different connotations: *Shame* involves
anxiety about social acceptance, whereas *guilt* is a more private, inward-looking emotion associated with morality.)

Identify one occasion when you felt ashamed. With other students, take turns
briefly explaining what happened and why you were ashamed. In whose eyes did you
feel the most shame? (Note that Brandt, for example, feels shame at being thought
of as a criminal by strangers in the shopping mall, but she feels even more ashamed
with her grandmother and perhaps most ashamed with her mother.)

Analyzing Writing Strategies

1. Reread the essay, paying particular attention to Brandt's use of dialogue—reconstructed conversation from the time of the event. What do you learn about the
   author from what she says and how she says it? What do you learn about her relationship with her parents?

2. The story begins and ends in a car, with the two car rides framing the story.
   Framing, a narrative device, echoes something from the beginning in the ending.
   Review what happens in each car ride. The writer assumes you might think of the
   beginning as you are reading the ending. What effect might this awareness have
   on your response to the ending car ride?

3. The Writer at Work section on pp. 66–73 includes some of Brandt's invention
   notes and her complete first draft. These materials show how her focus shifts
   gradually from the theft and subsequent arrest in her first draft to her emotional
   confrontation with her parents in the final version.

   Read over her notes and first draft, and then comment on this shift in focus.
   Why do you think Brandt decides to stress her confrontation with her parents?
   Why do you think she decides, against the advice of the student who commented
   on her draft, to cut the scenes in the police car and station? Notice, in particular,

For more on dialogue, see
Chapter 14, pp. 580–81.

that she leaves out of the final version the vivid image of herself handcuffed to the table (see p. 71, paragraph 5).

Commentary: A Vivid Presentation of Places and People

For more on dialogue, see Chapter 14, pp. 580–81.

To present the people involved in the event and especially to dramatize her relationship with her parents, Brandt depends on **dialogue.** We can see from her use of dialogue the two ways writers typically present remembered conversations: quoting and summarizing. Compare the two examples that follow. In the first example, Brandt quotes a brief exchange between herself and her sister as they were leaving the store (paragraphs 3 and 4):

> A few seconds later, my sister appeared and asked, "So, did you decide to buy the button?"
> "No, I guess not." I hoped my voice didn't quaver.

In this second example, Brandt summarizes what the store manager said to her as she left the store (paragraphs 5 and 6):

> An unexpected tap on my shoulder startled me. I whirled around to find a middle-aged man, dressed in street clothes, flashing some type of badge and politely asking me to empty my pockets. . . .
> Next thing I knew, he was talking about calling the police and having me arrested. . . .

As these examples indicate, writers usually summarize rather than quote when they need to give only the gist of what was said. Brandt apparently decides that the manager's actual words and way of speaking are not important for her purpose. However, presenting her response to her sister's question is important because it shows how she felt at the time. When you write a remembered event essay, you too will have to decide what to summarize and what to quote in light of your overall purpose.

While we are looking at Brandt's quoted dialogue, you should note a few of the conventions readers expect writers to follow when quoting dialogue. Use quotation marks for quoted dialogue but not for summarized dialogue. If you include one or two exact words in a summarized dialogue and want to call attention to the fact that they were actually spoken, put quotes only around those particular words. Indicate each change of speaker with a new paragraph. Put a concluding period, question mark, or exclamation point that is part of the quotation inside the quotation marks; otherwise, place it after the closing quotation marks. Do not conclude a sentence with one punctuation mark inside the quotation marks and a second one outside the marks.

Considering Topics for Your Own Essay

Think of a few occasions when you did something uncharacteristic. Perhaps you acted on impulse or took a chance you would not ordinarily take. The events do not have to be reckless, dangerous, or illegal; they could be quite harmless or even pleasant.

Pick one occasion you might like to write about. What would you want your readers to recognize about you on the basis of reading your story?

■ PURPOSE AND AUDIENCE

Writers have various reasons for writing about their experiences. Reminiscing makes it possible for writers to relive moments of pleasure and pain, but it also helps them gain insight, to learn who they are now by examining who they used to be and the forces that shaped them. Reflecting on the past can lead a writer to significant self-discovery. Nevertheless, writing about personal experience is public, not private. The autobiographer writes to be read and is therefore as much concerned with self-presentation as with self-discovery. Writers present themselves to readers in the way they want to be perceived. The rest they keep hidden, though readers may read between the lines.

We read about others' experiences for much the same reason that we write about our own—to learn how to live our lives. Reading autobiography can validate our sense of ourselves, particularly when we see our own experience reflected in another's life. Reading about others' lives can also challenge our complacency and help us appreciate other points of view. It can enlarge our sympathies by awakening our humanity. When we read about other people's lives, we are invited to empathize with their values and feelings and thus break the shell of our own isolation.

A Well-Told Story

An essay about a remembered event should tell an interesting story. Whatever else the writer may attempt to do, he or she must shape the experience into a story that is entertaining and memorable. This is done primarily by building suspense, leading readers to wonder, for example, whether Tobias Wolff will shoot the rifle or Jean Brandt will get caught for shoplifting. The principal technique for propelling the narrative and heightening suspense is specific narrative action with its action verbs and their tense markers. Suspense increases, for instance, when Wolff gives a detailed close-up of his play with the rifle. In addition, writers use time markers or temporal transitions to cue readers and move the narrative through time, as when Rick Bragg begins paragraphs with "In the summer of 1976," "That first weekend," and "On Saturday night." Finally, writers often use dialogue to convey immediacy and drama, as Brandt does to dramatize her confrontation with her mother on the phone.

A Vivid Presentation of Places and People

Instead of giving a generalized impression, skillful writers attempt to re-create the place where the event occurred and let us hear what people say. Vivid language and specific details make the writing memorable. By moving in close, a writer can name specific objects at a place, such as when Brandt catalogs the store's knickknacks, calendars, and buttons. A writer may also provide details about some of the objects, as when Brandt describes the coveted "75-cent Snoopy button." Finally, writers use similes and metaphors to draw comparisons and thereby help readers understand the point. For example, when Brandt says she felt "like Hester Prynne being put on public display," readers familiar with *The Scarlet Letter* can imagine how embarrassed Brandt must have felt.

To present people who played an important role in a remembered event, autobiographers often provide some descriptive details and a snatch of dialogue. They may detail the person's appearance, as Annie Dillard does by describing her mother sitting "with her knees crossed, in blue slacks, smoking a Chesterfield." Dialogue can be an especially effective way of giving readers a vivid impression of someone. Wolff, for example, describes his mother by combining specific narrative actions with her empathetic words: "She took a cellophane bag off a loaf of bread and we went outside and looked at the squirrel. 'Poor little thing,' she said. She stuck her hand in the wrapper and picked up the squirrel, then pulled the bag inside out away from her hand."

An Indication of the Event's Significance

There are two ways a writer can communicate an event's autobiographical significance: by showing us that the event was important or by telling us directly what it meant. Most writers do both. Showing is necessary because the event must be dramatized for readers to appreciate its importance and understand the writer's feelings about it. Seeing the important scenes and people from the writer's point of view naturally leads readers to identify with the writer. We can well imagine what that "unexpected tap on [the] shoulder" must have felt like for Brandt, how Dillard felt running upstairs to tell her parents about her great discovery, and what Bragg was thinking as he hung upside down in his overturned car.

Telling also contributes to a reader's understanding, so most writers comment on the event's meaning and importance. Readers expect to understand the significance of the event, but they do not expect the essay to begin with the kind of thesis statement typical of argumentative writing. Instead, as the story moves along, writers tell us how they felt at the time or how they feel now as they look back on the experience. Often writers do both. Wolff, for example, tells us some of his remembered feelings when he recalls feeling "like a sniper" and delighting in the "ecstasy" of power. He also tells us what he thinks looking back on the experience: "Because I did not know who I was, any image of myself, no matter how grotesque, had power over me. This much I understand now." Telling is the main way that writers interpret the event for readers, but skillful writers are careful not to append these reflections artificially, like a moral tagged on to a fable.

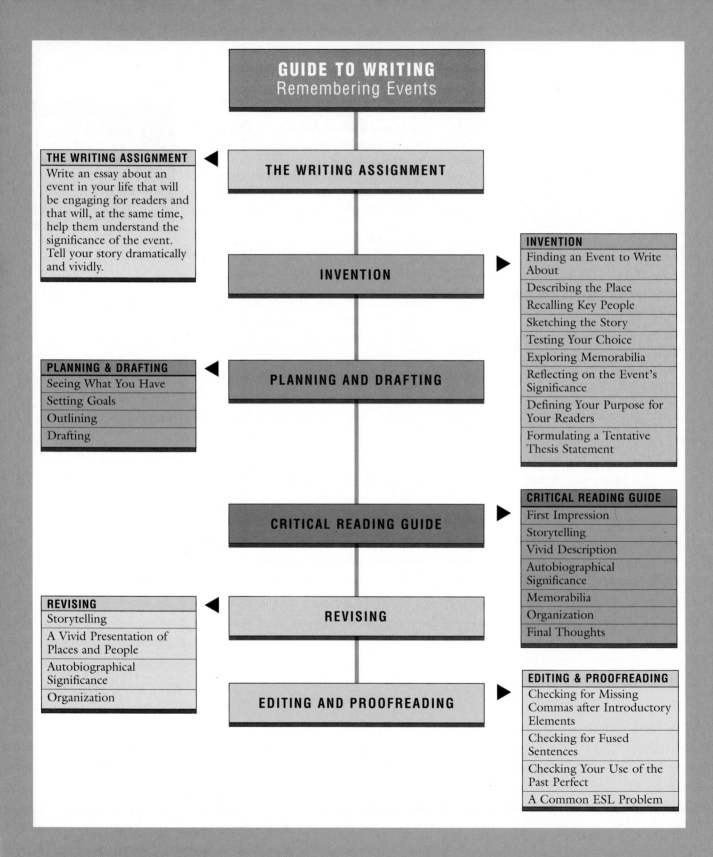

GUIDE TO WRITING
Remembering Events

THE WRITING ASSIGNMENT

Write an essay about an event in your life that will be engaging for readers and that will, at the same time, help them understand the significance of the event. Tell your story dramatically and vividly.

THE WRITING ASSIGNMENT

INVENTION

INVENTION

Finding an Event to Write About

Describing the Place

Recalling Key People

Sketching the Story

Testing Your Choice

Exploring Memorabilia

Reflecting on the Event's Significance

Defining Your Purpose for Your Readers

Formulating a Tentative Thesis Statement

PLANNING & DRAFTING

Seeing What You Have

Setting Goals

Outlining

Drafting

PLANNING AND DRAFTING

CRITICAL READING GUIDE

CRITICAL READING GUIDE

First Impression

Storytelling

Vivid Description

Autobiographical Significance

Memorabilia

Organization

Final Thoughts

REVISING

Storytelling

A Vivid Presentation of Places and People

Autobiographical Significance

Organization

REVISING

EDITING AND PROOFREADING

EDITING & PROOFREADING

Checking for Missing Commas after Introductory Elements

Checking for Fused Sentences

Checking Your Use of the Past Perfect

A Common ESL Problem

▓ THE WRITING ASSIGNMENT

Write an essay about an event in your life that will be engaging for readers and that will, at the same time, help them understand the significance of the event. Tell your story dramatically and vividly.

▓ INVENTION

The following invention activities will help you choose an appropriate event, recall specific details, sketch out the story, test your choice, and explore the event's auto-biographical significance. Each activity is easy to do and takes only a few minutes. If you can spread out the activities over several days, it will be easier for you to recall details and to reflect deeply on the event's meaning in your life. Keep a written record of your invention work to use when you draft the essay and later when you revise it.

Finding an Event to Write About

To find the best possible event to write about, consider several possibilities rather than choosing the first event that comes to mind.

Listing Remembered Events. *Make a list of significant events from your past.* Include only those events about which you can recall details, people, and activities. Begin your list now and add to it over the next few days. Include possibilities suggested by the Considering Topics for Your Own Essay activities following each reading in this chapter. Make your list as complete as you can. The following categories may give you some more ideas:

- An occasion when you realized you had a special skill, ambition, or problem

- A time when you became aware of injustice, selflessness, heroism, sexism, racism

- A difficult situation, such as when you had to make a tough choice, when someone you admired let you down (or you let someone else down), or when you struggled to learn or understand something hard

- An occasion when things did not turn out as expected, such as when you expected to be praised but were criticized or ignored, or when you were convinced you would fail but succeeded

- An incident charged with strong emotion, such as love, fear, anger, embarrassment, guilt, frustration, hurt, pride, happiness, or joy

- An incident that you find yourself thinking about frequently or occasionally or one you know you will never forget

Listing Events Related to Identity and Community. Whenever you write about events in your life, you are likely to reveal important aspects of your sense of identity and your relationships with others. The suggestions that follow, however, will help you recall events that are particularly revealing of your efforts to know yourself and to discover your place in the communities to which you belong.

- An event that shaped you in a particular way or revealed an aspect of your personality you had not seen before, such as your independence, insecurity, ambitiousness, or jealousy
- An incident that made you reexamine one of your basic values or beliefs, such as when you were expected to do something that went against your better judgment or when your values conflicted with someone else's values
- An occasion when others' actions led you to consider seriously a new idea or point of view
- An incident that made you feel the need to identify yourself with a particular community, such as an ethnic group, a political or religious group, or a group of co-workers
- An event that made you realize that the role you were playing did not conform to what was expected of you as a student, as a male or female, as a parent or sibling, as a believer in a particular religious faith, or as a member of a particular community
- An incident in which a single encounter with another person changed the way you view yourself or changed your ideas about how you fit into a particular community

Listing Events Related to Work and Career. The following suggestions will help you think of events involving your work experiences as well as your career aspirations.

- An event that made you aware of your capacity for or interest in a particular kind of work or career, or an event that convinced you that you were not cut out for a particular kind of work or career
- An incident of harassment or mistreatment at work
- An event that revealed to you other people's assumptions, attitudes, or prejudices about you as a worker, your fitness for a particular job, or your career goals
- An incident of conflict or serious misunderstanding with a customer, fellow employee, supervisor, or someone you supervised

Choosing an Event. *Look over your list of possibilities and choose one event that you think will make an interesting story.* You should be eager to explore the significance of the event and comfortable about sharing the event with your instructors and classmates, who will be your first readers. You may find the choice easy to make, or you may have several equally promising possibilities from which to choose.

It may help you in choosing an event if you tentatively identify your ultimate readers, the people with whom you most want to share the story. They could include, for example, your personal friends, members of your family, people you work with, members of a group with which you identify or of an organization to which you belong, your classmates, an instructor, or even the public at large.

Make the best choice you can now. If this event does not work out, you can try a different one later.

Describing the Place

The following activities will help you decide which places are important to your story and what you remember about them. Take the time now to explore your memory and imagination. This exploration will yield descriptive language you can use in your essay.

Listing Key Places. *Make a list of all the places where the event occurred, skipping a few lines after each entry on your list.* Your event may have occurred in one or more places. For now, list all the places you remember without worrying about whether they should be included in your story.

Describing Key Places. *In the space after each entry on your list, make some notes describing each place.* As you remember each place, what do you see (excluding people for the moment)? What objects stand out? Are they large or small, green or brown, square or oblong? What sounds do you hear? Do you detect any smells? Does any taste come to mind? Do you recall anything soft or hard, smooth or rough?

Recalling Key People

These activities will help you remember the people who played a role in the event—what they looked like, did, and said.

Listing Key People. *List the people who played more than a casual role in the event.* You may have only one person to list or you may have several.

Describing Key People. *Write a brief description of the people who played major roles in the event.* For each person, name and detail a few distinctive physical features or items of dress. Describe the person's way of talking or gesturing.

Re-Creating Conversations. *Reconstruct any important conversations you had during the event.* Also try to recall any especially memorable comments, any unusual choice of words, or any telling remarks that you made or were made to you. You may not remember exactly what was said during an entire conversation, but try to re-create it so that readers will be able to imagine what was going on.

Sketching the Story

Write for a few minutes, telling what happened. You may find it easier to outline what happened rather than writing complete sentences and paragraphs. Any way you can put the main action on paper is fine. Over the next few days you may want to add to this rough sketch.

Testing Your Choice

Now you need to decide whether you recall enough detail to write a good story about this particular event. Reread your invention notes to see whether your initial memories seem promising. If you can recall clearly what happened and what the important scenes and people were like, then you have probably made a good choice. If at any point you lose confidence in your choice, return to your list and choose another event.

Testing Your Choice: A Collaborative Activity

At this point, you will find it useful to get together with two or three other students to try out your story. Their reactions to your story will help you determine whether you have chosen an event you can present in an interesting way.

> *Storytellers:* Take turns telling your story briefly. Try to make your story dramatic (by piquing your listeners' curiosity and building suspense) and vivid (by briefly describing the place and key people).

> *Listeners:* Briefly tell each storyteller what you found most intriguing about the story. For example, were you eager to know how the story would turn out? Were you curious about any of the people? Were you able to identify with the story-teller? Could you imagine the place? Could you understand why the event is so memorable and significant for the storyteller?

Exploring Memorabilia

For an illustration of memorabilia in a remembered event essay and for suggestions for choosing and placing memorabilia in your writing, turn to the box on pp. 72–73.

Memorabilia are visual images, sounds, and objects that can help you remember details and understand the significance of an event. Examples include photographs, newspaper or magazine clippings, recordings of popular music, souvenirs, medals or trophies, and even items not necessarily designated as mementoes (restaurant menus and movie, theater, or concert stubs). *If you can easily obtain access to relevant memorabilia, take time to do so now. Add to your invention notes any details about the period, places, or people the memorabilia suggest. Consider using one or more pieces of memorabilia in your essay.*

Reflecting on the Event's Significance

You should now feel fairly confident that you can tell an interesting story about the event you have chosen. The following activities will help you understand the meaning the event holds in your life and develop ways to convey this significance to your readers.

Recalling Your Remembered Feelings and Thoughts. *Write for a few minutes about your feelings and thoughts during and immediately after the event.* The following questions may help stimulate your memory:

- What were my expectations before the event?
- What was my first reaction to the event as it was happening and right after it ended?
- How did I show my feelings? What did I say?
- What did I want the people involved to think of me? Why did I care what they thought of me?
- What did I think of myself at the time?
- How long did these initial feelings last?
- What were the immediate consequences of the event for me personally?

Pause now to reread what you have written. *Then write another sentence or two about the event's significance at the time it occurred.*

Exploring Your Present Perspective. *Write for a few minutes about your current feelings and thoughts as you look back on the event.* These questions may help you get started:

- Looking back, how do I feel about this event? If I understand it differently now than I did then, what is the difference?
- What do my actions at the time of the event say about the kind of person I was then? How would I respond to the same event if it occurred today?
- Can looking at the event historically or culturally help explain what happened? For example, did I upset gender expectations? Did I feel torn between two cultures or ethnic identities? Did I feel out of place?
- Do I now see that there was a conflict underlying the event? For example, did I struggle with contradictory desires within myself? Did I feel pressured by others or by society in general? Were my desires and rights in conflict with someone else's? Was the event about power or responsibility?

Pause now to reflect on what you have written about your present perspective. *Then write another sentence or two, commenting on the event's significance as you look back on it.*

Defining Your Purpose for Your Readers

Write a few sentences, defining your purpose in writing about this particular event for your readers. Use these questions to focus your thoughts:

- Who are my readers? (Remember that in choosing an event, you considered several possible readers: your personal friends, members of your family, people you work with, members of a group with which you identify or of an organization to which you belong, your classmates, an instructor, even the public at large.)
- What do my readers know about me?
- What do my readers expect when they read autobiography?
- How do I expect my readers to understand or react to the event?
- How do I want my readers to feel about what happened? What is the dominant impression or mood I want my story to create?
- What specifically do I want my readers to think of me? What do I expect or fear they might think?

It is unlikely, but you may decide at this point that you feel uncomfortable disclosing this event. If so, choose another event to write about.

Formulating a Tentative Thesis Statement

Review what you wrote for Reflecting on the Event's Significance and add another two or three sentences, not necessarily summarizing what you already have written but extending your insights into the significance of the event, what it meant to you at the time, and what it means now. These sentences must necessarily be speculative and tentative because you may never fully understand the event's significance in your life.

Keep in mind that readers do not expect you to begin your essay with the kind of explicit thesis statement typical of argumentative or explanatory writing. If you do decide to tell readers explicitly why the event was meaningful or significant, you will most likely do so as you tell the story, by commenting on or evaluating what happened, instead of announcing it at the beginning. Keep in mind that you are not obliged to tell readers the significance, but you should show it through the way you tell the story.

■ PLANNING AND DRAFTING

This section will help you review your invention writing and get started on your first draft.

Seeing What You Have

You have now done a lot of thinking and writing about the basic elements of a remembered event essay: what happened, where it happened, who was involved, what was said, and how you felt. You have also begun to develop your understanding of why the event is so important to you. Reread what you have written so far to see what you have. Watch for specific narrative actions, vivid descriptive details, choice bits of dialogue. Note also any language that resonates with feeling or that seems especially insightful. Highlight any writing you think could be used in your draft. Then ask yourself the following questions:

- Do I remember enough specific details about the event to describe it vividly?
- Do I understand how the event was significant to me?
- Does my invention material provide what I need to convey that significance to my readers?
- Does my present perspective on this event seem clear to me?
- Does the dominant impression I want to create in my essay seem relevant?

If you find little that seems promising, you are not likely to be able to write a good draft. Consider starting over with another event.

If, however, your invention writing offers some promising material, the following activities may help you develop more:

- To remember more of what actually happened, discuss the event with someone who was there or who remembers having heard about it at the time.
- To recall additional details about a person who played an important role in the event, look at any available photographs or letters, talk with the person, or talk with someone who remembers the person. If that is impossible, you might imagine having a conversation with the person today about the event: What would you say? How do you think the person would respond?
- To remember how you felt at the time of the event, try to recall what else was happening in your life during that period. What music, television shows, movies, sports, books, and magazines did you like? What concerns did you have at home, school, work, play?
- To develop your present perspective on the event, try viewing your experience as a historical event. If you were writing a news story or documentary about the event, what would you want people to know?
- To decide on the dominant impression you want your story to have on readers, imagine that you are making a film based on this event. What would your film look like? What mood or atmosphere would you try to create? Alternatively, imagine writing a song or poem about the event. Think of an appropriate image or refrain. What kind of song would you write—blues, hip-hop, country, ranchera, rock?

Setting Goals

Before starting to draft, set goals that will help you make decisions and solve problems as you draft and revise. Here are some questions that will help you set your goals:

Your Purpose and Readers

- What do I want my readers to think of me and my experience? Should I tell them how I felt and what I thought at the time of the event? Should I tell them how my perspective has changed, as Bragg does?

- If my readers are likely to have had a similar experience, how can I convey the uniqueness of my experience or its special importance in my life? Should I tell them more about my background or the particular context of the event, as Bragg does? Should I give them a glimpse, as Dillard does, of its impact years later?

- If my readers are not likely to have had a similar experience, how can I help them understand what happened and appreciate its importance? Should I reveal the cultural influences acting on me, as Wolff and Bragg do?

The Beginning

- What can I do in the opening sentences to arouse readers' curiosity? Should I begin with a surprising announcement, as Dillard and Wolff do, or should I establish the setting and situation, as Brandt does?

- How can I get my readers to identify with me? Should I tell them a few things about myself, as Bragg does?

- Should I do something unusual, such as begin in the middle of the action or with a funny bit of dialogue?

The Story

For more on narrative structure, see Chapter 14.

- What should be the climax of my story, the point readers anticipate with trepidation or eagerness?

- What specific narrative actions or dialogue would intensify the drama of the story?

- Should I follow strict chronological order? Or would flashback (referring to an event that occurred earlier) or flashforward (referring to an event that will occur later) make the narrative more interesting?

- How can I use vivid descriptive detail to dramatize the story?

The Ending

- If I conclude with some reflections on the meaning of the experience, how can I avoid tagging on a moral or being too sentimental?

- If I want readers to think well of me, should I conclude with a philosophical statement, as Wolff does? Should I be satirical? Should I be self-critical to avoid seeming smug?

- If I want to underscore the event's continuing significance in my life, can I show that the conflict was never fully resolved, as Brandt does? Could I contrast my remembered and current feelings and thoughts?

- Should I frame the essay by echoing something from the beginning to give readers at least a superficial sense of closure, as Brandt does by setting the last scene, like the first, in a car?

Outlining

The goals you have set should help you draft your essay, but first you might want to make a quick scratch outline to refocus on the basic story line. List the main actions in order. You could also note on your outline where you plan to describe the place, introduce particular people, present dialogue, and insert remembered or current feelings and thoughts. Use this outline to guide your drafting, but do not feel tied to it. As you draft, you may find a better way to sequence the action and integrate these features.

For an example of a paragraph scratch outline, turn to the Commentary following Annie Dillard's essay on p. 29. For more information on scratch outlining, see Chapter 12, p. 540.

Drafting

Start drafting your essay, keeping in mind the goals you have set for yourself, especially the goal of telling the story dramatically. Refer to your outline to help you sequence the action. If you get stuck while drafting, either make a note of what you need to fill in later or see if you can use something from your invention writing.

As you read over your first draft, you may see places where you can add new material to make the story dramatic. Or you may even decide that after this first draft you can finally see the story you want to write and set out to do so in a second draft.

Now is the time to get a good critical reading of your draft. Your instructor may schedule readings of drafts as part of your coursework. If not, ask a classmate, friend, or family member to read your draft. You could also seek comments from a tutor at your campus writing center. The guidelines in this section can be used by *anyone* reviewing an essay about a remembered event. (If you are unable to have someone read your draft, turn ahead to the Revising section, where you will find guidelines for reading your own draft critically.)

■ CRITICAL
READING
GUIDE

▶ **If You Are the Writer.** In order to provide focused, helpful comments, your reader must know your essay's intended audience, your purpose, and a problem in the draft that you need help solving. Briefly write out this information at the top of your draft.

- *Readers.* Identify the intended readers of your essay.
- *Purpose.* What do you hope to achieve in writing this remembered event essay? What features of your story do you hope will most interest readers? What do you want to disclose about yourself?

- *Problem.* Ask your reader to help you solve the single most important problem with your draft. Describe this problem briefly.

▶ **If You Are the Reader.**   Use the following guidelines to help you give critical comments to others on remembered event essays.

1. *Read for a First Impression.* Begin by reading the draft quickly, to enjoy the story and to get a sense of its significance. Then, in just a few sentences, describe your first impression. If you have any insights about the meaning or importance of the event, share your thoughts.

   Next, consider the problem the writer identified. If the problem will be covered by one of the other questions listed here, deal with it there. Otherwise, respond to the writer's concerns now.

2. *Analyze the Effectiveness of the Storytelling.* Review the story, looking at the way the suspense builds and resolves itself. Point to any places where the drama loses intensity—perhaps where the suspense slackens, where specific narrative action is sparse or action verbs are needed, where narrative transitions would help readers, or where dialogue could be added to dramatize people's interactions.

3. *Consider How Vividly the Places and People Are Described.* Point to any descriptive details, similes, or metaphors that are especially effective. Note any places or people that need more specific description. Also indicate any descriptive details that seem unnecessary. Identify any quoted dialogue that might be summarized instead or any dialogue that does not seem relevant.

4. *Assess Whether the Autobiographical Significance Is Clear.* Explain briefly what you think makes this event significant for the writer. Point out any places in the draft where the significance might seem to the intended readers so overstated as to be sentimental or so understated as to be insignificant. If the event lacks significance, speculate about what you think the significance could be. Then point to one place in the draft where you think the significance could be brought forth by telling the story more fully or dramatically or by stating the significance.

5. *Assess the Use of Memorabilia.* If the writer makes use of memorabilia, evaluate how successfully each item is used. How is it relevant? Does it seem integrated into the event or merely appended? Is it placed in the most appropriate location? Does it make a meaningful contribution to the essay?

6. *Analyze the Effectiveness of the Organization.* Consider the *overall plan*, perhaps by making a scratch outline. Pay special attention to narrative transitions and verb tense markers so that you can identify any places where the order of the action is unclear. Also indicate any places where you think the description or background information interrupts the action. If you can, suggest other locations for this material.

- Look at the *beginning*. If it does not arouse curiosity, point to language elsewhere in the essay that might serve as a better opening—for example, a bit of dialogue, a striking image, or a remembered feeling.
- Look at the *ending*. Indicate whether the conflict in the story is too neatly resolved at the end, whether the writer has tagged on a moral, or whether the essay abruptly stops without really coming to a conclusion. If there is a problem with the ending, try to suggest an alternative ending, such as framing the story with a reference to something from the beginning or projecting into the future.

7. *Give the Writer Your Final Thoughts.* What is the draft's strongest part? What part is most in need of further work?

REVISING

Now you have the opportunity to revise your essay. Your instructor or other students may have given you advice. You may have begun to realize that your draft requires not so much revising as rethinking. For example, you may recognize that the story you told is not the story you meant to tell. Or maybe you realize only now why the incident is important to you. Consequently, you may need to reshape your story radically or draft a new version of it, instead of working to improve the various parts of your first draft. Many students—and professional writers—find themselves in this situation. Often a writer produces a draft or two and gets advice on them from others and only then begins to see what might be achieved.

However, if instead you feel satisfied that your draft achieves what you set out to do, you can focus on refining the various parts of it. Very likely you have thought of ways to improve your draft, and you may even have begun revising it. This section will help you get an overview of your draft and revise it accordingly.

Getting an Overview

Consider the draft as a whole, following these two steps:

1. *Reread.* If at all possible, put the draft aside for a day or two. When you do reread it, start by reconsidering your purpose. Then read the draft straight through, trying to see it as your intended readers will.

2. *Outline.* Make a quick scratch outline.

Charting a Plan for Revision.   Once you have an overview of your draft, you may want to make a double-column chart to keep track of any problems you need to solve. In the left-hand column, list the basic features of writing about remembered

Turn to pp. 48–49 to review the basic features.

events. As you analyze your draft and study any comments received from others, note the problems you want to solve in the right-hand column. Here is an example:

Basic Features	*Problems to Solve*
A well-told story	
A vivid presentation of places and people	
An indication of the event's significance	
The organization	

Analyzing the Basic Features of Your Own Draft.   Turn to the Critical Reading Guide on the preceding pages. Using this guide, identify problems you now see in your draft. Note the problems on your chart.

Studying Critical Comments.   Review all of the comments you have received from other readers. For each comment, refer to the draft to see what might have led the reader to make that particular point. Try to be objective about any criticism. Ideally, these comments will help you to see your draft as others see it (rather than as you hoped it would be) and to identify specific problems.

Carrying Out Revisions

Having identified problems in your draft, you now need to figure out solutions and—most important—to carry them out. Basically, there are three ways to find solutions:

1. Review your invention and planning notes for material you can add to your draft.
2. Do additional invention writing to provide material you or your readers think is needed.
3. Look back at the readings in this chapter to see how other writers have solved similar problems.

The following suggestions, which are organized according to the basic features on your revision chart, will get you started solving some common writing problems.

A Well-Told Story

- ***Is the climax difficult to identify?*** Check to be sure your story has a climax. Perhaps it is the point when you get what you were striving for (Dillard), when you do what you were afraid you might do (Wolff), when something frightening happens (Bragg), or when you get caught (Brandt). If you cannot find a climax in your story or reconstruct your story so that it has one, then you may have a major problem. If this is the case, you should discuss with your instructor the possibility of starting over with another event.

- ***Does the suspense slacken instead of building to the climax?*** Try showing people moving or gesturing, adding narrative transitions to propel the action, or substituting quoted dialogue for summarized dialogue.

A Vivid Presentation of Places and People

- ***Do any places or people need more specific description?*** Try naming objects and adding sensory details to help readers imagine what the objects look, feel, smell, taste, or sound like. For people, describe a physical feature or mannerism that shows the role the person plays in your story.

- ***Does any dialogue seem irrelevant or poorly written?*** Eliminate any unnecessary dialogue or summarize quoted dialogue that has no distinctive language or dramatic purpose. Liven up quoted dialogue with faster repartee to make it more dramatic. Instead of introducing each comment with the dialogue cue "he said," describe the speaker's attitude or personality with phrases like "she gasped" or "he jokingly replied."

- ***Do any descriptions weaken the dominant impression?*** Omit extraneous details or reconsider the impression you want to make. Add similes and metaphors that strengthen the dominant impression you want your story to have.

- ***Do readers question any visuals you used?*** Might you move a visual to a more appropriate place? Could you make clear the relevance of a visual by mentioning it in your text? Consider replacing an ineffective visual with a more appropriate one.

An Indication of the Event's Significance

- ***Are readers getting a different image of you from the one you want to make?*** Look closely at the language you use to express your feelings and thoughts. If you project an aspect of yourself you did not intend to, reconsider what the story reveals about you. Ask yourself again why the event stands out in your memory. What do you want readers to know about you from reading this essay?

- ***Are your remembered or current feelings and thoughts about the event coming across clearly and eloquently?*** If not, look in your invention writing for more expressive language. If your writing seems too sentimental, try to express your feelings more directly and simply. Let yourself show ambivalence or uncertainty.

- ***Do readers appreciate the event's uniqueness or special importance in your life?*** If not, consider giving them more insight into your background or cultural heritage. Also consider whether they need to know what has happened since the event took place to appreciate why it is so memorable for you.

The Organization

- ***Is the overall plan ineffective or the story hard to follow?*** Look carefully at the way the action unfolds. Fill in any gaps. Eliminate unnecessary digressions. Add or clarify narrative transitions. Fix confusing verb tense markers.

- *Does description or other information disrupt the flow of the narrative?* Try integrating this material by adding smoother transitions. Or consider removing the disruptive parts or placing them elsewhere.

- *Is the beginning weak?* See whether there is a better way to start. Review the draft and your notes for an image, a bit of dialogue, or a remembered feeling that might catch readers' attention or spark their curiosity.

- *Does the ending work?* If not, think about a better way to end—with a memorable image, perhaps, or a provocative assertion. Consider whether you can frame the essay by referring back to something in the beginning.

■ EDITING AND PROOFREADING

Now is the time to check your revised draft for errors in grammar, punctuation, and mechanics and to consider matters of style. Our research has identified several errors that occur often in essays about remembered events: missing commas after introductory elements, fused sentences, and misused past-perfect verbs. The following guidelines will help you check your essay for these common errors.

Checking for Missing Commas after Introductory Elements. Introductory elements in a sentence can be words, phrases, or clauses. A comma tells readers that the introductory information is ending and the main part of the sentence is about to begin. If there is no danger of misreading, you can omit the comma after single words or short phrases or clauses, but you will never be wrong to include the comma. Remembered event essays require introductory elements, especially those showing time passing. The following sentences, taken from drafts written by college students using this book, show several ways to edit introductory sentence elements:

▶ **Through the nine-day run of the play⌃ the acting just kept getting better and better.**

▶ **Knowing that the struggle was over⌃ I felt through my jacket to find tea bags and cookies the robber had taken from the kitchen.**

▶ **As I stepped out of the car⌃ I knew something was wrong.**

Checking for Fused Sentences. Fused sentences occur when two independent clauses are joined with no punctuation or connecting word between them. When you write about a remembered event, you try to re-create a scene. In so doing, you might write a fused sentence like this one:

Sleet glazed the windshield the wipers were frozen stuck.

There are several ways to edit fused sentences:

- Make the clauses separate sentences.

  The
  ► Sleet glazed the windshield⊙~~the~~ wipers were frozen stuck.

- Join the two clauses with a comma and *and, but, or, nor, for, so,* or *yet.*

  ⌃ and
  ► Sleet glazed the windshield the wipers were frozen stuck.

- Join the two clauses with a semicolon.

  ► Sleet glazed the windshield⸴ the wipers were frozen stuck.

- Rewrite the sentence, subordinating one clause.

  As sleet   became
  ► ~~Sleet~~ glazed the windshield⸴ the wipers ~~were~~ frozen stuck.

Checking Your Use of the Past Perfect.   Verb tenses indicate the time an action takes place. As a writer, you will generally use the present tense for actions occurring at the time you are writing (we *see*), the past tense for actions completed in the past (we *saw*), and the future tense for actions that will occur in the future (we *will see*). When you write about a remembered event, you will often need to use various forms of the past tense: the past perfect to indicate an action that was completed at the time of another past action (she *had finished* her work when we saw her) and the past progressive to indicate a continuing action in the past (she *was finishing* her work). One common problem in writing about a remembered event is the failure to use the past perfect when it is needed. For example:

  had
► I had three people in the car, something my father told me not to do on

  several occasions.

In the following sentence, the meaning is not clear without the past perfect:

  had run
► Coach Kernow told me I ~~ran~~ faster than ever before.

A Common ESL Problem.   It is important to remember that the past perfect is formed with *had* followed by a past participle. Past participles usually end in *-ed, -d, -en, -n,* or *-t: worked, hoped, eaten, taken, bent.*

  spoken
► Before Tania went to Moscow last year, she had not really ~~speak~~ Russian.

A WRITER AT WORK

■ FROM INVENTION TO DRAFT TO REVISION

In this section, we look at the writing process that Jean Brandt follows in composing her essay, "Calling Home." You will see some of her invention writing and her complete first draft, which you can then compare to the final draft printed on pp. 42–45.

Invention

Brandt's invention work produced about nine handwritten pages, but it took her only two hours, spread out over four days, to complete. Here is a selection of her invention writings. She begins by choosing an event and then recalling specific sensory details of the scene and the other people involved. She writes two dialogues, one with her sister Sue and the other with her father. Following is the one with her sister:

Re-Creating Conversations

SUE: Jean, why did you do it?

ME: I don't know. I guess I didn't want to wait in that long line. Sue, what am I going to tell Mom and Dad?

SUE: Don't worry about that yet, the detective might not really call the police.

ME: I can't believe I was stupid enough to take it.

SUE: I know. I've been there before. Now when he comes back try crying and act like you're really upset. Tell him how sorry you are and that it was the first time you ever stole something but make sure you cry. It got me off the hook once.

ME: I don't think I can force myself to cry. I'm not really that upset. I don't think the shock's worn off. I'm more worried about Mom.

SUE: Who knows? Maybe she won't have to find out.

ME: God, I hope not. Hey, where's Louie and Grandma? Grandma doesn't know about this, does she?

SUE: No, I sort of told Lou what was going on so he's just taking Grandma around shopping.

ME: Isn't she wondering where we are?

SUE: I told him to tell her we would meet them in an hour.

```
ME:  How am I ever going to face her? Mom and Dad might possi-
     bly understand or at least get over it, but Grandma? This
     is gonna kill her.
SUE: Don't worry about that right now. Here comes the detec-
     tive. Now try to look like you're sorry. Try to cry.
```

This dialogue helps Brandt to recall an important conversation with her sister. Dialogues are an especially useful form of invention, for they enable writers to remember their feelings and thoughts.

Brandt writes this dialogue quickly, trying to capture the language of excited talk, keeping the exchanges brief. She includes a version of this dialogue in her second draft but excludes it from her revision. The dialogue with her father does not appear in any of her drafts. Even though she eventually decides to feature other completely different conversations, these invention dialogues enable her to evaluate how various conversations would work in her essay.

Next, Brandt makes her first attempt to bring the autobiographical significance of the event into focus. She explores her remembered as well as her current feelings and thoughts about the experience:

```
Being arrested for shoplifting was significant because it
changed some of my basic attitudes. Since that night I've
never again considered stealing anything. This event would
reveal how my attitude toward the law and other people has
changed from disrespectful to very respectful.
```

Brandt begins by stating tentatively that the importance of the event was the lesson it taught her. Reading this statement might lead us to expect a moralistic story of how someone learned something the hard way. As we look at the subsequent invention activities and watch the draft develop, however, we will see how her focus shifts to her relations with other people.

Recalling Remembered Feelings and Thoughts

```
     I was scared, humiliated, and confused. I was terrified
when I realized what was happening. I can still see the man-
ager and his badge and remember what I felt when I knew who he
was. I just couldn't believe it. I didn't want to run. I felt
there wasn't anything I could do--I was afraid, embarrassed,
worried, mad that it happened. I didn't show my feelings at
all. I tried to look very calm on the outside, but inside I
was extremely nervous. The nervousness might have come through
in my voice a little. I wanted the people around me to think
```

```
I was tough and that I could handle the situation. I was
really disappointed with myself. Getting arrested made me
realize how wrong my actions were. I felt very ashamed. After-
ward I had to talk to my father about it. I didn't say much
of anything except that I was wrong and I was sorry. The
immediate consequence was being taken to jail and then later
having to call my parents and tell them what happened. I hated
to call my parents. That was the hardest part. I remember how
much I dreaded that. My mom was really hurt.
```

Brandt's exploration of her first reaction is quite successful. Naming specific feelings, she focuses on the difference between what she felt and how she acted. She remembers her humiliation at being arrested as well as the terrible moment when she had to tell her parents. As we will see, this concern with her parents' reaction, more than her own humiliation, becomes the focus of her remembered feelings and thoughts.

In exploring her first response to the event, Brandt writes quickly, jotting down memories as they come to mind. Next, she rereads this first exploration and attempts to state briefly what the incident really reveals about her:

```
I think it reveals that I was not a hard-core criminal.
I was trying to live up to Robin Files's (supposedly my best
girlfriend) expectations, even though I actually knew that
what I was doing was wrong.
```

Stopping to focus her thoughts like this helps Brandt see the point of what she has just written in her longer pieces of exploratory writing. Specifically, it helps her connect diverse invention writings to her main concern: discovering the autobiographical significance of the event. She reflects on what her remembered feelings of the event reveal about the kind of person she was at the time: not a hard-core criminal. She identifies a friend, who will disappear from the writing after one brief mention. Next, she looks at her present perspective on the event.

Exploring Present Perspectives

```
At first I was ashamed to tell anyone that I had been
arrested. It was as if I couldn't admit it myself. Now I'm
glad it happened, because who knows where I'd be now if I
hadn't been caught. I still don't tell many people about it.
Never before have I written about it. I think my response was
appropriate. If I'd broken down and cried, it wouldn't have
helped me any, so it's better that I reacted calmly. My
actions and responses show that I was trying to be tough. I
thought that that was the way to gain respectability. If I
```

```
were to get arrested now (of course it wouldn't be for
shoplifting), I think I'd react the same way because it
doesn't do any good to get emotional. My current feelings are
ones of appreciation. I feel lucky because I was set straight
early. Now I can look back on it and laugh, but at the same
time know how serious it was. I am emotionally distant
now because I can view the event objectively rather than
subjectively. My feelings are settled now. I don't get upset
thinking about it. I don't feel angry at the manager or the
police. I think I was more upset about my parents than about
what was happening to me. After the first part of it was over
I mainly worried about what my parents would think.
```

By writing about her present perspective, Brandt reassures herself that she feels comfortable enough to write for class about this event. Having achieved a degree of emotional distance, she no longer feels humiliated, embarrassed, or angry. Reassessing her reaction at the time, she is obviously pleased to recall that she did not lose control and show her true feelings. Staying calm, not getting emotional, looking tough—these are the personal qualities Brandt wants others to see in her. Exploring her present perspective seems to have led to a new, "respectable" self-image she can proudly display to her readers:

```
      My present perspective shows that I'm a reasonable
person. I can admit when I'm wrong and accept the punishment
that was due me. I find that I can be concerned about others
even when I'm in trouble.
```

Next, Brandt reflects on what she has written in order to express the meaning of the event for her.

Defining the Event's Autobiographical Significance

```
      The event was important because it entirely changed one
aspect of my character. I will be disclosing that I was once a
thief, and I think many of my readers will be able to identify
with my story, even though they won't admit it.
```

After the first set of invention work, completed in about forty-five minutes on two separate days, Brandt is confident she has chosen an event with personal significance. She knows what she will be disclosing about herself and feels comfortable doing it. In her brief focusing statements she begins by moralizing ("my attitude . . . changed") and blaming others (Robin Files) but concludes by acknowledging what she did. She is now prepared to disclose it to readers ("I was once a thief"). Also, she thinks readers will like her story because she suspects many of them will recall doing something illegal and feeling guilty about it, even if they never got caught.

The First Draft

The day after completing the invention writing, Brandt reviews her invention and writes her first draft. It takes her about an hour to write the draft, which is handwritten and contains few erasures or other changes, indicating that she writes steadily. She knows this will not be her only draft.

Before you read Brandt's first draft, reread the final draft, "Calling Home," in the Readings section of this chapter. Then, as you read the first draft, consider what part it plays in the total writing process.

It was two days before Christmas and my older sister and brother, my grandmother, and I were rushing around doing last-minute shopping. After going to a few stores we decided to go to Lakewood Center shopping mall. It was packed with other frantic shoppers like ourselves from one end to the other. The first store we went to (the first and last for me) was the General Store. The General Store is your typical gift shop. They mainly have the cutesy knick-knacks, posters, frames and that sort. The store is decorated to resemble an old-time western general store but the appearance doesn't quite come off.

We were all browsing around and I saw a basket of buttons so I went to see what the different ones were. One of the first ones I noticed was a Snoopy button. I'm not sure what it said on it, something funny I'm sure and besides I was in love with anything Snoopy when I was 13. I took it out of the basket and showed it to my sister and she said "Why don't you buy it?" I thought about it but the lines at the cashiers were outrageous and I didn't think it was worth it for a 75 cent item. Instead I figured just take it and I did. I thought I was so sly about it. I casually slipped it into my pocket and assumed I was home free since no one pounced on me. Everyone was ready to leave this shop so we made our way through the crowds to the entrance.

My grandmother and sister were ahead of my brother and I. They were almost to the entrance of May Co. and we were about 5 to 10 yards behind when I felt this tap on my shoulder. I turned around already terror struck, and this man was flashing

1

2

3

some kind of badge in my face. It happened so fast I didn't
know what was going on. Louie finally noticed I wasn't with
him and came back for me. Jack explained I was being arrested
for shoplifting and if my parents were here then Louie should
go find them. Louie ran to get Susie and told her about it
but kept it from Grandma. By the time Sue got back to the
General Store I was in the back office and Jack was calling
the police. I was a little scared but not really. It was sort
of exciting. My sister was telling me to try and cry but I
couldn't. About 20 minutes later two cops came and handcuffed
me, led me through the mall outside to the police car. I was
kind of embarrassed when they took me through the mall in
front of all those people.

When they got me in the car they began questioning me,   4
while driving me to the police station. Questions just to fill
out the report--age, sex, address, color of eyes, etc.

Then when they were finished they began talking about   5
Jack and what a nuisance he was. I gathered that Jack had
every single person who shoplifted, no matter what their age,
arrested. The police were getting really fed up with it
because it was a nuisance for them to have to come way out to
the mall for something as petty as that. To hear the police
talk about my "crime" that way felt good because it was like
what I did wasn't really so bad. It made me feel a bit
relieved. When we walked into the station I remember the desk
sergeant joking with the arresting officers about "well we got
another one of Jack's hardened criminals." Again, I felt my
crime lacked any seriousness at all. Next they handcuffed me
to a table and questioned me further and then I had to phone
my mom. That was the worst. I never was so humiliated in my
life. Hearing the disappointment in her voice was worse
punishment than the cops could ever give me.

Brandt's first draft establishes the main sequence of actions. About a third of it is
devoted to the store manager, an emphasis that disappears by the final draft. What is
to have prominence in the final draft—Brandt's feelings about telling her parents and
her conversations with them—appears here only in a few lines at the very end. But
mentioning the interaction suggests its eventual importance, and we are reminded of
its prominence in Brandt's invention writing.

Brandt writes a second draft for another student to read critically. In this draft,
she includes dialogues with her sister and with the police officers. She also provides

more information about her actions as she considered buying the Snoopy button and then decided to steal it instead. She includes visual details of the manager's office. This draft is not much different in emphasis from the first draft, however, still ending with a long section about the police officers and the station. The parents are mentioned briefly only at the very end.

The reader tells Brandt how much he likes her story and admires her frankness. However, he does not encourage her to develop the dramatic possibilities in calling her parents and meeting them afterward. In fact, he encourages her to keep the dialogue with the police officers about the manager and to include what the manager said to the police.

DESIGNING YOUR WORK

As the student and rancher were working on the text of the local history project described earlier in this chapter (see p. 26), they considered design elements appropriate to writing about remembered events, including black-and-white and color photographs, other memorabilia, and quotations from the rancher's tape-recorded story.

Selecting Visuals

To begin, they discussed what visuals might accompany the final written piece and how photographs could enhance the telling of the rancher's story. The student found old snow-day photographs from the local newspaper's archives, and the rancher selected a family photograph taken the spring following the great snowstorm of 1938. As alternatives to these visuals, the student and the rancher also considered including a painting of an isolated homestead and an early snapshot that the rancher had taken of his house in 1941. For their final product, they narrowed their selections to pictures that gave read-

The Rocky Valley Times

SPECIAL SUPPLEMENT

Vol. XCII, No 2   January 14, 1999

This Sunday marks the sixty-first anniversary of the legendary "Storm of the Century" that blitzed the Rocky Valley area with up to eight feet of snow in just a few hours. In this era of cell phones and fax machines, it's all too easy to forget the danger and difficulties the regions' widely scattered settlers faced at that time. In this special eight-page supplement, we salute the resourceful individuals who "made it through" and helped to establish our community as we know it today   —THE EDITOR

INSIDE

• At the General Store 2
• An Engineer's Tale 2
• Local Women Saved Lives 2
• Photos from the Times Archive 3
• Born During the Storm 4
• Where the Forecast Went Wrong 5
• A Logger's Perspective 6
• Could It Happen Again Today? 7

RANCHER REMEMBERS THE STORM OF THE CENTURY

By George Valentino

"It was only a few days, but it seemed like a lifetime."

Jim and Anne Austin were new to Rocky Valley, and when it became clear that a major blizzard was imminent, relatives urged the couple and their two young children to stay in town lest supplies should become scarce. But Austin and Anne had lived off the land for a long time and had weathered storms before, and felt safest returning to their ranch to tend to the livestock. They were confident that they had enough food, water, and candles at the ranch to carry them through any storm.

Nothing in their past experience had prepared the couple, however, for the onslaught of what quickly came to be known as "the storm of the century." In a recent interview for the *Times*, Austin unfolded an inspiring tale of resourcefulness and courage in a desperate situation.

The date was January 1938. Young Jim Jr. was only two and Mark was just a few months old. Austin remembers that, despite the frigid temperature, the children were happy and excited on the ride home from town as the first few flakes of snow started to fall—innocently enough, it seemed at first. While Anne put the children to bed, Austin went about his usual evening chores. "Within the span of a few hours, the wind started to blow quite a bit harder," he recalls, "but the animals were calm and comfortable in their quarters. Anne and I retired for the night without a suspicion about what was to come."

The Austins in 1938 (a few months after the storm)

Anne checked on Mark "at about 2:45 in the morning, not that I remember it exactly," Austin recalls wryly, "and when she came back down the hall, I knew something was wrong just from the look on her face. She said—and this is what I'll never forget—that Mark was crying because snow was coming into his room, that there were snowdrifts up to the windowsills. She said we'd have to start plowing right away if we wanted to get the door open in the morning." That ended Austin's sleep for the night, and he recalls climbing out the kitchen window to start clearing the way to the other buildings. Anne, too, stayed awake, dividing her time between quieting restless little Mark, shoveling the walk near the house, and keeping hot beverages ready for Austin during his frequent breaks. As the sun rose, the snow continued to fall, although the wind died down for a while. "It wasn't a

Brandt's revision shows that she does not take her reader's advice. She reduces the role of the police officers, eliminating any dialogue with them. She greatly expands the role of her parents: The last third of the essay is now focused on her remembered feelings about calling them and seeing them afterward. In terms of dramatic importance, the phone call home now equals the arrest. When we recall Brandt's earliest invention writings, we can see that she was headed toward this conclusion all along, but she needed invention, three drafts, a critical reading, and about a week to get there.

ers the strongest basis for becoming involved in and imagining the rancher's story. They decided that black-and-white photographs would best emphasize that the event took place in a time and place without modern conveniences. In choosing the pictures of the dramatic snowstorm and the rancher's family, the student writer and the rancher hoped to show readers the central idea of the story—the importance of community in the face of adversity.

Remember that visuals do not have to be photographs, drawings, or graphics but may also be any objects that can be connected to the remembered event being described. The rancher and the student also might have included a previously published copy of the weather forecast from the day of the storm or a schedule for the train that ran through the rancher's town.

Pulling Revealing Quotations

After reviewing what they had written, the student and the rancher recommended to the newspaper two quotes from the story to highlight. They wanted to pull short passages that would capture readers' attention and convey some of the story's drama. The idea was not to summarize the rancher's story in these quotes but to emphasize to readers the significance of the event as well as to leave readers with a good understanding of the event as they finished reading the piece.

Chapter 22, "Using and Acknowledging Sources," offers guidelines on selecting quotations for research essays.

THINKING CRITICALLY ABOUT WHAT YOU HAVE LEARNED

Now that you have worked extensively in autobiography—reading it, talking about it, writing it—take some time to reflect on what you have learned: What problems did you have while you were writing, and how did you solve them? How did reading about events in other people's lives help you write about a remembered event in your own life? Finally, you might stop to think critically about autobiography as a genre of writing: How does it influence the way we think about ourselves?

Reflecting on Your Writing

Write a page or so telling your instructor about a problem you encountered in writing your essay and how you solved it. Before you begin, gather all of your writing—invention and planning notes, outlines, drafts, critical comments, revision plans, and final revision. Review these materials as you complete this writing task.

1. *Identify* one *problem you needed to solve as you wrote about a remembered event.* Do not be concerned with grammar and punctuation; concentrate on problems unique to writing a story about your experience. For example: Did you puzzle over how to present a particular place or person? Was it difficult to structure the narrative so it held readers' interest? Did you find it hard (or uncomfortable) to convey the event's autobiographical significance?

2. *Determine how you came to recognize the problem.* When did you first discover it? What called it to your attention? Did you notice it yourself, or did another reader point it out? Can you now see hints of it in your invention writing, your planning notes, or an earlier draft? If so, where specifically?

3. *Reflect on how you went about solving the problem.* Did you work on a particular passage, cut or

add details, or reorganize the essay? Did you reread one of the essays in the chapter to see how another writer handled similar material? Did you look back at the invention guidelines? Did you discuss the problem with another student, a tutor, or your instructor? If so, how did talking about it help, and how useful was the advice you got?

4. *Write a brief explanation of the problem and your solution.* Be as specific as possible in reconstructing your efforts. Quote from your invention notes or early drafts, from readers' comments, from your revision plan, and from your final revision to show the various changes your writing underwent as you worked to solve the problem. Taking the time now to think about how you recognized and solved a real writing problem will help you become more aware of what works and does not work, making you a more confident writer.

Reviewing What You Learned from Reading

Write a page or so explaining to your instructor how the readings in this chapter influenced your final draft. Your own essay about a remembered event has no doubt been influenced by the essays you have read in this chapter. These readings may have helped you decide which of your own experiences would seem significant to your readers, or they may have given you ideas about how to evoke a vivid sense of place or how to convey your feelings about the event. Write a page or so explaining to your instructor how the readings in this chapter influenced your essay. Before you start, take some time to reflect on what you have learned from the four reading selections.

1. *Reread the final revision of your essay; then review the selections you read before completing*

your own essay, looking for specific influences. If you were impressed, for example, with the way one of the readings described a place, used dialogue, dramatized the action, or conveyed autobiographical significance, look to see where you might have been striving for similar effects in your own essay. Look also for ideas you got from your reading: writing strategies you were inspired to try, specific details you were led to include, effects you sought to achieve.

2. *Write a page or so explaining these influences.* Did a single reading selection influence you, or were you influenced by several selections? Quote from the selections and your final revision to show how your essay was influenced by the other essays. If, in reviewing the selections, you have found another way to improve your own essay, indicate briefly what you would change and which of the selections inspired the change.

Considering the Social Dimensions of Essays about Remembered Events

Writing about events that have special significance for you can lead you to recognize personal strengths and weaknesses and to clarify your beliefs and values. At the same time, reading others' autobiographical writing can help forge connections between you and other people. Another person's life often reflects our own experience, enabling us to identify and empathize. Just as often, however, another person's life does not resemble ours, and we learn that people can have radically different experiences, even within the same society. Think of the dramatic contrast between Rick Bragg's experience and Annie Dillard's, or between Dillard's and Tobias Wolff's.

Wolff's experience, for example, gives us insight into how the American myth of the cowboy has defined manliness partly in terms of guns and power. Reading about such events in other people's lives may not completely bridge the differences that separate us, but it can help us better understand one another and the circumstances affecting our lives. Striving as readers and as writers to forge connections with other people is important, but so is recognizing the differences.

These ideas about autobiographical writing lead to some basic questions about how we understand ourselves and our relationships with others.

Autobiography and Self-Discovery. If autobiography leads to self-discovery, what do we mean by the "self"? Should we think of the self as our "true" essence or as the different roles we play in different situations?

If we accept the idea of an essential self, autobiographical writing helps us in the search to discover who we truly are. Given this idea of the self, we might see Tobias Wolff, for example, as searching to understand whether he is the kind of person who shoots squirrels or the kind of person who cries over dead animals. If, on the other hand, we accept the idea that the various roles we play are what create the self, then autobiographical writing allows us to reveal the many sides of our personalities. This view of the self assumes that we present different self-images to different people in different situations. Given this idea, we might see Wolff as presenting his sympathetic side to his mother but keeping his aggressive, "manly" side hidden from her.

Also recall Wolff's comment in the headnote prior to the reading: that autobiography for him is "part memory, part invention," that "the very act of writing has transformed the original experience into another experience more 'real' to me than what I started with." Here he brings up another essential question about autobiography and self-discovery: How "true" is autobiography? Surely when we relate past experience through the lens of memory, there may be discrepancies between what we write and what "actually" happened. Moreover, in the interest of telling a good story—or presenting a particular image of themselves—autobiographers may edit or embellish the event in some way, whether consciously or not.

1. *Consider how your remembered event essay might be considered an exercise in self-discovery.* Planning and writing your essay, did you see yourself as discovering your true self or examining

how you reacted in a particular situation? Do you think your essay reveals your single, essential, true self, or does it show only one aspect of the person you understand yourself to be?

2. *Reflect on how true your essay is.* Does it seem to you that your essay captures what actually happened? Or does it seem that your memory has created a somewhat different reality colored by your current thoughts and feelings about the incident? In the interests of telling a dramatic, vivid story and presenting yourself in a certain way, could you have embellished reality? If so or if any of your classmates did so, do you think it matters?

3. *Write a page or so explaining your ideas about self-discovery and truth in remembered event essays.* Connect your ideas to your own essay and to the readings in this chapter.

Ways of Interpreting Our Experience. How might we interpret autobiography? Should we view it psychologically—in terms of personal feelings, relationships, conflicts, and desires—or more publicly—in terms of the social, political, and cultural conditions of our lives? You can understand these different perspectives by applying them to the selections in this chapter. Wolff's essay, for example, could be seen in psychological terms as the story of an adolescent boy trying to assert his manhood. Or it could be seen in political terms as a critique of power and war. Brandt's essay could be interpreted psychologically, either in terms of her childish desire to have what she wants when she wants it, or socially in terms of her relationship with her mother.

1. *Consider how you have generally interpreted other people's essays about remembered events.* Have you understood the essays primarily in personal, psychological terms? Or in social or possibly political terms? Or in some of both? When you read Annie Dillard's essay, for example, did you wonder why she was so intent on finding the amoeba? Did you see her behavior as obsessive or her need for approval as indicating low self-esteem? Or did you think of her essay more in social terms: perhaps seeing Dillard's childhood as privileged, or thinking about her parents' style of child-raising, or whether they would have encouraged her scientific curiosity more if she had been a boy?

2. *Reflect on whether you adopted a psychological or social perspective when you were writing about your own life.* How did you think about your experience? Did you see yourself as being motivated by certain personal needs or fears? Or did you see yourself as being influenced more by external forces?

3. *Write a page or so about whether you find yourself interpreting autobiography psychologically or socially.* Neither is preferred over the other; they are simply quite different perspectives. Try to connect your ideas to readings in the chapter and to your experience writing your essay. What do you think we gain or lose by looking at experience in these different ways?

Remembering People

When you describe someone who played an important role in your life, you very likely have two aims: to portray the person vividly so that readers can imagine what he or she was like, and to give readers insight into the person's significance in your life. To give readers a vivid impression of the person, you need to describe the person's physical appearance, mannerisms, ways of speaking, and typical behavior toward you and others. To convey the person's significance in your life, you need to relate specific anecdotes that illustrate the person's character and reveal the nature of your relationship.

A temptation in writing about others is to oversimplify, to remember only the very best or the very worst about people. We may idealize those who have helped or inspired us and demonize those who have mistreated or frustrated us. When you search your memory for descriptive details and illustrative anecdotes, you should strive to go beyond caricature and stereotype and to portray your subject as a complex individual with both shortcomings and strengths. As you do so, you may discover qualities in the person you had overlooked and better understand your own contribution to the relationship.

You will encounter writing about a remembered person in many different contexts, as the following examples suggest.

Writing in Your Other Courses

- For an education class, a student writes about an unusually effective high school literature teacher. He describes the teacher as so enthusiastic about her teaching and about literature that she is able to win over even the most resistant students. To show how the teacher inspires her students, he relates what happened when the class compared key scenes in two film versions of *Romeo and Juliet* and then staged its own versions of the same scenes.

- For a history paper on immigration, a student interviews her grandfather and then writes an essay about his experience coming to the United States as a young boy. She begins by describing the major waves of Eastern European immigration during the late nineteenth and early twentieth centuries. Then she relates several anecdotes her grandfather told her. One anecdote tells how her grandfather, who attended school and learned English, had to act as an interpreter for his mother, who had great difficulty learning the language. Another anecdote illustrates the family tensions caused by the grandfather's efforts to assimilate and hide his ethnic roots. She concludes with the observation that recent immigrants from places around the world face many of the same problems her grandfather did nearly a century earlier.

Writing in the Community

- As part of a community service project, a student volunteers to help an eighty-year-old man write an essay about his grandfather for his grandchildren who live in another state. The student tape-records the man's stories and later transcribes them on the computer. He also uses a computer scanner to create images of old photographs and war medals. At a later visit, the two of them work together to organize and revise the essay, which they decide to put up on the student's home page so that the grandchildren can access it.

For more detail on the decisions these writers made about document design, see pp. 123–24.

- For a branch library display about residents who have helped shape the neighborhood, a volunteer helps a woman write about a diner owner for whom she used to work as a waitress. In a meeting with the woman, he takes notes as she tells him about the diner and about what was memorable about the owner. He later writes up her description of the restaurant as a popular gathering place for high school kids, a place where she used to hang out with friends before getting a job there. The writer includes several anecdotes to show that the owner was a tyrant to kids he did not like but a friend and mentor to those he did like, including the woman who worked for him.

Writing in the Workplace

- Invited to contribute an article to the upcoming theater program on someone who influenced her career, the lead actor in one of the plays decides to write about her high school drama teacher. She focuses the essay on her first encounters with the teacher, who had a reputation for being brilliant but harsh. She tells what happened when she tried out for her first role, got the part, but then struggled with the teacher, who she thought was squelching her talent. Only after opening night did she realize how much she had learned from the drama instructor.

- For their manager's retirement celebration, several employees write brief essays about their most memorable experiences working with her. One male employee writes about the difficulties he had when he first started working for her, explaining that he had never worked for a woman before. He writes humorously about what happened and how she quickly helped him fit in.

The preceding scenarios suggest some occasions for writing about a remembered person. Think of someone important in your life, someone you would feel comfortable describing to your classmates. The only requirements are that you remember the person well enough to write a description and that your relationship with the person seems important to you now as you look back on it.

Part 1. Consider the possibilities and choose a person. Then make notes about what you could say in only a few minutes to give others a sense of what this person was like and why your relationship was important.

Now, get together with two or three other students and take turns presenting the person you have chosen. Each of you should take just three or four minutes to present your person.

Part 2. As a group, spend ten to fifteen minutes discussing what happened when you presented a remembered person:

- Take turns telling each other what impression you wanted your classmates to get of the person and of your relationship with the person. Then see whether your listeners got those impressions or different ones.

- Review the kinds of details, events, and other memories each of you decided to include in your brief presentation.

- Conclude by reflecting on what each of you sees as the easiest part and the hardest part of presenting a remembered person—and why.

READINGS

The readings in this chapter illustrate the features of essays about remembered people and the strategies writers rely on to realize the features. No two essays in this genre are much alike, and yet they share defining features. The section Analyzing Writing Strategies and the Commentary following each reading touch on a few features best illustrated by that essay, capturing its special qualities and strengths. Together, the four essays cover many of the possibilities of the genre. Consequently, you will want to read as many of the essays as possible and, if time permits, complete the activities in Analyzing Writing Strategies and read the Commentaries. Following the readings is a section called Basic Features, which offers a concise summary of the features and strategies commonly used in writing about remembered people and provides examples from all of the readings.

Maya Angelou, a poet and an autobiographer, has also been an actress, a singer, an editor, a professor, and an administrator of the Southern Christian Leadership Conference. She has said of her writing: "I speak to the black experience, but I am always talking about the human condition."

Angelou grew up during the 1930s in the small Arkansas town of Stamps, where she lived with her brother Bailey; her grandmother, the "Momma" mentioned in this selection; and her Uncle Willie. Momma and Willie operated a small grocery store. In this selection, from I Know Why the Caged Bird Sings *(1970), Angelou writes about her childhood memories of her uncle, from her perspective as an adult of forty. As you read, notice how she describes him and tells brief stories about him to reveal their relationship.*

Uncle Willie

Maya Angelou

When Bailey was six and I a year younger, we used to rattle off the times tables with the speed I was later to see Chinese children in San Francisco employ on their abacuses. Our summer-gray pot-bellied stove bloomed rosy red during winter, and became a severe disciplinarian threat if we were so foolish as to indulge in making mistakes.

Uncle Willie used to sit, like a giant black Z (he had been crippled as a child), and hear us testify to the Lafayette County Training Schools' abilities. His face pulled down on the left side, as if a pulley had been attached to his lower teeth, and his left hand was only a mite bigger than Bailey's, but on the second mistake or on the third hesitation his big overgrown right hand would catch one of us behind the collar, and in the same moment would thrust the culprit toward the dull red heater, which throbbed like a devil's toothache. We were never burned, although once I might have been when I was so terrified I tried to jump onto the stove to remove the possibility of its remaining a threat. Like most children, I thought if I could face the worst danger voluntarily, and *triumph,* I would forever have power over it. But in my case of sacrificial effort I was thwarted. Uncle Willie held tight to my dress and I only got close enough to smell the clean dry scent of hot iron. We learned the times tables without understanding their grand principle, simply because we had the capacity and no alternative.

The tragedy of lameness seems so unfair to children that they are embarrassed in its presence. And they, most recently off nature's mold, sense that they have only narrowly missed being another of her jokes. In relief at the narrow escape, they vent their emotions in impatience and criticism of the unlucky cripple.

Momma related times without end, and without any show of emotion, how Uncle Willie had been dropped when he was three years old by a woman who was minding him. She seemed to hold no rancor against the baby-sitter, nor for her just God who allowed the accident. She felt it necessary to explain over and over again to those who knew the story by heart that he wasn't "born that way."

In our society, where two-legged, two-armed strong Black men were able at best to eke out only the necessities of life, Uncle Willie, with his starched shirts, shined shoes and shelves full of food, was the whipping boy and butt of jokes of the underemployed and underpaid. Fate not only disabled him but laid a double-tiered barrier in his path. He was also proud and sensitive. Therefore he couldn't pretend that he wasn't crippled, nor could he deceive himself that people were not repelled by his defect.

Only once in all the years of trying not to watch him, I saw him pretend to himself and others that he wasn't lame. 6

Coming home from school one day, I saw a dark car in our front yard. I rushed in to find a strange man and woman (Uncle Willie said later they were school teachers from Little Rock) drinking Dr. Pepper in the cool of the Store. I sensed a wrongness around me, like an alarm clock that had gone off without being set. 7

I knew it couldn't be the strangers. Not frequently, but often enough, travelers pulled off the main road to buy tobacco or soft drinks in the only Negro store in Stamps. When I looked at Uncle Willie, I knew what was pulling my mind's coattails. He was standing erect behind the counter, not leaning forward or resting on the small shelf that had been built for him. Erect. His eyes seemed to hold me with a mixture of threats and appeal. 8

I dutifully greeted the strangers and roamed my eyes around for his walking stick. It was nowhere to be seen. He said, "Uh . . . this this . . . this . . . uh, my niece. She's . . . uh . . . just come from school." Then to the couple—"You know . . . how, uh, children are . . . th-th-these days . . . they play all d-d-day at school and c-c-can't wait to get home and pl-play some more." 9

The people smiled, very friendly. 10

He added, "Go on out and pl-play, Sister." 11

The lady laughed in a soft Arkansas voice and said, "Well, you know, Mr. Johnson, they say, you're only a child once. Have you children of your own?" 12

Uncle Willie looked at me with an impatience I hadn't seen in his face even when he took thirty minutes to loop the laces over his high-topped shoes. "I . . . I thought I told you to go . . . go outside and play." 13

Before I left I saw him lean back on the shelves of Garret Snuff, Prince Albert and Spark Plug chewing tobacco. 14

"No, ma'am . . . no ch-children and no wife." He tried a laugh. "I have an old m-m-mother and my brother's t-two children to l-look after." 15

I didn't mind his using us to make himself look good. In fact, I would have pretended to be his daughter if he wanted me to. Not only did I not feel any loyalty to my own father, I figured that if I had been Uncle Willie's child I would have received much better treatment. 16

The couple left after a few minutes, and from the back of the house I watched the red car scare chickens, raise dust and disappear toward Magnolia. 17

Uncle Willie was making his own way down the long shadowed aisle between the shelves and the counter—hand over hand, like a man climbing out of a dream. I stayed quiet and watched him lurch from one side, bumping to the other, until he reached the coal-oil tank. He put his hand behind that dark recess and took his cane in the strong fist and shifted his weight on the wooden support. He thought he had pulled it off. 18

I'll never know why it was important to him that the couple (he said later that he'd never seen them before) would take a picture of a whole Mr. Johnson back to Little Rock. 19

He must have tired of being crippled, as prisoners tire of penitentiary bars and the   20
guilty tire of blame. The high-topped shoes and the cane, his uncontrollable muscles and
thick tongue, and the looks he suffered of either contempt or pity had simply worn him
out, and for one afternoon, one part of an afternoon, he wanted no part of them.

I understood and felt closer to him at that moment than ever before or since.   21

Connecting to Culture and Experience: Self-Image

Angelou concludes her essay with an anecdote about the one time she saw Uncle
Willie "pretend to himself and others that he wasn't lame" (paragraph 6). According
to Angelou, Uncle Willie not only presented a different image of himself to the
visiting strangers, but also pretended to himself that he was different. Uncle Willie's
actions suggest the possibility that people sometimes can present to others different
images of themselves, images that can influence how people see themselves.

Explore these possibilities with other students in your class. Begin by telling each
other about an occasion when you tried to project a different image of yourself—
such as when you moved to a new neighborhood or city, started out in a new school,
logged on to an Internet chat room, tried out for a new job or a team. The image
you presented may have been only a little different or it may have been radically
different. In what ways did you act differently? How did people respond to you? How
did acting differently or receiving different responses from others make you feel
about yourself?

With your classmates, reflect on what your experiences suggest about how our
sense of who we are can be influenced or changed by how we present ourselves to
others and how others' responses influence how we see ourselves.

Analyzing Writing Strategies

1. At the beginning of this chapter, we make several generalizations about writing about remembered people. Consider which of these assertions are true of
   Angelou's essay:

   - It focuses on a person with whom the writer had a significant, rather than
     casual, relationship.
   - It tries to convey the person's significance without oversimplifying or senti-
     mentalizing.
   - It vividly describes the person's appearance, mannerisms, ways of speaking,
     and typical behavior.
   - It relates specific anecdotes that reveal important aspects of the person and of
     his or her relationship to the writer.

2. **Dialogue** is a key element in many essays about remembered people. To see how
   Angelou uses dialogue to give readers an understanding of Uncle Willie, reread
   paragraphs 9–15. Notice how Angelou follows the conventions for presenting

For more on dialogue, see
Chapter 14, pp. 580–81.

dialogue—for example, she begins a new paragraph for each speaker and uses quotation marks to distinguish the spoken words from her own description of the speakers.

Reflect on the role that dialogue plays in the reading as a whole. What does it enable you to learn about Uncle Willie and about Angelou's feelings toward him?

Commentary: A Vivid Portrait

Angelou presents a vivid portrait of Uncle Willie by using three describing strategies: **naming, detailing,** and **comparing.** Notice, for example, how this bit of description from paragraph 2 incorporates all three strategies:

> Uncle Willie used to sit, *like a giant black Z* (he had been crippled as a child), and hear us testify to the Lafayette County Training Schools' abilities. His **face** <u>pulled down on the left side,</u> *as if a pulley had been attached to his lower teeth,* and <u>his left</u> **hand** was *only a mite bigger than Bailey's,* but on the second mistake or on the third hesitation his <u>big overgrown right</u> **hand** would catch one of us behind the collar, and in the same moment would thrust the culprit toward the <u>dull red</u> **heater,** which *throbbed like a devil's toothache.*

Angelou uses naming (shown here in **bold** type) to point to some notable features of Uncle Willie's appearance (his face and hands) as well as to an object in the room (the heater) that looms large in her memory. Detailing (<u>underlined</u> in the passage) combines with naming to particularize the description, to make it apply only to this one person, her uncle. The details identify what distinguishes Uncle Willie's face and hands: His face looks lopsided and his hands are of unequal size. This combination of naming and detailing gives readers a vivid and memorable picture of Uncle Willie.

The third describing strategy—comparing (indicated by *italics* in the passage)—adds another important dimension to the picture. Angelou uses comparing, for example, when she describes the shape of her uncle's "crippled" body "like a giant black Z." The comparison used here is a simile, an explicit comparison announced by the word *like* or *as*. Angelou also uses a metaphor, an indirect comparison, when she calls herself a "culprit" for making a math mistake. Skilled writers like Angelou employ similes and metaphors not to decorate their writing but to create surprising images that enable readers to understand the writer's feelings. The simile describing the heater throbbing "like a devil's toothache" associates Uncle Willie with the devil, an association that adds to the impression of him as all-powerful and threatening.

To create a vivid portrait, Angelou also uses an important narrating strategy—**specific narrative action.** Narrative action uses active verbs and modifying phrases and clauses to show a person's movements and gestures. Here is an example with the actions underlined:

> Uncle Willie <u>was making his own way</u> down the long shadowed aisle between the shelves and the counter—<u>hand over hand,</u> like a man <u>climbing out of a dream.</u> I stayed quiet and watched him <u>lurch from one side,</u> <u>bumping to the other</u> . . . (paragraph 18)

These concrete narrative actions help readers imagine Uncle Willie's movements.

For more on these describing strategies, see Chapter 15.

For more on specific narrative action, see Chapter 14, pp. 579–80.

Considering Topics for Your Own Essay

Consider writing about an adult who has significantly influenced your life. Think about someone who is outside your immediate family—perhaps a grandparent, aunt or uncle, teacher, or coach. Begin by listing two or three possibilities. Choose one, and then consider the following questions: How might you engage your readers' interest and disclose the person's significance in your life? What details might you include? What anecdotes might you relate? What photographs or other memorabilia might you include with your essay to help readers get a sense of the person and your relationship?

For more information on including memorabilia, see p. 108.

Gerald Haslam, a professor of English at Sonoma State University in California, has published several short-story collections, including Okies: Selected Stories *(1973) and* Hawk Flights: Visions of the West *(1983). In this remembered person essay, from* California Childhood *(1988), Haslam writes about his great-grandmother. Notice how he helps readers see her as he did when he was a young child.*

Grandma
Gerald Haslam

"*Expectoran su sangre!*" exclaimed Great-grandma when I showed her the small horned toad I had removed from my breast pocket. I turned toward my mother, who translated: "They spit blood." 1

"*De los ojos,*" Grandma added. "From their eyes," mother explained, herself uncomfortable in the presence of the small beast. 2

I grinned, "Awwwwww." 3

But my Great-grandmother did not smile. "*Son muy tóxicos,*"[1] she nodded with finality. Mother moved back an involuntary step, her hands suddenly busy at her breast. "Put that thing down," she ordered. 4

"His name's John," I said. 5

"Put John down and not in your pocket, either," my mother nearly shouted. "Those things are very poisonous. Didn't you understand what Grandma said?" 6

I shook my head. 7

"Well . . ." mother looked from one of us to the other—spanning four generations of California, standing three feet apart—and said, "of course you didn't. Please take him back where you got him, and be careful. We'll all feel better when you do." The tone of her voice told me that the discussion had ended, so I released the little reptile where I'd captured him. 8

I later learned that my great-grandmother—whom we simply called "Grandma"—had been moving from house to house within the family, trying to find a place she'd accept. She hated the city, and most of the aunts and uncles lived in Los Angeles. Our house in Oildale was much closer to the open country where she'd dwelled all her life. She had wanted to come to our place right away because she had raised my mother 9

---

[1] They're very poisonous.

from a baby when my own grandmother died. But the old lady seemed unimpressed with Daddy, whom she called *"ese gringo."*

In truth, we had more room, and my dad made more money in the oil patch than almost anyone else in the family. Since my mother was the closest to Grandma, our place was the logical one for her, but Ese Gringo didn't see it that way, I guess, at least not at first. Finally, after much debate, he relented.

10

In any case, one windy afternoon, my Uncle Manuel and Aunt Toni drove up and deposited four-and-a-half feet of bewigged, bejeweled Spanish spitfire: a square, pale face topped by a tightly-curled black wig that hid a bald head—her hair having been lost to typhoid nearly sixty years before—her small white hands veined with rivers of blue. She walked with a prancing bounce that made her appear half her age, and she barked orders in Spanish from the moment she emerged from Manuel and Toni's car. Later, just before they left, I heard Uncle Manuel tell my dad, "Good luck, Charlie. That old lady's dynamite." Daddy only grunted.

11

She had been with us only two days when I tried to impress her with my horned toad. In fact, nothing I did seemed to impress her, and she referred to me as *el malcriado,*[2] causing my mother to shake her head. Mom explained to me that Grandma was just old and lonely for Grandpa and uncomfortable in town. Mom told me that Grandma had lived over half a century in the country, away from the noise, away from clutter, away from people. She refused to accompany my mother on shopping trips, or anywhere else. She even refused to climb into a car, and I wondered how Uncle Manuel had managed to load her up in order to bring her to us.

12

She disliked sidewalks and roads, dancing across them when she had to, then appearing to wipe her feet on earth or grass. Things too civilized simply did not please her. A brother of hers had been killed in the great San Francisco earthquake and that had been the end of her tolerance of cities. Until my Great-grandfather died, they lived on a small rancho near Arroyo Cantua, north of Coalinga. Grandpa, who had come north from Sonora as a youth to work as a *vaquero,*[3] had bred horses and cattle, and cow-boyed for other ranchers, scraping together enough of a living to raise eleven children.

13

He had been, until the time of his death, a lean, dark-skinned man with wide shoul-ders, a large nose, and a sweeping handlebar mustache that was white when I knew him. His Indian blood darkened all his progeny so that not even I was as fair-skinned as my Great-grandmother, Ese Gringo for a father or not.

14

As it turned out, I didn't really understand very much about Grandma at all. She was old, of course, yet in many ways my parents treated her as though she were younger than me, walking her to the bathroom at night and bringing her presents from the store. In other ways—drinking wine at dinner, for example—she was granted adult privileges. Even Daddy didn't drink wine except on special occasions. After Grandma moved in, though, he began to occasionally join her for a glass, sometimes even sitting with her on the porch for a premeal sip.

15

---

[2]the brat
[3]cowboy

She held court on our front porch, often gazing toward the desert hills east of us or   16
across the street at kids playing on the lot. Occasionally, she would rise, cross the yard
and sidewalk and street, skip over them, sometimes stumbling on the curb, and wipe her
feet on the lot's sandy soil, then she would slowly circle the boundary between the open
middle and the brushy sides, searching for something, it appeared. I never figured out
what.

One afternoon I returned from school and saw Grandma perched on the porch as   17
usual, so I started to walk around the house to avoid her sharp, mostly incomprehensible, tongue. She had already spotted me. *"Venga aquí!"*[4] she ordered, and I understood.

I approached the porch and noticed that Grandma was vigorously chewing some-   18
thing. She held a small white bag in one hand. Saying *"Qué deseas tomar?"*[5] she with-
drew a large orange gumdrop from the bag and began slowly chewing it in her toothless
mouth, smacking loudly as she did so. I stood below her for a moment trying to remember the word for candy. Then it came to me: *"Dulce,"* I said.

Still chewing, Grandma replied, *"Mande?"*   19

Knowing she wanted a complete sentence, I again struggled, then came up with   20
"Deseo dulce."

She measured me for a moment, before answering in nearly perfect English, "Oh,   21
so you wan' some candy. Go to the store an' buy some."

I don't know if it was the shock of hearing her speak English for the first time, or the   22
way she had denied me a piece of candy, but I suddenly felt tears warm my cheeks and
I sprinted into the house and found Mom, who stood at the kitchen sink. "Grandma just
talked English," I burst between light sobs.

"What's wrong?" she asked as she reached out to stroke my head.   23

"Grandma can talk English," I repeated.   24

"Of course she can," Mom answered. "What's wrong?"   25

I wasn't sure what was wrong, but after considering, I told Mom that Grandma had   26
teased me. No sooner had I said that than the old woman appeared at the door and
hiked her skirt. Attached to one of her petticoats by safety pins were several small
tobacco sacks, the white cloth kind that closed with yellow drawstrings. She carefully
unhooked one and opened it, withdrawing a dollar, then handed the money to me. *"Para
su dulce,"*[6] she said. Then, to my mother, she asked, "Why does he bawl like a mother-
less calf?"

"It's nothing," Mother replied.   27

"Do not weep, little one," the old lady comforted me, "Jesus and the Virgin love you."   28
She smiled and patted my head. To my mother she said as though just realizing it, "Your
baby?"

Somehow that day changed everything. I wasn't afraid of my Great-grandmother   29
any longer and, once I began spending time with her on the porch, I realized that my
father had also begun directing increased attention to the old woman. Almost every

---

[4] Come here!
[5] What do you want to take?
[6] For your candy.

evening Ese Gringo was sharing wine with Grandma. They talked out there, but I never did hear a real two-way conversation between them. Usually Grandma rattled on and Daddy nodded. She'd chuckle and pat his hand and he might grin, even grunt a word or two, before she'd begin talking again. Once I saw my mother standing by the front window watching them together, a smile playing across her face.

No more did I sneak around the house to avoid Grandma after school. Instead, she 30 waited for me and discussed my efforts in class gravely, telling mother that I was a bright boy, *"muy inteligente,"* and that I should be sent to the nuns who would train me. I would make a fine priest. When Ese Gringo heard that, he smiled and said, "He'd make a fair-to-middlin' Holy Roller preacher, too." Even Mom had to chuckle, and my great-grandmother shook her finger at Ese Gringo. "Oh you debil, Sharlie!" she cackled.

Frequently, I would accompany Grandma to the lot where she would explain that no 31 fodder could grow there. Poor pasture or not, the lot was at least unpaved, and Grandma greeted even the tiniest new cactus or flowering weed with joy. "Look how beautiful," she would croon. "In all this ugliness, it lives." Oildale was my home and it didn't look especially ugly to me, so I could only grin and wonder.

Because she liked the lot and things that grew there, I showed her the horned toad 32 when I captured it a second time. I was determined to keep it, although I did not discuss my plans with anyone. I also wanted to hear more about the bloody eyes, so I thrust the small animal nearly into her face one afternoon. She did not flinch. *"Hola señor sangre de ojos,"*[7] she said with a mischievous grin. *"Qué tal?"*[8] It took me a moment to catch on.

"You were kidding before," I accused. 33

"Of course," she acknowledged, still grinning. 34

"But why?" 35

"Because the little beast belongs with his own kind in his own place, not in your 36 pocket. Give him his freedom, my son."

I had other plans for the horned toad, but I was clever enough not to cross 37 Grandma. "Yes, Ma'am," I replied. That night I placed the reptile in a flower bed cornered by a brick wall Ese Gringo had built the previous summer. It was a spot rich with insects for the toad to eat, and the little wall, only a foot high, must have seemed massive to so squat an animal.

Nonetheless, the next morning when I searched for the horned toad it was gone. I 38 had no time to explore the yard for it, so I trudged off to school, my belly troubled. How could it have escaped? Classes meant little to me that day. I thought only of my lost pet —I had changed his name to Juan, the same as my Great-grandfather—and where I might find him.

I shortened my conversation with Grandma that afternoon so I could search for 39 Juan. "What do you seek?" the old woman asked me as I poked through flower beds beneath the porch. "Praying mantises," I improvised, and she merely nodded, surveying me. But I had eyes only for my lost pet, and I continued pushing through branches and brushing aside leaves. No luck.

---

[7] Hello mister bloody eyes.

[8] What's up?

Finally, I gave in and turned toward the lot. I found my horned toad nearly across 40
the street, crushed. It had been heading for the miniature desert and had almost made
it when an automobile's tire had run over it. One notion immediately swept me: if I had
left it on its lot, it would still be alive. I stood rooted there in the street, tears slicking my
cheeks, and a car honked its horn as it passed, the driver shouting at me.

Grandma joined me, and stroked my back. "The poor little beast," was all she said, 41
then she bent slowly and scooped up what remained of the horned toad and led me out
of the street. "We must return him to his own place," she explained, and we trooped, my
eyes still clouded, toward the back of the vacant lot. Carefully, I dug a hole with a piece
of wood. Grandma placed Juan in it and covered him. We said an Our Father and a Hail
Mary, then Grandma walked me back to the house. "Your little Juan is safe with God, my
son," she comforted. We kept the horned toad's death a secret, and we visited his small
grave frequently.

Grandma fell just before school ended and summer vacation began. As was her 42
habit, she had walked alone to the vacant lot but this time, on her way back, she tripped
over the curb and broke her hip. That following week, when Daddy brought her home
from the hospital, she seemed to have shrunken. She sat hunched in a wheelchair on
the porch, gazing with faded eyes toward the hills or at the lot, speaking rarely. She still
sipped wine every evening with Daddy and even I could tell how concerned he was
about her. It got to where he'd look in on her before leaving for work every morning and
again at night before turning in. And if Daddy was home, Grandma always wanted him
to push her chair when she needed moving, calling, "Sharlie!" until he arrived.

I was tugged from sleep on the night she died by voices drumming through the walls 43
into darkness. I couldn't understand them, but was immediately frightened by the
uncommon sounds of words in the night. I struggled from bed and walked into the living
room just as Daddy closed the front door and a car pulled away.

Mom was sobbing softly on the couch and Daddy walked to her, stroked her head, 44
then noticed me. "Come here, son," he gently ordered.

I walked to him and, uncharacteristically, he put an arm around me. "What's wrong?" 45
I asked, near tears myself. Mom looked up, but before she could speak, Daddy said,
"Grandma died." Then he sighed heavily and stood there with his arms around his weep-
ing wife and son.

The next day my Uncle Manuel and Uncle Arnulfo, plus Aunt Chintia, arrived and 46
over food they discussed with my mother where Grandma should be interred. They
argued that it would be too expensive to transport her body home and, besides, they
could more easily visit her grave if she was buried in Bakersfield. "They have such nice,
manicured grounds at Greenlawn," Aunt Chintia pointed out. Just when it seemed they
had agreed, I could remain silent no longer. "But Grandma has to go home," I burst. "She
has to! It's the only thing she really wanted. We can't leave her in the city."

Uncle Arnulfo, who was on the edge, snapped to Mother that I belonged with the 47
other children, not interrupting adult conversation. Mom quietly agreed, but I refused. My
father walked into the room then. "What's wrong?" he asked.

"They're going to bury Grandma in Bakersfield, Daddy. Don't let 'em, please." 48

"Well, son . . ." 49

"When my horny toad got killed and she helped me to bury it, she said we had to 50
return him to his place."

"Your horny toad?" Mother asked. 51

"He got squished and me and Grandma buried him in the lot. She said we had to 52
take him back to his place. Honest she did."

No one spoke for a moment, then my father, Ese Gringo, who stood against the 53
sink, responded: "That's right . . . " he paused, then added, "We'll bury her." I saw a
weary smile cross my mother's face. "If she wanted to go back to the ranch then that's
where we have to take her," Daddy said.

I hugged him and he, right in front of everyone, hugged back. 54

No one argued. It seemed, suddenly, as though they had all wanted to do exactly 55
what I had begged for. Grown-ups baffled me. Late that week the entire family, hundreds
it seemed, gathered at the little Catholic church in Coalinga for mass, then drove out to
Arroyo Cantua and buried Grandma next to Grandpa. She rests there today.

Connecting to Culture and Experience: Caring for the Elderly

Haslam's family seems to assume that Grandma should live with one of them (she
"had been moving from house to house within the family, trying to find a place she'd
accept"). Taking care of elderly family members poses a challenge for many families,
especially since nursing home and health care costs are rising. In addition to these
costs, a family's decisions about its older members may be influenced by its ethnic,
cultural, or religious traditions.

With other students in your class, discuss the situation of the elderly in each of
your families in light of your family traditions. Identify the older family members and
their current living situations. If elderly relatives are in daily contact with your immediate family, what roles do they play in your life? If elderly relatives live far away from
your immediate family, how often do you see and communicate with them? Also consider what degree of responsibility your immediate family takes for the health and
well-being of elderly family members. (You may need to interview family members to
get this information.)

Analyzing Writing Strategies

1. Reread paragraph 11 and identify the describing strategies of **naming, detailing,**
    and **comparing** that Haslam uses to present a vivid portrait of Grandma. Circle
    the words that name Grandma's features (such as "face"). Underline the details
    that particularize these features (such as "square"). Also place brackets around
    comparisons Haslam employs to give readers his impression of how Grandma
    looked and acted. (*Similes* make a direct comparison using the word *as* or *like*,
    while *metaphors* make an indirect comparison.) What impression of Grandma do
    you get from these describing strategies?

For more on these describing strategies, see Chapter
15.

For more on narrating
events, see Chapter 14.

2. **Anecdotes** play a central role in Haslam's portrait of Grandma. In the margins of the essay, mark where each anecdote (narration of a brief incident or onetime event) begins and ends. To get you started, the first anecdote occupies paragraphs 1–8. Review all of the anecdotes in the reading; then choose one to analyze closely. First, summarize what happens in the anecdote, being sure to identify the people involved. Next, explain what the anecdote reveals about Grandma and her relationship with young Haslam.

Commentary: Autobiographical Significance

Writers convey a person's significance in their lives by telling how they felt at the time as well as how they feel now as they look back on their relationship with the person. Haslam presents his remembered feelings about Grandma ("I suddenly felt tears warm my cheeks" [paragraph 22]) as well as his remembered thoughts about her ("I didn't really understand very much about Grandma at all" [paragraph 15]). These childhood memories give readers an idea of the young Haslam's initial attitude toward and developing relationship with his great-grandmother.

Although Haslam relies predominantly on presenting remembered feelings and thoughts, he occasionally expresses what he is thinking and feeling as he writes about Grandma—what we call *present perspective*. Sometimes he employs language that only an adult would use, such as "She held court on our front porch" (paragraph 16). At other times he gives adult judgments and insights, such as when he uses the word *uncharacteristically* to describe his father's putting an arm around him (paragraph 45). In the following passage, notice how Haslam describes what he saw as a child before giving his adult analysis of what his great-grandmother's actions meant:

> She disliked sidewalks and roads, dancing across them when she had to, then appearing to wipe her feet on earth or grass. Things too civilized simply did not please her. (paragraph 13)

Haslam interprets Grandma for his readers, but he is careful not to oversimplify by labeling her in a stereotypical way. Instead, he lets readers see and hear Grandma interacting with him and with others. Through a combination of his remembered feelings and present perspective, readers get an impression of who Grandma was and why she is still such a significant person for Haslam.

Considering Topics for Your Own Essay

Recall two or three adults who influenced you during early childhood and then, for whatever reason, passed out of your life. You might consider, for example, neighbors, parents of friends, teachers, camp counselors, or relatives. Choose one person and think about the following questions: What anecdotes might reveal the important characteristics of this person? List these anecdotes and jot down what each one reveals. Which anecdote should you develop more fully because it promises to reveal an important aspect of your relationship with the person?

Amy Wu wrote this essay in 1993, when she was seventeen years old, just before becoming a student at New York University, where she majored in political science and journalism. She has worked for news organizations, Internet companies, and as a freelance writer, publishing articles in the New York Times, the New York Daily News, Asian Week, and other publications. This essay was published in Chinese American Forum, a quarterly magazine.

As you read, notice the way Wu relies on contrasts between her mother and other kinds of mothers to help readers understand her special relationship with her mother.

A Different Kind of Mother

Amy Wu

Amy Wu and her mother

My best friend once asked me what it was like being brought up by a Chinese mother. Surprisingly, I could find no answer. I found myself describing my mother's beauty—the way my mother's hair was so silky and black, how her eyes were not small and squinty, but shaped like perfect almonds. How her lips and cheeks were bright red even if she put on no makeup. 1

But unlike my friends, who see my mother as a Chinese mother, I see my mother as simply "my" mother. The language between any mother and daughter is universal. Beyond the layers of arguments and rhetoric, and beyond the incidents of humiliation and misunderstandings, there is a love that unites every mother and daughter. 2

I am not blind, however, to the disciplinary differences between a culture from the west and a culture from the east. Unlike American mothers, who encourage their young children to speak whatever is on their mind, my mother told me to hold my tongue. Once, when I was 5 or 6, I interrupted my mother during a dinner with her friends and told her that I disliked the meal. My mother's eyes transformed from serene pools of blackness into stormy balls of fire. "Quiet!" she hissed, "do you not know that silent waters run deep?" She ordered me to turn my chair to the wall and think about what I had done. I remember throwing a red-faced tantrum before my mother's friends, pounding my fists into the rug, and throwing my utensils at the steaming dishes. Not only did I receive a harsh scolding, but a painful spanking. By the end of that evening, I had learned the first of many lessons. I learned to choose my words carefully before I opened my undisciplined mouth. 3

Whenever my friends and I strike up conversations about our mothers in the cafeteria or at slumber parties, I find myself telling them this story. Nevertheless, they respond to my story with straight and pale faces. "How," one of my friends asked, "can a mother be so cruel?" "You mean she beat you in front of other people?" another asked. My best friend told me that her mother disciplined her children wisely instead of abusing them. She sat them on her lap, patiently explaining what they had done wrong. She didn't believe in beating children into submission. 4

What my American friends cannot understand, however, is how my mother's lessons have become so embedded within me, while my friends have easily forgotten their mother's words. My mother's eyes are so powerful, her fists so strong, that somehow I cannot erase her words of advice. To this day, I choose my words carefully before I speak, unlike so many of my friends whose words spill out aimlessly when they open their mouths. My mother says that American girls are taught to squabble like chickens, but a Chinese girl is taught how to speak intelligently.   5

Only lately have I also discovered that Chinese mothers show their love in different ways. Ever since I was a little girl, my mother has spent hours cooking intricate dishes. I remember Friday evenings she would lay out the precious china her mother had given her as a wedding present—how she laid down the utensils and glasses so meticulously, how she made sure there was not a crease in the tablecloth.   6

She would spend the entire day steaming fish, baking ribs, cutting beef into thin strips, and rolling dough to make dumplings. In the evening, her work of labor and art would be unveiled. My father and I and a few Chinese neighbors and friends would be invited to feast on my mother's work of art.   7

I remember how silent my mother was as she watched her loved ones devour her labor of love. She would sit back, with a small smile on her face. She would nibble at the food in her dish while urging others to eat more, to take seconds, and thirds and fourths. "Eat, eat!" she would order me. I dared not tell her I was too full.   8

She would fill my bowl with mounds of rice and my dish with endless vegetables, fish, and fried delicacies. A Chinese mother's love flows from the time and energy she puts into forming a banquet. A Chinese mother's love comes through her order to eat more.   9

My American friends laugh so hard that tears come out of their eyes, when I tell them how my Chinese mother displays her love. "So she wants you to get fat!" one screamed. They said that their mothers showed love by hugging them tightly, buying them clothes, and kissing them on the cheeks.   10

Deep inside, I know that my mother does show her love, except she does it when she thinks I am asleep. Every so often, she will tiptoe into my dark room, sit on the edge of my bed, and stroke my hair. When I am awake, however, she is like a professor constantly hounding her prize student and expecting only the best. All throughout my childhood, she drilled me on lessons of cleanliness and respect.   11

A few years ago at my Grandpa Du's 67th birthday party, I ran up to my grandfather and planted a wet, juicy kiss on his right cheek. To this day, I can easily remember the horrified looks on my relatives' faces. My grandfather turned pale for a second and then smiled meekly. He nodded his head and quickly sat down.   12

Later that evening, my mother cornered me against the wall. "Do you not know that respect to elderly is to bow!" she screamed. Her face turned bright purple. My excuses of "I didn't know . . . " were lost in her powerful words.   13

From that day on, I bowed to anyone Chinese and older than I. I have learned that respect for the elderly earns a young person a different kind of respect. These days, my grandfather points to me and tells my little cousins to follow my example. "She has been taught well," he tells them.   14

It saddens me that my Chinese mother is so often misunderstood. After she threw   15
my friends out during my twelfth birthday party, because they refused to take off their
shoes, they saw her as a callous, cruel animal. One of my friends went home and told
her father that I had an abusive mother. Her father even volunteered to call the child welfare department. They never dared to step foot in my house again.

My mother has given me so many fine values and morals because of her way of   16
teaching me. I choose words carefully before I speak. I am careful to speak and act
toward the elderly a certain way. Without my mother's strong words and teachings, I
believe that I would be a rather undisciplined person who didn't value life greatly. I would
most likely have been spoiled and callous and ignorant. I have also learned that there is
more than one definition of love between a mother and a daughter.

Connecting to Culture and Experience: Cultural Differences

Wu's essay suggests that ethnic differences may be especially apparent when we look at
how parents raise their children—both in how they discipline and how they show their
love. To her friends, for example, Wu's mother seems "callous" and "cruel." Wu's
mother is similarly critical of the way her daughter's friends are being raised by their
parents. Paragraph 15 probably presents the most graphic example of ethnic difference:
Not only do Wu's friends refuse to respect Chinese tradition by taking off their shoes
when entering the house, but a friend's father threatens to call the child welfare department to report Wu's mother as "abusive" for throwing the friends out of her house.

With other students in your class, discuss your reactions to the ethnic differences
Wu writes about. You may want to begin by taking turns describing your family's
cultural background, possibly including your own and your ancestors' nationalities,
religious affiliations, and racial identifications. Then discuss some of your family's
traditions and values to see if there are any notable cultural differences among the
people in your class.

Analyzing Writing Strategies

1. To convey her mother's significance, Wu tells readers directly what she now thinks
   and feels about their relationship. For example, she begins and ends the opening
   anecdote by stating what she learned from the experience (paragraph 3). Reread
   the rest of the essay, looking for places where Wu expresses her present perspective and putting brackets around them. Then reflect on how effectively these present perspective comments help you understand Wu's relationship with her mother.

2. In addition to telling readers how she feels about her mother, Wu tries to create
   a vivid portrait so that readers can imagine what her mother looks like. Reread
   paragraphs 1, 3, and 5, where Wu describes her mother. Underline the features
   she **names** and the **details** she gives. For example, in paragraph 1, she calls attention to her mother's "hair" being "silky and black."

For more on naming and
detailing, see Chapter 15,
pp. 589–93.

Commentary: Anecdotes and Recurring Events

To present her mother, Wu uses two related but different narrating strategies—**onetime events** (also called *anecdotes*) and **recurring events.** In paragraph 3, for instance, Wu relates an anecdote that shows what happened the one time she told her mother she did not like the food prepared for dinner. Wu uses the temporal transition "Once" to signal readers that she is telling an anecdote. She uses another temporal transition ("when I was 5 or 6") to locate the event at a particular point in time. Wu presents the event in a simple chronological sequence of actions and reactions: the young Wu interrupts her mother to complain about the food, she is reprimanded and told to face the wall, she throws a tantrum, and she suffers the consequences of a scolding and spanking.

For more on narrating strategies, see Chapter 14.

In contrast, paragraphs 6–9 present a recurring event that takes place every Friday: banquets for family and friends. Wu uses the verb tense marker "would" to signal readers that her mother's activities are recurring and not onetime events ("Friday evenings she would lay out the precious china. . . . She would spend the entire day steaming fish. . . . She would fill my bowl. . . ."). The Friday banquet is an important family ritual—the same china and utensils set out in the same way, the same dishes prepared in the same way. The mother always behaves predictably, as does Wu. There is not a hint that anything unusual ever happened at one of these banquets. Nevertheless, this recurring event helps readers see what Wu ultimately came to appreciate: the nonverbal way her mother expresses her love for her family.

In addition to showing what happened through anecdotes and recurring events, Wu lets us hear what was said on these occasions. She reconstructs dialogue, either by quoting to emphasize the words that were used (" 'Quiet!,' she hissed . . .") or by summarizing conversations to focus on their substance ("She ordered me to turn my chair to the wall . . .").

For more on dialogue, see Chapter 14, pp. 580–81.

Dialogue reveals important aspects of Wu's relationship with her mother. Since effective dialogue captures the mood as well as the content of a conversation, it gives readers an immediate impression of the person's character and reveals how he or she relates to others. Since writers recalling something in the past are unlikely to remember precisely what was said, they often must invent or reconstruct dialogue. They usually try to use words the person would have used. In the quoted dialogue in paragraph 3, for example, the words Wu quotes may have been a saying her mother used on many occasions: " 'Quiet!' she hissed, 'do you not know that silent waters run deep?' "

Considering Topics for Your Own Essay

Consider writing about a parent, guardian, counselor, minister, or another older person who has influenced you deeply, for good or ill. Choose one person and think for a few moments about what you would want readers to know about this person and your relationship. What details of appearance, style, or movement might you select? Which anecdotes would be memorable for readers and most revealing of your relationship with the person?

Notice that Wu does not give us many of her mother's words, but what her mother does say—and especially how she says it—is revealing. We know how she sounds because Wu details her mother's tone of voice with the description, "she hissed." Because Wu uses quotation marks, readers can easily distinguish what might have been said at the time from what Wu thought and felt. Writers, like Wu, tend to quote sparingly, choosing words that will leave a strong impression with readers. Seldom does a dialogue present a long speech unless the writer wants to emphasize the person's ideas or idiosyncratic way of talking.

In addition to reconstructing the dialogue with her mother, Wu reconstructs conversations with others about her mother. In paragraph 4, for example, Wu combines quoted and summarized dialogue to relate what her friends said about her mother in response to stories Wu told them. This strategy allows her to sharpen the contrast between what she calls her "Chinese" mother and her friends' "American" mothers. **Comparison** and **contrast** can be effective tools in presenting a person. We see them used in the following essay by Jan Gray as well, which is organized around two comparable anecdotes.

For more on comparing and contrasting, see Chapter 18.

Jan Gray *was a first-year college student when she wrote the following essay about her father, a man toward whom she has ambivalent but mostly angry feelings. As you read, notice how Gray uses description to convey these feelings.*

Father

Jan Gray

My father's hands are grotesque. He suffers from psoriasis, a chronic skin disease that covers his massive, thick hands with scaly, reddish patches that periodically flake off, sending tiny pieces of dead skin sailing to the ground. In addition, his fingers are permanently stained a dull yellow from years of chain smoking. The thought of those swollen, discolored, scaly hands touching me, whether it be out of love or anger, sends chills up my spine. 1

By nature, he is a disorderly, unkempt person. The numerous cigarette burns, food stains, and ashes on his clothes show how little he cares about his appearance. He has a dreadful habit of running his hands through his greasy hair and scratching his scalp, causing dandruff to drift downward onto his bulky shoulders. He is grossly overweight, and his pullover shirts never quite cover his protruding paunch. When he eats, he shovels the food into his mouth as if he hasn't eaten for days, bread crumbs and food scraps settling in his untrimmed beard. 2

Last year, he abruptly left town. Naturally, his apartment was a shambles, and I offered to clean it so that my mother wouldn't have to pay the cleaning fee. I arrived early in the morning anticipating a couple hours of vacuuming and dusting and scrubbing. The minute I opened the door, however, I realized my task was monumental: Old yellowed newspapers and magazines were strewn throughout the living room; moldy and rotten food covered the kitchen counter; cigarette butts and ashes were everywhere. The pungent aroma of stale beer seemed to fill the entire apartment. 3

As I made my way through the debris toward the bedroom, I tried to deny that the 4 man who lived here was my father. The bedroom was even worse than the front rooms, with cigarette burns in the carpet and empty bottles, dirty dishes, and smelly laundry scattered everywhere. Looking around his bedroom, I recalled an incident that had occurred only a few months before in my bedroom.

I was calling home to tell my mother I would be eating dinner at a girlfriend's house. 5 To my surprise, my father answered the phone. I was taken aback to hear his voice because my parents had been divorced for some time and he was seldom at our house. In fact, I didn't even see him very often.

"Hello?" he answered in his deep, scratchy voice. 6

"Oh, umm, hi Dad. Is Mom home?" 7

"What can I do for you?" he asked, sounding a bit too cheerful. 8

"Well, I just wanted to ask Mom if I could stay for dinner here." 9

"I don't think that's a very good idea, dear." I could sense an abrupt change in the 10 tone of his voice. "Your room is a mess, and if you're not home in ten minutes to straighten it up, I'll really give you something to clean." Click.

Pedalling home as fast as I could, I had a distinct image of my enraged father. I 11 could see his face redden, his body begin to tremble slightly, and his hands gesture nervously in the air. Though he was not prone to physical violence and always appeared calm on the outside, I knew he was really seething inside. The incessant motion of those hands was all too vivid to me as I neared home.

My heart was racing as I turned the knob to the front door and headed for my bed- 12 room. When I opened my bedroom door, I stopped in horror. The dresser drawers were pulled out, and clothes were scattered across the floor. Everything on top of the dresser —a perfume tray, a couple of baskets of hair clips and earrings, and an assortment of pictures—had been strewn about. The dresser itself was tilted on its side, supported by the bed frame. As I stepped in and closed the door behind me, tears welled up in my eyes. I hated my father so much at that moment. Who the hell did he think he was to waltz into my life every few months like this?

I was slowly piecing my room together when he knocked on the door. I choked 13 back the tears, wanting to show as little emotion as possible, and quietly murmured, "Come in." He stood in the doorway, one hand leaning against the door jamb, a cigarette dangling from the other, flicking ashes on the carpet, very smug in his handling of the situation.

"I want you to know I did this for your own good. I think it's time you started taking 14 a little responsibility around this house. Now, to show you there are no hard feelings, I'll help you set the dresser back up."

"No thank you," I said quietly, on the verge of tears again. "I'd rather do it myself. 15 Please, just leave me alone!"

He gave me one last look that seemed to say, "I offered. I'm the good guy. If you 16 refuse, that's your problem." Then he turned and walked away. I was stunned at how he could be so violent one moment and so nonchalant the next.

As I sat in his bedroom reflecting on what he had done to my room, I felt the utmost   17
disgust for this man. There seemed to be no hope he would break his filthy habits. I
could come in and clean his room, but only he could clean up the mess he had made of
his life. But I felt pity for him, too. After all, he is my father—am I not supposed to feel
some responsibility for him and to love and honor him?

Connecting to Culture and Experience: Ambivalence

Jan Gray admits that her disgust for her father is mixed with pity. Ambivalence—
mixed feelings—is fundamental to our relationships with others. We normally do not
feel only hatred toward other people. On the other hand, we usually do not feel only
unqualified love and devotion, either. Feelings tend to be influenced by our most
recent or memorable interactions with a person. Additionally, our experiences with
other people—or simply distance in space and time—can affect our understanding
of a relationship and alter our feelings about the person.

With students in your class, discuss ambivalence in human relationships. Identify
someone for whom you have notably ambivalent feelings—a family member, friend,
employer, or anyone else—someone you feel comfortable talking about with your
classmates. Your feelings may be mainly negative, mainly positive, or evenly balanced.
Take turns describing your relationship with the person you have chosen and speculating about how your ambivalent feelings emerged. Explain also how you have been
able to sustain the relationship, if you have.

As a group, what can you conclude about ambivalence in relationships? On the
basis of your individual experiences, does it seem that ambivalence is inevitable? Do
you think that accepting ambivalence would make families more stable and people in
general more tolerant? If so, try to explain how.

Analyzing Writing Strategies

1. Reread the **dialogue** in paragraphs 6–10 and 13–16, paying attention to what
   Gray's father says and how each conversation develops. Notice also how Gray
   comments on what her father says and how she shows his actions as he talks to
   her. Then consider these questions: What does each conversation reveal about
   the father and Gray's relationship with him? Do the conversations confirm what
   you learn about the father and the relationship elsewhere in the essay, or do they
   offer new information? If they offer something new, what do you think they
   reveal?

For more on dialogue, see Chapter 14, pp. 580–81.

2. Gray presents two **anecdotes** that take place at different times and places. Notice
   that instead of putting these anecdotes in a simple chronological order, one
   after the other, she embeds one anecdote within the other. She uses a narrating
   strategy called *flashback*, commonly used in movies and television. Find where

For more on anecdotes (onetime events), see Chapter 14, p. 576.

each anecdote begins and ends. Note especially how Gray makes the transition from one time in the past to another time in the past. How smooth is this transition? Then look at her overall purpose. What do you think Gray is trying to achieve with this anecdote within an anecdote? How effective do you think it is?

3. The Writer at Work section later in this chapter presents the first draft of Gray's essay. Compare the two versions by making a scratch outline of the draft and the revision. How did Gray change the organization? Why do you think she made these changes, and what effect do they have?

Commentary: Autobiographical Significance

Instead of telling what she remembers feeling about her father or what she feels now about their relationship, Gray shows his significance through descriptive details and actions. For example, her description of his skin condition and personal slovenliness reveals how repulsive she finds him. The way he leaves his apartment shows how irresponsible he is. Most important, the way he threatens her and wrecks her bedroom shows how cruel and violent he can be. Through description, anecdotes, and recurring activities, Gray creates a **dominant impression** that clearly conveys to readers what she thinks and feels about her father.

For more on creating a dominant impression, see Chapter 15, p. 599.

Although Gray seeks to create an impression that is consistent throughout the essay, she expresses her contradictory feelings at the end. She admits that she "felt the utmost disgust for" her father, but at the same time she acknowledges that she also "felt pity for him." Her final sentence poses a rhetorical question, one that readers are not expected to answer, and that she probably cannot answer either. She feels that she should and apparently wants very much "to love and honor" her father. But his behavior makes it nearly impossible for her to do so. One reason we choose, like Gray, to write about difficult relationships is to come to terms with our contradictory feelings. While the writing process may not resolve our ambivalence, it can help us to understand why we feel as we do.

Considering Topics for Your Own Essay

Imagine writing about someone with whom you have had a serious conflict. How would you present this person? Which anecdotes might be most revealing? What conversations might you reconstruct that would dramatize the conflict? What impression of this person would you attempt to convey to readers?

■ PURPOSE AND AUDIENCE

A writer of an essay about a remembered person may have several possible purposes in mind. Perhaps the most prominent is to gain a better understanding of the remembered person and of the writer's relationship with the person. To achieve this purpose, the writer needs to see the complexity of the relationship so as to avoid either demonizing or idealizing the person.

Another purpose is to entertain readers with a vivid portrait of an unusual or engaging person. To achieve this goal, writers present a remembered person through description, dialogue, recurring events, and anecdotes. All of these strategies are carefully coordinated to create a dominant impression that will enable readers to readily imagine the person and understand why he or she is significant for the writer. By using many concrete, revealing details, writers try to make their portraits come alive. Finally, writers may hope that readers will come to reflect on people who have been important in their own lives.

A Vivid Portrait

At the center of an essay about a remembered person is a vivid portrait. Writers of remembered person essays rely on the full range of descriptive strategies—naming, detailing, and comparing—to present a person to their readers. But they tend to be selective, choosing only one or two distinctive features of the person's appearance to emphasize. Maya Angelou, for example, uses naming, detailing, and comparing to describe Uncle Willie's lopsided face "pulled down on the left side, as if a pulley had been attached to his lower teeth." Similarly, Gray focuses attention on her father's "massive, thick hands with scaly, reddish patches that periodically flake off, sending tiny pieces of dead skin sailing to the ground."

Writers also use specific narrative action to describe people moving and gesturing. Haslam, for example, shows his mother's alarm on learning that the toad he is holding is poisonous: "Mother moved back an involuntary step, her hands suddenly busy at her breast." Wu's description of her grandfather's reaction when she kisses him ("My grandfather turned pale for a second and then smiled meekly") is punctuated by her mother's contrasting reaction ("my mother cornered me against the wall . . . she screamed. Her face turned bright purple").

Besides presenting their subjects visually, writers let us hear their subjects speak. All the readings in this chapter include some dialogue, usually a combination of quoted and summarized dialogue. Angelou uses quoted dialogue to present a stuttering, yet proud Uncle Willie ("I have an old m-m-mother and my brother's t-two children to l-look after") but summarizes the math quiz her uncle gives her and her brother ("on the second mistake or third hesitation . . ."). Haslam uses quoted dialogue to show how his relationship with Grandma deepened, but basically summarizes conversations between other family members.

Revealing Anecdotes and Recurring Events

In portraying significant relationships, writers may narrate anecdotes or recurring events. Many writers do both. In her brief essay about Uncle Willie, Angelou presents a onetime incident (when strangers came to the store) and a recurring event (doing math homework). Similarly, Wu shows us both what happened once when she complained about her mother's food and what happened every Friday at the ritual family banquets. Gray focuses on anecdotes depicting two specific events ("last year" when she cleaned her father's apartment and "a few months" earlier when he had wrecked her bedroom), but she also refers to recurring activities ("When he eats . . ."). Haslam presents a series of anecdotes and recurring events.

Writers use the whole panoply of narrating strategies to present anecdotes and recurring events. To create the dynamic quality of time passing and to orient readers, for example, they use calendar and clock time (*next day, Friday evenings, 67th birthday party*), temporal transitions (*when, used to, finally*), and verb tense markers (*would,* to signal recurring activities).

An Indication of the Person's Significance

Portrait writers choose as their subjects people they consider significant and they try to convey that autobiographical significance to their readers. Readers expect to understand the person's significance; however, they do not expect the essay to begin with the kind of explicit thesis statement typical of argumentative writing. Some writers, like Wu and Gray, begin their essays with statements about the person and their relationship, but these statements tell only part of what they have to say. The rest comes in the writers' comments and evaluations as they describe the person and narrate the events. Wu, for example, frames her essay at the beginning and end with statements about love between mothers and daughters. But she also sprinkles insights throughout the essay. After the anecdote about interrupting her mother, Wu comments that she "had learned the first of many lessons." After describing her mother's banquet preparations, she observes that a "Chinese mother's love flows from the time and energy she puts into forming a banquet."

Whether or not writers state this significance explicitly, they show it through anecdotes, recurring events, dialogue, descriptive details, and narrative actions. For example, Haslam never tells us directly that he learned to love Grandma. Instead, he shows us through anecdotes and recurring events how they grew close and how she helped him cope with death. The most explicit statement he makes is, "I wasn't afraid of my Great-grandmother any longer." Similarly, Angelou ends by commenting on what she understood after witnessing her uncle presenting a "whole Mr. Johnson" to the strangers from Little Rock.

The subjects writers choose are significant to them, but their feelings about those subjects often involve ambivalence. Angelou's relationship with Uncle Willie is highly ambivalent, for example, as is Gray's with her father. Neither writer tries to force a neat resolution by reducing deep and contradictory feelings to simple love or hate. They acknowledge the ambivalence and accept it. In many portraits, the significance seems to lie in this inevitable complexity of close relationships. Similarly, good writers avoid sentimentalizing their relationships, neither damning nor idealizing their subjects. Gray comes close to damning her father but stops just short of it by admitting her feelings of pity and responsibility. Angelou sympathizes with Uncle Willie's shame about his lameness and stuttering, but she does not present him as a long-suffering saint.

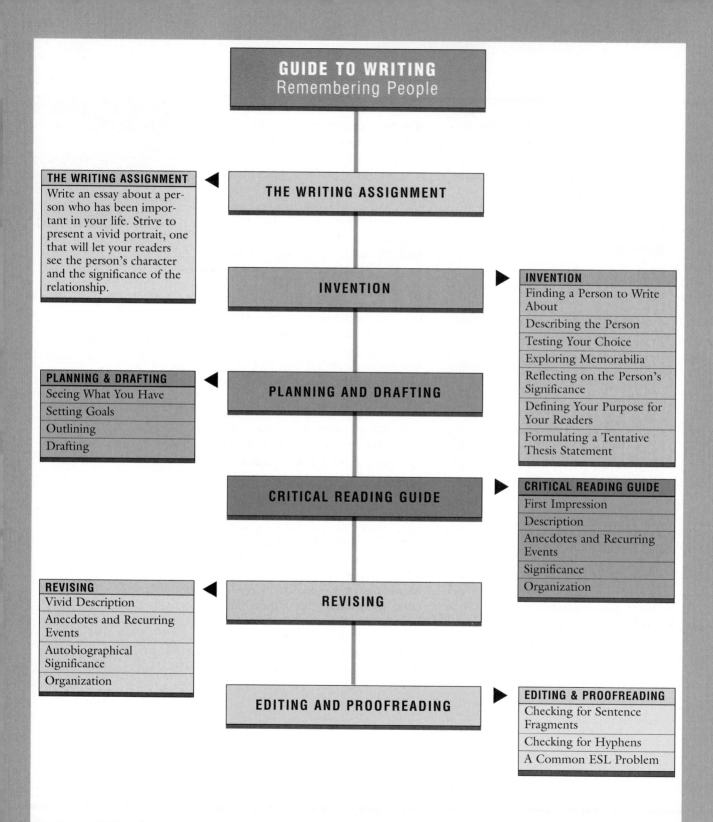

GUIDE TO WRITING
Remembering People

THE WRITING ASSIGNMENT

THE WRITING ASSIGNMENT
Write an essay about a person who has been important in your life. Strive to present a vivid portrait, one that will let your readers see the person's character and the significance of the relationship.

INVENTION

INVENTION
Finding a Person to Write About
Describing the Person
Testing Your Choice
Exploring Memorabilia
Reflecting on the Person's Significance
Defining Your Purpose for Your Readers
Formulating a Tentative Thesis Statement

PLANNING AND DRAFTING

PLANNING & DRAFTING
Seeing What You Have
Setting Goals
Outlining
Drafting

CRITICAL READING GUIDE

CRITICAL READING GUIDE
First Impression
Description
Anecdotes and Recurring Events
Significance
Organization

REVISING

REVISING
Vivid Description
Anecdotes and Recurring Events
Autobiographical Significance
Organization

EDITING AND PROOFREADING

EDITING & PROOFREADING
Checking for Sentence Fragments
Checking for Hyphens
A Common ESL Problem

THE WRITING ASSIGNMENT

Write an essay about a person who has been important in your life. Strive to present a vivid portrait, one that will let your readers see the person's character and the significance of the relationship.

INVENTION

The following activities will help you to choose a person, to describe this person, to explore your relationship, and to define the significance of the relationship. Each activity takes no more than a few minutes. Together, they enable you to search your memory and to think deeply about the person you choose to write about. Done one by one over several days' time, they provide a record of your thinking and put you in a strong position for drafting your essay.

Finding a Person to Write About

You may already have a person in mind. Even if you do, however, it is a good idea to consider other people in order to choose the best possible subject. The following activities will help you to make a good choice.

Listing People You Remember. *Make a list of people you could write about.* List only those people about whom you can recall specific details and stories. Include relatives, teachers, coaches, employers, friends, neighbors, and others. Also include people suggested by the Considering Topics for Your Own Essay activities following each reading in this chapter. Make your list as complete as you can, including people you knew for a long time and those you knew briefly, people you knew long ago and those you knew recently, people you liked and those you disliked. The following categories may give you some ideas:

- Anyone who had authority over you or, conversely, anyone over whom you had authority
- Anyone who helped you in difficult times or made life difficult for you
- Anyone whose advice or actions influenced you
- Anyone who taught you something important about yourself
- Anyone who inspired strong emotions in you—admiration, envy, disapproval, fascination, surprise, disappointment
- Anyone whose behavior or values led you to question your own

Listing People Related to Identity and Community. Think about people who helped you to explore your own identity and sense of community. List only people you remember vividly, people you knew very well over a period of time. Do not overlook the importance of people outside your immediate family.

- Someone who helped you develop a previously unknown side of yourself or play a role you had not played before
- Someone who led you to redefine your sense of identity, perhaps by making you think about your appearance, gender, age, financial status, cultural traditions, or family background
- Someone who caused you to reflect on whether you or anyone else can really change
- Someone who led you to question assumptions or stereotypes you had about other people
- Someone who made you feel you were part of a larger community or that you had something worthwhile to contribute or, conversely, someone who made you feel alienated, like an outsider

Listing People Related to Work and Career.   The following categories should help you to recall people who have influenced your thoughts about work and career.

- Someone who competed with you at work or someone with whom you learned to work collaboratively
- Someone who served as a positive or negative role model, perhaps leading you to change your attitudes toward work, your willingness to be supervised, or your ability to lead others
- Someone who helped you reevaluate your attitudes about a career—for example, about the pursuit of money or happiness, about focusing all of your energy in one direction in order to increase your chances of success, or about the value of helping people or protecting the environment
- Someone who helped you evaluate your choice of a college major or your attitude toward school in light of your career goals

Choosing a Person.   *Look over your list of possibilities and choose one person you can describe vividly and whose significance in your life you feel comfortable sharing with your readers.* Your instructors and classmates will be your first readers, but it may help to identify a group of other potential readers—friends, family members, fellow workers, teammates—who would be interested in knowing about your relationship with this person. Remember that in writing about the person, you also are writing about yourself. Make the best choice you can for now. If you become uncomfortable with this choice as you explore your memory, you can make another choice later.

Describing the Person

The following activities will help you to recall specific information that you can use to describe the person. If you complete each activity thoughtfully, you will have a wealth of remembered detail to draw on in drafting your essay. Even after you start drafting, you can return to these lists to capture fleeting memories that can be incorporated as you need them.

Appearance.   *Describe with naming, detailing, and comparing the person's appearance.* You might start at the top, with the person's hair and face, and work down to the feet. Or you might start with the person's typical way of dressing. Try to remember as much as you can.

Actions.   *Describe with specific narrative actions the way the person looked while moving and gesturing.* Detail any habits or typical mannerisms you recall. Depict the person in action: talking, eating, driving, playing sports, and so on.

Anecdotes and Recurring Events.   *List three or more anecdotes (onetime events) and recurring events that show something important about the person and your relationship.* For each anecdote or recurring event, write for several minutes telling what happened, who was there, what was said, and what you think it would show readers about the person and your relationship.

Dialogues.   *Reconstruct one or two conversations you had with the person or with someone else about the person.* Think of the first, last, or most memorable thing the person said to you. You may not remember exactly what was said, but try to re-create the conversation so that readers can imagine what was going on. Include any memorable words or phrases the person typically used and describe the person's tone of voice. Set up each conversation as a dialogue, with each person's words starting a new line.

Testing Your Choice

Now you need to decide whether you recall enough detail to give readers a vivid impression of this particular person. Reread your invention notes to see whether your memories seem promising. If you remember specific descriptions and stories you can use in an essay, then you have probably made a good choice. Consider also your intended readers and what you would want them to understand about the person and your relationship. As you go on to explore your feelings and thoughts, you will have to decide whether you still feel comfortable writing to these particular readers about this person. If at any point you lose confidence in your choice, return to your list and choose another person to write about.

At this point, you may find it useful to get together with two or three other students and describe your remembered person. This collaborative activity will help you determine whether you can present the person in a way that informs and interests others.

Testing Your Choice: A Collaborative Activity

Presenters: Take turns briefly identifying the role the person played in your life. Give a few key details describing the person's appearance and manner, and relate an anecdote or recurring activity that reveals something important about the person and your relationship.

Listeners: After each presenter speaks, tell him or her what impression you got of the person and the relationship. Note one thing the presenter said that you found especially vivid or surprising.

Exploring Memorabilia

For an illustration of memorabilia in a remembered person essay and suggestions for designing your document, turn to pp. 123–24.

Memorabilia are visuals, sounds, and objects associated with the person. Examples include photographs, homemade videos, postcards, songs, movie ticket stubs, souvenirs from trips or amusement parks, old clothes, and books. Memorabilia can help you remember details about the person. They might also be included—whole or in snippets—as visual or aural elements with your essay, multimedia presentation, or Web site.

You may or may not know about any relevant memorabilia. If you can easily get access to any, take time now to do so. Add to your invention notes any details about the person the memorabilia suggest. Consider using one or more in your essay.

Reflecting on the Person's Significance

Now you should consider what significance the person has had in your life. The following activities can help you discover this significance and find a way to share it with your readers.

Recalling Your Remembered Feelings and Thoughts.   *Write for five minutes about your memories of the person.* Use the following questions to stimulate your memory:

If You Have Known This Person All or Most of Your Life

- What are my earliest memories of the person?
- What was our relationship like initially? What did we do together and say to each other?
- How did we influence each other at various stages of our relationship?
- What were my feelings about the person?

If You Knew This Person for a Limited Time

- What do I remember about our first meeting—the place, time, occasion, other people, words exchanged? What did I expect and what was my first impression of the person?
- What did we do together and say to each other?

- How did we influence each other at various stages of our relationship?
- What were my feelings about the person?

Pause now to focus your thinking about your remembered feelings and thoughts. *Add a couple of sentences, indicating what you most remember thinking and feeling about the person and your relationship.*

Exploring Your Present Perspective. *Write for a few minutes reflecting on your relationship with this person.* Try to express your insights and feelings about the person's importance in your life. Use these questions to expand your ideas:

- Looking back on our relationship, in what ways do I understand it differently now than I did at the time?
- Would I have wanted the person to act differently toward me? How?
- How do I feel about the way I acted toward the person? Would I have behaved any differently had I known then what I know now? Why?
- If my feelings toward the person were ambivalent, how would I describe them? Were there any underlying tensions, outright disagreements, or unexpressed resentments?
- Do I see now that we differed in our values, attitudes, or goals?
- Did certain historical events in our community or in the country affect our relationship? Did differences between us (such as age, gender, cultural traditions, family background, or money) affect our relationship?
- Has looking at an old photograph or other memorabilia reminded me of anything about my relationship with the person?

Pause now to focus your thinking about your present perspective. *Add two or three sentences describing what you think and feel now as you look back on your relationship with the person.*

Defining Your Purpose for Your Readers

Write a few sentences, defining your purpose in writing about this particular person for your readers. Use these questions to focus your thoughts:

- Who are my readers? Remember that in choosing a person, you considered several possible readers: your instructors and classmates, friends, family members, fellow workers, teammates.
- What do my readers know about me?
- What, if anything, do they know about the person I am writing about?
- What do I want my readers to learn about the person and our relationship from reading my essay?
- What do I want to convey to readers about the person's significance in my life?

For more on thesis statements, see Chapter 13, pp. 557–58.

Formulating a Tentative Thesis Statement

Review what you wrote for Reflecting on the Person's Significance and add another two or three sentences that will help you tell readers what you understand about the person and what the relationship means to you. Try to write sentences that do not summarize what you have written, but that extend your insights and reflections. These sentences may be contradictory because they express ambivalent feelings. They also must necessarily be partial and speculative because you may never understand fully the person's significance in your life.

Keep in mind that readers do not expect you to begin your essay with the kind of explicit thesis statement typical of argumentative essays. If you decide to tell readers why the person was significant, you will most likely do so through interpretive or evaluative comments as you describe the person, present dialogue, and relate anecdotes and recurring activities. You are not obliged to tell readers the significance, but you should show it through the way you present the person and portray your relationship.

■ PLANNING AND DRAFTING

This section will help you review your invention writing and get started on your first draft.

Seeing What You Have

You have now produced a lot of writing for this assignment: descriptions of the person's appearance and behavior, recollections of anecdotes and recurring events, memorable conversations with the person and with others about the person, reflections on the person's significance. Before going on to plan and draft your essay, reread what you have already written.

If you make any new discoveries, add them. Also note any material you definitely will use in your draft. Then ask yourself the following questions:

- Do I remember enough specific details about the person to describe him or her vividly?
- Do I understand how the person was significant to me?
- Do my anecdotes, recurring events, and dialogues capture the person's character and portray our relationship effectively?
- Relationships tend to be complex. Will I be able to avoid sentimentality, oversimplifications, or stereotyping?

If your invention writing seems too general or superficial, or if you have discovered you feel uncomfortable writing about your relationship with this person, then choose another person to write about. As frustrating as it is to start over, it is far better to do so now than later.

If your invention writing looks thin but promising, you may be able to fill it out by doing one or more of the following:

- Discuss your relationship with a friend or family member to see if you can better understand why the person was significant to you.
- Recall additional anecdotes, recurring events, or conversations that would show readers other sides of the person or your relationship.
- Look at photographs, letters, or other memorabilia to recall additional descriptive details about the person and your relationship.
- Talk with the person about your past relationship, or with someone who remembers the person.

Setting Goals

Before actually beginning to draft, set goals to guide the decisions you will make as you draft and revise. Here are some questions that should help you set your goals:

Your Purpose and Readers

- How can I help readers to see the significance this person has for me?
- If my readers are likely to know someone like this person, how can I help them imagine the particular person I am writing about and avoid generalizing?
- If my readers are likely to be surprised by this person or by our relationship, how can I break through their preconceptions to get them to see the person as I do?

The Beginning

- What can I do in the opening sentences to awaken readers' interest? Should I begin with a surprising statement, as Wu does, or with an anecdote, as Angelou does? Should I first present myself, or should I let readers see the person right away, as Gray does, or let them hear the person, as Haslam does?
- Should I provide some background or context, as Wu and Gray do, or jump right into the action, as Angelou and Haslam do?

Describing the Person

- Which descriptive details will give readers a strong visual image of the person? What impression will these details convey to readers? How can I use photographs, letters, or other memorabilia to help readers imagine the person?
- Which anecdotes, recurring events, and conversations will best convey the values, attitudes, and character traits I want to emphasize?
- To help readers understand my relationship with the person, what anecdotes or recurring events will show them about how we interacted with one another? What dialogues would best capture the way we spoke to one another?
- What will my stories and conversations reveal about my remembered thoughts and feelings and about my present perspective? Do I need to insert any direct statements about how I felt at the time or how I feel now?

The Ending

- What do I want the ending to accomplish? Should it sum things up? Fix a particular image in readers' minds? Provide a sense of completion? Open up new possibilities?
- How shall I end? With my present perspective, as Gray and Wu do? With the person's words or with speculation about the person's feelings, as Angelou does? With an anecdote, as Haslam does?

Outlining

After you have set goals for your draft, you might want to make a scratch outline of your essay, indicating a tentative sequence for the material you will include. Note briefly how you plan to begin; list in order possible anecdotes, recurring events, descriptions, conversations; and note how you might end. As you draft, you may well diverge from your outline if you discover a better way to organize your essay.

Drafting

Start drafting your essay, keeping in mind the goals you set while you were planning. As you write, try to describe your subject in a way that makes his or her importance in your life clear to your readers. If you get stuck while drafting, explore the problem by using some of the writing activities in the Invention section of this chapter. You may want to review the general drafting advice on pp. 110–12.

As you read over your first draft, you may see places where you can add new material to reveal more about your relationship with the person. Or you may even decide that after this first draft, you can finally understand the complexity of the relationship, and you may set out to do so in a second draft.

■ CRITICAL READING GUIDE

Now is the time to get a good critical reading of your draft. Writers usually find it helpful to have someone else read and comment on their drafts, and all writers know how much they learn about writing when they read other writers' drafts. Your instructor may schedule readings of drafts as part of your coursework. If not, you can ask a classmate, friend, or family member to read your draft. You could also seek comments from a tutor at your campus writing center. The guidelines in this section can be used by *anyone* reviewing an essay about a remembered person. (If you are unable to have someone else read your draft, turn ahead to the Revising section, where you will find guidelines for reading your own draft critically.)

▶ **If You Are the Writer.** In order to provide focused, helpful comments, your reader must know your essay's intended audience, your purpose, and a problem in the draft that you need help solving. Briefly write out this information at the top of your draft.

- *Readers.* Identify the intended readers of your essay. How do you assume they will react to your writing?

- *Purpose.* What impression do you want the readers of your essay to have of the person? What do you want them to understand about the person's significance in your life?

- *Problem.* Ask your draft reader to help you solve the single most important problem you see with your draft. Describe this problem briefly.

▶ **If You Are the Reader.** The following guidelines can be useful for approaching a draft with a well-focused, questioning eye.

1. *Read for a First Impression.* Begin by reading the draft straight through to get a general impression. Read for enjoyment, ignoring spelling, punctuation, and usage errors for now. Try to imagine the person and to understand his or her significance for the writer.

   When you have finished this first quick reading, write a few sentences about your overall impression. Summarize the person's significance as you understand it. If you have any insights about the person or the relationship, write down these thoughts as well. Next, consider the problem the writer identified. If the problem will be covered by one of the other guidelines listed here, deal with it there. Otherwise, respond to the writer's concerns now.

2. *Consider How Vividly the Person Is Described.* Praise particularly effective descriptions and point out any descriptions that seem vague or contradict the dominant impression of the person given by the rest of the essay. Note where naming, detailing, or comparing could be added to help describe the person's appearance or where specific narrative actions could show the person's typical ways of moving, gesturing, and talking. If visuals are included, let the writer know whether you think they add valuable information.

3. *Consider the Effectiveness of Anecdotes and Recurring Events.* Praise especially effective anecdotes and recurring events. Also point out ones that seem confusing or that do not contribute to your understanding of the person or the relationship. Praise dialogue that seems helpful and identify any that seems not to add anything or to be poorly written.

4. *Assess Whether the Significance Is Clear.* Point out the passages that help you understand the significance and any that do not aid your understanding. If you think the essay sentimentalizes the person or oversimplifies the relationship, tell the writer why you think so.

5. *Analyze the Effectiveness of the Organization.* Consider the *overall plan,* perhaps by making a scratch outline. Decide whether the writer might

strengthen the essay by shifting parts around, changing the order of anecdotes, or moving the descriptions of the person.

- Look again at the *beginning* of the essay to see whether it sets up the right expectations. Point out any description, anecdote, recurring event, or dialogue that might make a better beginning.
- Look at the *ending*. Comment on its effectiveness, noting if it repeats what you already know or oversimplifies or reduces the meaning of the relationship. Point out any description, anecdote, recurring event, or dialogue that would work better at the end.
- Look again at any *memorabilia* the writer has incorporated. Assess how well the memorabilia are integrated into the essay. Point to any items that do not help you visualize the person or understand the relationship.

REVISING

This section will help you get an overview of your draft and revise it accordingly.

Getting an Overview

Consider your draft as a whole, following these two steps:

1. *Reread.* If at all possible, put the draft aside for a day or two. When you do reread it, start by reconsidering your purpose. Then read the draft straight through, trying to see it as your intended readers will.

2. *Outline.* Make a quick scratch outline, indicating the basic features as they appear in the draft.

Charting a Plan for Revision. You may want to make a double-column chart like the following one to help you keep track of any problems you need to solve. In the left-hand column, list the basic features of writing about remembered people. As you analyze your draft and study any comments you have received from others, note the problems you want to solve in the right-hand column.

Basic Features	*Problems to Solve*
Portrait of the person	
Anecdotes and recurring events	
Indication of significance	
Organization	

Analyzing the Basic Features of Your Draft. Turn to the Critical Reading Guide on the preceding pages. Using this guide, identify problems you now see in your draft. Note the problems on the chart.

Studying Critical Comments. Review all of the comments you have received from other readers. For each comment, look at the draft to determine what might have led the reader to make that particular point. Try to be objective about any criticism. Ideally, these comments will help you to see your draft as others see it (rather than as you hoped it would be) and to identify specific problems.

Carrying Out Revisions

Having identified problems in your draft, you now need to figure out solutions and—most important—to carry them out. Basically, you have three options for finding solutions:

1. Review your invention and planning notes for material you can add to your draft.

2. Do additional invention writing to provide material you or your readers think is needed.

3. Look back at the readings in this chapter to see how other writers have solved similar problems.

The following suggestions, which are organized according to the basic features on your revision chart, will get you started solving common writing problems.

Vivid Description

- *Do you need more visual description?* Try naming features of the person's appearance and style of dress and adding these details to help readers imagine what the person looked like. Think, for example, of Wu's mother's "silky and black" hair or Gray's father's "massive, thick hands with scaly, reddish patches." Consider adding a vivid comparison, like Wu's metaphor describing her mother's eyes transforming "from serene pools of blackness into stormy balls of fire" or Angelou's simile visualizing Uncle Willie sitting "like a giant black Z." Look through your invention notes for descriptive language you might add to your draft.

- *Can you add specific narrative actions?* Look back at your invention notes to see what specific gestures or mannerisms you described. Show what the person looked like while in action—while arguing, laughing, or playing a game.

- *Do any descriptions weaken the dominant impression?* Omit extraneous descriptions or reconsider the impression you want to make.

Anecdotes and Recurring Events

- ***Do any of the anecdotes or recurring events seem confusing?*** Try adding signals—such as clock time and transitional words—to clarify when each action occurred in relation to the other actions.

- ***Could the essay use more anecdotes or recurring events?*** Look over your invention notes for other onetime or recurring events worth telling about. Try to think of events that will help readers understand the person and your relationship.

- ***Does any dialogue seem irrelevant or poorly written?*** Eliminate any dialogue that does not help readers imagine the person or understand the relationship. Liven up quoted dialogue with actual words and phrases the person typically used. Summarize other parts of the conversation. Instead of relying on "he said" or "she said," describe the person's tone of voice or attitude with phrases like "she hissed" and "I said quietly, on the verge of tears."

Autobiographical Significance

- ***Do you need to clarify the significance this person has had in your life?*** Try to make the dialogues, anecdotes, and recurring events show readers something important about your relationship. Consider stating directly how you felt at the time or showing your feelings through description or by your actions. Also try letting readers know your present perspective by choosing words that convey a particular tone or by making direct statements. If any of the anecdotes, conversations, or descriptive details seem to contradict the overall impression you are trying to create, cut them or reconsider the significance you are trying to show.

- ***Is your essay too sentimental or reductive?*** Consider acknowledging any ambivalent feelings you may have had or still have about the person or the relationship. Think of ways to introduce some complexity into your presentation—for example, by showing different, contradictory sides of the person's character or by showing lows as well as highs in the relationship.

Organization

- ***Is the beginning weak?*** See whether there is a better way to begin. Consider an engaging dialogue, an intriguing anecdote, or a colorful description. Try to find something that will capture readers' attention.

- ***Is the ending flat?*** Review your draft to see if there is a better place to end your essay. You might try ending with a question to leave readers with something to ponder. Or there might be something at the outset that you could refer to again at the end to frame the essay.

- ***If you have included memorabilia as part of your document's design, are the items well chosen and effectively integrated?*** Indicate where in the essay a bit of memorabilia could be described or mentioned. Think about what other memorabilia could be added.

▨ EDITING AND PROOFREADING

Now is the time to check your revised draft for grammar, punctuation, and mechanics. According to our research, essays about remembered people frequently display problems with sentence fragments, missing hyphens in compound adjectives that precede nouns, and subject + pronoun repetition. The following guidelines will help you locate and correct these errors.

Checking for Sentence Fragments.   A sentence fragment is a group of words that is punctuated as a sentence but that lacks some necessary sentence element, usually either a subject or a verb. Writing about a remembered person seems to encourage sentence fragments such as the following:

> I felt sorry for Lucy. Not because of her weight problem but because of her own discomfort with herself.

The first five words are a sentence, containing a subject (*I*) and a verb (*felt*). The next fourteen words constitute a fragment; although they are punctuated like a sentence, beginning with a capital letter and ending with a period, they include neither a subject nor a verb. Sentence fragments seem to occur when writers try to present many specific details so that readers can imagine the person. The following examples have been edited to attach the fragment to the sentence preceding it.

▶ I felt sorry for Lucy./ ~~Not~~ _{, not} because of her weight problem but because of her own discomfort with herself.

▶ Frank turned over the tarot cards one at a time/ ~~Each~~ _{, each} time telling me something about my future.

▶ There she stood at the door to our summer cabin/ ~~The~~ _{, the} spare, dimly lit space where we were to become closest friends and then bitter enemies.

Checking for Hyphens.   When you use compound adjectives (two adjectives together) that are not in a dictionary as a single entry, you have to decide whether you need to use a hyphen. In general, you should hyphenate most compound adjectives that precede a noun but not those that follow a noun.

> Coach Braga was a feared but well-respected man.

> Coach Braga was feared but well respected.

You may have used some compound adjectives as you were adding vivid details to your essay. Check your draft carefully to see that you have hyphenated compound adjectives correctly. Here are some more examples taken from student essays about remembered people:

▶ The intruder turned out to be a fifteen year old runaway.

▶ One of my musician friends had a four channel mixing board.

▶ I bought a high powered Honda CRX.

A Common ESL Problem.   Unlike some other languages, English does not allow a subject to be repeated by a pronoun (*he, she, it, you, we, they*).

▶ Great-Aunt Sonia ~~she~~ taught me to pick mushrooms.

▶ The person I miss the most from my country ~~he~~ is Luis Paulo.

▶ In Rio, the rivalry between Flamengo and Fluminense ~~it~~ is as strong as the one here between the Yankees and the Red Sox.

A WRITER AT WORK

■ REVISING A DRAFT AFTER A CRITICAL READING

In this section we look at the way Jan Gray's essay about her father evolved from draft to revision. Included here are her first draft and a written critique of it by one of her classmates. Read the draft and critique, and then reread her final version, "Father," printed on pp. 97–99.

The First Draft

Gray drafted her essay after spending a couple of hours on the invention and planning activities. She had no difficulty choosing a subject, since she had such strong feelings about and vivid memories of her father. She wrote the draft quickly in one sitting, not worrying about punctuation or usage. Though she wrote in pencil, her draft appears here typed.

```
        My father is a large intelligent, overpowering man. He's    1
    well-respected in the food-processing trade for his clever
    but shrewd business tactics but I find his manipulative
    qualities a reflection of the maturity that he lacks. For as
```

long as I can remember he's always had to be in control, decision-maker of the family and what he said was law. There was no compromising with this man and for that reason I've always feared him.

When I was little and he used to still live with us, every time he came home from work I avoided him as best I could. If he came in the kitchen I went in the living room and if he came into the living room I went upstairs to my bedroom just to avoid any confrontation.

Family trips were the worst. There was nowhere to go, I was locked up with him in a camper or motel for 1 week, 2 weeks or however long the vacation lasted. I remember one trip in particular. It was the summer after my 12th Birthday and the whole family (5 kids, 2 adults and one dog) were going to go "out west" for a month. We travelled through Wyoming, North and South Dakota, Colorado and other neighboring states were on the agenda. My father is the type who thinks he enjoys these family outings because as a loyal husband and father that's what he should do. Going to the state parks and the wilderness was more like a business trip than a vacation. He had made the agenda so no matter what we were to stick to it. That meant at every road sign like Yellowstone Nat'l Park we had to stop, one or more of the kids would get out stand by the sign and he'd take a picture just so he could say we've been there. Get in and get out as quick as possible was his motto to cover as much ground in as little time as he could. I hated having to take those pictures because it seemed so senseless--who cares about the dumb signs anyway? But dad is a very impatient man and any sign of non conformity was sure to put him in a rage. Not a physical violence, no, my father never did get violent but you always knew when he was boiling up inside. I could sense it in the tone of his voice and the reddish glaze that would cover his eyes. He would always stay very calm yet he was ready to explode. He never physically hurt anyone of us kids--sure we've all been spanked before but only when we were younger. Although he constrained himself from inflicting harm on people he didn't hold back from damaging objects.

I remember one time I was calling my mother from a girl-friend's house to ask if I could stay over for dinner when my father unexpectedly answered the phone. "Hello?" he said, in his usually gruffy manner.

"Oh, hi dad. Is Mom around?"   5

"What can I do for you?"   6

"Well, I just wanted to ask her if I could eat dinner   7
over here at Shana's."

"I don't think that's a very good idea. Your room is a   8
shambles and if your not home in 10 minutes I'm really going
to make a mess for you to clean up." Click.

I was in shock. I hadn't expected him to be there because   9
at this time my parents were divorced but I knew he was serious so I jumped on my bike and pedalled home as fast as I
could. I know I was there within ten minutes but apparently
he didn't think so. I walked in the front door and headed
straight for my room. When I opened my bedroom door I couldn't
believe what I saw. My dresser drawers were all pulled out and
clothes strewn about the room, the dresser was lying on its
side and everything on top of the dresser had been cast aside
in a fit of anger. I closed my door and tears began to well up
in my eyes. I hated him so much at the moment. All those years
of fear suddenly turned to anger and resentment. Who the hell
was this man to do this when he didn't even live in the house
anymore? I was slowly piecing my room back together when he
knocked on the door. I choked back the tears because I didn't
want him to know that his little outrage had gotten to me and
quietly said, "Come in."

He opened the door and stood in the doorway one arm   10
leaning on the door jamb and a cigarette with ashes falling on
the carpet dangling from his other hand.

"I want you to know I did this for your own good" He   11
said. "I think its time you started taking a little responsibility around this house. Now let me help you put the dresser
back up."

"No thanks. I'd rather do it myself."   12

"Aw, come on. Let's not have any hard feelings now."   13

"Please, I said. I'd rather do it myself so would you   14
please leave me alone." By this time I was shaking and on the
verge of breaking out in tears. He gave me one last look that
seemed to say, "I offered, I did the right thing, I'm the good
guy and she refused me so now it's her problem" and he walked
out.

I was so upset that he could be so violent one moment and   15
then turn around and patronize me by offering to help clean up

```
what he had done. That one incident revealed his whole charac-
ter to me.

     My father is a spiteful, manipulative, condescending,      16
malicious man and from that day on I knew I would never under-
stand him or want to.
```

Gray opens her draft with a series of direct statements, describing her father's character and stating her feelings about him. The second paragraph illustrates what she tells us in the first. Paragraph 3 also serves as illustration, showing her father's domination over the family and concluding with a physical description and a suggestion of his potential for violence.

In paragraphs 4–15, Gray relates an anecdote. Though long, it is fast-paced and dramatic. She uses dialogue to show us her father's character and description to help us visualize the damage he did to her room. Then she ends as she began—with a series of statements explicitly disclosing her feelings.

Critical Comments

A classmate named Tom Schwartz read Gray's draft. He read it through once and quickly wrote down his general impression. Following the Critical Reading Guide in this chapter, Schwartz then reread the draft to analyze its features closely. It took him a little more than half an hour to complete a full written critique, which appears here. Note that each point corresponds to a step in the Critical Reading Guide (see pp. 112–14).

1. Read for a First Impression

```
Your dad sure seems crazy. I can see he's impossible to live
with. Because he's your dad he's naturally significant. You
say you hate him and you call him a lot of names. But you also
say he thought of himself as a loyal father. Was there anytime
he was ok?
```

2. Consider How Vividly the Person Is Described

```
I can't picture him. What did he look like? I like the
description of your messed up room. I'd like even more detail,
like what clothes were thrown around and where. Did he break
anything when he tipped the dresser? Was the whole room a
wreck or just the dresser? Oh yeah, the detail of his ciga-
rette ashes falling on the carpet is great. He's the one who's
making the mess, not you.
```

You make a lot of statements. Most need illustration. I don't get it about there being no compromising with him. What do you expect him to do? My dad is pretty strict too. But he doesn't wreck my room.

3. Consider the Effectiveness of Anecdotes and Recurring Events

I don't get the vacation. Was it a birthday trip? Didn't you go to Yellowstone? Or did you just take pictures of signs? Sounds weird. The room anecdote is the best. It's really dramatic. The dialogue works as a frame, I think. He had some nerve offering to help pick up the dresser. How smug and self-satisfied. Patronizing is right. Great anecdote.

4. Assess Whether the Significance Is Clear

I just said you might have more feelings than you're admitting. You certainly have every reason to hate him. You say he never really hit you. But he certainly was violent, like you said.

I'm not sure why you wrote about your dad. Maybe you just feel strongly about him and need to figure him out. Maybe because he's colorful--unusual, unpredictable, not like other fathers, even divorced ones. I think he was a great choice for an essay. You disclose a lot of unpleasant stuff about your family. You certainly seem honest.

5. Analyze the Effectiveness of the Organization

The beginning doesn't lead me to expect the room anecdote. The stuff about his business seems out of place. You're writing about your relationship with him, not about his business. I don't have any suggestions.

The ending may be going too far now that I think of it. Also, even though you say you don't want to understand him, here you are writing about him. Maybe there's more to it than you're admitting. You could end with the paragraph before. The anecdote sure does reveal his character.

This critique helped Gray a great deal in revising her draft. Reread her revision now to see what she changed; it is obvious that many of her changes were suggested by Schwartz.

In writing about what she learned from writing this essay, Gray remarked:

Tom's criticism helped me a lot. He warned me against making too many statements without illustrating them. He said I needed more showing and less telling. He also questioned the vacation anecdote. I guess it didn't have much of a point. And the incident with my room seemed to work so well I decided to add the part about my dad's apartment.

Gray realized that the heart of her essay was in the anecdote about her room. She also saw, from Schwartz's comments, that the opening paragraphs were not working. Responding to his request for more physical description of her father, Gray returned to the invention activity in which she listed important details about her father's appearance. From this exploration, she came up with the detailed description that opens her revised essay. As she was describing her father, she remembered the incident of cleaning his apartment and decided to use the description of his filthy apartment to frame the description of her own ransacked room.

Perhaps Schwartz's greatest contribution was to help Gray reexamine her father's real significance in her life. Specifically, Schwartz made her realize that her feelings were more complicated than she let on in her first draft. In writing about what she learned, Gray concluded, "The feelings I wanted to express didn't come across. I had a hard time writing the paper because I held back on a lot of things. I'm pretty ambivalent in my feelings toward my father right now." Gray discovered she could disclose her ambivalent feelings by showing her father, his room, and the confrontation over her room. Gray's portrait of her father turned out to be more sympathetic than her comments about him, expressing some ambivalence—pity as well as fury.

DESIGNING YOUR WORK

For the library display described earlier in this chapter (see p. 80), the volunteer and the waitress chose several artifacts to accompany their written narrative. They looked for photographs and objects that could be displayed in the space they had available—two glass cases and a bulletin board—and that would convey the flavor of the neighborhood during the years the diner and its owner played such an important role in the community. They chose a variety of items to accompany their written text, which provided the overall structure for the display. Enlarged photocopies of the typed document were cut apart, pasted on boards, and positioned so that viewers could easily read one section of the text, look at the artifacts, and then move on to the next part of the display.

Selecting Artifacts

Many of the artifacts that the volunteer and the waitress selected showed how the diner and the nearby high school had changed over time. Copies of menus, spanning over thirty years' time, showed that though many favorites on the menu had remained the same, prices had inevitably increased. Pennants from the high school football team showed different designs over the years, but collectively reminded viewers how many generations of teammates had celebrated their winning games by eating at the diner afterward. Records from the jukebox showed how teenagers' tastes had changed. Yearbooks, opened to pages with student photographs (including the waitress in her high school days), illustrated how styles and attitudes changed during the decades the diner was open. In choosing these memorabilia, the volunteer and waitress contrasted the changes that come with time with the constant presence of the restaurant and the owner as part of the neighborhood. In this way, they illustrated the old adage, "the more things change, the more they stay the same."

Incorporating Letters and Other Primary Documents

The diner owner had saved a great many letters and postcards from former neighborhood children. The volunteer and the waitress included some of these often casual and conversational notes (along with a selection of informal snapshots) to show how many of the diner's patrons had considered the owner to be something of a friend and mentor. The writers clearly wanted to keep the owner apprised of the changes and advances in their lives because he had been such a friendly figure in their formative years.

Primary documents, which are original materials written by an author rather than texts that reproduce or encompass other texts, often contain nuances and illustrate feelings that can be difficult to summarize. The exact words used by speakers and writers are sometimes the best ones to convey a sense of immediacy; when paraphrases or summaries are not enough to capture everything of importance, sections of or complete primary documents can often speak for themselves. In the library display, the letters not only showed how many people felt affection toward the diner's owner but also echoed the waitress's claims that he served as a significant mentor.

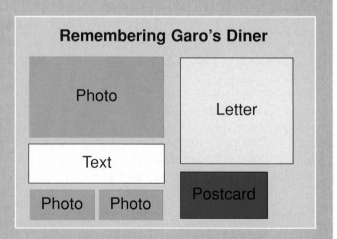

Layout showing the combination of text, photos, and other memorabilia used in part of the library display

THINKING CRITICALLY ABOUT
WHAT YOU HAVE LEARNED

Now that you have spent considerable time reading and discussing essays about remembered people, and writing such an essay yourself, you should reflect on what you have learned. What problems did you have as a writer, and how did you solve them? How did reading other essays influence your own essay? What ideas do you have about the social and cultural dimensions of this kind of writing?

Reflecting on Your Writing

Write a one-page explanation, telling your instructor about a problem you encountered in writing your essay and how you solved it. Before you begin, gather all of your writing—invention and planning notes, drafts, critical comments, revising notes and plans, and final revision. Review these materials as you complete this writing task.

1. *Identify* **one** *writing problem you needed to solve as you wrote about a remembered person.* Do not be concerned with grammar and punctuation; concentrate on problems unique to developing an essay in this genre. For example: Did you puzzle over how to create a vivid portrait or present revealing anecdotes and scenes? Was it difficult for you to probe the significance of the relationship?

2. *Determine how you came to recognize the problem.* When did you first discover it? What called it to your attention? If someone else pointed out the problem to you, can you now see hints of it in your invention writings? If so, where specifically? When you first recognized the problem, how did you respond?

3. *Reflect on how you went about solving the problem.* Did you change the wording of a passage, cut or add details, or move paragraphs around? Did you reread one of the essays in this chapter to

see how another writer handled a similar problem, or did you look back at the invention suggestions? If you talked about your writing problem with another student, a tutor, or your instructor, did talking about it help? How useful was the advice you received?

4. *Write a brief explanation of the problem and your solution.* Be as specific as possible in reconstructing your efforts. Quote from your invention notes or draft essay, others' critical comments, your revision plan, or your revised essay to show the various changes in your writing as you solved the problem. This is time well spent. If you can identify a particular problem, explain how you solved it, and understand what you learned from the experience, you will be able to solve future writing problems more easily.

Reviewing What You Learned from Reading

Write a page or so explaining to your instructor how the readings in this chapter influenced your final draft. Your own essay about a remembered person has been influenced to some extent by the essays in this chapter as well as by classmates' essays that you have read. These other essays may have helped you to choose your subject, suggested ideas for using anecdote and dialogue, shown you how to reveal ambivalence, or assisted you in some other way. Before you write, take some time to think about what you have learned from these selections.

1. *Reread the final revision of your essay; then look back at the selections you read before completing it.* Do you see any specific influences? For example, if you were impressed with the way one of the readings avoided sentimentality, acknowledged ambivalent feelings, detailed a scene, or

compared two people, look to see where you might have been striving for similar effects in your own writing. Also look for ideas you got from your reading: writing strategies you were inspired to try, specific details you were led to include, effects you sought to achieve.

2. *Write an explanation of these influences.* Did one selection have a particularly strong influence on your essay, or were several selections influential in different ways? Quote from the other essays and from your final revision to show how your portrait was influenced by the other selections. Finally, point out anything you would now do to improve your own essay, based on reviewing the reading selections again.

Considering the Social Dimensions of Essays about Remembered People

Writing about a person who played a significant role in your life can help you understand how you usually respond in certain types of relationships and what you need and expect from other people. Moreover, writing about significant people requires that you look at yourself as a participant in dynamic, reciprocal relationships. Thus, such writing encourages you to acknowledge that you are not solely responsible for all of your achievements or all of your failings. It shows you how others have helped as well as hindered you, taught as well as thwarted you.

Because they focus on interpersonal relationships, reading and writing essays about remembered people also can help us to understand other points of view. Maya Angelou, for example, writes about an incident that helped her to understand Uncle Willie's deepest feelings. When she senses his vulnerability, she begins to see him not simply in terms of how he treats her but also in terms of his own needs and frustrations. Her empathy allows her to feel closer to him, but it does not erase her other feelings of anger and resentment. Similarly, Amy Wu's essay shows us that how we understand and evaluate other people may depend on cultural expectations. Instead of seeing others as simple stereotypes, reading and writing about remembered people can help us to recognize people as

complex human beings. Moreover, it can make us aware of the influences that help shape our thinking about other people and our assumptions about relationships.

These ideas about relationships lead to some basic questions about how we use writing about remembered people to understand others and ourselves. Following are two topics for discussion. Note your thoughts as you read the questions or discuss them in class. Then write a page or so for your instructor exploring your ideas and conclusions.

Ways of Understanding Other People.   As we read and write essays about remembered people, we are influenced by other factors, such as whether we tend to understand people *psychologically*—in terms of personal feelings, conflicts, and desires—or more *socially*—in terms of the public cultural, economic, and political conditions of our lives. You can understand these different perspectives by applying them to the selections in this chapter. For example, Maya Angelou's portrait of Uncle Willie could be understood psychologically, as demonstrating a child's resentment of a father-figure or an adult's inability to show affection. But it also could be explained in terms of the larger social and political context. Uncle Willie's behavior toward Angelou and her brother might be connected to his position as an oppressed African American man in the segregated South of the 1930s and 1940s. Or we could easily attribute his behavior to the fact that he has a marked physical disability in a society intolerant of physical differences. Depending on how you interpret behavior, you could see Uncle Willie's bullying of Angelou and her brother either as a neurotic assertion of power or as an effort to fulfill societal expectations of him as a substitute father seeing that his children do their homework.

1. *Consider how you have generally interpreted other people's essays about remembered people.* Have you understood the essays primarily in personal, psychological terms? Or in more public— social, cultural, or political—terms? A little of both?

2. *Consider how you thought of the person when you were writing about a significant person in your own life.* Did you see the person as being motivated by certain personal needs or fears? Or did you see the person as being affected more by external social forces and pressures?

3. *Reflect on what these two ways of understanding people make possible.* What kinds of insights does psychological understanding of people lead to? What kinds of insights does social or political understanding of people lead to?

Views of the Self. If we assume that reading and writing about remembered people can contribute to self-discovery, we must consider how the "self" is defined and how it may be affected by significant relationships. Many people think that the self is formed early in life and remains basically unchanged by later circumstances. If you accept this view, then you are likely to see people as fundamentally unaffected by personal relationships. For example, you might see Jan Gray as emotionally independent of her father, secure in her own sense of herself: She seems neither to need his praise nor to care about his criticism. On the other hand, you may think of the self as more fluid and variable, believing that the various roles we play constitute different aspects of the self and that we change when we interact with other people. If you read Gray's essay from this perspective, you might see her relationship with her father as changing over time and Gray herself as different at various stages in the relationship. You might conclude that after her father wrecked her room, she was not the same person, that she was changed by the experience. You might also speculate that seeing her father's pathetic apartment was a turning point, enabling her to distance herself from him emotionally.

1. *Draw some conclusions about the impact of relationships on the self.* Do relationships provide an opportunity for us to act out who we already are? Or do they change us by giving us different roles to play?

2. *Consider your own views of the Gray essay.* Do you think Gray changes as her relationship with her father evolves, or do you see her as basically staying the same throughout? What in the essay makes you think so? (If you have read Gray's first draft in the Writer at Work section, think about what it reveals about her childhood.)

3. *Think about your own essay in the same terms.* Does it reveal a single, unified self or one that is marked by different sides and changes over time?

Writing Profiles

Much of what we know about people and the world we learn from profiles based on firsthand observation and interviews. Profiles tell about people, places, and activities. Some profiles give us a glimpse of the inner workings of familiar places. Others introduce us to the exotic—peculiar hobbies, unusual professions, bizarre personalities.

Whatever their subject, profile writers strive first and foremost to enable readers to visualize the person, place, or activity that is the focus of the profile. Writers succeed only by presenting many concrete details: how the person dresses, gestures, and talks; what the place looks, sounds, and smells like; what the activity involves and how it progresses. Not only must the details be vivid, but they also must help to convey the subject's significance—what makes the subject interesting and meaningful.

Because profiles share many features with essays about remembered events and people—such as description, narration, dialogue, and significance—you may use many of the strategies learned in Chapters 2 and 3 when you write your profile. Yet profiles differ from writing that reflects on personal experience in that profiles present newly acquired knowledge. To write a profile, you need to learn new strategies for researching, analyzing, synthesizing, and presenting information. Taking a questioning approach to even the most familiar subjects, you practice the field research methods of observing, interviewing, and notetaking. These research activities, combined with thoughtful analysis and imaginative synthesis, form the basic strategies of learning in many areas of study, including anthropology, sociology, and psychology.

The scope of your profile may be large or small, depending on your assignment and your subject. You could attend a single event such as a parade or tournament and write up your observations of the place, people, and activities. Or you might conduct an interview with a person who has an unusual occupation and write up a profile based on your interview notes. If you have the time to do more extensive research, you might write a full-blown profile based on several observations and interviews with various people.

Writing in Your Other Courses

- For a research essay in an education course, a student who has been studying collaborative learning principles incorporates a profile of a group of sixth-grade students working together on an Internet project. The college student observes

For a look at some of the decisions this student makes about document design, see pp. 177–78.

and takes extensive notes on the collaboration, and to learn what the sixth graders think about working together, interviews them individually and as a group. She also talks with the classroom teacher about how students were prepared to do this kind of work and how their collaboration will be evaluated.

- For an anthropology assignment, a student plans to research and write an ethnography about football at the local high school. He models his project on Clifford Geertz's groundbreaking research on Balinese cockfighting. Like Geertz, he writes a "thick description" that alternates observational details with his own ideas about what football means to this particular high school community. He focuses his profile on the way football confers status on the players, their parents, and friends.

Writing in the Community

- An art history student profiles a local artist recently commissioned to paint an outdoor mural for the city. The student visits the artist's studio and talks with him about the process of painting murals. The artist invites the student to spend the following day with a team of local art students and neighborhood volunteers working on the mural under his direction. This firsthand experience helps the student describe the process of mural painting almost from an insider's point of view. She organizes her profile around the main stages of this collaborative mural project, from conception to completion. As she describes each stage, she weaves in details about the artist, his helpers, and the site of their work, seeking to capture the civic spirit that pervades the mural project.

- For a small-town newspaper, a writer profiles a community activist who appears regularly at city council meetings to speak on various problems in the neighborhood. The writer interviews the activist as well as two of the council members. He also observes the activist speaking at one particular council meeting on the problem of trash being dumped in unauthorized areas. At this meeting, the activist describes an all-night vigil he made to capture on videotape a flagrant act of illegal dumping in an empty lot near his home. The writer uses the activist's appearance at this meeting as a narrative framework for the profile; he also integrates details of the activist's public life along with images from the videotape.

Writing in the Workplace

- A social worker preparing to write a probation report on a teenager convicted of a crime interviews the teenager and his parents and observes the interactions among the family members. Her report describes in detail what she saw and heard, concluding with a recommendation that the teenager return to his parents' home.

- For a company newsletter, a personnel officer writes a day-in-the-life type of profile of the new CEO. He follows the CEO from meeting to meeting, interviewing her between meetings about her management philosophy and her plans for handling the challenges facing the company. The CEO, who adopts a personal management style, invites the writer to visit her at home and meet her family. The profile is illustrated by two photographs—one showing the CEO in an intense business conference, and the other showing her at home with her family.

 The preceding scenarios suggest some occasions for writing profiles. Imagine that you have been assigned to write a profile of a person, a place, or an activity on your campus, in your community, or at your workplace. Think of subjects that you would like to know more about.

Practice Choosing a Profile Subject: A Collaborative Activity

Part 1. List several subjects. Consider interesting people (store owner, distinguished teacher, newspaper columnist, public defender, CEO, radio talk show host), places (student health center, research center, machine shop, police department, student newspaper office, day-care center, exercise or sports facility, women's resource center, campus tour office, office of telecommunications services), and businesses or activities (comic-book store, auto wrecking company, motorcycle dealer, commercial fishing boat, local brewery or winery, eating disorder treatment center, building contractor, dance studio, private tutoring service, dog kennel).

Now get together with two or three other students and take turns reading your lists of subjects to one another. The other group members will tell you which item on your list they personally find most interesting and discuss with you briefly any questions they have about it.

Part 2. After you have all read your lists and received responses, discuss these questions as a group:

- Are you surprised by which items on your list the other members of the group find most interesting?
- Are you surprised by any of their questions about this subject?
- How might these questions influence your approach to the subject?

READINGS

The readings in this chapter illustrate the features of profiles and the strategies writers rely on to realize the features. No two essays in this genre are much alike, and yet they share defining features. The section Analyzing Writing Strategies and the Commentary following each reading touch on a few features best illustrated by that essay, capturing its special qualities and strengths. Together, the four essays cover many of the possibilities of the genre. Consequently, you will want to read as many of the

131

essays as possible and, if time permits, complete the activities in Analyzing Writing Strategies and read the Commentaries. Following the readings is a section called Basic Features, which offers a concise description of the features of profiles and provides examples from all of the readings.

"Soup" is an unsigned profile that initially appeared in the "Talk of the Town" section of the New Yorker *magazine (January 1989). The* New Yorker *regularly features brief, anonymous profiles like this one, whose subject is the fast-talking owner/chef of a takeout restaurant specializing in soup. In 1995, Albert Yeganeh, the subject of this profile, also inspired an episode of the television series* Seinfeld. *As you read, notice the prominence given to dialogue.*

comfortable tone ←

Soup

The New Yorker

When Albert Yeganeh says "Soup is my lifeblood," he means it. And when he says "I am extremely hard to please," he means that, too. Working like a demon alchemist in a tiny storefront kitchen at 259-A West Fifty-fifth Street, Mr. Yeganeh creates anywhere from eight to seventeen soups every weekday. His concoctions are so popular that a wait of half an hour at the lunchtime peak is not uncommon, although there are strict rules for conduct in line. But more on that later.

"I am psychologically kind of a health freak," Mr. Yeganeh said the other day, in a lisping staccato of Armenian origin. "And I know that soup is the greatest meal in the world. It's very good for your digestive system. And I use only the best, the freshest ingredients. I am a perfectionist. When I make a clam soup, I use three different kinds of clams. Every other place uses canned clams. I'm called crazy. I am not crazy. People don't realize why I get so upset. It's because if the soup is not perfect and I'm still selling it, it's a torture. It's *my* soup, and that's why I'm so upset. First you clean and then you cook. I don't believe that ninety-nine per cent of the restaurants in New York know how to clean a tomato. I tell my crew to wash the parsley *eight* times. If they wash it five or six times, I scare them. I tell them they'll go to jail if there is sand in the parsley. One time, I found a mushroom on the floor, and I fired the guy who left it there." He spread his arms, and added, "This place is the only one like it in . . . in . . . the whole earth! One day, I hope to learn something from the other places, but so far I haven't. For example, the other day I went to a very fancy restaurant and had borscht. I had to send it back. It was *junk.* I could see all the chemicals in it. I never use chemicals. Last weekend, I had lobster bisque in Brooklyn, a very well-known place. It was *junk.* When I make a lobster bisque, I use a whole lobster. You know, I never advertise. I don't have to. All the big-shot chefs and the kings of the hotels come here to see what *I'm* doing."

As you approach Mr. Yeganeh's Soup Kitchen International from a distance, the first thing you notice about it is the awning, which proclaims "Homemade Hot, Cold, Diet Soups." The second thing you notice is an aroma so delicious that it makes you want to take a bite out of the air. The third thing you notice, in front of the kitchen, is an electric signboard that flashes, say, "Today's Soups . . . Chicken Vegetable . . . Mexican Beef Chili . . . Cream of Watercress . . . Italian Sausage . . . Clam Bisque . . . Beef Barley . . . Due to Cold Weather . . . For Most Efficient and Fastest Service the Line Must . . . Be

1

2

3

Kept Moving . . . Please . . . Have Your Money . . . Ready . . . Pick the Soup of Your Choice . . . Move to Your Extreme . . . Left After Ordering."

"I am not prejudiced against color or religion," Mr. Yeganeh told us, and he jabbed an index finger at the flashing sign. "Whoever follows that I treat very well. My regular customers don't say anything. They are very intelligent and well educated. They know I'm just trying to move the line. The New York cop is very smart—he sees everything but says nothing. But the young girl who wants to stop and tell you how nice you look and hold everyone up—*yah!*" He made a guillotining motion with his hand. "I tell you, I hate to work with the public. They treat me like a slave. My philosophy is: The customer is always wrong and I'm always right. I raised my prices to try to get rid of some of these people, but it didn't work."

The other day, Mr. Yeganeh was dressed in chefs' whites with orange smears across his chest, which may have been some of the carrot soup cooking in a huge pot on a little stove in one corner. A three-foot-long handheld mixer from France sat on the sink, looking like an overgrown gardening tool. Mr. Yeganeh spoke to two young helpers in a twisted Armenian-Spanish barrage, then said to us, "I have no overhead, no trained waitresses, and I have the cashier here." He pointed to himself theatrically. Beside the doorway, a glass case with fresh green celery, red and yellow peppers, and purple eggplant was topped by five big gray soup urns. According to a piece of cardboard taped to the door, you can buy Mr. Yeganeh's soups in three sizes, costing from four to fifteen dollars. The order of any well-behaved customer is accompanied by little waxpaper packets of bread, fresh vegetables (such as scallions and radishes), fresh fruit (such as cherries or an orange), a chocolate mint, and a plastic spoon. No coffee, tea, or other drinks are served.

"I get my recipes from books and theories and my own taste," Mr. Yeganeh said. "At home, I have several hundreds of books. When I do research, I find that I don't know anything. Like cabbage is a cancer fighter, and some fish is good for your heart but some is bad. Every day, I should have one sweet, one spicy, one cream, one vegetable soup —and they *must* change, they should always taste a little different." He added that he wasn't sure how extensive his repertoire was, but that it probably includes at least eighty soups, among them African peanut butter, Greek moussaka, hamburger, Reuben, B.L.T., asparagus and caviar, Japanese shrimp miso, chicken chili, Irish corned beef and cabbage, Swiss chocolate, French calf's brain, Korean beef ball, Italian shrimp and eggplant Parmesan, buffalo, ham and egg, short rib, Russian beef Stroganoff, turkey cacciatore, and Indian mulligatawny. "The chicken and the seafood are an addiction, and when I have French garlic soup I let people have only one small container each," he said. "The doctors and nurses love that one."

A lunch line of thirty people stretched down the block from Mr. Yeganeh's doorway. Behind a construction worker was a man in expensive leather, who was in front of a woman in a fur hat. Few people spoke. Most had their money out and their orders ready.

At the front of the line, a woman in a brown coat couldn't decide which soup to get and started to complain about the prices.

"You talk too much, dear," Mr. Yeganeh said, and motioned to her to move to the left. "Next!"

"Just don't talk. Do what he says," a man huddled in a blue parka warned.   10

"He's downright rude," said a blond woman in a blue coat. "Even abusive. But you   11
can't deny it, his soup is the best."

Connecting to Culture and Experience: Standards of Excellence

A popular book urges American business executives to "search for excellence," claiming that profit will follow. Albert Yeganeh is a prime example of this philosophy.

Discuss with two or three other students your experiences with excellence as a worker and student. How have your work values been shaped by the situations in which you have worked? On the job, for example, what kinds of attitudes encourage—or discourage—high-quality work? In school, what has inspired you to do your best work or prevented or discouraged you from doing it? Focus on specific examples of school and work experiences.

Analyzing Writing Strategies

1. At the beginning of this chapter, we make several generalizations about profile essays. Consider which of these assertions are true of "Soup":
   * It is based on a writer's newly acquired observations.
   * It takes readers behind the scenes of familiar places or introduces them to unusual places and people.
   * It is informative and entertaining.
   * It presents scenes and people vividly through description, action, and dialogue.
   * It conveys the subject's significance—what makes it interesting and meaningful.

For more on detailing, see Chapter 15, pp. 591–93.

2. In addition to profiling a person, "Soup" describes a place of business. Reread paragraphs 1, 3, and 5, underlining **details** that describe the soup restaurant itself, inside and outside. For example, in paragraph 3, you would underline *awning* as well as what is written on the awning: *"Homemade Hot, Cold, Diet Soups."* You need not worry about whether you are underlining too many or too few details. Try to catch every detail that expands your image of the place.

Commentary: A Specific Focus and Informative Plan

A profile focuses on a person, place, or activity. Often, as in "Soup," a profile focuses on one element—a person—while also presenting a good deal of information about the place and activity associated with the person. "Soup" begins and ends with Albert Yeganeh, the creative and rather demanding owner/chef of a small restaurant called Soup Kitchen International. Much of what we learn about him—his attitudes, ideas, and business methods—comes from Mr. Yeganeh himself, through the comments he made during interviews with the *New Yorker* writer. In addition, we are given the writer's firsthand observations and a few comments from customers.

Profile writers not only need to focus their observations, but they also need to plan how best to present the bits and pieces of information they accumulate from observations and interviews. Most profiles are organized in one of two ways: chronologically, as a story, or topically, as groups of related information. "Soup" is organized topically.

The following scratch outline of "Soup" shows at a glance the topics the writer has chosen and how they are sequenced:

Introduction to Yeganeh and his soup kitchen (paragraph 1)

Yeganeh's perfectionism (2)

An outside view of the soup kitchen (3)

Yeganeh's attitudes toward customers (4)

Yeganeh at work and his rules of the house (5)

Yeganeh's soup-making repertoire (6)

Customers and their interactions with Yeganeh (7–11)

This plan alternates interview segments with observations of the soup kitchen. There are three interview topics: perfectionism (paragraph 2), attitudes toward customers (4), and soup-making repertoire (6). Observational topics present the soup kitchen from three different vantage points: outside, approaching from a distance (3); inside the kitchen (5); and within the line of customers waiting to be served (7–11). Instead of organizing the information chronologically by telling a story of one visit to the soup kitchen, the writer reports topic by topic what is learned on several visits. The writer probably first grouped related topics and then came up with a sensible plan of alternating them, perhaps assuming that readers would remain more engaged if the relatively large blocks of quoted material alternated with descriptions of the soup kitchen. When you plan your profile essay, you will have to decide whether to organize your first draft topically or chronologically.

Considering Topics for Your Own Essay

List three to five unusual people or places on campus or in your community that you could profile. Then think of a few questions you or your readers might want answered about each of these possible subjects. Finally, choose the subject you think would be most interesting to research. What makes this choice interesting for you?

You will see an example of chronological organization in the following profile, "The Daily Grind," by Peggy Orenstein.

Peggy Orenstein has been a managing editor of Mother Jones, *a founding editor of the award-winning magazine* 7 days, *and a member of the editorial boards of* Esquire *and* Manhattan, inc. *Her own essays have appeared in the* New York Times Magazine, New Yorker, Vogue, *and other nationally known publications. This profile, which takes place primarily in Mrs. Richter's math class, comes from the opening chapter of her book,* School Girls: Young Women, Self-Esteem, and the Confidence Gap *(1994), a winner of the New York*

Times Notable Book of the Year Award. Orenstein undertook the extensive research for this book after reading a study conducted by the American Association of University Women in 1991, which identified a gender gap between male and female students in America. Her research "concentrated on the ways in which the educational system—often unwittingly— inhibits, restricts, diminishes, and denies girls' experience." As you read the profile, think about whether the story it tells is one you have witnessed firsthand.

The Daily Grind: Lessons in the Hidden Curriculum

Peggy Orenstein

Amy Wilkinson has looked forward to being an eighth grader forever—at least for the last two years, which, when you're thirteen, seems like the same thing. By the second week of September she's settled comfortably into her role as one of the school's reigning elite. Each morning before class, she lounges with a group of about twenty other eighth-grade girls and boys in the most visible spot on campus: at the base of the schoolyard, between one of the portable classrooms that was constructed in the late 1970s and the old oak tree in the overflow parking lot. The group trades gossip, flirts, or simply stands around, basking in its own importance and killing time before the morning bell. 1

At 8:15 on Tuesday the crowd has already convened, and Amy is standing among a knot of girls, laughing. She is fuller-figured than she'd like to be, wide-hipped and heavy-limbed with curly, blond hair, cornflower-blue eyes, and a sharply upturned nose. With the help of her mother, who is a drama coach, she has become the school's star actress: last year she played Eliza in Weston's production of *My Fair Lady*. Although she earns solid grades in all of her subjects—she'll make the honor roll this fall—drama is her passion, she says, because "I love entertaining people, and I love putting on characters." 2

Also, no doubt, because she loves the spotlight: this morning, when she mentions a boy I haven't met, Amy turns, puts her hands on her hips, anchors her feet shoulder width apart, and bellows across the schoolyard, "Greg! Get over here! You have to meet Peggy." 3

She smiles wryly as Greg, looking startled, begins to make his way across the schoolyard for an introduction. "I'm not exactly shy," she says, her hands still on her hips. "I'm *bold*." 4

Amy is bold. And brassy, and strong-willed. Like any teenager, she tries on and discards different selves as if they were so many pairs of Girbaud jeans, searching ruthlessly for a perfect fit. During a morning chat just before the school year began, she told me that her parents tried to coach her on how to respond to my questions. "They told me to tell you that they want me to be my own person," she complained. "My mother *told* me to tell you that. I do want to be my own person, but it's like, you're interviewing me about who *I* am and she's telling me what to say—that's not my own person, is it?" 5

When the morning bell rings, Amy and her friends cut off their conversations, scoop up their books, and jostle toward the school's entrance. Inside, Weston's hallways smell chalky, papery, and a little sweaty from gym class. The wood-railed staircases at either 6 end of the two-story main building are worn thin in the middle from the scuffle of hundreds of pairs of sneakers pounding them at forty-eight-minute intervals for nearly seventy-five years. Amy's mother, Sharon, and her grandmother both attended this school. So will her two younger sisters. Her father, a mechanic who works on big rigs, is a more recent Weston recruit: he grew up in Georgia and came here after he and Sharon were married.

Amy grabs my hand, pulling me along like a small child or a slightly addled new student: within three minutes we have threaded our way through the dull-yellow hallways to her locker and then upstairs to room 238, Mrs. Richter's math class.

7

The twenty-two students that stream through the door with us run the gamut of physical maturity. Some of the boys are as small and compact as fourth graders, their legs sticking out of their shorts like pipe cleaners. A few are trapped in the agony of a growth spurt, and still others cultivate downy beards. The girls' physiques are less extreme: most are nearly their full height, and all but a few have already weathered the brunt of puberty. They wear topknots or ponytails, and their shirts are tucked neatly into their jeans.

8

Mrs. Richter, a ruddy, athletic woman with a powerful voice, has arranged the chairs in a three-sided square, two rows deep. Amy walks to the far side of the room and, as she takes her seat, falls into a typically feminine pose: she crosses her legs, folds her arms across her chest, and hunches forward toward her desk, seeming to shrink into herself. The sauciness of the playground disappears, and, in fact, she says hardly a word during class. Meanwhile, the boys, especially those who are more physically mature, sprawl in their chairs, stretching their legs long, expanding into the available space.

9

Nate, a gawky, sanguine boy who has shaved his head except for a small thatch that's hidden under an Oakland A's cap, leans his chair back on two legs and, although the bell has already rung, begins a noisy conversation with his friend, Kyle.

10

Mrs. Richter turns to him, "What's all the discussion about, Nate?" she asks.

11

"He's talking to *me,"* Nate answers, pointing to Kyle. Mrs. Richter writes Nate's name on the chalkboard as a warning toward detention and he yells out in protest. They begin to quibble over the justice of her decision, their first—but certainly not their last— power struggle of the day. As they argue, Allison, a tall, angular girl who once told me, "My goal is to be the best wife and mother I can be," raises her hand to ask a question. Mrs. Richter, finishing up with Nate, doesn't notice.

12

"Get your homework out, everyone!" the teacher booms, and walks among the students, checking to make sure no one has shirked on her or his assignment. Allison, who sits in the front row nearest both the blackboard and the teacher, waits patiently for another moment, then, realizing she's not getting results, puts her hand down. When Mrs. Richter walks toward her, Allison tries another tack, calling out her question. Still, she gets no response, so she gives up.

13

As a homework assignment, the students have divided their papers into one hundred squares, color-coding each square prime or composite—prime being those numbers which are divisible only by one and themselves, and composite being everything else. Mrs. Richter asks them to call out the prime numbers they've found, starting with the tens.

14

Nate is the first to shout, "Eleven!" The rest of the class chimes in a second later.   15
As they move through the twenties and thirties, Nate, Kyle, and Kevin, who sit near one
another at the back of the class, call out louder and louder, casually competing for both
quickest response and the highest decibel level. Mrs. Richter lets the boys' behavior
slide, although they are intimidating other students.

"Okay," Mrs. Richter says when they've reached one hundred. "Now, what do you   16
think of one hundred and three? Prime or composite?"

Kyle, who is skinny and a little pop-eyed, yells out, "Prime!" but Mrs. Richter turns   17
away from him to give someone else a turn. Unlike Allison, who gave up when she was
ignored, Kyle isn't willing to cede his teacher's attention. He begins to bounce in his chair
and chant, *"Prime! Prime! Prime!"* Then, when he turns out to be right, he rebukes the
teacher, saying, *"See,* I told you."

When the girls in Mrs. Richter's class do speak, they follow the rules. When Allison   18
has another question, she raises her hand again and waits her turn; this time, the
teacher responds. When Amy volunteers her sole answer of the period, she raises her
hand, too. She gives the wrong answer to an easy multiplication problem, turns crimson,
and flips her head forward so her hair falls over her face.

Occasionally, the girls shout out answers, but generally they are to the easiest,   19
lowest-risk questions, such as the factors of four or six. And their stabs at public recognition depend on the boys' largesse: when the girls venture responses to more complex
questions the boys quickly become territorial, shouting them down with their own
answers. Nate and Kyle are particularly adept at overpowering Renee, who, I've been
told by the teacher, is the brightest girl in the class. (On a subsequent visit, I will see her
lay her head on her desk when Nate overwhelms her and mutter, "I hate this class.")

Mrs. Richter doesn't say anything to condone the boys' aggressiveness, but she   20
doesn't have to: they insist on—and receive—her attention even when she consciously
tries to shift it elsewhere in order to make the class more equitable.

After the previous day's homework is corrected, Mrs. Richter begins a new lesson,   21
on the use of exponents.

"What does three to the third power mean?" she asks the class.   22

"I know!" shouts Kyle.   23

Instead of calling on Kyle, who has already answered more than his share of ques-   24
tions, the teacher turns to Dawn, a somewhat more voluble girl who has plucked her
eyebrows down to a few hairs.

"Do you know, Dawn?"   25

Dawn hesitates, and begins "Well, you count the number of threes and. . . ."   26

"But I know!" interrupts Kyle. *"I know!"*   27

Mrs. Richter deliberately ignores him, but Dawn is rattled: she never finishes her   28
sentence, she just stops.

"I know! ME!" Kyle shouts again, and then before Dawn recovers herself he blurts,   29
"It's three times three times three!"

At this point, Mrs. Richter gives in. She turns away from Dawn, who is staring   30
blankly, and nods at Kyle. "Yes," she says. "Three times three times three. Does everyone get it?"

"*YES!*" shouts Kyle; Dawn says nothing. 31

Mrs. Richter picks up the chalk. "Let's do some others," she says. 32

"Let me!" says Kyle. 33

"I'll pick on whoever raises their hand," she tells him. 34

Nate, Kyle, and two other boys immediately shoot up their hands, fingers squeezed 35
tight and straight in what looks like a salute.

"Don't you want to wait and hear the problem first?" she asks, laughing. 36

They drop their hands briefly. She writes 8^4 on the board. "Okay, what would that 37
look like written out?"

Although a third of the class raises their hands to answer—including a number of 38
students who haven't yet said a word—she calls on Kyle anyway.

"Eight times eight times eight times eight," he says triumphantly, as the other 39
students drop their hands.

When the bell rings, I ask Amy about the mistake she made in class and the embar- 40
rassment it caused her. She blushes again.

"Oh yeah," she says. "That's about the only time I ever talked in there. I'll never do 41
that again."

Connecting to Culture and Experience: Gender Equality

The "hidden curriculum," according to Orenstein, teaches girls that boys have more
power and authority than they do. Discuss your own experience and observation to
see whether you agree with Orenstein about gender inequality in middle school and
high school. Also consider whether school culture fosters other kinds of inequality—
for example, based on money, cultural background, success in sports or academics.

Analyzing Writing Strategies

1. What do you think is the focus of Orenstein's observations—a person, a place,
   or an activity? This profile (like most profiles) includes all three elements, but
   which one seems to be at the center of Orenstein's attention? Consider how you
   know. What in the essay, for example, enables you to identify the primary focus
   of the observations?

2. Whereas the author of "Soup" organizes the information topically, Orenstein
   organizes her profile chronologically. Reread the essay and underline the time
   markers: **calendar time** ("By the second week of September" [paragraph 1]) and
   clock time ("At 8:15" [2]), as well as **temporal transitions** ("when" [6]). Then
   reflect on how well these time markers help you follow the profile's chronological organization.

For more on these narrating
strategies, see Chapter 14,
pp. 573–77.

Commentary: Significance

Profiles, like essays about remembered events or people, do more than merely present information; they also indicate what is significant or interesting about the person, place, or activity that is the focus of the profile. To convey this significance, profile writers either tell what they think or try to show it through description, action, and dialogue.

For more on comparison and contrast, see Chapter 18.

In "The Daily Grind," Orenstein relies predominantly on showing. She uses the strategies of **comparison and contrast** to show how girls like Amy Wilkinson fail to thrive in classrooms like Mrs. Richter's. The opening paragraphs present Amy as a confident, outgoing teenager: She is "one of the school's reigning elite" (paragraph 1) and the "school's star actress" (2). Not only do we hear Amy describe herself as "bold" (4), but we also see her acting boldly toward Greg. Here Orenstein also uses **specific narrative actions** to show Amy's movements: "Amy turns, puts her hands on her hips, anchors her feet shoulder width apart, and bellows across the schoolyard, 'Greg! Get over here!'" (3). This image of Amy, however, contrasts sharply with the image we get of her in math class, where she appears shy and retiring, sitting on the "far side of the room" (9). Her posture and movements seem anything but bold: "she crosses her legs, folds her arms across her chest, and hunches forward toward her desk, *seeming to shrink into herself*" (9). Here Orenstein says directly what she thinks Amy's body language means when she labels Amy's pose "typically feminine." To support her interpretation, Orenstein lets us see what happens when Amy gives a wrong answer (18) and, at the end, hear what Amy has to say about her mistake (41).

For more on specific narrative action, see Chapter 14, pp. 579–80.

In addition to contrasting the two sides of Amy, Orenstein contrasts the behavior of the boys and girls in the math class. Whereas Amy seems to shrink into herself, for example, the boys "sprawl . . . expanding into the available space" (9). While the girls raise their hands, the boys shout out their answers louder and louder (15). Orenstein points out that when the girls do shout out questions or answers, they are not recognized by the teacher, allowed by the boys to respond only to easy questions, or shouted down by the boys. These contrasts between the boys and girls and between the self-confident and self-effacing Amy help to convey to readers Orenstein's ideas without her having to explain at length what she thinks.

Considering Topics for Your Own Essay

Consider profiling a group of people who interact with each other for a specific purpose—such as a teacher and students interacting in a classroom, a group of actors rehearsing for a play, a basketball team practicing for an upcoming game, employees working collaboratively on a project, or a family celebrating a birthday.

David Noonan, *author of* Neuro-: Life on the Frontlines of Brain Surgery and Neurological Medicine *(1989), wrote this essay profiling a team of brain surgeons as they perform a complicated operation. His profile, originally published in* Esquire *in 1983, provides a direct look* *at something very few of us are likely ever to see—the human brain. Noonan had to handle this subject with delicacy to avoid making readers uncomfortable with overly explicit description or excessive technical terminology. Think about your own response as you read this piece: Are you made uneasy by any of the graphic detail? Are you overwhelmed by any of the terminology?*

Inside the Brain

David Noonan

The patient lies naked and unconscious in the center of the cool, tiled room. His head is shaved, his eyes and nose taped shut. His mouth bulges with the respirator that is breathing for him. Clear plastic tubes carry anesthetic into him and urine out of him. Belly up under the bright lights he looks large and helpless, exposed. He is not dreaming; he is too far under for that. The depth of his obliviousness is accentuated by the urgent activity going on all around him. Nurses and technicians move in and out of the room preparing the instruments of surgery. At his head, two doctors are discussing the approach they will use in the operation. As they talk they trace possible incisions across his scalp with their fingers.

It is a Monday morning. Directed by Dr. Stein, Abe Steinberger is going after a large tumor compressing the brainstem, a case that he describes as "a textbook beauty." It is a rare operation, a suboccipital craniectomy, supracerebellar infratentorial approach. That is, into the back of the head and over the cerebellum, under the tentorium to the brainstem and the tumor. Stein has done the operation more than fifty times, more than any other surgeon in the United States.

Many neurosurgeons consider brainstem tumors of this type inoperable because of their location and treat them instead with radiation. "It's where you live," says Steinberger. Breathing, heartbeat, and consciousness itself are some of the functions connected with this primary part of the brain. Literally and figuratively, it is the core of the organ, and operating on it is always very risky. . . .

The human skull was not designed for easy opening. It takes drills and saws and simple force to breach it. It is a formidable container, and its thickness testifies to the value of its contents. Opening the skull is one of the first things apprentice brain surgeons get to do on their own. It is sometimes called cabinet work, and on this case Steinberger is being assisted in the opening by Bob Solomon.

The patient has been clamped into a sitting position. Before the first incision is made he is rolled under the raised instrument table and he disappears beneath sterile green drapes and towels. The only part of him left exposed is the back of his head, which is orange from the sterilizing agent painted on it. Using a special marker, Steinberger draws the pattern of the opening on the patient's head in blue. Then the first cut is made into the scalp, and a thin line of bright-red blood appears.

The operation takes place within what is called the sterile field, a small germfree zone created and vigilantly patrolled by the scrub nurses. The sterile field extends out and around from the surgical opening and up over the instrument table. Once robed and gloved, the doctors are considered sterile from the neck to the waist and from the hands up the arms to just below the shoulders. The time the doctors must spend scrubbing their hands has been cut from ten minutes to five, but this obsessive routine is still the most striking of the doctor's preparations. Leaning over the trough-like stainless-steel sink with their masks in place and their arms lathered to the elbow, the surgeons carefully attend to each finger with the brush and work their way up each arm. It is the final pause, the last thing they do before they enter the operating room and go to work. Many at NI are markedly quiet while they scrub; they spend the familiar minutes running through the operation one more time. When they finish and their hands are too clean for anything but surgery they turn off the water with knee controls and back through the OR door, their dripping hands held high before them. They dry off with sterile towels, step into long-sleeved robes, and then plunge their hands down into their thin surgical gloves, which are held for them by the scrub nurse. The gloves snap as the nurse releases them around the doctors' wrists. Unnaturally smooth and defined, the gloved hands of the neurosurgeons are now ready; they can touch the living human brain.

"Drill the hell out of it," Steinberger says to Solomon. The scalp has been retracted and the skull exposed. Solomon presses the large stainless-steel power drill against the bone and hits the trigger. The bit turns slowly, biting into the white skull. Shavings drop from the hole onto the drape and then to the floor. The drill stops automatically when it is through the bone. The hole is about a half inch in diameter. Solomon drills four holes in a diamond pattern. The skull at the back of the head is ridged and bumpy. There is a faint odor of burning bone. 7

The drilling is graphic and jarring. The drill and the head do not go together; they collide and shock the eye. The tool is too big; its scale and shape are inappropriate to the delicate idea of neurosurgery. It should be hanging on the wall of a garage. After the power drill, a hand drill is used to refine the holes in the skull. It is a sterilized stainless-steel version of a handyman's tool. It is called a perforator, and as Solomon calmly turns it, more shavings hit the floor. Then, using powerful plierlike tools called Leksell rongeurs, the doctors proceed to bite away at the skull, snapping and crunching bone to turn the four small holes into a single opening about three inches in diameter. This is a *craniectomy;* the hole in the skull will always be there, protected by the many layers of scalp muscle at the back of the head. In a *craniotomy* a flap of bone is preserved to cover the opening in the skull. 8

After the scalp and the skull, the next layer protecting the brain is the dura. A thin, tough, leathery membrane that encases the brain, the dura (derived from the Latin for *hard*) is dark pink, almost red. It is rich with blood vessels and nerves (when you have a headache, it's the dura that aches), and now it can be seen stretching across the expanse of the opening, pulsing lightly. The outline of the cerebellum bulging against the dura is clear. With a crease in the middle, the dura-sheathed cerebellum looks oddly like a tiny pair of buttocks. The resemblance prompts a moment's joking. "Her firm young cerebellum," somebody says. . . . 9

The dura is carefully opened and sewn back out of the way. An hour and fifteen minutes after the drilling began, the brain is exposed. 10

The brain exposed. It happens every day on the tenth floor, three, four, and five times a day, day after day, week in and week out, month after month. The brain exposed. Light falls on its gleaming surface for the first time. It beats lightly, steadily. It is pink and gray, the brain, and the cerebellar cortex is covered with tiny blood vessels, in a web. In some openings you can see the curve of the brain, its roundness. It does not look strong, 11 it looks very soft, soft enough to push your finger through. When you see it for the first time you almost expect sparks, tiny sparks arcing across the surface, blinking lights, the crackle of an idea. You stare down at it and it gives nothing back, reveals nothing, gives no hint of how it works. As soon as they see it the doctors begin the search for landmarks. They start talking to each other, describing what they both can see, narrating the anatomy.

In the operating room the eyes bear much of the burden of communication. With their surgical masks and caps in place, the doctors and nurses resort to exaggerated stares and squints and flying eyebrows to emphasize what they are saying. After more than two decades in the operating room, Dr. Stein has developed this talent for nonverbal punctuation to a fine art. His clear blue eyes narrow now in concentration as he listens to Abe explain what he wants to do next. They discuss how to go about retracting the cerebellum. "Okay, Abe," Stein says quietly. "Nice and easy now." 12

The cerebellum (the word means *little brain*) is one of the most complicated parts of the brain. It is involved in the processing of sensory information of all kinds as well as balance and motor control, but in this case it is simply in the way. With the dura gone the cerebellum bulges out of the back of the head; it can be seen from across the room, protruding into space, striated and strange-looking. 13

When the cerebellum is retracted, the microscope is rolled into place and the operation really begins. It is a two-man scope, with a cable running to a TV monitor and a videotape machine. Sitting side by side, looking through the scope into the head, Steinberger and Stein go looking for the tumor. 14

It is a long and tedious process, working your way into the center of the human brain. The joke about the slip of the scalpel that wiped out fifteen years of piano lessons is no joke. Every seen and unseen piece of tissue does something, has some function, though it may well be a mystery to the surgeon. In order to spend hour after hour at the microscope, manipulating their instruments in an area no bigger than the inside of a juice can, neurosurgeons must develop an awesome capacity for sustained concentration. 15

After two hours of talking their way through the glowing red geography of the inner brain, Stein and Steinberger come upon the tumor. "Holy Toledo, look at that," exclaims Steinberger. The tumor stands out from the tissue around it, purple and mean-looking. It is the end of order in a very small, orderly place. It does not belong. They pause a moment, and Abe gives a quick tour of the opening. "That's tumor, that's the brainstem, and that's the third ventricle," he says. "And that over there, that's memory." 16

A doctor from the pathology department shows up for a piece of the tumor. It will be analyzed quickly while the operation is under way so the surgeons will know what they are dealing with. The type of tumor plays an important part in decisions about how much to take out, what risks to take in the attempt to get it all. A more detailed tissue analysis will be made later. 17

It turns out to be a brainstem glioma, an invasive intrinsic tumor actually growing up out of the brainstem. It is malignant. They get a lot of it but it will grow back. With radiation the patient could live fifteen years or even longer, and he will be told so. Abe Steinberger, in fact, will tell him. More than six hours after the first incision, the operation ends. 18

When the operation is over it is pointed out to Steinberger that he is the same age   19
as the patient. "Really?" he says. "It's funny, I always think of the patients as being older
than me."

How they think of the patients is at the center of the residents' approach to neuro-   20
surgery. It is a sensitive subject, and they have all given it a lot of thought. They know
well the classic preconceived notion of the surgeon as a cold and arrogant technican.
"You think like a surgeon" is a medical-school insult. Beyond that, the residents actually
know a lot of surgeons, and though they say most of them don't fit the stereotype, they
also say that there are some who really do bring it to life.

In many ways the mechanics of surgery itself create a distance between the sur-   21
geon and the patient. A man with a tumor is a case, a collection of symptoms. He is
transformed into a series of X rays, CAT scans, and angiograms. He becomes his tumor,
is even referred to by his affliction. "We've got a beautiful meningioma coming in tomorrow," a doctor will say. Once in the operating room the patient disappears beneath
the drapes and is reduced to a small red hole. Though it is truly the ultimate intimacy,
neurosurgery can be starkly impersonal.

"The goal of surgery is to get as busy as you can doing good cases and making   22
people *better* by operating on them," says Phil Cogen. "That automatically cuts down
the time you spend with patients." Though this frustrates Cogen, who has dreams and
nightmares about his patients "all the time," he also knows there is a high emotional
price to pay for getting too close. "One of the things you learn to do as a surgeon in
any field is disassociate yourself from the person you're operating on. I never looked
under the drapes at the patient until my third year in neurosurgery, when it was too late
to back out."

While Cogen prides himself on not having a "surgical personality," Abe Steinberger   23
believes that his skills are best put to use in the operating room and doesn't worry too
much about the problems of patient relations. "I sympathize with the patients," he says,
"I feel very bad when they're sick and I feel great when they're better. But what I want to
do is operate. I want to get in there and do it."

Connecting to Culture and Experience: Dissociation

At the end of "Inside the Brain," Noonan raises the issue of how surgeons cope with
their own feelings as well as with those of their patients, an issue that has broader
implications. He quotes Cogen as saying, "'One of the things you learn to do as a
surgeon in any field is disassociate yourself from the person you're operating on'"
(paragraph 22). Dissociation may be useful and sometimes even necessary, as this
profile suggests, but it may also have costs, both psychological and social. From a psychological perspective, because dissociation denies feelings, it may become habitual,
turning people into automatons. From a social perspective, dissociation may lead
practitioners to think of others as objects rather than people: "'We've got a beautiful
meningioma coming in tomorrow,' a doctor will say" (21). Dissociating from your
own and others' emotions may reflect a denial of feeling, rather than a practical

strategy for dealing with feelings. There is no reason to believe, however, that people who can dissociate in certain situations, like the surgeons in this profile, are incapable of normal feelings in other situations.

Think of a time when you felt the need to put aside your feelings in order to get on with the task before you. For example, has there ever been a time in school, during a sporting activity, or at work when you had to cut off your feelings in order to get something important done? Were you conscious at the time of what you were doing? What were the advantages and disadvantages of dissociating from your feelings?

Analyzing Writing Strategies

1. "Inside the Brain" shows how a profile can present part of the information chronologically and part topically. To examine Noonan's plan, make a quick scratch outline to indicate which paragraphs primarily tell what happened and which present information. To get you started, note that paragraph 1 begins the narrative, paragraphs 2–4 present information about the surgery, and paragraph 5 resumes the narrative.

For more on scratch outlining, see Chapter 12, pp. 540–41.

   Review your outline and then answer these questions:

   - How many paragraphs are primarily narrative, with most of their sentences describing the scene in the operating room and detailing the operation, and how many primarily give information about the brain or the surgery in general?
   - How successful do you think Noonan is in striking a balance between engaging readers with a dramatic story and informing them about a complex subject?

2. Noonan quotes both Dr. Stein and Dr. Steinberger, letting us hear what the surgeons say during the operation (paragraphs 3, 7, 12, and 16). What does this quoted **dialogue** add to the profile? How might the essay have been different had Noonan paraphrased or summarized rather than quoted the surgeons' comments?

For more on dialogue, see Chapter 14, pp. 580–81.

Commentary: Information

"Inside the Brain" illustrates how profile writers use the strategies of **definition** and **process narrative** to present information. Noonan does not hesitate to use technical vocabulary, but he nearly always gives his nonspecialist readers a quick definition. In paragraph 2, for example, he uses the term *brainstem* to identify the location of the tumor. In the next paragraph, he defines the term in a way that helps readers understand the importance and difficulty of the operation: "'It's where you live,' says Steinberger. Breathing, heartbeat, and consciousness itself are some of the functions connected with this primary part of the brain. Literally and figuratively, it is the core of the organ, and operating on it is always very risky. . . ." Here are two additional examples that show two ways Noonan introduces definitions of technical terms:

For more on defining, see Chapter 16.

The operation takes place within what is called the sterile field, a small germfree zone created and vigilantly patrolled by the scrub nurses. (6)

A thin, tough, leathery membrane that encases the brain, the dura (derived from the Latin for *hard*) is dark pink, almost red. (9)

For more on process narratives, see Chapter 14, pp. 582–87.

Noonan also explains procedures in a way that nonspecialists can understand. Look, for example, at paragraph 8 to see how he explains what is involved in performing a craniectomy, the process by which the surgeons use drills and "plierlike tools" to remove part of the skull. Notice how he graphically describes the process, identifying the tools, defining technical terms, and presenting each step in the order it occurs. Even though Noonan gives readers a great deal of information (more than some readers may want), he does not bog them down in specialized knowledge. Instead, he presents the information in a way that enhances readers' appreciation of the unfolding drama.

Considering Topics for Your Own Essay

If you were asked to profile a highly skilled specialist at work, what specialty would you choose? Who would you need to talk with and how would you gain access to the specialist? What kind of information would you need to gather? How might you go about getting it?

Brian Cable wrote the following selection when he was a first-year college student. Cable's profile of a mortuary combines both seriousness and humor. He lets readers know his feelings as he presents information about the mortuary and the people working there. As you read, notice in particular the way Cable uses his visit to the mortuary as an occasion to reflect on death.

The Last Stop
Brian Cable

> Let us endeavor so to live that when we come to die even the undertaker will be sorry.
>
> —MARK TWAIN

Death is a subject largely ignored by the living. We don't discuss it much, not as children (when Grandpa dies, he is said to be "going away"), not as adults, not even as senior citizens. Throughout our lives, death remains intensely private. The death of a loved one can be very painful, partly because of the sense of loss, but also because someone else's mortality reminds us all too vividly of our own. 1

Thus did I notice more than a few people avert their eyes as they walked past the dusty-pink building that houses the Goodbody Mortuaries. It looked a bit like a church—tall, with gothic arches and stained glass—and somewhat like an apartment complex—low, with many windows stamped out of red brick. 2

It wasn't at all what I had expected. I thought it would be more like Forest Lawn, serene with lush green lawns and meticulously groomed gardens, a place set apart from 3 the hustle of day-to-day life. Here instead was an odd pink structure set in the middle of a business district. On top of the Goodbody Mortuaries sign was a large electric clock. What the hell, I thought, mortuaries are concerned with time, too.

I was apprehensive as I climbed the stone steps to the entrance. I feared rejection or, worse, an invitation to come and stay. The door was massive, yet it swung open easily on well-oiled hinges. "Come in," said the sign. "We're always open." Inside was a cool and quiet reception room. Curtains were drawn against the outside glare, cutting the light down to a soft glow.   4

I found the funeral director in the main lobby, adjacent to the reception room. Like most people, I had preconceptions about what an undertaker looked like. Mr. Deaver fulfilled my expectations entirely. Tall and thin, he even had beady eyes and a bony face. A low, slanted forehead gave way to a beaked nose. His skin, scrubbed of all color, contrasted sharply with his jet black hair. He was wearing a starched white shirt, gray pants, and black shoes. Indeed, he looked like death on two legs.   5

He proved an amiable sort, however, and was easy to talk to. As funeral director, Mr. Deaver ("call me Howard") was responsible for a wide range of services. Goodbody Mortuaries, upon notification of someone's death, will remove the remains from the hospital or home. They then prepare the body for viewing, whereupon features distorted by illness or accident are restored to their natural condition. The body is embalmed and then placed in a casket selected by the family of the deceased. Services are held in one of three chapels at the mortuary, and afterward the casket is placed in a "visitation room," where family and friends can pay their last respects. Goodbody also makes arrangements for the purchase of a burial site and transports the body there for burial.   6

All this information Howard related in a well-practiced, professional manner. It was obvious he was used to explaining the specifics of his profession. We sat alone in the lobby. His desk was bone clean, no pencils or paper, nothing—just a telephone. He did all his paperwork at home; as it turned out, he and his wife lived right upstairs. The phone rang. As he listened, he bit his lips and squeezed his Adam's apple somewhat nervously.   7

"I think we'll be able to get him in by Friday. No, no, the family wants him cremated."   8

His tone was that of a broker conferring on the Dow Jones. Directly behind him was a sign announcing "Visa and Master Charge Welcome Here." It was tacked to the wall, right next to a crucifix.   9

"Some people have the idea that we are bereavement specialists, that we can handle the emotional problems which follow a death: Only a trained therapist can do that. We provide services for the dead, not counseling for the living."   10

Physical comfort was the one thing they did provide for the living. The lobby was modestly but comfortably furnished. There were several couches, in colors ranging from earth brown to pastel blue, and a coffee table in front of each one. On one table lay some magazines and a vase of flowers. Another supported an aquarium. Paintings of pastoral scenes hung on every wall. The lobby looked more or less like that of an old hotel. Nothing seemed to match, but it had a homey, lived-in look.   11

"The last time the Goodbodies decorated was in '59, I believe. It still makes people feel welcome."   12

And so "Goodbody" was not a name made up to attract customers but the owners'   13
family name. The Goodbody family started the business way back in 1915. Today, they
do over five hundred services a year.

"We're in *Ripley's Believe It or Not,* along with another funeral home whose owners'   14
names are Baggit and Sackit," Howard told me, without cracking a smile.

I followed him through an arched doorway into a chapel that smelled musty and old.   15
The only illumination came from sunlight filtered through a stained glass ceiling. Ahead
of us lay a casket. I could see that it contained a man dressed in a black suit. Wooden
benches ran on either side of an aisle that led to the body. I got no closer. From the red
roses across the dead man's chest, it was apparent that services had already been held.

"It was a large service," remarked Howard. "Look at that casket—a beautiful work   16
of craftsmanship."

I guess it was. Death may be the great leveler, but one's coffin quickly reestablishes   17
one's status.

We passed into a bright, fluorescent-lit "display room." Inside were thirty coffins, lids   18
open, patiently awaiting inspection. Like new cars on the showroom floor, they gleamed
with high-gloss finishes.

"We have models for every price range."   19

Indeed, there was a wide variety. They came in all colors and various materials.   20
Some were little more than cloth-covered cardboard boxes, others were made of wood,
and a few were made of steel, copper, or bronze. Prices started at $400 and averaged
about $1,800. Howard motioned toward the center of the room: "The top of the line."

This was a solid bronze casket, its seams electronically welded to resist corrosion.   21
Moisture-proof and air-tight, it could be hermetically sealed off from all outside elements.
Its handles were plated with 14-karat gold. The price: a cool $5,000.

A proper funeral remains a measure of respect for the deceased. But it is expen-   22
sive. In the United States the amount spent annually on funerals is about $2 billion.
Among ceremonial expenditures, funerals are second only to weddings. As a result,
practices are changing. Howard has been in this business for forty years. He remembers a time when everyone was buried. Nowadays, with burials costing $2,000 a shot,
people often opt instead for cremation—as Howard put it, "a cheap, quick, and easy
means of disposal." In some areas of the country, the cremation rate is now over 60 percent. Observing this trend, one might wonder whether burials are becoming obsolete.
Do burials serve an important role in society?

For Tim, Goodbody's licensed mortician, the answer is very definitely yes. Burials   23
will remain in common practice, according to the slender embalmer with the disarming
smile, because they allow family and friends to view the deceased. Painful as it may be,
such an experience brings home the finality of death. "Something deep within us
demands a confrontation with death," Tim explained. "A last look assures us that the person we loved is, indeed, gone forever."

Apparently, we also need to be assured that the body will be laid to rest in comfort   24
and peace. The average casket, with its inner-spring mattress and pleated satin lining,
is surprisingly roomy and luxurious. Perhaps such an air of comfort makes it easier for

the family to give up their loved one. In addition, the burial site fixes the deceased in the survivors' memory, like a new address. Cremation provides none of these comforts.

Tim started out as a clerk in a funeral home but then studied to become a mortician. 25 "It was a profession I could live with," he told me with a sly grin. Mortuary science might be described as a cross between pre-med and cosmetology, with courses in anatomy and embalming as well as in restorative art.

Tim let me see the preparation, or embalming, room, a white-walled chamber about 26 the size of an operating room. Against the wall was a large sink with elbow taps and a draining board. In the center of the room stood a table with equipment for preparing the arterial embalming fluid, which consists primarily of formaldehyde, a preservative, and phenol, a disinfectant. This mixture sanitizes and also gives better color to the skin. Facial features can then be "set" to achieve a restful expression. Missing eyes, ears, and even noses can be replaced.

I asked Tim if his job ever depressed him. He bridled at the question: "No, it 27 doesn't depress me at all. I do what I can for people and take satisfaction in enabling relatives to see their loved ones as they were in life." He said that he felt people were becoming more aware of the public service his profession provides. Grade-school classes now visit funeral homes as often as they do police stations and museums. The mortician is no longer regarded as a minister of death.

Before leaving, I wanted to see a body up close. I thought I could be indifferent after 28 all I had seen and heard, but I wasn't sure. Cautiously, I reached out and touched the skin. It felt cold and firm, not unlike clay. As I walked out, I felt glad to have satisfied my curiosity about dead bodies, but all too happy to let someone else handle them.

Connecting to Culture and Experience: Death

"Death," Cable announces in the opening sentence, "is a subject largely ignored by the living. We don't discuss it much, not as children (when Grandpa dies, he is said to be 'going away'), not as adults, not even as senior citizens." Yet when a family member dies, every family is forced to mark death in some way.

Discuss with other students the various ways your families and friends prepare for and arrange a memorial or funeral service. Think of a funeral you attended or ask a family member to describe how your family traditionally marks the death of a loved one. Consider the following questions, for example: Is there a formal service? If so, where does it take place—in a house of worship, a funeral home, a private home, a cemetery, or somewhere else? Who typically attends? Do people dress formally or informally? Who speaks and what kinds of things are said? What kind of music, if any, is played? Is the body cremated or buried? Is there usually a gathering after the formal service? If so, what is its purpose compared to the formal service?

Compare the different family traditions described by the members of your group. What do you think the service accomplishes for each family? If you have attended a service yourself, what did it accomplish for you?

Analyzing Writing Strategies

1. How does the opening quotation from Mark Twain shape your expectations as a reader? Compare Cable's opening (the quotation and paragraphs 1 and 2) against the openings of the three other profile essays in this chapter. What can you conclude about the opening strategies of these profile writers? Given each writer's subject, materials, and purpose, which opening do you find most effective and why?

2. During his visit to the mortuary, Cable focuses on four rooms: the lobby (paragraph 11), the chapel where funeral services are conducted (15), the casket display room (18–21), and the embalming room (26). Reread Cable's descriptions of these four rooms, and then underline the details he uses to describe each room. What impression do you get of each room? What does Cable gain by contrasting them so sharply? How do these descriptions work together to convey Cable's ideas about the mortuary, what we call its significance?

3. The Writer at Work section later in this chapter presents Cable's interview notes and preliminary write-up. Turn to pp. 173–77 to read these items now. Then consider how Cable integrates quotations from the interviews and descriptive details from his observations into his final essay. What do the quotations reveal about Cable's impressions of Howard and Tim? What do the descriptive details tell you about the effect the mortuary had on him? How do the quotations and descriptive details shape your reaction to the essay?

Commentary: Significance and Vivid Presentation

By organizing the profile essay as a narrative of his tour of the mortuary, Cable can present himself directly (using the first-person pronoun *I*) and tell readers what he thinks and feels about the mortuary and the people who work there. He begins with some general ideas about death and how people tend to deal with death basically by ignoring it. Then, in paragraphs 3 and 4, he discusses his expectations and confesses his apprehensions about the initial visit.

Cable reports what he learned from Howard and Tim, describing them and commenting on what they said as he quotes and summarizes their words. His descriptions and comments express his judgments about these people and the kinds of work they do. Look at paragraphs 5–10, for example, where Cable introduces Howard Deaver, the funeral director. He begins by comparing Deaver to his "preconceptions about what an undertaker looked like." Then he describes Deaver, no doubt emphasizing his stereotypical features:

> Tall and thin, he even had beady eyes and a bony face. A low, slanted forehead gave way to a beaked nose. His skin, scrubbed of all color, contrasted sharply with his jet black hair. He was wearing a starched white shirt, gray pants, and black shoes. Indeed, he looked like death on two legs. (5)

In this example, Cable uses all of the describing strategies: naming features (such as "eyes" and "face"), detailing the features ("beady" and "bony"), and comparing ("he looked like death on two legs"). The description creates an image that reinforces the stereotype of an undertaker. But Cable quickly replaces this stereotype with a different one when he describes Howard's tone on the telephone with a client as "that of a broker conferring on the Dow Jones" (paragraph 9). To make sure readers get the idea that mortuaries are a big business, Cable points out that on the wall directly behind Howard "was a sign announcing 'Visa and Master Charge Welcome Here.'"

Considering Topics for Your Own Essay

Think of a place or an activity about which you have strong preconceptions. Then imagine how you would go about writing a profile about that place or activity. What would you choose to tell about? How might you use your preconceptions to capture readers' attention?

■ PURPOSE AND AUDIENCE

A profile writer's primary purpose is to inform readers about the subject of the profile. Readers expect a profile to present information in an engaging way, however. Whether profiling people (a soup kitchen owner, an eighth-grade student), places (a mortuary), or activities (brain surgery), the writer must engage as well as inform readers. Readers of profiles expect to be surprised by unusual subjects. If the subject is familiar, they expect it to be presented from an unusual perspective. When writing a profile, you will have an immediate advantage if your subject is a place, an activity, or a person that is likely to surprise and intrigue your readers. For example, the writer of "Soup" has the double advantage of both a colorful person and an unusual place. Even when your subject is very familiar, however, you can still engage your readers by presenting it in a way they have never before considered.

A profile writer has one further concern: to be sensitive to readers' knowledge of a subject. Since readers must imagine the subject profiled and understand the new information offered about it, the writer must carefully assess what readers are likely to have seen and to know. For a profile of a brain operation, the decisions of a writer whose readers have little medical expertise will be different from those of a writer whose readers are primarily doctors and nurses. Given Noonan's attention to detail, he is clearly writing for a general audience that has never before seen a high-tech operating room.

Profile writers must also consider whether readers are familiar with the terminology they want to use. Because profiles are intended to be informative, they inevitably require definitions and illustrations. For example, Noonan carefully defines many terms: *craniectomy, craniotomy, dura, cerebellum*. However, he does not bother to define other technical terms such as *angiogram* and *meningioma*. Since profile writers are not writing technical manuals or textbooks, they can choose to define only those terms that readers will need to know to follow what is going on. Some concepts or activities will require extended illustrations, as when Noonan describes in detail what is involved in "opening the brain" or scrubbing up before entering the operating room.

A Specific Focus

The focus of a profile is typically a specific person, place, or activity. In this chapter, the *New Yorker* writer shows us Albert Yeganeh, soup cook extraordinaire; Peggy Orenstein shows us two sides of eighth-grader Amy Wilkinson; Brian Cable describes a place of business, Goodbody Mortuaries; and David Noonan presents an activity, brain surgery. Although they focus on a person, a place, or an activity, all of these profiles contain all three elements: certain people performing a certain activity at a particular place.

Whatever they examine, profile writers try to bring attention to the uniqueness of their subject, showing what is remarkable about it. In "Soup" and "The Daily Grind," we are shown something familiar in a new light. "Inside the Brain" and "The Last Stop" take a behind-the-scenes look at an activity and a place few of us have explored.

A Vivid Presentation

A profile particularizes its subject—one student's life, a surgical operation, an opinionated chef, a mortuary—rather than generalizing about the subject. Because profile writers are interested more in presenting individual cases than in making generalizations, they present the subject vividly and in detail.

Successful profile writers master the strategies of description—naming, detailing, and comparing. The profiles in this chapter, for example, evoke all the senses: sight (a "dusty-pink building" that "looked a bit like a church—tall, with gothic arches and stained glass —and somewhat like an apartment complex—low, with many windows stamped out of red brick"), touch ("a thin, tough, leathery membrane"), smell ("a faint odor of burning bone"), and hearing ("snapping and crunching bone"). Similes ("their legs sticking out of their shorts like pipe cleaners") and metaphors ("Soup is my lifeblood") also abound.

Profile writers often describe people in graphic detail ("The patient lies naked and unconscious in the center of the cool, tiled room. His head is shaved, his eyes and nose taped shut. His mouth bulges with the respirator that is breathing for him"). They reveal personal habits and characteristic poses ("As he listened, he bit his lips and squeezed his Adam's apple somewhat nervously"). They use dialogue to reveal character ("He spread his arms and added, 'This place is the only one like it in . . . in . . . the whole earth! One day, I hope to learn something from the other places, but so far I haven't'"). Dialogue also helps to dramatize power struggles and other relationships:

> Kyle . . . yells out, "Prime!" but Mrs. Richter turns away from him to give someone else a turn. . . . Kyle isn't willing to cede his teacher's attention. He begins to bounce in his chair and chant, *"Prime! Prime! Prime!"* Then, when he turns out to be right, he rebukes the teacher, saying *"See,* I told you."

An Indication of the Significance

Profile writers do not simply present their observations of a subject; they also convey what they think is significant or interesting about the person, place, or activity being profiled. After having spent time observing and interviewing people, profile writers formulate ideas and insights about the subject. David Noonan, for instance, points out the startling discrepancy between the impersonality of neurosurgery and the intimacy of such an operation. Brian Cable shares his realization that Americans seem to capitalize on death as a way of coping with it. Profile writers may also make evaluations, as the writer of "Soup" does in expressing admiration for Mr. Yeganeh, and as Peggy Orenstein does in expressing concern for Amy.

Profile writers may show their ideas, interpretations, and evaluations through such means as detail, actions, dialogue, and contrast, or they may tell readers directly what they think. Readers expect to understand the profile's significance, but do not expect the essay to begin with the kind of explicit thesis statement typical of argumentative writing. Some writers, like Cable and the author of "Soup," begin their essays with statements about significance, but these statements tell only part of what they have to say. The rest comes in the writers' comments and evaluations as they describe people, places, and activities.

An Engaging, Informative Plan

Successful profile writers know that if they are to maintain their readers' attention, they must engage as well as inform. For this reason, they tell their stories dramatically, describe people and places vividly, and also control the flow of unfamiliar information carefully. Whether the overall plan is topical or chronological, writers give much thought to where unfamiliar information is introduced and how it is introduced.

Profiles present a lot of factual detail about their subject. Noonan tells us about the brain's parts (dura, cerebellum, brainstem), surgical procedures (preparation of the patient, the difference between craniectomy and craniotomy), and the attitudes of surgeons toward brain surgery. But this information is woven into the essay in bits and pieces—conveyed in dialogue, interspersed throughout the narrative, given in description—rather than presented in one large chunk.

Parceling out information in this way enables readers to master one part of the information before going on to the next. Perhaps even more important, such control injects a degree of surprise and thus makes readers curious to know what will come next. Controlling the information flow may, in fact, keep readers reading, especially when the essay is organized topically, as it is in "Soup." Profiles organized chronologically tend to be easier to follow. Some even read like stories. Noonan, Orenstein, and Cable organize their profiles as narratives, using suspense and drama to maintain readers' interest.

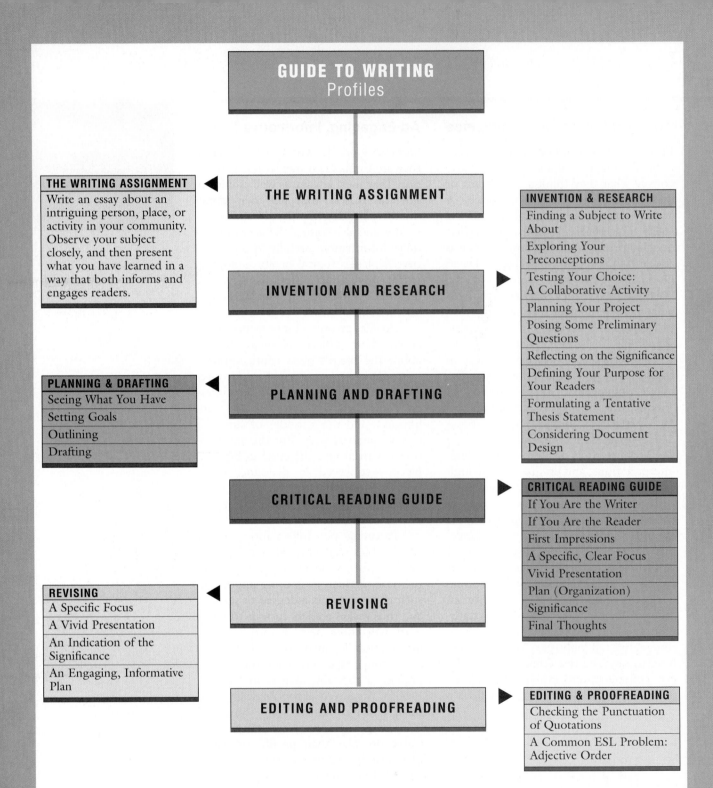

GUIDE TO WRITING
Profiles

THE WRITING ASSIGNMENT

THE WRITING ASSIGNMENT

Write an essay about an intriguing person, place, or activity in your community. Observe your subject closely, and then present what you have learned in a way that both informs and engages readers.

INVENTION AND RESEARCH

INVENTION & RESEARCH

Finding a Subject to Write About

Exploring Your Preconceptions

Testing Your Choice: A Collaborative Activity

Planning Your Project

Posing Some Preliminary Questions

Reflecting on the Significance

Defining Your Purpose for Your Readers

Formulating a Tentative Thesis Statement

Considering Document Design

PLANNING AND DRAFTING

PLANNING & DRAFTING

Seeing What You Have

Setting Goals

Outlining

Drafting

CRITICAL READING GUIDE

CRITICAL READING GUIDE

If You Are the Writer

If You Are the Reader

First Impressions

A Specific, Clear Focus

Vivid Presentation

Plan (Organization)

Significance

Final Thoughts

REVISING

REVISING

A Specific Focus

A Vivid Presentation

An Indication of the Significance

An Engaging, Informative Plan

EDITING AND PROOFREADING

EDITING & PROOFREADING

Checking the Punctuation of Quotations

A Common ESL Problem: Adjective Order

THE WRITING ASSIGNMENT

Write an essay about an intriguing person, place, or activity in your community. Observe your subject closely, and then present what you have learned in a way that both informs and engages readers.

INVENTION AND RESEARCH

Preparing to write a profile involves several activities, such as finding a subject, exploring your preconceptions about it, planning your project, posing some preliminary questions, and reflecting on the significance of the subject. Each step takes no more than a few minutes, yet together these activities will enable you to anticipate problems likely to arise in a complex project like a profile, arrange and schedule your interviews wisely, and take notes and gather materials in a productive way. There is much to learn about observing, interviewing, and writing about what you have learned, and these activities will support your learning.

Finding a Subject to Write About

When you choose a subject, you consider various possibilities, select a promising one, and check that particular subject's accessibility.

Listing Subjects. *Make a list of subjects to consider for your essay.* Even if you already have a subject in mind for your profile, take a few minutes to consider some other possible subjects. The more possibilities you consider, the more confident you can be about your choice. Do not overlook the subjects suggested by the Considering Topics for Your Own Essay activities following each reading in this chapter.

Before you list possible subjects, consider realistically the time you have available and the amount of observing and interviewing you will be able to accomplish. Whether you have a week to plan and write up one observational visit or interview or a month to develop a full profile will determine what kinds of subjects will be appropriate for you. Consult with your instructor if you need help defining the scope of your profile project.

Here we present some ideas you might use as starting points for a list of subjects. Try to extend your list to ten or twelve possibilities. Consider every subject you can think of, even unlikely ones. People like to read about the unusual.

People

- Anyone with an unusual or intriguing job or hobby—a private detective, beekeeper, classic-car owner, dog trainer

- A prominent local personality—a parent of the year, labor organizer, politician, consumer advocate, television or radio personality, community activist
- A campus personality—an ombudsman, coach, distinguished teacher
- Someone recently recognized for outstanding service or achievement—a volunteer, mentor, therapist

Places

- A weight-reduction clinic, martial arts or body-building gym, health spa
- A small-claims court, juvenile court, consumer fraud office
- A used-car lot, old movie house, used-book store, antique shop, historic site, auction hall, flower or gun show, farmers' or flea market
- A hospital emergency room, hospice, birthing center, psychiatric unit
- A local diner; the oldest, biggest, or quickest restaurant in town; a coffeehouse
- A campus radio station, computer center, agricultural research facility, student center, faculty club, museum, newspaper office, health center
- A book, newspaper, or Internet publisher; florist shop, nursery, or greenhouse; pawnshop; boatyard; automobile restorer or wrecking yard
- A recycling center; fire station; airport control tower; theater, opera, or symphony office; refugee center; orphanage; convent or monastery

Activities

- A citizens' volunteer program—a voter registration service, public television auction, meals-on-wheels project, tutoring program, election campaign
- A sports event—a marathon, Frisbee tournament, chess match, wrestling or boxing meet
- A hobby—folk dancing, roller blading, rock climbing, poetry reading

Listing Subjects Related to Identity and Community.   Writing a profile about a person or a place in your community can help you learn more about particular individuals in your community and about institutions and activities fundamental to community life. By "community" we mean both geographic communities, such as towns and neighborhoods, and institutional and temporary communities, such as religious congregations, college students majoring in the same subject, volunteer organizations, and sports teams. The following suggestions will enable you to list several possible subjects.

People

- Someone who has made or is currently making an important contribution to a community

- Someone who, as a prominent member of one of the communities you belong to, can help you define and understand that community
- Someone in a community who is generally not liked or respected but tolerated, such as a homeless person, gruff store owner, or unorthodox church member, or someone who has been or is in danger of being shunned or exiled from a community
- Someone who has built a successful business, succeeded in overcoming a disability or setback, supported a worthy cause, served as a role model, won respect from co-workers or neighbors

Places

- A facility that provides a needed service in a community, such as a legal advice bureau, child-care center, medical clinic, mission or shelter offering free meals
- A place where people of different ages, genders, ethnic groups, or some other attribute have formed a kind of ongoing community, such as a chess table in the park, political or social action headquarters, computer class, local coffeehouse, barber or beauty shop
- A place where people come together because they are of the same age, gender, or ethnic group, such as a seniors-only housing complex, a boathouse for a men's crew team, a campus women's center, an African American or Asian American student center
- An Internet site where people form a virtual community, such as a chat room, game parlor, or bulletin board

Activities

- A team practicing a sport or other activity (one you can observe as an outsider, not as a participant)
- A community improvement project, such as graffiti cleaning, tree planting, house repairing, church painting, highway litter pickup
- A group of researchers working collaboratively on a project

Listing Subjects Related to Work and Career. The following categories will help you consider work- and career-related subjects. Writing a profile on one of these possibilities can help you learn more about your attitudes toward your own work and career goals by examining how others do their work and pursue their careers.

People

- A college senior or graduate student in a major you are considering
- Someone working in the career you are thinking of pursuing
- Someone who trains people to do the kind of work you would like to do

Places

- A place on campus where students work—the library, computer center, cafeteria, bookstore, office, tutoring or learning center
- A place where you could learn more about the kind of career you would like to pursue—a law office, medical center, veterinary hospital, research institute, television station, newspaper, school, software manufacturer, engineering firm
- A place where people do a kind of work you would like to know more about—a clothing factory, coal mine, dairy farm, racetrack, restaurant, bakery, commercial fishing boat, gardening nursery, nursing home, delicatessen
- A place where people are trained for a certain kind of work or career—a police academy, cosmetology program, video repair course, truck drivers' school

Activities

- The actual activities performed by someone doing a kind of work represented on television, such as that of a police detective, judge, attorney, newspaper reporter, taxi driver, novelist, or emergency room doctor
- The activities involved in preparing for a particular kind of work, such as a boxer preparing for a fight, an attorney preparing for a trial, a teacher or professor preparing a course, an actor rehearsing a role, or a musician practicing for a concert

Choosing a Subject.   *Look over your list of possibilities and choose a subject that you find you want to know more about and that your readers will find interesting.*

Note, too, that most profile writers report the greatest satisfaction and the best results when they profile an unfamiliar person, place, or activity. If you choose a subject with which you are somewhat familiar, try to study it in an unfamiliar setting. For example, if you are a rock climber and decide to write a profile on rock climbing, do not rely exclusively on your own knowledge of and authority on the subject. Seek out other rock-climbing enthusiasts, even interview some critics of the sport to get another perspective, or visit a rock-climbing event or training class where you could observe without participating. By adopting an outsider's perspective on a familiar subject, you can make writing your profile a process of discovery for yourself as well as for your readers.

Stop now to focus your thoughts. *In a sentence or two, identify the subject you have chosen and explain why you think it is a good choice for you and your readers.*

Checking on Accessibility.   *Take steps to ensure that your subject will be accessible to you.* Having chosen a subject, you need to be certain you will be able to make observations and conduct interviews to learn more about it. Find out who might be able to give you information by making some preliminary phone calls. Explain that you need information for a school research project. You will be surprised how helpful people can be when they have the time. If you are unable to contact knowledgeable people or get access to the place you need to observe, you may not be able to write on this subject. Therefore, try to make these initial contacts early.

Exploring Your Preconceptions

Explore your initial thoughts and feelings about your subject in writing before you begin observing or interviewing. Take ten minutes to write about your thoughts, using the following questions as a guide:

What I already know about this subject

- How can I define or describe it?
- What are its chief qualities or parts?
- Do I associate anyone or anything with it?
- What is its purpose or function?
- How does it compare with other, similar subjects?

My attitude toward this subject

- Why do I consider it intriguing?
- What about it most interests me?
- Do I like it? Respect it? Understand it?

My own and my readers' expectations

- How do my preconceptions of this subject compare with my readers'?
- What might be unique about my preconceptions?
- What attitudes about this subject do I share with my readers?
- How is this subject represented in the media?
- What values and ideas are associated with subjects of this kind?

At this point, you will find it useful to get together with two or three other students and describe the subject you have chosen to profile. This collaborative activity will help you decide whether you have chosen a good subject to write about, one that will allow you to proceed confidently as you develop your profile.

Testing Your Choice: A Collaborative Activity

Presenters: Take turns identifying your subjects. Explain your interest in the subject and speculate about why you think it will interest your readers.

Listeners: Briefly tell each presenter what you already know about his or her subject, if anything, and what would make it interesting to readers.

Planning Your Project

Set up a tentative schedule for your observational and interview visits. Whatever the scope of your project—a single observation, an interview with follow-up, or multiple observations and interviews—you will want to get the most out of your time with your subject. Chapter 20 offers guidance in observing and interviewing and will give you an idea of how much time you will need to plan, carry out, and write up an observation or interview.

Take time now to consult Chapter 20. Figure out first the amount of time you have to complete your essay; then decide what visits you will need to make, whom you will need to interview, and what library or Internet research you might want to do, if any. Estimate the time necessary for each. You might use a chart like the following one:

Date	Time Needed	Purpose	Preparation
10/23	1 hour	Observe	Bring map, directions, paper
10/25	2 hours	Library research	Bring references, change or copycard for copy machine
10/26	45 minutes	Interview	Read brochure and prepare questions
10/30	3 hours	Observe and interview	Confirm appointment; bring questions and extra pen

You will probably have to modify your plan once you actually begin work, but it is a good idea to keep some sort of schedule in writing.

If you are developing a full profile, your first goal is to get your bearings. Some writers begin by observing; others start with an interview. Many read up on the subject before doing anything else, to get a sense of its main elements. You may also want to read about other subjects similar to the one you have chosen. Save your notes.

Posing Some Preliminary Questions

Write questions to prepare for your first visit. Before beginning your observations and interviews, try writing some questions for which you would like to find answers. These questions will orient you and allow you to focus your visits. As you work, you will find answers to many of these questions. Add to this list as new questions occur to you, and delete any that come to seem irrelevant.

Each subject invites its own special questions, and every writer has particular concerns. Consider, for example, how one student writing a profile on a local center of the Women's Health Initiative, a nationwide fifteen-year study of women's health, goes about preparing interview questions. After reading about the study in her local newspaper, she calls the local center to get further information. The center administrator faxes her a fact sheet on the study and the local center's special part in it. The student knows that she will need to report on the study within her profile of the local center and key people who work there. She also hopes to interview women who come to the center to participate in the research. Consequently, she devises these questions to launch her research and prepare for her first visit to the center to interview the director:

For more on interviewing techniques, see Chapter 20, pp. 645–48.

- Why has so little research been done until now on women's health?
- How did the study come about, and what is the role of the National Institutes of Health?
- Why does the study focus only on women between the ages of fifty and eighty?
- Will women from all income levels be involved?
- Why will it take fifteen years to complete the study?
- When was this center established, and what role does it play in the national study?
- Does the center simply coordinate the study, or does it also provide health and medical advice to women participating in the study?
- Who works at the center, and what are their qualifications to work there?
- Will I be able to interview women who come to the center to participate in the research?
- Will I be permitted to take photographs of the location?
- Would it be appropriate to take photographs of the researchers and participants, if they give their consent?

Reflecting on the Significance

Write for five to ten minutes, reflecting on what you now think is interesting and meaningful about the person, place, or activity you have chosen for your profile. Consider how you would answer these questions about your subject:

- What visual or other sensory impression is most memorable?
- What does this impression tell me about the person, place, or activity?
- What mood do I associate with my subject?
- What about my subject is most striking and likely to surprise or interest my readers?
- What is the most important thing I have learned about my subject? Why is it important?
- If I could find out the answer to one more question about my subject, what would that question be? Why is this question important?
- What about my subject says something larger about our culture and times?
- Which of my ideas, interpretations, or judgments do I most want to share with readers?

Defining Your Purpose for Your Readers

Write a few sentences, defining your purpose in writing about this particular person, place, or activity for your readers. Use these questions to focus your thoughts:

- Who are my readers? Apart from my instructors and classmates, who would be interested in reading an essay about this particular subject? If I were to try to publish my essay, what magazine, newspaper, newsletter, or Web site might want a profile on this particular subject? Would people who work in a particular kind of business or who pursue certain kinds of hobbies or sports be interested in the essay?

- What do I want my readers to learn about the person, place, or activity from reading my essay?

- What do I want my readers to understand about the significance I see in this particular person, place, or activity?

Formulating a Tentative Thesis Statement

Review what you wrote for Reflecting on the Significance and add another two or three sentences that will help you tell readers what you understand about the person, place, or activity on which you are focusing. Try to write sentences that do not summarize what you have already written, but that extend your insights and interpretations.

Keep in mind that readers do not expect you to begin a profile essay with the kind of explicit thesis statement typical of argumentative essays. If you do decide to tell readers why the person, place, or activity is significant, you will most likely do so through interpretive or evaluative comments as you describe people and places, present dialogue, and narrate what you observed. You are not obliged to tell readers the significance, but you should show it through the way you profile the subject.

Considering Document Design

For more on document design, see Chapter 25.

Think about whether visual or audio elements—photographs, postcards, menus, or snippets from films, television programs, or songs—would strengthen your profile. These are not at all a requirement of an effective profile, but they could be helpful. Consider also whether your readers might benefit from design features such as headings, bulleted or numbered lists, or other typographic elements that can make an essay easier to follow.

■ PLANNING AND DRAFTING

This section will help you review your invention writing and research notes and get started on your first draft.

Seeing What You Have

Read over your invention materials to see what you have. You probably have
deal of material—notes from observational and interview visits or from
research; some idea of your preconceptions; a list of questions, perhaps
answers. You should also have a tentative interpretation. Your goals at th
to digest all of the information you have gathered; to pick out the prom
details, anecdotes, and quotations; and to see how it all might come together to p
sent your subject and your interpretation of it to readers.

As you sort through your material, try asking yourself the following questions to
help clarify your focus and interpretation:

- How do my preconceptions of the subject contrast with my findings about it?
- Can I compare or contrast what different people say about my subject? Do I see
  any discrepancies between people's words and their behavior?
- How do my reactions compare with those of the people directly involved?
- How could I consider the place's appearance in light of the activity that occurs
  there?
- If I examine my subject as an anthropologist or archaeologist would, what evi-
  dence could explain its role in society at large?
- Could I use an illustration to complement the text?

Setting Goals

The following questions will help you establish goals for your first draft. Consider
each question briefly now, and then return to them as necessary as you draft and
revise.

Your Purpose and Readers

- Are my readers likely to be familiar with my subject? If not, what details do I need
  to provide to help them understand and visualize it?
- If my readers are familiar with my subject, how can I present it to them in a new
  and engaging way? What information do I have that is likely to be unfamiliar or
  entertaining to them?
- What design elements might make my writing more interesting or easier for
  readers to understand?

The Beginning

The opening is especially important in a profile. Because readers are unlikely to
have any particular reason to read a profile, the writer must arouse their curiosity and interest. The best beginnings are surprising and specific; the worst are
abstract. Here are some strategies you might consider:

- Should I open with a striking image, as Noonan does, an emphatic statement, as Orenstein does, or an intriguing epigraph, as Cable does?
- Do I have any dialogue to open with, as in "Soup"?
- Can I start with an amazing fact, anecdote, or question that would catch readers' attention?

A Vivid Presentation

- Where might I use naming and detailing to give readers a strong visual image of people and places?
- Can I think of a simile or metaphor that would help me present an evocative image?
- Which bits of dialogue would convey information about my subject as well as a vivid impression of the speaker?
- What specific narrative actions can I include to show people and activities?

An Informative Plan

Profile writers use two basic methods of organizing information, arranging it chronologically in a narrative or topically by grouping related materials.

If You Use a Chronological Plan

- How can I make the narrative interesting, perhaps even dramatic?
- What information should I present through dialogue and what information should I interrupt the narrative to present?
- How much space should I devote to describing people and places and to showing what happened?
- Can I set up comparisons or contrasts that would dramatize the significance?
- If I have the option of including design elements, how might I use them effectively: perhaps to clarify the chronology, highlight a dramatic part of the narrative, illustrate how the people and places in the profile changed over time?

If You Use a Topical Plan

- Which topics will best inform my readers and hold their interest?
- How can I sequence the topics to bring out significant comparisons or contrasts?
- What transitions will help readers make connections between topics?
- Where and how should I describe the subject vividly?
- If I have the option of including design elements, are there ways I can use them effectively to reinforce the topical organization?

The Ending

- Should I try to frame the essay by repeating an image or phrase from the beginning or by completing an action begun earlier in the profile?

- Would it be effective to end by stating or restating my interpretation or evaluation?

- Should I end with a telling image, anecdote, or bit of dialogue, or with a provocative question or connection?

Outlining

If you plan to arrange your material chronologically, plot the key events on a timeline. If you plan to arrange your material topically, you might use clustering or topic outlining to help you divide and group related information.

To learn about these mapping strategies, see Chapter 11, pp. 516–20.

The following outline suggests one possible way to organize a chronological profile of a place:

Begin by describing the place from the outside.

Present background information.

Describe what you see as you enter.

Introduce the people and activities.

Tour the place, describing what you see as you move from room to room.

Fill in information and comment about the place or the people.

Conclude with reflections on what you have learned about the place.

Here is a suggested outline for a topical profile about a person:

Begin with a vivid image of the person in action.

Use dialogue to present the first topic.

Narrate an anecdote or a procedure to illustrate the first topic.

Present the second topic.

Describe something related to it.

Evaluate or interpret what you have observed.

Present the third topic . . .

Conclude with a bit of action or dialogue.

All of the material for these hypothetical essays would come from observations, interviews, and background reading. The plan you choose should reflect the possibilities in your material as well as your purpose and readers. At this point, your decisions must be tentative. As you begin drafting, you will almost certainly discover new ways of organizing your material. Once you have written a first draft, you and others may see better ways to organize the material for your particular audience.

Drafting

You may want to review the general advice on planning and drafting in Chapter 1, pp. 16–17.

Start drafting your essay, keeping in mind the goals you set while you were planning. As you write, try to describe your subject in a way that makes its significance clear to your readers. If you get stuck while drafting, explore the problem by using some of the writing activities in the Invention and Research section of this chapter.

As you read over your first draft, you may see places where you can add new material to reveal more about the person, place, or activity. You may even decide that after this first draft, you can finally understand the complexity of your subject, and set out to convey it more fully in a second draft.

■ **CRITICAL READING GUIDE**

Now is the time to get a good critical reading of your draft. Writers usually find it helpful to have someone else read and comment on their drafts, and all writers know how much they learn about writing when they read other writers' drafts. Your instructor may schedule readings of drafts as part of your coursework. If not, you can ask a classmate, friend, or family member to read your draft. You could also seek comments from a tutor at your campus writing center. The guidelines in this section can be used by *anyone* reviewing a profile. (If you are unable to have someone else read your draft, turn ahead to the Revising section, where you will find guidelines for reading your own draft critically.)

▶ **If You Are the Writer.** In order to provide focused, helpful comments, your reader must know your essay's intended audience, your purpose, and a problem in the draft that you need help solving. Briefly write out this information at the top of your draft:

- *Readers.* Identify the intended readers of your essay. How do you assume they will react to your writing?

- *Purpose.* What effect do you want your profile to have on readers? What do you want them to discover?

- *Problem.* Ask your reader to help you solve the single most important problem you see with your draft. Describe this problem briefly.

▶ **If You Are the Reader.** Use the following guidelines to help you give critical comments to others on profile essays.

1. *Read for a First Impression.* Begin by reading the draft straight through to get a general impression. Read for enjoyment, ignoring spelling, punctuation, and sentence problems for now. When you have finished this first quick reading, write a few sentences about what seems most interesting to you about the person, place, or activity that is the focus of the profile. If you have any

insights or questions about the subject, write down these thoughts as well. Next, consider the problem the writer identified. If the problem will be covered by one of the other items below, deal with it there. Otherwise, respond to the writer's concerns now.

2. ***Consider Whether the Focus Is Specific and Clear.*** Consider whether the essay clearly focuses on a particular person, place, or activity. Point to any passages where the focus seems to shift to something else. Also let the writer know if the essay seems too much about the writer's general ideas and not enough about the specific person, place, or activity.

3. ***Assess the Vividness of the Presentation.*** Find the descriptions of people, places, and activities and let the writer know if any need enlivening. Point to passages where additional features could be named and detailed, or where the sense of smell or touch could be added to the visual description. Also indicate if you have difficulty seeing people in action or imagining what is involved in the activity.

4. ***Evaluate the Plan.*** Point out any places where you feel bogged down or overwhelmed with information or where information is not clearly presented or is inadequate. If the profile is organized chronologically, point out any places where the narrative seems to drag as well as where it seems most compelling. If the profile is organized topically, note whether the writer presents too little or too much material for a topic and whether topics might be sequenced differently or connected more clearly.

   - ***Look at the opening*** to see if it captures your attention. If not, is there a quotation, a fact, or an anecdote elsewhere in the draft that might make a better opening?

   - ***Look at the ending*** to see if it leaves you hanging, seems too abrupt, or oversimplifies the material. If it does, suggest another way of ending, possibly by moving a passage or a quotation from elsewhere in the essay.

   - ***Assess the design features.*** Comment on the contribution of any design features such as photographs, song lyrics, or headings. Help the writer think of design features that could be added.

5. ***Consider Whether the Significance Is Clear.*** Point to any comments, judgments, interpretations, or ideas that seem vague or unrelated to what you are shown in the profile. Tell the writer what you take to be significant and most interesting about the person, place, or activity that is the focus of the profile. Indicate any details that seem especially meaningful and explain why you think so.

6. ***Give the Writer Your Final Thoughts.*** What is the draft's strongest part? What part is most memorable? What part is weak or most in need of further work?

■ REVISING

This section will help you get an overview of your draft and revise it accordingly.

Getting an Overview

Consider your draft as a whole, following these two steps:

1. *Reread.* If at all possible, put the draft aside for a day or two. When you do reread it, start by reconsidering your purpose. Then read the draft straight through, trying to see it as your intended readers will.

For more on scratch
outlines, see Chapter 11,
pp. 518–19.

2. *Outline.* Make a quick scratch outline, indicating the basic features as they appear in the draft.

Charting a Plan for Revision.   Preparing a two-column list is a good way to start plotting out the course of your revision. In the left-hand column list the basic features of profiles; in the right-hand column list any problems that you or other readers identified with that feature.

Basic Features	*Problems to Solve*
A specific focus	
A vivid presentation	
An indication of the significance	
An engaging, informative plan	

Analyzing the Basic Features of Your Own Draft.   Turn to the Critical Reading Guide on the preceding pages. Using this guide, identify problems you now see in your draft. Note the problems on the chart.

Studying Critical Comments.   Review all of the comments you have received from other readers. For each comment, look at the draft to determine what might have led the reader to make that particular point. Try to be objective about any criticism. Ideally, these comments will help you see your draft as others see it (rather than as you hoped it would be) and to identify specific problems.

Carrying Out Revisions

Having identified problems in your draft, you now need to figure out solutions and—most important—to carry them out. Basically, you have three options for finding solutions:

1. Review your observation or interview notes for other information and ideas.

2. Do additional observations or interviews to answer questions you or other readers raised.

3. Look back at the readings in this chapter to see how other writers have solved similar problems.

The following suggestions, which are organized according to the basic features on your revision chart, will get you started solving some problems common to profiles.

A Specific Focus

- **Does the essay fail to focus clearly on a particular person, place, or activity?** Make explicit the focus of your profile. Add more description or bring the description together in one paragraph closer to the beginning of the essay.

- **Does the essay seem too general?** Break up long stretches of commentary. Interweave your ideas, interpretations, and evaluations into your presentation of the person, place, or activity. Try to present background information through dialogue rather than through your own comments.

A Vivid Presentation

- **Can the description of the person who is the focus of the profile be improved?** Add details to help readers see the person. Think, for example, of Orenstein's description of Amy's "curly, blond hair, cornflower-blue eyes, and [. . .] sharply upturned nose." Consider adding a vivid comparison, as the *New Yorker* writer does to describe Mr. Yeganeh as "working like a demon alchemist." Insert specific narrative actions to show the person's gestures and mannerisms. Recall, for example, how after giving a wrong answer Amy "turns crimson, and flips her head forward so her hair falls over her face."

- **Should other people be described briefly?** Consider naming and detailing a few physical features of each person. Recall, for example, Orenstein's quick descriptive phrases: "Kyle, who is skinny and a little pop-eyed" and "Mrs. Richter, a ruddy, athletic woman with a powerful voice." Add comparisons, as Cable does when he says Howard Deaver "looked like death on two legs." Also consider adding specific narrative action. Think of Howard again on the phone: "As he listened, he bit his lips and squeezed his Adam's apple."

- **Can you enliven the description of the place?** Add to visual description other senses. Recall, for example, these sensory descriptions from the readings: sound ("a lisping staccato of Armenian origin"), texture (the "tough, leathery membrane that encases the brain"), smell (the "faint odor of burning bone"), and taste ("sweet" or "spicy").

- **Do readers have difficulty seeing people in action or imagining what is involved in the activity?** Add specific narrative actions to show people moving, gesturing, or talking. For example, recall from Noonan's profile the "plierlike tools" that "bite away at the skull, snapping and crunching bone." Explain a procedure or use dialogue to narrate what the activity involved.

An Indication of the Significance

For more on creating a dominant impression, see Chapter 15, p. 599.

- *Do any comments seem vague or unrelated to what is being profiled?* Try stating your ideas more directly. Be sure that the **dominant impression** you create through descriptive and narrative details reinforces the significance you want to convey.

- *Do your readers have different ideas about the person, place, or activity being profiled?* Consider whether you can incorporate any of their ideas into your essay or use them to develop your own ideas.

- *Do critical readers point to any details that seem especially meaningful?* Consider what these details suggest about the significance of the person, place, or activity.

An Engaging, Informative Plan

- *Do readers feel bogged down by information?* Look for ways to reduce information or to break up long blocks of informational text with description of scenes or people, narration of events, lists, or other design elements. Consider presenting information through dialogue, as the "Soup" author and Cable do.

- *Does your chronologically arranged essay seem to drag or ramble?* Try adding drama through dialogue or specific narrative action. Try using comparison and contrast, as Orenstein does.

- *Does your topically arranged essay seem disorganized or out of balance?* Try rearranging topics to see if another order makes more sense. Add clearer, more explicit transitions or topic sentences. Move or condense information to restore balance.

- *Does the opening fail to engage readers' attention?* Consider alternatives. Think of questions you could open with, or look for an engaging image or dialogue later in the essay to move to the beginning. Go back to your observation or interview notes for other ideas. Recall how the writers in this chapter open their profile essays: the "Soup" author begins with an arresting quotation, Orenstein tells us how Amy felt, Noonan describes the patient awaiting surgery, Cable combines a quote by Mark Twain with comments about how people try to ignore death.

- *Are transitions between stages in the narrative or between topics confusing or abrupt?* Add appropriate words or phrases or revise sentences to make transitions clearer or smoother.

- *Does the ending seem weak?* Consider ending at an earlier point or moving something striking to the end. Review your invention and research notes to see if you overlooked something that would make for a strong ending. Consider ending your essay with a quotation, as many of the writers in this chapter do.

- *Are the design features effective?* Consider adding textual references to any visual elements in your essay or positioning visuals more effectively. Think of other possible design features you might incorporate to enhance your profile.

EDITING AND PROOFREADING

Now is the time to check your revised draft for errors in grammar, punctuation, and mechanics. Our research has identified several errors that occur often in profiles, including problems with the punctuation of quotations and the order of adjectives. The following guidelines will help you check your essay for these common errors.

Checking the Punctuation of Quotations. Because most profiles are based in part on interviews, you probably have quoted one or more people in your essay. When you quote someone's exact words, you must enclose those words in quotation marks and observe strict conventions for punctuating quotations. Check your revised draft for your use of the following specific punctuation marks.

All quotations should have quotation marks at the beginning and the end.

▶ "What exactly is civil litigation?" I asked.

Commas and periods go *inside* quotation marks.

▶ "I'm here to see Anna Post," I replied nervously.

▶ Tony explained, "Fraternity boys just wouldn't feel comfortable at the Chez Moi Café."

Question marks and exclamation points go *inside* closing quotation marks if they are part of the quotation, *outside* if they are not.

▶ After a pause, the patient asked, "Where do I sign?"

▶ Willie insisted, "You can *too* learn to play Super Mario!"

▶ When was the last time someone you just ticketed said to you, "Thank you, Officer, for doing a great job"?

Use commas with signal phrases (*he said, she asked,* etc.) that accompany direct quotations.

▶ "This sound system costs only four thousand dollars," Jorge said.

▶ I asked, "So where were these clothes from originally?"

A Common ESL Problem: Adjective Order. In trying to present the subject of your profile vividly and in detail, you probably have included many descriptive adjectives. When you include more than one adjective in front of a noun, you may have difficulty sequencing them. For example, do you write *a large old ceramic pot* or *an old large ceramic pot?* The following list shows the order in which adjectives are ordinarily arranged in front of a noun.

1. *Amount:* a/an, the, a few, six
2. *Evaluation:* good, beautiful, ugly, serious
3. *Size:* large, small, tremendous
4. *Shape, length:* round, long, short
5. *Age:* young, new, old
6. *Color:* red, black, green
7. *Origin:* Asian, Brazilian, German
8. *Material:* wood, cotton, gold
9. *Noun used as an adjective:* computer (as in *computer program*), cake (as in *cake pan*)
10. *The noun modified*

A WRITER AT WORK

■ THE INTERVIEW NOTES AND WRITE-UP

Most profile writers take notes when interviewing people. Later, they may summarize their notes in a short write-up. In this section, you will see some of the interview notes and a write-up that Brian Cable prepares for his mortuary profile, "The Last Stop," printed on pp. 146–49.

Cable arranged to tour the mortuary and conduct interviews with the funeral director and mortician. Before each interview, he wrote out a few questions at the top of a sheet of paper and then divided it into two columns; he used the left-hand column for descriptive details and personal impressions and the right-hand column for the information he got directly from the person he interviewed. Following are Cable's notes and write-up for his interview with the funeral director, Howard Deaver.

Cable used three questions to guide his interview with Howard and then took brief notes during the interview. He did not concern himself too much with note-taking because he planned to spend a half-hour directly afterward to complete his notes. He focused his attention on Howard, trying to keep the interview comfortable and conversational and jotting down just enough to jog his memory and catch especially meaningful quotations. A typescript of Cable's interview notes follows.

The Interview Notes

QUESTIONS

1. How do families of the deceased view the mortuary business?
2. How is the concept of death approached?
3. How did you get into this business?

DESCRIPTIVE DETAILS & PERSONAL IMPRESSIONS	INFORMATION
weird-looking tall long fingers big ears low, sloping forehead Like stereotype--skin colorless	Howard Deaver, funeral director, Goodbody Mortuaries "Call me Howard" How things work: Notification, pick up body at home or hospital, prepare for viewing, restore distorted features-- accident or illness, embalm, casket-- family selects, chapel services (3 in bldg.), visitation room--pay respects, family & friends.
	Can't answer questions about death-- "Not bereavement specialists. Don't handle emotional problems. Only a trained therapist can do that." "We provide services for dead, not coun- seling for the living." (great quote) Concept of death has changed in last 40 yrs (how long he's been in the business) Funeral cost: $500-$600, now $2,000
plays with lips blinks plays with Adam's apple desk empty--phone, no paper or pen angry disdainful of the Neptune Society	Phone call (interruption) "I think we'll be able to get him in on Friday. No, no, the family wants him cremated." Ask about Neptune Society--cremation Cremation "Cheap, quick, easy means of disposal." Recent phenomenon. Neptune Society-- erroneous claim to be only one.

```
DESCRIPTIVE DETAILS &
PERSONAL IMPRESSIONS          INFORMATION

                              "We've offered them since the
                              beginning. It's only now it's come
                              into vogue."
                              Trend now back toward burial.
                              Cremation still popular in
                              sophisticated areas
                              60% in Marin Co. and Florida
                              Ask about paperwork--does it upstairs,
                              lives there with wife, Nancy.


musty, old stained glass      Tour around (happy to show me around)
sunlight filtered             Chapel--large service just done,
                              Italian.


man in black suit             "Not a religious institution--a
roses                         business."
wooden benches                casket--"beautiful craftsmanship"--
                              admires, expensive


contrast brightness           Display room--caskets, about 30 of
fluorescent lights            them
Plexiglas stands              Loves to talk about caskets
                              "models in every price range"
                              glossy (like cars in a showroom)
                              cardboard box, steel, copper, bronze
                              $400 up to $1,800. Top of line:
                              bronze, electronically welded, no
                              corrosion--$5,000
```

Cable's interview notes include many descriptive details of Howard as well as of various rooms in the mortuary. Though most entries are short and sketchy, much of the language found its way into the final essay. In describing Howard, for example, Cable noted that he fits the stereotype of the cadaverous undertaker, a fact that Cable emphasized in his essay.

He put quotation marks around Howard's actual words, some of them written in complete sentences, others in fragments. We will see how Cable filled these quotes in when he wrote up the interview. In only a few instances did he take down more than he could use. Even though profile writers want good quotes, they should not use quotes to present information that can be more effectively expressed in their own words. In profiles, writers use direct quotation both to provide information and to capture the mood or character of the person speaking.

As you can see, Howard was not able to answer Cable's questions about the families of the deceased and their attitudes toward death or mortuaries. The gap between these questions and Howard's responses led Cable to recognize one of his own misperceptions about mortuaries—that they serve the living by helping people adjust to the death of loved ones. This misperception would become an important theme of his essay.

Immediately after the interview, Cable filled in his notes with details while they were still fresh in his mind. Next, he took some time to reflect on what he had learned from his interview with Howard. Here are some of his thoughts:

```
I was surprised by how much Howard looked like the undertakers
in scary movies. Even though he couldn't answer some of my
questions, he was friendly enough. It's obviously a business
for him (he loves to talk about caskets and to point out all
their features, like a car dealer kicking a tire). Best quote:
"We offer services to the dead, not counseling to the living."
I have to bring up these issues in my interview with the
mortician.
```

The Interview Write-Up

Writing up an account of the interview a short time afterward helped Cable fill in more details and reflect further on what he had learned. His write-up shows him already beginning to organize the information he had gained from his interview with the funeral director.

```
I. His physical appearance.
     Tall, skinny, with beady blue eyes embedded in his
bony face. I was shocked to see that he looks just like the
undertakers in scary movies. His skin is white and colorless,
from lack of sunshine. He has a long nose and a low, sloping
forehead. He was wearing a clean white shirt. A most unusual
man--have you ever seen those Ames Home Loan commercials? But
he was friendly, and happy to talk with me. "Would I answer
some questions? Sure."
II. What people want from a mortuary.
     A. Well first of all, he couldn't answer my second
question, about how families cope with the loss of a loved
one. "You'd have to talk to a psychologist about that," he
said. He did tell me how the concept of death has changed over
the last ten or so years.
```

B. He has been in the business for forty years(!). One look at him and you'd be convinced he'd been there at least that long. He told me that in the old times, everyone was buried. Embalmed, put in a casket, and paid final homage before being shipped underground forever. Nowadays, many people choose to be cremated instead. Hence comes the success of the Neptune Society and others specializing in cremation. You can have your ashes dumped anywhere. "Not that we don't offer cremation services. We've offered them since the beginning," he added with a look of disdain. It's just that they've become so popular recently because they offer a "quick, easy, and efficient means of disposal." Cheap too--I think it is a reflection of a "no nonsense" society. The Neptune Society has become so successful because it claims to be the only one to offer cremations as an alternative to expensive burial. "We've offered it all along. It's just only now come into vogue."

Sophisticated areas (I felt "progressive" would be more accurate) like Marin County have a cremation rate of over 60 percent. The phone rang. "Excuse me," he said. As he talked on the phone, I noticed how he played with his lips, pursing and squeezing them. He was blinking a lot, too. I meant to ask him how he got into this business, but I forgot. I did find out his name and title: Mr. Howard Deaver, funeral director of Goodbody Mortuaries (no kidding, that's the real name). He lives on the premises, upstairs with his wife. I doubt if he ever leaves the place.

III. It's a business!

Some people have the idea that mortuaries offer counseling and peace of mind--a place where everyone is sympathetic and ready to offer advice. "In some mortuaries, this is true. But by and large, this is a business. We offer services to the dead, not counseling to the living." I too had expected to feel an awestruck respect for the dead upon entering the building. I had also expected green lawns, ponds with ducks, fountains, flowers, peacefulness--you know, a "Forest Lawn" type deal. But it was only a tall, Catholic-looking building. "Mortuaries do not sell plots for burial," he was saying. "Cemeteries do that, after we embalm the body and select a casket. We're not a religious institution." He seemed hung up on caskets--though maybe he was just trying to impress upon me the differences between caskets. "Oh, they're very important. A good casket is a sign of respect. Sometimes if the family doesn't have enough money, we rent them a nice one. People pay for what they get just like any other business." I wondered when you had to return the casket you rented.

     I wanted to take a look around. He was happy to give me a tour. We visited several chapels and visiting rooms--places where the deceased "lie in state" to be "visited" by family and friends. I saw an old lady in a "fairly decent casket," as Mr. Deaver called it. Again I was impressed by the simple businesslike nature of it all. Oh yes, the rooms were elaborately decorated, with lots of shrines and stained glass, but these things were for the customers' benefit. "Sometimes we have up to eight or nine corpses here at one time, sometimes none. We have to have enough rooms to accommodate." Simple enough, yet I never realized how much (trouble?) people were after they died. So much money, time, and effort go into their funerals.

     As I prepared to leave, he gave me his card. He'd be happy to see me again, or maybe I could talk to someone else. I said I was going to interview the mortician on another day. I shook his hand. His fingers were long and his skin was warm.

Writing up the interview helped Cable probe his subject more deeply. It also helped him express a humorous attitude toward his subject. Cable's interview notes and write-up were quite informal; later, he integrated this material more formally into his full profile of the mortuary.

DESIGNING YOUR WORK

The education student working on a paper about collaborative learning principles (see pp. 129–30) published her paper on the Web so that her classmates and other interested people could read her work. Internet publishing is becoming an increasingly popular medium for students to share their work not just with their peers but with a wider audience as well. For this student, whose paper was based on her field research in a sixth-grade classroom, Web-based publishing allowed her to show her final product to the sixth graders and the teacher she had profiled.

    Web documents can be more visually complex and interactive than most other written pieces. In her Web-based essay, the education student incorporated photographs, links, color highlights, and quotations to make the material both more interesting and helpful to her readers. As the accompanying illustration shows, she also took advantage of the multiple frames and navigational tools Web publishing provides. She also included the list of scholarly essays about collaborative learning that served as background reading for her own work in two formats: as a traditional works-cited list at the end of her essay and as a pop-up window—a multimedia equivalent of a sidebar. While the works-cited list lent credibility to her work academically, the window was designed to provide content and links that might immediately attract casual visitors and encourage them to read the student's own writing more closely. When writers publish on the Web, they are much less bound by space constraints than they are when they generate conventional print documents. Duplication of information is also less of a concern, as readers can be expected to skip around and view the site selectively. The student organized the information in a way that enabled her to provide several different points of entry into her site.

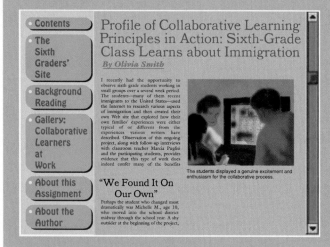

Opening page of student's paper published on the Web

In the main essay, the student writer included links to the sixth-grade class's Web site. Included on this site were the final projects that resulted from the Internet research she had watched the students perform. She encouraged readers to view the variety and quality of these projects as evidence of the significance of collaborative learning as a classroom tool.

The student decided to display one photograph of the sixth graders in action to give her readers a sense of what collaborative learning looks like and how the layout of the classroom she visited differed from the traditional setup. She included a button allowing readers to access other photos she had taken with her subjects' permission as part of her field research. By leaving viewing choices in her readers' hands, she helped ensure that they would not be forced to sit through a lengthy period of downloading.

At key points in her essay, the student writer also included quotes from the sixth graders themselves. She used these quotes as subtitles for individual sections of her essay, and to draw more attention to the quotes, she used a font larger than the body of the essay—a technique borrowed from print publishing. The availability of color, graphics, and animated or scrolling text in Web publishing has expanded the possibilities for creating visually exciting documents. In their capacity as Web page designers, however, writers must avoid bombarding readers with meaningless visual effects. In this example, the student made effective use of color and space on the Web page to help organize the key points she was making and to draw attention to the sixth graders' own voices and thoughts. In doing so, she clearly conveyed the students' love for school and made their quest for learning come alive.

THINKING CRITICALLY ABOUT
WHAT YOU HAVE LEARNED

Now that you have spent several days discussing profiles and writing one of your own, take some time to reflect on what you have learned about this genre. What problems did you encounter while you were writing your profile, and how did you solve them? How did what you learned as a reader of profiles help you write your own profile? Finally, explore the social dimensions of profiles: In what ways do they influence your thinking about yourself and the society we live in?

Reflecting on Your Writing

Write a one-page explanation, telling your instructor about a problem you encountered in writing your profile and how you solved it. Before you begin, gather all of your writing—invention material, planning and interview notes, drafts, critical comments, revision notes and plans, and final revision. Review these materials as you complete this writing task.

1. *Identify one writing problem you needed to solve as you worked on your profile.* Do not be concerned with grammar or punctuation; concentrate instead on problems unique to developing a profile. For example: Did you puzzle over how to organize your diverse observations into a coherent essay? Was it difficult to convey the significance? Did you have any concerns about presenting your subject vividly or controlling the flow of information?

2. *Determine how you came to recognize the problem.* When did you first discover it? What called it to your attention? If someone else pointed out the problem to you, can you now see hints of it in your invention writings? If so, where specifically? When you first recognized the problem, how did you respond?

3. *Reflect on how you went about solving the problem.* Did you work on the wording of a passage,

cut or add details about your subject, or move paragraphs or sentences around? Did you reread one of the essays in this chapter to see how another writer handled a similar problem, or did you look back at the invention suggestions? If you talked about the problem with another student, a tutor, or your instructor, did talking about it help? How useful was the advice you received?

4. *Write a brief explanation of the problem and your solution.* Reconstruct your efforts as specifically as possible. Quote from your invention notes or draft essay, others' critical comments, your revision plan, or your revised essay to show the various changes your writing underwent as you tried to solve the problem. When you have finished, consider how explaining what you have learned about solving this writing problem can help you solve future writing problems.

Reviewing What You Learned from Reading

Write a page or so explaining to your instructor how the readings in this chapter influenced your final essay. Before you write, take time to reflect on what you have learned from the readings in this chapter and how your reading has influenced your writing.

1. *Reread the final revision of your profile essay; then look back at the selections you read before completing it.* Do you see any specific influences? For example, if you were impressed with the way one of the readings presented a place through concrete details, made an ordinary activity seem interesting, focused all of the materials around a compelling and unexpected interpretation, or reconstructed dialogue from interview notes, look to see where you might have been striving for similar effects in your own writing. Also, look for ideas you got from your reading: writing

strategies you were inspired to try, specific details you were led to include, effects you sought to achieve.

2. *Write an explanation of these influences.* Did one selection in particular influence you, or were you influenced by several readings in different ways? Quote from the readings and from your final revision to show how your profile essay was influenced by the selections in this chapter. Finally, now that you have reviewed the other readings again, point out any ways in which you might further improve your profile.

Considering the Social Dimensions of Profiles

Profiles offer some of the same pleasures as auto-biographies, novels, and films—good stories, memorable characters, exotic places or familiar places viewed freshly, vivid images of people at work and play. They divert and entertain. They may even shock or fascinate. In addition, they offer information that may surprise and should interest readers. This special combination of entertainment and information makes profiles unique among all the kinds of reading and writing available to us.

Like travel writing and natural history, profiles nearly always take us to a particular place, usually a place we have never been. For example, Cable provides many visual details of Goodbody Mortuaries, with its gothic arches and stained glass, its hotel-like lobby with couches and coffee tables, aquarium, and pastoral paintings. The author of "Soup" describes Soup Kitchen International's appearance from the street so well that we could easily find it even if we did not know its number on West Fifty-fifth Street.

But the larger appeal of profiles is that they present real people most readers will never have a chance to meet. Often, profiles present people the writer admires—and assumes readers will admire—for their achievements, endurance, dedication, skill, or unselfishness. For example, we may find it easy to admire Mr. Yeganeh for his commanding knowledge

of the world's soups and his devotion to quality, just as we may be in awe of the brain surgeons in Noonan's profile for their great skill and extraordinary concentration. Profiles also present less admirable people; these people may occasionally be shown as cruel, greedy, or selfish, but more often they are people, such as Amy Wilkinson, with whom we can empathize. The strongest profiles present us not with saints, monsters, or helpless victims but with people of mixed motives, human failings, and some resources even in dire situations. Noonan invites us to admire the brain surgeons but also to question their apparent absence of feeling for their patients, while Orenstein suggests that Amy herself bears some responsibility for her lack of assertiveness in school.

Entertain Readers or Show the Whole Picture?
Profiles broaden our view of the world by entertaining and informing us with portraits of unusual people in particular places. It is important to recognize, however, that profiles sometimes offer a more limited view of their subjects than they seem to. For example, the impulse to entertain readers may lead a profile writer to focus exclusively on the dramatic, bizarre, colorful, or humorous aspects of a person, place, or activity, ignoring the equally important humdrum, routine, or even disturbing aspects. Imagine a profile of a travel agent focusing on the free trips he or she enjoys as part of the job but ignoring the everyday demands of dealing with clients, the energy-draining precision required by computerized airline reservation systems, and the numbing routine of addressing envelopes and mailing tickets to clients. Such a profile would provide a limited and distorted picture of a travel agent's work. While hardly distorted, Noonan's profile of a brain operation does skip over the more tedious parts of the procedure (the two-hour navigation through the brain before the tumor is found, for example) as a way of keeping readers involved in the drama of the moment.

In addition, by focusing on the dramatic or glamorous aspects of a subject, profile writers tend to ignore economic or social consequences and to slight "supporting players." Profiling the highly praised chef in a trendy new restaurant, a writer might not ask whether the chef participates in the city's leftover-food-collection program for the homeless or find out who the kitchen workers and wait staff are, how the chef treats them, or how much they are paid. Profiling the campus bookstore, a writer might become so entranced by the details of ordering books for hundreds of courses, shelving them so that they can be found easily, and selling them efficiently to hordes of students during the first week of a semester that he or she could forget to ask about textbook costs, pricing policies, profit margins, and payback on used textbooks. (Note that Noonan quotes only the surgeons; the nurses and other technicians involved in the brain operation remain anonymous. Neither do the costs of so elaborate a procedure—and who pays for it and profits from it—concern him.)

1. *Consider whether any of the profiles you have read glamorize or sensationalize their subjects.* Do they ignore less colorful but centrally important everyday activities? Is this a problem with your own profile?

2. *Single out a profile you read that seems to overlook potential social or economic consequences.* What is overlooked? Why do you think the writer omits these aspects?

3. *Write a page or so explaining what the omissions signify.* What do they suggest about the readers' desires to be entertained and profile writers'

reluctance to present the subject as boring or disturbing in some way?

Be Aware of the Writer's Viewpoint. Though profiles may seem impartial and objective, they inevitably reflect the views of their writers. The choice of subject, the details observed, the questions asked, the ultimate focus and presentation—all are influenced by the writer's interests and values, gender and ethnicity, and assumptions about social and political issues. For example, we would expect a vegetarian to write a very different profile of a cattle ranch than a beef-lover would. Consequently, profiles should be read critically, particularly because the writer's values are likely to be unstated.

1. *Consider the attitudes, values, and views of the profile writers in this chapter.* Are their attitudes obvious or hidden? How can you tell?

2. *Consider your own profile essay in the same terms.* Are your attitudes obvious or hidden? If obvious, how did you make them so, and did you feel as though you were taking a risk? If hidden, why did you think it best to keep your personal views out of sight?

3. *Write a page or so about how your viewpoint influenced your writing.* How have your own assumptions, values, gender, and ethnicity influenced your choice of a subject to profile, your approach to learning about it, and your attitudes toward it?

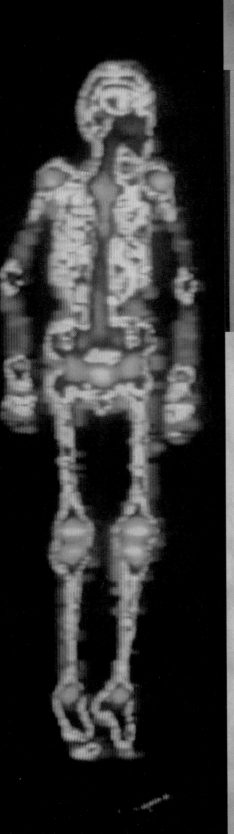

Explaining a Concept

5

Explanatory writing serves to inform readers. In general, it does not feature its writers' experiences or feelings, as autobiography does (see Chapters 2 and 3). Instead, successful explanatory writing presents information, confidently and efficiently, with the purpose of educating the reader about a subject. This type of writing, required almost every day in nearly every profession, may be based on firsthand observation (Chapter 4), but it always moves beyond describing specific objects and events to explain general principles and patterns of behavior. Since it deals almost exclusively with established information, explanatory writing tends not to present an argument but to present information as if everyone assumes it were true. It does not aspire to be more than it is: a way for readers to find out about a particular subject. Much of what we find in newspapers, encyclopedias, instruction manuals, reference books, and research reports is explanatory writing.

This chapter focuses on one important kind of explanatory writing, explanations of concepts. The chapter readings explain the concepts "love," "Internet addiction," "the new terrorism," and "cannibalism." These concepts name processes and phenomena under study. Scientists in various fields have studied the body's chemistry during both new romances and long-term relationships to create a "neurochemistry of love." Psychologists have borrowed the concept of "addiction" from their studies of other compulsive behaviors like alcohol and drug addiction to understand why some Internet users spend many hours every day online. Political scientists and security experts have sought to explain the activities of terrorists today by creating a concept that they call "the new terrorism." Anthropologists continue to learn more about the situations and cultural practices that lead humans to eat other humans, a phenomenon known as "cannibalism."

Every field of study has its concepts: physics has "entropy," "mass," and "fission"; literature has "irony," "romanticism," and "bildungsroman"; music has "harmony"; art has "perspective"; mathematics has "probability"; and so on. You can see from this brief list that concepts are central to the understanding of virtually every subject. Moreover, when you enter a new field, you are expected to learn a new set of concepts. That is why introductory courses and their textbooks teach a whole new vocabulary of technical terms and specialized jargon. When you read the opening chapter of this textbook, for example, you were introduced to many concepts important to the study of writing, such as "genre," "writing process," "invention," and "revision."

Learning to explain a concept is especially important to you as a college student. It will help you read textbooks (which themselves exist to explain concepts); it will prepare you to write a common type of exam and paper assignment; and it will acquaint you with the basic strategies common to all types of explanatory writing—definition, classification, comparison and contrast, cause and effect, and process narration.

You will encounter writing that explains concepts in many different contexts, as the following examples suggest:

Writing in Your Other Courses

- For a linguistics course, a student writes a term paper tracing children's gradual control of sentences (or syntax, as linguists say) from about eighteen months to five or six years of age. The student first explains how researchers go about studying children's syntax, using several well-known studies as examples. Then he presents the widely accepted classification of stages that children go through as they gain control of snytax. As he presents each stage, he gives examples of children's syntax in both their spoken monologues and their conversations in different situations, examples chosen from many possibilities in the published research studies. Even though he writes for his instructor, who is an expert in child language development, he carefully defines key terms to show that he understands what he is writing about.

- For a history of religion course, a student writes a term paper on religious fundamentalism. To explain this concept, she relies primarily on a book by a noted religious scholar. She follows the scholar in classifying the ways fundamentalist religious groups are similar and organizes her paper around these similarities, which include a sense of threat and an organized reaction to the threat, a reliance on authoritative texts, a resistance to ambiguity and ambivalence, an inclination to behave aggressively toward unbelievers, an allegiance to a grand past, and a belief in a bright future. She illustrates each of these features of fundamentalism with examples from the beliefs and histories of fundamentalist groups around the world. She concludes by pointing out that religious fundamentalism has become a major political force at the end of the twentieth century.

Writing in the Community

- "Community policing" has just been adopted by the police department in a mid-sized city, and a writer in the department's public relations division has been assigned the task of writing and producing a brochure explaining the new approach. The brochure will be mailed to all homes in the city. The writer designs a small, fold-out, six-panel, two-sided brochure that will feature both text and photographs. The text explains briefly the major features of community policing, for example, neighborhood-focused crime control and prevention, neighborhood involvement in deciding on crime-control priorities, the long-term assignment of officers to neighborhoods, increased reliance on foot and bicycle patrols and decreased reliance on car patrols, and the establishment of neighborhood mini-police stations. Working with a photographer, the writer arranges to get photographs taken that represent the different features of community policing explained in the text.

- As part of her firm's plan to encourage managers to volunteer in the community for a few hours each month, the manager at a marketing research firm has been tutoring fifth-grade students in math. Learning of the manager's expertise in surveys, the teacher encourages the manager to plan a presentation to the class about surveying, a concept and important research method in the social sciences. The manager agrees to do so and begins her lesson by having students fill out a brief questionnaire on their television-watching habits. She explains that she is not collecting data for marketing purposes, but rather introducing them to surveys. With the students helping, she tabulates the results on a computer, separating the results by sex, time of week (weekdays or weekends), and kinds of television shows. Using a PowerPoint program, she projects the data onto a large screen so that everyone can see how the tables represent the survey results. The manager first guides a brief discussion of the survey and the results, helping students understand its purpose, form, and graphic representation. Then she shows them on the screen examples of questions from other surveys and explains who gives such surveys, what they hope to learn, and how they report and use the results. She explains that the state tests the students take every year are a form of survey. Finally, she passes out a short-answer quiz so that she and each student can find out how much has been learned about surveys.

For more detail on some of the decisions the manager makes in designing her presentation, see p. 233.

Writing in the Workplace

- Returning from a small invitational seminar on the national security implications of satellite photography, the CEO of a space-imaging company prepares a report to his employees on the international debate about symmetrical transparency, the concept of using satellite photography to make everything on the planet visible to everyone on the planet at one-meter resolution—enough detail to reveal individual cars in parking lots, small airplanes on runways, backyard swimming pools, and individual shrubs and trees planted in parks. Aware of the financial implications for his company of the outcome of the debate, the executive carefully organizes his information and prepares a written text to read aloud to his employees, a one-page handout that lists key issues in the debate, and a transparency to project on a large screen during his presentation. He begins by reminding employees that the company's cameras already provide high-resolution images to government and corporate purchasers. Addressing the question of whether symmetrical transparency and the multinational monitoring it makes possible compromise national security—or promise greater worldwide security and peace—the CEO gives a brief overview of key issues in the debate. These issues include differing impacts on closed societies (like those of North Korea and Iraq) and more open ones, whether global terrorism will be reduced or become more prevalent or more effective, and whether the chance of a nuclear standoff will be lessened. He concludes by pointing out that the big question for the U.S. government to answer soon is whether it must attempt to control space or insist that it be open to everyone.

- Legislation in a western state defines a new concept in tourism—agri-tourism. In one area where farmers, vineyard owners, and ranchers might be most affected, a university-extension farm adviser calls a meeting to explain the concept as defined in the legislation. To prepare for the meeting, he writes a four-page summary of the legislation and prepares a one-page list of the main points in his presentation for everyone to pick up and read before the meeting begins. Assuming his listeners have all visited a bed and breakfast, the farm adviser compares the rules in the new law with the rules governing bed and breakfasts. He emphasizes that in agri-tourism, guests must be able to tour the farm or ranch and even participate in carefully supervised chores. Whoever prepares and serves the meals, which must be offered three times a day, has to be certified through coursework at a community college. He also explains that the greatest beneficiaries of agri-tourism will be small and middle-sized farms and ranches, where income is relatively low and varies greatly from year to year.

Practice Explaining a Concept: A Collaborative Activity

The preceding scenarios suggest some occasions for writing about concepts. Think of concepts you are currently studying or have recently studied or concepts connected to a sport or hobby you know a lot about. Here are some possibilities: "hip hop," "squeeze play," "ambition," "creativity," "friendship," "success," "hypertext," "interval training," "job satisfaction," "photosynthesis," "maturity," "community," "civil rights," "manifest destiny."

Part 1. Choose one concept to explain to two or three other students. When you have chosen your concept, think about what others in the group are likely to know about it and how you can inform them about it in two or three minutes. Consider how you will define the concept and what other strategies you might use—description, comparison, and so on—to explain it in an interesting, memorable way.

Get together with two or three other students and explain your concepts to one another. You might begin by indicating where you learned the concept and in what area of study or work or leisure it is usually used.

Part 2. When all group members have explained their concepts, discuss what you learned from the experience of explaining a concept. Begin by asking one another a question or two that would elicit further information you need to understand each concept more fully. Then, consider these questions:

- How did you decide what to include in your explanation and what to leave out?

- How successfully did you estimate listeners' prior knowledge of your concepts?

- If you were to repeat your explanation to a similar group of listeners, what would you add, subtract, or change?

READINGS

The readings in this chapter illustrate the features of essays that explain concepts and the strategies writers rely on to realize the features. No two essays in this type of writing are much alike, and yet they share defining features. The Analyzing Writing Strategies and the Commentary following each reading touch on a few features best illustrated by that essay, capturing its special qualities and strengths. Together, the four essays cover many of the possibilities of explanatory writing. Consequently, you will want to read as many of the essays as possible and, if time permits, complete the activities in Analyzing Writing Strategies and read the Commentary. Following the readings is a section called Basic Features, which offers a concise description of the features of concept explanations and provides examples from all of the readings.

Anastasia Toufexis, *for many years an associate editor at* Time, *has written major reports, including some best-selling cover stories, for nearly every section of the magazine: medicine, health and fitness, law, environment, education, science, and national and world news. Toufexis received her bachelor's degree in premedicine from Smith College in 1967 and spent several years reporting for medical and pharmaceutical magazines. She has won a number of awards for her work at* Time *and has lectured on newsmagazine journalism and science writing at Columbia University, the University of North Carolina, and the School of Visual Arts in New York. The following essay was originally published in a 1993 issue of* Time. *As you read, notice how Toufexis brings together a variety of sources of information to present a neurochemical perspective on love.*

Love: The Right Chemistry

Anastasia Toufexis

Love is a romantic designation for a most ordinary biological —or, shall we say, chemical?—process. A lot of nonsense is talked and written about it.
— GRETA GARBO to Melvyn Douglas in *Ninotchka*

O.K., let's cut out all this nonsense about romantic love. Let's bring some scientific precision to the party. Let's put love under a microscope. 1

When rigorous people with Ph.D.s after their names do that, what they see is not 2 some silly, senseless thing. No, their probe reveals that love rests firmly on the foundations of evolution, biology and chemistry. What seems on the surface to be irrational, intoxicated behavior is in fact part of nature's master strategy—a vital force that has helped humans survive, thrive and multiply through thousands of years. Says Michael Mills, a psychology professor at Loyola Marymount University in Los Angeles: "Love is our ancestors whispering in our ears."

It was on the plains of Africa about 4 million years ago, in the early days of the human 3 species, that the notion of romantic love probably first began to blossom—or at least that the first cascades of neurochemicals began flowing from the brain to the bloodstream to produce goofy grins and sweaty palms as men and women gazed deeply into each other's eyes. When mankind graduated from scuttling around on all fours to walking on two legs, this change made the whole person visible to fellow human beings for the first time. Sexual organs were in full display, as were other characteristics, from the color of eyes to the span of shoulders. As never before, each individual had a unique allure.

When the sparks flew, new ways of making love enabled sex to become a roman- 4 tic encounter, not just a reproductive act. Although mounting mates from the rear was, and still is, the method favored among most animals, humans began to enjoy face-to-face couplings; both looks and personal attraction became a much greater part of the equation.

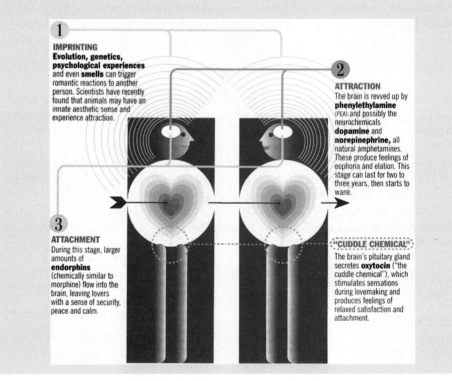

1 IMPRINTING
Evolution, genetics, psychological experiences and even **smells** can trigger romantic reactions to another person. Scientists have recently found that animals may have an innate aesthetic sense and experience attraction.

2 ATTRACTION
The brain is revved up by **phenylethylamine** (PEA) and possibly the neurochemicals **dopamine** and **norepinephrine,** all natural amphetamines. These produce feelings of euphoria and elation. This stage can last for two to three years, then starts to wane.

3 ATTACHMENT
During this stage, larger amounts of **endorphins** (chemically similar to morphine) flow into the brain, leaving lovers with a sense of security, peace and calm.

"CUDDLE CHEMICAL"
The brain's pituitary gland secretes **oxytocin** ("the cuddle chemical"), which stimulates sensations during lovemaking and produces feelings of relaxed satisfaction and attachment.

Romance served the evolutionary purpose of pulling males and females into long-term partnership, which was essential to child rearing. On open grasslands, one parent would have a hard—and dangerous—time handling a child while foraging for food. "If a woman was carrying the equivalent of a 20-lb. bowling ball in one arm and a pile of sticks in the other, it was ecologically critical to pair up with a mate to rear the young," explains anthropologist Helen Fisher, author of *Anatomy of Love.*

While Western culture holds fast to the idea that true love flames forever (the movie *Bram Stoker's Dracula* has the Count carrying the torch beyond the grave), nature apparently meant passions to sputter out in something like four years. Primitive pairs stayed together just "long enough to rear one child through infancy," says Fisher. Then each would find a new partner and start all over again.

What Fisher calls the "four-year itch" shows up unmistakably in today's divorce statistics. In most of the 62 cultures she has studied, divorce rates peak around the fourth year of marriage. Additional youngsters help keep pairs together longer. If, say, a couple have another child three years after the first, as often occurs, then their union can be expected to last about four more years. That makes them ripe for the more familiar phenomenon portrayed in the Marilyn Monroe classic *The Seven-Year Itch.*

If, in nature's design, romantic love is not eternal, neither is it exclusive. Less than 5% of mammals form rigorously faithful pairs. From the earliest days, contends Fisher, the human pattern has been "monogamy with clandestine adultery." Occasional flings upped the chances that new combinations of genes would be passed on to the next generation. Men who sought new partners had more children. Contrary to common assumptions, women were just as likely to stray. "As long as prehistoric females were secretive about their extramarital affairs," argues Fisher, "they could garner extra resources, life insurance, better genes and more varied DNA for their biological futures. . . ."

Lovers often claim that they feel as if they are being swept away. They're not mistaken; they are literally flooded by chemicals, research suggests. A meeting of eyes, a touch of hands or a whiff of scent sets off a flood that starts in the brain and races along the nerves and through the blood. The results are familiar: flushed skin, sweaty palms, heavy breathing. If love looks suspiciously like stress, the reason is simple: the chemical pathways are identical.

Above all, there is the sheer euphoria of falling in love—a not-so-surprising reaction, considering that many of the substances swamping the newly smitten are chemical cousins of amphetamines. They include dopamine, norepinephrine and especially phenylethylamine (PEA). Cole Porter knew what he was talking about when he wrote, "I get a kick out of you." "Love is a natural high," observes Anthony Walsh, author of *The Science of Love: Understanding Love and Its Effects on Mind and Body.* "PEA gives you that silly smile that you flash at strangers. When we meet someone who is attractive to us, the whistle blows at the PEA factory."

But phenylethylamine highs don't last forever, a fact that lends support to arguments that passionate romantic love is short-lived. As with any amphetamine, the body builds up a tolerance to PEA; thus it takes more and more of the substance to produce love's special kick. After two to three years, the body simply can't crank up the needed amount of PEA. And chewing on chocolate doesn't help, despite popular belief. The candy is high in PEA, but it fails to boost the body's supply.

Fizzling chemicals spell the end of delirious passion; for many people that marks the end of the liaison as well. It is particularly true for those whom Dr. Michael Liebowitz of the New York State Psychiatric Institute terms "attraction junkies." They crave the intoxication of falling in love so much that they move frantically from affair to affair just as soon as the first rush of infatuation fades.   12

Still, many romances clearly endure beyond the first years. What accounts for that? Another set of chemicals, of course. The continued presence of a partner gradually steps up production in the brain of endorphins. Unlike the fizzy amphetamines, these are soothing substances. Natural pain-killers, they give lovers a sense of security, peace and calm. "That is one reason why it feels so horrible when we're abandoned or a lover dies," notes Fisher. "We don't have our daily hit of narcotics."   13

Researchers see a contrast between the heated infatuation induced by PEA, along with other amphetamine-like chemicals, and the more intimate attachment fostered and prolonged by endorphins. "Early love is when you love the way the other person makes you feel," explains psychiatrist Mark Goulston of the University of California, Los Angeles. "Mature love is when you love the person as he or she is." It is the difference between passionate and compassionate love, observes Walsh, a psychobiologist at Boise State University in Idaho. "It's Bon Jovi vs. Beethoven."   14

Oxytocin is another chemical that has recently been implicated in love. Produced by the brain, it sensitizes nerves and stimulates muscle contraction. In women it helps uterine contractions during childbirth as well as production of breast milk, and seems to inspire mothers to nuzzle their infants. Scientists speculate that oxytocin might encourage similar cuddling between adult women and men. The versatile chemical may also enhance orgasms. In one study of men, oxytocin increased to three to five times its normal level during climax, and it may soar even higher in women. . . .   15

Chemicals may help explain (at least to scientists) the feelings of passion and compassion, but why do people tend to fall in love with one partner rather than a myriad of others? Once again, it's partly a function of evolution and biology. "Men are looking for maximal fertility in a mate," says Loyola Marymount's Mills. "That is in large part why females in the prime childbearing ages of 17 to 28 are so desirable." Men can size up youth and vitality in a glance, and studies indeed show that men fall in love quite rapidly. Women tumble more slowly, to a large degree because their requirements are more complex; they need more time to check the guy out. "Age is not vital," notes Mills, "but the ability to provide security, father children, share resources and hold a high status in society are all key factors."   16

Still, that does not explain why the way Mary walks and laughs makes Bill dizzy with desire while Marcia's gait and giggle leave him cold. "Nature has wired us for one special person," suggests Walsh, romantically. He rejects the idea that a woman or a man can be in love with two people at the same time. Each person carries in his or her mind a unique subliminal guide to the ideal partner, a "love map," to borrow a term coined by sexologist John Money of Johns Hopkins University.   17

Drawn from the people and experiences of childhood, the map is a record of whatever we found enticing and exciting—or disturbing and disgusting. Small feet, curly hair. The way our mothers patted our head or how our fathers told a joke. A fireman's uniform, a doctor's stethoscope. All the information gathered while growing up is imprinted in the brain's circuitry by adolescence. Partners never meet each and every requirement, but a sufficient number of matches can light up the wires and signal, "It's love." Not every partner will be like the last one, since lovers may have different combinations of the characteristics favored by the map. 18

O.K., that's the scientific point of view. Satisfied? Probably not. To most people—with or without Ph.D.s—love will always be more than the sum of its natural parts. It's a commingling of body and soul, reality and imagination, poetry and phenylethylamine. In our deepest hearts, most of us harbor the hope that love will never fully yield up its secrets, that it will always elude our grasp. 19

Connecting to Culture and Experience: Love Maps

The chemistry of love is easily summarized: Amphetamines fuel romance; endorphins and oxytocin sustain lasting relationships. As Toufexis makes clear, however, these chemical reactions do not explain why people are initially attracted to each other. Toufexis observes that an initial attraction occurs because each of us carries a "unique subliminal guide" or "love map" that leads us unerringly to a partner. Moreover, she explains that men look for maximal fertility, whereas women look for security, resources, status, and a willingness to father children.

Discuss these explanations for attraction between the sexes. Consider where your love map comes from and how much it may be influenced by your family, ethnicity, or images in the media or advertising. Consider whether it is possible for an individual's love map to change over time—from adolescence to adulthood, for example.

Analyzing Writing Strategies

1. At the beginning of this chapter, we made several generalizations about essays explaining concepts. Consider which of these assertions are true of Toufexis's essay:

   - It seeks to inform readers about a specific subject.
   - It presents information confidently and efficiently.
   - It relies almost exclusively on established information.
   - It does not feature its writer's experiences or feelings.
   - It tends not to argue for its points.

2. To explain a concept, you have to **classify** the information; that is, group or divide it into meaningful categories. Otherwise, you struggle to write about a jumble of information, and your readers quickly give up trying to make sense of it. For example, a writer setting out to explain testing in American colleges to a

To learn more about classifying, turn to Chapter 17.

For illustrations of scratch outlining, turn to pp. 518–19 in Chapter 11 and to the Commentary following Linh Ngo's essay in this chapter.

college student in Thailand would first try to classify the subject by dividing it into categories like the following: short-answer, essay, multiple-choice, lab demonstration, artistic performance. To understand more about how Toufexis divides her information, make a scratch outline of paragraphs 9–15, where she presents the centrally important information on specific chemicals. How is the information divided and sequenced in these paragraphs? What cues does Toufexis provide to help you follow the sequence? What do you find most and least successful about the division?

Commentary: A Focused Concept and Careful Use of Sources

Unless they are writing an entire book on the subject, writers explaining concepts must focus their attention on some particular aspect of the concept. A relatively brief essay or magazine article offers limited space for approaching a concept from several different angles or attempting to survey everything known about it. Consequently, after getting an overview of what is known about a concept, writers must choose a focus and select information related only to that focus. For instance, Toufexis focuses on the chemistry of love between adult human mates. She excludes parents' love for their children, dogs' love for their masters, views on love by the Catholic Church, the history of romance as revealed in literature, courtship rituals in the United States in the 1990s, and dozens of other possible subjects related to love. Toufexis holds to her chemical focus throughout the essay, except for a brief but relevant digression about "love maps" toward the end. When they finish the essay, readers have learned nothing new about love in general, but they are well informed about the neurochemistry of love. By keeping to this narrow focus Toufexis is able to present information that is likely to be new to most readers, and therefore has a better chance of holding readers' attention.

Besides holding to a well-chosen concept focus, concept explanations rely on authoritative, expert sources, on established material gleaned from reputable publications or interviews. Toufexis uses both these kinds of sources. She apparently arranged telephone or in-person interviews with six different professors specializing in diverse academic disciplines: psychology, anthropology, psychiatry, and sexology. (She does not immediately identify the discipline of one professor—Walsh, in paragraph 10—but from the title of his book, we might guess that he is a biochemist, and in paragraph 14 we are not surprised to learn that he is a psychobiologist.) We assume that Toufexis read at least parts of the two books she names in paragraphs 5 and 10, and perhaps she also read other sources, which may have led her to some of the professors she interviewed.

What is obvious about Toufexis's use of sources is that she does not indicate precisely where she obtained all the information she includes. For example, she does not cite the source of the anthropological information in paragraphs 3–5, although a reader might guess that she summarized it from *Anatomy of Love,* cited at the end of paragraph 5. We cannot be certain whether the quote at the end of paragraph 5 comes from the book or from an interview with its author. These liberties in citing sources are acceptable in newspapers and magazines, including the leading ones educated readers count on to keep them up to date on developments in various fields. Experienced readers know that reporters, who write about surprisingly diverse topics as part of their jobs, rely entirely on sources for their articles and essays. They understand that Toufexis is not an expert on the neurochemistry of love; they accept her role as synthesizer and summarizer of authoritative sources. In most college writing situations, however, you will be expected to cite formally all of your sources.

Observing an important requirement of essays explaining concepts, Toufexis provides several different kinds of cues to keep readers on track. In addition to paragraph-opening transitions, Toufexis carefully forecasts the topics and direction of her essay in her second paragraph: "their probe reveals that love rests firmly on the foundations of evolution, biology and chemistry." This forecast helps readers anticipate the types of scientific information Toufexis has selected for her special focus on love and the sequence in which she will introduce them.

For more help with keeping readers on track, see Chapter 13.

Considering Topics for Your Own Essay

Like Toufexis, you could write an essay about love or romance, but with a different focus: on its history (how and when did it develop as an idea in the West?), its cultural characteristics (how is love regarded presently among different American ethnic groups or world cultures?), its excesses or extremes, its expression between parent and child, or the phases of falling in and out of love. Also consider writing about other concepts involving personal relationships, such as "jealousy," "codependency," "idealization," "stereotyping," or "homophobia."

Carol Potera, *a freelance writer living in Great Falls, Montana, writes about topics and issues in medicine and science. She has worked as a researcher and writer in the Department of Human Oncology, University of Wisconsin, Madison, and at the Eleanor Roosevelt Institute for Cancer Research in Denver. Her awards include a 1990 Deems Taylor Award sponsored by the American Society of Composers, Authors, and Publishers for a profile of an academic chemist who studies the materials and sound qualities of the famous Stradivarius violins and a 1999 science writing fellowship at the Molecular Biological Laboratory, Woods Hole, Massachusetts. In this 1998 essay from* Psychology Today, *Potera explains a relatively new concept—Internet addiction. She identifies an addict as someone who spends around forty hours a week on the Internet, most of it in chat rooms or at interactive game sites, and who is experiencing personal, social, academic, or occupational problems as a result. Like all the authors in this chapter, Potera relies on experts for the information she needs. As you read, think about your own use of the Internet. How much of it is for academic or personal purposes and how much for diversion or entertainment?*

Internet Addiction

Carol Potera

Frustration with the sluggish speed of a browser is about the most serious psychological pitfall that most of us face when surfing the World Wide Web. But for as many as five million Americans, experts say, the Internet has become a destructive force, its remarkable benefits overshadowed by its potential to disrupt the lives of those who can't resist the lure of round-the-clock social opportunities, entertainment, and information. For such people, work, friends, family, and sleep are replaced by a virtual world of chat rooms and games.

Take Judy and Bob, a Seattle couple who were saving to buy their first house—until monthly credit card bills started arriving with $350 charges for online services. Bob was "pissing away all our money on the Internet," says Judy. And soon he was doing likewise to their marriage. Every evening Bob came home from work and headed straight for the computer; he stopped joining Judy for dinner or helping with household chores. At 10 P.M. each night Judy hit the sack, while Bob stumbled to bed some five hours later. Before long he was sucked into cyberspace 40 or 50 hours a week. When it became clear after six months that Bob had chosen his online world over his real one, Judy left.

Such tales became increasingly common in the early 1990s, when the growing popularity of commercial providers made the Internet affordable and accessible to anyone with a personal computer, modem, and phone. Only recently, however, have psychologists begun devising strategies to wean online addicts from their endless browsing and chatting. And while it's too soon to say how successful their efforts have been, their hope is that the extent of the problem will be recognized before it becomes even more widespread.

Cybertrouble

One of the first experts to notice that some people were spending an unhealthy amount of time on the Internet was Kimberly Young, Ph.D., an assistant professor of psychology at the University of Pittsburgh, Bradford. In 1994, Young launched the first major study of the problem, surveying nearly 500 avid Internet users about their online habits. Because there was no formal definition for the disorder—which she quickly christened "Internet addiction"—Young classified study participants as "dependent" or "nondependent" Internet users based on their answers to seven questions she adapted from those used to diagnose pathological gambling. (Sample question: Do you experience withdrawal symptoms—depression, agitation, moodiness—when not online?) Those who answered "yes" to three or more questions were classified as dependent.

On average, Young found, dependents spent an astonishing 38 hours a week online, compared with just five hours a week for nondependents. And usually they were not cruising the information highway to enrich their knowledge of El Niño or the Russian space station. Instead, dependents sought contact with other people: their favorite activities were chat rooms (35 percent) and Multi User Dungeon games (28 percent), while nondependents were most likely to use the Internet for electronic mail (30 percent) and searching the World Wide Web (25 percent). Similarly, a 1996 survey of 530 college students by Kathy Scherer, Ph.D., a psychologist at the University of Texas at Austin, found that dependents and nondependents spent similar amounts of time exchanging email and searching the Web, but dependents spent twice as much time in chat rooms and playing games.

None of the nondependents in Young's study reported academic, personal, financial, or occupational problems caused by their Internet use. But about half of dependents reported problems in all of these areas. Yet many dependents insisted they couldn't give up the Internet; a few even tossed out their modems, but their Internet cravings led them to buy a new one to get their cyberspace fix. In fact, the smokers in the study reported that their cravings for the Internet were stronger than the urge to light up a cigarette.   6

Who's at Risk?

Most Internet users don't become addicted. Among people who gamble or drink alcohol, about 5 to 10 percent develop problem behaviors, and Young believes that the figures are similar for pathological Internet behavior. With an estimated 47 million people currently online, as many as two to five million could be addicted. Especially vulnerable, Young believes, are those who are lonely, bored, depressed, introverted, lack self-esteem, or have a history of addictions.   7

Perhaps the most surprising—and widely reported—finding in Young's original study was that the majority (60 percent) of dependent users were middle-aged women, particularly housewives, not young male computer geeks. But this has not held up in later studies, which give men a slight edge. Young suspects a bias occurred in her first study, perhaps because women are more likely to admit and talk about their problems. Still, she understands the appeal that chat rooms hold for these women and others in her sample. "You never worry about how you look or how nice a house you have, and you talk to people all over the world. It's instant gratification without having to reveal yourself." Lonely housewives or shy sophomores can feel like exciting people when online. "It's novel and unique, and they get attached to the people they meet online," Young says.   8

Indeed, like alcoholics with favorite drinking buddies, Internet addicts form close bonds that fuel their compulsions. Dan, a college student, earned a 3.2 grade point average his freshman year. Then he moved in with roommates who played an interactive Multi User Dungeon computer game as a team from separate computers, and soon began logging on 50 to 60 hours a week. Dan's grade point average nose-dived to 1.6. His fiancée began to complain that he spent too much time with his computer friends; they, in turn, griped when he signed off to spend time with her. Faced with the reality that he might not graduate or get married, Dan tried to cut back, a goal that grew easier after his roommates graduated. A year later, his use was down to 10 hours per week. "I still get high on the Internet," he admits, "but I'm in control."   9

Get high? Internet addiction? Time was when the word "addiction" referred to drug and alcohol problems—period. Today, so-called addictions are everywhere: sex, exercise, work, chocolate, TV, shopping, and now the Internet. Have we been, well, abusing the word?   10

An Addiction? Really?

"Addiction," notes Young, "is a layman's term, not a clinical one." In fact, the DSM-IV[1] doesn't even mention the word. Young chose the label "Internet addiction" because it's readily understandable by the public. When writing for clinical journals, however, she refers to "pathological Internet use," modeling the term after that for pathological gambling in the DSM-IV.

Other experts shun the term addiction altogether because it means too many things to too many people. "It's a sloppy word," says pharmacologist Carlton Erickson, Ph.D., head of the Addiction Science Research and Education Center at the University of Texas at Austin. In the drug abuse field, he notes, "dependence" has replaced "addiction." "In dependence, people can't stop because they have developed a brain chemistry that does not allow them to stop," explains Erickson. Excessive behavior that hasn't quite reached full-fledged dependency, meanwhile, is called "abuse." If Internet abusers cannot stop for a month, suggests Erickson, then "Internet dependence" would be the appropriate term. Others believe that the problem is best described as a compulsion, suggesting the phrase "compulsive Internet use." And many psychologists question whether excessive Internet use should be pathologized at all: John Grohol, Ph.D., who directs the Web site "Mental Health Net," says that by the same logic, bookworms should be diagnosed with "book addiction disorder."

Perhaps the controversy will be definitively resolved when researchers determine whether behaviors like pathological gambling or Internet addiction produce chemical changes in the brain similar to those found in drug abusers. In the meantime, Young believes that the often severe personal consequences of Internet addiction justify popular use of the term. "Internet addiction does not cause the same physical problems as other addictions," she says, "but the social problems parallel those of established addictions."

Treatments for Internet addiction are beginning to emerge. Trouble is, not all mental health specialists recognize the problem or know how to treat it. Internet dependents have been told by uninformed therapists to simply "turn off the computer." That's like telling a heroin addict to just say no to drugs—and just as unsuccessful. What's more, HMOs and insurance companies do not pay for Internet addiction therapy because it's not recognized by the DSM-IV.

Among those developing treatments for the problem is Maressa Hecht Orzack, Ph.D., a psychologist at Harvard University's McLean Hospital in Belmont, Massachusetts. Orzack founded Harvard's Computer Addiction Services in Fall 1996, after seeing first-hand the fallout from Internet-related problems: divorce, child neglect, job termination, debt, flunking out of school, legal trouble. One client, she says, had separated from his wife but couldn't afford to move out because he spent so much money on computer services. He moved his bed into the computer room and started an affair with an online sweetheart.

11

12

13

14

15

---

[1]The *Diagnostic and Statistical Manual of Mental Disorders: DSM-IV* used by medical professionals

A cognitive therapist, Orzack likens Internet addiction to such impulse control dis- 16
orders as pathological gambling and kleptomania. However, "gamblers have a choice to
gamble or not," she notes. "People addicted to the Internet often do not have that choice,
since so many activities require people to use a computer."

Like Binge-Eating

So the best approach for excessive Internet use, Orzack believes, will be to treat it like 17
binge eating, where the individual frequently engages in the activity to be restricted. She
treats both by teaching clients how to set limits, balance activities, and schedule time,
without having to go cold turkey. "People often change in six or eight sessions," she says.

Unfortunately, the afflicted rarely admit to the problem, and it usually takes a crisis 18
with a job, relationship, or school to spur an Internet addict to seek treatment. More
often, it's loved ones who turn to the experts. "Families notice things and call me," says
Orzack. And she receives letters like this: "We got divorced one year after we got the
computer. My wife was in chat rooms all the time and ignored our young daughter. She
spent hundreds of dollars on phone bills . . . [and] had an affair online that turned into a
real affair. . . . Then she left. I don't know what to do. Please help." Now lawyers and
family courts call Orzack and Young wanting them to testify about Internet addiction in
divorce and custody battles. (In October, a Florida woman lost custody of her kids when
her ex-husband convinced a judge that the woman was addicted to the Internet and thus
incapable of properly caring for their children.)

College students are often vulnerable to Internet addiction because many universi- 19
ties provide free, unlimited access. At the University of Texas Counseling and Mental
Health Center at Austin, Scherer and her computer scientist husband Jacob Kornerup
created a workshop, called It's 4 A.M. and I Can't—Uh, Won't—Log Off, to help students
recognize harmful Internet habits. Scherer and Kornerup recommend keeping a chart
sorting weekly Internet time into academic/professional and leisure/personal use. If a
large part of your leisure time is spent on the Internet, she says, ask what you get out of
it, what you're giving up, and why you're finding online time so much more pleasurable
than other activities. Take note if your personal relationships are suffering.

Next, set a goal of how many hours a week you want to use the Internet. If your 20
actual usage exceeds it, remind yourself to log off after a period of time. Set a kitchen
timer and turn off the computer—no excuses—when it rings.

It's particularly important to separate work and play when online, says Jane Morgan 21
Bost, Ph.D., assistant director of the University of Texas Counseling and Mental Health
Center. Stay focused, visit only sites needed to complete work, and don't detour. Also,
she says, cut back mailing list memberships and sort play e-mail from work e-mail.

None of the experts *Psychology Today* spoke with demonize the Internet; they use 22
it extensively themselves and applaud the benefits of rapid communication and information exchange. But, they add, the Internet is here to stay, and problems with excessive
use need to be addressed. . . .

Are You Addicted to the Internet?

Psychologist Kimberly Young, Ph.D., has identified several warning signs of excessive Internet use. Behaviors that signal concern include:

- Staying online longer than you intended
- Admitting that you can't stop from signing on
- Neglecting loved ones, chores, sleep, reading, television, friends, exercise, hobbies, sex, or social events because of the Internet
- Spending 38 hours or more a week online
- Failing to cut down on time online
- Feeling anxious, bored, sad, lonely, angry, or stressed before going online, but feeling happy, excited, loved, calmed, or confident while on the Internet
- Favoring chat rooms, games, and Multi User Dungeons over other Internet activities

Connecting to Culture and Experience: Wasting Time Online

From researcher Kimberly Young's definition of nondependent Internet users, readers might infer that nondependents are always purposeful and efficient when they are online. Our own experience, however, tells us that it is nearly impossible to avoid wasting any time on the Internet, given the ease of writing email notes to friends, checking out advertised products, playing games, following more tangents at a site than are necessary to fulfill our purpose researching some subject, checking out sites that promise entertainment and diversion, and so on. Is there an Internet saint somewhere who has never wasted a moment on the Internet? Probably not. As Potera points out, unlike gambling addiction, which requires that you drive or get other transportation to a casino, Internet addiction is easily satisfied by a push of a button —the one that powers up your ever-present personal computer. Computers with Internet access have become as much a part of daily life as a toothbrush. How do you manage this new electronic element of your life?

Discuss the features of the Internet that seem to make occasional time-wasting inevitable. Tell about one or two recent instances when you relied on the Internet for diversion. What was the situation? Did you go online looking for diversion, or did you pursue it while doing research, seeking information, or responding to messages that called for a reply? How long did the diversion last? Did you have the feeling you had unwisely spent too much time online? How do these experiences help you understand Internet addiction, as Potera and the researchers define it?

Analyzing Writing Strategies

1. Like the other writers in this chapter, Potera relies on sources for the information she needs to explain her subject, and like Anastasia Toufexis, she acknowledges those sources informally within the sentences of her essay. Skim the essay and list all of the experts she relies on (text, interview, and Internet sources). Write down

the last name of each expert, along with brief phrases identifying that person's primary academic focus (for example, psychology) and key professional qualification. Include the paragraph numbers where each expert is mentioned. Some will be mentioned only one time, others more than one time.

Then consider these questions: How many different experts and academic specialties does Potera refer to? Given her purpose and readers, does Potera refer to enough experts? Too many? How does Potera establish the authority of each professional? Given the facts Potera presents about each expert, do you think they all seem equally well qualified? Do any seem unqualified or clearly less qualified than the others? Does one expert stand out as better qualified than the others? Which one does Potera most rely on—and why? Is there an expert you would like to have heard more from? If so, explain why briefly.

For more information on evaluating sources with a critical eye, see Chapter 21, pp. 689–91.

2. Potera makes good use of causes and effects to explain Internet addiction. Given her focus on Internet addiction as a problem needing a solution, it is appropriate and even essential for her to rely on these two strategies: She wants readers to know what causes this addiction and what its effects are on those addicted. Potera presents the effects through both cases (paragraphs 2 and 9) and explanation (paragraphs 4–6). She presents the causes of Internet addiction in paragraphs 7 and 8.

In these paragraphs, underline specific effects and causes. Then consider whether Potera presents enough effects and causes to explain Internet addiction to readers unfamiliar with it. Can you think of any effects or causes she has overlooked? Why do you think she uses both personal anecdotes (paragraphs 2 and 9) and research findings (paragraphs 4–6) to present effects? Given her purpose and readers, how well do you think she covers possible causes for the addiction?

Commentary: Defining an Emerging Phenomenon

Definitions are important to an essay explaining a concept. Even though a concept can be examined and illustrated in various ways, at some point it must be defined. With an emerging phenomenon—one that researchers and writers are trying to understand fully—there may not yet be agreement on how to define it and what to call it. Nevertheless, if the concept is to become widely understood, it has to have an agreed-upon name. Potera's essay well illustrates the struggle to name a new phenomenon. She reports on the struggle, but at the same time she selects a favorite name for the concept and defines it clearly.

For more on writing definitions, see Chapter 16.

Potera reports that experts are divided over what to call a behavior that occupies forty or more hours a week and usually results in personal problems of various kinds. One expert, psychologist Kimberly Young, prefers the term "Internet addiction" when writing for the general public but relies on the term "pathological Internet use" when writing for academic journals in her field. Pharmacologist Carlton Erickson prefers the term "Internet dependence," making a distinction between dependency and "abuse," which he would use to identify behavior that "hasn't quite reached full-fledged dependency." Other specialists Potera does not identify prefer the term "compulsion," leading her to suggest the term "compulsive Internet disorder." Psychologist Maressa Orzack likes the term "impulse control disorder" (paragraphs 10–16). For readers, Potera's explanation of the experts' division over what to call this new Internet-related behavior provides different perspectives on a troublesome phenomenon: Should we consider it an addiction, a pathology, a dependency, a compulsion, or an impulse-control disorder? It also allows Potera to demonstrate near-universal agreement among experts that the phenomenon exists and should be taken seriously. It even allows her to quote one expert who says, in effect, if we are not worried about people reading too much, why should we be worried about people being online too much? This expert would say that the phenomenon is none of the above.

Potera would lose authority with readers if she took sides in this dispute, and yet in order to explain her subject, she must settle on a name for it. Her subject is not the dispute itself but the phenomenon, whatever it may eventually be called by the experts and the general public. She uses Kimberly Young to resolve this problem, quoting Young as saying that for now the most sensible term to use is "Internet addiction," the term that best suggests "the often severe personal consequences" and "the social problems" of alcohol and drug addiction.

Potera relies on two anecdotes (in paragraphs 2 and 9) and the research findings of Young and psychologist Kathy Scherer to define Internet addiction. Instead of attempting a one- or two-sentence definition, she provides in paragraphs 1–9 a full profile of the Internet addict.

Toward the end of her essay, Potera focuses on treatments for Internet addiction. She does not, however, describe any one treatment at length or argue that one treatment is more effective than the others. Therefore, she does not propose a solution to the problem of Internet addiction. Instead, she merely surveys briefly several approaches to treatment that reflect the different approaches to understanding Internet addiction she has presented earlier in her essay.

Considering Topics for Your Own Essay

Consider writing an essay that would explain and help you learn about another type of addictive behavior or illness that can strain interpersonal relationships, such as drug or alcohol abuse or dependence, binge-eating, pathological gambling, domestic violence, hypochondriasis, mood disorders, or phobic behaviors. You can find introductions to these conditions in professional reference books such as the *Diagnostic and Statistical Manual of Mental Disorders: DSM-IV.* You would also want to look for current research and popular articles on your topic.

This essay was written in 1998 by an unnamed staff writer of the Economist, *a weekly magazine published in Great Britain that describes itself as an "international journal of news, ideas, opinion, and analysis." In newspapers, magazines, and journals it is not unusual for an article or a column to appear without credit being given to a particular writer. As you read, notice how the writer explains "the new terrorism" by contrasting it to the types of terrorism with which all readers are already aware.*

The New Terrorism
The Economist

A cloud of anthrax germs, designed to inflict a horrible death within five days on anyone who breathes it, is unleashed in the main shopping mall of a small American town. At first, the 500 or so victims think they have mild influenza, which recedes after a day or two; only when their symptoms return, and their lungs start filling with fluid, does anyone realize that a terrorist attack has occurred. For every actual sufferer, at least ten panic-stricken people—many with acute but purely psychosomatic pain—besiege local hospitals, demanding treatment; medical services quickly run out of drugs, and the police are overwhelmed by angry mobs.

That was one of the scenarios discussed last month at a high-powered brainstorming session near Washington, D.C., attended by ten of the country's leading germwarfare experts, as well as doctors and law-enforcement officers. The experts had been asked to describe the sort of biological terror which stood a reasonable chance of being attempted in America within the next few years; and the hypothesis they came up with was by no means the worst that could be imagined.

They assumed, for example, that the perpetrators would be some small, isolated group, without access to technical help from foreign governments; and they also guessed that the germ involved would not be of the contagious variety—capable of causing an epidemic—which was developed in Soviet laboratories during the 1980s. But even in a situation well short of Armageddon, the meeting concluded, the federal authorities might be unable to cope. Apart from the immediate human tragedy, such an attack would have dire long-term effects on America's political and social fabric—by eroding people's trust in the competence of their government. Indeed, that could well be the attackers' intention, whether they come from the Middle East or America's Middle West.

Such gloomy speculation in the conference rooms of Washington might seem a world away from the real bloodshed witnessed in two African cities last week.[1] In technical terms, the bombs in Kenya and Tanzania were of the old-fashioned variety; they involved big quantities of high explosive, rather than a few drops of some lethal potion from a test tube. Africa, with its ramshackle policing and infrastructure, may be one of the few places on earth where it is very easy for terrorists to cross borders without fear of electronic screening, and then hump explosives around a city center.

But for security experts, both the African carnage and the biological or poison-gas attacks which are now feared in the American heartland are examples of the same phenomenon: a "new terrorism" which will prove more deadly—and probably more elusive—than the hijackings and gelignite blasts of previous decades. In its latest mutation, politically motivated violence is vague about its long-term aims but utterly ruthless in its short-term intentions.

---

[1] The U.S. embassies in Nairobi, Kenya, and Dar es Salaam, Tanzania, were attacked by terrorists on August 7, 1998.

Attack for Attack's Sake

It used to be said of terrorists that "they want a lot of people watching and not a lot of people dead"; but the new variety of killers apparently see destruction as an end in itself. Where old terrorism sought to change the world—however misguidedly—the new sort is often practiced by those who believe the world is beyond redemption. According to Bruce Hoffman, an American specialist on political violence, the hallmarks of the new terror include "amorphous religious and millenarian aims" and "vehemently anti-government forms of populism, reflecting far-fetched conspiracy notions."   6

Already, there has been one instance of new terrorists using weapons of mass destruction—the generic term for biological, chemical and nuclear arms. That was in March 1995, when members of the Aum Shinrikyo (Supreme Truth) sect—preaching a bizarre distortion of Hindu, Buddhist and Judeo-Christian beliefs—unleashed a nerve gas called sarin in the Tokyo subway, killing 12 people and injuring several thousand. The attack was botched, and intended to inflict far greater casualties. Police later found enough sarin in the sect's possession to kill millions of people. There was no reason to make light of Aum's founder, a half-blind herbalist and mystic called Shoko Asahara, when he pledged to "eradicate major cities" by using the substance. With assets of up to a billion dollars, the sect had shopped in Russia's chaotic arms bazaar. Its purchases included a helicopter equipped to spray deadly chemicals, and training from special forces in the assembly and use of rifles and rocket-launchers. The movement's ideology has elements in common with the ultra-rightist militias of the United States: fear of world conspiracies of Jews, freemasons and financiers, and a fascination with Hitler. It was banned only in December 1995, and is believed to be reconstituting itself.   7

Mr. Hoffman, who helps run a terrorism research center at the University of St. Andrew's in Scotland, has argued that ultra-rightist militias in America, millenarian sects in Japan and Islamic fundamentalists in the Middle East are all representatives of the same trend: towards a sort of insatiable fanaticism which has no agenda other than destruction and revenge.   8

Old terrorism generally had a specific manifesto: the overthrow of a colonial power, or the capitalist system, and it was keen to draw attention to those aims in lengthy communiqués. It was carried out by well-organized clandestine networks and often sponsored by radical governments who hardly bothered to hide the fact that they viewed guerrilla violence as a sort of foreign policy by other means. While the old terrorists were not shy about planting bombs or diverting aircraft, their desire for political legitimacy set some limit to their brutality: killing too many innocent people could put their natural supporters off.   9

In this sense, the Red Brigades, the intellectual revolutionaries who turned the 1970s, for Italy, into a "decade of lead" were of the old school; so was the Palestine Liberation Organization, in its militant heyday, along with the African National Congress and the Irish Republican Army. A couple of dozen of the governments that now hold respected places at the United Nations came to power as a result of "old terrorist" campaigns.   10

New terrorism, by contrast, has no explicit agenda, and its perpetrators have no 11
realistic program for taking power themselves. It is often just a cacophonous cry of
protest against the West in general, and American government in particular—fueled by
impotent rage over the Great Satan's cultural and geopolitical supremacy. Its perpetrators may be religious fanatics, or simply diehard opponents of the federal government—
who might come from inside, as well as outside, American territory. They see no reason
to show restraint; they are simply intent on inflicting the maximum amount of pain on the
enemy.

By this definition, both the bombing of New York's World Trade Center in 1993 (by 12
Middle Easterners) and the Oklahoma City bombing in 1995 (by American ultra-rightists)
were products of the same, nihilist brand of fanaticism. If the new terrorists of the Islamic
world have any links with governments, they are shadowy ones—possibly restricted to
certain rogue elements in the sponsor state. After all, an important source of official suc-
cor disappeared with the collapse of the Soviet empire—for most international revolutionaries could be sure of a warm welcome in Moscow, East Berlin or Sofia. But the end
of communism also made it easier to start terrorist movements without government help,
as a significant part of the Warsaw Pact's arsenal—tons of Semtex, the Czech-made
explosive, and tens of thousands of Kalashnikovs—found their way on to the international black market. The American government still identifies seven states as sponsors
of terrorism—but it acknowledges that several of them, including Cuba and North
Korea, have become less active of late.

So far Aum—whose weird beliefs, huge wealth and murky Russian connections are 13
almost a paperback-writer's caricature—provides the only example of weapons of mass
destruction being used by a subversive group. Japan, which has local police forces rather
than a real national one and is hesitant, for historical reasons, about interfering with religious groups, may be the only industrial democracy where a sect like Aum Shinrikyo

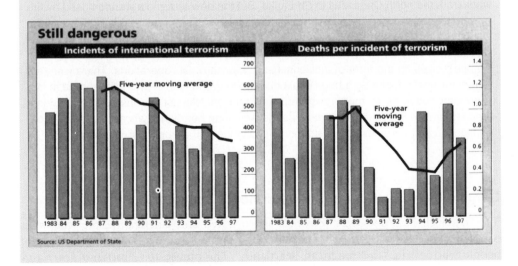

Still dangerous

Incidents of international terrorism — Five-year moving average

Deaths per incident of terrorism — Five-year moving average

1983 84 85 86 87 88 89 90 91 92 93 94 95 96 97

Source: US Department of State

could have gathered so much destructive power. But every western government is worried about the natural affinity between non-conventional weapons and non-conventional terrorists. Sooner or later, they fear, devout believers in mass destruction will acquire the means to bring it about.

As the recent brain-storming session indicated, it is biological terror—more than the chemical or nuclear sort—that keeps American security chiefs awake at night. Both chemical weapons—in other words, man-made poisons—and biological ones are relatively easy for anyone with a science degree to produce. But killing large numbers of people with chemical weapons would require a big stockpile of deadly substances—which would be difficult to accumulate without attracting suspicion. With germ warfare, tiny quantities could be enough to inflict tens of thousands of casualties.   14

The other difference is that there is no mistaking a chemical attack when it happens, because its victims die almost instantly. But biological attacks may not take effect for several days—making it much harder to mount an emergency response and cope with the mass hysteria among those who fear contamination.   15

Nuclear-armed subversives are perhaps the worst nightmare of all; but at least for now, it is considered very unlikely that terrorists could acquire the necessary quantities of plutonium or highly-enriched uranium to assemble a nuclear bomb. Unlikely, but perhaps not impossible. Alexander Lebed, Russia's former national security chief, prompted shudders in many defense ministries—and loud public denials in Washington and Moscow—when he said last year that up to 100 mini-nuclear weapons or "suitcase bombs," designed for use for Soviet special forces, had gone missing.   16

The Favorite Target

Versions of the old sort of terror—car-bombs, massacres, kidnappings—have been used by and against almost every side in the world's lengthening list of civil and ethnic wars, from the north Caucasus to Sri Lanka. But the new terror is a weapon used by the powerless and desperate against the all-powerful—so its main target is likely to be the United States. Granted, the distinction is not a precise one. The old terror that has been practiced on a horrifying scale in Algeria's internecine war may yet spill over into Europe's cities, in the form of indiscriminate, "new terrorist" operations. There was real fear of terrorist attacks on a huge scale during the World Cup—prompting police in five European countries to make a coordinated raid on Islamist groups. But the biggest magnet for new terrorists will always be the American heartland, whose prosperity, self-confidence and openness are a continual challenge to the frustrated and fanatical.   17

Connecting to Culture and Experience: Fanaticism

The writer characterizes new terrorists as frustrated and fanatical people who want to destroy people who are prosperous, self-confident, and tolerant—the kinds of people who live in "the American heartland." The phrase *the American heartland* usually refers to the Midwest. Nevertheless, the *Economist* writer discusses not only the 1995 Oklahoma City bombing of a federal office building, but also the 1993 bombing of New York's World Trade Center as examples of the new terrorism. The writer probably does not believe that new terrorist attacks are most likely to occur in the Midwest, but anywhere in—or associated with—the United States.

With other students, discuss this new terrorist threat to America. Clarify first what it means to be fanatical and what new terrorist fanatics are frustrated about. Discuss whether it seems more likely that new terrorists will come from within the United States or from other countries. Then consider what the United States might be able to do to prevent further terrorism—without violating its current immigration laws or its own citizens' civil rights.

Analyzing Writing Strategies

1. The *Economist* writer makes excellent use of a fundamentally important strategy writers use when explaining things: **comparison and contrast.** Throughout the explanation of the new terrorism, the writer contrasts it with the old terrorism. The writer also contrasts biological with chemical terrorism. Begin by analyzing the brief comparison and contrast of biological and chemical terrorism in paragraphs 14 and 15. Underline the specific points of likeness and difference. Then consider these questions: In each comparison and contrast, does the writer consistently lead with the same kind of terrorism? If so, what advantages might this consistency provide readers? Coming as it does toward the end of the essay, is this strategy clear, and does it offer enough points of likeness and difference for readers to understand the explanation?

   For more on comparing and contrasting, see Chapter 18.

   Next, analyze the primary contrast between the old terrorism and the new terrorism, especially in paragraphs 8–13. Reread these paragraphs and list the main features of the old and new faces of terrorism, using words and phrases from the essay. How much space does the writer give to each kind of terrorism? Does the writer define each kind of terrorism separately or weave them together or both? What parts of the contrast are clearest and most memorable? In general, how successful is the author in setting up this contrast? Included in this extended contrast is a comparison of Islamic fundamentalists and American ultra-rightists. How does the author attempt to show that these seemingly unlike groups are actually alike, and how successful do you find this comparison?

2. In an attempt to appeal to readers' interest, the writer opens the essay with a brief scenario about something that might happen. As an introduction to a concept explanation, a scenario must engage readers, seem plausible or believable, be relevant in a general way to the explanation, and prepare readers to understand the concept by introducing actual content. Use these criteria to evaluate the *Economist* writer's opening scenario.

Commentary: Clear Definitions

For help with writing definitions, turn to Chapter 16.

In an essay explaining a concept, readers expect to find a clear definition of the concept. The concept may be illustrated and contrasted with other concepts at length, but at some point the writer must offer a clear—and even relatively concise—**definition** of the concept. The *Economist* writer offers a concise definition in paragraphs 5 and 6. Toward the end of paragraph 5, for example, the new terrorism is characterized as "vague about its long-term aims but utterly ruthless in its short-term intentions." That is, its perpetrators have neither long-term goals nor a specific political agenda, but they intend to kill as many people as possible. In paragraph 6, the new terrorists are said to "see destruction as an end in itself" because they apparently "believe the world is beyond redemption." We also learn that these new terrorists are driven by religious aims and hatred of government. There are many more details in paragraphs 5 and 6, and together these paragraphs offer a clear—though general and abstract—definition of the phenomenon the author characterizes as "the new terrorism." Paragraphs 8 and 11 go on to restate in various ways the general features of the concept.

Other materials in the essay complement this general definition and make it more concrete. For example, paragraph 1 presents a scenario about a possible anthrax germ attack in the American Midwest, and paragraph 7 describes a typical new terrorist group, Japan's Aum Shinrikyo, which launched a 1995 chemical gas attack in Tokyo's subway system.

Through statement, restatement, and concrete examples, the *Economist* author responsibly defines the "new terrorism" concept and does so clearly. Proof is that working from the definition offered and relying on its key terms, you could easily construct a definition of your own of the new terrorism. Similarly, you will want to provide readers of your own essay explaining a concept with enough information so that they can make their own definitions.

Considering Topics for Your Own Essay

Consider explaining some new phenomenon such as tabloidization of television news, one-newspaper towns and cities, corporate downsizing, globalization of manufacturing, unequal access to preparation for college, Web pages, virtual relationships, chat rooms, sports utility vehicles, body modification (tattooing, piercing, and so on), or extreme sports.

Linh Kieu Ngo wrote this essay as a first-year college student. In it, he defines a concept of importance in anthropology and of wide general interest—cannibalism, the eating of human flesh by other humans. Most Americans know about survival cannibalism but few may know about the importance historically of dietary and ritual cannibalism. Ngo explains all of these types in his essay. As you read, notice how he relies on examples to illustrate the types.

Cannibalism: It Still Exists

Linh Kieu Ngo

Fifty-five Vietnamese refugees fled to Malaysia on a small fishing boat to escape communist rule in their country following the Vietnam War. During their escape attempt, the captain was shot by the coast guard. The boat and its passengers managed to outrun the coast guard to the open sea, but they had lost the only person who knew the way to Malaysia, the captain.

The men onboard tried to navigate the boat, but after a week fuel ran out and they drifted farther out to sea. Their supply of food and water was gone; people were starving, and some of the elderly were near death. The men managed to produce a small amount of drinking water by boiling salt water, using dispensable wood from the boat to create a small fire near the stern. They also tried to fish, but had little success.

A month went by, and the old and weak died. At first, the crew threw the dead overboard, but later, out of desperation, the crew turned to human flesh as a source of food. Some people vomited as they attempted to eat it, while others refused to resort to cannibalism and see the bodies of their loved ones sacrificed for food. Those who did not eat died of starvation, and their bodies in turn became food for others. Human flesh was cut out, washed in salt water, and hung to dry for preservation. The liquids inside the cranium were eaten to quench thirst. The livers, kidneys, heart, stomach, and intestines were boiled and eaten.

Five months passed before a whaling vessel discovered the drifting boat, looking like a graveyard of bones. There was only one survivor.

Cannibalism, the act of human beings eating human flesh (Sagan 2), has a long history and continues to hold interest and create controversy. Many books and research reports offer examples of cannibalism, but a few scholars have questioned whether cannibalism was ever practiced anywhere, except in cases of ensuring survival in times of famine or isolation (Askenasy 43–54). Recently, some scholars have tried to understand why people in the West have been so eager to attribute cannibalism to non-westerners (Barker, Hulme, and Iversen). Cannibalism has long been a part of American popular culture. For example, Mark Twain's "Cannibalism in the Cars" tells a humorous story about cannibalism by well-to-do travelers on a train stranded in a snowstorm, and cannibalism is still a popular subject for jokes ("Cannibal Jokes").

If we assume there is some reality to the reports about cannibalism, how can we best understand this concept? Cannibalism can be broken down into two main categories: exocannibalism, the eating of outsiders or foreigners, and endocannibalism, the eating of members of one's own social group (Shipman 70). Within these categories are several functional types of cannibalism, three of the most common being survival cannibalism, dietary cannibalism, and religious and ritual cannibalism.

Survival cannibalism occurs when people trapped without food have to decide "whether to starve or eat fellow humans" (Shipman 70). In the case of the Vietnamese refugees, the crew and passengers on the boat ate human flesh to stay alive. They did not kill people to get human flesh for nourishment, but instead waited until the people had died. Even after human carcasses were sacrificed as food, the boat people ate only enough to survive. Another case of survival cannibalism occured in 1945, when General Douglas MacArthur's forces cut supply lines to Japanese troops stationed in the Pacific Islands. In one incident, Japanese troops were reported to have sacrificed the Arapesh people of northeastern New Guinea for food in order to avoid death by starvation (Tuzin 63). The most famous example of survival cannibalism in American history comes from the diaries, letters, and interviews of survivors of the California-bound Donner Party, who in the winter of 1846 were snowbound in the Sierra Nevada Mountains for five months. Thirty-five of eighty-seven adults and children died, and some of them were eaten (Hart 116–117; Johnson).

Unlike survival cannibalism, in which human flesh is eaten as a last resort after a person has died, in dietary cannibalism, humans are purchased or trapped for food and then eaten as a part of a culture's traditions. In addition, survival cannibalism often involves people eating other people of the same origins, whereas dietary cannibalism usually involves people eating foreigners.   8

In the Miyanmin society of the west Sepik interior of Papua, New Guinea, villagers do not value human flesh over that of pigs or marsupials because human flesh is part of their diet (Poole 7). The Miyanmin people observe no differences in "gender, kinship, ritual status, and bodily substance"; they eat anyone, even their own dead. In this respect, then, they practice both endocannibalism and exocannibalism; and to ensure a constant supply of human flesh for food, they raid neighboring tribes and drag their victims back to their village to be eaten (Poole 11). Perhaps, in the history of this society, there was at one time a shortage of wild game to be hunted for food, and because people were more plentiful than fish, deer, rabbits, pigs, or cows, survival cannibalism was adopted as a last resort. Then, as their culture developed, the Miyanmin may have retained the practice of dietary cannibalism, which has endured as a part of their culture.   9

Similar to the Miyanmin, the people of the Leopard and Alligator societies in South America eat human flesh as part of their cultural tradition. Practicing dietary exocannibalism, the Leopard people hunt in groups, with one member wearing the skin of a leopard to conceal the face. They ambush their victims in the forest and carry their victims back to their village to be eaten. The Alligator people also hunt in groups, but they hide themselves under a canoelike submarine that resembles an alligator, then swim close to a fisherman's or trader's canoe to overturn it and catch their victims (MacCormack 54).   10

Religious or ritual cannibalism is different from survival and dietary cannibalism in that it has a ceremonial purpose rather than one of nourishment. Sometimes only a single victim is sacrificed in a ritual, while at other times many are sacrificed. For example, the Bangala tribe of the Congo River in central Africa honors a deceased chief or leader by purchasing, sacrificing, and feasting on slaves (Sagan 53). The number of slaves sacrificed is determined by how highly the tribe members revered the deceased leader.   11

Ritual cannibalism among South American Indians often serves as revenge for the dead. Like the Bangalas, some South American tribes kill their victims to be served as part of funeral rituals, with human sacrifices denoting that the deceased was held in high honor. Also like the Bangalas, these tribes use outsiders as victims. Unlike the Bangalas, however, the Indians sacrifice only one victim instead of many in a single ritual. For   12 example, when a warrior of a tribe is killed in battle, the family of the warrior forces a victim to take the identity of the warrior. The family adorns the victim with the deceased warrior's belongings and may even force him to marry the deceased warrior's wives. But once the family believes the victim has assumed the spiritual identity of the deceased warrior, the family kills him. The children in the tribe soak their hands in the victim's blood to symbolize their revenge of the warrior's death. Elderly women from the tribe drink the victim's blood and then cut up his body for roasting and eating (Sagan 53–54). By sacrificing a victim, the people of the tribe believe that the death of the warrior has been avenged and the soul of the deceased can rest in peace.

In the villages of certain African tribes, only a small part of a dead body is used in ritual cannibalism. In these tribes, where the childbearing capacity of women is highly valued, women are obligated to eat small, raw fragments of genital parts during fertility rites. Elders of the tribe supervise this ritual to ensure that the women will be fertile. In the Bimin-Kuskusmin tribe, for instance, a widow eats a small, raw fragment of flesh from the penis of her deceased husband in order to enhance her future fertility and reproductive capacity. Similarly, a widower may eat a raw fragment of flesh from his deceased wife's vagina along with a piece of her bone marrow; by eating her flesh, he hopes to strengthen the fertility capacity of his daughters borne by his dead wife, and by eating her bone marrow, he honors her reproductive capacity. Also, when an elder woman of the village who has shown great reproductive capacity dies, her uterus and the interior parts of her vagina are eaten by other women who hope to further benefit from her reproductive power (Poole 16–17). 13

Members of developed societies in general practice none of these forms of cannibalism, with the occasional exception of survival cannibalism when the only alternative is starvation. It is possible, however, that our distant-past ancestors were cannibals who through the eons turned away from the practice. We are, after all, descended from the same ancestors as the Miyanmin, the Alligator, and the Leopard people, and survival cannibalism shows that people are capable of eating human flesh when they have no other choice. 14

Works Cited

Askenasy, Hans. *Cannibalism: From Sacrifice to Survival.* Amherst, NY: Prometheus, 1994.

Barker, Francis, Peter Hulme, and Margaret Iversen, eds. *Cannibalism and the New World.* Cambridge: Cambridge UP, 1998.

Brown, Paula, and Donald Tuzin, eds. *The Ethnography of Cannibalism.* Washington: Society of Psychological Anthropology, 1983.

"Cannibal Jokes." The Loonie Bin of Jokes. <http://www.looniebin.mb.ca/cannibal.html> (22 Sept. 1999).

Hart, James D. *A Companion to California.* Berkeley: U of California P, 1987.

Johnson, Kristin. "New Light on the Donner Party." <http://www.metrogourmet.com/crossroads.KJhome.htm> (28 Sept. 1999).

MacCormack, Carol. "Human Leopard and Crocodile." Brown and Tuzin 54–55.

Poole, Fitz John Porter. "Cannibals, Tricksters, and Witches." Brown and Tuzin, 11, 16–17.

Sagan, Eli. *Cannibalism*. New York: Harper, 1976.

Shipman, Pat. "The Myths and Perturbing Realities of Cannibalism." *Discover* Mar. 1987: 70+.

Tuzin, Donald. "Cannibalism and Arapesh Cosmology." Brown and Tuzin 61–63.

Twain, Mark. "Cannibalism in the Cars." *The Complete Short Stories of Mark Twain*. Ed. Charles Neider. New York: Doubleday, 1957. 9–16.

Connecting to Culture and Experience: Taboos

The author of a respected book on the Donner Party has this to say about the fact that some members of the party ate other members after they had died:

> Surely the necessity, starvation itself, had forced them to all they did, and surely no just man would ever have pointed at them in scorn, or assumed his own superiority. . . . Even the seemingly ghoulish actions involved in the story may be rationally explained. To open the bodies first for the heart and liver, and to saw apart the skulls for the brain were not acts of perversion. We must remember that these people had been living for months upon the hides and lean meat of half-starved work oxen; their diet was lacking not only in mere quantity, but also in all sorts of necessary vitamins and mineral constituents, even in common salt. Almost uncontrollable cravings must have assailed them, cravings which represented a real deficiency in diet to be supplied in some degree at least by the organs mentioned.
>
> —GEORGE R. STEWART, *Ordeal by Hunger*

With other students, discuss this author's argument and his unwillingness to pass judgment on the Donner Party's cannibalism. Individually, are you inclined to agree or disagree with the author? Give reasons for your views. Keep in mind that no one, perhaps with one exception toward the very end of the Donner Party's isolation, was murdered in order to be eaten. Therefore, the issue is not murder but humans' eating other humans' flesh and body parts in order to remain alive. Humans do eat many other animals' flesh and body parts for nourishment. Where do you think the taboo against human cannibalism comes from in our society? Do you believe it should be observed in all circumstances? Do you think the taboo should be extended to the consumption of animal flesh?

Analyzing Writing Strategies

For more on defining, see Chapter 16.

1. Ngo organizes his explanation around two categories and three types of cannibalism. Review this classification in paragraph 6. Then analyze how Ngo **defines** the five terms of the classification. Begin by underlining the definitions in paragraphs 6–8 and 12. Some definitions are given in a single phrase, and others are made up of several phrases, not always contiguous. Exclude the examples from your underlining. Then look over the definitions you have underlined with the following questions in mind: What makes these definitions easy or hard for you

to understand? In what ways does the example that begins the essay (paragraphs 1–4) prepare you to understand the definitions? How do the examples that follow the definitions help you understand each concise definition?

2. As he explains the different types of cannibalism, Ngo makes good use of examples in paragraphs 7–13. Choose *one* of the longer examples in paragraph 9, 12, or 13 and analyze how it is put together and how effective it is. How many sentences long is the example? What kinds of information does it offer? What sources does the writer rely on? What seems most memorable or surprising to you in the example? How does it help you understand the type of cannibalism being illustrated? In general, how effective does it seem to you as an example of the concept?

Commentary: A Logical Plan

Writers face special challenges in planning essays that explain concepts. First they gather a lot of information about a concept. Then they find a focus for the explanation. With the focus in mind, they research the concept further, looking just for information to develop the focus. At this point they have to find a way to collect the information into logically related topics. This process is known formally as **classifying.** Sometimes, as in Ngo's research, one of the sources provides the classification, but sometimes the writer has to create it. This borrowing or creation allows writers to plan their essays—to identify the topics in the order in which they will present them. Ngo's explanation of cannibalism well illustrates the importance of a logical plan. The following topical scratch outline of the essay will help you see Ngo's classification and plan:

For more information on classifying and its role in planning an essay, see Chapter 17.

- Narration of a specific recent incident of cannibalism (paragraphs 1–4)
- Context for the concept (5)
- Definition of cannibalism and introduction of its two main categories and three types (6)
- Definition of survival cannibalism, with two brief examples (7)
- Definition of dietary cannibalism (8)
- Two extended examples of dietary cannibalism (9 and 10)
- Definition of ritual cannibalism, with one brief example (11)
- Two extended examples of ritual cannibalism (12 and 13)
- Conclusion (14)

For more on scratch outlines, see Chapter 12, p. 540.

Ngo presents the classification in paragraph 6. It has two levels. In the first level the information is divided into exocannibalism and endocannibalism. In the second level each of the first two divisions is divided into three parts: survival, dietary, and ritual cannibalism. That is, in each of these three types of cannibalism, either outsiders or members of one's own group can be eaten. Ngo relies on the three types of cannibalism to create a plan for his essay. First he explains survival cannibalism, then dietary cannibalism, and finally, ritual cannibalism. This plan may be considered logical in at least two ways: it moves from most to least familiar and from least to most complex. Perhaps Ngo assumes his readers will know about the Donner Party, an unfortunate group of 1846 immigrants to California who were trapped high in the Sierra Nevada Mountains by early, heavy snowstorms and ended up practicing survival endocannibalism. Therefore, Ngo explains this type of cannibalism first and then moves on to the less-familiar types. It seems that these two less-familiar types are also the most complex in that their practice takes different forms around the world. Ngo devotes two or three times more space to explaining dietary and ritual cannibalism than he does to explaining survival cannibalism, and he presents the examples in more detail.

For more about forecasting, see p. 559 in Chapter 13.

Ngo does more than adopt a classification and put it to use to plan his essay. He helps readers anticipate and follow the plan by forecasting it and then providing obvious cues to the steps in the plan. At the end of paragraph 6, Ngo forecasts the types of cannibalism he will focus on: "survival cannibalism, dietary cannibalism, and religious and ritual cannibalism." It is considered a **forecast** because it introduces the names or terms Ngo will use consistently throughout the explanation and because Ngo presents these types of cannibalism in the order he lists them here. Readers are thereby prepared for the step-by-step plan of the explanation.

For more about transitions, turn to pp. 561–62 in Chapter 13.

Ngo lets readers know when he is leaving one type of cannibalism and addressing the next type by constructing visible **transitions** at the beginnings of paragraphs. Here are the three key transition sentences:

> Survival cannibalism occurs when people trapped without food have to decide "whether to starve or eat fellow humans. . . ." (paragraph 7)

> Unlike survival cannibalism, in which human flesh is eaten as a last resort after a person has died, in dietary cannibalism, humans are purchased or trapped for food and then eaten as a part of a culture's traditions. (8)

> Religious or ritual cannibalism is different from survival and dietary cannibalism in that it has a ceremonial purpose rather than one of nourishment. (11)

You can feature these types of cues—forecasts and transitions—in your essay explaining a concept. Whereas forecasting is optional, transitions are essential; without them, your readers will either stumble along resentfully or throw up their hands in confusion and irritation.

Considering Topics for Your Own Essay

Consider writing about some other well-established human taboo or practice such as ostracism, incest, pedophilia, murder, circumcision, celibacy or virginity, caste systems, a particular religion's dietary restrictions, adultery, stealing, gourmandism, or divorce.

■ PURPOSE AND AUDIENCE

Though it often seeks to engage readers' interests, explanatory writing gives prominence to the facts about its subject. It aims at readers' intellect rather than their imagination, determined to instruct rather than entertain or argue.

To set out to teach readers about a concept is no small undertaking. To succeed, you must know the concept so well that you can explain it simply, without jargon or other confusing language. You must be authoritative without showing off or talking down. You must also estimate what your readers already know about the concept in order to decide which information will be truly new to them. You want to define unfamiliar words and pace the information carefully so that your readers are neither bored nor overwhelmed.

This assignment requires a willingness to cast yourself in the role of expert, which may not come naturally to you at this stage in your development as a writer. Students are most often asked to explain things in writing to readers who know more than they do—their instructors. When you plan and draft this essay, however, you will be aiming at readers who know less—maybe much less—than you do about the concept you will explain. Like Toufexis and Potera, you could write for a general audience of adults who regularly read a newspaper and subscribe to a few magazines. Even though some of them may be highly educated, you can readily and confidently assume the role of expert after a couple of hours of research into your concept. Your purpose may be to deepen your readers' understanding of a concept they may already be familiar with. You could also write for upper elementary or secondary school students, introducing them to an unfamiliar concept, or to your classmates, demonstrating to them that a concept in an academic discipline they find forbidding can actually be made both understandable and interesting. Even if you are told to consider your instructor your sole reader, you can assume that your instructor is eager to be informed about nearly any concept you choose.

You have spent many years in school reading explanations of concepts: Your textbooks in every subject have been full of concept explanations. Now, instead of receiving these explanations, you will be delivering one. To succeed, you will have to accept your role of expert. Your readers will expect you to be authoritative and well informed; they will also expect that you have limited the focus of your explanation but that you have not excluded anything essential to their understanding.

A Focused Concept

The primary purpose for explaining a concept is to inform readers, but writers of explanatory essays do not hope to say everything there is to say about a concept. Instead, they make choices about what to include, what to emphasize, and what to omit. Most writers focus on one aspect of the concept. Anastasia Toufexis, for example, focuses on the neurochemistry of love, and Linh Kieu Ngo focuses on types of cannibalism.

An Appeal to Readers' Interests

Most people read explanations of concepts for work or study. Consequently, they do not expect the writing to be entertaining, but simply informative. Yet readers appreciate explanations that both make clear the concept's importance and keep them awake with lively writing and vivid detail. The essays in this chapter show some of the ways in which writers may appeal to readers— for example, by using humor and unaffected, everyday language; by giving readers reasons for learning about the concept; by showing how the concept might apply personally to them.

A Logical Plan

Since concept explanations present information that is new to readers and can therefore be hard to understand, writers need to develop a plan that presents new material step by step in a logical order. The most effective explanations are carefully organized and give readers all the obvious cues they need, such as forecasting statements, topic sentences, transitions, and summaries. In addition, the writer may try to frame the essay for readers by relating the ending to the beginning. We have seen these features repeatedly in the readings in this chapter. For example, Toufexis frames her essay with references to Ph.D.s, forecasts the three sciences from which she has gleaned her information about the neurochemistry of love, and begins nearly all of her paragraphs with a transition sentence.

Good writers never forget that their readers need clear signals. Because writers already know the information and are aware of how their essays are organized, it can be difficult for them to see the essay the way someone reading it for the first time would. That is precisely how it should be seen, however, to be sure that the essay includes all the necessary cues.

Clear Definitions

Essays explaining concepts depend on clear definitions. To relate information clearly, a writer must be sensitive to readers' knowledge; any key terms that are likely to be unfamiliar or misunderstood must be explicitly defined, as Toufexis defines *attraction junkies* (paragraph 12) and *endorphins* (paragraph 13) and as Ngo defines the *categories* of cannibalism (paragraph 6) and *types* of cannibalism (at the beginnings of paragraphs where he illustrates them). In a sense, all the readings in this chapter are extended definitions of concepts, and all the authors offer relatively concise, clear definitions of their concepts at some point in their essays.

Appropriate Writing Strategies

Many writing strategies are useful for presenting information. The strategies a writer uses are determined by the way he or she focuses the essay and the kind of information available. The following strategies are particularly useful in explaining concepts.

Classification. One way of presenting information is to divide it into groups and discuss the groups one by one. For example, Toufexis divides the chemicals she discusses into those associated with falling in love and those associated with lasting relationships.

Process Narration. Process narration typically explains how something is done. Many concepts involve processes that unfold over time, such as the geologic scale, or over both time and space, such as bird migration. Process narration involves some of the basic storytelling strategies covered in Chapters 2 and 3: narrative time signals, actors and action, and connectives showing temporal relationships. For example, Ngo briefly narrates one process of ritual cannibalism (paragraph 12).

Comparison and Contrast. The comparison-and-contrast strategy is especially useful for explaining concepts because it helps readers understand something new by showing how it is similar to or different from things they already know. Every essayist in this chapter makes use of comparison and contrast. For example, the *Economist* writer contrasts the new terrorism with the old and chemical with biological ter-

rorism. Potera contrasts dependent with nondependent Internet users.

Cause and Effect. Another useful strategy for explaining a concept is to report its causes or effects. Toufexis explains the evolutionary benefits of romantic love, and Potera explores both the causes and effects of Internet addiction.

Note that writers of explanatory essays ordinarily either report established causes or effects or report others' speculated causes or effects as if they were established facts. They usually do not themselves speculate about possible causes or effects.

Careful Use of Sources

To explain concepts, writers usually draw on information from many different sources. Although they often draw on their own experience and observation, they almost always do additional research into what others have to say about their subject. Referring to expert sources always lends authority to an explanation.

How writers treat sources depends on the writing situation. Certain formal situations, such as college assignments or scholarly papers, have rules for citing and documenting sources. Students and scholars are expected to cite their sources formally because readers judge their writing in part by what they have read and how they have used their reading. For more informal writing—magazine articles, for example—readers do not expect page references or publication information, but they do expect sources to be identified; this identification often appears within the text of the article.

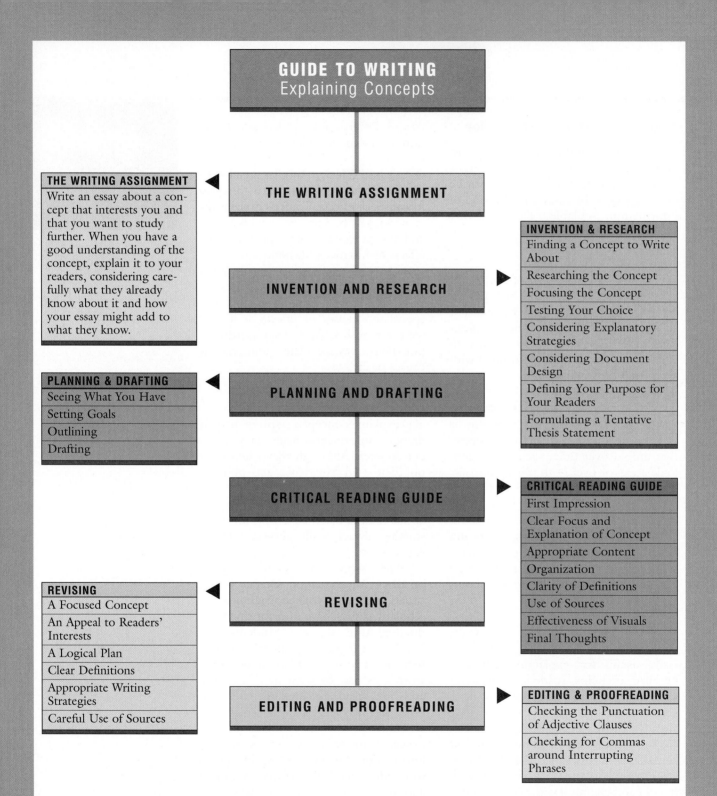

GUIDE TO WRITING
Explaining Concepts

THE WRITING ASSIGNMENT

THE WRITING ASSIGNMENT

Write an essay about a concept that interests you and that you want to study further. When you have a good understanding of the concept, explain it to your readers, considering carefully what they already know about it and how your essay might add to what they know.

INVENTION AND RESEARCH

INVENTION & RESEARCH

Finding a Concept to Write About

Researching the Concept

Focusing the Concept

Testing Your Choice

Considering Explanatory Strategies

Considering Document Design

Defining Your Purpose for Your Readers

Formulating a Tentative Thesis Statement

PLANNING & DRAFTING

Seeing What You Have

Setting Goals

Outlining

Drafting

PLANNING AND DRAFTING

CRITICAL READING GUIDE

CRITICAL READING GUIDE

First Impression

Clear Focus and Explanation of Concept

Appropriate Content

Organization

Clarity of Definitions

Use of Sources

Effectiveness of Visuals

Final Thoughts

REVISING

A Focused Concept

An Appeal to Readers' Interests

A Logical Plan

Clear Definitions

Appropriate Writing Strategies

Careful Use of Sources

REVISING

EDITING AND PROOFREADING

EDITING & PROOFREADING

Checking the Punctuation of Adjective Clauses

Checking for Commas around Interrupting Phrases

THE WRITING ASSIGNMENT

Write an essay about a concept that interests you and that you want to study further. When you have a good understanding of the concept, explain it to your readers, considering carefully what they already know about it and how your essay might add to what they know.

INVENTION AND RESEARCH

The following guidelines will help you find a concept, understand it fully, select a focus appropriate for your readers, test your choice, and devise strategies for presenting what you have discovered in a way that will be truly informative for your particular readers. Each activity is easy to do and takes only a few minutes. If you can spread out the activities over several days, you will have adequate time to understand the concept and decide how to present it. Keep a written record of your invention work to use when you draft the essay and later when you revise it.

Finding a Concept to Write About

Even if you already have a concept in mind, completing the following activities will help you to be certain of your choice.

Listing Concepts.   *Make a list of concepts you could write about.* The longer your list, the more likely you are to find just the right concept for you. And should your first choice not work out, you will have a ready list of alternatives. Include concepts you already know something about as well as some you know only slightly and would like to research further. Also include concepts suggested by the Considering Topics for Your Own Essay activities following each reading in this chapter.

Your courses provide many concepts you will want to consider. Here are some typical concepts from a number of academic and other subjects. Your class notes or textbooks will suggest many others.

- *Literature:* hero, antihero, picaresque, the absurd, canon, representation, figurative language, modernism
- *Philosophy:* existentialism, nihilism, logical positivism, determinism
- *Business management:* autonomous work group, quality circle, cybernetic control system, management by objectives, zero-based budgeting, liquidity gap
- *Psychology:* Hawthorne effect, assimilation/accommodation, social cognition, moratorium, intelligence, divergent/convergent thinking, operant conditioning, short-term memory, tip-of-the-tongue phenomenon, sleep paralysis

- *Government:* majority rule, minority rights, federalism, popular consent, exclusionary rule, political party, political machine, interest group, political action committee
- *Biology:* photosynthesis, morphogenesis, ecosystem, electron transport, plasmolysis, phagocytosis, homozygosity, diffusion
- *Art:* cubism, Dadaism, surrealism, expressionism
- *Math:* polynomials, boundedness, null space, permutations and combinations, factoring, Rolle's theorem, continuity, derivative, indefinite integral
- *Physical sciences:* matter, mass, weight, energy, gravity, atomic theory, law of definite proportions, osmotic pressure, first law of thermodynamics, entropy
- *Public health:* alcoholism, seasonal affective disorder, contraception, lead poisoning, prenatal care
- *Environmental studies:* acid rain, recycling, ozone depletion, toxic waste, endangered species
- *Sports:* squeeze play, hit and run (baseball); power play (hockey); nickel defense, wishbone offense (football); serve and volley offense (tennis); setup (volleyball); pick and roll, inside game (basketball)
- *Personal finance:* mortgage, budget, insurance, deduction, revolving credit
- *Law:* tort, contract, garnishment, double indemnity, liability, reasonable doubt
- *Sociology:* norm, deviance, role conflict, ethnocentrism, class, social stratification, conflict theory, functionalist theory

Listing Concepts Related to Identity and Community.   Many concepts are important in understanding identity and community. As you consider the following concepts, try to think of others in this category: self-esteem, character, personality, autonomy, individuation, narcissism, multiculturalism, ethnicity, race, racism, social contract, communitarianism, community policing, Social Darwinism, identity politics, special-interest groups, diaspora, colonialism, public space, the other, agency, difference, yuppie, generation X.

Listing Concepts Related to Work and Career.   Concepts like the following enable you to gain a deeper understanding of your work experiences and career aspirations: free enterprise, minimum wage, affirmative action, stock option, sweatshop, glass ceiling, downsizing, collective bargaining, service sector, market, entrepreneur, bourgeoisie, underclass, working class, middle class, division of labor, monopoly, automation, robotics, management style, deregulation, multinational corporation.

Choosing a Concept.   *Look over your list of possibilities and select one concept to explore.* Pick a concept that interests you, one you feel eager to learn more about. Consider also whether it might interest others. You may know very little about the concept now, but the guidelines that follow will help you research it and understand it fully.

Researching the Concept

Considering What You Already Know. *Take a few minutes to write out whatever you know about the concept.* Also say why you have chosen the concept and why you find it interesting and worth knowing about. Write quickly, without planning or organizing. Write phrases or lists as well as sentences. You might also want to make drawings or charts. Ask questions that you hope to answer.

Gathering Information. *Learn more about your concept by taking notes or making copies of relevant material and keeping careful records of your sources.* Check any materials you already have at hand that explain your concept. If you are considering a concept from one of your academic courses, you will find explanatory material in your textbook or lecture notes.

To acquire a comprehensive, up-to-date understanding of your concept and to write authoritatively about it, you may also need to know how experts other than your textbook writer and instructor define and illustrate the concept. To find this information, you might locate relevant articles or books in the library, search for resources or make inquiries on the Internet, or consult experts on campus or in the community.

As you get a better understanding of the concept and decide which aspect of it you will focus your essay on, you may need to do additional research to get answers to specific questions.

If you can, make photocopies or print out information you download from CD-ROMs or the Internet. If you must rely on notes, be sure to copy the language exactly so that later you can quote sources accurately.

Since you do not know what information you will ultimately use, keep a careful record of the author, title, publication date, and page numbers for all the source material you gather. Check with your instructor about whether you should follow the Modern Language Association (MLA) or American Psychological Association (APA) style of acknowledging sources. In this chapter, the Ngo essay follows the MLA style.

For more on search strategy and specific sources for researching your concept, see Chapter 21.

For MLA and APA guidelines, see Chapter 22, pp. 703–25.

Focusing the Concept

Once you have done some research on your concept, you must choose a way to focus your essay. Because more is known about most concepts than you can include in an essay and concepts can be approached from so many perspectives (for example, history, definition, significance), you must limit your explanation. Doing so will help you avoid the common problem of trying to explain too much.

Because the focus must reflect both your special interest in the concept and your readers' likely knowledge and interest, you will want to explore both.

Exploring Your Own Interests. *Make a list of different aspects of the concept that could become a focus for your essay, and evaluate what you know about each aspect.* To consider which aspect of the concept most interests you, review what you know about the concept. As you review this information, make a list of different aspects of the concept, skipping a few lines after each item in the list.

Under each item in your list, indicate whether you know enough to begin writing about that aspect of the concept, what additional questions you would need to answer, and what is important or interesting to you about that particular aspect.

Analyzing Your Readers.   *Take a few minutes to analyze your readers in writing.* To decide what aspect of the concept to focus on, you also need to think about who your prospective readers are likely to be and to speculate about their knowledge of and interest in the concept. Even if you are writing only for your instructor, you should give some thought to what he or she knows and thinks about the concept.

The following questions are designed to help you with your analysis:

- Who are my readers, and what are they likely to know about this concept?
- What, if anything, might they know about the field of study to which this concept applies?
- What could I point out that would be useful for them to know about this concept, perhaps something that could relate to their life or work?
- What connections could I make between this concept and others that my readers are likely to be familiar with?

Choosing a Focus.   *With your interests and those of your readers in mind, choose an aspect of your concept on which to focus, and write a sentence justifying its appropriateness.*

Testing Your Choice

Pause now to test whether you have chosen a workable concept and focused it appropriately. As painful as it may be to consider, starting fresh with a new concept is better than continuing with an unworkable one. The following questions can help you test your choice:

- Do I understand my concept well enough to explain it?
- Have I discovered a focus for writing about this concept?
- Have I found enough information for an essay with such a focus?
- Do I see possibilities for engaging my readers' interest in this aspect of my subject?

If you cannot answer yes to all four questions, consider choosing another focus or selecting another concept to write about.

Testing Your Choice: A Collaborative Activity

Get together with two or three other students to find out what your readers are likely to know about your subject and what might interest them about it.

Presenters: Take turns briefly explaining your concept, describing your intended readers, and identifying the aspect of the concept you will focus on.

Listeners: Briefly tell the presenter whether the focus sounds appropriate and interesting for the intended readers. Share what you think readers are likely to know about the concept and what might be especially interesting and informative for them to learn about.

Considering Explanatory Strategies

Before you move on to plan and draft your essay, consider some possible ways of presenting the concept. Try to answer each of the following questions in a sentence or two. Questions that you can answer readily may identify strategies that can help you explain your concept.

- What term is used to name the concept, and what does it mean? (definition)
- How is this concept like or unlike related concepts? (comparison and contrast)
- How can an explanation of this concept be divided into parts? (classification)
- How does this concept happen, or how does one go about doing it? (process narration)
- What are this concept's known causes or effects? (cause and effect)

For more on these writing strategies, see Part 3.

Considering Document Design

Think about whether visual elements—tables, graphs, drawings, photographs—would make your explanation clearer. These are not at all a requirement of an essay explaining a concept, but they could be helpful. Consider also whether your readers might benefit from design features such as headings, bulleted or numbered lists, or other elements that would present information efficiently or make your explanation easier to follow. You could construct your own graphic elements, download materials from the Internet, copy images from television or other sources, or scan into your document visuals from books and magazines.

For more on document design, see Chapter 25.

Defining Your Purpose for Your Readers

Write a few sentences, defining your purpose in writing about this particular concept for your readers. Remember that you have already identified and analyzed your readers, and you have begun to research and develop your explanation with these readers in mind. Given these readers, try now to define your purpose in explaining the concept to them. Use these questions to focus your thoughts:

- Are my readers familiar with the concept? If not, how can I overcome their resistance or puzzlement? Or, if so, will my chosen focus allow my readers to see the familiar concept in a new light?
- If I suspect that my readers have misconceptions about the concept, how can I correct the misconceptions without offending readers?

- Do I want to arouse readers' interest in information that may seem at first to be less than engaging?
- Do I want to get readers to see that the information I have to report is relevant to their lives, families, communities, work, or studies?

Formulating a Tentative Thesis Statement

Write one or more sentences that could serve as a thesis statement. State your concept and focus. You might also want to forecast the topics you will use to explain the concept.

Anastasia Toufexis begins her essay with this thesis statement:

> O.K., let's cut out all this nonsense about romantic love. Let's bring some scientific precision to the party. Let's put love under a microscope.
>
> When rigorous people with Ph.D.s after their names do that, what they see is not some silly, senseless thing. No, their probe reveals that love rests firmly on the foundations of evolution, biology and chemistry.

Toufexis's concept is love, and her focus is the scientific explanation of love, specifically the evolution, biology, and chemistry of love. In announcing her focus, she forecasts the order in which she will present information from the three most relevant academic disciplines—anthropology (which includes the study of human evolution), biology, and chemistry. These discipline names become her topics.

In his essay on cannibalism, Linh Kieu Ngo offers his thesis statement in paragraph 6:

> Cannibalism can be broken down into two main categories: exocannibalism, the eating of outsiders or foreigners, and endocannibalism, the eating of members of one's own social group (Shipman 70). Within these categories are several functional types of cannibalism, three of the most common being survival cannibalism, dietary cannibalism, and religious and ritual cannibalism.

Ngo's concept is cannibalism and his focus three common types of cannibalism. He carefully forecasts how he will divide the information to create topics and the order in which he will explain each of the topics, the common types of cannibalism.

As you draft your own tentative thesis statement, take care to make the language clear and unambiguous. Although you may want to revise your thesis statement as you draft your essay, trying to state it now will give your planning and drafting more focus and direction. Keep in mind that the thesis in an explanatory essay merely announces the subject; it never asserts a position that requires an argument to defend it.

■ PLANNING AND DRAFTING

The following guidelines will help you get the most out of your invention notes, determine specific goals for your essay, and write a first draft.

Seeing What You Have

Reread everything you have written so far. This is a critically important time for reflection and evaluation. Before beginning the actual draft, you must decide whether your subject is worthwhile and whether you have sufficient information for a successful essay.

It may help, as you read, to annotate your invention writings. Look for details that will help you explain the concept in a way that your readers can grasp. Underline or circle key words, phrases, or sentences; make marginal notes. Your goal is to identify the important elements in what you have written so far.

Be realistic. If at this point your notes do not look promising, you may want to choose a different focus for your concept or select a different concept to write about. If your notes seem thin but promising, do further research to find more information before continuing.

Setting Goals

Successful writers are always looking beyond the next sentence to larger goals. Indeed, the next sentence is easier to write if you keep larger goals in mind. The following questions can help you set these goals. Consider each one now, and then return to them as necessary while you write.

Your Purpose and Readers

- How can I build on my readers' knowledge?
- What new information can I present to them?
- How can I organize my essay so that my readers can follow it easily?
- What tone would be most appropriate? Would an informal tone like Toufexis's or a formal one like Ngo's be more appropriate to my purpose?

The Beginning

- How shall I begin? Should I open with a provocative quotation, as Toufexis does? With an incident illustrating the concept, as Ngo does? With a nightmare scenario, as the *Economist* writer does? With a question?
- How can I best forecast the plan my explanation will follow? Should I offer a detailed forecast, as Toufexis and Ngo do? Or should I begin with general statements, as Potera does?

Writing Strategies

- What terms do I need to define? Can I rely on brief sentence definitions, or will I need to write extended definitions?
- Are there ways to categorize the information?
- What examples can I use to make the explanation more concrete?

- Would any comparisons or contrasts help readers understand the information?
- Do I need to explain any processes or known causes or effects?

The Ending

- Should I frame the essay by relating the ending to the beginning, as Toufexis does?
- Should I offer leads to further relevant information?
- Should I end with a speculation about the past, as Ngo does?
- Should I end with a prediction about the future, as the *Economist* writer does?

Outlining

An essay explaining a concept is made up of four basic parts:

1. An attempt to engage readers' interest in the explanation
2. The thesis statement, announcing the concept, its focus, and its topics
3. An orientation to the concept, which may include a description or definition of the concept
4. Information about the concept

These parts nearly always appear in the order listed above. Parts 1, 2, and 3 are relatively brief, sometimes no more than two or three paragraphs.

Here is a possible outline for an essay explaining a concept:

An attempt to gain readers' interest in the concept

Thesis statement

Definition of the concept

Topic 1 with illustration

Topic 2 with illustration

(etc.)

Conclusion

An attempt to gain readers' interest could take as little space as two or three sentences or as much as four or five paragraphs. The thesis statement and definition are usually quite brief, sometimes only a few sentences. A topic illustration may occupy one or several paragraphs, and there can be few or many topics, depending on how the information has been divided up. A conclusion might summarize the information presented, give advice about how to use or apply the information, or speculate about the future of the concept.

Consider tentative any outlining you do before you begin drafting. Never be a slave to an outline. As you draft, you will usually see ways to improve on your original plan. Be ready to revise your outline, shift parts around, or drop or add parts as you draft.

Drafting

Begin drafting your essay, keeping your focus in mind. Remember also the needs and expectations of your readers; organize, define, and explain with them in mind. Work to increase readers' understanding of your concept.

You may want to review the general advice on drafting in Chapter 1, pp. 16–19.

■ **CRITICAL READING GUIDE**

Now is the time to get a good critical reading of your draft. Your instructor may arrange such a reading as part of your coursework. If not, you can ask a classmate, friend, or family member to read your draft using this guide. If your campus has a writing center, you might ask a tutor there to read and comment on your draft. (If you are unable to have someone else review your draft, turn ahead to the Revision section for help reading your own draft with a critical eye.)

▶ **If You Are the Writer.** In order to provide focused, helpful comments, your reader must know your essay's intended audience, your purpose, and a problem in the draft that you need help solving. Briefly write out this information at the top of your draft.

- *Readers.* To whom are you directing your concept explanation? What do you assume they know about the concept? How do you plan to engage and hold their interest?
- *Purpose.* What do you hope to achieve with your readers?
- *Problem.* Ask your reader to help you solve the single most important problem you see in the draft. Describe this problem briefly.

▶ **If You Are the Reader.** Use the following guidelines to help you give constructive, helpful comments to others on essays explaining concepts.

1. *Read for a First Impression.* Read first to get a sense of the concept. Then briefly write out your impressions. What in the draft do you think will especially interest the intended readers? Where might they have difficulty in following the explanation? Next, consider the problem the writer identified. If the problem will be covered by one of the other items below, deal with it there. Otherwise, respond to the writer's concerns now.

2. *Assess Whether the Concept Is Clearly Explained and Focused.* Restate, in one sentence, what you understand the concept to mean. Indicate any confusion or uncertainty you have about its meaning. Given the concept, does the focus seem appropriate, too broad, or too narrow for the intended readers? Can you think of a more interesting aspect of the concept on which to focus the explanation?

3. *Consider Whether the Content Is Appropriate for the Intended Readers.* Does it tell them all that they are likely to want to know about the concept?

Can you suggest additional information that should be included? What unanswered questions might readers have about the concept? Point out any information that seems either superfluous or too predictable.

For an illustration of scratch outlining, see Chapter 12, pp. 540–41.

4. *Evaluate the Organization.* Look at the way the essay is organized by making a scratch outline. Does the information seem to be logically divided? If not, suggest a better way to divide it. Also consider the order or sequence of information. Can you suggest a better way of sequencing it?

   - Look at the *beginning*. Does it pull readers into the essay and make them want to continue? Does it adequately forecast the direction of the essay? If possible, suggest a better way to begin.
   - Look for obvious *transitions* in the draft. Tell the writer how they are helpful or unhelpful. Try to improve one or two of them. Look for additional places where transitions would be helpful.
   - Look at the *ending*. Explain what makes it particularly effective or less effective than it might be, in your opinion. If you can, suggest a better way to end.

5. *Assess the Clarity of Definitions.* Point out any definitions that may be unclear or confusing to readers. Identify any other terms that may need to be defined for the intended readers.

6. *Evaluate the Use of Sources.* If the writer has used sources, review the list of sources cited. Given the purpose, readers, and focus of the essay, does the list seem balanced, and are the selections appropriate? Try to suggest concerns or questions about sources that readers knowledgeable about the concept might raise. Then consider the use of sources within the text of the essay. Are there places where summary or paraphrase would be preferable to quoted material or vice versa? Note any places where the writer has placed quotations awkwardly into the text, and recommend ways to smooth them out.

7. *Evaluate the Effectiveness of Visuals.* If charts, graphs, tables, or other visuals are included, let the writer know if they help you understand the concept or if you find them confusing. Suggest ideas you have for changing, adding, moving, or deleting visuals.

8. *Give the Writer Your Final Thoughts.* Which part needs the most work? What do you think the intended readers will find most informative or memorable? What do you like best about the draft essay?

▦ REVISING

Now you are ready to revise your essay. Your instructor or other students may have given you advice on improving your draft. Nevertheless, you may have begun to realize that your draft requires not so much revision as rethinking. For example, you may recognize that the focus you chose is too broad to be explained adequately in a few pages, that you need to make the information more engaging or interesting for your intended readers, or that you need substantially more information to present the concept adequately. Consequently, instead of working to improve parts of the draft, you may need to write a new draft that radically reenvisions your explanation. It is not unusual for students—and professional writers—to find themselves in this situation. Seek your instructor's advice if you must plan a radical revision.

On the other hand, you may feel quite satisfied that your draft achieves most, if not all, of your goals. In that case, you can focus on refining specific parts of your draft. Very likely you have thought of ways to improve your draft, and you may even have begun improving it. This section will help you get an overview of your draft and revise it accordingly.

Getting an Overview

Consider your draft as a whole. It may help to do so in two steps:

For an illustration of scratch outlining, turn to the Commentary following Linh Kieu Ngo's essay in this chapter. For more information on making a scratch outline, see Chapter 12, pp. 540–41.

1. *Reread.* If at all possible, put the draft aside for a day or two before rereading it. When you return to it, start by reconsidering your readers and purpose. Then read the draft straight through, trying to see it as your intended readers will.
2. *Outline.* Make a scratch outline to get an overview of the essay's development.

Charting a Plan for Revision.   After you gain an overview of your draft, you may want to make a two-column chart like the following one to keep track of the work you need to do as you revise. In the left-hand column, list the basic features of concept explanations, skipping several lines between each feature. As you analyze your draft and study any comments from other readers, note any problems you need to solve in the right-hand column.

Turn to pp. 214–15 to review the basic features.

Basic Features	*Problems to Solve*
A focused concept	
An appeal to readers' interests	
A logical plan	
Clear definitions	
Appropriate writing strategies	
Careful use of sources	

Analyzing the Basic Features of Your Own Draft.   Using the Critical Reading Guide on the preceding pages, reread the draft to identify problems you need to solve. Note the problems on your revision chart.

Studying Critical Comments.   Review all of the comments you have received from other readers, and add to your chart any commentary that you intend to act on. Try not to react defensively. For each comment, look at the draft to determine what might have led the reader to make the comment. By letting you see how others respond to your draft, these comments provide valuable information about how you might improve it.

Carrying Out Revisions

Having identified problems in your draft, you now need to come up with solutions and—most important—to carry them out. Basically, there are three ways to find solutions:

1. Review your invention and planning notes and your sources for information and ideas to add to the draft.
2. Do further invention or research to answer questions your readers raised.
3. Look back at the readings in this chapter to see how other writers have solved similar problems.

The following suggestions, which are organized according to the basic features on your revision chart, will get you started solving some writing problems common to explanatory essays.

A Focused Concept

- **Is the focus too broad?** Consider limiting it further so that you can explain one part of the concept in more depth. If readers were uninterested in the aspect you focused on, consider focusing on some other aspect of the concept.
- **Is the focus too narrow?** You may have isolated too minor an aspect. Go back to your invention and research notes and look for larger or more significant aspects.

An Appeal to Readers' Interests

- **Do you fail to connect to readers' interests and engage their attention throughout the essay?** Help readers see the significance of the information to them personally. Eliminate superfluous or too-predictable content. Open with an unusual piece of information that would catch readers' interest.
- **Do you think readers will have unanswered questions?** Review your invention writing and sources for further information to satisfy your readers' needs or answer their concerns and questions.

A Logical Plan

- **Does the beginning successfully orient readers to your purpose and plan?** Try making your focus obvious immediately. Forecast the plan of your essay.
- **Is the explanation difficult to follow?** Look for a way to reorder the parts so that the essay is easier to follow. Try constructing an alternative outline. Add transi-

tions or summaries to help keep readers on track. Or consider ways you might classify and divide the information to make it easier to understand or provide a more interesting perspective on the topic.

- *Is the ending inconclusive?* Consider moving important information there. Try summarizing highlights of the essay or framing it by referring to something in the beginning. Or you might speculate about the future of the concept or assert its usefulness.

Clear Definitions

- *Do readers need a clearer or fuller definition of the concept?* Add a concise definition early in your essay, or consider adding a brief summary that defines the concept later in the essay (in the middle or at the end). Remove any information that may blur readers' understanding of the concept.

- *Are other key terms inadequately defined?* Supply clear definitions, searching your sources or checking a dictionary if necessary.

Appropriate Writing Strategies

- *Does the content seem thin or the definition of the concept blurred?* Consider whether any other writing strategies would improve the presentation.
  - Try comparing or contrasting the concept with a related one that is more familiar to readers.
  - Add some information about its known causes or effects.
  - See whether adding examples enlivens or clarifies your explanation.
  - Tell more about how the concept works or what people do with it.
  - Add design features such as charts, headings, drafts, drawings, photographs.

Careful Use of Sources

- *Do readers find your sources inadequate?* Return to the library or the Internet to find additional ones. Consider dropping weak or less reliable sources. Make sure that your sources provide coverage in a comprehensive, balanced way.

- *Do you rely too much on quoting, summarizing, or paraphrasing?* Change some of your quotations to summaries or paraphrases, or vice versa.

- *Does quoted material need to be more smoothly integrated into your own text?* Revise to make it so.

- *Are there discrepancies between your in-text citations and list of sources?* Compare each in-text citation against the examples of your chosen citation style given in Chapter 22. Be sure that all of the citations and sources follow the style you are using exactly. Check to see that your list of sources has an entry for each in-text citation.

See Chapter 22, pp. 695–97 for advice on integrating quotations into your text.

■ EDITING AND PROOFREADING

Now is the time to check your revised draft carefully for errors in usage, punctuation, and mechanics and to consider matters of style. Our research on students' writing has identified several errors that are especially common in writing that explains concepts. The following guidelines will help you check and edit your essay for these errors.

Checking the Punctuation of Adjective Clauses.   Adjective clauses include both a subject and a verb. They give information about a noun or a pronoun. They often begin with *who, which,* or *that.* Here is an example from a student essay explaining the concept of schizophrenia, a type of mental illness:

> **It is common for schizophrenics to have delusions** *that they are being persecuted.*

Because adjective clauses add information about the nouns they follow—defining, illustrating, or explaining—they can be useful in writing that explains a concept. Adjective clauses may or may not need to be set off with a comma or commas. To decide, first you have to determine whether or not the clause is essential to the meaning of the sentence. Clauses that are essential to the meaning of a sentence should not be set off with a comma; clauses that are not essential to the meaning must be set off with a comma. Here are two examples from the student essay about schizophrenia:

ESSENTIAL   **It is common for schizophrenics to have delusions** *that they are being persecuted.*

The adjective clause defines and limits the word *delusions.* If the clause were removed, the basic meaning of the sentence would change, saying that schizophrenics commonly have delusions of all sorts.

NONESSENTIAL   **Related to delusions are hallucinations,** *which are very common in schizophrenics.*

The adjective clause gives information that is not essential to understanding the main clause *(Related to delusions are hallucinations).* Taking away the adjective clause *(which are very common in schizophrenics)* in no way changes the basic meaning of the main clause.

To decide whether an adjective clause is essential or nonessential, mentally delete the clause. If taking out the clause changes the basic meaning of the sentence or makes it unclear, the clause is probably essential and should not be set off with commas. If the meaning of the main part of the sentence or the main clause does not change enormously, the clause is probably nonessential and should be set off with commas.

► Postpartum neurosis, which can last for two weeks or longer, can adversely affect a mother's ability to care for her infant.

► The early stage starts with memory loss, which usually causes the patient to forget recent life events.

► Seasonal affective disorders are mood disturbances, that occur with a change of season.

► The coaches, who do the recruiting should be disciplined.

Adjective clauses following proper nouns always require commas.

► Nanotechnologists defer to K. Eric Drexler, who speculates imaginatively about the uses of nonmachines.

Checking for Commas around Interrupting Phrases.   When writers are explaining a concept, they need to supply a great deal of information. They add much of this information in phrases that interrupt the flow of a sentence. Words that interrupt are usually set off with commas. Be especially careful with interrupting phrases that fall in the middle of a sentence—such phrases must be set off with two commas, one at the beginning and one at the end:

► People on the West Coast, especially in Los Angeles, have always been receptive to new ideas.

► Alzheimer's disease, named after the German neuropathologist Alois Alzheimer, is a chronic degenerative illness.

► These examples, though simple, present equations in terms of tangible objects.

A WRITER AT WORK

■ SELECTING AND INTEGRATING INFORMATION FROM SOURCES

This section describes how student writer Linh Kieu Ngo selected information from a source and integrated it into one part of his essay on cannibalism.

One paragraph from Ngo's essay illustrates a sound strategy for integrating sources into your essay, relying on them fully—as you nearly always must do in explanatory writing—and yet making them your own. Here is paragraph 9 from Ngo's essay (the sentences are numbered for ease of reference):

> (1) In the Miyanmin society of the west Sepik interior of Papua, New Guinea, villagers do not value human flesh over that of pigs or marsupials because human flesh is part of their diet (Poole 7). (2) The Miyanmin people observe no differences in "gender, kinship, ritual status, and bodily substance"; they eat anyone, even their own dead. In this respect, then, they practice both endocannibalism and exocannibalism; and to ensure a constant supply of human flesh for food, they raid neighboring tribes and drag their victims back to their village to be eaten (Poole 11). (3) Perhaps, in the history of this society, there was at one time a shortage of wild game to be hunted for food, and because people were more plentiful than fish, deer, rabbits, pigs, or cows, survival cannibalism was adopted as a last resort. (4) Then, as their culture developed, the Miyanmin may have retained the practice of dietary cannibalism, which has endured as a part of their culture.

Most of the information in this paragraph comes from a twenty-six-page research report by an anthropologist, Fitz John Porter Poole. Given Ngo's purpose in this paragraph—to illustrate some forms of dietary cannibalism—he selects only a limited amount of information from small sections of text on two different pages of the Poole report. Notice first that Ngo quotes only once (sentence 2, a phrase that emphasizes what indiscriminate dietary cannibals the Miyanmin people are). Otherwise, Ngo paraphrases information from Poole. (When you **paraphrase,** you construct your own sentences and phrases but rely necessarily on the key words in your source.) For example, in his sentence 1, Ngo paraphrases this sentence: "For Miyanmin, they claim, humans do indeed become food in an ordinary sense and are seen as comparable to pigs and marsupials." Toward the end of sentence 2, Ngo again paraphrases Poole. By contrast, Ngo's sentences 3 and 4 seem to be his own specu-

For more on paraphrasing, see Chapter 12, pp. 541–42.

lations about the possible origins of Miyanmin cannibalism because this information does not appear in Poole.

The paragraph illustrates a careful balance between a writer's ideas and information gleaned from sources. Ngo is careful not to let the sources take over the explanation. The paragraph also illustrates judicious use of quotations and paraphrases. Ngo avoids stringing quotes together to illustrate an explanation.

In the successful presentation made by the marketing manager who volunteers to teach fifth graders about the concept of surveys (see the community writing project described on p. 185), effective document design is an important factor. Much of the preparation the researcher makes beforehand involves creating a questionnaire for the students to fill out.

She recognizes that students will need to be interested in the questionnaire, not intimidated by its appearance, and that they will need to be able to fill it out quickly, without much thought. After first drafting the questionnaire so that it fits on a single page, she realizes that it would be easier and faster for the students to fill out if there were more space around each question. She then refers to workbooks and other printed material designed for ten- and eleven-year-olds for guidance in deciding how much space they'd need to write out their answers. In this case, the convenience of her audience outweighs the time and expense of photocopying multiple pages.

The appearance of the questionnaire itself is not her only design consideration, however. The marketing researcher is savvy enough to know that information from the questionnaire has to be easy to represent graphically, so that the students will understand and appreciate the results when they are projected on a large screen, and she keeps this goal in mind as she drafts the language for the questionnaire. For instance, by asking separate questions about television-watching habits on weekdays and weekends, the researcher ensures that she has two categories of data to tabulate.

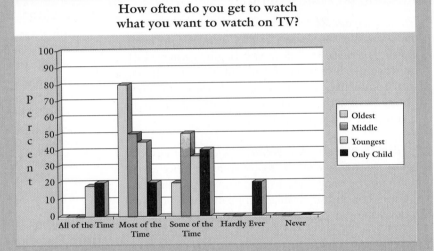

How often do you get to watch what you want to watch on TV?

Because of the time constraints and the need to maintain the audience's interest during an oral presentation, the researcher also makes sure that the questions are phrased in a way that will permit her to input some of the students' answers into the computer right there in the classroom. Thus she writes multiple-choice questions and short fill-ins.

For more on oral presentations, see Chapter 26.

Finally, the marketing researcher makes sure she knows how to use her PowerPoint program to display the results clearly.

THINKING CRITICALLY ABOUT WHAT YOU HAVE LEARNED

Now that you have read and discussed several essays that explain concepts and written one of your own, take some time to reflect on the act of reading and writing concept essays and to think critically about how explanations of concepts influence the way we think about ourselves and our culture.

Reflecting on Your Writing

Write a one-page explanation, telling your instructor about a problem you encountered in writing your essay and how you solved it. Before you begin, gather all of your writing—invention and planning notes, drafts, critical comments, revision notes and plans, and final revision. Review these materials and refer to them as you complete this writing task.

1. *Identify* **one** *writing problem you had to solve as you worked to explain the concept in your essay.* Do not be concerned with grammar and punctuation; concentrate instead on problems unique to developing a concept explanation. For example: Did you puzzle over how to focus your explanation? Did you worry about how to appeal to your readers' interests or how to identify and define the terms your readers would need explained? Did you have trouble integrating sources smoothly?

2. *Determine how you came to recognize the problem.* When did you first discover it? What called it to your attention? If you did not become aware of the problem until someone else pointed it out, can you now see hints of it in your invention writings? If so, where specifically? How did you respond when you first recognized the problem?

3. *Reflect on how you went about solving the problem.* Did you work on the wording of a particular passage, cut or add information, move paragraphs or sentences around, add transitions or forecasting statements, experiment with differ-

ent writing strategies? Did you reread one of the essays in this chapter to see how another writer handled the problem, or did you look back at the invention suggestions? If you talked about the writing problem with another student, a tutor, or your instructor, did talking about it help? How useful was the advice you received?

4. *Write a brief explanation of how you identified the problem and how you solved it.* Be as specific as possible in reconstructing your efforts. Quote from your invention notes and draft essay, others' critical comments, your revision plan, or your revised essay to show the various changes your writing underwent as you tried to solve the problem. If you are still uncertain about your solution, say so. Thinking in detail about how you identified a particular problem, how you went about solving it, and what you learned from this experience can help you solve future writing problems more easily.

Reviewing What You Learned from Reading

Write a page or so explaining to your instructor how the readings in this chapter influenced your final draft. To some extent, your own essay has been influenced by the concept explanations you have read in this chapter and by classmates' essays that you have read. Your reading may have helped you choose a topic, suggested that you needed to do research, or shown you how to structure your essay or how to use examples or comparisons. Before you write, take time to reflect on what you have learned about concept explanations from the readings in this chapter and how the readings have influenced your own writing.

1. *Reread the final revision of your essay; then look back at the selections you read before completing*

your essay. Name any specific influences. For example, if you were impressed by the way one of the readings described the origins or originators of the concept, organized the information, or connected to the readers' knowledge through analogy or comparison, look in your revised essay to see where you might have been striving for similar effects in your own writing. Also look for ideas you got from your reading: writing strategies you were inspired to try, specific details you were led to include, effects you sought to achieve.

2. *Write an explanation of these influences.* Did one reading have an especially strong influence on your essay, or were several readings influential in different ways? Quote from the readings and from your final revision to show how your essay explaining a concept was influenced by the readings in this chapter. Finally, based on this review of the chapter's readings, briefly explain any further improvements you would now make in your essay.

Considering the Social Dimensions of Concept Explanations

Concepts are the building blocks of knowledge, essential to its creation and acquisition. We use concepts to name and organize ideas and information in areas as diverse as snowboarding and psychiatry. Academic disciplines and most professions are heavily concept-based, enabling newcomers to be introduced efficiently, if abstractly, to the basic knowledge they need to begin to work in a field.

The Nature of Knowledge. As you have learned from your reading, research, and writing for this chapter, writers explaining concepts present knowledge as established and uncontested. They presume to be unbiased and objective, and they assume that readers will not doubt or challenge the truth or the value of the knowledge they present. This stance encourages readers to feel confident about the validity of the explanation.

However, explanatory writing should not always be accepted at face value. Textbooks and reference materials, in particular, sometimes present a limited view of knowledge in an academic discipline. Because introductory textbooks must be highly selective, they necessarily leave out certain sources of information and types of knowledge.

1. *Consider the claim that concept explanations attempt to present their information as uncontested truths.* Identify a reading in this chapter that particularly seems to support this claim, and then think about how it does so. Do the same for a chapter or section in a textbook you are reading for another course.

2. *Reflect on how concept explanations present established knowledge.* How do you think knowledge gets established in academic disciplines such as biology, psychology, and history? How might the prominent researchers and professors in a discipline go about deciding what is to be considered established knowledge for now? How might they decide when that established knowledge needs to be revised? If possible, ask these questions of a professor in a subject you are studying.

3. *Write a page or so explaining your initial assumptions about the knowledge or information you presented about a concept in your essay.* When you were doing research on the concept, did you discover that some of the information was being challenged by experts? Or did the body of knowledge seem settled and established? Did you at any point think that your readers might question any of the information you were presenting? How did you decide what information might seem new or even surprising to readers? Did you feel comfortable in your roles as the selector and giver of knowledge?

Arguing a Position

You may associate arguing with quarreling or with the in-your-face debating we hear so often on radio and television talk shows. These ways of arguing may let us vent strong feelings, but they seldom lead us to consider seriously other points of view, let alone to look critically at our own thinking or learn anything new.

This chapter presents a more deliberative way of arguing that we call *reasoned argument* because it depends on giving reasons rather than raising voices. It demands that positions be supported rather than merely asserted. It also commands respect for the right of others to disagree with you as you may disagree with them. Reasoned argument requires more thought than quarreling, but no less passion or commitment, as you will see when you read the essays in this chapter arguing about controversial issues.

Controversial issues are, by definition, issues about which people feel strongly and sometimes disagree vehemently. The issue may involve a practice that has been accepted for some time, like fraternity hazing, or it may concern a newly proposed or recently instituted policy, like the "Peacekeeper" school program. People may agree about goals but disagree about the best way to achieve them, as in the perennial debate over how to guarantee adequate health care for all citizens. Or they may disagree about fundamental values and beliefs, as in the debate over euthanasia.

As you can see from these examples, controversial issues have no obvious "right" answer, no truth that everyone accepts, no single authority on which everyone relies. Writers cannot offer absolute proof in debates about controversial issues because they are matters of opinion and judgment. Simply gathering information—finding the facts or learning from experts—will not settle disputes like these, although the more that is known about an issue, the more informed the positions will be. To some extent, people decide such matters by considering factual evidence, their own experience, and the opinions of people they trust, but they also base their positions on less objective factors such as values and principles, assumptions and preconceptions about how the world works and how it should work.

Although it is not possible to prove that a position on a controversial issue is right or wrong, it is possible through argument to convince others to accept or reject a particular position. To be convincing, not only must an argument present plausible reasons and solid support for its position, but it also should anticipate readers' likely objections and opposing arguments, conceding those that are reasonable and refuting those that are not. Vigorous debate that sets forth arguments and counter-arguments on all sides of an issue can advance everyone's thinking.

Learning to make reasoned arguments on controversial issues and to think critically about our own as well as others' arguments is not a luxury; it is a necessity if our increasingly diverse society is to survive and flourish. As citizens in a democracy, we have a special duty to inform ourselves about pressing issues and to participate constructively in the public debate. Honing our thinking and arguing skills also has practical advantages in school, where we are often judged by our ability to write convincingly, and in the workplace, where we often need to recommend or defend controversial decisions. You will encounter writing that argues a position in many different contexts, as the following examples suggest.

Writing in Your Other Courses

- For a sociology class, a student writes an essay on surrogate mothering. She finds several newspaper and magazine articles and checks the Internet for surrogate mothering Web sites. In her essay, she acknowledges that using *in vitro* fertilization and a surrogate may be the only way some couples can have their own biological children. Although she respects this desire, she argues that from a sociological perspective surrogate mothering does more harm than good. She gives two reasons—that the practice has serious emotional consequences for the surrogates and their families, and that it exploits poor women by creating a class of professional breeders. She supports her argument with anecdotes from surrogates and their families as well as with quotations from sociologists and psychologists who have studied surrogate mothering.

- For a business course, a student writes an essay arguing that the "glass ceiling" that prevents women from advancing up the corporate ladder still exists at the highest executive levels. She acknowledges that in the twenty years since the phrase "glass ceiling" was coined by a writer at the *Wall Street Journal,* the percentage of corporate officers who are women has grown. Nevertheless, she argues, the statistics are misleading. Because it is good business to claim gender equity, many companies define to their own advantage the positions counted as corporate officers. The student cites statistics from the Catalyst research group indicating that only 7 percent of the corporate officers in "line" positions—those responsible for the bottom line and therefore most likely to be promoted to chief executive positions—are women.

For a look at some of the decisions this student makes about document design, see p. 286–87.

Writing in the Community

- For the campus newspaper, a student writes an editorial condemning the practice of fraternity hazing. He acknowledges that most hazing is harmless but argues that hazing can get out of hand and even be lethal. He refers specifically to two incidents reported in the national news in which one student died of alcohol poisoning after being forced to drink too much liquor and another student had a heart attack after being made to run too many laps. To show that the potential for a similar tragedy exists on his college campus, the writer recounts several anecdotes told to him by students about their experiences pledging for campus fraternities. He concludes with a plea to the fraternities on campus to curtail—or at least, radically change—their hazing practices before someone is seriously hurt or killed.

- In a letter to the school board, parents protest a new "Peacekeepers" program being implemented at the local middle school. The writers acknowledge that the aim of the program—to teach students to avoid conflict—is worthwhile. But they argue that the program's methods unduly restrict students' freedoms. Moreover, they claim that the program teaches children to become passive rather than thinking adults ready to fight for what is right. To support their argument, they list some of the rules that have been instituted: students must wear uniforms to school, must keep their hands clasped behind their backs when walking down the halls, are not permitted to raise their voices in anger or to use obscenities, and cannot play aggressive games like dodgeball or contact sports like basketball and football.

Writing in the Workplace

- For a business magazine, a corporate executive writes an essay arguing that protecting the environment is not only good citizenship, but also good business. She supports her position with examples of two companies that became successful by developing innovative methods of reducing hazardous wastes. She also reminds readers of the decisive action taken in the late 1980s by established corporations to help solve the problem of ozone depletion, such as DuPont's decision to discontinue production of chlorofluorocarbons (CFCs) and McDonald's elimination of styrofoam cartons. Finally, she points out that *Fortune* magazine agrees with her position, noting that its annual ranking of "America's Most Admired Corporations" includes "community and environmental responsibility" alongside "financial soundness" among the eight deciding factors.

- In a memo to the director of personnel, a loan company manager argues that written communication skills should be a more important factor in hiring. He acknowledges that math skills are necessary, but tries to convince the director that mistakes in writing are too costly to ignore. To support his argument, he cites examples when bad writing in letters and memos cost the company money and time. For additional examples and suggestions on solving the problem, he refers the personnel director to an ongoing discussion about writing on a listserv to which the manager subscribes.

Practice Arguing a Position: A Collaborative Activity

The preceding scenarios suggest some occasions for arguing a position. To construct an effective argument, you must assert a position and offer support for it. This activity gives you a chance to practice constructing an argument with other students.

Part 1. Get together with two to three other students and choose an issue. You do not have to be an expert on the issue, but you should be familiar with some of the arguments people typically make about it. If you do not have an issue in mind, the following list might help you think of possibilities.

- Should all students be required to wear uniforms in school?
- Should college athletes be paid a portion of the money the school gains from sports events?
- Should community service be a requirement for graduation from high school or college?

In your group, spend two to three minutes quickly exchanging your opinions and then agree together to argue for the same position on the issue, whether you personally agree with the position or not. Also decide who you would want to read your argument and what you expect these readers to think about the issue. Choose someone in the group to write down the results of your discussion like this:

Issue. Should grades in college be abolished?

Position. Grades should be abolished.

Readers. Teachers who think grades measure learning accurately and efficiently.

Take another ten to fifteen minutes to construct an argument for your position, giving several reasons and noting the kinds of support you would need. Also try to anticipate one or two objections you would expect from readers who disagree with your position. Write down what you discover under the following headings: *Reasons, Support Needed,* and *Likely Objections.* Following is an example of this work for the position that grades should be abolished.

Reasons

1. Tests are not always the best way to judge students' knowledge because some students do poorly on tests even though they know the material.
2. Tests often evaluate only what is easily measurable, such as whether students remember facts, rather than whether students can use facts to support their ideas.

Support Needed

1. Research on testing anxiety

2. Anecdotes from students' experience with testing anxiety

3. Teachers' comments on why they rely on tests and how they feel about alternatives to testing (such as group projects)

Likely Objections

1. Tests are efficient—for teachers and for students, especially in comparison with research papers.

2. Tests are evaluated strictly on what students have learned about the subject, not on how well they write or how well a group collaborates.

Part 2. Discuss for about five minutes what you did as a group to construct an argument:

Reasons. What did you learn about giving reasons? If you thought of more reasons than you needed, how did you choose? If you had difficulty thinking of reasons, what could you do?

Support. What did you learn about supporting an argument? How many different kinds of support (such as quotations, examples, or anecdotes) did you consider? Which reasons seemed the easiest to support? Which the hardest?

Objections. What did you learn about anticipating objections to your argument? How did you come up with these objections? Given your designated readers, was it easy or hard to think of their likely objections? How could you learn more about your readers' likely objections?

READINGS

The readings in this chapter illustrate the features of essays that argue a position on a controversial issue and the strategies writers rely on to realize the features. No two essays in this genre are much alike, and yet they share defining features. The Analyzing Writing Strategies and Commentary following each reading touch on a few features best illustrated by that essay, capturing its special qualities and strengths. Together, the four essays cover many of the possibilities of writing that argues a position. Consequently, you will want to read as many of the essays as possible and, if time permits, complete the activities in Analyzing Writing Strategies and read the Commentaries. Following the readings, the Basic Features section offers a concise description of the features of writing that argues a position and gives examples from all of the readings.

Richard Estrada wrote a syndicated column for the Dallas Morning News. *He wrote this essay, "Sticks and Stones and Sports Team Names," in late October 1995 during the World Series in which the Atlanta Braves played the Cleveland Indians. The series, which was televised, drew attention to the practice of dressing team mascots like Native Americans on the warpath and encouraging fans to rally their team with gestures like the "tomahawk chop" and pep yells like the "Indian chant." The controversy over these practices ignited a long-standing debate over sports teams using names associated with Native Americans. Various high schools and at least one university, Stanford, have changed the names of their sports teams because of this ongoing controversy.*

The title, as you may know, refers to a children's chant: "Sticks and stones will break my bones, but words will never hurt me." As you read, consider why Estrada and his newspaper editor thought this title was appropriate.

Sticks and Stones and Sports Team Names

Richard Estrada

When I was a kid living in Baltimore in the late 1950s, there was only one professional sports team worth following. Anyone who ever saw the movie *Diner* knows which one it was. Back when we liked Ike, the Colts were the gods of the gridiron and Memorial Stadium was their Mount Olympus. 1

Ah, yes: The Colts. The Lions. Da Bears. Back when defensive tackle Big Daddy Lipscomb was letting running backs know exactly what time it was, a young fan could easily forget that in a game where men were men, the teams they played on were not invariably named after animals. Among others, the Packers, the Steelers and the distant 49ers were cases in point. But in the roll call of pro teams, one name in particular always discomfited me: the Washington Redskins. Still, however willing I may have been to go along with the name as a kid, as an adult I have concluded that using an ethnic group essentially as a sports mascot is wrong. 2

The Redskins and the Kansas City Chiefs, along with baseball teams like the Atlanta Braves and the Cleveland Indians, should find other names that avoid highlighting ethnicity. 3

By no means were such names originally meant to disparage Native Americans. The noble symbols of the Redskins or college football's Florida Seminoles or the Illinois Illini are meant to be strong and proud. Yet, ultimately, the practice of using a people as mascots is dehumanizing. It sets them apart from the rest of society. It promotes the politics of racial aggrievement at a moment when our storehouse is running over with it. 4

The World Series between the Cleveland Indians and the Atlanta Braves reignited the debate. In the chill night air of October, tomahawk chops and war chants suddenly became far more familiar to millions of fans, along with the ridiculous and offensive cartoon logo of Cleveland's "Chief Wahoo." 5

The defenders of team names that use variations on the Indian theme argue that tradition should not be sacrificed at the altar of political correctness. In truth, the nation's No. 1 P.C. [politically correct] school, Stanford University, helped matters some when it changed its team nickname from "the Indians" to "the Cardinals." To be sure, Stanford 6 did the right thing, but the school's status as P.C. without peer tainted the decision for those who still need to do the right thing.

Another argument is that ethnic group leaders are too inclined to cry wolf in alleging racial insensitivity. Often, this is the case. But no one should overlook genuine cases of political insensitivity in an attempt to avoid accusations of hypersensitivity and political correctness. 7

The real world is different from the world of sports entertainment. I recently heard a father who happened to be a Native American complain on the radio that his child was being pressured into participating in celebrations of Braves baseball. At his kid's school, certain days are set aside on which all children are told to dress in Indian garb and celebrate with tomahawk chops and the like. 8

That father should be forgiven for not wanting his family to serve as somebody's mascot. The desire to avoid ridicule is legitimate and understandable. Nobody likes to be trivialized or deprived of their dignity. This has nothing to do with political correctness and the provocations of militant leaders. 9

Against this backdrop, the decision by newspapers in Minneapolis, Seattle and Portland to ban references to Native American nicknames is more reasonable than some might think. 10

What makes naming teams after ethnic groups, particularly minorities, reprehensible is that politically impotent groups continue to be targeted, while politically powerful ones who bite back are left alone. How long does anyone think the name "Washington Blackskins" would last? Or how about "the New York Jews"? 11

With no fewer than 10 Latino ballplayers on the Cleveland Indians' roster, the team could change its name to "the Banditos." The trouble is, they would be missing the point: Latinos would correctly object to that stereotype, just as they rightly protested against Frito-Lay's use of the "Frito Bandito" character years ago. 12

It seems to me that what Native Americans are saying is that what would be intolerable for Jews, blacks, Latinos and others is no less offensive to them. Theirs is a request not only for dignified treatment, but for fair treatment as well. For America to ignore the complaints of a numerically small segment of the population because it is small is neither dignified nor fair. 13

Connecting to Culture and Experience: Name-Calling

As children, we may say, "Sticks and stones will break my bones, but words will never hurt me." Most children, however, recognize the power of words, especially words that make us feel different or inferior.

Discuss with other students your experience of name-calling. List the names given to groups with which you identify based on your ethnicity, religion, gender, interests, geographic region, or any other factor. Which of these names, if any, do you consider insulting? Why? What does the name connote? Would you consider someone who uses names like these insensitive, as Estrada suggests, or do you think that someone who takes offense at the use of names like these is being hypersensitive? Or if you think the issue is a matter not of sensitivity but of something else, what terms would you use to describe the issue? Consider, for example, the relationship between who is doing the naming and who is being named. Who has the power in this relationship?

Analyzing Writing Strategies

1. At the beginning of this chapter, we discuss several features of essays that argue a position. Consider which of these is true of Estrada's essay:
   - It presents a controversial issue.
   - It asserts a clear position on the issue.
   - It argues for the position by presenting plausible reasons and support.
   - It anticipates readers' objections and arguments, either conceding or refuting them.

For more on using examples to support an argument, see Chapter 19, pp. 627–28.

2. Reread paragraphs 11–13, where Estrada offers hypothetical **examples** of team names for ethnic groups such as the "Washington Blackskins" and "New York Jews." Underline the sentence that most clearly states the reason he is supporting with these examples. What do you think is the logical connection between the reason and the examples supporting it? How effective do you think this part of Estrada's argument is likely to be for his readers?

Commentary: Presenting the Issue and Plausible Reasons

Although the essay's title lets readers infer what the piece is about, Estrada does not identify the issue explicitly until the end of the second paragraph. He begins the essay by remembering his childhood experience as a football fan and explaining that, even as a child, he was "discomfited" by the practice of naming sports teams for Native Americans. In paragraphs 2–4, he lists team names (Washington Redskins, Kansas City Chiefs, Atlanta Braves, Cleveland Indians, Florida Seminoles, Illinois Illini) to remind readers how common the practice is. Then, in paragraph 8, he relates an anecdote about a boy who not only feels "discomfited" by the practice, but as a Native American feels personally ridiculed as well. Estrada uses this anecdote to demonstrate that the issue is important and worth taking seriously.

Estrada presents the issue in this way to appeal to the readers of his column in the politically conservative *Dallas Morning News*. He apparently assumes that unless he can convince his readers that the issue of sports teams' names is significant, many readers would dismiss it as unimportant or as advancing a liberal agenda. Therefore, Estrada tries to make his readers empathize with what he calls a "real world" issue, one that actually hurts kids (paragraph 8). When you present the issue in your own essay, you also may need to help readers understand why it is important and for whom. In the next reading, for example, Alan I. Leshner tries to present the issue of treating drug addiction as affecting not only the addicts themselves, but the rest of society as well.

Presenting the issue is just a beginning. To convince readers, Estrada has to give reasons why he believes naming sports teams for ethnic groups is detrimental. He gives two: because (1) it treats people like team mascots and (2) it singles out a politically weak group. Moreover, to be convincing, the reasons have to seem plausible to readers. The position (naming sports teams for Native Americans is wrong) has to follow logically from the reason: If readers accept the reason, then they also should accept the position. In other words, if readers are convinced by the support Estrada provides to show the effects of treating people like mascots, then they will be inclined to agree with Estrada that the practice is wrong. Similarly, if readers are convinced also that naming sports teams for Native Americans unfairly singles out a politically weak group, then they would be even more likely to agree with Estrada's conclusion. Of course, if readers do not think that these reasons outweigh reasons for the opposing position, then they will not be persuaded by Estrada's argument. That is why essays arguing a position cannot simply argue for a position; they must also anticipate opposing arguments and counterargue.

Considering Topics for Your Own Essay

List some issues that you could write about involving cultural diversity. For example, should a law be passed to make English the "official language" in this country, requiring that ballots and driver's tests be in English only? Should elementary schools continue bilingual education to help non-English-speaking students learn subjects like math, science, and history while they are learning to read and write fluently in English? Should there be some form of affirmative action in college admissions for underrepresented groups?

Alan I. Leshner *is the director of the National Institute on Drug Abuse (NIDA), one of the National Institutes of Health (NIH). NIDA supports worldwide research on drug abuse, prevention, and treatment. In addition to his administrative duties, Leshner advises the president and Congress on drug policy and informs the public about policy issues and research developments. Before coming to NIDA, Leshner was acting director of the National Institute of Mental Health and served at the National Science Foundation. A former professor of psychology, Leshner's scientific research has focused on the biological bases of behavior. He has received many awards for his national leadership in substance abuse and addiction, science education, and mental health. In 1996, President Clinton gave him the Presidential Distinguished Executive Rank Award, the highest recognition for federal service.*

In his role as NIDA director, Leshner writes and speaks to a wide range of audiences, from research scientists to schoolchildren. As this reading demonstrates, he also writes syndicated newspaper columns intended to influence public opinion. "Why Shouldn't Society Treat Substance Abusers?" first appeared in the Los Angeles Times *(June 11, 1999). As you read, notice that Leshner refers to scientific research but, following newspaper convention, does not cite specific sources.*

Why Shouldn't Society Treat Substance Abusers?

Alan I. Leshner

Imagine a debilitating disease for which there are effective treatments. Imagine that this treatable disease costs society $110 billion a year. Can you imagine not using the treatments? It seems unfathomable, but that often is the case with the treatment of drug addiction.

Addicts are frequently denied treatment that would not only improve their lives, but also would improve our own lives—by cutting crime, reducing disease and improving the productivity of employees and the economy.

People are polarized on the issue of treatment: They are either strong advocates for treating addiction or they hate the idea. People debate with passion whether treatment works or not, which approaches are best and whether treatments such as methadone simply substitute one addiction for another.

From my observation post, the core of the issue cannot be simply whether drug treatments are effective or not, since there already is abundant scientific data showing that they are. In fact, research shows that drug treatments are as, or more, effective than treatments for other chronic disorders, such as forms of heart disease, diabetes and some mental illness.

The central issue for many people is whether addicts should be treated at all. I frequently hear people ask: Do they really deserve to be treated? Didn't they just do it to themselves? Why should we coddle people who cause so much societal disruption? Shouldn't they be punished, rather than treated? Even many people who recognize addiction as a disease still get hung up on whether it is a "no-fault" illness.

Science has brought us to a point where we should no longer focus the drug treatment question simply on these kinds of unanswerable moral dilemmas. From a practical perspective, benefits to society must be included in the decision equations. The very same body of scientific data that demonstrates the effectiveness of treatments in reducing an individual's drug use also shows the enormous benefits that drug treatment can have for the patient's family and the community.

A variety of studies from the National Institutes of Health, Columbia University, the University of Pennsylvania and other institutions all have shown that drug treatment reduces use by 50% to 60%, and arrests for violent and nonviolent criminal acts by 40% or more. Drug abuse treatment reduces the risk of HIV infection, and interventions to prevent HIV are much less costly than treating AIDS. Treatment tied to vocational services improves the prospects for employment, with 40% to 60% more individuals employed after treatment.

The case is just as dramatic for prison and jail inmates, 60% to 80% of whom have serious substance abuse problems. Science shows that appropriately treating addicts in prison reduces their later drug use by 50% to 70% and their later criminality and resulting arrests by 50% to 60%. These data make the case against warehousing addicts in prison without attending to their addictions.

Successful drug treatment takes a person who is now seen as only a drain on a community's resources and returns the individual to productive membership in society. Best estimates are that for every $1 spent on drug treatment, there is a $4 to $7 return in cost savings to society. This means that dwelling on moralistic questions, such as who deserves what kind of help, blocks both the individual and society from receiving the economic and societal benefits that can be achieved from treating addicts.

It is true that the individual initially made the voluntary decision to use drugs. But 10 once addicted, it is no longer a simple matter of choice. Prolonged drug use changes the brain in long-lasting and fundamental ways that result in truly compulsive, often uncontrollable, drug craving, seeking and use, which is the essence of addiction. Once addicted, it is almost impossible for most people to stop using drugs without treatment.

It is clearly in everyone's interest to rise above our moral outrage that addiction 11 results from a voluntary behavior. If we are ever going to significantly reduce the tremendous price that drug addiction exacts from every aspect of our society, drug treatment for all who need it must be a core element of our society's strategies.

Connecting to Culture and Experience: Addiction

In this essay, Leshner focuses on drug addiction, but there are other kinds of addiction—such as addiction to chocolate, dieting, exercise, video games, work, shopping. For many of us, the word *addiction* carries negative connotations because of its association with drug and alcohol abuse. But some addictions may not be bad for us, and it is possible that certain addictions actually might be good. Before making judgments, we need to determine what we mean by addiction, and whether we should distinguish among kinds or intensities of addiction. For example, would jogging two miles every morning, always picking up cans and bottles, or playing poker every Friday night qualify as an addiction? Is a sports fan who goes to every game of his favorite team addicted? Is a person who attends city council meetings as a self-appointed public watchdog addicted?

With two or three other students, begin exploring your understanding of addiction by taking turns either telling about your own experience with addiction or about the experience of someone you know. Or if you have no personal experience, describe the image you have of someone with an addiction and where you think that image comes from.

Then, as a group, try to define *addiction* based on your experiences as well as on popular cultural images and stereotypes. Do you think some addictions are socially acceptable and should be encouraged?

Analyzing Writing Strategies

1. To see how Leshner uses hypothetical examples or scenarios in his essay, reread the first paragraph. What do you think Leshner is trying to accomplish with these hypotheticals? How well does his strategy work for you as a reader? Instead of hypothetical examples, what could he have done to create a similar effect on readers?

For more on anticipating objections, see counter-arguing in Chapter 19, pp. 634–37.

2. In paragraph 3, Leshner **anticipates objections** and questions that readers might raise about the effectiveness of different treatments for drug addiction. Reread paragraph 4, where he responds to these objections. Decide whether he responds by acknowledging, conceding, or refuting the objections. Then consider how convincing his response is likely to be for his audience of newspaper readers.

Commentary: Convincing Support

For more on using statistics and authorities, see Chapter 19, pp. 628–31.

To support his argument in paragraphs 7–9 that drug treatment can not only help drug users but also benefit the community, Leshner uses a combination of **statistics** and **authorities.** In paragraph 7, for example, he cites statistics on the effects of treatment on reducing drug use and crime and of increasing the prospects for employment. In paragraph 8, he uses much the same strategy in discussing inmates. And in paragraph 9, he uses statistics to show how much society would save from treating drug addicts.

For this statistical support to be convincing, Leshner's readers must accept it as fact. But most critical readers are appropriately skeptical about statistics. They need to know whether the statistics come from reliable sources and whether they are current, relevant, and accurate. Leshner, as we pointed out in the headnote, wrote his essay for a newspaper, so he cannot document it as he would a research report. To overcome this difficulty, he uses authorities to bolster the credibility of his statistics. He tries to establish the authority of his sources in three ways: by invoking the authority of the research institutions where the studies were conducted, by invoking his own authority, and by invoking the authority of science itself. He begins by simply naming the institutions, two respected research universities most readers will have heard of, and his own National Institutes of Health (paragraph 7). He tries to establish his own authority both by displaying his wide knowledge of the subject and by letting readers know his credentials, which appeared originally in a box at the end of the essay. Finally, Leshner invokes the authority of science itself in sentences that begin like this: "Science has brought us to a point" and "Science shows" (paragraphs 6 and 8). Some readers may question the ultimate authority of science, but as a researcher himself and director of an institute that, according to Leshner's own Director's Page at the NIDA Web site, "supports 85% of the world's research on the health aspects of drug abuse and addiction," it is not surprising that he expects readers to have faith in scientists and scientific research.

Leshner, as we said, is prevented by newspaper convention from citing his sources. The NIDA Web site at <http://www.nida.nih.gov> contains links to various research studies, so we can infer that, in another context, it would have been easy for Leshner to support his statistics by referring to specific reports.

The next two essays in this chapter, an excerpt from a book by Mariah Burton Nelson and an academic essay by Jessica Statsky, illustrate two different citation styles. The style used in the excerpt from Nelson is based on the *Chicago Manual of Style* (often used in books published for general audiences), whereas Statsky uses the Modern Language Association (MLA) style (often used in academic writing). These two systems use different types of citations in the text and different formats for the references collected in a list at the end.

For guidance on using and acknowledging sources, see Chapter 22.

Considering Topics for Your Own Essay

Consider other controversial issues that involve public policy. For example, should individuals be able to sell videotapes they have copied from commercial broadcasts? Should prime-time television programs be permitted to show nudity? Should store owners be prohibited from selling recordings with "Parental Advisory" stickers to people under eighteen? Should there be censorship on the Internet? Select one issue on which you have a position; then consider how you would construct a reasoned argument for your position.

Mariah Burton Nelson is a sports reporter and writer who has written extensively on sports and gender. As a former Stanford University star athlete and professional basketball player, Nelson is highly critical of the unequal funding of men's and women's college sports programs, the issue addressed in this reading from her controversial book, The Stronger Women Get, the More Men Love Football: Sexism and the American Culture of Sports *(1994). Her latest book is called* Embracing Victory: How Women Can Compete Joyously, Compassionately, and Successfully in the Workplace and on the Playing Field *(1999).*

As you read this excerpt from The Stronger Women Get, the More Men Love Football, *which we have titled "Adventures in Equality" after the cartoon from her book, notice how Nelson uses the journalistic convention of quoting people and presenting information without specifying her sources. For college essays, however, readers expect every source to be cited consistently.*

Adventures in Equality

Mariah Burton Nelson

In the early 1990s, as female athletes and coaches sued dozens of universities for equal opportunities and as judges consistently ruled in favor of the women, football coaches and administrators waged what one woman called "an offensive" against athletic feminists, claiming that women were attacking the sacred football cow. 1

Women weren't, in fact, attacking football. They just wanted to swim, row, play soccer, play tennis, or golf, and to coach and direct programs, as men do. They just wanted equal salaries, uniforms, travel schedules, scholarships, and facilities. 2

In fact, football—or, rather, male support of football and lack of support of women's sports—is responsible for much of the disparity between male and female college sports opportunities. Football "requires" oodles of athletes (108, on average, in Division I), scores of scholarships (75, on average), excessive coaching salaries ($81,574 is the average "base"), and exorbitant operating expenses (more than for all other women's and men's sports combined). 3

Inevitably, if women are to have half of all sports allocations, as they are entitled to by law, football will have to change. Some schools will trim football's bloated budgets. Others will drop football altogether, as the University of Wisconsin, Superior; Wichita State; the University of Southern Colorado; and Northeastern Illinois University have 4 already done. Others will leave football alone and add several large-squad women's sports, market women's programs to increase revenue, or find other creative ways to stop discriminating. But football defenders fear that their glory days are limited, and they blame women.

"What I'm afraid of is that somebody is trying to put a bull's eye on football's chest," said Oregon Athletic Director Bill Byrne, former president of the National Association of Collegiate Directors of Athletics.[1]

The Reverend Edmund P. Joyce, former executive vice-president at the University of Notre Dame, accused "militant women" of waging a "strident, irresponsible, and irrational campaign" against football. "Never have our football programs been in such jeopardy as they are today," Joyce said. "I think we are fighting for our lives and had better act accordingly."[2]

The fight for college football's life includes arguing that football is the cash cow upon which all the women's programs suckle, even though this is a lie. "Revenue producing" —a term often used to justify discriminatory football and men's basketball programs— is not synonymous with "profit producing." Football programs that earn money almost always spend more—not on women's sports, but on football. In 91 percent of all colleges, the football program does not make enough money to pay for itself.[3] Even in the big, football-dominated universities (Division I-A), 45 percent of the football programs lose money. In the other three divisions (I-AA, II, and III), between 94 and 99 percent of the schools lose money on football.[4]

Besides, judges have ruled that "financial considerations cannot justify gender discrimination." 8

The fight for football's life includes arguing that football should be exempt from gender-discrimination calculations. Thomas Hearn, president of Wake Forest University, defended his school to Representative Cardiss Collins of Illinois during a congressional hearing by saying, "At Wake Forest, our athletic scholarship awards without football would approach parity, with 60 percent going to men and 40 percent to women." 9

University of New Haven football coach Mark Whipple has said, "Football shouldn't have anything to do with gender equity. If you don't count football, I think everyone would be happy."[5] 10

"I don't think football players are a third sex," Women's Sports Foundation executive director Donna Lopiano responded. The courts have agreed. 11

The fight for football's life includes arguing that women are being unAmerican, even communist, by depriving young men of their right to play football. Auburn University football coach Pat Dye has said, "To tell a kid he can't come out for college football as a walk-on because it creates a numbers problem with the women in another area, I mean that's almost like communism. That (isn't) what this country was built on, or what it stands for."[6] 12

University of Iowa women's athletic director Christine Grant's response: "Schools have had twenty years to think about this. It's unfortunate for the young men who get cut, but it's even more unfortunate for the millions of young women who have missed out for 100 years."[7] 13

The fight for football's life includes redefining "gender equity" to mean men get 60 percent, women get 40 percent. In what was hailed as a bold move, the Big Ten Conference recently approved a "gender equity" plan requiring 40 percent of its athletes to be women by 1997. Only the University of Iowa committed itself to a 50–50 split, which will make it the only Big Ten school to comply, finally, with the 1972 law. 14

The fight for football's life includes arguing that "progress" toward Title IX compliance is being made. In fact, if athletic directors had wanted to end discrimination during the wealthy eighties, they could have added women's programs while holding men's programs steady. Instead, over the ten-year period between the 1981–1982 season and the 1991–1992 season, for every two female participation slots created, 1.5 male slots were created.[8] 15

Representative Cardiss Collins has introduced a House bill called the "Equity in Athletics Disclosure Act" that would require school administrators to disclose participation rates and expenditures for male and female athletes. Football coaches and male athletic directors testified against the bill. 16

The fight for football's life includes contending that few women want to play sports. This is a last-ditch effort to deny women their rights based on a Title IX interpretation that allows unequal allocations if "the program fully and effectively accommodates the interests and abilities" of both sexes. Big Ten Commissioner Jim Delaney told me, "Not as many women are interested in playing sports as men. Look at field hockey versus football. Hundreds of men go out for football. It carries more status." 17

Collins's response: "Lower participation rates are the *result* of discrimination, and not an *excuse* for continued inequities."[9]   18

At the Division I-A level, only one out of 107 schools complies with Title IX. This is Washington State University (WSU), which was forced to do so by its own Supreme Court. In response to a class action suit filed by fifty-three female coaches and players, a judge ruled in 1982 that the number of WSU scholarships must be proportional to the ratio of women and men in the undergraduate student body. However, he exempted football from the count. But in 1987, the Supreme Court of Washington overruled the football exemption. The number of female athletes at WSU is now 44 percent, up from 29 percent in 1987. The female undergraduate student population is 46 percent.   19

"We were dragged kicking and screaming into the forefront," recalls Harold C. Gibson, Washington State's associate athletic director. People "thought the sky was falling."[10]   20

They still seem to think so. The College Football Association's Charles Neinas recently launched a public relations campaign with the slogan, "College football: More than just a game."[11]   21

In a surprisingly frank speech to his fellow football coaches and athletic directors, Neinas said, "Football may be the last bastion of male domination."[12]   22

Which explains a lot.   23

Notes

1. Ben Brown, "Law Gives Women Their Fair Share," *USA Today,* 9 June 1992, p. C1.

2. Buck Turnbull, "Notre Dame's Joyce Says Future of Game on Line vs. Militant Women," *USA Today,* 7 June 1993, p. 12C.

3. Mitchell H. Raiborn, "Revenues and Expenses of Intercollegiate Athletics Programs: Analysis of Financial Trends and Relationships 1985–89" (Mission, Kansas: National Collegiate Athletic Association, 1990). This data refers to NCAA member institutions, which includes most colleges and universities.

4. Ibid.

5. Woody Anderson, Greg Garber, and Lori Riley, "At Last, Title IX Gets Serious Look," *The Hartford Courant,* p. D4.

6. Pat Dye, quoted in the *Birmingham Post–Herald,* cited in "Fundamentals Apply in Education," *NCAA News,* 19 August 1992, p. 4.

7. Chris Grant, *Chicago Tribune,* cited in "Coaches Question Baseball Use of RPI," *NCAA News,* 23 June 1993, p. 4.

8. National Collegiate Athletic Association, 1993, cited in Donna Lopiano, "Statement Before the Subcommittee on Commerce, Consumer Protection, and Competitiveness" (Washington, D.C.: U.S. House of Representatives, 17 February 1993).

9. Cardiss Collins, "Opening Statement," Subcommittee on Commerce, Consumer Protection, and Competitiveness (Washington, D.C.: U.S. House of Representatives, 17 February 1993).

10. Mary Jordan, "Only One School Meets Gender Equity Goal," *Washington Post,* 21 June 1992, p. D1.

11. Debra E. Blum, "Officials of Big-Time College Football See Threat in Moves to Cut Costs and Provide Equity for Women," *The Chronicle of Higher Education,* 16 June 1993, p. A35.

12. Brown, 1992, p. C2.

Connecting to Culture and Experience: Equity

Nelson bases her argument on a fundamental value most Americans share: "equity."
As she explains in paragraph 2, "[Women] just wanted to swim, row, play soccer, play
tennis, or golf, and to coach and direct programs, as men do. They just wanted equal
salaries, uniforms, travel schedules, scholarships, and facilities." She makes equity
sound so simple, and yet legislation and court rulings requiring colleges to comply
with fairness guidelines have not had much effect. If equity is such a treasured American value, why do you suppose compliance with the Title IX law has been so hard to
achieve?

Discuss this question with two or three other students in your class. Begin by
exchanging your views on the issue. What values most concern you in regard to college sports? Is gender equity your highest priority, or do other competing values matter more to you than equal opportunity in sports for men and women? How do you
think Americans traditionally decide between competing values on issues like this?
How do you think Americans should decide?

Analyzing Writing Strategies

1. To examine how Nelson presents the issue, reread the first four paragraphs and
   note in the margin what she does to demonstrate to readers that the issue exists
   and is important. To get started, notice that she opens paragraph 1 with a brief
   history ("In the early 1990s . . ."). How does she use this history lesson to
   explain the issue? What else does she do, in paragraphs 1–4, to help her readers
   understand and appreciate what is at stake?

2. One of the ways Nelson supports her argument is by quoting **authorities.** Skim
   the essay and put brackets around each quotation. Some of the sources Nelson
   quotes share her opinion, while others take a different stand on the issue. Look
   at what Nelson tells readers in the text and in the list of references at the end
   about each source she quotes (such as the name, credentials, and affiliations);
   then consider how readers can use this information to help evaluate what the
   sources are saying.

For more on quoting authorities, see Chapter 19, pp.
629–31.

Commentary: Anticipating Opposing Positions

Successfully arguing a position usually requires the writer to be aware of widely held
positions others have taken on the issue and to respond in some way to their most
likely arguments. Writers have three options for **counterarguing:** merely acknowledging other positions, conceding valid points by accommodating or making room
for them in their own argument, or trying to refute them.

How writers choose to counterargue depends on their readers and purpose.
Nelson probably had two kinds of readers in mind: those who know very little about
the debate, and those who already know about the debate and basically agree with
her. Nelson's purpose in addressing the less knowledgeable readers is primarily
to convince them that there is no reason to delay implementing the Title IX law
requiring gender equity in spending for college sports. For her more knowledgable

For more on counterarguing,
see Chapter 19, pp. 634–37.

readers, Nelson may have had two aims: to remind them of the outrageous and unfounded reasons advanced by the opposition, and to inspire them to continue the fight for gender equity in collegiate sports.

The bulk of Nelson's essay (twelve of twenty-three paragraphs) is organized as a refutation in which she systematically describes and critiques six common reasons for the opposing position:

1. Gender equity should not be imposed on football programs because football supports other sports programs, including women's sports (paragraphs 7–8).

2. Gender equity should not be imposed on football programs because football is special and should not be included in gender-discrimination calculations (9–11).

3. Gender equity should not be imposed on football programs because college men in America have the "right" to play football (12–13).

4. Gender equity should not be imposed on football programs because a 50–50 split is an unfair goal (14).

5. Gender equity should not be imposed on football programs because "progress" is being made (15–16).

6. Gender equity should not be imposed on football programs because "few women want to play sports" anyway (17–18).

Nelson attempts to refute each of these points, supporting her counterargument with information, examples, statistics, and quotations from experts.

For more on cohesive devices, see Chapter 13, pp. 564–67.

You probably noticed that Nelson repeats the same language ("The fight for football's life includes. . . .") to announce each new point she refutes. This repetition has two purposes. Repeating an introductory phrase in this way enhances **cohesion** by making it easy for readers to follow the thread of the argument. It also may serve a rhetorical purpose by creating the impression that her opponents are desperately fighting for football's life, grasping at straws in search of any argument that will postpone the inevitable, and suggesting that women themselves had better continue fighting until funding equity is assured.

Considering Topics for Your Own Essay

Think of a political issue on which you could write an essay. You might consider a local campus issue (such as whether a particular instructor should get tenure or be fired, whether funds should be used for computer labs or parking spaces, or whether student athletes should be required to maintain a certain grade point average to participate in sports) or a local community issue (such as whether a new shelter for abused women and children should be opened, whether parents should be held responsible legally and financially for crimes committed by their children under age eighteen, or whether skateboarding should be permitted in a park). Choose an issue and then think about how you would go about getting information to support your argument.

Jessica Statsky wrote the following essay about children's competitive sports for her college composition course. Before reading, recall your own experiences as an elementary student playing competitive sports, either in or out of school. If you were not actively involved yourself, did you know anyone who was? Looking back, do you think that winning was unduly emphasized? What value was placed on having a good time? On learning to get along with others? On developing athletic skills and confidence?

Children Need to Play, Not Compete

Jessica Statsky

Over the past three decades, organized sports for children have increased dramatically in the United States. And though many adults regard Little League Baseball and Peewee Football as a basic part of childhood, the games are not always joyous ones. When overzealous parents and coaches impose adult standards on children's sports, the result can be activities that are neither satisfying nor beneficial to children.

I am concerned about all organized sports activities for children between the ages of six and twelve. The damage I see results from noncontact as well as contact sports, from sports organized locally as well as those organized nationally. Highly organized competitive sports such as Peewee Football and Little League Baseball are too often played to adult standards, which are developmentally inappropriate for children and can be both physically and psychologically harmful. Furthermore, because they eliminate many children from organized sports before they are ready to compete, they are actually counterproductive for developing either future players or fans. Finally, because they emphasize competition and winning, they unfortunately provide occasions for some parents and coaches to place their own fantasies and needs ahead of children's welfare.

One readily understandable danger of overly competitive sports is that they entice children into physical actions that are bad for growing bodies. Although the official Little League Web site acknowledges that children do risk injury playing baseball, they insist that severe injuries are infrequent, "far less than the risk of riding a skateboard, a bicycle, or even the school bus" ("What about My Child"). Nevertheless, Leonard Koppett in *Sports Illusion, Sports Reality* claims that a twelve-year-old trying to throw a curve ball, for example, may put abnormal strain on developing arm and shoulder muscles, sometimes resulting in lifelong injuries (294). Contact sports like football can be even more hazardous. Thomas Tutko, a psychology professor at San Jose State University and coauthor of the book *Winning Is Everything and Other American Myths,* writes:

> I am strongly opposed to young kids playing tackle football. It is not the right stage of development for them to be taught to crash into other kids. Kids under the age of fourteen are not by nature physical. Their main concern is self-preservation. They don't want to meet head on and slam into each other. But tackle football absolutely requires that they try to hit each other as hard as they can. And it is too traumatic for young kids. (qtd. in Tosches A1)

As Tutko indicates, even when children are not injured, fear of being hurt detracts from their enjoyment of the sport. Little League Online ranks fear of injury as the seventh of seven reasons children quit ("What about My Child"). One mother of an eight-year-old

Peewee Football player explained, "The kids get so scared. They get hit once and they don't want anything to do with football anymore. They'll sit on the bench and pretend their leg hurts . . ." (qtd. in Tosches A1). Some children are driven to even more desperate measures. For example, in one Peewee Football game, a reporter watched the following scene as a player took himself out of the game:

> "Coach, my tummy hurts. I can't play," he said. The coach told the player to get back onto the field. "There's nothing wrong with your stomach," he said. When the coach turned his head the seven-year-old stuck a finger down his throat and made himself vomit. When the coach turned back, the boy pointed to the ground and told him, "Yes there is, coach. See?" (Tosches A33)

Besides physical hazards and anxieties, competitive sports pose psychological dangers for children. Martin Rablovsky, a former sports editor for the *New York Times,* says that in all his years of watching young children play organized sports, he has noticed very few of them smiling. "I've seen children enjoying a spontaneous pre-practice scrimmage become somber and serious when the coach's whistle blows," Rablovsky says. "The spirit of play suddenly disappears, and sport becomes joblike" (qtd. in Coakley 94). The primary goal of a professional athlete—winning—is not appropriate for children. Their goals should be having fun, learning, and being with friends. Although winning does add to the fun, too many adults lose sight of what matters and make winning the most important goal. Several studies have shown that when children are asked whether they would rather be warming the bench on a winning team or playing regularly on a losing team, about 90 percent choose the latter (Smith, Smith, and Smoll 11). 5

Winning and losing may be an inevitable part of adult life, but they should not be part of childhood. Too much competition too early in life can affect a child's development. Children are easily influenced, and when they sense that their competence and worth are based on their ability to live up to their parents' and coaches' high expectations— and on their ability to win—they can become discouraged and depressed. Little League advises parents to "keep winning in perspective" (Little League Online, "Your Role"), noting that the most common reasons children give for quitting, aside from change in interest, are lack of playing time, failure and fear of failure, disapproval by significant others, and psychological stress (Little League Online, "What about My Child"). According to Dr. Glyn C. Roberts, a professor of kinesiology at the Institute of Child Behavior and Development at the University of Illinois, 80 to 90 percent of children who play competitive sports at a young age drop out by sixteen (Kutner C8). 6

This statistic illustrates another reason I oppose competitive sports for children: because they are so highly selective, very few children get to participate. Far too soon, a few children are singled out for their athletic promise, while many others, who may be on the verge of developing the necessary strength and ability, are screened out and discouraged from trying out again. Like adults, children fear failure, and so even those with good physical skills may stay away because they lack self-confidence. Consequently, teams lose many promising players who with some encouragement and experience might have become stars. The problem is that many parent-sponsored, out-of-school 7 programs give more importance to having a winning team than to developing children's physical skills and self-esteem.

Indeed, it is no secret that too often scorekeeping, league standings, and the drive to win bring out the worst in adults who are more absorbed in living out their own fantasies than in enhancing the quality of the experience for children (Smith, Smith, and Smoll 9). Recent newspaper articles on children's sports contain plenty of horror stories. *Los Angeles Times* reporter Rich Tosches, for example, tells the story of a brawl among seventy-five parents following a Peewee Football game (A33). As a result of the brawl, which began when a parent from one team confronted a player from the other team, the teams are now thinking of hiring security guards for future games. Another example is provided by an *L.A. Times* editorial about a Little League manager who intimidated the opposing team by setting fire to one of their team's jerseys on the pitching mound before the game began. As the editorial writer commented, the manager showed his young team that "intimidation could substitute for playing well" ("The Bad News" B6).

Although not all parents or coaches behave so inappropriately, the seriousness of the problem is illustrated by the fact that Adelphi University in Garden City, New York, offers a sports psychology workshop for Little League coaches, designed to balance their "animal instincts" with "educational theory" in hopes of reducing the "screaming and hollering," in the words of Harold Weisman, manager of sixteen Little Leagues in New York City (Schmitt B2). In a three-and-one-half-hour Sunday morning workshop, coaches learn how to make practices more fun, treat injuries, deal with irate parents, and be "more sensitive to their young players' fears, emotional frailties, and need for recognition." Little League is to be credited with recognizing the need for such workshops.

Some parents would no doubt argue that children cannot start too soon preparing to live in a competitive free-market economy. After all, secondary schools and colleges require students to compete for grades, and college admission is extremely competitive. And it is perfectly obvious how important competitive skills are in finding a job. Yet the ability to cooperate is also important for success in life. Before children are psychologically ready for competition, maybe we should emphasize cooperation and individual performance in team sports rather than winning.

Many people are ready for such an emphasis. In 1988, one New York Little League official who had attended the Adelphi workshop tried to ban scoring from six- to eight-year-olds' games—but parents wouldn't support him (Schmitt B2). An innovative children's sports program in New York City, City Sports for Kids, emphasizes fitness, self-esteem, and sportsmanship. In this program's basketball games, every member on a team plays at least two of six eight-minute periods. The basket is seven feet from the floor, rather than ten feet, and a player can score a point just by hitting the rim (Bloch C12). I believe this kind of local program should replace overly competitive programs like Peewee Football and Little League Baseball. As one coach explains, significant improvements can result from a few simple rule changes, such as including every player in the batting order and giving every player, regardless of age or ability, the opportunity to play at least four innings a game (Frank).

Authorities have clearly documented the excesses and dangers of many competitive sports programs for children. It would seem that few children benefit from these programs and that those who do would benefit even more from programs emphasizing fitness, cooperation, sportsmanship, and individual performance. Thirteen- and fourteen-year-olds may be eager for competition, but few younger children are. These younger children deserve sports programs designed specifically for their needs and abilities.   12

Works Cited

Bloch, Gordon B. "Thrill of Victory Is Secondary to Fun." *New York Times* 2 Apr. 1990, late ed.: C12.

"The Bad News Pyromaniacs?" Editorial. *Los Angeles Times* 16 June 1990: B6.

Coakley, Jay J. *Sport in Society: Issues and Controversies.* St. Louis: Mosby, 1982.

Frank, L. "Contributions from Parents and Coaches." CYB Message Board 8 July 1997, 14 May 1999 <http://members.aol.com/JohnHoelter/b-parent.html>.

Koppett, Leonard. *Sports Illusion, Sports Reality.* Boston: Houghton, 1981.

Kutner, Lawrence. "Athletics, through a Child's Eyes." *New York Times* 23 Mar. 1989, late ed.: C8.

Little League Online. "Your Role As a Little League Parent." Little League Baseball, Incorporated 1999. 30 June 1999 <http://www.littleleague.org/about/parents/yourrole.htm>.

———. "What about My Child." Little League Baseball, Incorporated 1999. 30 June 1999 <http://www.littleleague.org/about/parents/yourchild.htm>.

Schmitt, Eric. "Psychologists Take Seat on Little League Bench." *New York Times* 14 Mar. 1988, late ed.: B2.

Smith, Nathan, Ronald Smith, and Frank Smoll. *Kidsports: A Survival Guide for Parents.* Reading: Addison, 1983.

Tosches, Rich. "Peewee Football: Is It Time to Blow the Whistle?" *Los Angeles Times* 3 Dec. 1988: A1+.

Connecting to Culture and Experience: Competition versus Cooperation

Statsky makes the point that competition is highly valued in our culture, whereas cooperation tends to be downplayed. Discuss some of the ways in which our society encourages competition, especially among children and through sports or other forms of play. Consider also how cooperation is encouraged. Think about whether, in your own experience, the educational system has encouraged one more than the other.

Then expand your discussion to include the influence of cultural forces such as advertising, television, and movies. Which of the two, competition or cooperation, seems to be valued more highly in these areas? If you believe there is a cultural preference for competition or cooperation, reflect on who in society might benefit most from such a preference. Consider such factors as gender, age, ethnicity, class, and religion. Who loses most?

Analyzing Writing Strategies

1. **Anecdotes** can provide convincing support if they are clearly relevant to the point they support, believable, and vivid enough to enable readers to imagine what happened. In paragraph 4, Statsky presents one fully developed anecdote that includes dialogue and a detailed narrative. In paragraph 8, she offers two brief anecdotes that summarize rather than detail the events: one is about a brawl among parents and the other about a team manager who set fire to a jersey of the opposing team. Locate and reread these anecdotes in order to find out what each one contributes to Statsky's argument and to judge how convincing they are likely to be for her readers.

    For more on using anecdotes and authorities, see Chapter 19, pp. 629–32.

2. To support her argument, Statsky repeatedly quotes **authorities,** experts who agree with her position. Skim the essay, underlining each authority she cites. Note where she quotes whole sentences or individual words and phrases. Also try to determine where she summarizes the source instead of quoting it verbatim. Then pick one source you think adds something important to her argument, and briefly explain what it adds.

    For more on quoting and summarizing, see Chapter 22, pp. 693–701.

3. Read the Writer at Work section on pp. 283–85 to see how Statsky describes her prospective readers and anticipates opposing positions. Notice how she develops her **counterargument** with these readers in mind. Then review the essay to see how she incorporates counterargument into it. Has she left anything out or added anything new? Finally, how well do you think Statsky anticipates and responds to opposing arguments?

    For more on counterarguing, see Chapter 19, pp. 634–37.

Commentary: A Clear Position

Writers arguing a position must state their opinion clearly, but they also try not to overstate it. By avoiding absolute, unconditional language and carefully qualifying her position, Statsky makes clear her concerns without making enthusiasts overly defensive. Throughout the essay, she temporizes with words like *not always, can, maybe,* and *it would seem*—words that potentially have a major effect on readers, making Statsky's position seem reasonable without making her seem indecisive. Similarly, Statsky qualifies her position by focusing on a particular age group. To ensure that readers know the particular kind of sports she is talking about, she gives two familiar examples: Peewee Football and Little League Baseball.

For more on asserting a thesis, see Chapter 19, pp. 623–26.

Statsky's unambiguous **word choice** and appropriate **qualification** satisfy two of the three standards of an effective **thesis.** The third criterion, that the position be **arguable,** is indicated clearly in paragraph 2, where Statsky forecasts the three

For more on forecasting, see Chapter 13, p. 559.

reasons for opposing organized competitive sports for young children developed later in the essay:

Such sports are "physically and psychologically harmful" (developed in paragraphs 3–6)

They are "counterproductive for developing either future players or fans" (developed in paragraph 7)

They "emphasize competition and winning" (developed in paragraphs 8–9)

Inexperienced writers are sometimes reluctant to state their thesis and forecast their reasons as clearly and directly as Statsky does. They fear that being explicit would oversimplify or give away the whole argument. But we can see from Statsky's essay that the effectiveness of her argument is enhanced, not diminished, by her directness. Nor does explicitness prevent her from advancing a complex and thoughtful argument on an issue that is certain to arouse strong feelings in many readers.

Considering Topics for Your Own Essay

Make a list of issues related to childhood and adolescence. For example, should elementary and secondary schools be on a year-round schedule? Should children have the right to "divorce" their parents? Should adolescents who commit serious crimes be tried as adults? Then choose an issue that you think you could write about. What position would you take?

■ PURPOSE AND AUDIENCE

Purpose and audience are closely linked when you write an essay arguing a position. In defining your purpose, you also need to anticipate your readers. Most writers compose essays arguing for a position because they care deeply about the issue. As they develop an argument with their readers in mind, however, writers usually feel challenged to think critically about their own as well as their readers' feelings and thoughts about the issue.

Writers with strong convictions seek to influence their readers. Assuming that logical argument will prevail over prejudice, they try to change readers' minds by presenting compelling reasons and support based on shared values and principles. Nevertheless, they also recognize that in cases where disagreement is profound, it is highly unlikely that a single essay will be able to change readers' minds, no matter how well written it is. Addressing an audience that is completely opposed to their position, most writers are satisfied if they can simply win their readers' respect for their different point of view. Often, however, all that can be done is to sharpen the differences.

A Focused Presentation of the Issue

Writers use a variety of strategies to present the issue and prepare readers for their argument. For current, hotly debated issues, the title may be enough to identify the issue. Leshner, for example, frames the issue as a question ("Why Shouldn't Society Treat Substance Abusers?") and Estrada alludes to a familiar children's chant ("Sticks and Stones and Sports Team Names"). Leshner states explicitly that "people are polarized on the issue" and Statsky gives a brief history of the debate about competitive sports for children. Many writers provide concrete examples early on to make sure that readers can understand the issue. Statsky mentions Peewee Football and Little League Baseball as examples of the kind of organized sports she opposes. Leshner opens his essay with a hypothetical example, a scenario in which readers are asked to imagine a situation like the one he is writing about.

How writers present the issue depends on what they assume readers already know and what they want readers to think about the issue. Therefore, they try to define the issue in a way that promotes their position. Estrada defines the issue of naming sports teams after Native Americans in terms of how it affects individuals, especially children, rather than in terms of liberal or conservative politics. Similarly, Leshner presents the issue of treating drug addiction in terms of its practical impact on society.

A Clear Position

Very often writers declare their position in a thesis statement early in the essay. This strategy has the advantage of letting readers know right away where the writer stands. Statsky places her thesis in the opening paragraph, whereas Estrada, Leshner, and Nelson put it in the second paragraph. Moreover, they all restate the thesis at places in the argument where readers could lose sight of the central point. And they reiterate the thesis at the end.

In composing a thesis statement, writers try to make their position unambiguous, appropriately qualified, and clearly arguable. For example, to avoid ambiguity, Estrada uses common words like *wrong*. But because readers may differ on what they consider to be wrong, Estrada demonstrates exactly what he thinks is wrong about naming teams for ethnic groups. To show readers he shares their legitimate concerns about hypersensitivity, Estrada qualifies his thesis to apply only to "genuine cases of political insensitivity." Finally, to show that his position is not based solely on personal feelings, Estrada appeals to readers' common sense of right and wrong.

Plausible Reasons and Convincing Support

To argue for a position, writers must give reasons. Even in relatively brief essays, writers usually give more than one reason and make their reasons explicit. Leshner, for instance, supports treating drug addicts for four reasons:

doing so will improve lives, cut crime, reduce disease, and improve productivity.

Moreover, to make their reasons seem plausible to readers, writers try to logically connect each reason to the position it backs. This logical connection can be understood in terms of an "if . . . then" relationship. For example, if readers believe Leshner's argument that treatments for drug addiction are effective and that treating drug addicts will improve lives, cut crime, reduce disease, and enhance productivity, then readers will be more inclined to "rise above" their "moral outrage that addiction results from a voluntary behavior," as Leshner urges in the final paragraph. In other words, logic dictates that if the reason is true, then the position is also likely to be true. The truth of the reason, of course, depends on how convincing the support seems to individual readers.

Writers know they cannot simply assert their reasons. They must support them with examples, statistics, authorities, or anecdotes. We have seen all of these kinds of support used in this chapter. For instance, Statsky uses all of them in her essay—giving examples of common sports injuries children may incur, citing statistics indicating the percentage of children who prefer not to play on their team, quoting authorities on the physical and psychological hazards of competitive sports for young children, and relating an anecdote of a child vomiting to show the enormous psychological pressure competitive sports put on some children.

Anticipating Opposing Positions and Objections

Writers also try to anticipate other widely held positions on the issue as well as objections and questions readers might raise to their argument. The writers in this chapter counterargue by either accommodating or refuting opposing positions and objections. Estrada does both, implying that he shares his readers' objection to "political correctness," but arguing that naming sports teams after ethnic groups is a "genuine" case of "political insensitivity" and not an instance of "hypersensitivity."

Nelson takes up six different reasons often presented by opponents of Title IX gender equity requirements and devotes most of her argument to refuting them. For each, she first presents the opposing argument, summarizing and quoting what others have said or written. Then she counterargues briefly, often quoting an authority or citing statistics to undermine the argument.

Anticipating readers' positions and objections can enhance the writer's credibility and strengthen the argument. When readers holding an opposing position recognize that the writer takes their position seriously, they are more likely to listen to what the writer has to say. It can also reassure readers that they share certain important values and attitudes with the writer, building a bridge of common concerns among people who have been separated by difference and antagonism.

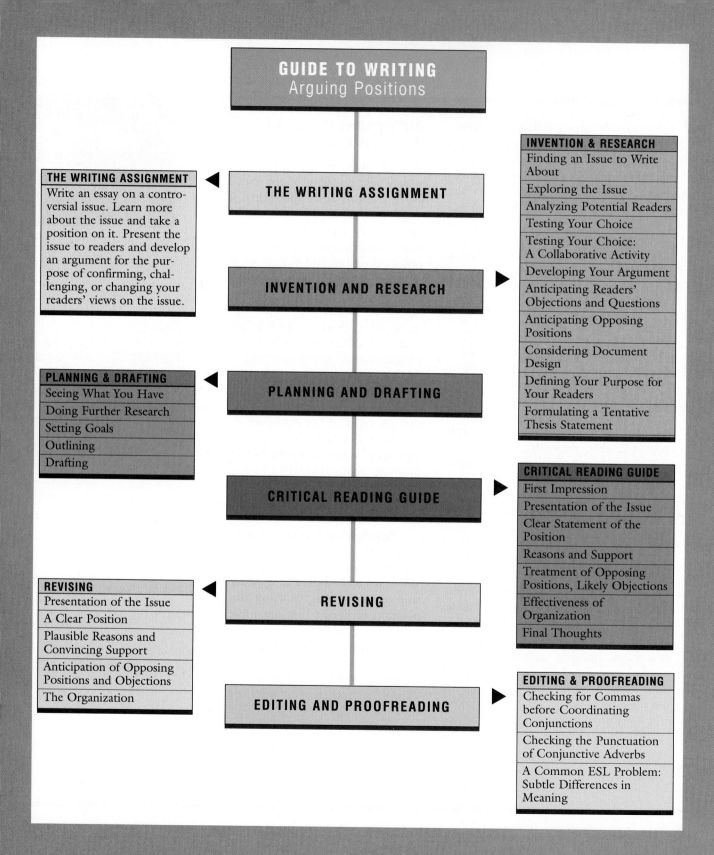

GUIDE TO WRITING
Arguing Positions

THE WRITING ASSIGNMENT

INVENTION AND RESEARCH

PLANNING AND DRAFTING

CRITICAL READING GUIDE

REVISING

EDITING AND PROOFREADING

THE WRITING ASSIGNMENT

Write an essay on a controversial issue. Learn more about the issue and take a position on it. Present the issue to readers and develop an argument for the purpose of confirming, challenging, or changing your readers' views on the issue.

PLANNING & DRAFTING

Seeing What You Have

Doing Further Research

Setting Goals

Outlining

Drafting

REVISING

Presentation of the Issue

A Clear Position

Plausible Reasons and Convincing Support

Anticipation of Opposing Positions and Objections

The Organization

INVENTION & RESEARCH

Finding an Issue to Write About

Exploring the Issue

Analyzing Potential Readers

Testing Your Choice

Testing Your Choice: A Collaborative Activity

Developing Your Argument

Anticipating Readers' Objections and Questions

Anticipating Opposing Positions

Considering Document Design

Defining Your Purpose for Your Readers

Formulating a Tentative Thesis Statement

CRITICAL READING GUIDE

First Impression

Presentation of the Issue

Clear Statement of the Position

Reasons and Support

Treatment of Opposing Positions, Likely Objections

Effectiveness of Organization

Final Thoughts

EDITING & PROOFREADING

Checking for Commas before Coordinating Conjunctions

Checking the Punctuation of Conjunctive Adverbs

A Common ESL Problem: Subtle Differences in Meaning

THE WRITING ASSIGNMENT

Write an essay on a controversial issue. Learn more about the issue and take a position on it. Present the issue to readers and develop an argument for the purpose of confirming, challenging, or changing your readers' views on the issue.

INVENTION AND RESEARCH

The following activities will help you find an issue, explore what you know about it, and do any necessary research to develop an argument and counterargument. Each activity is easy to do and in most cases takes only a few minutes. Spreading the activities over several days will help you think critically about your own as well as other people's positions on the issue. Keep a written record of your invention and research to use when you draft and revise your essay.

Finding an Issue to Write About

To find the best possible issue for your essay, list as many possibilities as you can. The following activities will help you make a good choice.

Listing Issues.   *Make a list of issues you might consider writing about.* Begin your list now, and add to it over the next few days. Include issues on which you already have a position and ones you do not know much about but would like to explore further. Do not overlook the issues suggested by the Considering Topics for Your Own Essay activities following each reading in this chapter.

Put the issues in the form of questions, like the following examples:

- Should local school boards be allowed to ban books (like *The Adventures of Huckleberry Finn* and *Of Mice and Men*) from school libraries?
- Should teenagers be required to get their parents' permission to obtain birth-control information and contraceptives?
- Should public libraries and schools be allowed to block access to selected Internet sites?
- Should undercover police officers be permitted to pose as high school students in order to identify sellers and users of drugs?
- Should training in music performance or art (drawing, painting, sculpting) be required of all high school students?
- Should college admission be based solely on academic achievement in high school?

- Should colleges be required to provide child-care facilities for children of students taking classes?
- Should students attending public colleges be required to pay higher tuition fees if they do not graduate within four years?
- Should sports officials rely on instant replay to settle disputed calls?
- Should elected state or national representatives vote primarily on the basis of their individual conscience, their constituents' interests, or the general welfare?
- Should scientists attempt to clone human beings as they have done with animals?

Listing Issues Related to Identity and Community. As the following suggestions indicate, many controversial issues will enable you to explore your understanding of identity and community. List issues that interest you.

- Can self-esteem be increased by workshops or counseling?
- Should students choose a college or courses that would confirm or challenge their beliefs and values?
- Should our schools continue to emphasize the history, philosophy, literature, and art of western European civilization, or should they give equal time to other cultural traditions (such as Native American, African, Asian, and Latin) that contribute to American civilization?
- Should high schools or colleges require students to perform community service as a condition for graduation?
- Should children of immigrants who do not speak English be taught in their native language while they are learning English?
- Should all materials related to voting, driving, and income-tax reporting be written only in English or in other languages read by members of the community?
- Should the racial, ethnic, or gender makeup of a police force parallel the makeup of the community it serves?

Listing Issues Related to Work and Career. Many current controversial issues will allow you to explore work and career topics. Identify issues that you would consider writing about.

- Should businesses remain loyal to their communities, or should they move to wherever labor costs, taxes, or other conditions are more favorable?
- Should companies be free to replace workers who go on strike for better wages or working conditions, or should they be required to negotiate with workers?
- When they choose careers, should people look primarily for jobs that are well paid or for jobs that are personally fulfilling, morally correct, or socially responsible?
- Should the state or federal government provide job training, temporary employment, or financial aid to people who are unemployed and willing to work?

- Should the primary purpose of a college education be job training?
- Should drug testing be mandatory for people in high-risk jobs such as bus drivers, heavy-equipment operators, and airplane pilots?

Choosing an Interesting Issue. *Select an issue from your list that you think would be interesting to explore further.* You may already have an opinion on the issue or you may have chosen it because you want to learn more about it.

Your choice may be influenced by whether you have time for research or whether your instructor requires you to do research. Issues that have been written about extensively make excellent topics for extended research projects. In contrast, you may feel confident writing about a local community or campus issue without doing much, if any, research. It also may help you in choosing an issue to identify your readers tentatively and to think about the kinds of arguments people usually make when debating the issue.

Exploring the Issue

To explore the issue, you need to define it, determine whether you need to do research, and decide tentatively on your position.

Defining the Issue. *To begin thinking about the issue, write for a few minutes explaining how you currently understand it.* If you have strong feelings about the issue, briefly explain why, but do not present your argument at this time. Focus on clarifying the issue by considering questions like these:

- Who has taken a position on this issue, and what positions have they taken?
- How does the issue affect different groups of people? What is at stake for them?
- What is the issue's history? How long has it been an issue? Has it changed over time? What makes it important now?
- How broad is the issue? What other issues are related to it? In what category (or categories) might the issue fit?

Doing Research. *If you do not know very much about the issue or the different views people have taken on it, do some research before continuing.* You can gather information by talking to others and by reading what others have written.

If you do not have time for research and lack confidence in your knowledge of the issue, you should switch to another issue about which you are better informed. Return to your list of possible issues and start over.

Exploring Your Opinion. *Write for a few minutes exploring your current thinking on the issue.* What is your current position? Why do you hold this position? What other positions on the issue do you know about? As you develop your argument and learn

Refer to Chapter 20 for advice on interviewing an expert or surveying opinion and to Chapter 21 for guidelines on doing library and Internet research.

more about the issue, you may change your mind. Your aim now is merely to record your thinking as of this moment.

Analyzing Potential Readers

Write several sentences describing the readers to whom you will be addressing your argument. Begin by briefly identifying your readers; then use the following questions to help you describe them.

- What position or positions will my readers take on this issue? How entrenched are these positions likely to be?

- What do my readers know about the issue? In what contexts are they likely to have encountered it? In what ways might the issue affect them personally or professionally?

- How far apart on the issue are my readers and I likely to be? What fundamental differences in worldview or experience might keep us from agreeing? Which of my readers' values might most influence their view of the issue?

- Why would I want to present my argument to these particular readers? What could I realistically hope to achieve—convincing them to adopt my point of view, getting them to reconsider their own position, confirming or challenging some of their underlying beliefs and values?

Testing Your Choice

Decide whether you should proceed with this particular issue. Review your invention notes to see whether you understand the issue well enough to continue working with it and whether you can feel confident that you will be able to construct a convincing argument for your prospective readers. To make these decisions, ask yourself the following questions:

- Have I begun to understand the issue and my own position well enough to begin constructing a well-reasoned, well-supported argument?

- Do I have a good enough sense of how my readers view this issue to begin formulating an argument that is appropriate for them?

- Do I now know enough about the issue or can I learn what I need to know in the time I have remaining?

If you cannot answer these questions affirmatively at this point in the process, it might be wise to consider a different issue. Giving up on a topic after you have worked on it is bound to be frustrating, but if you have little interest in the issue and do not have any idea how you could address your readers, starting over may be the wisest course of action. The following collaborative activity may help you decide whether to go on with this issue or begin looking for an alternative.

At this point in your invention work, you will find it helpful to get together with two or three other students to try out a bit of your argument. Their reactions will help you determine whether you will be able to construct a convincing argument for your position.

Arguers: Take turns briefly providing the context—the issue, purpose and readers, and your position—followed by one reason for your position. Choose a reason you think will carry weight with your readers and explain why you think so.

Listeners: Briefly tell each arguer how you think the intended readers are likely to respond to the reason. Also try to help the arguer by suggesting one way in which the reason could be made stronger—for example, by providing a clearer explanation of why readers should accept the position if they think the reason is plausible. Suggest an example, anecdote, or authority the writer could use to support the reason. If you think the reason is weak, explain the objections readers could raise.

Developing Your Argument

To construct a convincing argument, you need to list reasons for your position, choose the most plausible ones, and support them.

Listing Reasons. *Write down every reason you can think of to convince readers of your position.* Try stating your reasons as part of a tentative thesis statement with *because* or *that* clauses, as in "My position is X because . . ." or "A reason I believe X is that . . . ."

Choosing the Most Plausible Reasons. *Write several sentences on each reason to determine which reasons are most plausible; then identify your most plausible reasons.* To test the plausibility of your reasons, try to explain the logical *(if . . . then)* connection between each reason and your position. For each reason, draft a brief answer to this question: "Why do I think that *if* my readers accept this reason, *then* they also would accept my position?" If you decide that none of your reasons seems very plausible, you might need to reconsider your position, do some more research, or choose another issue.

Anticipating Readers' Objections and Questions

Listing Your Most Plausible Reasons. Review the choices you made at the end of the preceding activity and list your two or three most plausible reasons, skipping a few lines between the reasons.

Listing Objections and Questions.   *Under each reason, list one or more objections or questions that readers could raise.* You may know how readers will respond to some of your reasons. For others, you may need to be inventive. Imagining yourself as a critical reader, look for places where your argument is vulnerable to criticism. For example, think of an assumption you are making that others might not accept or a value others might not share. Imagine how people in different situations—different neighborhoods, occupations, age groups, living arrangements—might react to your argument.

Accommodating a Legitimate Objection or Question.   *Choose one objection or question that makes sense to you and write for a few minutes on how you could accommodate it into your argument.* You may be able simply to acknowledge an objection or answer a question and explain why you think it does not negatively affect your argument. If the criticism is more serious, try not to let it shake your confidence. Instead, consider how you can accommodate it, perhaps by conceding the point and qualifying your position or changing the way you argue for it.

If the criticism is so damaging that you cannot accommodate it into your argument, however, you may need to rethink your position or even consider writing on a different issue. If you arrive at such an impasse, discuss the problem with your instructor; do not abandon your issue unless it is absolutely necessary.

Refuting an Illegitimate Objection or Question.   *Choose one objection or question that you do not accept to try to refute, and write for a few minutes planning your response.* Do not choose to refute only the weakest objection (sometimes called a *straw man*) while ignoring the strongest one. Consider whether you can show that an objection is based on a misunderstanding or that it does not really damage your argument.

Anticipating Opposing Positions

Now that you have planned your argument, you need to consider how you can respond to the arguments for other positions on the issue.

Considering Other Positions.   *Identify one or more widely held positions other than your own that people take on the issue.* If you can, identify the individuals or groups who support the positions you list.

Listing Reasons for the Opposing Position.   *Choose the opposing position you think is likely to be most attractive to your readers (there may only be one), and list the reasons people give for it.* Given what you now know, try to represent the argument accurately and fairly. Later, you may need to do some research to find out more about this opposing position.

Accommodating a Plausible Reason.   *Choose* one *reason that makes sense to you and write for a few minutes on how you could accommodate it into your argument.* Consider whether you can concede the point and put it aside as not really damaging to your central argument. You may also have to consider qualifying your position or changing the way you argue for it.

Refuting an Implausible Reason.   *Choose one reason that you do not accept and write for a few minutes on how you will plan your refutation.* Do not choose to refute a position no one really takes seriously. Also be careful not to misrepresent other people's positions or to criticize people personally (sometimes called an *ad hominem* attack). Do try to get at the heart of your disagreement.

You may want to argue that the values on which the opposing argument is based are not widely shared or are just plain wrong. Or perhaps you can point out that the reasoning is flawed (for instance, showing that an example applies only to certain people in certain situations and cannot be generalized). Or maybe you can show that the argument lacks convincing support (for instance, that the opposition's statistics can be interpreted differently or that quoted authorities do not qualify as experts). If you do not have all the information you need, make a note of what you need and where you might find it. Later, you can do more research to develop this part of your argument.

Considering Document Design

Think about whether including visual or audio elements—cartoons, photographs, tables, graphs, or snippets from films, television programs, or songs—would strengthen your argument. These are not a requirement of an effective essay arguing a position, but could be helpful. Consider also whether your readers might benefit from design features such as headings, bulleted or numbered lists, or other elements that would make your essay easier to follow. You could construct your own graphic elements, download materials from the Internet, copy images and sounds from television or other sources, or scan into your document visuals from books and magazines; if you do so, be sure to acknowledge your sources.

Defining Your Purpose for Your Readers

Write a few sentences, defining your purpose in writing about your position on this issue for your particular readers. Remember that you already have analyzed your potential readers and developed your argument with these readers in mind. Given these readers, try now to define your purpose by considering the following possibilities and any others that might apply to your writing situation:

- If my readers are likely to be sympathetic to my point of view, what do I hope to achieve—give them reasons to commit to my position, arm them with ammunition to make their own arguments, or win their respect and admiration?

- If my readers are likely to be hostile to my point of view, what do I hope to accomplish—get them to concede that other points of view must be taken seriously, make them defend their reasons, show them how knowledgeable and committed I am to my position, or show them how well I can argue?

- If my readers are likely to take an opposing position but are not staunchly committed to it, what should I try to do—make them think critically about the reasons and the kinds of support they have for their position, give them reasons to change their minds, show them how my position serves their interests better, appeal to their values and sense of responsibility, or disabuse them of their preconceptions and prejudices against my position?

Formulating a Tentative Thesis Statement

Write several sentences that could serve as a thesis statement. Assert your position carefully. You might also forecast your reasons, listing them in the order in which you will take them up in your argument. In other words, draft a thesis statement that tells your readers simply and directly what you want them to think about the issue and why.

Estrada states his thesis at the end of the second paragraph: "Still, however willing I may have been to go along with the name as a kid, as an adult I have concluded that using an ethnic group essentially as a sports mascot is wrong." Leshner states his thesis and forecasts his argument in the second paragraph: "Addicts are frequently denied treatment that would not only improve their lives, but also would improve our own lives—by cutting crime, reducing disease and improving the productivity of employees and the economy."

Perhaps the most explicit and fully developed thesis statement in this chapter's readings is Jessica Statsky's. She asserts her thesis at the end of the first paragraph and then qualifies it and forecasts her reasons in the second paragraph:

> . . . When overzealous parents and coaches impose adult standards on children's sports, the result can be activities that are neither satisfying nor beneficial to children.
>
> I am concerned about all organized sports activities for children between the ages of six and twelve. The damage I see results from noncontact as well as contact sports, from sports organized locally as well as those organized nationally. Highly organized competitive sports such as Peewee Football and Little League Baseball are too often played to adult standards, which are developmentally inappropriate for children and can be both physically and psychologically harmful. Furthermore, because they eliminate many children from organized sports before they are ready to compete, they are actually counterproductive for developing either future players or fans. Finally, because they emphasize competition and winning, they unfortunately provide occasions for some parents and coaches to place their own fantasies and needs ahead of children's welfare.

As you formulate your own tentative thesis statement, pay attention to the language you use. It should be clear and unambiguous, emphatic but appropriately qualified, as well as arguable and based on plausible reasons. Although you will most probably refine this thesis statement as you work on your essay, trying now to articulate it will help give your planning and drafting direction and impetus.

■ PLANNING AND DRAFTING

You should now review what you have learned about the issue, do further research if necessary, and plan your first draft by setting goals and making an outline.

Seeing What You Have

Pause now to reflect on your invention and research notes. Reread everything carefully in order to decide whether you have enough plausible reasons and convincing support to offer readers and whether you understand the debate well enough to anticipate and respond to your readers' likely objections.

If your invention notes are skimpy, you may not have given enough thought to the issue or know enough at this time to write a convincing argument about it. You can do further research at this stage or begin drafting and later do research to fill in the blanks.

If you fear that you are in over your head, consult your instructor to determine whether you should make a radical change. For example, your instructor might suggest that you tackle a smaller, more doable aspect of the issue, perhaps one with which you have firsthand experience. It is also possible that your instructor will advise you to give up on this topic for the time being and to try writing on a different issue.

Doing Further Research

If you think you lack crucial information you will need to plan and draft your essay, this is a good time to do some further research. Consider possible sources, including people you could interview as well as library materials and Internet sites. Then do your research, making sure to note down all the information you will need to cite your sources.

For help with research, see Chapters 20–22.

Setting Goals

Before you begin writing your draft, consider some specific goals for your essay. The draft will not only be easier to write if you have some clear goals in mind, but also more focused. The following questions will help you set goals. You may find it useful to return to them while you are drafting, for they are designed to help you look at specific features and strategies of an essay arguing a position on a controversial issue.

Your Purpose and Readers

- Who are my readers and what can I realistically hope to accomplish by addressing them?
- Should I write primarily to change readers' minds, to get them to consider my arguments seriously, to confirm their opinions, to urge them to do something about the issue, or for some other purpose?

- How can I present myself so that my readers will consider me informed, knowledgeable, and fair?

The Beginning

- What opening would capture readers' attention? Should I begin as if I were telling a story, with phrases like "When I was" (Estrada), "In the early 1990s" (Nelson), or "Over the past three decades" (Statsky)? Should I open with rhetorical questions, as Leshner does? Should I start with an arresting quotation or surprising statistic?
- Should I make clear at the outset exactly what my concerns are and how I see the issue, as Statsky does?

Presentation of the Issue

- Should I place the issue in a historical context, as Nelson does, or in a personal context, as Estrada does?
- Should I use examples—real or hypothetical—to make the issue concrete for readers, as Leshner does?
- Should I try to demonstrate that the issue is important by citing statistics, quoting authorities, or describing its negative effects, as Statsky does?

Your Argument and Counterargument

- How can I present my reasons so that readers will see them as plausible, leading logically to my position? Should I assume readers will see the connection, as Leshner does, or do I need to spell it out for them, as Estrada does?
- If I have more than one reason, how should I sequence them?
- Should I forecast my reasons early in the essay, as Leshner and Statsky do?
- Which objections should I anticipate? Can I concede any objections without undermining my argument, as Estrada does?
- Which opposing positions should I anticipate?
- How can I support my counterargument? Should I cite authorities and statistics, as Nelson does, or use an anecdote, as Estrada does?

The Ending

- How can I conclude my argument effectively? Should I reiterate my thesis?
- Should I try to unite readers with different allegiances by reminding them of values we share, as Estrada and Leshner do?
- Could I conclude by looking to the future or by urging readers to take action or make changes, as Statsky does?

Outlining

An essay arguing a position on a controversial issue contains as many as four basic parts:

1. Presentation of the issue
2. A clear position
3. Reasons and support
4. Anticipating opposing positions and objections

These parts can be organized in various ways. If you expect some of your readers to oppose your argument, you might try to redefine the issue so that these readers can see the possibility that they may share some common values with you after all. To reinforce your connection to readers, you could go on to concede the wisdom of some aspect of their position before presenting the reasons and support for your position. You would conclude by reiterating the shared values upon which you hope to build agreement. In this case, an outline might look like this:

Presentation of the issue

Concession of some aspect of an opposing position

Thesis statement

First reason with support

Second reason with support (etc.)

Conclusion

If you have decided to write primarily for readers who agree rather than disagree with you, then you might choose to organize your argument as a refutation of opposing arguments in order to strengthen your readers' convictions. Begin by presenting the issue, stating your position, and reminding readers of your most plausible reasons. Then take up each opposing argument and try to refute it. You might conclude by calling your supporters to arms. Here's an outline showing what this kind of essay might look like:

Presentation of the issue

Thesis statement

Your most plausible reasons

First opposing argument with refutation

Second opposing argument with refutation

Conclusion

There are, of course, many other possible ways to organize an essay arguing for a position on a controversial issue, but these outlines should help you start planning your own essay.

Drafting

You may want to review the general advice on drafting in Chapter 1, pp. 16–17.

As you draft, keep in mind your goals and the following tips for writing a position paper:

- Accept the burden of proof by offering specific and credible support for your argument and counterargument.

- Remember that the basis for disagreement about controversial issues often depends on values as much as on credible support. Try to think critically about the values underlying your own as well as others' views so that your argument can take these values into account.

- Consider the tone of your argument and how you want to come across to readers.

- Remember that your outline is just a plan. Writers often make discoveries and reorganize as they draft. Be flexible.

- If you run into a problem as you draft, see whether any of your invention writing can help you solve it or whether it would help to return to one of the invention activities earlier in this chapter.

- If, as you draft, you find that you need more information, just make a note of what you have to find out and go on to the next point. When you are done drafting, you can go in search of the information you need.

CRITICAL READING GUIDE

Now is the time to get a good critical reading of your draft. Your instructor may arrange such a reading as part of your coursework; if not, you can ask a classmate, friend, or family member to read it over. If your campus has a writing center, you might ask a tutor there to read and comment on your draft using this guide to critical reading. (If you are unable to have someone else review your draft, turn ahead to the Revising section for help reading your own draft with a critical eye.)

▶ **If You Are the Writer.** To provide focused, helpful comments, your critical reader must know your essay's intended audience, your purpose, and a problem in the draft that you need help solving. Briefly write out this information at the top of your draft.

- *Readers.* To whom are you directing your argument? What do you assume they think about this issue? Do you expect them to be receptive, skeptical, resistant, antagonistic?

- *Purpose.* What effect do you realistically expect your argument to have on these particular readers?

- *Problem.* Ask your reader to help you solve the single most important problem you see in your draft. Describe this problem briefly.

▶ **If You Are the Reader.**   Use the following guidelines to help you give constructive, critical comments to others on their position papers.

1. *Read for a First Impression.* Tell the writer what you think the intended readers would find most and least convincing. If you personally think the argument is seriously flawed, share your thoughts. Then try to help the writer improve the argument for the designated readers.

   Next, consider the problem the writer identified. If the problem will be covered by one of the other items below, deal with it there. Otherwise, respond to the writer's concerns now.

2. *Analyze the Way the Issue Is Presented.* Look at the way the issue is presented and indicate if you think most readers would understand the issue differently. If you think that readers would need more information to grasp the issue and appreciate its importance, ask questions to help the writer fill in whatever is missing.

3. *Assess Whether the Position Is Stated Clearly.* Write a sentence or two summarizing the writer's position as you understand it from reading the draft. Then underline the sentence or sentences in the draft where the thesis is stated explicitly. (It may be restated in several places.) If you cannot find an explicit statement of the thesis, let the writer know. Given the writer's purpose and audience, consider whether the thesis statement is too strident or too timid and whether it needs to be better qualified, more sharply focused, or asserted more confidently. If you think that the thesis, as presented, is not really arguable — for example, if it asserts a fact no one questions or a matter of personal belief — let the writer know.

4. *Evaluate the Reasons and Support.* Underline the reasons. Tell the writer if you think any important reasons have been left out or any weak ones overemphasized. Indicate any contradictions or gaps in the argument. Point to any reasons that do not seem plausible to you, and briefly explain why. Then note any places where support is lacking or unconvincing. Help the writer think of additional support or suggest sources where more or better support might be found.

5. *Assess How Well Opposing Positions and Likely Objections Have Been Handled.* Find where opposing arguments or objections are mentioned and identify them in the margin. Consider whether the writer has ignored any important arguments or objections. Point to any places where the refutation could be strengthened or where shared assumptions or values offer the potential for concession.

6. *Consider Whether the Organization Is Effective.* Get an overview of the essay's organization and point out any places where more explicit cueing—

transitions, summaries, or topic sentences—would clarify the relationship between parts of the essay.

- Reread the *beginning*. Let the writer know if you think readers will find it engaging. If not, see if you can recommend something from later in the essay that might work as a better opening.
- Study the *ending*. Does the essay conclude decisively and memorably? If not, suggest an alternative. Could something be moved to the end?
- Assess the *design features*. Comment on the contribution of any headings, tables, cartoons, or other design features that may have been included. Help the writer think of additional design features that could make a contribution to the essay.

7. *Give the Writer Your Final Thoughts.* What is this draft's strongest part? What part is most in need of further work?

◼ REVISING

Now you are ready to revise your essay. Your instructor or other students may have given you advice on improving your draft. Nevertheless, you may have begun to realize that your draft requires not so much revising as rethinking. For example, you may recognize that your reasons do not lead readers to accept your position, that you cannot adequately support your reasons, or that you have been unable to refute damaging objections to your argument. Consequently, instead of working to improve parts of the draft, you may need to write a new draft that radically reenvisions your argument. It is not unusual for students—and professional writers—to find themselves in this situation. Learning to make radical revisions is a valuable lesson for all writers.

On the other hand, you may feel quite satisfied that your draft achieves most, if not all, of your goals. In that case, you can focus on refining specific parts of your draft. Very likely you have thought of ways of improving your draft, and you may even have begun improving it. This section will help you get an overview of your draft and revise it accordingly.

Getting an Overview

Consider your draft as a whole, following these two steps:

1. *Reread.* If at all possible, put the draft aside for a day or two before rereading it. When you return to it, start by reconsidering your purpose. Then read the draft straight through, trying to see it as your intended readers will.

2. *Outline.* Make a scratch outline, indicating the basic features as they appear in the draft.

For more on scratch outlining, see Chapter 12, pp. 540–41.

Charting a Plan for Revision.   Once you have an overview of your draft, you may want to make a two-column chart like the following one to keep track of the work you need to do as you revise. In the left-hand column, list the basic features of position papers. As you analyze your draft and study any comments from other readers, use the right-hand column for noting problems you need to solve. (If making a chart on the computer is difficult, simply list the basic features and under each heading, list the problems to solve.)

Basic Features	*Problems to Solve*
The issue	
Position	
Reasons and support	
Opposing arguments or objections	

Analyzing the Basic Features of Your Own Draft.   Using the questions presented in the Critical Reading Guide on the preceding pages, reread your draft to identify specific problems you need to solve. Note the problems on your revision chart.

Studying Critical Comments.   Review all of the comments you have received from other readers, and add to the chart any suggestions you intend to act on. For each comment, look at the draft to see what might have led the reader to make that particular point. Try to be receptive to any criticism. By letting you see how other readers respond to your draft, these comments provide valuable information about how you might improve it.

Carrying Out Revisions

Having identified problems in your draft, you now need to come up with solutions and—most important—to carry them out. Basically, you have three ways of finding solutions:

1. Review your invention and planning notes for information and ideas to add to your draft.

2. Do additional invention and research to provide material you or your readers think is needed.

3. Look back at the readings in this chapter to see how other writers have solved similar problems.

The following suggestions, which are organized according to the basic features on your revision chart, will help you get started solving some common writing problems in position papers.

Presentation of the Issue

- ***Do readers have difficulty summarizing the issue or do they see it differently than you do?*** Try to anticipate possible misunderstandings or other ways of seeing the issue.

- ***Do readers need more information?*** Consider adding examples, quoting authorities, or simply explaining the issue further.

- ***Does the issue strike readers as unimportant?*** State explicitly why you think it is important and why you think your readers should think so, too. Try to provide an anecdote, facts, or a quote from an authority that would demonstrate its importance.

A Clear Position

- ***Do readers have difficulty summarizing your position or finding your thesis statement?*** You may need to announce your thesis statement more explicitly or rewrite it to prevent misunderstanding.

- ***Do any words seem unclear or ambiguous?*** Use other words, explain what you mean, or add an example to make your position more concrete.

- ***Do you appear to be taking a position that is not really arguable?*** Consider whether your position is arguable. If you believe in your position as a matter of faith and cannot provide reasons and support, then your position probably is not arguable. Consult your instructor about changing your position or topic.

- ***Could you qualify your thesis to account for execeptions or strong objections to your argument?*** Add language that specifies when, where, under what conditions, or for whom your position applies.

Plausible Reasons and Convincing Support

For more on these cues for readers, see Chapter 13, pp. 559–63.

- ***Do readers have difficulty identifying your reasons?*** Announce each reason explicitly, possibly with **topic sentences.** Consider adding a **forecast** early in the essay so readers know what reasons to expect.

- ***Have you left out any reasons?*** Consider whether adding particular reasons would strengthen your argument. To fit in new reasons, you may have to reorganize your whole argument.

- ***Do any of your reasons seem implausible or contradictory?*** Either delete implausible reasons or show how they relate logically to your position or to your other reasons.

- ***Does your support seem unconvincing or scanty?*** Where necessary, explain why you think the support should lead readers to accept your position. Review your invention notes or do some more research to gather additional examples, statistics, anecdotes, or quotations from authorities.

Anticipation of Opposing Arguments or Objections

- *Do readers have difficulty finding your response to opposing arguments or objections?* Add transitions that call readers' attention to each response.

- *Do you ignore any important objections or arguments?* Consider adding to your response. Determine whether you should replace a response to a relatively weak objection with a new response to a more important one.

- *Are there any concessions you could make?* Consider whether you should acknowledge the legitimacy of readers' concerns or concede particular objections. Show on what points you share readers' values, even though you may disagree on other points.

- *Does your attempt at refutation seem unconvincing?* Try to strengthen it. Avoid attacking your opponents. Instead, provide solid support—respected authorities, accepted facts, and statistics from reputable sources—to convince readers that your argument is credible.

The Organization

- *Do readers have trouble following your argument?* Consider adding a brief forecast of your main reasons at the beginning of your essay and adding explicit topic sentences and transitions to announce each reason as it is developed.

- *Does the beginning seem vague and uninteresting?* Consider adding a striking anecdote or surprising quotation to open the essay or find something in the essay you could move to the beginning.

- *Does the ending seem indecisive or abrupt?* Search your invention notes for a strong quotation, or add language that will reach out to readers. Try moving your strongest point to the ending.

- *Can you add illustrations or any other design features to make the essay more interesting to read and to strengthen your argument?* Consider incorporating a visual you came across in your research or one you can create on your own.

▉ EDITING AND PROOFREADING

Now is the time to edit your revised draft for errors in grammar, punctuation, and mechanics and to consider matters of style. Our research has revealed several errors that are especially likely to occur in student essays arguing a position. The following guidelines will help you check and edit your draft for these common errors.

Checking for Commas before Coordinating Conjunctions. An independent clause is a group of words that can stand alone as a complete sentence. Writers often join two or more such clauses with coordinating conjunctions (*and, but, for, or, nor, so, yet*) in order to link related ideas in one sentence. Look at one example from Jessica Statsky's essay:

> Winning and losing may be an inevitable part of adult life, but they should not be part of childhood.

In this sentence, Statsky links two ideas: (1) that winning and losing may be part of adult life and (2) that they should not be part of childhood. In essays that argue a position, writers often join ideas in this way as they set forth the reasons and support for their positions.

When you join independent clauses, use a comma before the coordinating conjunction so that readers can easily see where one idea stops and the next one starts:

▶ The new immigration laws will bring in more skilled people, but their presence will take jobs away from other Americans.

▶ Sexually transmitted diseases are widespread, and many students are sexually active.

Do not use a comma when the coordinating conjunction joins phrases that are not independent clauses:

▶ Newspaper reports have visited pharmacies and observed pharmacists selling steroids illegally.

▶ We need people with special talents and diverse skills to make the United States a stronger nation.

Checking the Punctuation of Conjunctive Adverbs.   When writers take a position, the reasoning they need to employ seems to invite the use of conjunctive adverbs (*consequently, furthermore, however, moreover, therefore, thus*) to connect sentences and clauses. Conjunctive adverbs that open a sentence should be followed by a comma:

▶ Consequently, many local governments have banned smoking.

▶ Therefore, talented nurses will leave the profession because of poor working conditions and low salaries.

If a conjunctive adverb joins two independent clauses, it must be preceded by a semicolon and followed by a comma:

▶ The recent vote on increasing student fees produced a disappointing turnout; moreover, the presence of campaign literature on ballot tables violated voting procedures.

▶ Children watching television recognize violence but not its intention; thus, they become desensitized to violence.

Conjunctive adverbs that fall in the middle of an independent clause are set off with commas:

▶ Due to trade restrictions ⸴ however ⸴ sales of Japanese cars did not surpass sales of domestic cars.

A Common ESL Problem: Subtle Differences in Meaning. Because the distinctions in meaning among some common conjunctive adverbs are subtle, nonnative speakers often have difficulty using them accurately. For example, the difference between *however* and *nevertheless* is small; each is used to introduce statements that contrast with what precedes it. But *nevertheless* emphasizes the contrast, whereas *however* softens it. Check usage of such terms in an English dictionary rather than a bilingual one. *The American Heritage Dictionary of the English Language* has special usage notes to help distinguish frequently confused words.

A WRITER AT WORK

■ ANTICIPATING OBJECTIONS

In this section, we look at how Jessica Statsky tried to anticipate opposing positions and respond to them.

To understand Statsky's thinking about her possible counterargument, look first at the invention writing she did while analyzing her potential readers.

```
        I think I will write mainly to parents who are consider-
ing letting their children get involved in competitive sports
and to those whose children are already on teams and who don't
know about the possible dangers. Parents who are really into
competition and winning probably couldn't be swayed by my
arguments anyway. I don't know how to reach coaches (but
aren't they also parents?) or league organizers. I'll tell
parents some horror stories and present solid evidence from
psychologists that competitive sports can really harm children
under the age of twelve. I think they'll be impressed with
this scientific evidence.
        I share with parents one important value: the best inter-
ests of children. Competition really works against children's
best interests. Maybe parents' magazines (don't know of any
specific ones) publish essays like mine.
```

Notice that Statsky listed three potential groups of readers—parents, coaches, and league organizers. In her essay, she addressed concerns of coaches and organizers, but she focused primarily on parents. She divided parents into two camps: those new to organized sports and unaware of the adverse effects of competition, and those who are "really into" winning. Statsky decided against trying to change the minds of parents who place great value on winning. But, as you will see in the next excerpt from her invention writing, Statsky gave a lot of thought to the position these parents would likely favor.

Listing Reasons for the Opposing Position

Statsky lists the following reasons for the position that organized competitive sports teach young children valuable skills:

```
--Because competition teaches children how to succeed in later
  life
--Because competition--especially winning--is fun
--Because competition boosts children's self-esteem
--Because competition gives children an incentive to excel
```

This list appears to pose serious challenges to Statsky's argument, but she benefits considerably before she drafts her essay by facing up to the reasons her readers might give for opposing her position. By preparing this list, she gains insight into how she must develop her own argument in light of these predictable arguments, and she can begin thinking about which reasons she might accommodate and which she must refute. Her essay ultimately gains authority because she can demonstrate a good understanding of the opposing arguments that might be offered by her primary readers—parents who have not considered the dangers of competition for young children.

Accommodating a Plausible Reason

Looking over her list of reasons, Statsky decides that she can accommodate readers by conceding that competitive sports can sometimes be fun for children—at least for those who win. Here are her invention notes:

```
    It is true that children do sometimes enjoy getting
prizes and being recognized as winners in competitions adults
set up for them. I remember feeling very excited when our
sixth-grade relay team won a race at our school's sports day.
And I felt really good when I would occasionally win the candy
bar for being the last one standing in classroom spelling con-
tests. But when I think about these events, it's the activity
```

```
itself I remember as the main fun, not the winning. I think
I can concede that winning is exciting to six- to twelve-
year-olds, while arguing that it's not as important as adults
might think. I hope this will win me some friends among read-
ers who are undecided about my position.
```

We can see this accommodation in paragraph 5 of Statsky's revised essay (p. 256), where she concedes that sports should be fun. She quotes an authority who argues even fun is jeopardized when competition becomes intense.

Refuting an Implausible Reason

Statsky recognizes that she must attempt to refute the other objections in her list. She chooses one and tries out the following refutation to the first reason in her list:

```
        It irritates me that adults are so eager to make first
and second graders go into training for getting and keeping
jobs as adults. I don't see why the pressures on adults need
to be put on children. Anyway, both my parents tell me that
in their jobs, cooperation and teamwork are keys to success.
You can't get ahead unless you're effective in working with
others. Maybe we should be training children and even high
school and college students in the skills necessary for coop-
eration, rather than competition. Sports and physical activity
are important for children, but elementary schools should
emphasize achievement rather than competition--race against
the clock rather than against each other. Rewards could be
given for gains in speed or strength instead of for defeating
somebody in a competition.
```

This brief invention activity leads to the argument in paragraph 10 of the revised essay (p. 257), where Statsky acknowledges the importance of competition for success in school and work, but goes on to argue that cooperation is also important. To support this part of her argument, she gives examples in paragraph 11 of sports programs emphasizing cooperation over competition.

You can see from Statsky's revised essay that her refutation of this opposing argument runs through her entire essay. These invention activities advanced her thinking about her readers and purpose; they also brought an early, productive focus to her research on competition in children's sports.

In her essay arguing that the glass ceiling still exists for women in the corporate world (see the business course project described on p. 238), the student includes pie charts and a table comparing the percentages of women and men at the highest levels of corporate America. She decides to reinforce her written argument with the graphics because she believes her readers may have difficulty absorbing information from text that is densely packed with numerical data.

First, she considers downloading visuals from the Federal Glass Ceiling Commission Report (<http://www.ilr.cornell.edu/library /e_archive/glassceiling/Executive Summary .pdf>), but decides that its 1991 publication date makes its statistics out of date. Then, she tries the Catalyst Web site (<http://www .catalystwomen.org>) only to discover that she cannot access the report she's interested in without purchasing it. Eventually, she locates an article in *Business Week* (November 22, 1999) with several easy-to-read pie charts and tables.

She decides to include *Business Week*'s three pie charts showing the percentage of female and male corporate officers, corporate officers with line jobs, and top earners. The charts are simple because each compares only two items, women and men. But because she thinks the color helps readers easily distinguish between the two groups, she decides to make color photocopies at her local copy shop. Even though her essay acknowledges there has been some improvement in the representation of women in the corporate world, she keeps the title *Business Week* gave the charts because

STILL AN ALL BOY'S CLUB
HOW WOMEN AND MEN COMPARE IN THE 500 LARGEST COMPANIES, BY SALES*

■ WOMEN   ■ MEN

CORPORATE OFFICERS	CORPORATE OFFICERS WITH LINE JOBS	TOP EARNERS
12% / 88%	7% / 93%	3% / 97%
1,386 WOMEN 10,295 MEN	367 WOMEN 5,052 MEN	77 WOMEN 2,276 MEN

*AS OF MARCH 31, 1999   DATA: CATALYST

Now that you have read and discussed several essays that argue a position on a controversial issue and written one of your own, take some time to think critically about what you have learned. What problems did you encounter as you were writing your essay, and how did you solve them? How did reading other essays that argue a position influence your own essay? How does this type of writing reflect cultural attitudes about public debate and controversy?

it reinforces her own position: "Still an All Boy's Club."

The *Business Week* article features two tables: "Power Titles: Who Has Them" and "Women in Power: A Score Card." Although the student incorporates information from the first table into her written argument, she decides against reproducing the first table in her essay because the titles of corporate officers vary so much from one company to another as to be virtually meaningless. She does include the second table from the article, however, because she thinks her readers will be interested in knowing which companies have a high percentage of women officers.

Another reason the student finds the *Business Week* graphics appealing is that they indicate the actual numbers of women and men so that readers can see at a glance the relatively small numbers of women who have made it into the upper echelons.

WOMEN IN POWER: A SCORE CARD

The top 51* companies based on their percentages of women corporate officers

COMPANY	TOTAL WOMEN OFFICERS	TOTAL OFFICERS	PERCENT WOMEN OFFICERS	COMPANY	TOTAL WOMEN OFFICERS	TOTAL OFFICERS	PERCENT WOMEN OFFICERS
US WEST	6	14	42.9%	KELLY SERVICES	4	14	28.6%
PACIFICARE HEALTH SYSTEMS	15	35	42.9	NEW CENTURY ENERGIES	2	7	28.6
LINCOLN NATIONAL	6	14	42.9	HUMANA	6	22	27.3
AVON PRODUCTS	9	21	42.9	SBC COMMUNICATIONS	7	26	26.9
NORDSTROM	15	36	41.7	PNC BANK CORP.	4	15	26.7
FANNIE MAE	61	158	38.6	NEW YORK TIMES	5	19	26.3
WASHINGTON MUTUAL	3	8	37.5	TEXTRON	6	24	25.0
TIMES MIRROR	11	31	35.5	EDISON INTERNATIONAL	3	12	25.0
DAYTON HUDSON	8	23	34.8	GAP	5	20	25.0
VENATOR	8	23	34.8	WELLPOINT HEALTH NETWORKS	2	8	25.0
PAINEWEBBER GROUP	2	6	33.3	RALSTON PURINA	2	8	25.0
SOUTHWEST AIRLINES	8	24	33.3	SOLECTRON	2	8	25.0
BJ'S WHOLESALE CLUB	2	6	33.3	GPU	2	8	25.0
KNIGHT-RIDDER	8	24	33.3	BRUNSWICK	4	16	25.0
SLM HOLDING	4	12	33.3	BARNES & NOBLE	3	12	25.0
CARDINAL HEALTH	7	22	31.8	TRANS WORLD AIRLINES	5	21	23.8
MERCK	5	16	31.3	JOHN HANCOCK MUTUAL LIFE INS.	22	93	23.7
RYDER SYSTEM	5	16	31.3	SUPERVALU	4	17	23.5
MATTEL	5	16	31.3	SODEXHO MARRIOTT SERVICES	4	17	23.5
PITNEY BOWES	5	16	31.3	GANNETT	8	34	23.5
PHILIP MORRIS	4	13	30.8	PECO ENERGY	7	30	23.3
AMERITECH	10	33	30.3	CHASE MANHATTAN CORP.	6	26	23.1
CBS	3	10	30.0	COCA-COLA ENTERPRISES	6	26	23.1
TRANSAMERICA	6	20	30.0	UNICOM	3	13	23.1
HANNAFORD BROS.	8	27	29.6	3COM	12	52	23.1
ENRON	10	35	28.6				

*The list includes 51 companies because the last four companies are tied.

DATA FROM INFORMATION REPORTED BY THE 500 LARGEST PUBLIC CORPORATIONS, BASED ON REVENUE, IN 1998 ANNUAL REPORTS, PROXY STATEMENTS, AND 10-K STATEMENTS. ALL COMPANIES CONFIRMED INFORMATION BY MAIL, EXCEPT FOR SELECTRON AND COCA-COLA. REFLECTS OFFICERS AS OF MARCH 31, 1999, OR EARLIER.

Reflecting on Your Writing

Write a one-page explanation, telling your instructor about a problem you encountered in writing your essay and how you solved it. Before you begin, gather all of your invention and planning notes, drafts, critical comments, revision plan, and final revision. Review these materials as you complete this writing task.

1. *Identify* one *writing problem you needed to solve as you worked on the essay.* Do not be concerned with grammar and punctuation; concentrate instead on problems unique to developing an essay arguing for a position. For example: Did you puzzle over how to convince your readers that the issue is important? Did you have trouble asserting your position forcefully while acknowledging other points of view? Was it difficult to refute an important objection you knew readers would raise?

2. *Determine how you came to recognize the problem.* When did you first discover it? What called it to your attention? If you did not become aware of the problem until someone pointed it out to you, can you now see hints of it in your invention writings? If so, where specifically?

3. *Reflect on how you went about solving the problem.* Did you work on the wording of a passage, cut or add reasons or refutations, conduct further research, or move paragraphs or sentences around? Did you reread one of the essays in this chapter to see how another writer handled a similar problem, or did you look back at your invention writing? If you talked about the problem with another student, a tutor, or your instructor, did talking about it help? How useful was the advice you received?

4. *Write a brief explanation of how you identified the problem and tried to solve it.* Be as specific as possible in reconstructing your efforts. Quote from your invention notes and draft essay, others' critical comments, your revision plan, or your revised essay to show the various changes your writing—and thinking—underwent as you tried to solve the problem. If you are still uncertain about your solution, say so. Taking time to explain how you identified a particular problem, how you went about solving it, and what you learned from this experience can help you solve future writing problems more easily.

Reviewing What You Learned from Reading

Write a page or so explaining to your instructor how the readings in this chapter influenced your final essay. Your own essay has undoubtedly been influenced to some extent by one or more of the essays in this chapter as well as by classmates' essays that you may have read. These other essays may have helped you decide that you needed to do further research before you could argue responsibly for your position, that you could use a personal anecdote as part of your support, or that you should try to anticipate and effectively refute readers' objections. Before you write, take time to reflect on what you have learned from the readings and how they have influenced your own writing.

1. *Reread the final revision of your essay; then look back at the selections you read before completing it.* Do you see any specific influences? For ex-

ample, did any reading influence how you decided to present the issue, use authorities, make concessions, or refute objections? Also look for ideas you got from your reading: writing strategies you were inspired to try, specific details you were led to include, and goals you sought to achieve.

2. *Write an explanation of these influences.* Did one selection have a particularly strong influence or were several selections influential in different ways? Quote from the readings and from your final revision to show how your essay was influenced by the selections you read. Finally, based on your review of the chapter's readings, point out any further improvements you would now make in your essay.

Considering the Social Dimensions of Position Papers

Arguing positions on important social and political issues is essential in a democracy. Doing so gives us each a voice. Instead of remaining silent and on the margins, we can enter the ongoing debate. We can try to influence others, perhaps convincing them to change their minds or at least to take seriously our point of view. Airing our differences also allows us to live together in relative peace. Instead of brawling with each other at school board meetings, in legislative halls, on street corners, or in the classroom, we argue. We may raise our voices in anger and frustration, and our differences may seem insurmountable, but at least no one is physically hurt.

Anticipating the positions taken by our readers and their likely objections to our argument benefits us in another important way. It forces us to do more than merely assert our views; we must also give reasons why we think as we do. Anticipating readers' responses to our argument encourages us not only to think of reasons, but also to think critically about our reasons so that we can defend them against potential criticism. To refute objections, we need to support our reasons in ways that ground our opinions in something other than personal belief—for example, in facts that can be verified, in the authority of experts, in anecdotal experiences with which others can identify. Ideally, then, writing position papers fosters the kind of reasonable debate that enables a diverse society like ours to hold together.

Yet even though reasoned argument about controversial social issues is a highly valued activity in our society, cautious readers and writers need to be aware that this way of presenting an argument for a position may have serious shortcomings and problems.

The Illusion of Objectivity. Part of what we value about reasoned argument is that it seems to allow us to transcend personal bias and narrow self-interest. In other words, it enables us to be—or at least appear—objective because we are not merely saying what we think, but backing our opinions with reasons and support.

Many people, however, have begun to question this idea of objectivity. They suggest that objectivity is only an illusion because it is impossible to escape one's history and culture. Who we are and what we believe may be influenced by factors such as gender, ethnicity, family, religion, money, schooling, and exposure to the media (such as television, film, music, the Internet). Consequently, according to this point of view, the fact that we are able to give objective-sounding, seemingly logical reasons for our opinions does not guarantee that they are unbiased or even reasonable: What appears to be rational thought may be merely rationalization, a way of justifying fundamentally intuitive personal convictions. In other words, supporting a position with a "well-reasoned" argument may simply be a game we play to trick others—and ourselves—into believing that we are open-minded and our opinions are based on something other than personal bias.

1. *As a reader of others' essays arguing a position, do you think you are swayed by objective-sounding arguments?* Review the readings in this chapter to locate one reason you thought was objective or that seemed objective. What do you think makes this reason appear to be objective? What might lead readers to think it is?

2. *Consider the entire essay and how it reflects some aspect of the writer's history and culture.* Think of a factor that may have influenced the writer's point of view on the issue. For example, how do you imagine Nelson's experience as a college and professional athlete may influence her views on gender equity in college sports? How do you think the fact that Leshner is a scientist might influence his choice of reasons and support?

3. *Reflect on the opposition between objectivity and personal bias.* Do you think that reasoned argument should try to be objective? When you were writing your own position paper, were you trying to be objective? Which of your reasons would you now identify as objective-sounding, chosen because you thought your readers would find it convincing, not because you really believed it? If it is true that everyone has biases based on personal history and culture, does it necessarily follow that it is impossible to escape these biases or, at least, to set them aside? When Estrada anticipates the objection about political correctness, do you think he uses critical thinking to examine a bias he shares with readers, or do you think he's trying to trick readers and possibly also trick himself? Do any of the other writers in this chapter critically examine their underlying ideas or values? Did you do so in your own essay?

4. *Write a page or so explaining your ideas about objectivity and bias in essays arguing a position.* Connect your ideas to the readings in this chapter and to your own essay.

Suppressing Dissent. Some critics argue that society privileges reasoned argument over other ways of arguing in order to control dissent. Instead of expressing what may be legitimate outrage and inciting public concern through passionate language, dissenters are urged to be dispassionate and reasonable. They may even be encouraged to try to build their arguments on shared values even though they are arguing with people whose views they find repugnant. While it may help prevent violent confrontation, this emphasis on calmly giving reasons and support may also prevent an honest and open exchange of differences. In the end, trying to present a well-reasoned, well-supported argument may serve to maintain the status quo by silencing the more radical voices within the community.

1. *In your own experience of writing an essay arguing a position on a controversial issue, did having to give reasons and support discourage you from choosing any particular issue or from expressing strong feelings?* Reflect on the issues you listed as possible subjects for your essay and how you made your choice. Did you reject any issues because you could not come up with reasons and support for your position? When you made your choice, did you think about whether you could be dispassionate and reasonable about it?

2. *Consider the readings in this chapter and the essays you read by other students in the class.* Do you think any of these writers felt limited by the need to give reasons and support for their position? Which of the essays you read, if any, seemed to you to express strong feelings about the issue? Which, if any, seemed dispassionate?

3. *Consider the kind of arguing you typically witness in the media—radio, television, newspapers, magazines, the Internet.* We have said that society privileges reasoned argument, but in the media, has giving reasons and support and anticipating readers' objections been replaced with a more contentious, "in your face" style of arguing? Think of media examples of these two different ways of arguing. In the context of these examples, what can you conclude about reasoned argument stifling dissent?

4. *Write a page or so explaining your ideas about whether the requirement to give reasons and support suppresses dissent.* Connect your ideas to your own essay and to the readings in this chapter.

Proposing a Solution

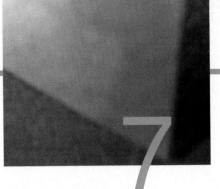

Proposals are vital to a democracy. They inform citizens about problems affecting their well-being and suggest actions that could be taken to remedy these problems. People write proposals every day in business, government, education, and the professions. Proposals are a basic ingredient of the world's work.

As a special form of argument, proposals have much in common with position papers, described in Chapter 6. Both analyze a subject about which there is disagreement and take a definite stand on it. Both make an argument, giving reasons and support and acknowledging readers' likely objections or questions. Proposals, however, go further: They urge readers to take specific action. They argue for a proposed solution to a problem, and they succeed or fail by the strength of that argument.

Problem-solving is basic to most disciplines and professions. For example, scientists use the scientific method, a systematic form of problem-solving; political scientists and sociologists propose solutions to troubling political and social problems; engineers employ problem-solving techniques in building bridges, automobiles, and computers; teachers make decisions about how to help students with learning problems; counselors devote themselves to helping clients solve personal problems; business owners and managers daily solve problems large and small.

Problem-solving depends on a questioning attitude—wondering about alternative approaches to bringing about change, puzzling over how a goal might be achieved, questioning why a process unfolds in a particular way, posing challenges to the status quo. In addition, it demands imagination and creativity. To solve a problem, you need to see it anew, to look at it from new angles and in new contexts.

Because a proposal tries to convince readers that its way of defining and solving the problem makes sense, proposal writers must be sensitive to readers' needs and expectations. Readers need to know details of the solution and to be convinced that it will solve the problem and can be implemented. If readers initially favor a different solution, knowing why the writer rejects it will help them decide whether to support or reject the writer's proposed solution. Readers may be wary of costs, demands on their time, and grand schemes.

As you plan and draft a proposal, you will have to determine whether your readers are aware of the problem and whether they recognize its seriousness, and you will have to consider their views on any other solutions. Knowing what your readers know

—their assumptions and biases, the kinds of arguments likely to appeal to them—is a central part of proposal writing.

The writing of proposals occurs in many different contexts, as the following examples suggest.

Writing in Your Other Courses

- For an economics class, a student writes an essay proposing a solution to the problem of inadequate housing for Mexican workers in the nearly three thousand maquiladora factories clustered along the Mexican side of the border with the United States. She briefly describes the binational arrangement that has produced over a million low-paying jobs for Mexican workers and increased profits for American manufacturers who own the assembly plants—along with job losses for thousands of American workers. She sketches the history of maquiladoras since the 1970s and then surveys some of the problems they have spawned. Focusing on inadequate housing, she argues that it, of all the problems, should be addressed first and is most amenable to modest, short-term solutions. The student argues that maquiladora owners must share with Mexican city and state governments the costs of planning and installing water delivery systems and minimal house plumbing installations, and provide low-interest loans to workers who want to buy indoor plumbing fixtures. Recognizing that this is only a first-stage solution to a major problem requiring long-term efforts, the student calls for an international competition to design entire maquiladora workers' communities, along with plans for adequate low-cost houses with plumbing and electricity. She rejects high-rise housing, arguing that it has failed to solve housing problems for the poor in U.S. cities and that land for housing developments in Mexico is relatively plentiful on the outskirts of border cities, if adequate bus service is provided for workers.

- For an education class, a student researches the history of educational television production and programming for two- to thirteen-year-old children, beginning with the 1969 production of Children's Television Workshop's *Sesame Street*. He also researches children's television in Australia, Great Britain, and Japan and learns that these countries provide much more support for children's television programming than the United States does. In an essay proposing a solution to this problem, he defines the problem as the absence of a plan to develop programming that might attract funding from the federal government and other sources. He presents the problem by reporting how far behind some other countries the United States has fallen in supporting children's television. Influenced by a book by the founder of Children's Television Workshop, the student proposes a solution that outlines conditions for developing new television programming for children. These conditions include demonstrating that television is the most efficient and effective way to teach particular skills or content, giving priority to the needs of children, making innovative educational television programming a national goal, aiming for calendar-year programming of at least one hour each weekday for children in three age groups, and planning to replace at least 25 percent of the content of every program each year. Arguing to support these conditions, the student concedes that attractive new programs continue to appear—for example, *Bill Nye, the Science Guy*—but argues that these are sporadic and cannot provide the amount or diversity of programming that is needed.

Writing in the Community

- A California high school junior enters an essay contest, "There Ought to Be a Law," sponsored by her state legislator. The goal of the contest is to encourage high school students to propose solutions to community problems. The student wins the contest with a proposal for a state law requiring school districts to replace textbooks every ten years. She presents the problem by describing her own battered, marked-up, dated textbooks, particularly a chemistry text older than she is. To gain a better understanding of the problems caused by outdated textbooks, she talks with several other students and with teachers. Recognizing that she lacks the expertise to outline a legislative solution, she speculates about the probable obstacles, chief among them the costs of implementing her solution. The legislator drafts a law based on the student's proposal, introduces the law at the opening of the next legislative session, and invites the student to attend the event.

- A social services administrator in a large northeastern city becomes increasingly concerned about the rise in numbers of adolescents in jail for minor and major crimes. From his observations and the research studies he reads, he becomes convinced that a partial solution to the problem would be to intervene at the first sign of delinquent behavior from eight- to twelve-year-olds. In developing a proposal to circulate among influential people in the local police department, juvenile justice system, school system, and business and religious communities, the administrator begins by describing the long-term consequences of jailing young criminals. Trying to make the problem seem significant and worth solving, he focuses mainly on the costs and the high rate of return to criminal activity after release from jail. He then lists and discusses at length the major components of his early intervention program. These components include assigning mentors and companions to young people who are beginning to fail in school, placing social workers in troubled families to help out daily before and after school, hiring neighborhood residents to work full-time on the streets to counter the influence of gangs, and encouraging businesses to hire high school students as paid interns. The administrator acknowledges that early intervention to head off serious criminal activity will require the cooperation of many city agencies. He offers to take the lead in bringing about this cooperation and in launching the program.

Writing in the Workplace

- Frustrated by what they see as the failure of schools to prepare students for the workplace, managers of a pharmaceuticals manufacturer in the Midwest decide to develop a proposal to move vocational and technical training out of ill-equipped high school vocational programs and onto the plant's floor. Seven division managers meet weekly for four months to develop a proposal for schools in the region. They are joined by one of the firm's experienced technical writers, who takes notes of discussions, writes progress reports, and eventually drafts the proposal. Their discussions begin with the published research and arguments of an academic consultant to their project. They define the problem as schools being unable to offer the modern equipment, motivation, tutorial instruction, efficiency, or accountability of on-the-job training. They eventually propose a vocational track that would begin in grade 10, with all of the job training taking place in businesses and industries. Each year students would spend more time on the job, and by grade 12 they would work thirty-two hours a week and spend ten hours a week in school, mainly in courses in English (reading and writing) and advanced math. As the managers detail their solution, develop a timetable for implementing it, and speculate about how current school budgets could be reworked to support the program, they seek advice on early drafts of their proposal from business leaders, school board members, school administrators, representatives of teachers' unions, newspaper editorial boards, and key members of the state legislature. The near-final draft incorporates suggestions from these advisers and attempts to refute known arguments against the proposal. This draft is reviewed by a small group of the most well-informed and creative advisers. The published proposal is directed primarily to state legislators and school board members.

For a look at some of the decisions this writer makes about document design, see pp. 345–46.

- A woman in her sixties who has been hauling asphalt and gravel in a double-bottom dump truck for sixteen years writes a proposal for trucking company owners and managers, who face a continual shortage of well-qualified drivers for heavy diesel tractor-and-trailer trucks, suggesting that the companies focus on recruiting more women. As she plans her proposal, she talks to the owner of the company she drives for and to the few women drivers she knows. She begins the proposal by describing her work briefly and explaining how she got a lucky break when her brother taught her how to drive his truck. She then points out the problem: that few women ever get the chance to learn this skill. She argues that the industry's starting salaries and equitable pay scales would appeal to many women, and that the seasonal nature of many trucking jobs would make them especially attractive to women who want to work only a few months a year. Then she proposes her solution to this problem: an in-house training program in which women recruits would be trained by company drivers on the job and after hours. Drivers would be paid for their after-hours training contributions, and the students would be paid a small stipend after agreeing to drive for the company for a certain number of months at a reduced salary. She argues that her proposal would succeed only if trucking companies sponsor a well-designed recruitment program relying on advertisements published on Web sites and in magazines read by working women, and she lists titles of several such publications. She attempts to refute the alternative solution of relying on already established truck-driving schools by arguing that many women cannot afford the tuition. Her proposal is first published in her company's internal newsletter and later, in slightly revised form, in a leading magazine read by trucking company owners and managers.

The preceding scenarios suggest some occasions for writing proposals to solve problems. To get a sense of the complexities and possibilities involved in proposing solutions, think through a specific problem, and try to come up with a feasible proposal.

Practice Proposing a Solution to a Problem: A Collaborative Activity

Part 1. Form a group with two or three other students, and select one person to take notes during your discussion.

- First, identify two or three problems within your college or community, and select one that you all recognize and agree needs to be solved.

- Next, consider possible solutions to this problem, and identify one solution that you can all support. You need not all be equally enthusiastic for this solution.

- Finally, determine which individual or group has the authority to take action on your proposed solution and how you would go about convincing this audience that the problem is serious and must be solved and that your proposed solution is feasible and should be supported. Make notes also about questions this audience might have about your proposal and what objections the audience might raise.

Part 2. As a group, discuss your efforts at proposing a solution to a problem. What surprised or pleased you most about this activity? What difficulties did you encounter in coming up with arguments that the problem must be solved and that your proposed solution would solve it? How did the objections you thought of influence your confidence in your proposed solution?

READINGS

The readings in this chapter illustrate the features of essays proposing solutions to problems and the strategies writers rely on to realize the features. No two essays in this type of writing are alike, and yet they share defining features. The Analyzing Writing Strategies and Commentary following each reading touch on a few features best illustrated by that essay, capturing its special qualities and strengths. Together, the four essays cover many of the possibilities of proposals. Consequently, you will want to read as many of the essays as possible and, if time permits, complete the activities in Analyzing Writing Strategies and read the Commentaries. Following the readings, the Basic Features section offers a concise description of the features of proposals and provides examples from all of the readings.

Rob Ryder writes screenplays and directs movies. Because of his experience playing and coaching basketball, he has served as an adviser on several recent hoop-related movies.

Ryder's proposal to turn basketball into an eight-player game was published in 1998, in the sports section of the New York Times. *His style is informal, like that of a sports announcer at work. His sentences and paragraphs tend to be short, and his words are familiar ones, except for a few technical terms from basketball. Ryder mentions several professional basketball players and coaches, but you need not recognize them or know much about the game to follow his proposal. Your experience with any sport will help you understand Ryder's attempt to make basketball a more challenging and interesting game.*

Ten Is a Crowd, So Change the Game
Rob Ryder

1 Along with about a billion other people on this planet, I've had a lifelong love affair with basketball. I've known the game as a player (Princeton), as a coach (Hollywood Y.M.C.A. 5- to 8-year-olds), and as a basketball supervisor for the movies (*White Men Can't Jump, Blue Chips,* and *Eddie* among others).

2 So, it is with deep regret that I must finally go public with the truth: Basketball is a mess. A muddled, boring, chaotic, overcrowded, utterly predictable game of slapping, clawing, double and triple-teaming, endless stoppages, timeouts, whistles, whining, and countless trips to the free-throw line where players continue to stupefy us with their ineptitude.

3 Yet the game is still punctuated by enough moments of pure poetry, grace, power and creativity to keep us coming back for more.

4 So, now that we can admit the game is flawed, let's fix it.

5 I'm not tinkering here—this is no "raise the rim," "widen the lane" Band-Aid I'm proposing. Rather, I'm going straight to the heart of the problem. It's just too crowded out there. Basketball is meant to be played four on four.

6 Too radical? You're forgetting your American heritage. It's our game. We invented it; we can change it if we want to. (I'm sure there was a lot of groaning when the forward pass was introduced to football.)

7 When I ran the concept of four-on-four basketball, or 8-Ball, by Doc Rivers during the filming of *Eddie,* his eyes lighted up.

8 "Guards would rule," he said. Not necessarily, but we'll get to that later. Working on another movie, *The Sixth Man,* I proposed the change to Jerry Tarkanian, who replied: "I've been saying that for years. I've been saying that for years." When I asked Marty Blake, the crusty old N.B.A. war horse, he responded, "What, are you nuts?"

9 Yeah. And so was James Naismith. The man almost got it right. But how many realize that in the old days, there was a jump ball after every basket scored? Or that teams were allowed to hold the ball indefinitely? Or that there wasn't always a 3-point shot?

10 The new game will be a lean, sleek, fluid game—dominated by high-flying superbly coordinated athletes, with no room for defensive ends. Charles Oakley, I love your work ethic, but you're going to have trouble keeping up.

11 Kobe Bryant, Tim Duncan, Keith Van Horn, Ray Allen, the future is yours.

Lisa Leslie, Teresa Edwards, Venus Lacey, you too will love 8-Ball. As will all the 12 little kids out there whose Saturday morning games often resemble two swarms of bees fighting over a Rollo.

Remember the pick-and-roll?—now it's more commonly known as the pick-and- 13 collide-into-two-defenders-coming-from-the-weak-side. In 8-Ball, the pick-and-roll will rule. Help from the weak side leaves the defense much more vulnerable without the fifth defender there to rotate over the passing lane.

The old back-door play (which only Princeton seems to pull off regularly these days) 14 will be back. Only now, there will be a cleaner path to the basket. Defenders, deny your man the ball at your own peril.

But what about Doc Rivers's comment that guards would rule playing four on four? 15 Tell that to Hakeem Olajuwon, who cannot only run the floor but will now also have enough room for this dazzling array of post-up moves.

You see, everybody wins: The big men will finally have some space, the shooters 16 will get plenty of open looks from the 3-point line, and the slashers, like Eddie Jones, should have a field day with one fewer defender out there to clog the lane.

So just what are we sacrificing by going to four on four? 17

Well, the lumbering big man will go the way of the dinosaur. Sorry, George Mhuresan, 18 but no one's going to cover for you when your man releases and beats you downcourt. A four on three is infinitely tougher to defend than a five on four.

And for you little guys, if you can't shoot, you're a liability. 19

There'll be a lot less room for the role player out there because 8-Ball will demand 20 that every player on the floor polish his or her overall skills.

So where's the downside? Nolan Richardson knows—as Arkansas' 94-feet-of-hell 21 amoeba defense will be reduced to a quick detour through purgatory. It'll be a lot tougher to press full court with only four defenders. Any good ball-handler will be able to break the press, and this will definitely hurt the college and high school game.

For the pros, it's a moot point—full-court pressure disappeared years ago. Even 22 Rick Pitino's on his way to discovering how tough it is to ask pro athletes to press full court over an 82-game season.

But will this mean a reduction of the 12-man roster, reduced playing time and howls 23 from the N.B.A. Players' Association?

Not at all, for two reasons. One, 8-Ball will be a running game, and in some ways 24 may adopt the more exciting characteristics of hockey (yes, hockey). Coaches may actually find themselves injecting four new players into a game simultaneously (a line change)—a nifty way to ratchet up the action while giving your starters a rest.

And secondly, in the world of 8-Ball, the time of game will expand; in the pros, from 25 48 to 60 minutes. But how do you keep these games from running over three hours?

In 8-Ball, the time wasted on stupor-inducing foul shooting will be reduced by two- 26 thirds, allowing for extra minutes of real action. Whenever a player is fouled but not in the act of shooting, his team automatically gets the ball out of bounds. When fouled in the act of shooting, a player gets one free throw worth 2 points or 3 points, depending on the shot he was taking. But in both cases, the offensive team gets the option of skipping the foul line and taking the ball out of bounds.

This will eliminate the ugly strategy of intentional fouling, choke-induced shooting   27
and subhuman fan behavior all in one easy stroke.

A good basketball game is about rhythm, and 8-Ball will flow.   28

The substitutions will make for marvelous matchups. We'll see more fast breaks,   29
cleaner inside moves, purer shooting, more offensive rebounding, fewer turnovers, a lot
less standing around, more minutes of actual action, and more scoring.

Plus, 8-Ball would bring forth the elimination of what must be the stupidest addition   30
to N.B.A. rules: the illegal defense violation. Just try playing a four-man zone in 8-Ball.
It'll turn to a man-to-man real fast.

There it is, 8-Ball. Is there any realistic chance that the N.C.A.A. or the N.B.A. will   31
change over to four on four? "Never happen," Dick Vitale answered.

That's why a group of former Princeton players is launching a professional basket-   32
ball league—the "8BL." Look for it in '99 following a televised exhibition this fall. In the
meantime, all you rec league and intramural players out there—with your smaller courts
and running clocks and purists' love for the game—8-Ball's for you, too. Show us
the way.

Connecting to Culture and Experience: Obsession with Watching Sports

Nearly all Americans of all ages have somewhere between a tepid to hot interest in watching and following competitive team sports. Few people have no interest in watching competitive sports. Even fewer will *admit* to having no interest. It is difficult to avoid sports news in America. Most newspapers devote an entire section to sports but only an occasional page to religion or education. Regional newspapers report results from the lowest-ranked high school leagues in surrounding counties. Entire television channels are devoted to sports events and news. National and local television news programs pay attention to sports.

With several other students, discuss this American—and worldwide—obsession with watching other people play competitive sports. Begin by telling each other which competitive sport, if any, you most enjoy watching and which team or athlete is your favorite. Then speculate about where your interest originated and what sustains it. Then, more generally, speculate about why so many Americans seem eager to go to stadiums or sit in front of a television set to watch other people play a sport. Why do you think they prefer to watch others play a sport instead of engaging in some sort of physical activity themselves?

Analyzing Writing Strategies

1. At the beginning of this chapter, we make several generalizations about essays that propose solutions to problems. Consider which of these assertions are true of Ryder's proposal.

- It defines the problem.
- It helps readers realize the seriousness of the problem.
- It describes the proposed solution.
- It attempts to convince readers that the solution will solve the problem and can be implemented.
- It anticipates readers' likely questions and objections.
- It evaluates alternative solutions that readers may initially favor.
- It urges readers to take specific action.

2. Ryder sets out to define the problem and describe a solution. Reread paragraphs 1–3, where Ryder defines the problem. How does he define it? How does he establish his authority to do so? Given his readers' likely knowledge of sports in general and of basketball in particular, how successfully do you think Ryder defines the problem?

   Next, reread paragraphs 4–16, where Ryder describes a solution to the problem he sees with five-on-five basketball. Underline the major features of his proposal for four-on-four basketball. Do these features add up to an adequate description of the solution, given Ryder's purpose and readers? If not, what more do you think he might have included? Why do you think he quotes three basketball experts in paragraph 8?

Commentary: Anticipating Readers' Objections and Questions

To have any hope of readers' taking his advice seriously, Ryder has to anticipate readers' questions and objections. Ryder takes an imaginative and direct approach to anticipating readers' questions: He tries to guess what their questions might be and then poses four of them (see paragraphs 17, 21, 23, and 25). Both the questions and his answers are part of his counterargument.

When you counterargue, you may merely **acknowledge** that you are aware of readers' objections and questions; or you may **accommodate or concede** their usefulness or **refute** them. By posing the questions—something few writers do—Ryder acknowledges that some readers may be thinking of them. Then he either accommodates or refutes them. He accommodates the first two questions, treating readers considerately at the beginning, and refutes the last two, challenging readers more directly after he draws them into his argument. For example, in accommodating, or conceding, the wisdom of the first question—"So just what are we sacrificing by going to four on four?" (paragraph 17)—Ryder admits that the game will change but only in ways readers would surely support: big, slow players have to go, along with little, fast players who cannot shoot. He seems to assume that nearly all readers would concede the wisdom and logic of these improvements to the game.

Consider the third question—"But will this mean a reduction of the 12-man roster . . . ?" (23)—which Ryder refutes. Here the question is more specific, and he firmly challenges the possibility that any intelligent reader would answer "Yes." He answers "Not at all" (24), giving two reasons to support his answer: A hard-running game like 8-Ball will require at least as many players as 10-Ball in order to give tired

For more on these counter-arguing strategies, see Chapter 19, pp. 634–37.

players a break, and the game will expand to sixty minutes, placing even further demands on players' stamina. Ryder seems to be saying to readers that there may be some worrisome questions raised about his proposal, but this is not one of them.

Ryder demonstrates that refutation need not be dismissive. As he refutes the third and fourth questions, he gives reasons and support (24–27). Ryder knows that readers who feel insulted or even misunderstood are not likely to want to take action on his proposed solution. In planning and developing your own essay, your goals should be to anticipate a wide range of readers' inevitable questions and objections as well as to attempt to concede or refute these questions and objections convincingly but sensitively.

Considering Topics for Your Own Essay

Following Ryder's lead, consider proposing a way to improve a popular sport. Your proposal need not seek to revolutionize the sport, though it might. Or it could offer only a small refinement such as changing a rule or adding a feature to the game. Your proposal could seek to improve the safety of the game for participants, the way records are kept, the way athletes are recruited into the sport, the way athletes are treated, or the entertainment value of the game to spectators. There are many other possibilities. You could focus on either a professional or amateur sport, a team sport or individual competition, high school or college teams, or the National Hockey League. You could address your proposal to players, officials, fans, or the general public.

Another idea for writing is to identify a problem that needs to be solved in some activity or enterprise that no one seems to be questioning or that people would strongly resist changing. Possible topics include having big, expensive weddings, taking honeymoons after weddings, commuting to work or school by car, the youth programs run by religious organizations, high school sports competitions (Italian secondary schools sponsor no sports teams), studying a different subject every period for a semester in high school rather than focusing on one or two subjects for two to four weeks, requiring 17- and 18-year-olds to attend high school, giving senior citizens discounts, nine-to-five work schedules, four-year college programs, buying or leasing a car, ATMs, or pumping your own gasoline.

Adam Paul Weisman wrote this article in 1987 for the New Republic, *a national news and opinion magazine. It proposes a solution to the problem of teenage pregnancy. As you read the proposal, ask yourself how Weisman's admission that his solution is not original—that it has already been tried—affects your reaction to it.*

Birth Control in the Schools
Adam Paul Weisman

Should contraceptives be distributed to teenagers in public schools? A research panel of the National Academy of Sciences spent two years studying adolescent pregnancy in America, and decided they should. Its

1

1986 report, *Risking the Future,* prompted a new wave of angry debate about how to reduce the high rate of teenage pregnancy in the United States.

No one disputes the severity of the problem. Teen pregnancy ruins young lives and perpetuates a tragic cycle of poverty. According to the Alan Guttmacher Institute, the rate of pregnancy among American women aged 15 to 19 was almost ten percent in 1981. That far outstrips the next closest industrialized nation, England, where the rate is less than 5 percent. Guttmacher estimates that more than 80 percent of teenage pregnancies in the United States are unintended and unwanted. Every year about four in 100 women aged 15 to 19 have an abortion. But those looking for ways to reduce these statistics have divided into two distinct camps: one favoring contraception, the other, sexual abstinence.

The contraception advocates point out that a majority of teenagers have already rejected abstinence. In 1986, 57 percent of 17-year-olds [said] they have had sex. This camp believes that schools, as a central location in young people's lives, are a good place to make contraceptives available. Three recent studies (by the National Academy of Sciences, the Guttmacher Institute, and the Children's Defense Fund) have taken this view, while also calling for programs geared toward postponing adolescent sexual involvement and including parents in school sex education classes.

The abstinence advocates believe the answer lies in inculcating values based on a clear understanding that sex is simply wrong for teenagers. They say that moral lessons are best taught by parents in the home, but that schools should continue the job by teaching a chaste morality. Secretary of Education William Bennett[1] has been the most outspoken proponent of this view. Exposing students to "mechanical" means of pregnancy prevention, he says, encourages "children who do not have sexual intimacy on their minds to . . . be mindful of it."

Bennett concedes that "birth control clinics in schools may prevent some births." And indeed, whatever the drawbacks, the contraception advocates have one strong advantage in this debate: their approach works. The only rigorous study of a pregnancy prevention program for urban teenagers was conducted in Baltimore from 1982 to 1983 by researchers from Johns Hopkins Medical School. The Hopkins-run birth-control clinic, located across the street from one school and nearby another, reduced the pregnancy rate in the schools it served by 30 percent while pregnancy rates in control schools soared 58 percent.

"Why did this program work?" asks Dr. Laurie Zabin, the program's director, in her report on the experiment. "Access to high-quality, free services was probably crucial to its success. Professional counseling, education, and open communications were, no doubt, also important. All these factors appear to have created an atmosphere that allowed teenagers to translate their attitude into constructive preventive behavior." And what of those students who were virgins? According to Zabin, that group of girls (not very large) delayed initiation of sexual activity an average of seven months longer than those in the control groups, strong evidence that awareness of contraception is not directly linked to promiscuity.

---

[1] William Bennett was Secretary of Education during the Reagan administration.

But the existing school-based clinics that distribute or arrange for birth control are   7
not just rooms plastered with Planned Parenthood posters where contraceptives are
handed out. They are full-service health clinics that came into existence to provide
young people with comprehensive health care. Public health officials, including many
who have doubts about distributing contraceptives in schools, agree that in many
places, particularly the inner city, health care for adolescents is inadequate. The school-
based clinic, like the school lunch program, seeks to make all students healthy enough
to get the most out of education.

This is not to say that school-based clinics don't do a lot in the way of contracep-   8
tion. According to Douglas Kirby, director of research for the Center for Population
Options, a group that advocates and monitors school-based clinics, 15 percent to 20
percent of visits to clinics are for family planning. The majority are for general health
care. Twenty-eight percent of the clinics actually dispense contraceptives or other prescription drugs. About half of the clinics write prescriptions that are filled off-campus; the
rest diagnose and counsel teens before making referrals to outside health agencies.

The clinics also seem to help reduce unintended pregnancies. In St. Paul 33 per-   9
cent of girls made use of the clinic's contraceptive services, and birth rates dropped by
50 percent. Thanks to the clinic's counseling, four out of five of the girls who did have
children stayed in school, and only 1.4 percent of them had another pregnancy before
graduation. Nationally, about 17 percent of teenage mothers become pregnant again
within a year.

Bennett argues that distributing birth control is "not what school is for," and that   10
doing so represents "an abdication of moral authority." Many educators have similar concerns. They fear that communities and government are trying to dump another social
problem—like drug counseling and AIDS education—on the schools when they could
better be handled in the home. Diane Ravitch, an adjunct professor of history and education at Teachers College in New York, says, "Schools are increasingly being pushed
to be social service centers, and they don't do that well."

Yet clearly schools do more than teach students the three R's. Schools are where   11
many teenagers learn to drive, weld, and cook. And numerous surveys reveal that
over 80 percent of parents think it is a proper place for their children to learn about sex.
Dr. Stephen Joseph, health commissioner for New York City, explains that if it weren't
for the involvement of schools, the United States never could have achieved 100 percent immunization rates, a worthy goal that "wasn't perceived as the role of the school
either at that time."

If the pressing health crisis were non-sexual in nature—tuberculosis, for example   12
—it's hard to believe that educators such as Bennett wouldn't be the first to volunteer
schools as a locus for a solution. And of course, if the problem of teen pregnancy is one
that the schools shouldn't be expected to deal with, that would exclude any program of
anti-sex indoctrination as well as the distribution of contraceptives. Putting such indoctrination into the curriculum is, arguably, more intrusive on the schools' basic function
than the existence of a birth control or general health clinic. Bennett's speeches rule out

the very real possibility that schools could prosecute a moral agenda and also support a clinic.

Despite the success of Zabin's off-campus model, there is a good reason school-based clinics receive such wide support in the health services community: teenagers are notoriously lazy. As Cheryl Hayes, director of the NAS study, explains, "If teenagers have to wait in the rain for a bus to take them to a clinic, there is a good chance they will never make it to the clinic." If the goal is providing health care and family planning services to teenagers, it is unlikely that anything will work as well as locating those services where most teenagers are: at school.

Of course the real question that excites people isn't whether teenagers should get birth control at school, but whether they should get it at all. There is no hard evidence linking exposure to contraception with promiscuity, and it is unlikely any teenager who watches prime-time television is less than "mindful" (as Bennett puts it) of sexual intimacy. Although Bennett has dismissed the recommendations of *Risking the Future* as "stupid," the opponents of making contraception available to teenagers have yet to offer an effective alternative. As for the "parental authority" that birth control availability is said to undermine, a 1986 Planned Parenthood survey of 1,000 teenagers revealed that 31 percent of parents discuss neither sex nor birth control with their children. The failure of parental authority is manifest in the almost 900,000 unintended teenage pregnancies in 1983. *Risking the Future* only makes that failure painfully clear.

Connecting to Culture and Experience: Access to Contraception and Birth Control at School

Weisman points out that school-based clinics exist primarily to provide full-service health care. Some clinics also provide information about birth control and dispense contraceptives or prescriptions for drugs. In addition, some schools offer sex education classes. Dispensing contraceptives and, to a lesser extent, giving out information about birth control and offering sex education classes continue to be controversial policies.

With two or three students, discuss whether school-based health clinics should be permitted to distribute birth-control information and contraceptives. Begin by telling each other briefly whether your high school offered sex education classes and provided a health clinic. Summarize the major topics of the sex education curriculum and the services offered by the clinic at your school. How were your schools alike, or how were they different?

Then exchange views about whether you think it is appropriate for school-based clinics to give out birth-control information or contraceptives. If your school had a clinic, was it controversial? What are the advantages or dangers of schools' ensuring that all students have access to information about birth control and contraception? What are the advantages or dangers of distributing contraceptives?

Analyzing Writing Strategies

For more on counter-
argument, see Chapter
19, pp. 634–37.

1. In paragraphs 10–12, Weisman **counterargues** some readers' objections to his argument that school clinics should dispense contraceptives and information about birth control. Notice how he presents the objections in paragraph 10. Why do you think he quotes opponents? Decide whether his presentation seems adequate and fair.

    Next, look closely at his counterargument in paragraphs 10 and 11. How would you describe his strategy here? For his readers, what seems most and least convincing about Weisman's counterargument? Would you say that he shows respect for readers who might initially object to school clinics' giving out contraceptives? If so, how does he do so?

2. Weisman presents the problem to be solved in paragraphs 1–4. What exactly is the problem? Determine whether Weisman demonstrates that this problem actually exists and that it is serious. If you believe that he does, how does he go about it? In what way might the differing views of contraception and abstinence advocates in paragraphs 3 and 4 be part of the problem? Here Weisman presents these differing views impartially. Why do you think he would want to do so?

Commentary: Supporting the Proposed Solution

For more on supporting an
argument, see Chapter 19,
pp. 627–33.

The heart of an essay proposing a solution to a problem is the direct argument supporting the solution. Readers primarily want to know why they should take the proposed solution seriously. In making a special effort to present a convincing argument to **support** his solution, Weisman relies primarily on results from two research studies, one conducted by the prestigious Johns Hopkins Medical School in Baltimore, the other by an unidentified group in St. Paul, Minnesota. In paragraph 5, Weisman cites statistics from the Johns Hopkins study showing that the Hopkins-run birth-control clinic (located near two high schools) reduced the pregnancy rate by 30 percent. In paragraph 9, he cites statistics from the St. Paul study showing a pregnancy reduction of 50 percent. The St. Paul study supports Weisman's argument further in that follow-up counseling was very effective, keeping pregnant girls in school and reducing second pregnancies.

From the Johns Hopkins study Weisman quotes the director of the clinic program, who provides a concise answer to the question, "Why did this program work?" (paragraph 6). The director also gives evidence that the program influenced girls to delay their first sexual experiences, an outcome demonstrating that dispensing birth-control devices does not necessarily encourage promiscuity.

Weisman goes further. He reminds readers in paragraphs 7 and 8 that school clinics offer a wide range of services. In fact, as statistics he cites show, no more than 20 percent of students' visits to clinics are for the purpose of learning about contraception or picking up contraceptives. Most visits are for "general health care." He seems to recognize that his solution has no hope of being implemented unless he can convince readers that school clinics are indispensable. If readers accept that conclusion, then they are more likely to support giving clinics the authority to serve students in many ways, including giving them contraceptives. When you plan your essay you will have the opportunity to list reasons you think readers should support your solution, to think creatively about how to argue for your reasons, and to consider the most logical sequence for presenting the reasons to your readers.

Considering Topics for Your Own Essay

Teenagers are part of the problem addressed in Weisman's proposal, but they can also be part of the solution to social problems. For example, high school students can refurbish playgrounds and parks; tutor elementary-school students who need help with math, reading skills, or the English language; work to reduce violence in their schools; coach neighborhood children's teams; or train people to set up their computers, use the Internet, or design Web pages. Think of a problem teenagers might be able to solve. If you were to propose a solution to this problem, how might you define the problem? What specific solution would you propose? How might you go about convincing teenagers that they should participate?

Katherine S. Newman, an anthropology professor at Columbia University, published this proposal in 1995 in the Brookings Review, *a journal concerned with public policy. Addressing fast-food corporate executives and managers, Newman tries to convince them to adopt policies that would help their employees find better jobs. Her proposal comes out of her two-year study of fast-food workers in Harlem in which she learned that workers experience great difficulty finding better jobs because they lack the kinds of "social networks" that middle-class workers depend on for job information and referrals. As you read Newman's proposal, notice why the social networks that inner-city fast-food workers do have fail to lead to better jobs and evaluate whether you think the proposed solution—an "employer consortium" (a group of cooperating employers)—will provide the type of networks that the workers need.*

Dead-End Jobs: A Way Out
Katherine S. Newman

Millions of Americans work full-time, year-round in jobs that still leave them stranded in poverty. Though they pound the pavement looking for better jobs, they consistently come up empty-handed. Many of these workers are in our nation's inner cities.

I know, because I have spent two years finding out what working life is like for 200 employees—about half African-American, half Latino—at fast food restaurants in Harlem. Many work only part-time, though they would happily take longer hours if they could get them. Those who do work full-time earn about $8,840 (before taxes)—well below the poverty threshold for a family of four.

These fast food workers make persistent efforts to get better jobs, particularly in retail and higher-paid service-sector occupations. They take civil service examinations and apply for jobs with the electric company or the phone company. Sometimes their efforts bear fruit. More often they don't.

A few workers make their way into the lower managerial ranks of the fast food indus- 4
try, where wages are marginally better. An even smaller number graduate into higher
management, a path made possible by the internal promotion patterns long practiced
by these firms. As in any industry, however, senior management opportunities are limited. Hence most workers, even those with track records as reliable employees, are
locked inside a low-wage environment. Contrary to those who preach the benefits of
work and persistence, the human capital these workers build up—experience in food
production, inventory management, cash register operation, customer relations, minor
machinery repair, and cleaning—does not pay off. These workers are often unable to
move upward out of poverty. And their experience is not unusual. Hundreds of thousands of low-wage workers in American cities run into the same brick wall. Why? And
what can we do about it?

Stagnation in the Inner City

Harlem, like many inner-city communities, has lost the manufacturing job base that once 5
sustained its neighborhoods. Service industries that cater to neighborhood consumers,
coupled with now dwindling government jobs, largely make up the local economy. With
official jobless rates hovering around 18 percent (14 people apply for every minimum-
wage fast food job in Harlem), employers can select from the very top of the preference
"queue." Once hired, even experienced workers have virtually nowhere to go.

One reason for their lack of mobility is that many employers in the primary labor 6
market outside Harlem consider "hamburger flipper" jobs worthless. At most, employers
credit the fast food industry with training people to turn up for work on time and to fill out
job applications. The real skills these workers have developed go unrecognized. However inaccurate the unflattering stereotypes, they help keep experienced workers from
"graduating" out of low-wage work to more remunerative employment. . . .

As Harry Holzer, an economist at Michigan State University, has shown, "central- 7
city" employers insist on specific work experience, references, and particular kinds of
formal training in addition to literacy and numeracy skills, even for jobs that do not
require a college degree. Demands of this kind, more stringent in the big-city labor markets than in the surrounding suburbs, clearly limit the upward mobility of the working
poor in urban areas. If the only kind of job available does not provide the "right" work
experience or formal training, many better jobs will be foreclosed.

Racial stereotypes also weaken mobility prospects. Employers view ghetto blacks, 8
especially men, as a bad risk or a troublesome element in the workplace. They prefer
immigrants or nonblack minorities, of which there are many in the Harlem labor force,
who appear to them more deferential and willing to work harder for low wages. As Joleen
Kirshenman and Kathryn Neckerman found in their study of Chicago workplaces, stereotypes abound among employers who have become wary of the "underclass." Primary
employers exercise these preferences by discriminating against black applicants, particularly those who live in housing projects, on the grounds of perceived group characteristics. The "losers" are not given an opportunity to prove themselves. . . .

Social Networks

Social networks are crucial in finding work. Friends and acquaintances are far more use- 9
ful sources of information than are want ads. The literature on the urban underclass suggests that inner-city neighborhoods are bereft of these critical links to the work world. My
work, however, suggests a different picture: the working poor in Harlem have access to
two types of occupational social networks, but neither provides upward mobility. The first
is a homogeneous *lateral* network of age mates and acquaintances, employed and
unemployed. It provides contacts that allow workers to move sideways in the labor market—from Kentucky Fried Chicken to Burger King or McDonald's—but not to move to
jobs of higher quality. Lateral networks are useful, particularly for poor people who have
to move frequently, for they help ensure a certain amount of portability in the low-wage
labor market. But they do not lift workers out of poverty; they merely facilitate "churning"
laterally in the low-wage world.

Young workers in Harlem also participate in more heterogeneous *vertical* networks 10
with their older family members who long ago moved to suburban communities or better urban neighborhoods to become homeowners on the strength of jobs that were more
widely available 20 and 30 years ago. Successful grandparents, great-aunts and uncles,
and distant cousins, relatives now in their 50s and 60s, often have (or have retired from)
jobs in the post office, the public sector, the transportation system, public utilities, the
military, hospitals, and factories that pay union wages. But these industries are now
shedding workers, not hiring them. As a result, older generations are typically unable to
help job-hunting young relatives.

Although little is known about the social and business networks of minority business 11
owners and managers in the inner city, it seems that Harlem's business community, particularly its small business sector, is also walled off from the wider economy of midtown.
Fast food owners know the other people in their franchise system. They do business
with banks and security firms inside the inner city. But they appear less likely to interact
with firms outside the ghetto.

For that reason, a good recommendation from a McDonald's owner may represent 12
a calling card that extends no farther than the general reputation of the firm and a
prospective employer's perception—poor, as I have noted—of the skills that such work
represents. It can move someone from an entry-level job in one restaurant to the same
kind of job in another, but not into a good job elsewhere in the city.

Lacking personal or business-based ties that facilitate upward mobility, workers in 13
Harlem's fast food market find themselves on the outside looking in when it comes to the
world of "good jobs." They search diligently for them, they complete many job applications, but it is the rare individual who finds a job that pays a family wage. Those who do
are either workers who have been selected for internal promotion or men and women
who have had the luxury of devoting their earnings solely to improving their own educational or craft credentials. Since most low-wage service workers are under pressure to
support their families or contribute to the support of their parents' households, this kind
of human capital investment is often difficult. As a result, the best most can do is to churn
from one low-wage job to another.

The Employer Consortium

Some of the social ills that keep Harlem's fast food workers at the bottom of a short job   14
ladder—a poor urban job base, increasing downward mobility, discrimination, structural
problems in the inner-city business sector—are too complex to solve quickly enough to
help most of the workers I've followed. But the problem of poor social networks may be
amenable to solution if formal organizations linking primary and secondary labor market
employers can be developed. An "employer consortium" could help to move hard-
working inner-city employees into richer job markets by providing the job information and
precious referrals that "come naturally" to middle-class Americans.

How would an employer consortium function? It would include both inner-city   15
employers of the working poor and downtown businesses or nonprofit institutions with
higher-paid employees. Employers in the inner city would periodically select employees
they consider reliable, punctual, hard-working, and motivated. Workers who have successfully completed at least one year of work would be placed in a pool of workers
eligible for hiring by a set of linked employers who have better jobs to offer. Entry-level
employers would, in essence, put their own good name behind successful workers as
they pass them on to their consortium partners in the primary sector.

Primary-sector employers, for their part, would agree to hire from the pool and meet   16
periodically with their partners in the low-wage industries to review applications and
follow up on the performance of those hired through the consortium. Employers "up the
line" would provide training or educational opportunities to enhance the employee's
skills. These training investments would make it more likely that hirees would continue
to move up the new job ladders.

As they move up, the new hirees would clear the way for others to follow. First, their   17
performance would reinforce the reputation of the employers who recommended them.
Second, their achievements on the job might begin to lessen the stigma or fear their new
employers may feel toward the inner-city workforce. On both counts, other consortium-
based workers from the inner city would be more likely to get the same opportunities,
following in a form of managed chain migration out of the inner-city labor market. Meanwhile, the attractiveness of fast food jobs, now no better reputed among inner-city residents than among the rest of society, would grow as they became, at least potentially, a
gateway to something better.

Advantages for Employers

Fast food employers in Harlem run businesses in highly competitive markets. Constant   18
pressure on prices and profit discourage them from paying wages high enough to keep
a steady workforce. In fact, most such employers regard the jobs they fill as temporary
placements: they *expect* successful employees to leave. And despite the simple production processes used within the fast food industry to minimize the damage of turnover,
sudden departures of knowledgeable workers still disrupt business and cause considerable frustration and exhaustion.

An employer consortium gives these employers—who *can't* raise wages if they   19
hope to stay in business—a way to compete for workers who will stay with them longer

than usual. In lieu of higher pay, employers can offer access to the consortium hiring pool and the prospect of a more skilled and ultimately better-paying job upon graduation from this real world "boot camp." . . .

Consortiums would also appeal to the civic spirit of minority business owners, who often choose to locate in places like Harlem rather than in less risky neighborhoods because they want to provide job opportunities for their own community. The big franchise operations mandate some attention to civic responsibility as well. Some fast food firms have licensing requirements for franchisees that require demonstrated community involvement.   20

At a time when much of the public is voicing opposition to heavy-handed government efforts to prevent employment discrimination, employer consortiums have the advantage of encouraging minority hiring based on private-sector relationships. Institutional employers in particular—for example, universities and hospitals, often among the larger employers in East Coast cities—should find the consortiums especially valuable. These employers typically retain a strong commitment to workforce diversity but are often put off by the reputation of secondary-sector workers as unskilled, unmotivated, and less worthy of consideration.   21

The practical advantages for primary-sector managers are clear. Hirees have been vetted and tested. Skills have been assessed and certified in the most real world of settings. A valuable base of experience and skills stands ready for further training and advancement. The consortium assures that the employers making and receiving recommendations would come to know one another, thus reinforcing the value of recommendations—a cost-effective strategy for primary-sector managers who must make significant training investments in their workers.   22

Minimal Government Involvement

Despite the evident advantages for both primary and secondary labor market employers, it may be necessary for governments to provide modest incentives to encourage wide participation. Secondary-sector business owners in the inner city, for example, might be deterred from participating by the prospect of losing some of their best employees at the end of a year. Guaranteeing these employers a lump sum or a tax break for every worker they promote into management internally or successfully place with a consortium participant could help break down such reluctance.   23

Primary-sector employers, who would have to provide support for training and possibly for schooling of their consortium employees, may also require some kind of tax break to subsidize their efforts at skill enhancement. Demonstration projects could experiment with various sorts of financial incentives for both sets of employers by providing grants to underwrite the costs of training new workers.   24

Local governments could also help publicize the efforts of participating employers. Most big-city mayors, for example, would be happy to shower credit on business people looking to boost the prospects of the deserving (read working) poor.   25

Government involvement, however, would be minimal. Employer consortiums could probably be assembled out of the existing economic development offices of U.S.   26 cities, or with the help of the Chamber of Commerce and other local institutions that encourage private-sector activity. Industry- or sector-specific consortiums could probably be put together with the aid of local industry councils.

Moreover, some of the negative effects of prior experiments with wage subsidies for the "hard to employ"—efforts that foundered on the stigma assigned to these workers and the paperwork irritants to employers—would be reversed here. Consortium employees would be singled out for doing well, for being the cream of the crop. And the private-sector domination of employer consortiums would augur against extensive paperwork burdens.   27

Building Bridges

The inner-city fast food workers that I have been following in Harlem have proven themselves in difficult jobs. They have shown that they are reliable, they clearly relish their economic independence, and they are willing to work hard. Still, work offers them no escape from poverty. Trapped in a minimum-wage job market, they lack bridges to the kind of work that can enable them to support their families and begin to move out of poverty. For reasons I have discussed, those bridges have not evolved naturally in our inner cities. But where they are lacking, they must be created and fostered. And we can begin with employer consortiums, to the benefit of everyone, workers and employers alike.   28

Connecting to Culture and Experience:
The Value of Routine, Repetitive Work

Newman explains that one reason fast-food workers cannot find better jobs is that employers believe such workers learn only routine, repetitive skills that do not prepare them for other types of jobs.

With several students, discuss this possible limitation of fast-food jobs and other kinds of routine jobs. You may hold such a job now, or you may have held one in the past. Maybe you parked cars, delivered pizzas, ran a cash register, wiped down cars in a car wash, bagged and carried groceries or other merchandise, wrapped holiday packages, or did cleanup work. Tell each other about the routine jobs you have held. Then consider Newman's criticism of these jobs: that they only teach workers how to show up on time and follow rudimentary directions. Is this a fair criticism, do you think? Have critics overlooked certain important kinds of learning on these jobs? If so, what might these kinds of learning be, and how do they prepare students for the jobs they hope to have after college? Or if you agree that these jobs are as limiting as the critics contend, what is limiting about them? What other kinds of low-paying work might teach students skills of importance to their education or future work?

Analyzing Writing Strategies

1. Reread paragraphs 1–8, where Newman defines the problem she believes needs to be solved. In a sentence or two, state what you understand the problem to be.

   At the end of paragraph 4, Newman asks why this problem continues. Underline the main reasons she gives in paragraphs 6–8. For her purpose and readers, does she present a well-defined problem? Can you think of questions readers might have about her presentation of the problem? Most important, does her proposed solution (employer consortiums) address all of the reasons the problem continues?

2. Readers are often aware of previous attempts to solve the problem, or they might think of solutions they believe are better than the one the writer is proposing. We call these alternative solutions: they are alternatives to the solution the writer is proposing. Writers who hope to win readers' support must evaluate alternative solutions that readers are most likely to be aware of. To evaluate an alternative, writers may **acknowledge** that they are aware of it, but usually they go further and either **concede** that it has some merit or **refute** it as meritless and not worth further consideration.

   Newman evaluates an alternative solution in paragraphs 9–13. How would you define this alternative to the employer consortium as a way for fast-food workers to find better jobs outside the inner city? What are the main reasons Newman gives for not taking it seriously and encouraging readers to do the same? Do you think she successfully refutes this alternative to her proposed solution?

For more on these counter-arguing strategies, see Chapter 19, pp. 634–37.

Commentary: Describing the Proposed Solution

Newman describes her proposed solution relatively fully. In paragraphs 14–17, she provides many details about the employer consortium. She defines it at the end of paragraph 14 in terms of its purpose: to find better jobs for hardworking, ambitious fast-food workers. An employee consortium would provide information about jobs and referrals to specific available jobs, the two main resources inner-city fast-food employees lack.

Newman then describes how an employer consortium would function and points out some of its advantages for everyone involved (15–17). She outlines the responsibilities of the two key players in the consortium she envisions: the inner-city fast-food employers and the downtown employers with the better-paying jobs. Notice that she does not hesitate to specify criteria for eligible inner-city employees—they must be "reliable, punctual, hard-working, and motivated" and they must have completed one year of successful work (15). To make it clear that inner-city employers will not be doing all the work, she describes how downtown employers would meet with fast-food employers, review workers' job applications, and pay attention to workers once they are on the job. The downtown employers would also be required to offer on-the-job training for the new workers in order for them to be prepared to take better jobs (16).

As though anticipating inner-city employers' concern that they would be continually giving up their best workers, Newman speculates that employers' reputations would be enhanced and the image of fast-food work would change as the jobs came to be seen as a step to better jobs (17). Presumably, fast-food workers would be more committed to doing a good job if the quality of their work could lead to a better job downtown—and their employers would benefit as well.

Considering Topics for Your Own Essay

Think of barriers or obstacles you have met or expect to meet in realizing your goals and dreams. You might want to think specifically about obstacles to preparing for and entering the career of your choice, but you need not limit yourself to career goals. Perhaps you want to be a more effective speaker and writer but have been unable to find the instruction and support you think you need. Perhaps you are not able to get into an internship program that would give you some experience with the kind of work you hope to do. Perhaps your high school did not offer the courses you needed to prepare for the college major you are pursuing. Perhaps at some crucial point in your life you received inadequate medical care or counseling. Identify one of these obstacles and think of it as a general problem to be solved; that is, assume that other people have confronted the same obstacle. How would you define the problem? How might you propose to solve it? To be more than a personal complaint about bad luck or mistreatment, your proposal would need to appeal to readers who have experienced a similar obstacle or who would be able to remove the obstacle or give sound advice on getting around it.

Patrick O'Malley wrote the following proposal while he was a first-year college student. He proposes that college professors give students frequent brief examinations in addition to the usual midterm and final exams. After discussing with his instructor his unusual rhetorical situation—a student advising professors—he decided to revise the essay into the form of an open letter to professors at his college, a letter that might appear in the campus newspaper.

O'Malley's essay may strike you as unusually authoritative. This air of authority is due in large part to what O'Malley learned about the possibilities and problems of frequent exams as he interviewed two professors (his writing instructor and the writing program director) and talked with several students. As you read his essay, notice particularly how he anticipates professors' likely objections to his proposal and evaluates their preferred solutions to the problem he identifies.

More Testing, More Learning
Patrick O'Malley

It's late at night. The final's tomorrow. You got a *C* on the midterm, so this one will make or break you. Will it be like the midterm? Did you study enough? Did you study the right things? It's too late to drop the course. So what happens if you fail? No time to worry about that now—you've got a ton of notes to go over.

1

Although this last-minute anxiety about midterm and final exams is only too familiar to most college students, many professors may not realize how such major, infrequent, high-stakes exams work against the best interests of students both psychologically and intellectually. They cause unnecessary amounts of stress, placing too much importance on one or two days in the students' entire term, judging ability on a single or dual performance. They don't encourage frequent study, and they fail to inspire students' best performance. If professors gave additional brief exams at frequent intervals, students would be spurred to study more regularly, learn more, worry less, and perform better on midterms, finals, and other papers and projects.

Ideally, a professor would give an in-class test or quiz after each unit, chapter, or focus of study, depending on the type of class and course material. A physics class might require a test on concepts after every chapter covered, while a history class could necessitate quizzes covering certain time periods or major events. These exams should be given weekly, or at least twice monthly. Whenever possible, they should consist of two or three essay questions rather than many multiple-choice or short-answer questions. To preserve class time for lecture and discussion, exams should take no more than 15 or 20 minutes.

The main reason professors should give frequent exams is that when they do, and when they provide feedback to students on how well they are doing, students learn more in the course and perform better on major exams, projects, and papers. It makes sense that in a challenging course containing a great deal of material, students will learn more of it and put it to better use if they have to apply or "practice" it frequently on exams, which also helps them find out how much they are learning and what they need to go over again. A recent Harvard study notes students' "strong preference for frequent evaluation in a course." Harvard students feel they learn least in courses that have "only a midterm and a final exam, with no other personal evaluation." They believe they learn most in courses with "many opportunities to see how they are doing" (Light, 1990, p. 32). In a review of a number of studies of student learning, Frederiksen (1984) reports that students who take weekly quizzes achieve higher scores on final exams than students who take only a midterm exam and that testing increases retention of material tested.

Another, closely related argument in favor of multiple exams is that they encourage students to improve their study habits. Greater frequency in test taking means greater frequency in studying for tests. Students prone to cramming will be required—or at least strongly motivated—to open their textbooks and notebooks more often, making them less likely to resort to long, kamikaze nights of studying for major exams. Since there is so much to be learned in the typical course, it makes sense that frequent, careful study and review are highly beneficial. But students need motivation to study regularly, and nothing works like an exam. If students had frequent exams in all their courses, they would have to schedule study time each week and gradually would develop a habit of frequent study. It might be argued that students are adults who have to learn how to manage their own lives, but learning history or physics is more complicated than learning to drive a car or balance a checkbook. Students need coaching and practice in learning. The right way to learn new material needs to become a habit, and I believe that frequent exams are key to developing good habits of study and learning. The Harvard study concludes that "tying regular evaluation to good course organization enables students to plan their work more than a few days in advance. If quizzes and homework are scheduled on specific days, students plan their work to capitalize on them" (Light, 1990, p. 33).

By encouraging regular study habits, frequent exams would also decrease anxiety by reducing the procrastination that produces anxiety. Students would benefit psychologically if they were not subjected to the emotional ups and downs caused by major exams, when after being virtually worry-free for weeks they are suddenly ready to check into the psychiatric ward. Researchers at the University of Vermont found a strong relationship among procrastination, anxiety, and achievement. Students who regularly put off studying for exams had continuing high anxiety and lower grades than students who procrastinated less. The researchers found that even "low" procrastinators did not study regularly and recommended that professors give frequent assignments and exams to reduce procrastination and increase achievement (Rothblum, Solomon, & Murakami, 1986, pp. 393, 394).   6

Research supports my proposed solution to the problems I have described. Common sense as well as my experience and that of many of my friends support it. Why, then, do so few professors give frequent brief exams? Some believe that such exams take up too much of the limited class time available to cover the material in the course. Most courses meet 150 minutes a week—three times a week for 50 minutes each time. A 20-minute weekly exam might take 30 minutes to administer, and that is one-fifth of each week's class time. From the student's perspective, however, this time is well spent. Better learning and greater confidence about the course seem a good trade-off for another 30 minutes of lecture. Moreover, time lost to lecturing or discussion could easily be made up in students' learning on their own through careful regular study for the weekly exams. If weekly exams still seem too time-consuming to some professors, their frequency could be reduced to every other week or their length to 5 or 10 minutes. In courses where multiple-choice exams are appropriate, several questions could be designed to take only a few minutes to answer.   7

Another objection professors have to frequent exams is that they take too much time to read and grade. In a 20-minute essay exam, a well-prepared student can easily write two pages. A relatively small class of 30 students might then produce 60 pages, no small amount of material to read each week. A large class of 100 or more students would produce an insurmountable pile of material. There are a number of responses to this objection. Again, professors could give exams every other week or make them very short. Instead of reading them closely they could skim them quickly to see whether students understand an idea or can apply it to an unfamiliar problem; and instead of numerical or letter grades they could give a plus, check, or minus. Exams could be collected and responded to only every third or fourth week. Professors who have readers or teaching assistants could rely on them to grade or check exams. And the Scantron machine is always available for instant grading of multiple-choice exams. Finally, frequent exams could be given *in place of* a midterm exam or out-of-class essay assignment.   8

Since frequent exams seem to some professors to create too many problems, however, it is reasonable to consider alternative ways to achieve the same goals. One alter-   9 native solution is to implement a program that would improve study skills. While such a program might teach students how to study for exams, it cannot prevent procrastination or reduce "large test anxiety" by a substantial amount. One research team studying anxiety and test performance found that study skills training was "not effective in reducing anxiety or improving performance" (Dendato & Diener, 1986, p. 134). This team, which also reviewed other research that reached the same conclusion, did find that a combination of "cognitive/relaxation therapy" and study skills training was effective. This possible solution seems complicated, however, not to mention time-consuming and expensive. It seems much easier and more effective to change the cause of the bad habit rather than treat the habit itself. That is, it would make more sense to solve the problem at its root: the method of learning and evaluation.

Still another solution might be to provide frequent study questions for students to 10 answer. These would no doubt be helpful in focusing students' time studying, but students would probably not actually write out the answers unless they were required to. To get students to complete the questions in a timely way, professors would have to collect and check the answers. In that case, however, they might as well devote the time to grading an exam. Even if it asks the same questions, a scheduled exam is preferable to a set of study questions because it takes far less time to write in class, compared to the time students would devote to responding to questions at home. In-class exams also ensure that each student produces his or her own work.

Another possible solution would be to help students prepare for midterm and final 11 exams by providing sets of questions from which the exam questions will be selected or announcing possible exam topics at the beginning of the course. This solution would have the advantage of reducing students' anxiety about learning every fact in the textbook, and it would clarify the course goals, but it would not motivate students to study carefully each new unit, concept, or text chapter in the course. I see this as a way of complementing frequent exams, not as substituting for them.

From the evidence and from my talks with professors and students, I see frequent, 12 brief in-class exams as the only way to improve students' study habits and learning, reduce their anxiety and procrastination, and increase their satisfaction with college. These exams are not a panacea, but only more parking spaces and a winning football team would do as much to improve college life. Professors can't do much about parking or football, but they can give more frequent exams. Campus administrators should get behind this effort, and professors should get together to consider giving exams more frequently. It would make a difference.

References

Dendato, K. M., & Diener, D. (1986). Effectiveness of cognitive/relaxation therapy and study-skills training in reducing self-reported anxiety and improving the academic performance of test-anxious students. *Journal of Counseling Psychology, 33,* 131–135.

Frederiksen, N. (1984). The real test bias: Influences of testing on teaching and learning. *American Psychologist, 39,* 193–202.

For information on using and acknowledging sources, see Chapter 22.

Light, R. J. (1990). *Explorations with students and faculty about teaching, learning, and student life.* Cambridge, MA: Harvard University Graduate School of Education and Kennedy School of Government.

Rothblum, E. D., Solomon, L., & Murakami, J. (1986). Affective, cognitive, and behavioral differences between high and low procrastinators. *Journal of Counseling Psychology, 33,* 387–394.

Connecting to Culture and Experience: Experience with Frequent Exams

O'Malley advocates frequent brief exams as a solution to the problems of midterm- and final-exam anxiety, poor study habits, and disappointing exam performance.

With two or three other students, discuss O'Malley's proposal in light of your own experience in your courses. Which of your high school or college courses have included frequent exams? Describe these courses and the kinds of exams they offered. Did they offer the benefits O'Malley claims? Did you learn more because of them? Did courses without frequent exams produce the problems he identifies?

Analyzing Writing Strategies

For more on counterarguing and responding to readers' objections, see Chapter 19, pp. 634–37.

1. O'Malley devotes almost a third of his essay to **counterarguing** readers' likely objections to his proposal that frequent exams will increase student learning and achievement. This section of the essay begins in the middle of paragraph 5 (with the sentence "It might be argued . . .") and then resumes in paragraphs 7 and 8. Begin by underlining the three objections, one each in paragraphs 5, 7, and 8. Then make notes about what strategies and resources O'Malley brings to bear to counterargue. Finally, evaluate how successful each counterargument seems to be for its intended readers—college professors who are going to resist changing their practices. Does O'Malley show respect for readers while challenging them? If so, how does he manage that? What seems most and least convincing in each counterargument?

2. Nearly always readers of proposals are aware of solutions different from the one the writer is proposing, alternatives to the writer's solution. Readers may know of a solution someone has already proposed or one that has been tried with mixed results, or readers—as they have a tendency to do—may think of an alternative solution after learning about the writer's preferred one. Consequently, a proposal is rarely complete unless it evaluates one or more likely alternative solutions. O'Malley evaluates alternative solutions in paragraphs 9–10, a different one in each paragraph. Reread these counterarguments and notice two things: what strategies and resources O'Malley relies on and to what extent he concedes there may be some good ideas in each alternative or refutes it as unworkable. How do you think his intended readers will react to these paragraphs? What might they find most and least convincing?

3. Turn to this chapter's Writer at Work section (p. 343), where part of O'Malley's first draft appears. Compare the draft paragraph that begins "Lastly, with multiple exams . . ." with paragraph 4 of his final essay, and list specific changes he made from draft to revision. Knowing his purpose and readers, what advantages do you see in his changes?

Commentary: Supporting the Proposed Solution

O'Malley's essay demonstrates the importance of taking readers seriously. Not only does he interview both those who would carry out his proposal (professors) and those who would benefit from it (students), but he also features in his essay what he has learned from these interviews. Paragraphs 7–11 directly acknowledge professors' objections, their questions, and the alternative solutions they would probably prefer. These counterarguments, which may be essential to convincing readers to support a proposal, are only part of the overall argument, which centers on the writer's direct support of the proposed solution. Most of O'Malley's direct argument can be found in paragraphs 4–6, in which O'Malley presents three reasons professors should give frequent exams: (1) students will learn more and perform better on major exams, projects, and essays; (2) acquire better study habits; and (3) experience decreased anxiety and improved performance. He supports each reason with a combination of assertions based on his own experience and references to reputable research studies carried out at three universities. He **quotes** and **paraphrases** these studies.

For more on quoting and paraphrasing, turn to Chapter 22, pp. 693–701.

Argument and counterargument can be woven together in many different ways in an essay proposing a solution to a problem. Because O'Malley succeeds at balancing argument and counterargument, the organization of his proposal is worth noting. The following is a paragraph outline of his essay:

Opening: a scenario to introduce the problem (paragraph 1)

Presentation of the problem and introduction of the solution (2)

Details of the solution (3)

Reason 1: improved learning and performance (4)

Reason 2: improved study habits (5)

Refutation of objection 1: students as adults (5)

Reason 3: less procrastination and anxiety (6)

Accommodation of objection 2: limited class time (7)

Accommodation of objection 3: too much work (8)

Refutation of alternative solution 1: study-skills training (9)

Refutation of alternative solution 2: study questions (10)

Accommodation of alternative solution 3: sample exam questions (11)

Closing: reiteration of the proposed solution and advice on implementing it (12)

Except for a brief refutation in paragraph 5, O'Malley first presents the direct argument for frequent exams (paragraphs 4–6) and then counterargues (paragraphs

7–11). The outline reveals that counterargument takes up most of the space, a not unusual balance in proposals to solve problems. O'Malley might have counterargued first or counterargued as he presented his direct argument, as he does briefly in paragraph 5. The approach you take depends on what your readers know about the problem and their experience with other proposed solutions to it.

Considering Topics for Your Own Essay

Much of what happens in high school and college is predictable and conventional. Examples of conventional practices that have changed very little over the years are exams, group instruction, graduation ceremonies, required courses, and lowered admission requirements for athletes. Think of additional examples of established practices in high school or college; then select one that you believe needs to be improved or refined in some way. What changes would you propose? What individual or group might be convinced to take action on your proposal for improvement? What questions or objections should you anticipate? How could you discover whether others have previously proposed improvements in the practice you are concerned with? Whom might you interview to learn more about the practice and the likelihood of changing it?

■ PURPOSE AND AUDIENCE

Most proposals are calls to action. Because of this clear purpose, a writer must anticipate readers' needs and concerns more when writing a proposal than in any other kind of writing. The writer attempts not only to convince readers but also to inspire them, to persuade them to support or implement the proposed solution. What your particular readers know about the problem and what they are capable of doing to solve it determine how you address them.

Readers of proposals are often unaware of the problem. In this case, your task is clear: to present them with evidence that will convince them of its existence. This evidence may include statistics, testimony from witnesses or experts, and examples, including the personal experiences of people involved with the problem. You can also speculate about the cause of the problem and describe its ill effects.

Sometimes readers recognize the existence of a problem but fail to take it seriously. When readers are indifferent, you may need to connect the problem closely to their own concerns. For instance, you might show how much they have in common with the people directly affected by it or how it affects them indirectly. However you appeal to readers, you must do more than alert them to the problem; you must also make them care about it. You want to touch readers emotionally as well as intellectually.

At other times, readers concerned about the problem may assume that someone else is taking care of it and that they need not become personally involved. In this situation, you might want to demonstrate that the people they thought were taking care of the problem have failed. Another assumption readers might make is that a solution they supported in the past has already solved the problem. You might point out that the original solution has proved unworkable or that new solutions have become available through changed circumstances or improved technology. Your aim is to rekindle these readers' interest in the problem.

Perhaps the most satisfying proposals are addressed to parties who can take immediate action to remedy the problem. You may have the opportunity to write such a proposal if you choose a problem faced by a group to which you belong. Not only do you have a firsthand understanding of the problem but you also have a good idea what solution other members of the group will support. (You might informally survey some of them before you submit your proposal in order to test your definition of the problem and your proposed solution.) When you address readers who are in a position to take action, you obviously want to assure them that it is wise to do so. You must demonstrate that the solution is feasible—that it can be implemented and that it will work.

A Well-Defined Problem

A proposal is written to offer a solution to a problem. Before presenting the solution, the writer must be sure that readers know and understand what the problem is. Patrick O'Malley, for example, devotes the first three paragraphs of his essay to defining the problem of infrequent course exams. It is wise to define the problem explicitly, as all the writers in this chapter do. Rob Ryder states precisely how he thinks basketball is limited, and Adam Paul Weisman identifies the problem directly as teenage pregnancy.

Stating the problem is not enough, however; the writer also must establish the problem as serious enough to need solving. Sometimes a writer can assume that readers will recognize the problem and its seriousness. For example, Weisman can assume that readers are aware of the high rate of teenage pregnancy and acknowledge its seriousness, even if they disagree about a solution. At other times, readers may not be aware of the problem and will need to be convinced that it deserves their attention. Katherine S. Newman, for instance, does not assume her readers will understand how difficult it is for inner-city fast-food workers to find better jobs.

In addition to defining the problem and establishing its seriousness for readers, a proposal writer may have to analyze the problem, exploring its causes, consequences, history, and past efforts at dealing with it.

An Adequately Described Solution

Once the problem is defined and its existence established, the writer must describe the solution so that readers can readily imagine what it would be like. Because O'Malley assumes that his readers know what brief exams are like, he runs little risk in not describing them. He does, however, identify their approximate lengths and possible forms—brief essay, short answer, or multiple choice. In contrast, because Newman cannot assume her readers will know what she means by an "employer consortium," she describes it at length, focusing on who would be involved and the roles they would play.

A Convincing Argument in Support of the Proposed Solution

The main purpose of a proposal is to convince readers that the writer's solution is the best way of solving the problem. A writer must give reasons and support to show that the proposed solution will solve the problem. To this end, Weisman cites the Johns Hopkins study as evidence that the program he proposes will work, and O'Malley gives three reasons why he proposes more brief exams and supports each reason with published research studies as well as his own experience.

Writers must also argue that the proposed solution is feasible—that it can actually be implemented and that it will work. The easier it is to implement, the more likely it is to win readers' support. Therefore, writers sometimes set out the steps required to put the proposed solution into practice, an especially important strategy when the solution might seem difficult, time-consuming, or expensive to enact. All the writers in this chapter offer specific suggestions for implementing their proposals, though none outlines all the steps required. For example, O'Malley offers professors several specific ways to give their students frequent, brief exams, and Newman offers many details about how an employer consortium would function.

An Anticipation of Readers' Objections and Questions

The writer arguing for a proposal must anticipate objections or reservations that readers may have about the proposed solution. Weisman anticipates the objection that schools should not be used as "social service centers." He attempts to refute it by arguing that schools have provided health-related services in the past and that if birth-control information is banned from the schools, teaching sexual abstinence should also be banned. Similarly, Ryder addresses several questions that he knows his readers

will likely ask about four-on-four basketball, such as "So just what are we sacrificing by going to four on four?" and "But how do you keep these games from running over three hours?" He accommodates or concedes some questions and refutes others.

An Evaluation of Alternative Solutions

The writer of a proposal wants to convince readers that the proposed solution is preferable to other possible solutions. To do so, the writer evaluates the alternative solutions and demonstrates what is wrong with each one. O'Malley considers study-skills training, study questions, and sample exam questions as alternatives to frequent exams. The best way to reject an alternative solution is simply to demonstrate that it does not work, as Weisman does with the alternative solution of sexual abstinence. Another way to reject an alternative solution is to show that it solves only part of the problem. O'Malley uses this strategy in rejecting sample exam questions.

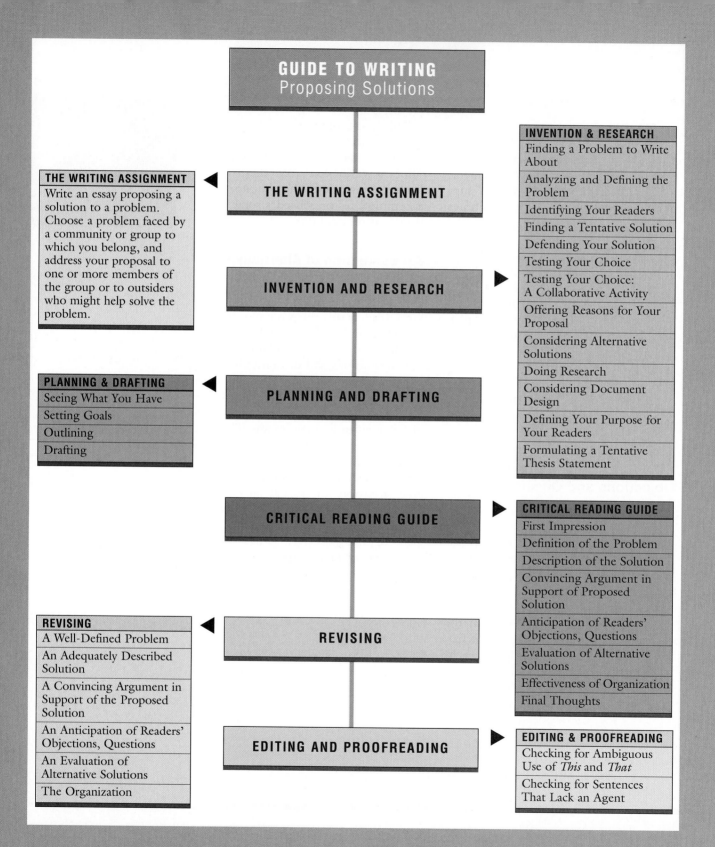

GUIDE TO WRITING
Proposing Solutions

THE WRITING ASSIGNMENT

THE WRITING ASSIGNMENT
Write an essay proposing a solution to a problem. Choose a problem faced by a community or group to which you belong, and address your proposal to one or more members of the group or to outsiders who might help solve the problem.

INVENTION AND RESEARCH

INVENTION & RESEARCH
Finding a Problem to Write About
Analyzing and Defining the Problem
Identifying Your Readers
Finding a Tentative Solution
Defending Your Solution
Testing Your Choice
Testing Your Choice: A Collaborative Activity
Offering Reasons for Your Proposal
Considering Alternative Solutions
Doing Research
Considering Document Design
Defining Your Purpose for Your Readers
Formulating a Tentative Thesis Statement

PLANNING AND DRAFTING

PLANNING & DRAFTING
Seeing What You Have
Setting Goals
Outlining
Drafting

CRITICAL READING GUIDE

CRITICAL READING GUIDE
First Impression
Definition of the Problem
Description of the Solution
Convincing Argument in Support of Proposed Solution
Anticipation of Readers' Objections, Questions
Evaluation of Alternative Solutions
Effectiveness of Organization
Final Thoughts

REVISING

REVISING
A Well-Defined Problem
An Adequately Described Solution
A Convincing Argument in Support of the Proposed Solution
An Anticipation of Readers' Objections, Questions
An Evaluation of Alternative Solutions
The Organization

EDITING AND PROOFREADING

EDITING & PROOFREADING
Checking for Ambiguous Use of *This* and *That*
Checking for Sentences That Lack an Agent

■ THE WRITING ASSIGNMENT

Write an essay proposing a solution to a problem. Choose a problem faced by a community or group to which you belong, and address your proposal to one or more members of the group or to outsiders who might help solve the problem.

■ INVENTION AND RESEARCH

The following activities will help you prepare to write a proposal. You will choose a problem you can write about, analyze and define the problem, identify your prospective readers, decide on and defend your proposed solution, test your choice, offer reasons and support for adopting your proposal, and consider readers' objections and alternative solutions, among other things. These activities are easy to complete. Doing them over several days will give your ideas time to ripen and grow. Be sure to keep a written record of your invention and research to use later when you draft and revise.

Finding a Problem to Write About

You may have already thought about a problem you could write about. Or you may have been drawn to one of the problems suggested by the Considering Topics for Your Own Essay activities following the readings in this chapter. Even so, you will want to consider several problems that need solving before making your final choice. The following activity will help you get started.

Listing Problems. *Make a list of problems you could write about.* Divide a piece of paper into two columns. In the left-hand column, list communities, groups, or organizations to which you belong. Include as many communities as possible: college, neighborhood, hometown, and cultural or ethnic groups. Also include groups you participate in: sports, musical, work, religious, political, support, hobby, and so on. In the right-hand column, list any problems that exist within each group. Here is how such a chart might begin:

Community	*Problem*
My college	Poor advising or orientation
	Shortage of practice rooms in music building
	No financial aid for part-time students
	Lack of facilities for disabled students
	Lack of enough sections of required courses
	Class scheduling does not accommodate working students or students with children

My neighborhood   Need for traffic light at dangerous intersection
Unsupervised children getting into trouble
Megastores driving away small businesses
Lack of safe places for children to play

See Chapter 28 if you are preparing a proposal as part of a service-learning project.

Listing Problems Related to Identity and Community.   Writing a proposal can give you special insight into issues of identity and community by helping you understand how members of a community negotiate their individual needs and concerns. You may already have made a chart of communities to which you belong and problems in those communities. The following categories may help you think of additional problems in those or other communities that you could add to your list:

- Disagreement over conforming to community standards
- Conflicting economic, cultural, or political interests within the community
- Problems with equity or fairness between men and women, rich and poor, different ethnic groups
- Lack of respect or trust among the members of the community
- Struggles for leadership of the community

Listing Problems Related to Work and Career.   Proposals are frequently written on the job and about the work people do. Based on your work experience, make a double-column chart like the following one. List the places you have worked in the left column and the problems you encountered on the job in the right column.

Workplace	*Problem*
Restaurant	Inadequate training
	Conflicts with supervisor
	Unfair shift assignments
Department store	Inadequate inventory
	Computer glitches
	Overcomplicated procedures
Office	Unfair workloads
	Changing requirements
	Inflexible work schedules
	Lack of information about procedures
	Difficulty in scheduling vacations
	Outdated technology

Choosing a Problem.   *Choose one problem from your list that seems especially important to you, that concerns others in the group or community, and that seems solvable. (You need not know the exact solution now.) The problem should also be one that you can explore in detail and are willing to discuss in writing.*

Proposing to solve a problem in a group or community to which you belong gives you an inestimably important advantage: You can write as an expert, an insider. You know about the history of the problem, have felt the urgency to solve it, and perhaps have already thought of possible solutions. Equally important, you will know precisely to whom to address the proposal, and you can interview others in the group to get their views of the problem and to understand how they might resist your solution. From such a position of knowledge and authority comes confident, convincing writing.

Should you want to propose a solution for a social problem of national scope, concentrate on one with which you have direct experience and for which you can suggest a detailed plan of action. Even better, focus on unique local aspects of the problem. For example, if you would like to propose a solution to the lack of affordable child care for children of college students or working parents, you have a great advantage if you are a parent who has experienced the frustration of finding professional, affordable child care. Moreover, it may well be that even though such a problem is national in scope, it can only be solved campus by campus, business by business, or neighborhood by neighborhood.

Analyzing and Defining the Problem

Before you can begin to consider the best possible solution, you must analyze the problem carefully and then try to define it. Keep in mind that you will have to demonstrate to readers that the problem exists, that it is serious, and that you have a more than casual understanding of its causes and consequences. If you find that you cannot do so, you will want to select some other problem to write about.

Analyzing. *Start by writing a few sentences in response to these questions:*

- Does the problem really exist? How can I tell?
- What caused this problem? Can I identify any immediate causes? Any deeper causes? Is the problem caused by a flaw in the system, a lack of resources, individual misconduct or incompetence? How can I tell?
- What is the history of the problem?
- What are the bad effects of the problem? How does it harm members of the community or group? What goals of the group are endangered by the existence of this problem? Does it raise any moral or ethical questions?
- Who in the community or group is affected by the problem? Be as specific as possible: Who is seriously affected? Minimally affected? Unaffected? Does anyone benefit from its existence?
- What similar problems exist in this same community or group? How can I distinguish my problem from these?

Defining. *Write a definition of the problem, being as specific as possible.* Identify who or what seems responsible for it, and give one recent, telling example.

Identifying Your Readers

In a few sentences, describe your readers, stating your reason for directing your proposal to them. Then take a few minutes to write about these readers. Whom do you need to address—everyone in the community or group, a committee, an individual, an outsider? You want to address your proposal to the person or group who can help implement it. The following questions will help you develop a profile of your readers:

- How informed are my readers likely to be about the problem? Have they shown any awareness of it?

- Why would this problem be important to my readers? Why would they care about solving it?

- Have my readers supported any other proposals to solve this problem? If so, what do those proposals have in common with mine?

- Do my readers ally themselves with any group, and would that alliance cause them to favor or reject my proposal? Do we share any values or attitudes that could bring us together to solve the problem?

- How have my readers responded to other problems? Do their past reactions suggest anything about how they might respond to my proposal?

Finding a Tentative Solution

Solving problems takes time. Apparent solutions often turn out to be impossible. After all, a solution has to be both workable and acceptable to the community or group involved. Consequently, you should strive to come up with several possible solutions whose advantages and disadvantages you can weigh. You may notice that the most imaginative solutions sometimes occur to you only after you have struggled with a number of other possibilities.

Look back at the way you defined the problem and described your readers. Then with these factors in mind, list as many possible solutions to the problem as you can think of. You might come up with only two or three possible solutions; but at this stage, the more the better. To come up with different solutions, use the following problem-solving questions:

- What solutions to this problem have already been tried?

- What solutions have been proposed for related problems? Might they solve this problem as well?

- Is a solution required that would disband or change the community or group in some way?

- What solution might eliminate some of the causes of the problem?

- What solution would eliminate any of the bad effects of the problem?

- Is the problem too big to be solved all at once? Can I divide it into several related problems? What solutions might solve one or more of these problems?

- If a series of solutions is required, which should come first? Second?
- What solution would ultimately solve the problem?
- What might be a daring solution, arousing the most resistance but perhaps holding out the most promise?
- What would be the most conservative solution, acceptable to nearly everyone in the community or group?

Give yourself enough time to let your ideas percolate as you continue to add to your list of possible solutions and to consider the advantages and disadvantages of each one in light of your prospective readers. If possible, discuss your solutions with those members of the community or group who can help you consider the advantages and disadvantages of each one.

Choosing the Most Promising Solution.   *In a sentence or two, state what you consider the best possible way of solving the problem.*

Determining Specific Steps.   *Write down the major stages or steps necessary to carry out your solution.* This list of steps will provide an early test of whether your solution can, in fact, be implemented.

Defending Your Solution

Proposals have to be feasible—that is, they must be both reasonable and practical. Imagine that one of your readers strongly opposes your proposed solution and confronts you with the following statements. *Write a few sentences refuting each one.*

- It would not really solve the problem.
- I am comfortable with things as they are.
- We cannot afford it.
- It would take too long.
- People would not do it.
- Too few people would benefit.
- I do not even see how to get started on your solution.
- We already tried that, with unsatisfactory results.
- You support this proposal merely because it would benefit you personally.

Answering these questions should help you prepare responses to possible objections. If you feel that you need a better idea of how others are likely to feel about your proposal, talk with a few people who are directly involved with or affected by the problem. The more you know about your readers' concerns, the better you will be able to anticipate their reservations and preferred alternative solutions.

Testing Your Choice

Now examine the problem and your proposed solution to see whether you can write a strong proposal. Start by asking yourself the following questions:

- Is this a significant problem? Do other people in the community or group really care about it, or can they be persuaded to care?
- Will my solution really solve the problem? Can it be implemented?
- Can I answer objections from enough people in the community or group to win support for my solution?

As you plan and draft your proposal, you will probably want to consider these questions again. If at any point you decide that you cannot answer them with a confident "Yes," you may want to consider proposing a different, more feasible solution to the problem; if none exists, you may need to choose a different problem to write about.

Testing Your Choice: A Collaborative Activity

At this point, you will find it useful to get together with two or three other students and present your plans to one another. This collaborative activity will help you determine whether you can write this proposal in a way that will interest and convince others.

Presenters: Take turns briefly defining the problem you hope to solve, identifying your intended readers, and describing your proposed solution.

Listeners: Tell the presenter whether the proposed solution seems appropriate and feasible for the situation and intended readers. Suggest objections and reservations you believe readers may have.

Offering Reasons for Your Proposal

To make a convincing case for your proposed solution, you must offer your readers good reasons for adopting your proposal.

Listing Reasons. *Write down every plausible reason you could give that might persuade readers to accept your proposal.* These reasons should answer your readers' key question: "Why is this the best possible solution?"

Choosing the Strongest Reasons. *Put an asterisk next to the strongest reasons—the reasons most likely to be convincing to your intended readers.* If you do not consider at least two or three of your reasons strong, you will probably have difficulty developing a strong proposal and should reconsider your topic.

Evaluating Your Strongest Reasons. *Now look at your strongest reasons and explain briefly why you think each one will be effective with your particular readers, the members of the group or community you are addressing.*

Considering Alternative Solutions

List alternative solutions members of the group or community might offer when they learn about your solution, and consider the advantages and disadvantages of each one relative to your solution. Even if members are likely to consider your proposal reasonable, they will probably want to compare your proposed solution with other possible solutions. You might find it helpful to chart the information as follows:

Possible Solutions	*Advantages*	*Disadvantages*
My solution		
Alternative solution 1		
Alternative solution 2		
Etc.		

Doing Research

So far you have relied largely on your own knowledge and experience for ideas about solving the problem. You may now feel that you need to do some research to learn more about the causes of the problem and to find more technical information about implementing the solution.

For guidelines on library and Internet research, see Chapter 21.

If you are proposing a solution to a problem about which others have written, you will want to find out how they have defined the problem and what solutions they have proposed. You may need to acknowledge these solutions in your essay, either accommodating or refuting them. Now is a good time—before you start drafting—to get any additional information you need. If you are proposing a solution to a local problem, you will want to conduct informal interviews with several people who are aware of or affected by the problem. Find out whether they know anything about its history and current ill effects. Try out your solution on them. Discover whether they have other solutions in mind.

For more on interviewing, see Chapter 20, pp. 645–48.

Considering Document Design

Think about whether your readers might benefit from design features, such as headings, numbered lists, or other elements that would make your presentation of the problem easier to follow and your solution more convincing. Earlier in this chapter's readings, for instance, Katherine S. Newman uses headings to introduce the major sections of her proposal. Consider also whether visuals—drawings, photographs, tables, or graphs—would strengthen your argument. These are not at all a requirement of

For more on document design, see Chapter 25.

an essay proposing a solution, but they could be helpful. You may come across promising visuals in your research and either download them from the Internet or make photocopies from library materials. When you reproduce visuals, make sure to acknowledge their sources.

Defining Your Purpose for Your Readers

Write a few sentences defining your purpose in proposing a solution to a problem of concern to the particular readers you have in mind. Remember that you have already identified your readers in the group or community you are addressing and developed your proposal with these readers in mind. Given these readers, try now to define your purpose by considering the following questions:

- Do I seek incremental, moderate, or radical change? Am I being realistic about what my readers are prepared to do? How can I overcome their natural aversion to change of any kind?

- How can I ensure that my readers will not remain indifferent to the problem?

- Who can I count on for support, and what can I do to consolidate that support? Who will oppose my solution? Shall I write them off or seek common ground with them?

- What exactly do I want my readers to do? To take my proposed solution as a starting point for further discussion about the problem? To take action immediately to implement my solution? To commit themselves to take certain preliminary steps, like seeking funding or testing the feasibility of the solution? To take some other action?

Formulating a Tentative Thesis Statement

For more on thesis and forecasting statements, see Chapter 13, pp. 557–59.

Write one or more sentences that could serve as your tentative thesis statement. In most essays proposing solutions to problems, the thesis statement is a concise assertion or announcement of the solution. Think about how emphatic you should make the thesis and whether you should include in it a forecast of your reasons.

Review the readings in this chapter to see how other writers construct their thesis statements. For example, recall that Rob Ryder moves from describing the problem to announcing his solution ("It's just too crowded out there. Basketball is meant to be played four on four" [paragraph 5]) to supporting his argument for the feasibility of this solution. His thesis statement is clear. With its surprising challenge to five-on-five basketball, it certainly calls for argument. Similarly, Patrick O'Malley states his thesis early in his essay: "If professors gave additional brief exams at frequent intervals, students would be spurred to study more regularly, learn more, worry less, and perform better on midterms, finals, and other papers and projects" (paragraph 2). O'Malley's thesis announces his solution—brief, frequent exams—to the problems created for students in courses limited to anxiety-producing, high-stakes midterms and finals. The thesis lists the reasons students will benefit from the solution in the order in which the benefits appear in the essay. A forecast is not a requirement of a thesis statement, but it does enable readers to predict the stages of the argument, thereby increasing their understanding.

As you draft your own thesis statement, pay attention to the language you use. It should be clear and unambiguous, emphatic but appropriately qualified. Although you will probably refine your thesis statement as you draft and revise your essay, trying now to articulate it will help give your planning and drafting direction and impetus.

For more on asserting a thesis, see Chapter 19, pp. 623–26.

■ PLANNING AND DRAFTING

This section will help you review your invention writing and research notes, determine specific goals for your essay, prepare a rough outline, and get started on your first draft.

Seeing What You Have

Reread your invention and research notes, asking yourself whether you have a good topic—an interesting problem with a feasible solution. If at this point you doubt the significance of the problem or question the success of your proposed solution, you might want to consider a new topic. If you are unsure about these basic points, you cannot expect to produce a persuasive draft.

However, if your invention material seems thin but promising, you may be able to strengthen it with additional invention writing. Ask yourself the following questions:

- Can I make a stronger case for the seriousness of the problem?
- Can I think of additional reasons for readers to support my solution?
- Are there any other ways of refuting alternative solutions to or troubling questions about my proposed solution?

Setting Goals

Before beginning to draft, think seriously about the overall goals of your proposal. Not only will the draft be easier to write once you have clear goals, but it will almost surely be more convincing as well.

Here are some questions that will help you set goals now. You may find it useful to return to them while drafting, for they are designed to help you focus on exactly what you want to accomplish with this proposal.

Your Purpose and Readers

- What do my readers already know about this problem?
- Are they likely to welcome my solution or resist it?
- Can I anticipate any specific reservations or objections they may have?

- How can I gain readers' enthusiastic support? How can I get them to want to implement the solution?
- How can I present myself so that I seem both reasonable and authoritative?

The Beginning

- How can I immediately engage my readers' interest? Should I open with a dramatic scenario, like O'Malley does? With statistics that highlight the seriousness of the problem, like Newman does? With a question (like Weisman) or a reference to personal experience (like Ryder)?
- What information should I give first? Next? Last?

Defining the Problem

- How much do I need to tell about the problem's causes or history?
- How can I show the seriousness of the problem? Should I use statistics, like Weisman does? Stress negative consequences, like O'Malley does?
- Is it an urgent problem? How can I emphasize its urgency? Should I redefine the problem?
- How much space should I devote to defining the problem? Only a little space (like O'Malley) or much space (like Newman)?

Describing the Proposed Solution

- How can I describe my solution so that it will look like the best way to proceed? Should I show how to implement it in stages, as Newman does? Or should I focus on my reasons to support it, as O'Malley does?
- How can I make the solution seem easy to implement? Or should I acknowledge that the solution may be difficult to implement and argue that it will be worth the effort?

Anticipating Readers' Objections

- Should I acknowledge every possible objection to my proposed solution? How might I choose among these objections?
- Has anyone already raised these objections? Should I name the person?
- Should I accommodate certain objections and refute others?
- What specific reasons can I give for refuting each objection? How can I support my refutations with reasons?
- How can I refute my readers' objections without seeming to attack anyone?

Evaluating Alternative Solutions

- How many alternative solutions do I need to mention? Which ones should I discuss at length? Should I indicate where each one comes from?

- What reasons should I give for rejecting the alternative solutions? Like O'Malley, can I offer any support for my reasons?
- How can I reject these other solutions without seeming to criticize their proponents? Weisman and O'Malley, for example, succeed at rejecting other solutions respectfully.

The Ending

- How should I conclude? Should I end by restating the problem and summarizing the solution? By arguing that some readers' preferred solution is sure to fail, as Weisman does? Or simply by summarizing my solution and its advantages, as O'Malley and Newman do?
- Is there something special about the problem that I should remind readers of at the end?
- Should I end with an inspiring call to action, like Ryder does, or with a scenario suggesting the consequences of a failure to solve the problem?
- Might a shift to humor or satire provide an effective way to end?

Outlining

After setting goals for your proposal, you are ready to make a working outline. The basic outline for a proposal is quite simple:

The problem

The solution

The reasons for accepting the solution

This simple plan is nearly always complicated by other factors, however. In outlining your material, you must take into consideration many other details, such as whether readers already recognize the problem, how much agreement exists on the need to solve the problem, how many alternative solutions are available, how much attention must be given to these other solutions, and how many objections should be expected.

Here is a possible outline for a proposal where readers may not understand the problem fully and other solutions have been proposed:

Presentation of the problem

    Its existence

    Its seriousness

    Its causes

Consequences of failing to solve the problem

Description of the proposed solution

List of steps for implementing the solution

See p. 319 for another
sample outline.

Reasons and support for the solution

    Acknowledgment of objections

    Accommodation or refutation of objections

Consideration of alternative solutions and their disadvantages

Restatement of the proposed solution and its advantages

Your outline will of course reflect your own writing situation. As you develop it, think about what your readers know and feel and about your own writing goals. Once you have a working outline, you should not hesitate to change it as necessary while drafting and revising. For instance, you might find it more effective to hold back on presenting your own solution until you have dismissed other possible solutions. Or you might find a better way to order the reasons for adopting your proposal. The purpose of an outline is to identify the basic features of your proposal and to help you organize them effectively, not to lock you into a particular structure.

For more on outlining, see
Chapter 11, pp. 518–21.

Most of the information you will need to develop each feature of a proposal can be found in your invention writing and research notes. How much space you devote to each feature is determined by the topic, not the outline. Do not assume that each entry on your outline must be given one paragraph. For example, each reason for supporting the solution may require a paragraph, but you might instead present the reasons, objections, and refutations all in one paragraph.

Drafting

You may want to review the
general advice on drafting in
Chapter 1, pp.16–19.

Start drafting your proposal, keeping in mind the goals you set while you were planning. Also keep in mind the two main goals of proposals: (1) to establish that a problem exists and is serious enough to require a solution, and (2) to demonstrate that your proposed solution is both feasible and the best possible alternative. Use your outline to guide you as you write, but do not hesitate to stray from it whenever you find that drafting takes you in an unexpected direction.

If you get stuck while drafting, explore the problem by using some of the writing activities in the Invention and Research section of this chapter. Perhaps the most important advice to remember about drafting is to write quickly without worrying about grammar and spelling. Later you can make corrections.

CRITICAL READING GUIDE

Now is the time to get a good critical reading of your draft. Writers usually find it helpful to have someone else read and comment on their drafts, and all writers know how much they learn when they read other writers' drafts. Your instructor may arrange such a reading as part of your coursework. If not, you can ask a classmate, friend, or family member to read your draft. You could also seek comments from a tutor at your campus writing center. (If you are unable to have someone

else read your draft, turn ahead to the Revising section, where you will find guidelines for reading your own draft critically.)

▶ **If You Are the Writer.**   In order to provide focused, helpful comments, your
reader must know your essay's intended audience, your purpose, and a problem in
the draft that you need help solving. Briefly write out this information at the top
of your draft.

- *Readers.* Identify the intended readers of your essay. How much do they
  know about the problem? How will they react to your proposed solution?

- *Purpose.* What do you want your readers to do or think as a result of reading
  your proposal?

- *Problem.* Ask your reader to help you solve the single most important problem you see with your draft. Describe this problem briefly.

▶ **If You Are the Reader.**   Reading a draft critically means reading it more than
once, first to get a general impression and then to analyze its basic features. Use
the following guidelines to help you give critical comments to others on essays that
propose solutions to problems.

1. *Read for a First Impression.* Read first to get a basic understanding of the
   problem and the proposed solution to it. After reading the draft, briefly write
   out your impressions. How convincing do you think the proposal will be
   for its particular readers? What do you notice about the way the problem is
   presented and the way the solution is argued for? Next, consider the problem
   the writer identified. If the problem will be covered by one of the other questions listed here, deal with it there. Otherwise, respond to the writer's concerns now.

2. *Evaluate How Well the Problem Is Defined.* Decide whether the problem is
   stated clearly. Does the writer give enough information about its causes and
   consequences? What more might be done to establish its seriousness? Is there
   more that readers might need or wish to know about it?

See pp. 322–23 to review
the basic features.

3. *Consider Whether the Solution Is Described Adequately.* Does the presentation of the solution seem immediately clear and readable? How could the presentation be strengthened? Has the writer laid out steps for implementation?
   If not, might readers expect or require them? Does the solution seem practical? If not, why?

4. *Assess Whether a Convincing Argument Is Advanced in Support of the Proposed Solution.* Look at the reasons offered for advocating this solution. Are
   they sufficient? Which are likely to be most and least convincing to the
   intended readers? What kind of support does the writer provide for each reason? How believable do you think readers will find it? Has the writer argued
   forcefully for the proposal without offending readers?

5. *Evaluate How Well the Writer Anticipates Readers' Objections and Questions.* Which accommodations and refutations seem most convincing? Which seem least convincing? Are there other objections or reservations that the writer should acknowledge?

6. *Assess the Writer's Evaluation of Alternative Solutions.* Are alternative solutions discussed and either accommodated or refuted? Which are the most convincing reasons given against other solutions? Which are least convincing, and why? Has the writer sought out common ground with readers who may advocate alternative solutions? Are such solutions accommodated or rejected without a personal attack on those who propose them? Try to think of other solutions that readers may prefer.

7. *Consider the Effectiveness of the Organization.* Evaluate the overall plan of the proposal, perhaps by outlining it briefly. Would any parts be more effectively placed earlier or later in the essay? Look closely at the way the writer orders the argument for the solution—the presentation of the reasons and the accommodation or refutation of objections and alternative solutions. How might the sequence be revised to strengthen the argument? Point out any gaps in the argument.

   - Look at the *beginning*. Is it engaging? If not, how might it be revised to capture readers' attention? Does it adequately forecast the main ideas and the plan of the proposal? Suggest other ways the writer might begin.
   - Look at the *ending*. Does it frame the proposal by echoing or referring to something at the beginning? If not, how might it do so? Does the ending convey a sense of urgency? Suggest a stronger way to conclude.
   - Look at any *design elements and visuals* the writer has incorporated. Assess how well they are incorporated into the essay. Point to any items that do not strengthen either the presentation of the problem or the argument in support of the solution.

8. *Give the Writer Your Final Thoughts.* What is the draft's strongest part? What part is most in need of further work?

▪ REVISING

Now you have the opportunity to revise your essay. Your instructor or other students may have given you advice on how to improve your draft. Or you may have begun to realize that your draft requires not so much revising as rethinking. For example, you may recognize that you are no longer convinced the problem is serious, that it is serious but cannot be solved now or anytime soon, that you cannot decide to whom to address the proposal, that you cannot come up with a set of convincing reasons why readers should support your solution, or that you have been unable to accommodate or refute readers' objections and questions or to evaluate alternative solutions. Consequently, instead of working to improve the various parts of your first draft, you may need to write a new draft that reshapes your argument. Many students —and professional writers—find themselves in this situation. Often a writer produces a draft or two and gets advice on them from others and only then begins to see what might be achieved.

If you feel satisfied that your draft achieves what you set out to do, you can focus on refining the various parts of it. This section will help you get an overview of your draft and revise it accordingly.

Getting an Overview

Consider your draft as a whole, following these two steps:

1. *Reread.* If at all possible, put the draft aside for a day or two before rereading it. When you do go back to it, start by reconsidering your audience and purpose. Then read the draft straight through, trying to see it as your intended readers will.

2. *Outline.* Make a quick scratch outline, indicating the basic features as they appear in the draft.

For more on scratch outlining, see Chapter 11, pp. 518–19.

Charting a Plan for Revision.   You may want to make a double-column chart like the following one to help you keep track of any problems you need to solve. In the left-hand column, list the basic features of proposals. As you analyze your draft and study any comments you have received from others, note the problems you want to solve in the right-hand column.

Turn to pp. 322–23 to review the basic features.

Basic Features	*Problems to Solve*
A well-defined problem	
An adequately described solution	
A convincing argument in support of the proposed solution	
An anticipation of readers' objections and questions	
An evaluation of alternative solutions	

Analyzing the Basic Features of Your Own Draft.   Turn to the Critical Reading Guide on the preceding pages. Using this guide, identify problems you now see in your draft. Note the problems on your chart.

Studying Critical Comments.   Review all of the comments you have received from other readers. For each comment, look at the draft to determine what might have led the reader to make that particular point. Try to be receptive to constructive criticism. Ideally, these comments will help you see your draft as others see it. Add to your revision chart any problems readers have identified.

Carrying Out Revisions

Having identified problems in your draft, you now need to find solutions and—most important—to carry them out. You have three ways of finding solutions:

1. Review your invention and planning notes for additional information and ideas.
2. Do further invention writing or research to provide material you or your readers think is needed.
3. Look back at the readings in this chapter to see how other writers have solved similar problems.

The following suggestions, which are organized according to the basic features on your revision chart, will get you started solving some common writing problems in essays proposing solutions. For now, focus on solving the problems identified on your chart. Avoid tinkering with grammar and punctuation; those tasks will come later, when you edit and proofread.

A Well-Defined Problem

- *Is the definition of the problem unclear?* Consider sketching out its history, including past attempts to deal with it, discussing its causes and consequences more fully, dramatizing its seriousness more vividly, or comparing it to other problems that readers may be familiar with.

An Adequately Described Solution

- *Is the description of the solution inadequate?* Try outlining the steps or phases involved in its implementation. Help readers see how easy the first step will be, or acknowledge the difficulty of the first step.

A Convincing Argument in Support of the Proposed Solution

- *Does the argument seem weak?* Try to think of more reasons for readers to support your proposal.
- *Is the argument hard to follow?* Try to put your reasons in a more convincing order—leading up to the strongest one rather than putting it first, perhaps.

An Anticipation of Readers' Objections and Questions

- *Does your refutation of any objection or question seem unconvincing?* Consider accommodating it by modifying your proposal.
- *Have you left out any likely objections to the solution?* Acknowledge those objections and either accommodate or refute them.

An Evaluation of Alternative Solutions

- *Have you neglected to mention alternative solutions that some readers are likely to prefer?* Do so now. Consider whether you want to accommodate or refute these alternatives. For each one, try to acknowledge its good points but argue that it is not as effective a solution as your own. You may in fact want to strengthen your own solution by incorporating into it some of the good points from alternatives.

The Organization

- **Is the beginning weak?** Think of a better way to start. Would an anecdote or an example of the problem engage readers more effectively?

- **Is the ending flat?** Consider framing your proposal by mentioning something from the beginning of your essay or ending with a call for action that expresses the urgency of implementing your solution.

- **Would design elements make the problem or proposed solution easier to understand?** Consider adding headings or visuals.

EDITING AND PROOFREADING

Now is the time to check your revised draft for errors in grammar, punctuation, and mechanics as well as to consider matters of style. Our research has identified several errors that are especially common in essays that propose solutions. The following guidelines will help you check and edit your essay for these common errors.

Checking for Ambiguous Use of *This* and *That*.   Using *this* and *that* vaguely to refer to other words or ideas can confuse readers. Because you must frequently refer to the problem and the solution in a proposal, you will often use pronouns to avoid the monotony or wordiness of repeatedly referring to them by name. Check your draft carefully for ambiguous use of *this* and *that*. Often the easiest way to edit such usage is to add a specific noun after *this* or *that*, as Patrick O'Malley does in the following example from his essay in this chapter:

> Another possible solution would be to help students prepare for midterm and final exams by providing sets of questions from which the exam questions will be selected or announcing possible exam topics at the beginning of the course. *This solution* would have the advantage of reducing students' anxiety about learning every fact in the textbook. . . .

O'Malley avoids an ambiguous *this* in the second sentence by repeating the noun *solution*. (He might just as well have used *preparation* or *action* or *approach*.)

The following sentences from proposals have been edited to avoid ambiguity:

▶ Students would not resist a reasonable fee increase of about $40 a year.

    increase
This would pay for the needed dormitory remodeling.
    ^

▶ Compared to other large California cities, San Diego has the weakest

                                         neglect
  programs for conserving water. This and our decreasing access to Colorado

  River water give us reason to worry.

▶ Compared to other proposed solutions to this problem, that is clearly the
                                                               one
  most feasible.

Checking for Sentences That Lack an Agent. A writer proposing a solution to a problem usually needs to indicate who exactly should take action to solve it. Such actors are called "agents." An agent is a person who is in a position to take action. Look at this sentence from O'Malley's proposal:

> To get students to complete the questions in a timely way, professors would have to collect and check the answers.

In this sentence, *professors* are the agents. They have the authority to assign and collect study questions, and they would need to take this action in order for this solution to be successfully implemented. Had O'Malley instead written "the answers would have to be collected and checked," the sentence would lack an agent. Naming an agent makes his argument convincing, demonstrating to readers that O'Malley has thought through one of the key parts of any proposal: who is going to take action.

The following sentences from student-written proposals illustrate how you can edit agentless sentences:

    Your staff should plan a survey
▶ ~~A survey could be planned~~ to find out more about students' problems in
  scheduling the courses they need.

    The registrar should extend
▶ ~~Extending~~ the deadline to mid-quarter ~~would make sense.~~

Sometimes it is appropriate to write agentless sentences, however. Study the following examples from O'Malley's essay:

> These exams should be given weekly, or at least twice monthly.

> Exams could be collected and responded to only every third or fourth week.

> Still another solution might be to provide frequent study questions for students to answer.

Even though these sentences do not name explicit agents, they are all fine because it is clear from the larger context who will perform the action. In each case, it is obvious that the action will be carried out by a professor.

■ STRENGTHENING THE ARGUMENT

This section focuses on student writer Patrick O'Malley's successful efforts to strengthen his argument for the solution he proposes in his essay, "More Testing, More Learning." Read the following three paragraphs from his draft; then compare them with paragraphs 4–6 of his final essay on pp. 315–16. As you read, take notes on the differences you observe between the draft and final versions.

The predominant reason students perform better with multiple exams is that they improve their study habits. Greater regularity in test taking means greater regularity in studying for tests. Students prone to cramming will be forced to open their textbooks more often, keeping them away from long, "kamikaze" nights of studying. Regularity prepares them for the "real world" where you rarely take on large tasks at long intervals. Several tests also improve study habits by reducing procrastination. An article about procrastination from the Journal of Counseling Psychology reports that "students view exams as difficult, important, and anxiety provoking." These symptoms of anxiety leading to procrastination could be solved if individual test importance was lessened, reducing the stress associated with the perceived burden.

With multiple exams, this anxiety decrease will free students to perform better. Several, less important tests may appear as less of an obstacle, allowing the students to worry less, leaving them free to concentrate on their work without any emotional hindrances. It is proven that "the performance of test-anxious subjects varies inversely with evaluation stress." It would also be to the psychological benefit of students if they were not subjected to the emotional ups and downs of large exams where they are virtually worry-free one moment and ready to check into the psychiatric ward the next.

Lastly, with multiple exams, students can learn how to perform better on future tests in the class. Regular testing allows them to "practice" the information they learned, thereby improving future test scores. In just two exams, they are not able to learn the instructor's personal examination

```
style, and are not given the chance to adapt their study
habits to it. The American Psychologist concludes: "It is
possible to influence teaching and learning by changing the
type of tests."
```

One difference you may have noted between O'Malley's draft and revision paragraphs is the sequencing of specific reasons readers should accept the solution and take action on it. Whereas the draft moves in three paragraphs from improving study habits to decreasing anxiety to performing better on future tests, the revision moves from learning more and performing better on major exams to improving study habits to decreasing anxiety. O'Malley made the change after a response from a classmate and a conference with his instructor helped him see that his particular readers (professors) would probably be most convinced by the improved quality of students' learning, not improvements in their study habits and feelings. As he continued thinking about his argument and discovering further relevant research, he shifted his emphasis from the psychological to the intellectual benefits of frequent exams.

You may also have noticed that the paragraphs of the revision are better focused than in the draft. The psychological benefits (reduced anxiety as a result of less procrastination) are now discussed mainly in a single paragraph (the third), whereas in the draft they are mixed in with the intellectual benefits in the first two paragraphs. O'Malley also uses more precise language in his revision; for example, changing "future tests" to "major exams, projects, and papers."

Another change you may have noticed is that all of the quoted research material in the draft has been replaced in the revision. Extending his library research to support his argument, O'Malley discovered the very useful Harvard report. As he found a more logical sequence, more precise terms, and fuller elaboration for his argument, he saw different ways to use the research studies he had turned up initially and quoted in the draft.

A final difference is that in the revision, O'Malley argues his reasons more effectively. Consider the draft and revised paragraphs on improved study habits. In the draft paragraph, O'Malley shifts abruptly from study habits to procrastination to anxiety. Except for study habits, none of these topics is developed, and the quotation adds nothing to what he has already said. By contrast, the revised paragraph focuses strictly on study habits. O'Malley keeps the best sentences from the draft for the beginning of the revised paragraph, but he adds several new sentences to help convince readers of the soundness of his argument that frequent exams improve students' study habits. These new sentences serve several functions: They anticipate a possible objection ("It might be argued . . ."), note a contrast between complex academic learning and familiar survival skills, and assert claims about the special requirements of regular academic study. The quotation from the Harvard report provides convincing support for O'Malley's claims and an effective way to conclude the paragraph.

The truck driver who wrote the proposal for recruiting and training more women (in the Writing in the Workplace project described on page 296) drafted and designed her document on her personal computer. Although she did not want to spend a lot of time on design, she did recognize the importance of her document's overall appearance. Using one of her grandson's college research papers as a model, she used double-spaced type, conventional paragraph indents, and one-inch margins. She told her grandson she hoped this "term-paperish format" would help persuade readers of the seriousness of the problem and the value of her proposed solution.

The driver also incorporated graphs and tables, which she gathered from several trucking industry magazines and newsletters that she had access to, to support and strengthen her proposal. To stress that carriers must increase their fleets in order to remain competitive within the industry, she used a line graph showing how the skyrocketing demand for motor carriers in the next five years will greatly exacerbate the current driver shortage. She used a second graph to demonstrate that recruiting minority-group men alone was unlikely to provide enough new drivers to fill the new positions. To show how the trucking industry can attract women on the basis of salary, she included a table contrasting the amount of money a woman truck driver could earn after one year, after five years, and so on, to how much women in other fields could earn over the same periods of time. In addition, she countered readers' possible preferred solution, established truck-driving schools, with a list comparing tuition rates with income statistics from the local newspaper—a comparison that clearly illustrated how difficult it would be for the region's divorced and single women to afford such training. In the accompanying text, the driver explained that although the proposed after-hours training program would require participating companies to spend some money up front, this solution had the added benefit of helping the community.

Finally, she used photographs as a framing device. Toward the beginning of the proposal, she scanned in a snapshot showing her alongside the double-bottom dump truck that she first learned to drive, which helped establish her authority as a trucker. Toward the end of the

The proposal incorporated photographs, such as this one, showing women truck drivers

proposal, she scanned in a variety of photographs showing women truck drivers competently performing their jobs; each of these images attested to the feasibility of her proposed solution.

THINKING CRITICALLY ABOUT WHAT YOU HAVE LEARNED

Now that you have worked extensively with essays that propose solutions to problems—reading them, talking about them, writing one of your own—take some time to reflect on what you have learned. What problems did you encounter while you were writing your essay, and how did you solve them? How did reading other essays proposing solutions influence your own essay? What ideas do you have about the social and cultural dimensions of this kind of writing?

Reflecting on Your Writing

Write a page or so telling your instructor about a problem you encountered in writing an essay that proposes a solution and how you solved it. Before you begin, gather all of your writing—invention and planning notes, drafts, critical comments, revision notes and plans, and final revision. Review these materials as you complete this writing task.

1. *Identify* one *writing problem you had to solve as you worked on your proposal essay.* Do not be concerned with grammar and punctuation; concentrate instead on problems unique to developing a proposal. For example: Did you puzzle over how to convince readers that your proposed solution would actually solve the problem you identified? Did you find it difficult to support the reasons you gave for recommending the solution?

Did you have trouble coming up with alternative solutions that your readers might favor?

2. *Determine how you came to recognize the writing problem.* When did you first discover it? What called it to your attention? If someone else pointed out the problem to you, can you now see hints of it in your invention writings? If so, where specifically? When you first recognized the problem, how did you respond?

3. *Reflect on how you went about solving the problem.* Did you reword a passage, cut or add details about the problem or solution, or move paragraphs or sentences around? Did you reread one of the essays in this chapter to see how another writer handled a similar problem, or did you look back at the invention suggestions? If you discussed the writing problem with another student, a tutor, or your instructor, did talking about it help? How useful was the advice you received?

4. *Write a page or so explaining the problem and your solution.* Be as specific as possible in reconstructing your efforts. Quote from your invention notes, draft essay, others' critical comments, your revision plan, and your revised essay to show the various changes your writing underwent as you tried to solve the problem. If you are still uncertain about your solution, say so. The point is not to prove that you have solved the problem perfectly but rather to show what you have learned

about solving problems when writing proposals. Taking time to explain how you identified a particular problem, how you went about trying to solve it, and what you learned from this experience can help you solve future writing problems more easily.

Reviewing What You Learned from Reading

Write a page or so explaining to your instructor how the readings in this chapter influenced your final essay. Your own essay has doubtless been influenced to some extent by one or more of the proposals you have read in this chapter as well as by classmates' essays that you have read. These other proposals may have helped you decide how to show your readers the seriousness of the problem you focused on, or they may have suggested how you could convince readers that they should support your proposed solution and ignore alternative solutions. Before you write, take some time to reflect on what you have learned from these selections.

1. *Reread the final revision of your essay; then look back at the selections you read before completing it.* Do you see any specific influences? For example, if you were impressed with the way one of the readings defined the problem, built a bridge of shared concerns with readers, detailed the steps in implementing the solution, argued against an alternative solution, or demonstrated that the solution would not cost too much, look to see where you might have been striving for similar effects in your own writing. Also look for ideas you got from your reading: writing strategies you were inspired to try, specific details you were led to include, and effects you sought to achieve.
2. *Write a page or so explaining these influences.* Did one reading have a particularly strong influence on your essay, or were several readings influential in different ways? Quote from the readings and from your final revision to show how your proposal was influenced by the selec-

tions you read. Finally, based on your review of the chapter's readings, point out any further improvements you would now make in your essay.

Considering the Social Dimensions of Essays Proposing Solutions

Proposals to solve problems are essential to our society. Businesspeople, school administrators, and government officials especially depend on proposals to decide where to direct resources and energy. Proposals enable us as individuals and as a society to make things better. We probably value this kind of thinking and writing because it makes us feel effective. It convinces us that difficulties can be overcome, that we can make practical, material changes that will improve our lives and the lives of others. We tell ourselves that with a little time, hard work, and ingenuity, we can make a difference. And this attitude has produced many positive changes in our culture—improvements in civil rights, in gender equality, in business and applied sciences as diverse as bridge building and environmental protection. Even so, thorny problems persist in the very areas where the most gains have been accomplished.

Who Defines the Problem?   First, when someone proposes a solution, that proposal shapes our thinking about some aspect of our own and others' lives by labeling it a problem. Yet the individuals most directly affected by the solution may not even accept this definition and may not want to see any change. Most basketball fans probably like basketball just the way it is; yet if Ryder's proposal became reality, they would have to learn how to watch and appreciate a somewhat different game. Similarly, not all students regard infrequent testing as a problem, but O'Malley's proposed solution would affect them nonetheless.

   This question of definition becomes particularly difficult when a relatively powerless constituency in our society—the homeless, illegal immigrants, unwed teenage mothers—is designated a "problem" by politicians and others in the mainstream. Writers (and readers) of proposals must exercise caution in such circumstances. For example, Newman proposes enabling inner-city fast-food workers to move to better-paying jobs downtown, but the workers remaining in the fast-food industry would not want to be seen as working "dead-end jobs," especially those who prefer taking on part-time work.

1. *How specifically would the proposals you have read and written actually make things better?* Whose interests would be served by these solutions? Who would be affected without their own stated interests being served?

2. *Do any of these proposals try to improve the status of a group that is not particularly powerful?* If so, what do you think is motivating the proposal writer? Is there any evidence that the writer is a member of this group or has consulted members of the group? What gives the writer authority to speak for them?

3. *Write a page or so explaining your ideas about defining social problems in essays that propose solutions to them.* Connect your ideas to your own essay and to the readings in this chapter.

The Frustrations of Effecting Real Change. No matter how well researched and well argued, many proposals are simply never carried out. The head of a personnel department might spend weeks drawing up a persuasive and feasible proposal for establishing a company day-care center, only to have upper management decide not to commit the necessary resources. A team of educators and social scientists might spend several years researching and writing a comprehensive, book-length proposal for dealing with the nation's drastic illiteracy rate but never see their solutions carried out because of a lack of coordination among the country's various educational institutions and governing bodies. In fact, it might be argued that the most successful proposals often operate on the smallest scale. For example, a proposal suggesting ways for a single community to increase literacy rates would probably have a better chance of implementation and ultimate success than the more far-reaching national proposal. (Yet this observation is not to rule out the value of the national proposal, on which the local proposal might, in fact, be based.)

Further, in choosing among competing alternative proposals, decision makers—who usually hold the power of the purse strings and necessarily represent a fairly conservative position—often go for the one that is cheapest, most expedient, and least disruptive. They may also choose small, incremental changes over more fundamental, radical solutions. While sometimes the most pragmatic choice, such immediately feasible solutions may also merely patch over a problem, failing to solve it structurally. They may even inadvertently maintain the status quo. Worse, they can cause people to give up all attempts to resolve a problem after superficial treatments fail.

1. *Consider how proposals invite writers to select problems that are solvable, and how they might inadvertently attempt to solve a minor problem that is actually only a small part of a major problem.* Do any of the proposals you have read and written reveal this misdirection? If so, which ones, and what do you think is the major problem in each case? Do you think the minor problem is worth solving as a first step toward solving the major problem, or is it perhaps an unfortunate diversion?

2. *Consider how the proposals you have read and written challenge the status quo.* What existing situation do they challenge, and just how do they challenge it? What roadblocks might deter these challenges? Might the proposals be more successfully carried out on a local scale?

3. *Reflect on commentators' argument that we should not try to solve fundamental social problems by "throwing money at them."* Do you think this objection is a legitimate criticism of most proposals to solve social problems? Or is it a manipulative justification for allowing the rich

and powerful to maintain the status quo? What else, besides money, is required to solve serious social problems? Where are these other resources to come from?

4. *Write a page or so explaining your ideas about the frustrations of effecting real change.* Connect your ideas to your own essay and to the readings in this chapter.

Justifying an Evaluation

Evaluation involves making judgments. Many times each day, we make judgments about subjects as diverse as the weather, food, music, computer programs, sports events, politicians, and films. In everyday conversation, we often express judgments casually ("I like it" or "I don't like it"), seldom giving our reasons (for example, "I hate cafeteria food because it is bland and overcooked") or supporting them with specific examples ("Take last night's spaghetti. That must have been a tomato sauce because it was red, but it did not have the tang of tomatoes. And the noodles were so overdone, they were mushy").

When we write an evaluation, however, we know most readers expect that instead of merely asserting a judgment, we will provide reasons and support to back it up. We know that unless we argue convincingly, readers who disagree will simply dismiss our judgments as personal preferences.

Evaluators can argue convincingly in several ways. One way is by making the reasons for your judgment explicit and by providing specific examples to support your reasons. You can also demonstrate knowledge of the particular subject being evaluated as well as the general category to which the subject belongs. For example, in an evaluation of a new Arnold Schwarzenegger action film, you would want to reassure readers that you are judging the particular film against your experience of other action films by Schwarzenegger and comparable films like those by Jean-Claude Van Damme and Sylvester Stallone. Showing readers you understand how the particular subject relates to other subjects in the same general category demonstrates that your judgment is based on standards that readers recognize as appropriate for judging that kind of subject. For example, most people would agree that taste and consistency are appropriate standards for judging spaghetti served in the school cafeteria, but they would reject the high noise level and uncomfortable seating in a cafeteria as appropriate reasons for evaluating cafeteria food (although these reasons would be appropriate for judging the cafeteria itself).

As you can see, reading and writing evaluations contributes to your intellectual growth by teaching you to develop reasoned, well-supported arguments for your judgments. Evaluations also require you to look critically at the standards underlying your own judgments as well as those of other people. In the process, you learn to appreciate how fundamentally important values are in determining what we think and how crucial it is for us to examine with a critical eye our cherished, but often unexamined values.

You will encounter evaluative writing in many different contexts, as the following examples suggest.

Writing in Your Other Courses

For a look at some of the decisions this writer makes about document design, see pp. 401–2.

- For an essay evaluating two films (*Emma* and *Clueless*) based on the Jane Austen novel, *Emma*, a student reads the novel, watches both films on videotape, and takes extensive notes. He also does an Internet search for reviews of the films. In his evaluation, the student argues that *Emma*, a period piece that faithfully follows the novel, is less successful than *Clueless*, a loose adaptation set in contemporary Beverly Hills, in capturing the spirit and romance of the novel. He supports his judgment with examples from the films and the novel as well as a few quotations from the movie reviews.

- For a political science course, a student writes a research paper evaluating the two major presidential candidates' performances during the first of their scheduled televised debates. Before watching the debate, she researches newspaper and newsmagazine reports on two previous presidential debates to see what kinds of standards others have used to evaluate televised debates. Then she watches the debate and records it so that she can review it later. As she views the debate, she makes notes evaluating each candidate's performance. Afterward, she copies the transcript of the debate from the newspaper and collects published, televised, and online reviews of the debate. She uses this material both to support her own judgment and to respond to possible objections and opposing judgments. Her final multimedia research paper includes downloaded Internet materials and videotaped excerpts from the debate.

Writing in the Community

- For the travel section of a local newspaper, a motorcycle enthusiast writes an article called "Hog Heaven" evaluating the tour at the Harley-Davidson factory and museum in York, Pennsylvania. He argues that Harley fans will enjoy the two dozen antique bikes on display and that people interested in business will be fascinated by the Harley plant because it includes both a classic assembly line (in which each worker performs an isolated operation on the motorcycles as they move along a conveyor belt) and a Japanese-inspired assembly team (in which three workers assemble an entire motorcycle from beginning to end in whatever way they think works best). He points out that, surprisingly, productivity is substantially higher for the assembly teams (forty-five minutes to assemble a motorcycle) than for the assembly-line workers (one hour and forty minutes). He concludes by emphasizing that the free tour offers something for everyone.

- For a campus publication, a college student writes an evaluation of a history course. She explains that the course includes three one-hour lectures per week by the professor plus a one-hour-per-week discussion led by a teaching assistant (TA). She states her judgment that although the lectures are boring, hard to follow, and seemingly unrelated to the assigned reading, the discussions are stimulating and help students grasp important information in each week's lectures and readings. To support her judgment, she describes a typical lecture and contrasts it to a typical discussion. She praises the TA for his innovative "term game," in which two teams of students compete to identify important concepts brought up in the week's lectures and reading, and for reviewing drafts via email. She concludes by recommending the course even though she wishes the TA could conduct the lectures as well as the discussions.

Writing in the Workplace

- In a written review of the work of a probationary employee, a supervisor judges the employee's performance as being adequate overall but still needing improvement in two key areas: completing projects on time and communicating effectively with others. To back up his judgment with specific examples and anecdotes, the supervisor explains that in one instance the employee's lateness derailed a team of workers, and tells how the employee's lack of tact and clarity in communicating with co-workers created a few serious misunderstandings during the six-month probation period.

- For a conference on innovations in education, an elementary school teacher evaluates *Schoolhouse Rock,* an animated educational television series developed in the 1970s and recently reinvented in several new formats: books, CD-ROM learning games, and music CDs. She praises the series as an entertaining and inventive way of presenting information, giving two reasons why the series is an effective teaching tool: Witty lyrics and catchy tunes make the information memorable, and cartoon-like visuals make the lessons painless. She supports each reason by showing and discussing videotaped examples of popular *Schoolhouse Rock* segments, such as "Conjunction Junction," "We the People," and "Three Is a Magic Number." She ends by expressing her hope that teachers and developers of multimedia educational software will learn from the example of *Schoolhouse Rock.*

Practice Evaluating a Subject: A Collaborative Activity

The preceding scenarios suggest some occasions for evaluating a subject. Think of several possible subjects that you know well enough to evaluate and consider the reasons you would give for evaluating each one.

Part 1. Get together with two or three other students to discuss possible subjects. Then choose one subject that everyone in your group knows well enough to evaluate (such as music, action movies, computer games, football, or science fiction novels). For example, if everyone in your group likes a particular style of music (such as country, blues, heavy metal, or rap), choose an artist or a recording with which you are all familiar. Note that for this activity you do not have to agree on a judgment. Instead, your aim is to see whether you can agree on appropriate reasons for evaluating the subject you choose.

Together, list all the reasons you can think of for evaluating the subject. For example, if your group decides to evaluate Me'shell Ndegéocello's second CD, *Peace beyond Passion* (1996), some possible reasons might include the following: the lyrics explore important social issues such as racism, religious intolerance, homophobia, and sexism; the bitter tone of the social commentary does not go with the slick, upbeat melodies of some of the songs; and some of the lyrics are hard to understand. Next, decide as a group which reasons are appropriate for evaluating the subject.

Part 2. As a group, spend ten to fifteen minutes discussing what happened when you tried to agree on appropriate reasons for evaluating the subject:

- First focus on the reasons your group found *easiest* to agree on. Discuss how you explained (or defended) their appropriateness or inappropriateness. For example, if you agreed on the value of social commentary in a recording like Ndegéocello's, why did you consider social commentary an appropriate standard for evaluating her music?

- Then focus on the reasons your group found *hardest* to agree on. Discuss why your group found these particular reasons so hard to agree on. For example, if you disagreed on the value of social commentary in a recording like Ndegéocello's, why did some group members consider it an appropriate standard while others considered it inappropriate? Where might your ideas about what was or was not an appropriate standard for evaluating the subject have come from?

READINGS

The readings in this chapter illustrate the features of essays that justify evaluations and the strategies writers rely on to realize the features. No two essays in this type of writing are much alike, and yet they share defining features. The Analyzing Writing Strategies and Commentary following each reading touch on a few features best illustrated by that essay, capturing its special qualities and strengths. Together, the four essays cover many of the possibilities of evaluative writing. Consequently, you will want to read as many of the essays as possible and, if time permits, complete the activities in Analyzing Writing Strategies and read the Commentaries. Following the readings, the Basic Features section offers a concise description of the features and strategies of evaluative essays and provides examples from all of the readings.

David Ansen, a senior editor at Newsweek, *has also worked as a film critic for the Associated Press Radio and various television programs. He has been honored by the Newspaper Guild of New York and has won the National Headliner Award. In his weekly movie reviews, Ansen usually can assume that his reviews will have some influence on whether his readers decide to see a movie. But, as Ansen acknowledges, his review of the first new* Star Wars *film in sixteen years is unlikely to influence many readers. Nevertheless, he takes seriously the assignment to think critically about the new film,* Star Wars: The Phantom Menace, *in this review, originally published in the May 17, 1999 issue of* Newsweek. *As you read, notice how Ansen gives readers specific examples from the film to support his judgment, while also encouraging readers to think critically about their own judgment.*

Star Wars: The Phantom Movie

David Ansen

A new menace: Darth Maul (Ray Park).

1   Twenty-two years ago *Star Wars* came out of nowhere, and changed the world. *Star Wars: Episode I, The Phantom Menace* comes out amid a cacophony of media hype, carrying on its shoulders the wildest hopes of several generations of worshipful moviegoers. It's been 16 years since *Return of the Jedi,* the last installment of George Lucas's trilogy. In a country with a notoriously short attention span, it's nothing less than miraculous that the passage of time made no dent in our appetite for this intergalactic adventure. It's not hype to say that *Phantom Menace* is the most eagerly awaited movie ever made. (Pilgrims started camping out in front of theaters a month before its May 19 opening.) You'll be hard pressed to find anyone who doubts for a moment that it will recoup its $115 million budget.

2   I will beat around the bush no longer. The movie is a disappointment. A big one. Will you take my word for it? Of course not. This massively marketed movie is virtually critic-proof. Everyone feels he must find out for himself.

3   The oddest thing about *Episode I*—which takes us back to the childhood of Anakin Skywalker, who as we know will later become Darth Vader, father of Luke Skywalker—is that it's a tale that didn't need to be told. Or that should have been told in 20 minutes, so that we could get on to the good stuff. What we want to know is how Anakin Skywalker, Jedi knight, turned to the Dark Side. You won't find that out in *The Phantom Menace.* Lucas presents us with a cute, towheaded 9-year-old (Jake Lloyd), a slave on the outlaw planet Tatooine (everyone's favorite sci-fi funkytown), who is discovered by the Jedi warriors Qui-Gon Jinn (Liam Neeson) and his apprentice Obi-Wan Kenobi (Ewan McGregor). The two Jedi are trying, and failing, to prevent a war between the powerful Trade Federation and the peaceful planet of Naboo, and they have stopped off on Tatooine to find a hyperdrive generator for their battle-damaged spacecraft. The war seems to be about commerce, but Qui-Gon Jinn intuits a

darker purpose behind it (just what *that* is also awaits in *Episode II*). Traveling with our Jedi heroes in Naboo's young Queen Amidala (Natalie Portman), who apparently is destined to marry Anakin (also in the next movie).

This boy, the Jedi instantly see, is special. It's even heavily hinted that he's been 4 immaculately conceived. Knowing what we know about his future, we want to see hints in this sweet child of his future monstrosity. Astonishingly, Lucas plants no seeds of evil. Instead, we are just told (by our old friend Yoda, in his pre-hermit days) that he senses a danger in him. What a rudimentary failure of storytelling. What was Lucas thinking when he turned Anakin into a banal youngster who, upon hearing he's going to leave home to train as a Jedi, proclaims, "Can I go, Mom? Yipee!" There is nothing strange, special or particularly interesting about the future Darth Vader here, and the casting of the conventionally adorable Lloyd, who looks like he should be hawking cereal on TV commercials, is no help. Neither is his good old-fashioned bad acting.

There's no shortage of action in *Phantom Menace*—lightsaber fights, attacking 5 armies, exploding spacecraft—but there's a curious lack of urgency. Our emotions are rarely engaged. It's been 22 years since Lucas directed a movie, and he's gotten rusty. His rhythm is off. Many of the scenes feel shapeless and flat—they're not ended, but abandoned. He doesn't seem to care about building a character. Ewan McGregor, one of the most vital and versatile young actors around, is completely wasted: Obi-Wan is given nothing interesting to do or say. Liam Neeson brings a grave, slightly weary dignity to Qui-Gon, but he's a rather somber character to carry what is meant to be a slam-bang adventure fantasy. There is no equivalent here to the irreverent, wise-cracking Han Solo, and his light touch is missed. For comic relief, we get the computer-generated Jar Jar Binks, a goofy, floppy-eared, vest-wearing toy serpent with a clumsy two-legged lope and an incomprehensible Caribbean accent. (He's a kind of extraterrestrial Stepin Fetchit.) Funny not he is, as Yoda would say. A more successful debut is made by the devilish Darth Maul, a horned, painted Sith lord who works for shrouded Evil Genius Darth Sidious. There's fresh menace in his mien.

The genuine magic in *Episode I* is all in its design. Conceptual artist Doug Chiang 6 and production designer Gavin Bocquet give us breathtaking vistas, fabulous imaginary cities that range from the Florentine splendor of Queen Amidala's domain to the teeming metropolis of Coruscan. The vaultlike Galactic Senate, whose box seats float through the air, is a triumph of baroque futurism. The sunset-drenched, open-air Jedi council chambers (shades of *Blade Runner*) glow like a remembered childhood picture book. (The art nouveau, glass-bubble undersea city, however, looks like a floating Lamps Plus showroom to me.) The massive, tree-crunching tanks of the droid armies have a brutal beauty; there's visual wit in the insectlike robot soldiers who do the Trade Federation's dirty work. Indeed, there's often so much to take in you wish Lucas would hold his shots longer, and let us feast on the details.

This is the impressive fruit of what Lucas calls his "digital backlot." *Phantom Men-* 7 *ace* uses more computer-generated shots than any movie in history (95 percent of the frames employ some digital work). The technical significance can't be denied—Lucas is blurring the line between live action and animation. When it works—in the spectacular pod-racing sequence on Tatooine, in which Anakin and his repulsive rival Sebulba fly like the wind through jagged desert canyons—the movie re-creates the buoyant adrenaline rush the original Star Wars so lightheartedly and consistently generated.

Lucas even uses digital techniques to tinker with the performances—seamlessly merging, for example, an actor's frown in take three upon his face in take six. This may be the first step toward a cinematic future in which virtual actors replace flesh-and-blood ones—and unfortunately it sometimes seems as if he's drained the flesh and blood from his own cast. The usually vibrant Portman is decked out in wonderful Kabuki-like makeup and dressed in beautifully bejeweled costumes, but most of the time she looks lost in space, stranded without a character to play. All the state-of-the-art technology in the world is no help to an actor saddled with Lucas's tinny dialogue. The original had its share of cheesy, B-movie performances: it was part of its retro "Buck Rogers" charm. But in these more extravagant settings, the lapses seem puzzling.

8

The arc of Anakin's story—a boy leaving home to become a Jedi and a hero, saving the day in battle—recapitulates Luke's story in *Star Wars.* You can understand why Lucas would want to carbon-copy his golden oldies—why tamper with the most successful formula in movie history? But you can't go home again. Lucas's sensibility, which was never particularly sophisticated to begin with, hasn't evolved in two decades. The *Phantom Menace* is more of the same, without the innocence and without the juice. And in the year of *The Matrix,* which offers a new style of special effects and a dystopian fantasy that hits closer to home, Lucas's childlike vision is beginning to look merely childish.

9

Connecting to Culture and Experience: Stereotypes

Some viewers of *The Phantom Menace* have complained about the ethnic stereotyping of certain characters. Lucas's "noseless leaders of the Galactic Trade Federation," reviewer Andrew Gumbel wrote online, "are clearly a throwback to the Yellow Peril characters popular in *Flash Gordon* and other series, but risk being interpreted as a racial slur" ("*Star Wars* Battles Charges of Racism" <http://www.freep.com/fun /starwars/nstar4.htm>). Ansen himself compares the digitized character Jar Jar Binks to a "kind of extraterrestrial Stepin Fetchit," referring to a 1930s actor who portrayed an African American stereotype now considered insulting, even racist (paragraph 5). Negative reaction to this character has been so strong that numerous Web sites have been created with titles like "The Jar Jar Hate Page" and "Die Jar Jar Binks, Die!"

With two or three other students, explore your views on ethnic, gender, or other stereotyping in films. Take turns trying to name movie characters that you think fit an ethnic stereotype. Then discuss as a group whether stereotyping should be taken into account when evaluating a film.

Analyzing Writing Strategies

1. At the beginning of this chapter, we make several generalizations about evaluative essays. Consider which of these statements is true of Ansen's essay:

   - It asserts a judgment.
   - It makes explicit the reasons for the judgment.
   - It provides specific support for the judgment.
   - It tries to demonstrate knowledge of the particular subject as well as the general category to which the subject belongs.

For more on using reasons to support an argument, see Chapter 19, pp. 627–33.

2. Reread paragraphs 3–5, where Ansen presents his **reasons** for judging *The Phantom Menace* as "disappointing," and underline each reason. To get started, underline the last part of sentence 1 in paragraph 3 that begins: "it's a tale that didn't need to be told."

Commentary: Subject and Judgment

Ansen identifies the subject by name in the title and twice in the first paragraph. Because the film is so widely anticipated, he can assume readers already know something about it. Nevertheless, he reminds them of its history as the latest installment in the *Star Wars* series by George Lucas. In subsequent paragraphs, Ansen identifies the actors, describes the main characters, and presents the story.

All of this information is necessary to give readers a context for the judgment. From the way Ansen addresses readers ("Anakin Skywalker, who as we know . . ." and "What we want to know is . . ." [paragraph 3]), he obviously expects them to know a great deal about the *Star Wars* films and even a little about *The Phantom Menace* from all the advance publicity. What readers cannot know, however, until they read his review, is his assessment of the film, which he announces in a clear, definitive **thesis statement**: "The movie is a disappointment" (paragraph 2). Ansen's thesis statement has two of the three qualities of a good thesis—that it be clear and arguable. The key word "disappointment" is clear in that everyone understands that it asserts an overall negative evaluation. Moreover, Ansen helps readers grasp what he means by showing them exactly what about the film he finds disappointing. The thesis is also obviously arguable since others disagree with his judgment. Ansen's thesis statement does not have the third quality—that the thesis be appropriately qualified. Instead of modifying his judgment, he makes it even more extreme by following the word "disappointment" with the phrase "A big one." Nevertheless, Ansen's essay is not all negative. In fact, he spends nearly as much space praising the film's "design" and "state-of-the-art technology" (paragraphs 6–8), as he does criticizing its "failure of storytelling" (paragraphs 3–5).

For more about thesis statements, see Chapter 19, pp. 623–26.

Considering Topics for Your Own Essay

List several movies that you would enjoy reviewing, and choose one from your list that you recall especially well. Of course, if you were actually to write about this movie, you would need to see it several times (on video) in order to develop your reasons and find supporting examples. For this activity, however, you do not have to view your film again. Just be sure it is one about which you have a strong judgment. Then, consider how you would argue for your judgment. Specifically, what reasons do you think you would give your readers? Why do you assume that your readers would recognize the standards these reasons reflect as appropriate for evaluating this particular film?

Amitai Etzioni is a sociology professor and former White House adviser. He has written many books and articles, including The Spirit of Community: Rights, Responsibilities, and the Communitarian Agenda *(1993),* The New Golden Rule: Community and Morality in a Democratic Society *(1997), for which he won the Simon Wiesenthal Center's annual Tolerance Book Award, and* The Limits of Privacy *(1999). He is also the founder of the journal* The Responsive Community.

This evaluative essay was first published in the Miami Herald. *According to the original headnote, Etzioni's teenage son Dari, one of his five children, helped him write this evaluation—although the headnote does not specify what Dari contributed. As you read the essay, notice that Etzioni also acknowledges learning from another of his children, Oren. Given that Etzioni is a respected professor and author, how do you think his credibility in this evaluation is affected by his admission that he got help from two of his children?*

Working at McDonald's

Amitai Etzioni

1   McDonald's is bad for your kids. I do not mean the flat patties and the white-flour buns; I refer to the jobs teen-agers undertake, mass-producing these choice items.

2   As many as two-thirds of America's high school juniors and seniors now hold down part-time paying jobs, according to studies. Many of these are in fast-food chains, of which McDonald's is the pioneer, trend-setter and symbol.

3   At first, such jobs may seem right out of the Founding Fathers' educational manual for how to bring up self-reliant, work-ethic-driven, productive youngsters. But in fact, these jobs undermine school attendance and involvement, impart few skills that will be useful in later life, and simultaneously skew the values of teen-agers—especially their ideas about the worth of a dollar.

4   It has been a longstanding American tradition that youngsters ought to get paying jobs. In folklore, few pursuits are more deeply revered than the newspaper route and the sidewalk lemonade stand. Here the youngsters are to learn how sweet are the fruits of labor and self-discipline (papers are delivered early in the morning, rain or shine), and the ways of trade (if you price your lemonade too high or too low . . .).

5   Roy Rogers, Baskin Robbins, Kentucky Fried Chicken, *et al.,* may at first seem nothing but a vast extension of the lemonade stand. They provide very large numbers of teen jobs, provide regular employment, pay quite well compared to many other teen jobs and, in the modern equivalent of toiling over a hot stove, test one's stamina.

6   Closer examination, however, finds the McDonald's kind of job highly uneducational in several ways. Far from providing opportunities for entrepreneurship (the lemonade

stand) or self-discipline, self-supervision and self-scheduling (the paper route), most teen jobs these days are highly structured—what social scientists call "highly routinized."

True, you still have to have the gumption to get yourself over to the hamburger stand, but once you don the prescribed uniform, your task is spelled out in minute detail. The franchise prescribes the shape of the coffee cups; the weight, size, shape and color of the patties; and the texture of the napkins (if any). Fresh coffee is to be made every eight minutes. And so on. There is no room for initiative, creativity, or even elementary rearrangements. These are breeding grounds for robots working for yesterday's assembly lines, not tomorrow's high-tech posts.

There are very few studies on the matter. One of the few is a 1984 study by Ivan Charper and Bryan Shore Fraser. The study relies mainly on what teen-agers write in response to questionnaires rather than actual observations of fast-food jobs. The authors argue that the employees develop many skills such as how to operate a food-preparation machine and a cash register. However, little attention is paid to how long it takes to acquire such a skill, or what its significance is.

What does it matter if you spend 20 minutes to learn to use a cash register, and then —"operate" it? What "skill" have you acquired? It is a long way from learning to work with a lathe or carpenter tools in the olden days or to program computers in the modern age.

A 1980 study by A. V. Harrell and P. W. Wirtz found that, among those students who worked at least 25 hours per week while in school, their unemployment rate four years later was half of that of seniors who did not work. This is an impressive statistic. It must be seen, though, together with the finding that many who begin as part-time employees in fast-food chains drop out of high school and are gobbled up in the world of low-skill jobs.

Some say that while these jobs are rather unsuited for college-bound, white, middle-class youngsters, they are "ideal" for lower-class, "non-academic," minority youngsters. Indeed, minorities are "over-represented" in these jobs (21 percent of fast-food employees). While it is true that these places provide income, work and even some training to such youngsters, they also tend to perpetuate their disadvantaged status. They provide no career ladders, few marketable skills, and undermine school attendance and involvement.

The hours are often long. Among those 14 to 17, a third of fast-food employees (including some school dropouts) labor more than 30 hours per week, according to the Charper-Fraser study. Only 20 percent work 15 hours or less. The rest: between 15 and 30 hours.

Often the stores close late, and after closing one must clean up and tally up. In affluent Montgomery County, Md., where child labor would not seem to be a widespread economic necessity, 24 percent of the seniors at one high school in 1985 worked as much as five to seven days a week; 27 percent, three to five. There is just no way such amounts of work will not interfere with school work, especially homework. In an informal survey published in the most recent yearbook of the high school, 58 percent of seniors acknowledged that their jobs interfere with their school work.

The Charper-Fraser study sees merit in learning teamwork and working under supervision. The authors have a point here. However, it must be noted that such learning is not automatically educational or wholesome. For example, much of the supervision in fast-food places leans toward teaching one the wrong kinds of compliance: blind obedience, or shared alienation with the "boss."

Supervision is often both tight and woefully inappropriate. Today, fast-food chains and other such places of work (record shops, bowling alleys) keep costs down by having teens supervise teens with often no adult on the premises.

There is no father or mother figure with which to identify, to emulate, to provide a role model and guidance. The work-culture varies from one place to another: Sometimes it is a tightly run shop (must keep the cash registers ringing); sometimes a rather loose pot party interrupted by customers. However, only rarely is there a master to learn from, or much worth learning. Indeed, far from being places where solid adult work values are being transmitted, these are places where all too often delinquent teen values dominate. Typically, when my son Oren was dishing out ice cream for Baskin Robbins in upper Manhattan, his fellow teen-workers considered him a sucker for not helping himself to the till. Most youngsters felt they were entitled to $50 severance "pay" on their last day on the job.

The pay, oddly, is the part of the teen work-world that is most difficult to evaluate. The lemonade stand or paper route money was for your allowance. In the old days, apprentices learning a trade from a master contributed most, if not all, of their income to their parents' household. Today, the teen pay may be low by adult standards, but it is often, especially in the middle class, spent largely or wholly by the teens. That is, the youngsters live free at home ("after all, they are high school kids") and are left with very substantial sums of money.

Where this money goes is not quite clear. Some use it to support themselves, especially among the poor. More middle-class kids set some money aside to help pay for college, or save it for a major purchase—often a car. But large amounts seem to flow to pay for an early introduction into the most trite aspects of American consumerism: flimsy punk clothes, trinkets and whatever else is the last fast-moving teen craze.

One may say that this is only fair and square; they are being good American consumers and spend their money on what turns them on. At least, a cynic might add, these funds do not go into illicit drugs and booze. On the other hand, an educator might bemoan that these young, yet unformed individuals, so early in life driven to buy objects of no intrinsic educational, cultural or social merit, learn so quickly the dubious merit of keeping up with the Joneses in ever-changing fads, promoted by mass merchandising.

Many teens find the instant reward of money, and the youth status symbols it buys, much more alluring than credits in calculus courses, European history or foreign languages. No wonder quite a few would rather skip school—and certainly homework— and instead work longer at a Burger King. Thus, most teen work these days is not providing early lessons in the work ethic; it fosters escape from school and responsibilities, quick gratification and a short cut to the consumeristic aspects of adult life.

Thus, parents should look at teen employment not as automatically educational. It is an activity—like sports—that can be turned into an educational opportunity. But it can also easily be abused. Youngsters must learn to balance the quest for income with the needs to keep growing and pursue other endeavors that do not pay off instantly—above all education.

Go back to school.

Connecting to Culture and Experience: Job Skills

Etzioni argues in this essay that McDonald's-type jobs do not teach the kinds of skills young people need to prepare for employment in a "high-tech" world, skills like entrepreneurship, self-discipline, and initiative (paragraphs 6 and 7).

With other students, discuss the skills you believe you need to learn for the kind of job or career you envision for yourself. Review the essay to make a complete list of the skills Etzioni mentions. Then discuss each skill to determine whether it is important to you. Add to Etzioni's list any other skills you think are important.

Analyzing Writing Strategies

1. To see how Etzioni presents the subject, reread the essay, underlining the factual details about who works at fast-food restaurants and what they do on the job. If you can, identify the source of Etzioni's information: his own firsthand observation, conversations with fast-food workers (such as his sons), or published research.

   Then, based on your own knowledge of fast-food restaurants, consider which details you accept and which you think may be inaccurate or only partly true. Also consider what Etzioni may have left out and why: Do you think he left out certain facts because he assumes his readers already know them, because they are not important, or because they would not support his judgment?

For more on these ways of supporting a thesis, see Chapter 19, pp. 627–29.

2. Etzioni provides several kinds of **support.** Find and underline the **examples** he offers in paragraph 7 to support his assertion in paragraph 6 that jobs at McDonald's do not teach teenagers to become self-disciplined entrepreneurs. Then find and underline the **statistics** he offers in paragraphs 12 and 13 to support his assertion in paragraph 11 that such jobs "undermine school attendance and involvement." Finally, speculate about whether these kinds of support are likely to be convincing for Etzioni's readers—parents who think that after-school jobs can teach teenagers valuable skills. How convincing are they for you?

Commentary: Counterarguing

Early in his essay, Etzioni acknowledges the alternative judgment he expects many of his readers to hold: that McDonald's-type jobs are good because they teach teenagers to become "self-reliant, work-ethic-driven, productive youngsters" (paragraph 3). Although he suggests that he shares with his readers these standards for evaluating jobs for teenagers, Etzioni makes clear that he disagrees with his readers' judgment about the type of fast-food jobs popularized by McDonald's.

For more on counterarguing, see Chapter 19, pp. 634–37.

In addition to anticipating readers' likely preference for the opposing judgment, Etzioni anticipates and **counterargues** readers' possible objections to his argument. For example, he acknowledges that Charper and Fraser's research finding that "employees develop many skills" (paragraph 8) directly contradicts his own claim that fast-food jobs "impart few skills that will be useful in later life" (paragraph 3). He handles this objection by accepting as fact Charper and Fraser's finding, but counterarguing that the kinds of skills learned by fast-food workers are the wrong skills. They are "highly routinized" skills that prepare young people to work on "yesterday's assembly lines, not tomorrow's high-tech posts" (paragraph 7).

Similarly, Etzioni acknowledges as "impressive" Harrell and Wirtz's statistic showing that students who work a lot in high school may be employed four years later at a higher rate than those who do not work in high school (paragraph 10). But he then counterargues by noting that "many who begin as part-time employees in fast-food chains drop out of high school and are gobbled up in the world of low-skill jobs." He concludes this refutation by condemning McDonald's-type jobs because they "perpetuate" the status quo. He compares fast-food jobs to the school tracking system that separates "non-academic" and "college-bound" students (paragraph 11). Instead of providing minority youngsters with an opportunity to advance, McDonald's-type jobs "perpetuate their disadvantaged status," providing "no career ladders, few marketable skills" and at the same time undermining "school attendance and involvement."

Etzioni has his readers very much in mind as he writes this essay. He anticipates how they are likely to evaluate the subject as well as how they might respond to his argument. Writers have three options in anticipating readers: they can simply acknowledge readers' concerns, they can accommodate them by making concessions, or they can try to refute them. Etzioni chooses this last option. As you plan your own essay, think about your readers and how you could anticipate and counterargue readers' concerns.

Considering Topics for Your Own Essay

In this essay, Etzioni evaluates a kind of job he thinks is inappropriate for high school students. List the kinds of jobs you know enough about to evaluate. Then choose one job from your list and consider the standards you would use to evaluate it. If you do not have sufficient firsthand knowledge to evaluate any particular job, consider what kind of work or career you might want to know more about. Etzioni gathered information about fast-food jobs from his children and from published research. How could you learn more about the job you have chosen?

Kristine Potter was a college student when she wrote this essay evaluating a Web site related to her son's medical condition. As you read, notice what she looks for in evaluating medical information on the Web. Then consider whether the standards Potter applies to the Web differ from those you would apply to research sources found in the library or through interviews and observations.

Asthma on the Web

Kristine Potter

The World Wide Web (or WWW) has served as a convenient starting point for much of my college research, but I was still not sure whether it would also be useful for researching questions concerning my personal life. Since my nine-year-old son, Jeremy, suffers from asthma, I am particularly interested in using the Web to learn about the most current treatments for the disease. The Web's up-to-date information and easy accessibility from my home make it an especially attractive research tool. However, I am also aware that Web-based material must be evaluated carefully because anyone with technological know-how can publish on the Web. I have found that when I research medical information on the Web, I need to consider the same basic questions I use when researching for my college courses: (1) Is the information easily accessible? (2) Is it helpful? and (3) Is it reliable? My evaluation of the Canadian Lung Association's *Asthma* Web site, located at <http://www.lung.ca/asthma>, led me to the conclusion that this site successfully meets my criteria for accessible, helpful, and reliable information.

I accessed the *Asthma* home page from a list of search results produced by Yahoo!, <http://www.yahoo.com>, a popular Internet search engine, and was happy to learn that one important criterion for Web site usefulness—speedy access to information—was immediately satisfied. Unlike my earlier visit to another asthma-related Web site where I spent an average of thirty seconds waiting for each new page to load, the Lung Association's *Asthma* home page loaded instantaneously and I could see at a glance that it might be useful for my needs. The page downloaded quickly because it does not use a lot of graphics to attract visitors. Although the information at the other site may have been useful in my research, graphic downloads took so long that I left in search of other sites that might more efficiently satisfy my research purposes. While the speed at which a Web page loads will vary from one computer to the next, according to Yale's *Web Style Guide,* "research has shown that for most computing tasks the threshold of frustration is around 10 seconds" (Lynch and Horton). Researchers, like myself, who access the Internet from home at less than ethernet speeds appreciate quick downloading of information more than fancy graphics. Therefore, the speed at which the Lung Association's *Asthma* home page appeared in my browser contributed largely to my decision to remain on the Web site.

The Canadian Lung Association's *Asthma* Web site seems well designed, incorporating a variety of links and other features that make it easy to navigate the site and find information quickly. As shown in Figure 1, for example, the *Asthma* home page includes several different links to additional pages of information at the site. At the top of the home page are three clickable buttons: "Home," for accessing the Canadian Lung Association home page; "Index," for accessing a list of the site's contents; and "Français," for giving users a choice between the French and English language versions of the Web site. On the left side of the screen are a "Quick Search" option and a lengthy menu of topics. The "Quick Search" option gives users an opportunity to search for information by keywords, while the menu organizes information under various topic headings with hyperlinks to available information at the Lung Association's Web site. In the center of the *Asthma*

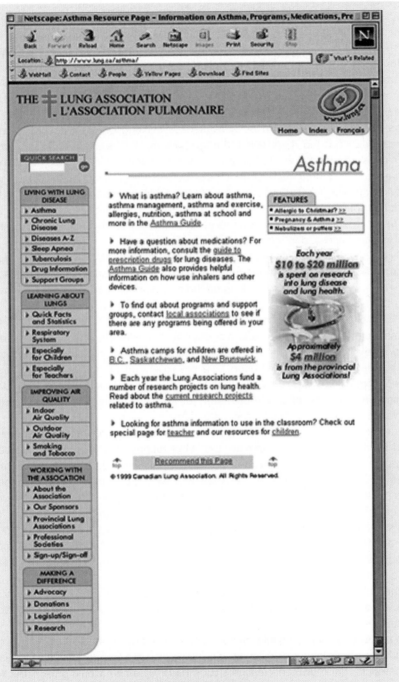

Fig. 1. The Lung Association's asthma home page.

home page are two additional sets of hyperlinks for accessing specific information about asthma: first, keywords, underlined and printed in red, within the easy-to-read bulleted text (such as "Asthma Guide") and, second, underlined double arrows in a "Features" box (for example, "Pregnancy & Asthma >>").

Other pages at the *Asthma* site also feature useful ways of accessing information. The most important of these is a site map, which displays large buttons as hyperlinks to important topics on asthma. As shown in Figure 2, the "Asthma Resource Guide" maps out the site's contents. It can be accessed by clicking on the underlined keywords "Asthma Guide" on the *Asthma* home page (Figure 1). The site map reappears at the bottom of every page within the Lung Association's *Asthma* Web site. Look, for example, at Figure 3, the "Asthma Management" page accessed by clicking on the "Management" button in Figure 2. As you can see, the "Asthma Management" page includes the site map at the bottom of the screen as well as the search and menu options at the top and left side of the screen. It also introduces yet another way of maneuvering within the Web site: "Go back" and "Go to" clickable arrows.

4

By giving users a variety of options, the designers of this Web site have made it very easy for users to access information. The site map, in particular, enables users to return to pages they visited earlier by clicking on the corresponding links, rather than having to retype the URL or rely on the "Back" button in their browsers to retrace their steps. I found only one problem in the site's system of hyperlinks: Two buttons, both labeled "Asthma," one in the site map and the other in the left-frame menu, lead to different pages. The site map "Asthma" button links to the *Asthma* home page (Figure 1), whereas the menu "Asthma" button links to a general information page on asthma adapted from a 1997 article by a Canadian doctor (see Figure 4). Apart from this one hyperlink problem, the Web site provides easy access to information about the Lung Association in general and asthma in particular.

5

Furthermore, the hyperlinks at the *Asthma* Web site offer quality information that helped in my research. For example, the "Medications" link on the site map leads to information on various drug treatments and their possible side effects. I was grateful to learn that Jeremy's doctor is not treating him with drugs that produce serious side effects. I also learned about the different causes of asthma and clarified a confusion I had gotten from visiting a different Web site, *Adult/Pediatric Allergy Asthma Center,* <http://www.allergies-asthma.com>, which had led me to misunderstand the importance of symptoms that asthma and allergies have in common (Dantzler). However, according to Jeremy's doctor, my son's asthmatic attacks are responses to viral infections, not allergic reactions to things like dust and pollen. The Lung Association's site confirmed what the doctor had told me. Now I know which symptoms indicate that Jeremy is having an asthmatic attack and which indicate he is having a harmless allergic reaction to high pollen counts.

6

In addition to confirming information that Jeremy's doctor had already given me, the *Asthma* site offers useful new information, including the suggestion that I collaborate with the doctor on a "Written 'Rescue' Action Plan." The plan would give instructions on what to do at each stage in an asthmatic attack so as to avoid a "full-blown episode" (Canadian Lung Association). I also learned about the Peak Flow Meter, a device that

7

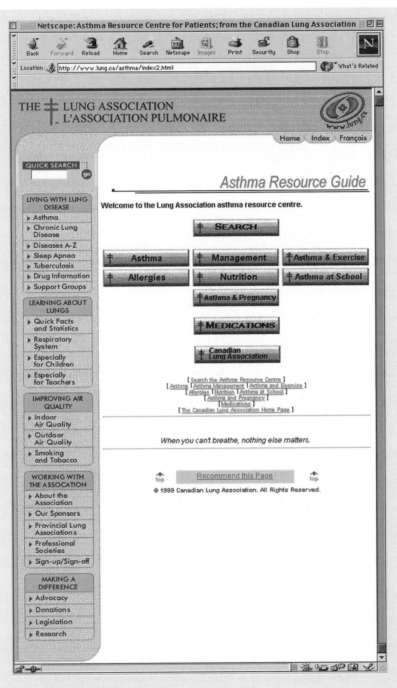

Fig. 2. The Asthma Resource Guide.

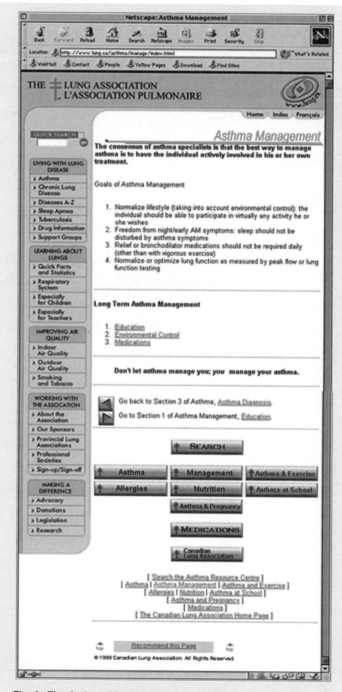

Fig. 3. The Asthma Management page accessed via the "Management" button shown in Fig. 2.

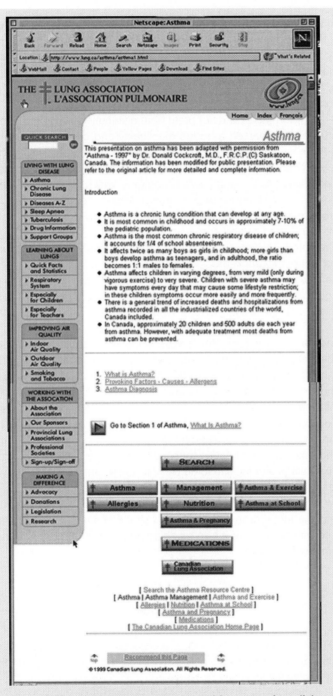

Fig. 4. General information page accessed from one of two links both labeled "Asthma."

can detect each stage in an asthmatic attack and that can help implement the action plan appropriately. Because I felt this new information might benefit Jeremy, I downloaded the pages to my hard drive and printed them out to bring to Jeremy's next doctor's appointment.

Not only is the Lung Association's *Asthma* Web site easy to access and full of helpful information, but it is also reliable. For a Web site to be reliable, it must have authoritative, up-to-date information and not profit from distributing that information. Although it can be difficult for a layperson to judge the quality and currency of information, most Web sites indicate who has sponsored and authored the site, as well as when it was last revised. The *Asthma* home page, for example, identifies itself as an official site of the Canadian Lung Association, <http://www.lung.ca>, which links to the American Lung Association, <http://www.lungusa.org> (and vice versa), completing a circle that shows that each organization considers the other to be a trustworthy source of information. Although both the Canadian and American Lung Association Web sites solicit donations to help fund research, the information on the *Asthma* site is free and meant to promote healthy lungs, not empty pocketbooks.

8

Because new research in medicine and health care constantly changes, it is important to seek out information that is up-to-date. Of course, currency is supposed to be one of the advantages of researching on the Web. Many Web designers indicate on a general information page when the information at a Web site was created or last updated. A copyright notice at the bottom of the pages at the *Asthma* site indicates it was created in 1999 by the Canadian Lung Association. The page I mentioned earlier (Figure 4) has the 1999 copyright but includes a headnote indicating that it is adapted from a 1997 article. The headnote also identifies the author by name, academic credentials, and professional affiliations.

9

The time I have spent at the *Asthma* Web site has been worthwhile. I consider the information there useful to my research because it provides answers to my questions concerning accessibility, helpfulness, and reliability. Despite the problem with the two "Asthma" hyperlinks, I find the site to be well organized and efficient (I can move quickly among pages). I also find the material helpful because it substantiates information I already knew about asthma and gives me new and practical ways to monitor Jeremy's health. Finally, the fact that the *Asthma* Web site is sponsored by the Canadian Lung Association convinces me that it is a reliable source of up-to-date information on successful treatments for asthma.

10

Works Cited

American Lung Association. 1998. 8 Nov. 1999 <http://www.lungusa.org>.

Canadian Lung Association. *Asthma*. 1999. 18 Nov. 1999 <http://www.lung.ca/asthma>.

Dantzler, Brian S. *Adult/Pediatric Allergy Asthma Center*. 5 July 1999 <http://www.allergies-asthma.com>.

Lynch, Patrick J., and Sarah Horton. *Web Style Guide*. 1997. Yale University. 5 July 1999 <http://info.med.yale.edu/caim/manual/interface/basic_interface2.html>.

Connecting to Culture and Experience: Responsibility

Access to medical information on the Web has increased at the same time that confidence in the quality of health care in the United States has declined. Like Potter, many people want to verify that their doctor is up-to-date and offering all of the available treatment options, not just those that the insurance company or HMO (health maintenance organization) wants to pay for. In the past, patients seemed to rely more on doctors not only for information, but for decision making as well. When doctors made diagnoses or prescribed particular treatments, patients usually would simply accept their doctors' decisions. Only in special cases would patients ask for a consultation with another doctor and seldom would patients try to do research themselves to learn about other possible diagnoses or treatment options. Now, however, more and more people are trying to inform themselves and take an active role in their own and their family's health care. Instead of granting all the authority to their doctors, they are taking on more responsibility for their own health care decisions.

With two or three other students, discuss how this change was brought about or accelerated by the widespread accessibility of medical information on the Web. Take turns telling about your own experience. Have you, your family, or your friends attempted to research a medical condition or treatment option? Do you normally rely on your doctor's expertise and authority, or do you try to take some responsibility for health care decisions?

In what other areas, besides health care, are individuals without special training informing themselves and trying to share responsibility with (or perhaps wrest authority from) the experts? Home schooling? Stock trading? Computer programming?

Analyzing Writing Strategies

1. Potter supports her argument with examples: figures displaying screen shots of Web pages she refers to in her essay. To see how they contribute to her argument, skim paragraphs 3–5, where the figures are referred to and discussed. Then choose *one* reference to examine closely. Look both at the sentences explaining what the figure is supposed to illustrate and at the figure itself. Consider whether the figure is really needed and whether the explanation is sufficient.

   Finally, notice that in paragraphs 6–8, Potter refers to particular Web sites but does not illustrate them with figures. In some cases, readers could look at a figure referred to earlier to see what she is referring to. But in a couple of cases, Potter would have to add new figures. If you were the author of this essay, how do you think you would decide which figures to include and which to leave out?

2. Reread paragraph 1 and underline Potter's **thesis statement,** the place where she asserts her overall judgment of the *Asthma* Web site. Then skim the essay, marking other places where she restates her judgment. Determine whether her thesis statement meets the three standards of a good thesis: Is it clear, arguable, and appropriately qualified? If you think it could be improved, indicate how you would revise it.

For more on asserting a thesis, see Chapter 19, pp. 623–26.

Commentary: Reasons

Potter gives three reasons in support of her judgment of the Canadian Lung Associ-ation's *Asthma* Web site: It is a useful site because the information it contains is acces-sible, helpful, and reliable. Although these reasons seem to be commonsensical, Potter assumes her readers need explanations in order to understand what she means by the key terms *accessible, helpful,* and *reliable* as well as why she thinks these reasons are appropriate for her evaluation. For example, in paragraph 2, she explains what she means by *accessible:* "speedy access to information" and "quick downloading" of pages. To support her reason, Potter relates her own experience with slow-loading pages, cites an expert, and describes in paragraphs 3–5 the features that make the *Asthma* Web site easy to navigate. Readers with frustrating experiences like hers will readily agree that accessibility is a plausible reason for judging a Web site being used for research. Similarly, to explain what she considers *helpful* information, Potter identifies and then discusses several categories of "quality information that helped in my research": Information that confirms (or presumably does not contradict) what her son's doctor has told her, information that clarifies confusion, and information that offers new and practical suggestions for monitoring an asthmatic attack (para-graphs 6 and 7).

For more on forecasting and topic sentences, see Chap-ter 13, pp. 559–63.

Because Potter wants her readers to understand her reasons, she tries to make her writing direct and clear. She **forecasts** her reasons in a series of questions at the end of the opening paragraph, and then takes up each reason in that order in her essay, as this scratch outline shows:

Paragraph 1 introduces the subject, states the thesis, and forecasts three reasons

Paragraphs 2–5 develop and support the first reason ("accessible")

Paragraphs 6–7 develop and support the second reason ("helpful")

Paragraphs 8–9 develop and support the third reason ("reliable")

Paragraph 10 concludes by summarizing the main points

Potter also tends to begin her paragraphs with a **topic sentence** announcing what she will discuss next; for example, "Furthermore, the hyperlinks at the *Asthma* Web site offer quality information that helped in my research" (paragraph 6). In some cases, the topic sentence serves as well to remind readers of the topic they just read about in the preceding paragraph, as in these examples: "In addition to confirming information that Jeremy's doctor had already given me, the *Asthma* site offers useful new information" (paragraph 7), and "Not only is the Lung Association's *Asthma* Web site easy to access and full of helpful information, but it is also reliable" (para-graph 8). The topic sentences help keep readers oriented; without these cues, read-ers might get lost in the details and examples Potter gives to support her reasons.

Considering Topics for Your Own Essay

Potter uses the Web for medical and academic research, but it has many other uses as well. Some people use the Web to keep up with information through Usenet groups or other specialized sites. Others like to shop online for certain kinds of products—computer equipment, music, books, and stocks—or play online games with other users. List some of the Web sites you use regularly; then note which *one* site you might want to evaluate. Look at the site itself and consider what makes a visit to it worthwhile. If you were to write an essay evaluating what you like and do not like about this Web site, which features of the site would you focus on in your evaluation?

Christine Romano wrote the following essay when she was a first-year college student. In it she evaluates an argument essay written by another student, Jessica Statsky's "Children Need to Play, Not Compete," which appears in Chapter 6 of this book (pp. 255–58). Romano focuses not on the writing strategies or basic features of an essay arguing a position but rather on its logic—on whether the argument is likely to convince its intended readers. She evaluates the logic of the argument according to the standards presented in Chapter 12. You might want to review these standards on pp. 550–52 before you read Romano's evaluation. Also, if you have not already read Statsky's essay, you might want to do so now, thinking about what seems most and least convincing to you about her argument that competitive sports can be harmful to young children.

"Children Need to Play, Not Compete," by Jessica Statsky: An Evaluation

Christine Romano

Parents of young children have a lot to worry about and to hope for. In "Children Need to Play, Not Compete," Jessica Statsky appeals to their worries and hopes in order to convince them that organized competitive sports may harm their children physically and psychologically. Statsky states her thesis clearly and fully forecasts the reasons she will offer to justify her position: Besides causing physical and psychological harm, competitive sports discourage young people from becoming players and fans when they are older and inevitably put parents' needs and fantasies ahead of children's welfare. Statsky also carefully defines her key terms. By *sports,* for example, she means to include both contact and noncontact sports that emphasize competition. The sports may be organized locally at schools or summer sports camps or nationally, as in the examples of Peewee Football and Little League Baseball. She is concerned only with children six to twelve years of age.

In this essay, I will evaluate the logic of Statsky's argument, considering whether the support for her thesis is appropriate, believable, consistent, and complete. While her logic *is* appropriate, believable, and consistent, her argument also has weaknesses. I will focus on two: Her argument seems incomplete because she neglects to anticipate parents' predictable questions and objections, and because she fails to support certain parts of it fully.

Statsky provides appropriate support for her thesis. Throughout her essay, she relies for support on different kinds of information (she cites eleven separate sources, including books, newspapers, and Web sites). Her quotations, examples, and statistics all support the reasons she believes competitive sports are bad for children. For example, in paragraph 3, Statsky offers the reason that "overly competitive sports" may damage children's growing bodies and that contact sports, in particular, may be especially hazardous. She supports this reason by paraphrasing Koppett that muscle strain or even lifelong injury may result when a twelve-year-old throws curve balls. She then quotes Tutko on the dangers of tackle football. The opinions of both experts are obviously appropriate. They are relevant to her reason, and we can easily imagine that they would worry many parents.

Not only is Statsky's support appropriate, but it is also believable. Statsky quotes or summarizes authorities to support her argument in paragraphs 3–6, 8, 9, and 11. The question is whether readers would find these authorities credible. Since Statsky relies almost entirely on authorities to support her argument, readers must believe these authorities for her argument to succeed. I have not read Statsky's sources, but I think there are good reasons to consider them authoritative. First of all, the newspaper authors she quotes write for two of America's most respected newspapers, the *New York Times* and the *Los Angeles Times*. These newspapers are read across the country by political leaders and financial experts and by people interested in the arts and popular culture. Both have sports reporters who not only report on sports events but also take a critical look at sports issues. In addition, both newspapers have reporters who specialize in children's health and education. Second, Statsky gives background information about the authorities she quotes, which is intended to increase the person's believability in the eyes of parents of young children. In paragraph 3, she tells readers that Thomas Tutko is "a psychology professor at San Jose State University and co-author of the book *Winning Is Everything and Other American Myths*." In paragraph 5, she announces that Martin Rablovsky is "a former sports editor for the *New York Times*," and she notes that he has watched children play organized sports for many years. Third, she quotes from two Web sites—the official Little League site and an AOL message board. Parents are likely to accept the authority of the Little League site and be interested in what other parents and coaches (most of whom are also parents) have to say.

In addition to quoting authorities, Statsky relies on examples and anecdotes to support the reasons for her position. If examples and anecdotes are to be believable, they must seem representative to readers, not bizarre or highly unusual or completely unpredictable. Readers can imagine a similar event happening elsewhere. For anecdotes to be believable, they should, in addition, be specific and true to life. All of Statsky's examples and anecdotes fulfill these requirements, and her readers would find them believable. For example, early in her argument, in paragraph 4, Statsky reasons that fear of being hurt greatly reduces children's enjoyment of contact sports. The anecdote comes from Tosches's investigative report on Peewee Football as does the quotation by the mother of an eight-year-old player who says that the children become frightened and pretend to be injured in order to stay out of the game. In the anecdote, a seven-year-old makes himself vomit to avoid playing. Because these echo the familiar "I feel bad" or "I'm sick" excuse children give when they do not want to go somewhere (especially school) or do something, most parents would find them believable. They could easily imagine their own children pretending to be hurt or ill if they were fearful or depressed. The anecdote is also specific. Tosches reports what the boy said and did and what the coach said and did.

Other examples provide support for all the major reasons Statsky gives for her position:

- That competitive sports pose psychological dangers—children becoming serious and unplayful when the game starts (paragraph 5)

- That adults' desire to win puts children at risk—parents fighting each other at a Peewee Football game and a coach setting fire to an opposing team's jersey (paragraph 8)

- That organized sports should emphasize cooperation and individual performance instead of winning—a coach banning scoring but finding that parents would not support him and a New York City basketball league in which all children play an equal amount of time and scoring is easier (paragraph 11)

All of these examples are appropriate to the reason they support. They are also believable. Together, they help Statsky achieve her purpose of convincing parents that organized, competitive sports may be bad for their children and that there are alternatives.

If readers are to find an argument logical and convincing, it must be consistent and complete. While there are no inconsistencies or contradictions in Statsky's argument, it is seriously incomplete because it neglects to support fully one of its reasons, it fails to anticipate many predictable questions parents would have, and it pays too little attention to noncontact competitive team sports. The most obvious example of thin support comes in paragraph 11, where Statsky asserts that many parents are ready for children's team sports that emphasize cooperation and individual performance. Yet the example of a Little League official who failed to win parents' approval to ban scores raises serious questions about just how many parents are ready to embrace noncompetitive sports teams. The other support, a brief description of City Sports for Kids in New York City, is very convincing but will only be logically compelling to those parents who are already inclined to agree with Statsky's position. Parents inclined to disagree with Statsky would need additional evidence. Most parents know that big cities receive special federal funding for evening, weekend, and summer recreation. Brief descriptions of six or eight noncompetitive teams in a variety of sports in cities, rural areas, suburban neighborhoods—some funded publicly, some funded privately—would be more likely to convince skeptics. Statsky is guilty here of failing to accept the burden of proof, a logical fallacy.

Statsky's argument is also incomplete in that it fails to anticipate certain objections and questions that some parents, especially those she most wants to convince, are almost sure to raise. In the first sentences of paragraphs 6, 9, and 10, Statsky does show that she is thinking about her readers' questions. She does not go nearly far enough, however, to have a chance of influencing two types of readers: those who themselves are or were fans of and participants in competitive sports and those who want their six- to twelve-year-old children involved in mainstream sports programs despite the risks, especially the national programs that have a certain prestige. Such parents might feel that competitive team sports for young children create a sense of community with a shared purpose, build character through self-sacrifice and commitment to the group, teach children to face their fears early and learn how to deal with them through the support of coaches and team members, and introduce children to the principles of social cooperation and collaboration. Some parents are likely to believe and to know from personal experience that coaches who burn opposing teams' jerseys on the pitching mound before the game starts are the exception, not the rule. Some young children idolize teachers and coaches, and team practice and games are the brightest moments in their lives. Statsky seems not to have considered these reasonable possibilities, and as a result her argument lacks a compelling logic it might have had. By acknowledging that she was aware of many of these objections—and perhaps even accommodating more of them in her own argument, as she does in paragraph 10, while refuting other objections—she would have strengthened her argument.

Finally, Statsky's argument is incomplete because she overlooks examples of non-contact team sports. Track, swimming, and tennis are good examples that some readers would certainly think of. Some elementary schools compete in track meets. Public and private clubs and recreational programs organize competitive swimming and tennis competitions. In these sports, individual performance is the focus. No one gets trampled. Children exert themselves only as much as they are able to. Yet individual performances are scored, and a team score is derived. Because Statsky fails to mention any of these obvious possibilities, her argument is weakened.

The logic of Stasky's argument, then, has both strengths and weaknesses. The support she offers is appropriate, believable, and consistent. The major weakness is incompleteness—she fails to anticipate more fully the likely objections of a wide range of readers. Her logic would prevent parents who enjoy and advocate competitive sports from taking her argument seriously. Such parents and their children have probably had positive experiences with team sports, and these experiences would lead them to believe that the gains are worth whatever risks may be involved. Many probably think that the risks Statsky points out can be avoided by careful monitoring. For those parents inclined to agree with her, Statsky's logic is likely to seem sound and complete. An argument that successfully confirms readers' beliefs is certainly valid, and Statsky succeeds admirably at this kind of argument. Because she does not offer compelling counter-arguments to the legitimate objections of those inclined not to agree with her, however, her success is limited.

Connecting to Culture and Experience: Team Sports and Community

Romano reasons in paragraph 8 that some parents "feel that competitive team sports for young children create a sense of community with a shared purpose, build character through self-sacrifice and commitment to the group, teach children to face their fears early and learn how to deal with them through the support of coaches and team members, and introduce children to the principles of social cooperation and collaboration."

With other students, discuss this view of the role of sports in developing a child's sense of community. Begin by telling one another about your own, your siblings', or your children's experiences with team sports between the ages of six and twelve. Explain how participating in sports at this young age did or did not help create a sense of community. If you think team sports failed to create community or had some other effect, explain the effect it did have. Then, discuss how each of you is defining the term *community,* and consider whether you are using it in the same way that Romano uses it in her essay.

Analyzing Writing Strategies

1. Reread Romano's essay to identify the reasons she gives for her judgment of Statsky's essay. As you read, put brackets around the sentences where she states each reason. Then make a paragraph-by-paragraph scratch outline like the one shown on p. 372 for Kristine Potter's essay.

    Finally, reflect on what you can learn from the way Romano presents her reasons. Are they clear and easy to follow? Do you think her intended readers—her instructor and parents of young children (the same audience Statsky is trying to convince)—are likely to consider her reasons plausible? In other words, are these reasons appropriate for evaluating an essay that argues a position?

2. Romano applies to Statsky's essay the ABC test for evaluating an argument, which is presented in Chapter 12 of this book on pp. 550–52. Choose *one* quality of a good argument—Appropriateness, Believability, or Consistency and Completeness—and use it to evaluate Romano's argument. Support your evaluation with one or two examples from her essay.

3. In paragraph 8, Romano observes that Statsky "fails to anticipate certain objections and questions" her readers "are almost sure to raise." Romano herself has analyzed her readers and tried to anticipate their likely objections and questions as well as the judgments they may be inclined to take on the subject. Turn to the Writer at Work section on pp. 399–400 to see how Romano uses the Guide to Writing in this chapter to help her anticipate her readers' concerns. Note what Romano changes when she revises her draft. Finally, reflect on why it is important for writers evaluating a subject to anticipate their readers' concerns, as Romano tries to do in this essay.

Commentary: Support

Because she is evaluating a written text, Romano uses **textual evidence** to support her argument. To provide textual evidence, writers can **quote, paraphrase,** or **summarize** passages from the text. Romano quotes selectively, usually brief phrases. In paragraph 4, for example, Romano supports her argument about the believability of Statsky's sources with a quote showing how Statsky presents authorities:

For more on using textual evidence as support, see Chapter 19, pp. 632–33.

> In paragraph 3, she tells readers that Thomas Tutko is "a psychology professor at San Jose State University and co-author of the book *Winning Is Everything and Other*

American Myths." In paragraph 5, she announces that Martin Rablovsky is "a former sports editor for the *New York Times.*"

For additional examples of paraphrasing and summarizing, see Chapter 12, pp. 541–43. For guidance on integrating quotations into your writing, see Chapter 22, pp. 695–97.

In addition to quoting, Romano paraphrases and summarizes passages from Statsky's essay. Summarizing, a distillation of the main ideas, tends to be briefer than paraphrasing. Paraphrasing, in contrast, tries to capture the rich detail of the original. A good example of paraphrasing appears in the opening paragraph, where Romano represents Statsky's argument. Compare Romano's paraphrase to the original passage from Statsky's essay:

Statsky's Original Version

Highly organized competitive sports such as Peewee Football and Little League Baseball are too often played to adult standards, which are developmentally inappropriate for children and can be both physically and psychologically harmful. Furthermore, because they eliminate many children from organized sports before they are ready to compete, they are actually counterproductive for developing either future players or fans. (paragraph 2)

Romano's Paraphrase

Besides causing physical and psychological harm, competitive sports discourage young people from becoming players and fans when they are older and inevitably put parents' needs and fantasies ahead of children's welfare. (paragraph 1)

Notice that in the paraphrase, Romano mostly uses her own words, with a few significant exceptions for key terms like *physical* and *psychological, players* and *fans.*

Romano uses summarizing primarily to describe parts of Statsky's argument, as in the following excerpt:

Romano's Summary

. . . in paragraph 3, Statsky offers the reason that "overly competitive sports" may damage children's growing bodies and that contact sports, in particular, may be especially hazardous. She supports this reason by paraphrasing Koppett that muscle strain or even lifelong injury may result when a twelve-year-old throws curve balls. She then quotes Tutko on the dangers of tackle football. (paragraph 3)

If you compare this summary with Romano's paraphrase, you will notice another important distinction between summarizing and paraphrasing. When summarizing, writers usually describe what the author is doing in the passage. In the summarized passage, for instance, Romano uses Statsky's name and the pronoun *she* to relate the different strategic moves Statsky makes in the paragraph being summarized. When paraphrasing, however, writers typically leave out references to the author and his or her moves. Like Romano does in the preceding sample paraphrase, they simply restate what the author has written.

Especially when you write an evaluation of a written document, a Web site (like Potter does), or a film (like Ansen does), these are the strategies you need to employ for citing textual evidence.

Considering Topics for Your Own Essay

List several written texts you would consider evaluating. For example, you might include in your list an essay from one of the chapters in this book. If you choose an argument from Chapters 6–10, you could evaluate its logic, its use of emotional appeals, or its credibility. You might prefer to evaluate a children's book you read when you were younger or one you now read to your own children, a magazine for people interested in a particular topic like computers or cars, a scholarly article you read for a research paper, or a short story from Chapter 10. You need not limit yourself to texts written on paper; also consider texts available online such as the Internet webzine *Slate*. Choose one possibility from your list, and come up with two or three reasons why it is a good or bad text.

■ PURPOSE AND AUDIENCE

When you evaluate something, you seek to influence readers' judgments and possibly their actions. Your primary aim is to convince readers that your judgment is well informed and reasonable and, therefore, that they can feel confident in making decisions based on it. Good readers do not simply accept reviewers' judgments, however, especially on important subjects. More likely they read reviews to learn more about a subject so that they can make an informed decision themselves. Consequently, most readers care less about the forcefulness with which you assert your judgment than about the reasons and support you give for it.

Effective writers develop an argumentative strategy designed for their particular readers. Your argumentative strategy determines every writing decision you make, from what you reveal about the subject to the way you construct your argument— which reasons you use, how you explain your reasoning, how much and what kind of support you give.

You may want to acknowledge directly your readers' knowledge of the subject, perhaps revealing that you understand how they might judge it differently. You might even let readers know that you have anticipated their objections to your argument. In responding to objections, reservations, or different judgments, you could agree to disagree on certain points but try to convince readers that on other points you do share the same or at least similar standards.

A Well-Presented Subject

The subject must be clearly identified if readers are to know what is being evaluated. Most writers name it explicitly. When the subject is a film, essay, or Web site, naming is easy. When it is something more general, naming may be difficult. Etzioni, for example, uses the name *McDonald's* to stand for the entire class of fast-food restaurant jobs he is evaluating.

Evaluations should provide only enough information to give readers a context for the judgment. However, certain kinds of evaluations—such as book, television, and movie reviews—usually require more information than other kinds of evaluations because reviewers have to assume that readers will be unfamiliar with the subject and are reading, in part, to learn more about it. Ansen tells readers who the actors and director of *The Phantom Menace* are, where and when the film's story takes place, and generally what happens in it. For a recently released film, the writer must decide how much of the plot to reveal—trying not to spoil the suspense while explaining how well or how poorly the suspense is managed. For a classic film, reviewers may be released from this constraint.

A Clear, Authoritative Judgment

Evaluation essays are built around a judgment—an assertion that the subject is good or bad or that it is better or worse than something else of the same kind. This judgment is the thesis of the essay. The thesis statement may appear in the first sentence, as it does in Etzioni's essay: "McDonald's is bad for your kids," or elsewhere in the essay. Potter asserts her thesis at the end of the first paragraph, whereas Ansen and Romano put theirs in the second paragraph. Writers also may restate the thesis at the end of the essay, summarizing their main points. Wherever the thesis appears, it must satisfy three requirements: that it be arguable, clear and unambiguous, and appropriately qualified.

Although readers expect a definitive judgment, they also appreciate a balanced one. All of the writers in this chapter acknowledge both good and bad qualities of the subject they are evaluating. Romano praises the strengths and criticizes the weaknesses of Statsky's logic. Ansen criticizes the storytelling but praises the design of *The Phantom Menace*. Potter is enthusiastic about the *Asthma* Web site, but points out a problem with hyperlinks. Even Etzioni, who is highly critical of fast-food jobs, admits that fast-food chains do "provide very large numbers of teen jobs, provide regular employment," and "pay quite well compared to many other teen jobs" (paragraph 5).

Appropriate Reasons and Convincing Support

Writers assert the reasons for their judgment, often explain their reasons in some detail, and provide support for their reasons. For example, one of the reasons Etzioni gives for his judgment that McDonald's-type jobs are bad for teenagers is that they "impart few skills that will be useful in later life." He then specifies the skills fast-food jobs teach young people and explains exactly why he thinks they are not useful, contrasting them to the kinds of skills learned in other types of jobs that are useful later in life. Etzioni's argument hinges on the key terms *skills* and *useful,* both of which he defines and illustrates for readers.

For an argument to be convincing, readers have to accept the reasons as appropriate for evaluating the subject. Romano applies as her reasons the ABC test suggested in this book for evaluating the logic of Statsky's argument: Appropriateness, Believability, Consistency and Completeness. Potter chooses reasons for evaluating the usefulness of a Web site on asthma, because they seem commonsensical to her and, she hopes, to most of her readers.

Evaluators not only give reasons but must also support their reasons. They may use various kinds of support. Romano and Ansen, for example, rely primarily on textual evidence to support their reasons, presenting it in quotations, paraphrases, and summaries. In evaluating a Web site, Potter supports her argument with examples (figures showing screen shots from the Web site).

Many writers also use comparisons to support an evaluative argument. For example, Ansen's references to other science-fiction films (such as *Blade Runner* and *The Matrix*) are designed to convince readers that he is an expert who knows what kinds of standards knowledgeable people normally apply when evaluating this kind of film. Potter briefly compares the *Asthma* Web site to another site on asthma.

Counterargument

Writers often try to anticipate readers' possible alternative judgments as well as likely questions and objections to the argument. Writers may counterargue by acknowledging, conceding, or trying to refute judgments and objections with which they disagree. Etzioni, for example, acknowledges the alternative judgment preferred by many readers— that fast-food jobs, like the old-fashioned lemonade stand and paper route, teach young people useful skills. While he suggests that he agrees with readers and shares their values, he also tries to refute their judgments. He bases his judgment on the same standards his readers use, so he needs to show them that McDonald's-type jobs do not meet their shared standards. Ansen begins his essay by anticipating readers' alternative judgment of *The Phantom Menace.* He then tries to refute this judgment by counterarguing that it is based more on the film's skillful advertising together with viewers' enthusiasm for the earlier *Star Wars* films than on an honest evaluation of the film itself.

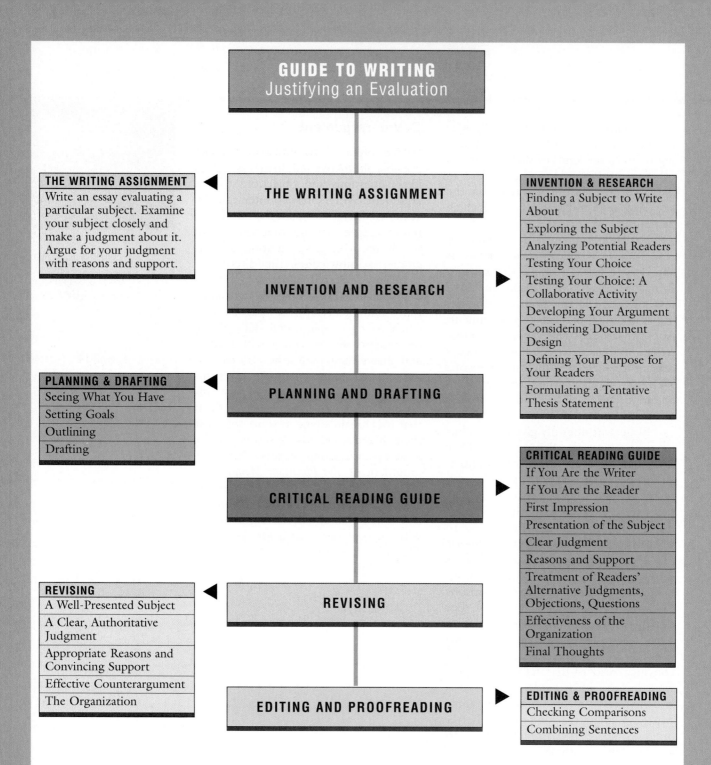

GUIDE TO WRITING
Justifying an Evaluation

THE WRITING ASSIGNMENT
Write an essay evaluating a particular subject. Examine your subject closely and make a judgment about it. Argue for your judgment with reasons and support.

THE WRITING ASSIGNMENT

INVENTION & RESEARCH
Finding a Subject to Write About
Exploring the Subject
Analyzing Potential Readers
Testing Your Choice
Testing Your Choice: A Collaborative Activity
Developing Your Argument
Considering Document Design
Defining Your Purpose for Your Readers
Formulating a Tentative Thesis Statement

INVENTION AND RESEARCH

PLANNING & DRAFTING
Seeing What You Have
Setting Goals
Outlining
Drafting

PLANNING AND DRAFTING

CRITICAL READING GUIDE
If You Are the Writer
If You Are the Reader
First Impression
Presentation of the Subject
Clear Judgment
Reasons and Support
Treatment of Readers' Alternative Judgments, Objections, Questions
Effectiveness of the Organization
Final Thoughts

CRITICAL READING GUIDE

REVISING
A Well-Presented Subject
A Clear, Authoritative Judgment
Appropriate Reasons and Convincing Support
Effective Counterargument
The Organization

REVISING

EDITING AND PROOFREADING

EDITING & PROOFREADING
Checking Comparisons
Combining Sentences

THE WRITING ASSIGNMENT

Write an essay evaluating a particular subject. Examine your subject closely and make a judgment about it. Argue for your judgment with reasons and support.

INVENTION AND RESEARCH

The following activities will help you choose and explore a subject, consider your judgment, and develop your argument. These activities are easy to complete. Doing them over several days will give your ideas time to ripen and grow. Keep a written record of your invention and research to use later when you draft and revise.

Finding a Subject to Write About

You may already have a subject in mind and some ideas on how you will evaluate it. Even so, it is wise to take a few minutes to consider some other possible subjects. That way you can feel confident not only about having made the best possible choice but also about having one or two alternative subjects in case your first choice does not work. The following activities will help you make a good choice.

Listing Subjects.   *Make a list of subjects you might be interested in evaluating.* Make your list as complete as you can, including, for example, the subjects suggested by the Considering Topics for Your Own Essay activity following each reading in this chapter. The following categories may give you some ideas.

- *Culture:* Television program, magazine or newspaper, computer game, band, songwriter, recording, film, actor, performance, dance club, coffeehouse, artist, museum exhibit, individual work of art
- *Written work:* Poem, short story, novel, magazine article, newspaper column, letter to the editor, textbook, autobiography, essay from this book
- *Education:* School, program, teacher, major department, library, academic or psychological counseling service, writing center, campus publication, sports team
- *Government:* Government department or official, proposed or existing law, agency or program, candidate for public office
- *Leisure:* Amusement park, museum, restaurant, resort, sports team, sports equipment, national or state park

   Listing Subjects Related to Identity and Community.   The following are ideas for an evaluative essay on issues of identity and community.

- Evaluate your performance as a student, athlete, musician, parent, sibling, or spouse.
- Evaluate how well one of the following meets the needs of residents of your town or city: a community center, public library, health clinic, college, athletic team, festival, neighborhood watch or block parent program, meals-on-wheels program, theater or symphony, school or school program.
- Evaluate how well one of the following serves the members of your religious community: a religious school, youth or senior group, religious leader, particular sermon, bingo, revival meeting, choir, building and grounds.
- Evaluate how well one of the following aspects of local government serves the needs of the community: a mayor, city council, police, courts, department of motor vehicles, social services, park system, zoning commission.

Listing Subjects Related to Work and Career.   Following are some suggestions for an evaluative essay on issues involving work and career.

- Evaluate a job you have had or currently have, evaluate yourself as a worker, or evaluate someone else you have observed closely, such as a co-worker or supervisor.
- Evaluate a local job training program, either one in which you have participated or one where you can observe and interview other students.
- Evaluate how well suited you may be for some career in which you are interested.
- Evaluate the work done by city or campus employees—the police, trash collectors, road repair workers, emergency service providers, class schedulers, advisers, cafeteria workers, dorm counselors.

Choosing a Subject.   *Review your list and choose the one subject that seems most promising.* Your subject should be one that you can evaluate with some authority, either one that you already know quite well or one that you could study. Although your judgment of this subject need not be fully formed at this point, you should have some sense of how you will evaluate it.

Exploring the Subject

To explore the subject, you need to reflect on what you know about it, determine whether you need to do research, and consider how you will evaluate the subject.

Reflecting on the Subject.   *To begin reflecting on the subject and how you will evaluate it, write for a few minutes to collect your thoughts.* Focus your thinking by considering questions like these:

- What do I like and/or dislike about the subject I am evaluating?

- What category of subject is this? What do I usually look for in evaluating a subject of this kind? What do other people look for? In other words, what standards of judgment are considered appropriate for evaluating this kind of subject?

- What details do I know about the subject that I could use in my essay? What details do I need to find out about the subject? (For example, if I were to evaluate the storytelling of a film, what details would I need to point out about the film?)

Planning Research.   *If you do not know very much about the subject or the standards people typically use when evaluating this kind of subject, make some notes about how you will go about doing research.* If you are writing about a film, for example, you may need to rent the film and view it, taking notes about the storytelling, special effects, acting, direction, or any other aspect of the film you think is important. If you do not know the standards usually used to evaluate this kind of film, you may want to read some reviews.

If you need to do more research than time permits or you cannot review your subject to find the details needed to support an evaluation of it, then you may need to consider choosing a different, more accessible subject.

Considering Your Judgment.   *Reread what you have written; then write a few sentences stating your best current judgment of the subject.* Your judgment may only be tentative at this stage, or you may feel quite confident in it. Or your judgment may be mixed: You may have a high regard for certain aspects of the subject and, at the same time, a rather low assessment of other aspects. As you consider your judgment, keep in mind that readers of evaluative essays not only expect writers to balance their evaluation of a subject by pointing out things they like as well as things they dislike; readers also expect writers to state a definitive judgment about the subject, not a vague, wishy-washy, or undecided judgment.

Analyzing Potential Readers

Write several sentences analyzing your readers, with the following questions in mind:

- What are my readers likely to know about my subject? Will I be introducing the subject to them (as in a film or book review), or will they already be familiar with it, and if so, how expert on the subject are they likely to be?

- How are my readers likely to judge my subject? What about it will they like, and what will they dislike?

- What reasons might they give for their judgment?

- On what standards is their judgment likely to be based? Do I share these standards, or at least recognize their appropriateness?

Testing Your Choice

Pause now to decide whether you have chosen a subject about which you can make a convincing evaluative argument. Reread your invention notes to see whether you know enough about your subject or can get the information you need by researching the subject. Also consider whether you feel confident in your judgment.

As you develop your argument, you should become even more confident. If, however, you begin to doubt your choice, consider doing further research or beginning again with a different subject selected from your list of possibilities. Before changing your subject, however, discuss your ideas with another student or your instructor to see whether they make sense to someone else.

Testing Your Choice: A Collaborative Activity

At this point in your invention work, you will find it helpful to get together with two or three other students to discuss your subjects and test out ways of evaluating them.

Presenters: Take turns briefly describing your subject without revealing your judgment. Take notes on your group's response.

Evaluators: Take turns explaining to the presenters how you would evaluate a subject of this kind. For example, would you judge a science-fiction film by the story, acting, ideas, special effects, or some other aspect of the film? Would you judge a lecture course by how interesting or entertaining the lectures are, how hard the tests are, how well the lectures are organized, or on some other basis? In other words, tell the presenter what standards you would apply to his or her particular subject.

Developing Your Argument

Listing Reasons. *Write down every reason you can think of to convince readers of your judgment.* Try stating your reasons as part of a tentative thesis statement with *because* or *that* clauses, like this: "My judgment is X because . . ." or "A reason I like (or dislike) X is that. . . ." Then look over your list to consider which reasons you regard most important and which would be most convincing to your readers, given the standards on which they ordinarily base their evaluations of subjects of this kind. *Put an asterisk by the reasons likely to be convincing for your readers.*

Finding Support. *Make notes about how to support your most promising reasons.* To evaluate a text such as an essay, Web site, recording, or film, you will need to find textual evidence—quotation, summary, or paraphrase—from your own close analysis of the subject. For other kinds of subjects, you may need to do research in the library or on the Internet for supporting authorities, statistics, or anecdotes.

Drawing Comparisons. *Write for five to ten minutes, trying to support one or more of your reasons with an argument based on comparisons and contrasts to related subjects.* Remember that comparisons and contrasts are often used to establish a writer's credibility by demonstrating not only that the writer is knowledgeable but also that the argument is based on standards that readers would agree are appropriate for judging that kind of subject.

Anticipating Readers' Alternative Judgments and Objections. *Assuming your readers might evaluate the subject differently or that they might have objections or questions about your argument, write for five to ten minutes trying out a counterargument.* To help you anticipate readers' concerns, look back at the notes you took for Testing Your Choice: A Collaborative Activity to see what your fellow students said about your reasons. Remember that a counterargument could involve simply acknowledging disagreement, accommodating readers' views by conceding certain points, or trying to refute readers' arguments by challenging the standards on which they are based or their reasons and support.

Considering Document Design

Think about whether visual or audio elements—cartoons, photographs, tables, graphs, or snippets from films, television programs, or songs—would strengthen your argument. These are not at all a requirement of an effective evaluation essay, but they could be helpful. Consider also whether your readers might benefit by such design features as headings, bulleted or numbered lists, or other elements that would make your essay easier to follow. You could construct your own graphic elements, download materials from the Internet, videotape images and sounds from television or other sources, or scan into your document visuals from books and magazine.

Defining Your Purpose for Your Readers

Write a few sentences, defining your purpose in writing this evaluation for your readers. Remember that you already have analyzed your potential readers and developed your argument with these readers in mind. Given these readers, try now to define your purpose by considering the following possibilities and any others that might apply to your writing situation:

- If my readers are likely to agree with my judgment, should I try to give them confidence in their own judgment? Can I help them refute others' judgments or suggest how they might respond to questions and objections?

- If my readers and I share certain standards for evaluating a subject of this kind, but we disagree on how to judge this particular subject, can I build a convincing argument based on these shared standards or, at least, get readers to acknowledge the legitimacy of my judgment?

- If my readers use different standards of judgment, what should I try to do—urge them to think critically about their own judgment, to consider seriously other ways of judging the subject, or to see certain aspects of the subject they might have overlooked?

Formulating a Tentative Thesis Statement

Write several sentences that could serve as your thesis statement. Think about how you should state your judgment—how emphatic you should make it, whether you should qualify it, and whether you should include in the thesis a forecast of your reasons and support.

Review the readings in this chapter to see how other writers construct thesis statements. For example, recall that Etzioni abruptly begins his essay with a surprising judgment: "McDonald's is bad for your kids." He then qualifies this assertion in the next sentence to make clear that he is focusing on the types of jobs at McDonald's, not the food. Like Etzioni, Ansen boldly asserts a judgment he knows will not be expected by his readers. His thesis statement is simple and direct: "The movie is a disappointment."

Potter and Romano use the thesis statement to forecast their reasons as well as to express their judgment. Both these writers begin by indicating the standards they think are appropriate for evaluating their subjects. Their thesis statements show that they base their reasons on these standards. Potter, for example, writes: "My evaluation of the Canadian Lung Association's *Asthma* Web site, located at <http://www.lung.ca/asthma>, led me to the conclusion that this site successfully meets my criteria for accessible, helpful, and reliable information" (paragraph 1). Romano's thesis statement lets readers know in advance what she likes about the subject she is evaluating as well as what she does not like: "While [Statsky's] logic is appropriate, believable, and consistent, her argument also has weaknesses" (paragraph 2). In contrast to Etzioni, who states his thesis rather dramatically, Romano makes her thesis statement seem thoughtful and balanced. There is no ambivalence or confusion, however, about Romano's judgment. She is clear and emphatic, not vague or wishy-washy.

As you draft your own tentative thesis statement, pay attention to the language you use. It should be clear and unambiguous, emphatic but appropriately qualified. Although you will most probably refine your thesis statement as you draft and revise your essay, trying now to articulate it will help give your planning and drafting direction and impetus.

■ PLANNING AND DRAFTING

This section will help you review what you have learned about evaluating your subject, determine specific goals for your essay, make a tentative outline, and get started on your first draft.

Seeing What You Have

Pause now to reread your invention and research notes. Consider whether you have enough reasons and support to offer readers and whether you understand—even if you do not share—your readers' standards for judging a subject of this kind. Highlight anything you think you will be able to use in your draft and note connections between ideas.

If your invention notes seem skimpy, you may need to do further research at this stage or you could begin drafting now and later do research to fill in the blanks.

If your confidence in your judgment has been shaken or if you are concerned that you will not be able to write an argument to support your judgment, consult your instructor to determine whether you should try evaluating a different subject.

Setting Goals

Before you begin drafting, set some specific goals to guide the decisions you will make as you draft and revise your essay. The draft will not only be easier to write, but also more focused if you start with clear goals in mind. The following questions will help you set goals. You may find it useful to return to them while you are drafting, for they are designed to help you focus on specific features and strategies of evaluative essays.

Your Purpose and Readers

- What do I want my readers to think about the subject after reading my essay? Do I want to show them how the subject I am evaluating fails (as Etzioni and Ansen do), how it succeeds (as Potter does) or demonstrate its strengths and weaknesses (as Romano does)?

- Should I assume that my readers are likely to have read other evaluations of the subject (perhaps like Ansen) or to have developed their own evaluation of it (like Etzioni and Romano)? Or should I assume that I am introducing readers to the subject (like Potter)?

- How should I present myself to my readers—as knowledgeable, balanced, impassioned, or in some other way?

The Beginning

- What opening would capture readers' attention? Should I open by abruptly stating my judgment, as Etzioni does? Or should I begin by giving readers a context for my evaluation, as Ansen and Potter do?

- Should I try to make clear to readers at the outset the standards I will apply, as Romano and Potter do? Should I begin by comparing my subject with a subject more familiar to readers, as Ansen does? Should I begin by describing the subject?

The Presentation of the Subject

- What should I name the subject? Should I name it after something readers will recognize, as Etzioni does in naming "McDonald's"? Should I name it after a recognized category or genre, as Ansen does in referring to science-fiction films?

- What about the subject should I describe? Can I use visuals to illustrate, as Potter does?

- Should I place the subject historically, as Etzioni does when he compares delivering newspapers to working at McDonald's?

- If the subject has a story, how much of it should I tell? Can I simply set the scene and identify the characters, as Ansen does, without giving away the story?

Your Evaluative Argument

- How should I state my thesis? Should I forecast my reasons early in the essay, as Potter and Romano do? Should I place my thesis at the beginning or wait until after I have provided a context?

- How can I convince readers to consider my judgment seriously even if they disagree with it? Should I build my argument on shared standards (like Etzioni) or defend my standards (like Potter and Romano)? Should I try to present a balanced judgment by praising some things and criticizing others?

- How can I present my reasons? Should I explain the standards on which I base my reasons, as Romano and Potter do?

- If I have more than one reason, how should I sequence them?

- How can I support my reasons? Can I find examples from the text to quote, paraphrase, or summarize, as Ansen and Romano do? Can I call on authorities, as Etzioni does? What examples, statistics, or other support could I use?

- What objections or questions should I counterargue? How should I respond— by merely acknowledging them, by conceding legitimate objections and qualifying my judgment, or by trying to refute objections I consider illegitimate or weak?

The Ending

- How should I conclude? Should I try to frame the essay by echoing something from the opening or from another part of the essay?

- Should I conclude by restating my judgment, as Romano and Potter do, or by comparing my subject to others, as Ansen does?

- Should I end by making a recommendation, as Etzioni does?

Outlining

An evaluative essay contains as many as four basic parts:

1. A presentation of the subject
2. A judgment of the subject
3. A presentation of reasons and support
4. A consideration of readers' objections and alternative judgments

These parts can be organized in various ways. If, for example, you expect readers to disagree with your judgment, you could try to show them what about the subject you think they have overlooked or misjudged. You could begin by presenting the subject; then you could assert your thesis, present your reasons and support, and anticipate readers' likely objections.

Presentation of the subject

Thesis statement (judgment)

First reason and support

Anticipation and refutation of objection

Second reason and support

Counterargument

Conclusion

If you expect some of your readers to disagree with your negative judgment even though they base their judgment on the same standard on which you base yours, you could try to show them that the subject really does not satisfy the standard. You could begin by reinforcing the standard you share, and then demonstrate how the subject fails to meet it.

Establish shared standard

Acknowledge alternative judgment

State thesis (judgment) that subject fails to meet shared standard

First reason and support showing how the subject fails standard

Second reason and support (etc.)

Conclusion

There are, of course, many other possible ways to organize an evaluative essay, but these outlines should help you start planning your own essay.

For more on outlining, see Chapter 11, pp. 518–21.

Drafting

Start drafting your essay, keeping in mind the goals you set while you were planning and these tips on writing an evaluative argument:

You may want to review the general advice on drafting in Chapter 1, pp. 16–17.

- Accept the burden of proof by offering reasons and support for your judgment.
- Remember that the basis for judgment often depends on standards as much as reasons and support. Try to think critically about the standards on which you

base your judgment as well as the standards others apply to subjects of the kind you are evaluating.

- Remember that your outline is just a plan. Writers often make discoveries and reorganize as they draft. Be flexible.

- If you run into a problem as you draft, see whether any of your invention writing can help you solve it or whether returning to one of the invention activities earlier in this chapter would help.

- If, as you draft, you discover that you need more information, just make a note of what you have to find out and go on to the next point. When you are done drafting, you can go in search of the information you need.

Perhaps the most important advice to remember about drafting is to write quickly without worrying abut grammar and spelling. Later you can make corrections.

■ CRITICAL READING GUIDE

Now is the time to get a good critical reading of your draft. Writers usually find it helpful to have someone else read and comment on their drafts, and all writers know how much they learn about writing when they read other writers' drafts. Your instructor may arrange such a reading as part of your coursework. If not, you can ask a classmate, friend, or family member to read your draft. You could also seek comments from a tutor at your campus writing center. (If you are unable to have someone else read your draft, turn ahead to the Revising section, where you will find guidelines for reading your own draft critically.)

▶ **If You Are the Writer.**   In order to provide focused, helpful comments, your reader must know your essay's intended audience, your purpose, and a problem in the draft that you need help solving. Briefly write out this information at the top of your draft.

- *Readers.* Identify the intended readers of your essay. What do you assume they think about your subject? Do you expect them to be receptive, skeptical, resistant, antagonistic?

- *Purpose.* What effect do you realistically expect your argument to have on these particular readers?

- *Problem.* Ask your reader to help you solve the single most important problem you see in your draft. Describe this problem briefly.

▶ **If You Are the Reader.**   Use the following guidelines to help you give constructive, critical comments to others on evaluation essays:

1. *Read for a First Impression.* Tell the writer what you think the intended readers would find most and least convincing. If you personally think the

argument is seriously flawed, share your thoughts. Then try to help the writer improve the argument for the designated readers.

Next, consider the problem the writer identified. If the problem will be covered by one of the other questions listed here, deal with it there. Otherwise, respond to the writer's concerns now.

2. *Analyze How Well the Subject Is Presented.* Locate where in the draft the subject is presented and ask questions that will help the writer fill in whatever is missing. If you are surprised by the way the writer has presented the subject, briefly explain how you usually think of this particular subject or subjects of this kind. Also indicate if any of the information about the subject seems unnecessary. Finally, and most important, let the writer know if any of the information about the subject seems inaccurate or only partly true.

3. *Assess Whether the Judgment Is Stated Clearly.* Write a sentence or two summarizing the writer's judgment as you understand it from reading the draft. Then underline the sentence or sentences in the draft where the thesis is stated explicitly. (It may be restated in several places.) If you cannot find an explicit statement of the thesis, let the writer know. Given the writer's purpose and audience, consider whether the thesis is arguable, clear, and appropriately qualified. If the judgment seems indecisive or too extreme, suggest how it might be made clearer or qualified to account for the subject's strengths and weaknesses.

4. *Evaluate the Reasons and Support.* Underline the reasons. Look closely at the reasons and support that seem most problematic, and briefly explain what bothers you—for example, that the reason does not seem appropriate for judging this kind of subject, that you do not fully understand the reason or how it applies to this particular subject, that the connection between a particular reason and its support is not clear or convincing to you, or that the support is too weak or there is not enough of it to hold up the argument. Be as specific and constructive as you can, not only pointing out what does not work but also suggesting what the writer might do to solve the problem. For example, if the reason seems inappropriate, explain why you think so, and indicate what kinds of reasons you expect the intended readers to recognize as acceptable for judging this kind of subject. If the support is lacking, suggest how it could be strengthened. Indicate whether any visual or audio elements that have been included fail to support the evaluation and offer suggestions for improvement.

5. *Assess How Well Readers' Alternative Judgments and Objections or Questions Have Been Handled.* Mark where the writer acknowledges, accommodates, or tries to refute readers' opposing judgments, objections, or questions. Point to any places where the counterargument seems superficial or dismissive and suggest how it could be strengthened. Help the writer anticipate any important objections or questions that have been overlooked, providing advice on

how to respond to them. Keep in mind that the writer may choose to acknowledge, accommodate, or refute opposing arguments.

6. ***Consider the Effectiveness of the Organization.*** Get an overview of the essay's organization and point out any places where more explicit cueing—transitions, summaries, or topic sentences—would clarify the relationship between parts of the essay.

- Look at the *beginning*. Let the writer know if you think readers will find it engaging. If not, suggest moving something from later in the essay that might work as a better opening.
- Look at the *ending*. Does the essay conclude decisively and memorably? If not, suggest an alternative. Could something be moved to the end?
- Look at the *design features*. Comment on the contribution of figures, headings, tables, and other design features. Help the writer think of additional visual or audio elements that could make a contribution to the essay.

7. ***Give the Writer Your Final Thoughts.*** What is this draft's strongest part? What part is most in need of further work?

▧ REVISING

Now you are ready to revise your essay. Your instructor or other students may have given you advice on improving your draft. Nevertheless, you may have begun to realize that your draft requires not so much revising as rethinking. For example, you may recognize that your reasons do not lead readers to accept your evaluation, that you cannot adequately support your reasons, or that you are unable to refute damaging objections to your argument. Consequently, instead of working to improve parts of the draft, you may need to write a new draft that radically reenvisions your argument. It is not unusual for students—and professional writers—to find themselves in this situation. Learning to make radical revisions is a valuable lesson for any writer.

If you feel satisfied that your draft achieves most, if not all, of your goals, you can focus on refining specific parts of your draft. Very likely you have thought of ways of improving your draft, and you may even have begun improving it. This section will help you get an overview of your draft and revise it accordingly.

Getting an Overview

Consider your draft as a whole, following these two steps:

1. ***Reread.*** If at all possible, put the draft aside for a day or two before rereading it. When you return to it, start by reconsidering your purpose. Then read the draft straight through, trying to see it as your intended readers will.

2. *Outline.* Make a quick scratch outline, indicating the basic features as they appear in the draft.

For an illustration of scratch outlining, see Chapter 12, pp. 540–41.

Charting a Plan for Revision.   Once you have an overview of your draft, you may want to make a two-column chart like the following one to keep track of any problems you need to solve. In the left-hand column, list the basic features of evaluation essays. As you analyze your draft and study any comments you have received from other readers, note the problems you need to solve in the right-hand column.

Turn to pp. 380–81 to review the basic features.

Basic Features	*Problems to Solve*
A well-presented subject	
A clear, authoritative judgment	
Appropriate reasons and convincing support	
Effective counterargument	

Analyzing the Basic Features of Your Own Draft.   Using the Critical Reading Guide on the preceding pages, identify problems you now see in your draft. Note them on your revision chart.

Studying Critical Comments.   Review all of the comments you have received from other readers and add to your chart any that you intend to act on. For each comment, look at the draft to determine what might have led the reader to make that particular point. Try to be objective about any criticism. Ideally, these comments will help you see your draft as others see it, providing valuable information about how you can improve it.

Carrying Out Revisions

Having identified problems in your draft, you now need to come up with solutions and—most important—to carry them out. Basically, you have three ways of finding solutions:

1. Review your invention and planning notes for information and ideas to add to your draft.
2. Do additional invention and research to provide additional material you or your readers think is needed.
3. Look back at the readings in this chapter to see how other writers have solved similar problems.

The following suggestions, which are organized according to the basic features on your revision chart, will help you solve some common writing problems in evaluation essays.

A Well-Presented Subject

- **Is the subject hard to find or unclear?** Try to give it a name or to identify the general category to which it belongs. If you need more information about the subject, review your invention writing to see if you have left out any details you could now add. You may also need to do further invention writing or research to answer questions your readers have raised or your intended readers might have.

- **Is the subject presented in too much detail?** Cut extraneous and repetitive details. If your subject is a film or book, try not to give away too much.

- **Is any of the information inaccurate or only partly true?** Reconsider the accuracy and completeness of the information you present. If any of the information will be surprising to readers, consider how you might reassure them that the information is accurate, perhaps by citing your sources.

A Clear, Authoritative Judgment

- **Is your overall judgment hard to find?** Announce your thesis explicitly. If your judgment is mixed—pointing out what you like and do not like about the subject—let readers know that from the beginning.

- **Does your judgment seem indecisive or too extreme?** If your readers do not know what your judgment is or if they think you are either too adulatory or too harsh, you may need to clarify your thesis statement or qualify it more carefully.

Appropriate Reasons and Convincing Support

- **Do any of the reasons or support seem inappropriate to readers?** Explain why you think the reason or support is appropriate. Consider using comparison or authorities to show that your argument employs a standard commonly used for evaluating subjects of this kind.

- **Are any of your reasons and support unclear?** To clarify them, you may need to explain your reasoning in more detail or use examples and comparisons to make your ideas understandable. You may need to do some additional exploratory writing or research to figure out how to explain your reasoning. Consider also whether any of the reasons should be combined, separated, or cut.

- **Are any of the reasons and support thin or unconvincing?** To find additional support, review your invention writing or reexamine the subject. You may also need to do library research to find information—examples, statistics, expert testimony—to support your argument.

Effective Counterargument

- **Do readers fail to recognize your counterargument?** Make your disagreement with readers or other evaluators explicit.

- **Are any important objections or questions overlooked?** Review your invention writing to see if you have left out something or do some more invention or research to develop a response to these objections and questions.

The Organization

- *Does the essay seem disorganized or confusing?* You may need to add a forecasting statement, transitions, summaries, or topic sentences. You may also need to do some major restructuring, such as moving your presentation of the subject or reordering your reasons.

- *Is the beginning weak?* See if there is a better place to start. Review your notes for an interesting quotation, comparison, or example to open with.

- *Is the ending weak?* See if you can frame the essay by echoing a point made earlier, restate your thesis, or summarize your argument.

- *Can you add any design features to make the essay more interesting to read and to strengthen your argument?* Consider adding features you came across in your research or creating visual or audio elements of your own.

EDITING AND PROOFREADING

Now is the time to check your revised draft for errors in grammar, punctuation, and mechanics and to consider matters of style. Our research has identified several errors that are especially likely to occur in evaluative writing. The following guidelines will help you check and edit your revised draft for these common errors.

Checking Comparisons. Whenever you evaluate something, you are likely to engage in comparison. You might want to show that a new recording is inferior to an earlier one, that one film is stronger than another, that this café is better than that one. Make a point of checking to see that all comparisons in your writing are complete, logical, and clear.

Editing to Make Comparisons Complete

▶ *Jazz* is as good ^*as*, if not better than, Morrison's other novels.

▶ I liked the Lispector story because it's so different/ ^*from anything else I've ever read.*

Editing to Make Comparisons Logical

▶ Chris Rock's Pookie is more serious than any ^*other* role he's played.

▶ Ohio State's offense played much better than ~~Michigan.~~ ^*Michigan's did.*

Check also to see that you say *different from* instead of *different than*.

▶ Carrying herself with a confident and brisk stride, Katherine Parker seems

different ~~than~~ *from* the other women in the office.

▶ Films like *Internal Affairs* that glorify violence for its own sake are different

~~than~~ *from* films like *New Jack City* that use violence to make a moral point.

Combining Sentences.   When you evaluate something, you generally present your subject in some detail—defining it, describing it, placing it in some context. Writers often give such details almost one by one, in separate sentences. Combining closely related sentences can make your writing more readable, helping readers to see how ideas relate.

▶ In paragraph 5, the details provide a different impression~~. It is~~, a comic or

perhaps even pathetic impression~~. This impression comes from~~ *based on* the boy's

attempts to dress up like a real westerner.

From three separate sentences, this writer combines details about the "different impression" into one sentence, using two common strategies for sentence-combining:

• Changing a sentence into an appositive phrase (a noun phrase that renames the noun or pronoun that immediately precedes it: "a comic or perhaps even pathetic impression")
• Changing a sentence into a verbal phrase (phrases with verbals that function as adjectives, adverbs, or nouns: "based on the boy's attempts to dress up like a real westerner")

Using Appositive Phrases to Combine Sentences

▶ "Something Pacific" was created by Nam June Paik~~. He is~~, a Korean artist who is considered a founder of video art.

▶ One of Dylan's songs ridiculed the John Birch Society. *"Talkin' John Birch Paranoid Blues"* ~~This song was called "Talkin' John Birch Paranoid Blues."~~

Using Verbal Phrases to Combine Sentences

▶ Batman's lifesaving ropes sprung from his wristbands and belt buckle~~.~~,

~~They carried~~ *carrying* Vicki Vale and him out of peril.

> *enticing*
> ► The coffee bar flanks the bookshelves/. ~~It entices~~ readers to relax with a
> book.
>   ^

A WRITER AT WORK

■ ANTICIPATING READERS' OBJECTIONS AND QUESTIONS

In this section, we look at how Christine Romano tried to anticipate her readers' objections and questions. The final revision of Romano's evaluation essay appears in this chapter on pp. 373–76; Statsky's argument essay (which Romano evaluates) appears in Chapter 6.

Because Romano was applying the standards for evaluating logical arguments from Chapter 12 of this textbook, she felt confident that the standards on which she based her judgment of Statsky's argument would also be important to her readers. Using the Analyzing Your Readers activity in this chapter's Guide to Writing, she identified two kinds of readers: her instructor, who she assumed would approve of her using the textbook standards, and parents of young children, the same audience Statsky addresses. Romano acknowledged that parents would not know the textbook standards, but she speculated that, like her, they also would be impressed by the way Statsky supports her position. Romano noted also that she expected parents to be sympathetic to Statsky's position because they would not want their children to get hurt playing sports.

After writing for a few minutes on the Testing Your Choice activity, Romano worked with a group of students in class on Testing Your Choice: A Collaborative Activity. One of her group's members told her that he had been hurt playing in a Little League game and had wanted to quit but that his dad had made him go back. He remembered crying and trying to get out of going to the next game. But looking back on the experience now, he said he was glad his father insisted because years later, when playing on the high school football team, he realized that being a serious athlete meant facing up to the fear and pain of injury. He said this was an important lesson, one that applied to everything in life, not just to playing sports. Therefore, the student told Romano, his standard for judging competitive sports for young children was based on how well the experience taught them to stick it out, to conquer their pain and fear.

This student's choice of standards made Romano realize that Statsky's argument does not adequately address this compelling alternative judgment. When Romano planned and wrote her first draft, she tried to accommodate this student's point of view and others like it. In addition to praising the appropriateness, believability, and consistency of Statsky's argument, she criticized the argument for being incomplete:

"[Statsky] neglects to anticipate parents' predictable questions and objections" (paragraph 2).

A few days later, Romano received some helpful advice from another student, who read her draft critically. Using the Critical Reading Guide in this chapter, the student noted (in response to item 3 in the Guide) that she could not find a clear statement of the thesis (judgment) in the draft. She guessed that it might be hinted at in the final paragraph, but she was not sure what Romano's judgment was and urged Romano to state it clearly. Here is the draft version of Romano's final paragraph that the student reader commented on:

```
     I have been able to point out both strengths and weak-
nesses in the logic of Statsky's support for her argument. The
strengths are appropriateness, believability, and consistency.
The major weakness is incompleteness--a failure to anticipate
more fully the likely objections of a wide range of readers.
I have been able to show that her logic would prevent certain
kinds of parents from taking her argument seriously, parents
whose experience and whose children's experience of team
sports lead them to believe that the gains are worth whatever
risks may be involved and who believe that many of the risks
Statsky points out can be avoided by careful monitoring. For
parents inclined to agree with her, however, her logic is
likely to seem sound and complete. An argument that success-
fully confirms readers' beliefs is certainly valid, and
Statsky succeeds admirably at this kind of argument.
```

In response to item 4 in the Critical Reading Guide, the student reader noted that she thought Romano's draft essay was well supported by textual evidence and examples. She also said she found the praise of the strengths of Statsky's argument convincing but found the criticism of its weaknesses equally convincing. Therefore, she concluded by asking Romano to clarify her evaluation.

This request hit home because Romano had been trying to give Statsky's essay a mixed review but was not sure how well her own judgment was coming across. Romano was reassured by her critical reader's judgment that her argument was convincing, but she saw that she needed to clarify which standards carried the most weight for her. She revised the last paragraph, adding this final sentence to make her thesis more explicit and let readers see exactly which standards were most important in her evaluation of Statsky's argument:

```
Because she does not offer compelling counterarguments to the
legitimate objections of those inclined not to agree with her,
however, her success is limited.
```

In his comparison of the films *Emma* and *Clueless,* the student author described on p. 352 of this chapter selected movie stills to accompany his written text. He collected a number of stills from each film and chose two contrasting images that would best illustrate his argument that *Emma,* the film, looks more like Austen's England, but *Clueless* captures the satirical spirit of the novel.

The writer used the still from *Emma* of Emma and Knightley dancing to emphasize the film's attention to aesthetics and romance. Details such as the hanging garlands, the ornate woodwork, the women's similar pale-toned dresses, the style of dancing and the musicians in the background create an image of aristocratic wealth and elegance that, the student argues, satisfies audience expectations for a romantic period piece, but obscures an important part of the novel's message.

To illustrate the flavor of *Clueless,* the student chose the picture of Cher descending the stairs in her minidress with shopping bags, water bottle in its holder, and cell phone. This over-the-top satiric image in *Clueless,* the student argued, was designed to emphasize the social and economic distinctions in the novel. The image captures the ridiculousness of Cher. While admired and well liked by her peers, she is also naïve and too well-off for her own good. Her interest in reforming Tai is a result of her confidence that she

Perrillo 3

Emma is, above all, a novel about class consciousness. Marriage is here, as in all of Austen's novels, a vehicle for exploring the rigidity of social class in nineteenth-century England. However, Emma the film (1996) is better at capturing the feel of the period than the intricacies of social dynamics. (See Fig. 1.) Though the characters come from a range of social classes, their homes and clothing look more similar than not. When Gwyneth Paltrow plays the occasionally lovable, occasionally irritating Emma, the focus on the heroine's failure at matchmaking overshadows the fact that she is obsessed not only with manners but also with wealth. For example, she has something that even her beloved Knightley does not, an estate that she will inherit from her father as long as she does not leave him. In the novel when Knightley agrees to live in the Woodhouse home after the two marry, he goes against traditional gender roles in order to make the most of the two characters' fortunes: his wealth and her property. As it does so many times, the film misses this cue, and instead focuses on Emma's emotional inability to leave her father. In the 1996 Emma, social distinctions get paved over for the audience's aesthetic expectations of a romance and of a period piece.

Fig. 1. This scene from Emma offers a typical example of the film's attention to aesthetics.

Perrillo 4

Clueless (1995), though it could not look less like Austen's England, better captures the spirit of the novel. Cher, who never leaves her cell phone at home and shops on Rodeo Drive, is both the consummate brat and the consummate charmer. (See Figure 2.) Cher does more than just try to find a suitable match for the obviously not as well-off or stylish Tai; she actually works on transforming her, much as Emma does with Harriet Smith in the novel. Cher encourages Tai to cut her hair, buy new clothes, exercise, and read more nonacademic books, and she takes pride in the new person that she has tried to create. In this way, the film parallels the novel's attention not only to Emma's preoccupation with social status but also to the way she tries to use Harriet to further elevate her own reputation.

Fig. 2. Clueless depicts Cher as a status-conscious consumer, echoing a significant theme in Austen's novel.

could help someone to become as stylish and savvy as herself. Just as the novel makes fun of Emma for her lack of critical self-awareness, the student argued, so does Clueless make fun of Cher.

THINKING CRITICALLY ABOUT WHAT YOU HAVE LEARNED

Now that you have read and discussed several evaluation essays and written one of your own, take some time to think critically about what you have learned. What problems did you encounter as you were writing your essay, and how did you solve them? How did reading other evaluation essays influence your own essay? How do evaluation essays in general reflect social or cultural attitudes about judgment?

Reflecting on Your Writing

Write a one-page explanation, telling your instructor about a problem you encountered in writing your essay and how you solved it. Before you begin, gather all of your writing—invention and planning notes, drafts, critical comments, revision plan, and final revisions. Review these materials as you complete this writing task.

1. *Identify* **one** *writing problem you needed to solve as you worked on the essay.* Do not be concerned with grammar and punctuation; concentrate instead on problems unique to developing an evaluation essay. For example: Did you puzzle over how to present your subject? Did you have trouble asserting an overall judgment while acknowledging what you liked as well as disliked? Was it difficult to refute an important objection you knew readers would raise?

2. *Determine how you came to recognize the problem.* When did you first discover it? What called it to your attention? If you did not become aware of the problem until someone else pointed it out to you, can you now see hints of it in your invention writings? If so, where specifically? When you first recognized the problem, how did you respond?

3. *Reflect on how you went about solving the problem.* Did you work on the wording of a passage,

cut or add reasons or refutations, conduct further research, move paragraphs or sentences around? Did you reread one of the essays in this chapter to see how another writer handled a similar problem, or did you look back at your invention writing? If you talked about the problem with another student, a tutor, or your instructor, did talking about it help? How useful was the advice you received?

4. *Write a brief explanation of the problem and your solution.* Be as specific as possible in reconstructing your efforts. Quote from your invention notes or draft essay, others' critical comments, your revision plan, or your revised essay to show the various changes your writing—and thinking—underwent as you tried to solve the problem. If you are still uncertain about your solution, say so. Taking time to explain how you identified a particular problem, how you went about trying to solve it, and what you learned from this experience can help you solve future writing problems more easily.

Reviewing What You Learned from Reading

Write a page or so explaining to your instructor how the readings in this chapter influenced your final draft. Your own essay may have been influenced to some extent by one or more of the essays in this chapter as well as by classmates' essays that you have read. These other essays may have helped you decide that you needed to do further research before you could argue responsibly for your judgment, that you could use comparisons as part of your support, or that you should try to anticipate and refute readers' objections. Before you write, take some time to reflect on what you have learned about writing evaluations from these selections.

1. *Reread the final revision of your essay; then look back at the selections you read before completing it.* Do you see any specific influences? For example, did any reading influence how you decided to present the subject, state your thesis, use authorities, or refute objections? Also look for ideas you got from your reading, writing strategies you were inspired to try, specific details you were led to include, and goals you sought to achieve.

2. *Write an explanation of these influences.* Did one selection have a particularly strong influence on your essay, or were several selections influential in different ways? Quote from the readings and from your final revision to show how your essay was influenced by other essays you read. Finally, based on your review of this chapter's readings, point out any further improvements you would now make in your essay.

Considering the Social Dimensions of Evaluations

The media or arts review—someone's judgment about the quality of movies, television programs, musical performances, books, and so forth—is a special kind of evaluation. We rely on such evaluations to help us decide what movies or performances to see, what books to buy, what exhibits to attend. They confirm or challenge our attraction to a particular television series or musical group. The best media reviewers develop impressive expertise. They come to be trusted by readers to set standards for movies, musical recordings, novels, or works of art. They educate readers, helping to shape their judgment and discrimination, building their confidence in recognizing a clumsy, passable, or outstanding work or performance. At their best, reviewers counterbalance advertising: Instead of enticing us to see every movie that comes to town, they help us choose among the advertised movies. A trusted media or arts reviewer for a local newspaper can come to influence a community's values, building a local consensus, for example, about what constitutes a successful musical performance and

encouraging tolerance or even appreciation for new kinds of music.

Excluding and Silencing. By deciding what to review and what to ignore, media and arts reviewers determine what receives public attention and what remains invisible, and their decisions may often be based to a large extent on economic factors: Which review is likely to sell more newspapers or bring in more advertising? (In this sense, reviewers are part of a larger publicity apparatus; indeed, in our age of giant media conglomerates, a movie or music reviewer in a national magazine may well work for the same parent company that produced or distributed the film or the recording being reviewed—a situation that may not encourage the most objective evaluations.) Local theater or musical groups without money to advertise their performances may only get a brief listing in the newspaper; but unless they are reviewed, they will be unlikely to attract enough ticket buyers to survive (and the less mainstream their offerings, the less likely they are to be reviewed). Similarly, a new artist is simply not likely to be reviewed as widely as a more established one.

For a long time, this sort of resistance to anything new and different kept many women and minority writers from being appreciated by reviewers—both in the universities and in the media—thus making it harder for them to earn a living by their work and effectively silencing their voices. This situation has changed in some ways, especially with the advent of the Internet, where people have wider access to reviews by professionals and by people who simply want to share their judgments with others. But reviewers who work for traditional media outlets such as newspapers and television still have great power to determine what is or is not considered a "successful" work of art.

1. *Reflect on your own experience reading reviews on the Internet, in magazines, and in newspapers (including your college newspaper), as well as on the television or radio.* Think of one film, television program, or live performance you decided to see because of a review you read or

one CD, book, or video you purchased after reading a review of it. Recall how the review influenced you, and explain its influence.

2. *Consider how you usually learn about new films, music, and books.* Do you read reviews or get your information some other way? Does your information come mainly from the mainstream media, from word of mouth, neighborhood or alternative newspapers, or from some other source? Where do you get information about nonmainstream music, books, or films?

3. *Reflect on Ansen's review of* **The Phantom Menace** *and any other media reviews you read in class or wrote yourself.* Consider these ideas about reviews excluding artists who do not make a lot of money or who express minority points of view in light of Ansen's review and the other reviews you read or the one you wrote.

4. *Write a page reflecting on the role of media reviews in excluding or silencing new, innovative, or minority performers and artists.* If possible, connect your ideas to the readings in this chapter and to your own essay.

Hidden Assumptions of Evaluators. Good evaluative writing provides readers with reasons and support for the writer's judgments. However, it is easy to overlook the fact that judgments also reflect the writer's personal experience, cultural background, and political ideology. Even the most fair-minded evaluators write from the perspective of their particular ethnicity, religion, gender, age, social class, sexual ori-

entation, academic discipline, and so on. Writers seldom make explicit their assumptions. Consequently, while the reasons for an evaluation may make it seem fair and objective, the writer's judgment may result from hidden assumptions that even the writer has not examined critically.

1. *Choose* **one** *reading from this chapter and try to identify one of its hidden assumptions.* Think of a personal or cultural factor that may have influenced the writer's judgment of the subject. For example, how do you imagine Romano's gender may have influenced her judgment of Statsky's essay on competitive sports for children? How do you think Etzioni's background as a college professor and a father of teenage sons might have influenced his negative evaluation of McDonald's-type jobs for teenagers?

2. *Reflect on your own experience of writing an evaluation essay.* How do you think factors such as gender, age, social class, ethnicity, religion, geographical region, or political perspective may have influenced your own evaluation? Recall the subjects you listed as possibilities for your essay and how you made your choice. Also recall how you arrived at your judgment and how you decided which reasons to use and which not to use in your essay.

3. *Write a page or so explaining your ideas about how hidden assumptions play a role in evaluation essays.* Connect your ideas to the readings in this chapter and to your own essay.

Speculating about Causes

We all quite naturally try to explain causes. Because we assume that everything has a cause, we predictably ask "Why?" when we notice something new or unusual or puzzling.

Many things can be fully and satisfactorily explained. When children ask, "Why is the sky blue in the day and black at night?" parents can provide an answer. But we can answer other questions only tentatively: Why in the 1980s and 1990s did the cost of college education increase faster than the cost of living? Why is there so much violence by young men? Why does poverty remain so widespread in America? Why have SAT scores declined? Questions such as these often have only plausible, not definitive, explanations because we cannot design a scientific experiment to identify the cause conclusively. The decline in SAT scores, for example, has been attributed to the rise in television viewing among children. Although this contention is plausible, we cannot know for certain that television viewing is indeed responsible for the drop in scores.

Much of what we want to know about can never be known definitively but can only be speculated about on the basis of the best available evidence and experience. To speculate means primarily to examine or ponder something, but it also means to question, to be curious, and even to take risks.

Writing that speculates about causes plays an important role in academic and professional life. Government specialists analyze the causes of unemployment or homelessness to design policies intended to solve social problems. Business executives study the reasons for increases in sales or declines in worker productivity. Educators look at why some teaching techniques work and others do not or how family problems affect students' performance in school.

This chapter presents several essays speculating about the causes of some phenomenon or trend. A phenomenon is something notable about the human condition or social order—fear of failure, for example, or the high rate of intermarriage among ethnic and racial groups in the United States. A trend is a significant change occurring over some period of time, generally months or years. It can be identified by an increase or decrease—for example, a rise in the number of babies born with AIDS or a decline in the percentage of men, relative to the percentage of women, attending college.

When you speculate about causes, you must first describe your subject and then propose some causes and argue for one (or more) as the best available explanation. You do not have to prove that your explanation is right, but you must attempt to convince readers that it is plausible by supporting your explanation with examples, statistics, or anecdotes. You will probably need to anticipate readers' questions or objections to your causal argument. You may show readers that you are aware of their resistance, concede the usefulness of their questions by accommodating your own argument to them, or attempt to refute readers' objections by arguing that they are not reasonable or cannot be supported by any known evidence. When you speculate about causes, you inevitably find yourself in a situation where some of your readers believe other causes to be more plausible than the ones you are arguing for. Here, too, you must either acknowledge that you are aware of causes readers may prefer, concede the likelihood of these alternative causes, or refute them.

Speculating about why things are the way they are or why things change will develop your creativity as you identify possible causes. It will refine your judgment as you evaluate these causes and choose the most plausible ones. It will exercise your reasoning as you argue to support your speculations.

You will encounter writing that speculates about causes in many different contexts, as the following examples suggest:

Writing in Your Other Courses

- For an anthropology course, a student writes an essay speculating about the cause of the "afternoon lull," the period of reduced activity after the midday meal. She cites research studies to reject two possible causes: the possibility that the lull is caused either by the biochemical effects of eating or by a change in body temperature. She also argues against the idea that the lull is due to laziness or a desire for diversion. She argues instead that it is most likely caused by a biological rhythm established during early human evolution in the tropics, where heat peaks in the early afternoon.

To see how this student uses a map and other visuals in his report, see pp. 459–60.

- For a biology course, a student writes a report describing the AIDS epidemic in the United States and sub-Saharan Africa and speculating about this question: Why is AIDS concentrated among homosexuals in this country but among heterosexuals in Africa? The student speculates that these differences could possibly be explained in part by such factors as sexual practices, attitudes toward courtship and marriage, and the impact of AIDS-prevention programs. The student relies on reports and speculations from hospice workers, medical doctors, and sociologists to support these speculations.

Writing in the Community

- For a report on her internship in a social agency, a nursing student interviews older people who have been abandoned or neglected by their relatives. She also reviews published studies of elder abuse and neglect. In her report, she describes the widespread and increasing trend of elder neglect and speculates about its possible causes. She recognizes early in her research that there is no widespread agreement on why relatives do not take responsibility for elder care. She speculates that there are possibly three major causes besides the obvious ones of caretakers' psychological or medical problems and poverty: some caretakers must divide their efforts between caring for young children and an elder; some caretakers have long commutes to work, spend long hours on the job, and consequently do not have time to care adequately for an elder; and some caretakers have no helpful family members nearby and lack a neighborhood support network. The nurse intern supports her speculations with quotes from caretakers and elders she interviewed and with information from the reports she read.

- For a national newspaper, a science reporter writes an article speculating about the increasing intolerance in the United States of boyish behavior. She describes the various types of disorders with which boys are being diagnosed at a higher rate than girls and muses that these days Tom Sawyer and Huckleberry Finn would have been diagnosed with conduct disorder and attention-deficit hyperactivity disorder and put on Ritalin. She acknowledges certain biological differences between boys and girls and argues that these alone cannot explain the increasing concern with boyish behavior. Instead, she argues that cultural expectations best explain it. For example, because adults are excessively fearful of crime, they attempt to stamp out any signs of early aggression in boys such as rowdy playground behavior. In addition, school classrooms are increasingly group-oriented, allowing no sympathy for the individualist or the jokester. Finally, boyish fidgetiness is seen as a threat to success in an economy that places such a high value on sitting still and concentrating for ten or more hours a day.

Writing in the Workplace

- Writing for a journal read by other school administrators, a high school principal speculates about conditions at a school site that make violence more likely. She reviews a few well-publicized recent examples of violence in high schools, focusing on conditions in those schools that made it too easy for students to bring in guns, knives, or explosives and to attack teachers and other students. She argues that a major cause of school violence is that spaces like bathrooms, cafeterias, hallways, and recreational spaces that once were monitored by teachers, counselors, and administrators are now monitored by people from the community whom students do not take seriously. She also argues that lockers contribute to violence because they permit reckless students to store weapons, ammunition, or explosives at school. Finally, she argues that diffidence about inspecting everything students bring into a school and take from it has contributed to violence. Recognizing that unpopular solutions are implied by the way she sees the problem—assigning teachers to monitor all school spaces, removing lockers, and installing backpack screening equipment—she anticipates reservations other school principals will have to her analysis of the problem. To support her causal argument, she quotes from educational research studies and from recent reports by other principals that imply or assert agreement with her analysis.

- The marketing executive of a large multistate supermarket chain must try to explain the failure of an expensive, long-running advertising campaign designed to attract more customers to the stores' delicatessens. As he goes over the analyses provided by the advertising firm team, he realizes that he does not believe any of the reasons the team advances to explain the failure of the campaign. He makes notes about what he believes to be the most likely causes for the failure and plans an oral presentation accompanied by visuals for the next executive committee meeting. At the meeting, he uses computer-generated images to review the goals, costs, and results of the advertising campaign. Then he reviews and refutes the reasons given by the advertising company. He argues that there are most likely two major causes for the failure of the ad campaign: the advertising company's inexperience in coordinating multimedia campaigns and his own failure to discover their inexperience before signing a contract with them.

Practice Speculating about Causes: A Collaborative Activity

The preceding scenarios suggest some occasions for writing causal speculations. To get a sense of this special kind of argument, choose a current trend, and speculate about its causes.

Part 1. Get together with two or three other students, and select one person to take notes.

1. Make a list of five or six trends—such as the decline in voter turnout in the United States, the increasing costs of a college education, or the increasing rate of smoking among young people—whose causes you are interested in speculating about. Choose one trend that interests all of you.

2. Come up with several likely causes of this trend. Just list as many as you can in different areas, including economic, cultural, or psychological causes.

3. Select three or four causes that seem most likely to provide a partial explanation for the trend. Discuss how you might support each of these causes; that is, how you would convince others that these causes are plausible or likely explanations for the trend.

Part 2. When you have finished speculating, take a few more minutes to reflect on the process you have been engaged in.

- Where did your ideas about causes come from—reading, television, your own imagination?

- How did you differentiate among the causes, rejecting some and accepting others as most likely?

• What kinds of support did you come up with? Where do you think you might find further support?

READINGS

The readings in this chapter illustrate the features of causal speculation and the strategies writers rely on to realize the features. No two essays in this type of writing are much alike, and yet they share defining features. The Analyzing Writing Strategies and the Commentary following each reading touch on a few features best illustrated by that essay, capturing its special qualities and strengths. Together, the four essays cover many of the possibilities of causal speculation. Consequently, you will want to read as many of the essays as possible and, if time permits, complete the activities in Analyzing Writing Strategies and read the Commentary. Following the readings, the Basic Features section offers a concise description of the features of essays speculating about causes and provides examples from all of the readings.

Stephen King *is America's best-known writer of horror fiction. In the following essay, excerpted from* Playboy, *King speculates about the popular appeal of horror movies. Before you begin reading, think about your own attitude toward horror films. Do you enjoy them? "Crave" them? Dislike them? Or are you indifferent?*

As you read, notice how assertively King presents his assumptions about people, such as the ones in the opening sentence. How does he try to get you to accept these assumptions? Is he successful?

Why We Crave Horror Movies

Stephen King

I think that we're all mentally ill; those of us outside the asylums only hide it a little better—and maybe not all that much better, after all. We've all known people who talk to themselves, people who sometimes squinch their faces into horrible grimaces when they believe no one is watching, people who have some hysterical fear—of snakes, the dark, the tight place, the long drop . . . and, of course, those final worms and grubs that are waiting so patiently underground. 1

When we pay our four or five bucks and seat ourselves at tenth-row center in a theater showing a horror movie, we are daring the nightmare. 2

Why? Some of the reasons are simple and obvious. To show that we can, that we are not afraid, that we can ride this roller coaster. Which is not to say that a really good horror movie may not surprise a scream out of us at some point, the way we may scream 3 when the roller coaster twists through a complete 360 or plows through a lake at the bottom of the drop. And horror movies, like roller coasters, have always been the special province of the young; by the time one turns 40 or 50, one's appetite for double twists or 360-degree loops may be considerably depleted.

We also go to re-establish our feelings of essential normality; the horror movie is innately conservative, even reactionary. Freda Jackson as the horrible melting woman in *Die, Monster, Die!* confirms for us that no matter how far we may be removed from the beauty of a Robert Redford or a Diana Ross, we are still light-years from true ugliness. 4

And we go to have fun. 5

Ah, but this is where the ground starts to slope away, isn't it? Because this is a very peculiar sort of fun, indeed. The fun comes from seeing others menaced—sometimes killed. One critic has suggested that if pro football has become the voyeur's version of combat, then the horror film has become the modern version of the public lynching. 6

It is true that the mythic, "fairy tale" horror film intends to take away the shades of gray. . . . It urges us to put away our more civilized and adult penchant for analysis and to become children again, seeing things in pure blacks and whites. It may be that horror movies provide psychic relief on this level because this invitation to lapse into simplicity, irrationality, and even outright madness is extended so rarely. We are told we may allow our emotions a free rein . . . or no rein at all. 7

If we are all insane, then sanity becomes a matter of degree. If your insanity leads you to carve up women like Jack the Ripper or the Cleveland Torso Murderer, we clap you away in the funny farm (but neither of those two amateur-night surgeons was ever caught, heh-heh-heh); if, on the other hand, your insanity leads you only to talk to yourself when you're under stress or to pick your nose on your morning bus, then you are left alone to go about your business . . . though it is doubtful that you will ever be invited to the best parties. 8

The potential lyncher is in almost all of us (excluding saints, past and present; but then, most saints have been crazy in their own ways), and every now and then, he has to be let loose to scream and roll around in the grass. Our emotions and our fears form their own body, and we recognize that it demands its own exercise to maintain proper muscle tone. Certain of these emotional muscles are accepted—even exalted—in civilized society; they are, of course, the emotions that tend to maintain the status quo of civilization itself. Love, friendship, loyalty, kindness—these are all the emotions that we applaud, emotions that have been immortalized in the couplets of Hallmark cards and in the verses (I don't dare call it poetry) of Leonard Nimoy. 9

When we exhibit these emotions, society showers us with positive reinforcement; we learn this even before we get out of diapers. When, as children, we hug our rotten little puke of a sister and give her a kiss, all the aunts and uncles smile and twit and cry, "Isn't he the sweetest little thing?" Such coveted treats as chocolate-covered graham crackers often follow. But if we deliberately slam the rotten little puke of a sister's fingers in the door, sanctions follow—angry remonstrance from parents, aunts, and uncles; instead of a chocolate-covered graham cracker, a spanking. 10

But anticivilization emotions don't go away, and they demand periodic exercise. We have such "sick" jokes as "What's the difference between a truckload of bowling balls and a truckload of dead babies?" (You can't unload a truckload of bowling balls with a pitchfork . . . a joke, by the way, that I heard originally from a ten-year-old.) Such a joke may surprise a laugh or a grin out of us even as we recoil, a possibility that confirms the thesis: If we share a brotherhood of man, then we also share an insanity of man. None of which is intended as a defense of either the sick joke or insanity but merely as an explanation of why the best horror films, like the best fairy tales, manage to be reactionary, anarchistic, and revolutionary all at the same time. 11

The mythic horror movie, like the sick joke, has a dirty job to do. It deliberately appeals to all that is worst in us. It is morbidity unchained, our most base instincts let free, our nastiest fantasies realized . . . and it all happens, fittingly enough, in the dark. For those reasons, good liberals often shy away from horror films. For myself, I like to see the most aggressive of them—*Dawn of the Dead,* for instance—as lifting a trap door in the civilized forebrain and throwing a basket of raw meat to the hungry alligators swimming around in that subterranean river beneath. 12

Why bother? Because it keeps them from getting out, man. It keeps them down there and me up here. It was Lennon and McCartney who said that all you need is love, and I would agree with that. 13

As long as you keep the gators fed. 14

Connecting to Culture and Experience: Media Violence

"The potential lyncher is in almost all of us," says Stephen King, ". . . and every now and then, he has to be let loose to scream and roll around in the grass" (paragraph 9). King seems to say that horror films perform a social function by allowing us to exercise (or possibly exorcise) our least civilized emotions.

Discuss this idea with two or three other students. Certain religious groups and politicians believe that violence like that shown in horror films inspires people, especially the impressionable young, to commit violence—a belief quite different from King's. Do you believe that media violence exorcises or inspires violence? You may find that the members of your group disagree on this issue. What reasons can you give for your positions? If you believe that media violence inspires real violence, do you support censorship of movies, television programs, books, or magazines that portray violence? For children or adults or both? If you oppose censorship, do you support movie rating systems or the television V-chip, which gives parents some control over what their children watch?

These questions identify important social and political issues: the role of the media in a democratic society, the right of free expression and access to media, and the need to control violence.

Analyzing Writing Strategies

1. At the beginning of this chapter, we make several generalizations about essays that speculate about causes. Consider which of these assertions is true of King's essay:

   - It presents or defines its subject.
   - It proposes specific causes to explain the subject.
   - It argues that these causes are likely or plausible, though not definitive, explanations for the subject.
   - It tries to support each cause with examples, statistics, or anecdotes.
   - It anticipates readers' concerns, objections, and ideas about alternative causes.

For more on supporting arguments, see Chapter 19, pp. 627–33.

2. King offers several kinds of **support** for the causes he proposes. For example, in paragraph 3, in the last sentence of paragraph 12, and in paragraphs 13 and 14, he provides analogies; in paragraph 4, an example; and in paragraph 6, a comparison. Analyze each kind of support: Notice what general statement King is trying to support in each case, and describe how the analogy, example, or comparison supports the general statement. Then evaluate whether the support is likely to be convincing for King's particular readers.

Commentary: Plausible Causes and Logical Sequence of Causes

King proposes four causes of our craving for horror movies:

> We go to horror movies to prove that we can sit through them. (paragraphs 2 and 3)
>
> We go to reassure ourselves that we are normal. (4)
>
> We go because we enjoy seeing others in danger. (5 and 6)
>
> We go for the psychological relief that comes from giving in to our emotions. (7)

Readers are likely to find the first cause plausible—likely, possible, or believable—because it seems obvious, but they may resist the other three, at least initially, because these causes are less predictable, even surprising. They are based on a psychology that goes back to Aristotle and is still popular in our times that says we engage all of the arts so readily, even horror movies, because they make us feel better. King's readers may not accept his psychology or they may find his less predictable causes implausible, but whatever their reaction, King has not bored them with causes so obvious that they could have predicted all of them before reading the argument.

King begins with a cause that seems obvious but is still worth mentioning: We go to horror films because we want to prove that we can sit through them, just as we ride roller coasters to show ourselves and others that we have the courage to do so (paragraph 3). We can surmise that King mentions this cause right away because he assumes that readers will be thinking of it. It enables him both to connect to a very common experience of his readers and to set an obvious cause aside in order to move on to the not-so-obvious causes, which are the heart of his argument.

King next entertains a very different cause: We go to horror movies "to re-establish our feelings of essential normality" (paragraph 4). This cause is much less predictable than the first. Although this cause is also plausible, it moves us from *obvious causes* toward the one *hidden* (unexpected, unlikely, risky) *cause* that King is to argue at length—that we "crave" horror movies (not just attend them casually) in order to manage our uncivilized emotions of fear, violence, and aggression.

In your own causal analysis essay, your first goal will be to speculate creatively about your subject so that you can come up with at least one not-so-obvious cause. Like King, you may want to place this cause last, after discussing other more obvious causes, and to argue for it at length and with ingenuity.

Considering Topics for Your Own Essay

Consider speculating about some popular cultural phenomenon that interests you. For instance, have you ever wondered why romance novels are so popular? Police shows or soap operas or MTV? Roller blading? Singles bars? Drive-through fast-food restaurants? You will think of other popular cultural phenomena. How might you present the phenomenon to your readers? What obvious and not-so-obvious causes might you propose to explain the popularity of the phenomenon?

Jill Neimark is a journalist and author living in New York City. She has contributed many articles to magazines, especially Psychology Today. *(Several of her* Psychology Today *articles are available on the Internet at <http://www.nyu.edu/classes/neimark>.) She has also published a novel,* Bloodsong *(1994). In addition to writing, she teaches a course in digital journalism in the Science and Environmental Reporting Division, Graduate School of Journalism, New York University.*

This essay was originally published in a 1998 issue of Psychology Today, *a publication of the American Psychological Association designed to translate research findings into useful information for general but educated readers who have no formal academic training in psychology. Relying for support on publications by academic specialists, Neimark speculates about why the annual Miss America contest remains so popular thirty years into the feminist revolution. She begins with the assumption that "Miss America informs us about our culture's ideals and conflicts" and in so doing mirrors America. Such an assumption requires that Neimark attempt to convince readers that particular ideals and conflicts are revealed by the Miss America contest. As you read, notice what ideals and conflicts she singles out as possible causes for why the Miss America contest remains so important to many Americans. These are easy to recognize because Neimark sets them off graphically (with bullets and italics).*

Why We Need Miss America

Jill Neimark

Miss America. For a skin show, she's been caught in the crossfire of colossal cultural battles: women's rights, pornography, changing racial and religious values. Feminist poet Robin Morgan claimed that the pageant inspired the formal launching of the women's movement in 1968, when a crowd of protesters burned their bras, torched host Bert Parks in effigy, stormed the exhibition hall, and accused the contest of being lily-white, racist, and pro-military. Since then, Miss America has changed with the times: she has been black, deaf, and a social activist with platforms ranging from AIDS prevention to children's self-esteem and aging with dignity—although she still struts in a bathing suit.

In the last decade, interest in the title has been flagging, and the pageant has had to offer gimmicks like viewer phone-in votes and two-piece swimsuits to boost television ratings. Still, every September, at least 20 million Americans stay home on a Saturday night to scorn or applaud the winner and see the kitschy crown passed on. If you're one who observes that annual ritual, you may watch out of simple nostalgia—Miss America as a kind of Proustian madeleine of days long gone, when you were a girl and she was a queen. Or you may watch for the treacly high camp of it all, or just out of an ambivalent blend of disgust and fascination. Yet somehow, at 78-years-old, this icon still lives. 2

The fact is, Miss America informs us about our culture's ideals and conflicts. That's what all beauty pageants do, according to Richard Wilk, professor of anthropology at Indiana University. "They're always about fundamental contradictions in the culture," he declares. "How else could you get millions of people to watch a bunch of relatively untalented women in bathing suits?" The Miss America contest has always knit together in its middle-class queen the deep schisms in American society. Whether her contestants flaunt pierced belly buttons or Ph.D.s in veterinary medicine, wear pants or ballgowns, Miss America is a mirror of America, even now. 3

So what *is* she really saying about us—and why do we need to know, anyway? 4

• *We're a big clubhouse, but we're not sure you should be a member.* We may be a melting pot of races and types, but we have a fairly inflexible standard of beauty. Almost all the Miss Americas have been white. According to Frank Deford, author of *There She Is,* the composite contestant in 1971 was 19 years old, 5 feet 6 inches, 119 pounds, with brown hair, blue eyes, and a fair complexion. And she hasn't changed much since then. "Miss America is the official standard of beauty, kind of like the dollar bill," observes Wilk. "The rest of us schlubs are not necessarily ugly. We may be beautiful, but by different standards." As an example, he cites Monica Lewinsky, with her plump curves and formerly big hair. "She is extremely beautiful by the small-town standards of the Midwest, and that big hair is the peak of fashion in southern Indiana where I live. But she does not look like a Miss America." 5

Give the pageant a bit of credit, though. The first black winner was chosen in 1984 —Vanessa Williams (and her replacement, Suzette Charles). Since then, three more African-Americans have worn the crown. Williams, with her fine-boned features, was said to match the "white" ideal, but Marjorie Vincent, the 1991 titleholder, with her very dark skin and full figure, represented a different, and more diverse, vision of beauty. In 1997, the contestant from Colorado was Hispanic and Miss Washington, D.C., was of Indian descent. 6

"More Latina young women and African-Americans are entering the contest, and those audiences are now watching," says New York City psychologist Elizabeth Debold, author of *Mother Daughter Revolution: From Good Girls to Great Women.* "The pageant may be providing a way for immigrant and outsider groups to enter the mainstream." 7

It is at the smaller local contest level that the clash of immigrant culture and mainstream America is most clearly seen. In fact, some local competitions seem to exist precisely on that fault line, providing a stage on which to battle out cultural assimilation in the arena of beauty. "These pageants let immigrants ask who they are," says Wilk, "how much of the American model they want, how much they're going to adapt, how to pass their culture's values on to the next generation." For instance, the Miss India America pageant, held in Atlanta, Georgia, offers teenagers of Asian Indian descent a chance to parade their own standards of beauty and their position in American society. One teen performs an acrobatic routine to disco music; another does a classical Indian dance.

Though such local contests don't feed directly into the Miss America pageant, the conflicts of the microcosm spread ripples that are felt in the macrocosm. Even so, the favored contestant hasn't altered all that much. If beauty does reflect cultural and social values, we—the great democracy—don't know how inclusive we really want to be. Bess Myerson, the first Jewish Miss America, was crowned in 1945. "She meant as much then to Jewish women as Vanessa Williams meant to blacks," says Vicki Gold Levi, co-author with Lee Eisenberg of *Atlantic City: 125 Years of Ocean Madness*. Myerson is still the only Jewish woman to wear the crown. And most of the finalists and winners are still white.

• *We're still a nation of Yankees and Southern belles.* Miss America unmasks the schism between the North and the South—it never went away—and the penumbra of the Southern belle still holds sway in our national psyche. Only one New England contestant has ever won the Miss America title, Connecticut's Marian Bergeron in 1933, while southern and western states have been overwhelmingly represented. New England women don't seem to cotton to beauty pageants. In Vermont, the Miss America organization has such a hard time dredging up contestants that a few years ago there were only 10 candidates for the state crown. One recent Miss Vermont flaunted a pierced navel—not exactly Miss America's brand of all-American.

• *Cinderella ought to come from the middle class and go to college.* Miss America gives us a capsule look at middle-class America and its values. After World War II, Miss America became part of the culture of middle-class civic boosterism. The girls who make it to the national pageant start out competing in county or state contests sponsored by community organizations like the Elks or the Rotary Club. "At the local level," says anthropologist Robert Lavenda, a professor at St. Cloud State University in Minnesota, "the community is looking for an appropriate representative. When a girl wins a small-town queen pageant she'll be announced as 'Mary Jo, the daughter of Frank and Suzanne.' The community knows these girls." These days, however, junior contestants are drawn from a different circle than earlier. Where once they came from cheerleading squads and drama clubs, nowadays they're picked off soccer fields and basketball courts.

The "bawdy" pageant initiated its scholarship program at the end of the War, and today the organization gives out $32 million in scholarships to young women every year. Many of the early winners of the crown vowed to use the money to enter college. Today's Miss America often has her sights set far higher. Older than earlier candidates, she's likely to already be in college and aiming for medical, law, or graduate school. In fact, many Miss America contestants now say the sole reason they enter the pageant is to finance their education. Practicality—what could be a more middle-class and American virtue?

• *We've got faith.* She reminds us of our bottomless sincerity and spirit. Miss Americas say things like "Mental attitude is so important" and "Every day is a gift from God." You might snicker at the platitudes, but who's buying all the self-help books that offer precisely that inspirational message? She comes out of the same cultural spout as that runaway bestseller, *Chicken Soup for the Soul.*

• *We've got pluck.* Miss America embodies our Horatio Alger can-do spirit. We believe that by dint of hard work we can overcome anything. It's the triumph of nurture over nature. So many aspects of being a beauty queen are beyond personal control— you've got to be between 5 feet 6 inches and 5 feet 10 inches, for instance. "On the other hand," notes Wilk, "everyone always talks about how hard these girls work."

Reflecting our preoccupation with fitness, today's Miss America is pumped and streamlined, whereas in 1921 she was soft and plump. Bodybuilding is practically a given for contestants as are strenuous sessions in the gym. One participant in the 1990 pageant, Karrie Mitchell of Colorado, admitted, "I was not a swimsuit winner a year ago, let me tell you." She worked out until she shrank from a size 12 to a size five.

Many contestants are willing to undergo extensive cosmetic surgery (which the state pageants sometimes pay for). They also resort to the old stand-bys, mummifying themselves with surgical tape to enhance their cleavage and the curve of their buttocks.

• *We're all equal, but we love royalty.* Sure, she's just an ordinary American girl, but she wears a crown and is cloaked in celebrity. Norman Rockwell was one of the pageant's original judges, others have ranged from Grace Kelly to Donald Trump. Miss America opens shopping centers and moves in power circles. As a *Boston Globe* editorial recently noted, "In a letter to the President, one icon to another, Miss America asked for federal funds for needle exchange programs [to prevent AIDS]." Icons, of course, gain status when they rub noses with other icons. She's got to be more than a bathing beauty, asking the president for federal funding.

Vanessa Williams is one of the few winners to gain fame.

Very few Miss Americas have gone on to lasting fame, but that makes perfect sense. To win, she has to be the ultimate paradox, everyday royalty, the thing that every American secretly believes he or she is.

• *We love to gossip.* It's the corollary to fame. Miss America lets us know we love knowing a secret, no matter how trivial. Journalists have asked competitors about the "firm grip gunk" they spray on their butts to keep their bathing suits from riding up; during one recent pageant, the press rooted out that 37 contestants had been arrested for speeding at some time in their life.

• *We love glitz.* Let's face it, America has always had a purple-spangled heart, 20
always been genuinely and even naively trashy. From its start, Miss America has been
high camp. "The pageant always manages to confuse the wholesome with the whole-
sale, a clean time with a good time," says Levi.

In the late 1940s, Miss Montana rode her horse onstage and almost fell into the 21
orchestra pit; after that animals were banned; Miss Nevada lamented, "You mean I won't
be able to have my cow perform?" Miss Nebraska tossed a flaming baton into the
judges' booth; flaming batons were banned. Later, a church choir member did a
striptease—and won the crown.

Alas, such glorious moments are gone. The highlight of the pageant, though, 22
remains: the declaration of the winner with her requisite burst of tears and careful stroll
down the runway, crown slipping from her head.

• *Superwoman is alive and well.* This pageant tells us what women are supposed 23
to be. "She's the cultural icon of the perfect girl," declares Debold. Today, Miss Americas
are asked to be beautiful, to achieve, and to serve. (In the pageant's official parlance,
she no longer "reigns.") She has a platform, and it's inevitably for social good. One
recent Miss America was a cancer survivor studying to be a musical therapist for the
gravely ill.

"It's a totally contradictory model," asserts Wilk. "She should be strong but weak, 24
aggressive but submissive, totally committed to her career and her family, have touches
of the social worker, and basically walk on water in high-heeled shoes and make it look
easy." Whew.

• *It's all for one and one for all.* Miss America tells us, finally, one last fact: that we 25
still believe a single person can serve as a living snapshot of an entire country. Like the
Mercury astronauts, like baseball's boys of summer, Miss America thrives, simply
because we believe in the best and the brightest. What could be brighter than her Vase-
lined smile, telling us, at the close of that special September evening every year, that we
still believe? We're a nation of believers. God Bless Miss America—and does anyone
have a handful of popcorn to throw at the TV?

Connecting to Culture and Experience: Contradictory Ideals

Neimark argues that we need Miss America the woman because she tells us something important about ourselves and our society. One thing Miss America tells us is
that "Superwoman is alive and well" (paragraph 23). Her goals are "to be beautiful,
to achieve, and to serve," ideals that seem contradictory. Neimark quotes an anthropologist: " 'She should be strong but weak, aggressive but submissive, totally committed to her career and her family, have touches of the social worker, and basically
walk on water in high-heeled shoes and make it look easy' " (paragraph 24).

Discuss these contradictory ideals with two or three other students. Test them
against your own experience as a woman (in terms of what it might be like to live this

contradiction) or as a man (in terms of your expectations of women). Also consider the following questions: Do you think it is possible to cherish an ideal without being aware of its contradictions and conflicts? Are people who are willing to live with contradictions simply unaware of the contradictions? Or do ideals like faithfulness, social service, high achievement, and loyalty always have built-in contradictions and conflicts? How could you know?

Analyzing Writing Strategies

1. For a causal argument to be convincing, it must be based on plausible causes. Review Neimark's ten causes (set off graphically with bullets and italics); then choose one cause that seems plausible and one that seems less plausible. What makes one of these causes more plausible to you than the other?

2. Evaluate Neimark's presentation of the subject. Neimark's subject seems to include both a cultural phenomenon—the Miss America pageant—and a particular way of thinking about the pageant—from the perspective of an academic specialty known as cultural studies. In paragraphs 1–3, what kinds of information does Neimark give readers about her subject? Is it enough information to orient you to her causal argument, which begins in paragraph 4? If not, what other information do you need?

Commentary: Convincing Support

To learn more about these criteria for convincing support, turn to Evaluating the Logic of an Argument in Chapter 12, pp. 550–52.

To learn more about conceding (or concession), see the section Accommodating Readers' Concerns in Chapter 19, pp. 635–36.

Neimark offers from one to five paragraphs of **support** for each of her ten causes. This material needs to be both interesting and convincing. It also must be appropriate or relevant, believable, and consistent—that is, it should not contradict itself. Support is necessary in causal argument because the causes are likely or possible causes, not definitive ones, and therefore must be supported thoughtfully, creatively, and convincingly in order to seem plausible to readers. In addition to coming up with plausible causes, then, writers of causal arguments must offer convincing support for those causes.

Neimark's first cause—we need Miss America because she reveals to us that even though we think we are democratically inclusive, we actually are quite exclusive, insisting on a very narrow definition of female beauty—is supported at length in paragraphs 5–9. She quotes four different authorities: Deford, Wilk, Debold, and Levi. In paragraph 6, Neimark **concedes** that there have been four African American Miss Americas and that in a recent pageant the contestants included a Hispanic woman and a woman of Indian descent. In paragraph 8, she describes local beauty contests that offer diverse images of beauty. Pursuing her theme of cultural conflict and contradiction in paragraph 9, she illustrates how, despite efforts at inclusivity, the national pageant continues to present finalists and winners who are nearly exclusively white.

By contrast, Neimark's second cause—that because nearly all the winners have been southerners, Miss America reveals that we are still a country divided between

North and South—is supported only briefly in paragraph 10. Neimark points out that in seventy-eight years only one New Englander has ever become a Miss America. Then she concedes that New Englanders do not seem to be much interested in beauty pageants. She seems to assume that readers will find this brief support convincing. She may be correct in this assumption because readers need to see only enough support to consider a cause plausible.

Considering Topics for Your Own Essay

Like Neimark, speculate about why something has remained popular or of compelling interest over time in your state or in the nation. Examples include *Star Wars* movies, stock-car racing, the Fourth-of-July barbecue, coffee shops, a state fair, Thanksgiving Day, state or national elections, the Academy Awards, sitcoms, and cop shows. If you were to write an essay speculating about "Why We Need _____," which subject would you choose and how would you present it to your readers? What causes might you come up with to explain its long-term popularity? Consider your own personal interest in the subject, but go beyond that to speculate about why you think the subject remains so widely popular. For example, *Star Wars* movies may be fun and entertaining to watch, but what deeper personal or social needs might they fulfill?

William S. Pollack, *professor of clinical psychiatry at Harvard University and codirector of the Center for Men at McLean Hospital/Harvard Medical School, has spent many years counseling boys and men. He has coauthored* In a Time of Fallen Heroes: The Re-Creation of Masculinity *(1993) and coedited* A New Psychology for Men *(1995) and* New Psychotherapy for Men *(1998). The following essay is excerpted from his most recent book,* Real Boys: Rescuing Our Sons from the Myths of Boyhood *(1999). About* Real Boys, *Pollack has written, "Through this book I would like to help families, communities, and boys themselves better understand what a real boy is and, most important, how to help boys flourish and succeed in our society."*

In this reading, Pollack focuses on the causes of depression in boys. As you read, notice that Pollack defines depression and describes its well-established biological causes before he speculates about its possible psychological causes. Read to understand the interactions between the biological and psychological causes of depression in boys and to evaluate the plausibility of the psychological causes Pollack proposes.

Why Boys Become Depressed

William S. Pollack

The Many Faces of Depression

Depression affects boys in a variety of ways. It may make them feel sad, anxious, or numb. The depressed boy may act sullen and withdrawn or . . . may become agitated, overly aggressive, and full of rage. He may misbehave in school or become dependent on drugs or alcohol. Or he may just seem glum.

Depression in boys is a syndrome involving a whole range of behavioral difficulties   2
and symptoms. While just about any adult who's been diagnosed with clinical depression will tell you that the experience is quite different from a "bad mood," it's essential,
especially in the case of boys, to see depression as this kind of wide-ranging syndrome
with symptoms that fall along a continuum from mild to extreme. I believe that if we dwell
merely on the most extreme—and obvious—instances of full-blown, or "clinical,"
depression, we risk failing to help boys cope with emotional states that, though less
intense on the surface, are actually very painful for them, emotional states that without
appropriate intervention may very well evolve into a major depression or provoke suicidal feelings. There's also a risk that by ignoring certain related behaviors, most notably
irritable conduct and the abuse of substances, we may also fail to recognize the onset
of a serious depression.

The Biology of Depression

We now know that in addition to psychological elements, depression can often be   3
caused by biological factors, most notably by an imbalance in certain neurotransmitters,
such as serotonin, that seem to directly affect emotional well-being. Medications that
correct these imbalances—so-called SSRIs (selective serotonin reuptake inhibitors)
such as Prozac (fluoxetine), Zoloft (sertraline), and Paxil (paroxetine)—have been
shown to be helpful to many people, including children, suffering depression. But neurotransmitter levels are also affected by psychological phenomena, such as daily stress,
loss of a loved one, or an early trauma, all of which may change the biological and
chemical workings of the brain, leaving it vulnerable to depression. Exercise levels
can change neurotransmitter levels in a different way, improving your mood and your
biology.

We are just beginning to understand the complex interrelationships between the   4
biological and psychological aspects of our emotional systems. As with the heart, some
people are born with a genetic predisposition to heart disease; they inherit a weak heart,
high blood pressure, or a tendency to atherosclerosis. Such individuals will have to work
hard to prevent heart disease. But heart disease doesn't have to come about through
genetics. If a previously strong heart receives enough abuse—a poor diet, chronic
smoking, or a habitual lack of exercise—it will become vulnerable to a heart attack.
Likewise, depression seems to run in some families, but a *vulnerability* to it can be
created at any point, through early deprivation, a lack of healthy loving relationships, or
repeated blows to one's self-esteem.

While I believe the biological, or "organic," components of clinical depression (and   5
the medical treatments for them) are of paramount importance and need to be carefully
studied, my primary focus here is on what other psychologists and I have discovered
about *external* psychological factors that can lead boys toward serious sadness or
depression—factors such as a boy's family life, how he's treated at school, the quality
of his friendships, and what kind of emotional support he gets on a regular basis.

The Cost . . . of Society's Disconnection

In my view, so many of the symptoms of depression that boys experience are caused by   6
gaps in how we, as a society, address the inner emotional worlds of our boys. . . . [B]oys
are often pushed too early to be independent of those people—their parents—who
have so far been their main source of comfort and nurturance. I believe that the pain of
being separated from and losing these people, in and of itself, is enough to depress just
about any boy. While neither the trauma of premature separation nor "abandonment"
leads all boys to become depressed, either may create a deep sadness in many boys,
making them vulnerable to depression later, either as boys or as men.

Further, I believe that many boys become susceptible to depression because of   7
the emotional scarring they receive through society's shame-based hardening process.
No matter how healthy a boy's emotional system was when he started life, it quickly
becomes compromised by the hardening he feels is necessary to avoid feelings of
shame, and by his denial (because of shame) of vulnerable emotional states such as
sadness, disappointment, and despair. Every boy needs to cry sometimes, to seek the
comfort of loving arms, to tell someone how much he hurts and to have them respond
with empathy. Yet because of the gender straitjacket that inhibits boys from ever completely *experiencing* these feelings (let alone expressing them) and insists that they
don't need help, boys actively repress feelings of sadness in an unhealthy way that can
lead them to feel lonely and frightened, or push them toward more severe forms of
depression.

But the straitjacket also brings about sadness and depression in boys in yet another   8
important way. . . . [O]ur gender-stereotyped myths about boys mislead us to believe that
boys do not care much about their relationships with friends and families and that boys
are generally tough, "cocky," and independent. Yet we've also learned that, in reality,
most boys experience all sorts of insecurities, feel tremendously dependent on their
friends and families, and in many areas (for example, at school or when dating) are
prone to large fluctuations in self-esteem. Boys yearn for connection—they care a lot
about their relationships and about how they are liked by others. But because we are so
often confused by the old myths, we may tend not to pay attention to the emotional ups
and downs in our sons' friendships and relationships and thus be unaware of the dev-
astating feelings of shame our sons may experience when these friendships or relationships are not going well or have come to an end. Such shame in a boy, if no one detects
it and explores it with him, can lead him to feel profoundly sad, afraid, and disconnected
from the rest of the world, and even to become clinically depressed.

Depression over Relationships

Yet researchers have perennially doubted the intensity or basic emotional importance of   9
boys' relationships and so have assumed that problems in them would be unlikely to
cause boys to become sad or depressed. Thus a study on depression in adolescent

boys and girls conducted by Joan Girgus and her colleagues at Princeton University hypothesized that "levels of depression in early adolescent girls are more closely related to their popularity with peers than in early adolescent boys"—an assumption based on "the frequent argument that women are more likely than men to base their self-esteem on their relationships with others and on the approval of others." But the results of the study were not as expected. "Surprisingly, the boys' depression scores were significantly correlated with both popularity and rejection, whereas the girls' depression scores were only significantly correlated with rejection. Thus, girls and boys are apparently equally vulnerable to depression as a function of poor peer relationships."

Another study, by Paul Rohde, John Seeley, and David Mace, in Eugene, Oregon, also found that boys suffer when they don't have healthy relationships. This study focused on the extent to which delinquent adolescents develop ideas about suicide, and it found that boys were more likely to think about suicide if they were suffering stressful life events and if they lacked social supports in situations such as when they were lonely and had few close relatives. The authors concluded that suicidal behavior for boys is closely linked to their social connections.   10

We now know that the opposite is also true—that strong relationships can *prevent*   11 boys from sliding into depression or engaging in risky, self-destructive behaviors in the first place. The National Longitudinal Study on Adolescent Health . . . found that teenagers who felt connected to their families were less likely to experience emotional distress. They were also less likely to engage in violence, attempt suicide, or use harmful substances. The key factors were parents who "shared activities" with teens, who were physically present at key times during the day, and, most important, who expressed warmth, love, and caring. Also . . . Blake Bowden, at Cincinnati Children's Hospital Medical Center . . . found that teens who ate dinner with their parents at least five nights a week were significantly better adjusted than classmates who dined alone.

In my opinion, we simply must resist being fooled by a boy's mask. Boys are not   12 Lone Rangers, and at all ages they need to be told that they're good, that they make good friends, that they're needed and loved. And, like all human beings, they particularly need caring support when their relationships are disrupted or come to an untimely end.

Connecting to Culture and Experience: Societal Expectations and Emotional Needs

Pollack argues that most people, including some psychologists who study adolescent development, wrongly believe that boys' relationships with family and friends are not so important to them as the same relationships are to girls. He also argues that most people believe boys need to be trained to be tough and independent. These arguments lead Pollack to conclude that too many people believe that boys' and girls' emotional lives and psychological needs are different, to the disadvantage of boys, whose emotional needs are widely ignored.

With two or three other students, discuss these ideas. Begin by describing a current close, personal, but nonromantic relationship you have with someone outside your family and speculating about how this relationship affects the way you feel about yourself. Then describe a close personal relationship you once had that came to an end for some reason or another and reflect on how you felt about losing that relationship. How did you feel at the time about talking about this loss? Was there someone you could express your feelings to? What short- and long-term effects did losing this relationship have on your psychological well-being?

Now focus on the cultural or societal expectation that boys and girls, men and women, have—or should be trained to have—different emotional needs. Do you think most people have this expectation? Do you think Pollack correctly assesses the danger this expectation presents to boys?

Analyzing Writing Strategies

1. To analyze and evaluate Pollack's causes, make a **scratch outline** of paragraphs 6–8, where Pollack proposes three causes to explain why boys become depressed. In a phrase or sentence, identify the cause in each of these paragraphs. Then decide whether each cause is likely to be considered plausible by Pollack's intended readers—parents and educators. Which cause is likely to be considered more or less plausible than the others? Why do you think so?

   For more on scratch outlining, see Chapter 12, pp. 540–41.

   Finally, analyze the logical sequence of these causes. How would you describe the relationship among the causes? Why do you think Pollack sequences them the way he does? Does one cause lead logically to the next and depend on the meaning of the previous cause, or do the causes seem only loosely related? If you believe they are sequenced meaningfully and logically, what evidence do you find for your view in the essay? What might make the sequence effective for the intended readers?

2. Unlike King and Neimark, Pollack devotes a large part of his essay to a presentation of the subject—depression in boys. Reread paragraphs 1–5, noticing how Pollack presents the subject and evaluating how well he does so for his particular readers. What does he seem to be trying to accomplish in paragraphs 1 and 2? What would you say is the purpose of the last two sentences in paragraph 2, in light of the causal argument Pollack goes on to make? What contribution do paragraphs 3 and 4 make? Why might paragraph 5 be important to readers? Finally, how effective do you think Pollack's presentation of the subject is for his intended readers?

Commentary: Anticipating Readers' Objections and Alternative Causes

When you anticipate your readers' objections and alternative causes, you have three options: to merely acknowledge that you are aware of them, to accommodate or concede them by approving of them or making them part of your own argument, or to refute them by trying to show that they are limited or implausible. While attempting to support his preferred causes for depression in boys in paragraphs 6–8, Pollack at least one time anticipates readers' objections. In the last sentence of paragraph 6, he anticipates what some readers will be thinking and concedes that "neither the trauma of premature separation nor 'abandonment' leads all boys to become depressed." But he then goes on to insist that "either may create a deep sadness in many boys, making them vulnerable to depression later." This strategy of conceding to the wisdom of part of an objection and refuting the rest is common in counterargument.

Pollack refutes another objection in paragraphs 9–11. He begins paragraph 9 by acknowledging that some researchers have always doubted that personal relationships are important to boys. Because this objection poses a serious challenge to his argument, Pollack must try to refute it convincingly. To do so, he draws support from four published studies. The first is especially useful because the researchers in the study assumed that boys would not be much influenced by their relationships. To the researchers' surprise—and, Pollack probably assumes, to some readers' surprise—boys who felt unpopular were more vulnerable to depression than girls who felt the same way. Pollack devotes almost a third of his argument to **counterargument**—to conceding and refuting readers' likely objections to his own argument.

For more information on anticipating readers' objections, turn to the section on counterarguing in Chapter 19, pp. 634–37.

Considering Topics for Your Own Essay

For your own essay, you could, like Pollack, speculate about why a certain group behaves the way it does. For example, you might speculate about why young boys tend to like a type of toy, why young girls like to play with Barbie dolls, why older girls are increasingly involved in competitive sports, why some high school teachers are more effective than others, why accomplished musicians of any age devote much of their lives to mastering their craft, why some students begin but never complete college, or why fewer unmarried teenage girls become pregnant or fewer young men attempted suicide or committed violence in the 1990s than in the 1980s. You could rely on your personal experience to identify causes and argue to support them. Or, in addition to using what you know from experience, you could research your subject in the library, on the Internet, or by interviewing experts. Try to move beyond obvious causes to hidden or unexpected causes. Consider both immediate and background causes for a group's behavior.

For more on research strategies, see Chapters 20–22.

Sarah West wrote this causal speculation essay for her first-year college composition course. Unlike Stephen King, Jill Neimark, and William S. Pollack, who speculate about the causes of phenomena, West speculates about the causes of a trend: a sharp increase in reported incidents of workplace sexual harassment over a four-year period. She begins by establishing that the trend exists. Notice that her concern is not whether workplace sexual harassment is increasing but whether reported incidents of it are increasing. (She recognized, during her invention and research, that it would be too difficult to prove that actual acts of harassment *are increasing or decreasing; she also recognized that such acts are very likely decreasing as reported incidents increase and receive wide publicity.) West then launches her speculations about the causes for the increasing number of reports.*

As you read, keep in mind that the U.S. Supreme Court has defined illegal sexual harassment as "sufficiently severe or pervasive to alter the conditions of the victim's employment." In other words, it is not a casual or unthreatening onetime incident, but several incidents that create a hostile work environment and undermine a victim's trust in a co-worker and ability to work effectively.

The Rise of Reported Incidents of Workplace Sexual Harassment

Sarah West

1   To those students who recently graduated from high school, it may sound like the Dark Ages, but it wasn't: Until 1964, an employee who refused to give in to his or her employer's sexual advances could be fired— legally. An employee being constantly humiliated by a co-worker could be forced either to deal with the lewd comments, the stares, and the touching or to just quit his or her job. It is truly strange to think that sexual harassment was perfectly legal in the United States until Congress passed the Civil Rights Act of 1964.

2   But even after 1964, sexual harassment still persisted. It was not widely known exactly what sexual harassment was or that federal laws against it existed. Often when an employee was sexually harassed on the job, he or she felt too alienated and humiliated to speak out against it (Martell and Sullivan 6). During the 1970s and 1980s, however, sexual harassment victims began coming forward to challenge their harassers. Then suddenly in the 1990s, the number of sexual harassment complaints and lawsuits sharply rose. According to a 1994 survey conducted by the Society for Human Resource Management, the percentage of human resource professionals who have reported that their departments handled at least one sexual harassment complaint rose from 35 percent in 1991 to 65 percent in 1994 *(Sexual)*. Why did this large increase occur in such a short amount of time? Possible answers to this question surely would include growing awareness of the nature of workplace sexual harassment, government action, efforts of companies to establish anti-harassment policies and encourage harassed employees to come forward, and prominence given by the media to many cases of workplace harassment.

3   One significant cause of the rise in reported incidents of sexual harassment was most likely the increased awareness of what constitutes sexual harassment. There are two distinct types of sexual harassment, and although their formal names may be unfamiliar, the situations they describe will most certainly ring a bell. *Hostile environment* sexual harassment occurs when a supervisor, or co-worker gives the victim "unwelcome sexual attention" that "interferes with (his or her) ability to work or creates an intimidating or offensive atmosphere" (Stanko and Werner 15). *Quid pro quo* sexual harassment occurs when "a workplace superior demands some degree of sexual favor" and either threatens to or does retaliate in a way that "has a tangible effect on the working conditions of the harassment victim" if he or she refuses to comply (Stanko and Werner 15).

A fundamental cause of the rise in reports of workplace harassment was government action in 1964 and again in 1991. After the passage of the Civil Rights Act of 1991, which allowed, among other things, larger damage awards for sexually harassed employees, many more employees began coming forward with complaints. They realized that sexual harassment was not legal and they could do something about it. Suddenly, it became possible for a company to lose millions in a single sexual harassment case. For example, Rena Weeks, a legal secretary in San Francisco, sued the law firm of Baker & McKenzie for $3.5 million after an employee, Martin Greenstein, "dumped candy down the breast pocket of her blouse, groped her, pressed her from behind and pulled her arms back to 'see which one (breast) is bigger'" ("Workplace"). The jury awarded Weeks $7.1 million in punitive damages, twice what she sought in her lawsuit ("Workplace"). In addition, research revealed that the mere existence of sexual harassment in a company could lead to "hidden costs" such as absenteeism, lower productivity, and loss of valuable employees (Stanko and Werner 16). These "hidden costs" could add up to $6 or $7 million a year for a typical large company, according to one survey of Fortune 500 companies (Stanko and Werner 16).

Concerned about these costs, most companies decided to develop and publicize sexual harassment policies, making every employee aware of the problem and more likely to come forward as early as possible so that employers have a chance to remedy the situation before it gets out of hand. Prior to 1991, sexual harassment victims were often asked by their employers simply to remain silent (Martell and Sullivan 8). These new policies and procedures, along with training sessions, made it much more likely that employees would report incidents of sexual harassment. And we should not be surprised that the Internet has provided independent information to employees about dealing with workplace sexual harassment ("Handling"; "Sexual").

The media have also contributed to the rise of reports of workplace sexual harassment by giving great attention to a few prominent cases. In 1991, Supreme Court Justice Clarence Thomas in Senate hearings on his nomination had to defend himself from sexual harassment charges by his former colleague Anita Hill. Later that same year, U.S. male navy officers were accused of sexually harassing female navy officers at the infamous Tailhook Convention, a yearly gathering of navy aviators (Nelton 24). During the late 1990s, Paula Jones's sexual harassment charges against President Clinton dominated the national news on many days. Jones was an Arkansas state employee at the time she said Clinton, who was then governor, harassed her. These three highly publicized cases made sexual harassment a much-discussed public issue that sparked debate and encouraged victims to come forward.

Not everyone believes that there has been an increase in reports of workplace sexual harassment. One journalist, writing in 1995, has argued that the rise in reported sexual harassment complaints is actually a sort of illusion caused by insufficient research, since "research on this topic has only been undertaken since the 1970s" (Burke 23). This journalist seems to be the one suffering from an illusion or an unwillingness to read the research. Clearly, as the Society for Human Resource Management shows, there was a sharp rise in complaints between 1991, when the Civil Rights Act was passed, and the mid-1990s. Has there been a steady increase in reported incidents since 1964? I do not know and am not focusing on that period. The noticeable increase in complaints from 1991 to 1994—from 35 percent to 65 percent *(Sexual)*—is enough to establish a trend.

It has also been suggested that the trend is the result of a greater percentage of women in the workplace (Martell and Sullivan 5). This may be a sufficient argument since women report sexual harassment in a significantly greater number of cases than men do (men report roughly one-tenth of what women report). It has been noted, however, that there has been a rise in sexual harassment complaints reported by male victims as well recently. According to the Equal Employment Opportunity Commission, the number of sexual harassment complaints filed annually by men more than doubled from 1989 to 1993 (Corey). Sexual harassment is by no means a new occurrence. It has most likely existed since workplace environments have existed. Yet, that there are more women in the workplace today has likely increased the percentage of women workers being sexually harassed, but it is also very plausible that the rise in reported incidents of sexual harassment is because of increased awareness of sexual harassment and the steps that one can legally take to stop it.

It has taken thirty years, but American society seems to be making significant progress in bringing a halt to a serious problem. *Sexual harassment,* a phrase that was unfamiliar to most of us only a few years ago, is now mentioned almost daily on television and in newspapers. We can only hope that the problem will end if we continue to hear about, read about, and, most importantly, talk about sexual harassment and its negative consequences as we educate each other about sexual harassment. Then, perhaps someday, sexual harassment can be stopped altogether.

8

9

Works Cited

Burke, Ronald J. "Incidence and Consequences of Sexual Harassment in a Professional Services Firm." *Employee Counselling Today* Feb. 1995: 23–29.

Corey, Mary. "On-the-Job Sexism Isn't Just a Man's Sin Anymore." *Houston Chronicle* 30 Aug. 1993: D1.

"Handling Sexual Harassment Complaints." *Employer and Employee.* 1997. 8 Jan. 1998 <http://www.employer-employee.com/sexhar1.html>.

Martell, Kathryn, and George Sullivan. "Strategies for Managers to Recognize and Remedy Sexual Harassment." *Industrial Management* May–June 1994: 5–8.

Nelton, Sharon. "Sexual Harassment: Reducing the Risks." *Nation's Business* Mar. 1995: 24–26.

"Sexual Harassment: FAQ." *Employment: Workplace Rights and Responsibilities.* 1998. 8 Jan. 1998 <http://www.nolo.com/ChunkEMP/emp7.html>.

Sexual Harassment Remains a Workplace Problem, but Most Employers Have Policies in Place, SHRM Survey Finds. Alexandria: Society for Human Resource Management, 26 June 1994: 1.

Stanko, Brian B., and Charles A. Werner. "Sexual Harassment: What Is It? How to Prevent It." *National Public Accountant* June 1995: 14–16.
"Workplace Bias Lawsuits." *USA Today* 30 Nov. 1994: B2.

Connecting to Culture and Experience: Sexual Harassment or Romantic Relationship?

West speculates about possible causes for an increase in reported incidents of workplace sexual harassment. She does not mention consensual sex or romance in the workplace. And yet everyone knows that affairs and romances can begin at work. Sometimes they lead to marriage. Finding a spouse on the job is a common experience, and surely it is an experience few if any managers or workers would want to discourage or preclude, even if it were possible to do so. Similarly, at college, romance can blossom and lifetime partners may find each other. Moreover, as you are probably aware, colleges publish strict and punishing sexual harassment policies. What might be the effects on ordinary romantic relationships of sexual harassment policies? Do such policies make trying to initiate a romantic relationship riskier? What if one's advances are misinterpreted? What if a sour romance leads the rejected partner to recriminate by bringing false sexual harassment charges? What might "consensual" mean legally, and why has it not been so carefully defined as harassment? If there is no well-defined or widely understood line between consent and harassment, might this uncertainty lead to misunderstandings, if not trouble?

Discuss with two or three other students the line between consent and harassment. First get a copy of your college's sexual harassment policies. If you work for an organization with a published sexual harassment policy, bring in a copy. Decide whether these policies are clear and unambiguous. Do they mention consensual relationships or attempt to make a distinction between consent and harassment? How might they influence your attempts to start a relationship with someone at college or work? Tell about anyone you know who has complained of harassment or been accused of it. Describe what happened and the outcome.

Analyzing Writing Strategies

1. In paragraphs 3–6, West advances her causes for the increase in reports of sexual harassment in the workplace. She also attempts to support those causes—to argue for them so that readers will find them plausible. Analyze how she attempts to provide convincing **support,** and evaluate how successful she is.

   In each paragraph, find West's assertion of a cause early in the paragraph, and then look closely at the kind of support she provides. You will find that in different paragraphs she makes good use of definitions, examples, statistics, and other information she has gathered from published sources. Notice also the amount of space she devotes to support in these paragraphs.

For more information on supporting an argument, see Chapter 19.

Finally, evaluate how successful West is in providing convincing support for her particular readers. Is her support relevant and believable? Do her sources seem reliable and authoritative? Where might the support seem most convincing and least convincing? Try to explain why.

2. Reread paragraphs 7 and 8, where West anticipates readers' objections and alternative causes. In each paragraph, decide whether West is anticipating a reader's (or published author's) objection to her argument or anticipating a cause some reader (or published author) might prefer. Then notice her strategy of **counterargument.** Does she **acknowledge, accommodate,** or **refute?** Finally, evaluate how convincing West's counterarguments are likely to be for her intended readers. Do they seem informed, responsible, and believable? Which parts seem most and least convincing—and why?

For more on counterarguing, turn to Chapter 19, pp. 634–37.

Commentary: Presenting the Subject

West presents her subject in paragraphs 1–3. She begins by trying to engage readers' interests and declaring the significance of her subject. She points out that protections from sexual harassment are surprisingly recent. For readers who are aware of the rich two-hundred-year history of efforts to guarantee all Americans basic personal rights and freedoms, West seems justified in inviting them to be amazed that legal freedom from sexual harassment at work had to wait so long for legislative and legal protection. She explains that the Civil Rights Act of 1964 made sexual harassment illegal, and then singles out the Civil Rights Act of 1991 as the crucial event causing the sharp rise in the number of sexual harassment complaints.

Because West is presenting a trend, she has a special responsibility to document changes over time—in this case, an increase. She does so very successfully by relying on a report by a respected professional association of personnel managers who work in government and business, the Society for Human Resource Management. This report, which is included in her list of works cited, gives statistics supporting her claim that there has been a sharp increase in reports of sexual harassment on the job.

Notice that West takes care to make readers aware that she intends to speculate not about an increase in workplace sexual harassment, but about an increase in *reported incidents* of workplace sexual harassment. Perhaps no one knows whether workplace sexual harassment is increasing or decreasing. Because it is not always reported and for other reasons, it would be difficult to collect evidence that it is increasing or decreasing. West has solid evidence, however, that *reports* of harassment increased sharply between the early 1990s and the mid-1990s. Once she establishes that this trend exists, she turns to her defining question: "Why did this large increase occur in such a short amount of time?" (paragraph 2). Readers are then fully prepared for a causal argument.

Before beginning her causal argument, however, West orients readers to how her argument will unfold. In a **forecast** at the end of paragraph 2, she names the causes in the order she will take them up in her argument.

For more on forecasting, see Chapter 13, p. 559.

Considering Topics for Your Own Essay

West speculates about the causes of a trend—the rise of reported incidents of work-place sexual harassment—but she could have speculated about the phenomenon of sexual harassment itself, asking why it happens at all or why there seems to be so much of it in the workplace. Following her lead, you could speculate about the causes of some other important social phenomenon or trend that influences how people live and work and what their opportunities in life may be. Here are some examples: the increase in students working part time or full time to get a college degree; the increase in specific standards to be met before admission to college; the increase in the cost of a college education; the decline of neighborhood or community cohesion; the rise of influence of the political right; the growing gap in wealth between the rich and the rest; the increasing reliance by technology companies on workers trained in other countries; or the stagnant wages over two decades for most American workers.

■ PURPOSE AND AUDIENCE

The fundamental purpose of writing a causal argument is to engage readers in a profoundly important way of making sense of the world. The possible causes of puzzling phenomena or trends are worth thinking about and irresistibly interesting. Indeed, humans are probably unable not to speculate about causes since so much of what we want to understand can never be known definitively.

If we assume we can engage readers in our subject and our speculations about it, then our purpose becomes to help them understand their world better, to show them a new way to think about a subject. For example, like King, you might hope to lead readers to think about popular culture in new ways. Like Pollack, your purpose might be to subvert myths about human development. Or, like West, you might want readers to appreciate the significance of a major social change.

The chief purpose of an essay speculating about causes is to convince readers that the proposed causes are plausible. Therefore, you must construct a coherent, logical, authoritative argument that readers will take seriously. Sometimes, like Neimark, you may want readers to look at a phenomenon in a new way or to go beyond obvious or familiar explanations. At other times, you may, like Pollack and West, hope to influence policy decisions regarding a social problem.

Your audience will also affect your purpose. If you think that your readers are only mildly curious about the subject and know little about it, you might write partly to stimulate their interest in the subject itself. You could then concentrate on convincing them of the plausibility of your proposed causes. If you expect that readers will know about the subject and be strongly opposed to your speculations or very skeptical of them, you could devote a lot of attention to conceding and refuting what you assume to be their preferred causes. If you believe that the distance between you and them is unbridgeable, you could even accentuate your differences, forcefully refuting their likely objections to your causes and refuting their preferred causes.

A Presentation of the Subject

First, it is necessary to describe the subject. Depending on what readers know or need to know, writers sometimes may devote a large portion of the essay to presenting the subject—describing it with specific details and examples and establishing that it actually exists (or existed) by citing statistics and statements by authorities.

In writing about a phenomenon he knows will be familiar to his readers, Stephen King simply asserts in his title that horror movies are widely popular. In contrast, William S. Pollack's less familiar and not-so-immediately engaging subject—depression in boys—requires considerable detail. Pollack devotes almost a third of his essay to describing how depression affects boys, how depression is caused by biological factors, how biological and psychological factors interreact, and how important external psychological factors are in bringing on depression.

In an essay about a trend, a writer must always demonstrate that the trend exists. Sarah West, for example, demonstrates that the trend exists by citing statistics that document a dramatic four-year increase in reports of sexual harassment on the job.

In some cases, a writer may have to show that the subject is an established, significant trend as opposed to a fad, a fluctuation, or a superficial change. For example, a new form of exercise might become a fad if many people try it out for a few months. This brief popularity would not make it a trend, but it might be part of a trend—a general increase in health consciousness perhaps.

Plausible Causes

No matter how well presented the subject may be, a causal argument goes nowhere unless it offers plausible causes as a possible explanation. In many causal arguments, readers first encounter the proffered causes in a forecast, a list of causes in the order in which they will be taken up in the argument.

Speculating about the rise of reported incidents of workplace sexual harassment, Sarah West comes up with four plausible causes based on what she learned through research. The first is increased awareness and condemnation of sexual harassment through the landmark Civil Rights Act of 1964. The second is the sharp impetus given to reporting sexual harassment by the 1991 Civil Rights Act, which imposed severe penalties on businesses that failed to protect employees. The third is businesses' increased efforts to inform employees about their rights to do their jobs without being sexually harassed. The fourth is increased media attention to prominent cases of sexual harassment (not all of them proved). At first glance, even without West's arguments to support them, these causes seem likely and worth taking seriously. They do not immediately arouse readers' resistance or skepticism. They are, in short, plausible.

A Logical Sequence of Causes

Causes must be presented in a logical sequence. The reader needs to be aware of a meaningful step-by-step sequence of causes: the second cause follows from the first in some meaningful way, the third from the second, and so forth.

Maybe an obvious cause prepares for a hidden cause, as in Stephen King's essay, or one cause creates a necessary condition for the next cause, as in William Pollack's essay, or every cause is a consequence of the preceding cause and predates the following cause, as in Sarah West's essay. West's logical sequence may seem complicated when it is outlined, but to readers making their way through the argument the sequence seems inevitable. Such a logical sequence is sometimes referred to as a *line of reasoning*.

Convincing Support

The support for every cause is the heart of causal speculation. A list of causes is not an argument. Writers of essays speculating about causes know that argument—or support—is required because a definitive, unarguable explanation for the subject is not available. Causal speculation is quintessentially argumentative; every cause must be argued for—or supported—if readers are going to be convinced that the explanation, though tentative, throws some light on the subject.

To provide convincing support for a cause requires both knowledge and creativity. Stephen King supports his causes with his understanding of psychology and his many years of involvement with horror novels and movies. Jill Neimark supports her argument with the work of scholars who have devised a theory that popular entertainment reveals the conflicts and contradictions in our culture and with analyses of the Miss America contest.

A Consideration of Readers' Objections and Alternative Causes

Writers of causal speculation choose plausible causes and convincing support and sequence them logically in the essay. However, in nearly every writing situation requiring causal argument, writers must also imaginatively anticipate readers' objections and possible alternative causes and then acknowledge, concede, or refute these points in the counterargument. It is not enough to be aware that readers may have objections or alternative causes they prefer over the writer's. These objections must be addressed within and become part of the argument, making it complete.

Stephen King anticipates that some readers will be skeptical that horror movies are popular because they appeal to and help us control the dark, dangerous side within us. He devotes roughly half of his essay to trying to convince readers that this cause is plausible. Similarly, Pollack devotes about a third of his essay to refuting the widely held belief that boys' relationships with family and friends are not so important to them as these same relationships are to girls.

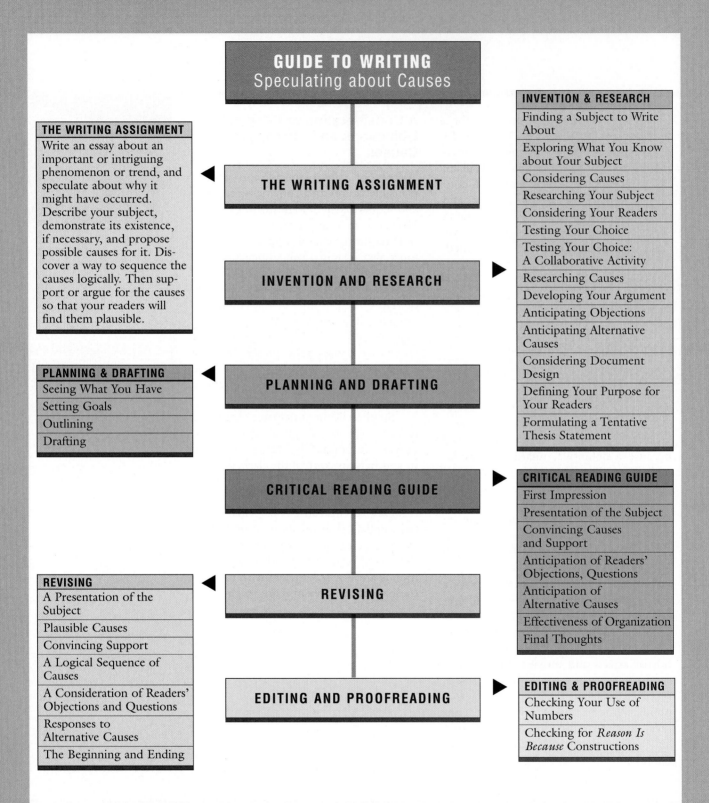

GUIDE TO WRITING
Speculating about Causes

THE WRITING ASSIGNMENT

Write an essay about an important or intriguing phenomenon or trend, and speculate about why it might have occurred. Describe your subject, demonstrate its existence, if necessary, and propose possible causes for it. Discover a way to sequence the causes logically. Then support or argue for the causes so that your readers will find them plausible.

THE WRITING ASSIGNMENT

INVENTION AND RESEARCH

INVENTION & RESEARCH

Finding a Subject to Write About

Exploring What You Know about Your Subject

Considering Causes

Researching Your Subject

Considering Your Readers

Testing Your Choice

Testing Your Choice: A Collaborative Activity

Researching Causes

Developing Your Argument

Anticipating Objections

Anticipating Alternative Causes

Considering Document Design

Defining Your Purpose for Your Readers

Formulating a Tentative Thesis Statement

PLANNING & DRAFTING

Seeing What You Have

Setting Goals

Outlining

Drafting

PLANNING AND DRAFTING

CRITICAL READING GUIDE

CRITICAL READING GUIDE

First Impression

Presentation of the Subject

Convincing Causes and Support

Anticipation of Readers' Objections, Questions

Anticipation of Alternative Causes

Effectiveness of Organization

Final Thoughts

REVISING

A Presentation of the Subject

Plausible Causes

Convincing Support

A Logical Sequence of Causes

A Consideration of Readers' Objections and Questions

Responses to Alternative Causes

The Beginning and Ending

REVISING

EDITING AND PROOFREADING

EDITING & PROOFREADING

Checking Your Use of Numbers

Checking for *Reason Is Because* Constructions

GUIDE TO WRITING

■ THE WRITING ASSIGNMENT

Write an essay about an important or intriguing phenomenon or trend, and speculate about why it might have occurred. Describe your subject, demonstrate its existence, if necessary, and propose possible causes for it. Discover a way to sequence the causes logically. Then support or argue for the causes so that your readers will find them plausible.

■ INVENTION AND RESEARCH

The following activities will help you find a subject, explore what you know about it, do any necessary research, and develop the parts of your causal argument. These activities are easy to complete. Doing them over several days will give your ideas time to ripen and grow. Be sure to keep a written record of your invention and research to use later when you draft and revise.

Finding a Subject to Write About

You may already have a subject in mind and some ideas about what might have caused it to occur. Even so, you should take some time to consider other possible subjects in order to ensure the best possible choice. Remember to consider both phenomena and trends as possible subjects for this writing assignment. A *phenomenon* is something notable about the human condition or the social order—fear of speaking to a group, for example, or opposition to gun-control legislation. A *trend* is a significant change extending over many months or years. It can be identified by some sort of increase or decrease—a rise in the birthrate, a decline in test scores. Some subjects can be approached as either phenomena or trends. For example, you could speculate about the causes of the changing suicide rate among young people (a trend), or you could ignore the change and simply speculate about the causes of such suicides (a phenomenon).

The following activities will help you choose a subject for your essay. Make your lists of possible phenomena and trends as complete as possible, including, for example, the subjects suggested by the Considering Topics for Your Own Essay activity following each reading in this chapter.

Listing Phenomena.   *Make a list of current phenomena that you could write about.* Here are some possibilities to consider. Start with a few of them, and see whether they bring to mind other topics of interest to you.

- *College:* A noisy library, insufficient parking, an instructor's skill or popularity, cheating on exams, a successful or unsuccessful class or course, women as the majority of college students

- *Personal life:* Competitiveness, idealism, creativity, popularity, jealousy, laziness, workaholism, high achievement, contentiousness, rage
- *Politics and government:* Hostility toward politicians, low voter turnout, satisfactions of jury duty, stability of our system of government, negative campaigning, percentage of minority inmates in U.S. prisons
- *Environment:* Pollution, garbage crisis, recycling programs, food safety
- *Life stages:* The "terrible twos," teenage alienation or rebellion, postponement of motherhood, midlife crisis, abrupt career changes
- *The arts:* Popularity of rap or jazz, decline of musical theater, impulse to censor the arts
- *Culture:* Continuing influence or popularity of a book, movie, actor, novelist, social activist, athlete, politician, religious leader, or television program

Listing Trends.   *Make a list of several trends, from the past as well as the present, that you would like to understand better.* Consider both trends you have studied and can research and ones you know about firsthand. Be sure that the possibilities you list are trends, not fads or short-term fluctuations. To start, consider the following possibilities:

- *Shifting patterns in education:* Increasing interest in computer science or in teaching as a career; increases in home schooling or in community college enrollments; declining numbers of math and science majors; increase in the number of African American students attending historically black colleges
- *Changes in patterns of leisure or entertainment:* Increasing consumption of fast food, declining interest in a particular style of music, increase in competitive cycling, increase or decrease in a magazine's circulation
- *Shifts in religious practices:* Decreasing support for television evangelists, increasing incidence of women ministers or rabbis, increasing interest in Asian religions, increased membership in fundamentalist churches
- *New patterns of political behavior:* Increase in conservatism or liberalism, a growing desire for isolation from world affairs, developing power of minorities and women
- *Societal changes:* Increases in the number of working women with children, single-parent households, telecommunicators, ethnic intermarriages in the United States, or grandparents raising their grandchildren
- *Changes in political or world affairs:* Spreading influence of capitalism, increasing terrorist activity, increasing numbers of women elected to political office, growing ethnic or religious conflicts
- *Changes in economic conditions:* Increasing cost of medical care, decline in real median wage for families and individuals since 1973, increasing gap between wealthiest and poorest Americans, decreasing family savings rate
- *Noteworthy artistic movements or historical trends:* Impressionism, pop art, female suffrage, industrialization

Listing Subjects Related to Identity and Community. These suggestions may bring to mind topics related to identity and community.

Phenomena

- A particular conflict in a community to which you belong
- The popularity of athletes or other groups of students in high school
- The lack of understanding and sympathy between the young and the old
- The obsession of many young women and men with their weight and body image
- The continued high level of teenage pregnancy despite the widespread availability of birth control

Trends

- Increasing prejudice against new immigrants
- Increasing incidence of people abandoning or abusing aged relatives
- Increasing incidence of domestic violence—against spouses or children
- Increasing popularity of twelve-step, self-help programs
- Increasing popularity of sororities and fraternities on college campuses
- Increasing use of plastic surgery to enhance self-image
- Increasing numbers of young people choosing to remain virgins until they marry
- Increasing rate of cigarette smoking among young people

Listing Subjects Related to Work and Career. The following suggestions will help you to think of subjects related to work and career.

Phenomena

- Students expecting to have less financial success than their parents
- People preferring to own their own businesses even though they must work harder for more hours each day
- Students holding part-time jobs while attending college
- Students aspiring to careers in business
- The importance or difficulty of arranging working internships while in college
- Older students attending college

Trends

- Rise in employment rate among young people
- Increase in number of full-time and part-time temporary or contingent workers
- Increase in types of service-related careers

Choosing a Subject.   *Look over your list of possibilities, and choose one subject to write about.* Describe the subject in two or three sentences. You may or may not already have some ideas about why this phenomenon or trend occurred. As you analyze it in detail, you will have the opportunity to consider possible causes and to decide which ones are the most plausible.

Of the two types of subjects—a phenomenon or trend—a trend may be more challenging because you must nearly always do research to demonstrate that it actually exists, that something has been increasing or decreasing over an extended period of time. (Usually one or two references will be adequate.) Since a trend begins at a specific point, you must take care that the causes you propose as the sources of the trend actually precede its onset. You may also need to differentiate between causes that launched the trend and those that perpetuate it.

It may help you in choosing a subject if you tentatively identify your ultimate readers. They could be either a general adult readership or adult readers who already have some special interest or stake in your subject. They could be instructors or administrators on campus or people you work with or for. They could be members of a particular community or region. They could be your classmates or even a particular instructor.

Exploring What You Know about Your Subject

Write for several minutes about the subject you have chosen. Note everything you know about it. Try to describe why you are interested in this trend or phenomenon, and speculate about where you might find more information about it.

Considering Causes

Think now about what might have caused your selected phenomenon or trend to occur. List possible causes and then analyze the most promising ones.

Listing Possible Causes.   *Write down all the things you can think of that might have caused the phenomenon or trend.* Consider each of the following:

- Immediate causes (those responsible for making the phenomenon or trend begin when it did)
- Remote, background causes (those from before the phenomenon or trend began)
- Perpetuating causes (those that may have contributed to sustaining or continuing the phenomenon or trend)
- Obvious causes
- Hidden causes

Selecting the Most Promising Causes.   *Review your list; then select five or six causes that seem to you to provide a plausible explanation of your subject.* Since you will next need to analyze these causes, it might be helpful to list them in table form. List the causes, leaving five or six lines of space between each cause.

Analyzing Promising Causes.   *Below each cause in your list, explain why you think it is real and important.* Consider the following questions as you analyze each cause:

- Is it a necessary cause? Without it, could the phenomenon or trend have occurred anyway?
- Is it a sufficient cause? Could it alone have caused this phenomenon or trend?
- Would this cause affect everybody the same way?
- Would this cause always lead to phenomena or trends like this one?
- What particular anecdotes or examples might demonstrate the importance of the cause?
- Have any authorities suggested that it is an important cause?
- Is the cause a *result* of the subject rather than an actual *cause*?
- Is it a remote or background cause or an immediate cause?
- Is it a perpetuating cause, sustaining the trend?
- Is it an obvious cause or a hidden cause?

Researching Your Subject

In exploring your subject, you may have found that you already know enough to describe or define it adequately for your readers. If not, you will need to consult library and Internet sources or interview a faculty or community expert to learn more about the subject.

If you are speculating about the causes of a *trend,* you will also need to do some research to confirm that it actually is a trend and not just a fluctuation or a fad. To do so, you will need to find examples, and probably statistics that support an increase or decrease in the trend over time and that indicate the date when this change began. (For example, recall that West cites dates and statistics to demonstrate that there actually was an increase in reported incidents of sexual harassment on the job.) If you are unable to find evidence to confirm that a trend actually exists, then it is probably just a fad or short-term fluctuation. In this case, you will have to choose a different subject for your essay.

Considering Your Readers

Write a careful analysis of your readers. Because you will be trying to make a convincing case for some particular readers, you should know as much as possible about them. Only after you have analyzed your readers can you confidently decide how to present these causes in your essay—which causes you will emphasize, which causes will require the most convincing evidence, which causes will be obvious or not so obvious. Take a few minutes to answer the following questions:

- Who are my readers? (Describe them briefly.)
- What do my readers know about my subject? Will I have to prove its existence to them? How extensively will I have to define or describe it for them?
- What attitudes do my readers have about my subject? Do they care about it? Are they indifferent to it? Might they understand it differently from the way I understand it?
- What causes would they be most likely to think of?

Testing Your Choice

Now that you have explored your subject, considered its possible causes, and confirmed its existence, take some time to review your material and decide whether your subject is workable. Start by asking the following questions:

- Does the subject still interest me?
- Do I believe I can describe and define it in a way that will interest readers and show them that it is a phenomenon or a trend?
- Have I been able to come up with several possible causes?
- Do any of the causes I have come up with go beyond the simply obvious ones?
- Do I want to research the subject further?

If your subject does not seem promising, return to your list of possible subjects to select another.

**Testing
Your Choice:
A Collaborative
Activity**

At this point, you will find it helpful to get together with two or three other students to discuss and get feedback on your subject and list of causes. This collaborative activity will help you determine whether you are ready to start developing your causal argument.

Presenters: Briefly identify your subject, and ask the listeners what causes immediately come to their minds as plausible explanations for your subject. Make a list of these causes as the listeners talk. Finally, tell the listeners the causes you propose to argue for, and ask them whether they accept these as likely or plausible. Take notes about their objections and questions. (When you plan and draft your essay, these lists and notes may suggest further causes you will want to argue for, and they will help you anticipate your readers' likely questions and objections to your proposed causes.)

Listeners: Respond imaginatively to the presenter's request for causes that you think initially explain the subject. When the presenter tells you the causes he or she proposes to argue for, praise those that seem plausible, but also ask all the questions and raise all the objections you can think of. In this way, you will help the presenter anticipate readers' likely questions and objections.

Researching Causes

Some causal arguments can be made fully and convincingly on the basis of your own knowledge and intuition. In fact, you may have to rely on your own ideas to explain very recent phenomena or emerging trends. Most subjects, however, will have already been noticed by others, and you will want to learn what they have said about the causes. Doing research can be helpful in several ways:

- To confirm or challenge your own ideas
- To identify further causes to add to your own explanation
- To provide support for causes you want to argue for
- To identify causes your readers may prefer to the ones you find plausible
- To reveal some of the reservations readers may have about the causes you suggest

As you discover causes others have proposed, add the most interesting or most plausible ones to your list. Analyze these as you did your own proposed causes. In your essay, you may want to accommodate them—integrate them in full or in part into your own argument.

As you gather evidence about causes, remember to record the information you will need to acknowledge your sources.

For guidelines on acknowledging sources, see Chapter 22.

Developing Your Argument

Try out an argument in writing to support a key cause. Once you have figured out what to expect of your readers, review your list of causes and analyses, and make a new, shorter list of all the causes that you believe provide a plausible explanation of your subject. Then try out an argument for one of these causes, the one you think readers may find the most plausible or interesting or unexpected. Write at least a page, making use of some of the support you have found. Begin by identifying the cause; then try to make it seem plausible or likely to your readers. As part of your argument to support this cause, you may want to respond to readers' likely questions or objections.

Anticipating Objections

Try responding to the most likely objections to your causes. You should expect readers to evaluate your essay critically, considering each cause and your support for it carefully before deciding that you have devised a plausible explanation. It would be wise, therefore, to account for any possible objections your readers could raise. Consider

For more information on these strategies, turn to Chapter 19, pp. 634–37.

the two most likely objections, and think about how you would **acknowledge, concede,** or **refute** them. Write several sentences, trying out your response.

Anticipating Alternative Causes

Try responding to alternative causes your readers may prefer to your own proposed causes. As they read your essay, your readers may think of other causes that seem more plausible to them than your causes. Try to think of two or three such causes now, and write several sentences about each one, explaining why you do not consider it important, why you specifically reject it, and why you think it is less plausible than your causes.

Considering Document Design

Think about whether your readers might benefit from design features, such as headings, numbered lists, or other design elements that would make the development of your causal argument easier to follow. Consider also whether visuals—drawings, photographs, tables, or graphs—would strengthen your argument. These are not at all a requirement for an essay speculating about causes, but they could be helpful. You may come across promising visuals in your research and either download them from the Internet or make photocopies from library materials. Or you may find statistics that you can use to construct your own visuals, such as tables or graphs.

Defining Your Purpose for Your Readers

Write a few sentences defining your purpose in devising this argument speculating about causes. Recall that in an earlier invention activity you identified your readers and considered what they know about your subject. Given these readers, try now to define your purpose by considering the following questions:

- How can I interest readers in my subject, establishing its significance for them personally, so that they will care about my speculations about its possible causes?

- Do I attempt to give my readers a fresh, new way of thinking about a phenomenon or trend that they may not have strong feelings about, or must I dissuade them from their present way of thinking about a phenomenon or trend that is already of significant concern to them?

- How much resistance should I expect from my readers to each of the causes I want to propose? Will the readers be largely receptive? Skeptical but convinceable? Resistant and perhaps even antagonistic?

- How can I best respond to my readers' likely questions and objections and to the alternative causes they may prefer to my own? Shall I concede where I can or refute at every opportunity, and how can I refute without seeming dismissive of my readers' ideas?

Formulating a Tentative Thesis Statement

Write a sentence or more that could serve as your thesis statement. In an essay speculating about causes the thesis statement refocuses on the subject and announces the causes to be argued for. You will already have described the trend or phenomenon that is your subject. As readers approach your causal speculations, they need to know what causes you consider plausible and want them to take seriously; and, though it is optional, they would benefit from knowing how you have sequenced the causes.

Readings in this chapter illustrate effective thesis statements. For instance, West presents her thesis this way: "Why did this large increase [in reported incidents of workplace sexual harassment] occur in such a short amount of time? Possible answers to this question surely would include growing awareness of the nature of workplace sexual harassment, government action, efforts of companies to establish anti-harassment policies and encourage harassed employees to come forward, and prominence given by the media to many cases of workplace harassment." (paragraph 2) West reiterates her subject and then lists all of the causes she believes best explain it. Furthermore, she lists the causes in exactly the order she will argue for them in the essay, helpfully forecasting for readers the sequence of the argument.

Similarly, after describing his subject—depression in boys—but before launching his causal speculations, Pollack asserts his thesis: "While I believe the biological, or 'organic,' components of clinical depression (and the medical treatments for them) are of paramount importance and need to be carefully studied, my primary focus here is on what other psychologists and I have discovered about *external* psychological factors that can lead boys toward serious sadness or depression—factors such as a boy's family life, how he's treated at school, the quality of his friendships, and what kind of emotional support he gets on a regular basis." In clear and unambiguous language he announces that he intends to speculate about the psychological causes of boys' depression. He then forecasts the causes he believes to be most plausible.

■ PLANNING AND DRAFTING

This section will help you review your invention writing, determine specific goals for your essay, make a tentative outline, and get started on your first draft.

Seeing What You Have

Pause now to reflect on your invention and research notes. Reread everything carefully in order to decide whether you can prove that your subject exists (or existed) and that you can offer a plausible explanation of its causes. Ask yourself the following questions:

- Could I research my subject more fully in order to make it seem more significant and worth speculating about?

- If I am speculating about the causes of a trend, do I have enough information to establish convincingly that the trend is (or was) increasing or decreasing over time?
- Will I be able to sequence my causes logically and argue for them convincingly?
- Have I been able to anticipate a wide range of readers' likely questions and objections?
- Have I been able to identify a few alternative causes readers may prefer over my causes?

Setting Goals

Before you begin drafting, set some specific goals to guide the decisions you will make as you draft and revise your essay. The draft will not only be easier to write, but also more convincing if you start with clear goals in mind. The following questions will help you set goals. You may find it useful to return to them while you are drafting, for they are designed to help you focus on specific elements of causal speculation essays.

Your Purpose and Readers

- What are my readers likely to know about my subject?
- How can I interest them in understanding its causes?
- How can I present myself so that my readers will consider me informed and authoritative?

The Beginning

- What opening would make readers take this subject seriously and really want to think about its causes? Should I declare its cultural significance, as Neimark does? Assert its seriousness and importance, as Pollack does? Provide a historical perspective, as West does?
- Should I personalize my subject by connecting it to my firsthand experience? Should I begin with an anecdote? Should I cite surprising statistics, as West does?

The Presentation of the Subject

- Do I need to demonstrate that my subject really exists, as Pollack and West do?
- If I am analyzing a trend, do I need to demonstrate that it is not just a fluctuation or a fad, as West does?
- How much and what kind of support do I need for these points?

The Causal Argument

- How many causes should I propose?
- How can I present my proposed causes in the most effective sequence? Should I arrange them from most to least important or vice versa? From most obvious to

least obvious, as King does, or vice versa? From immediate to remote or vice versa?

- Do I need to make other distinctions among causes, such as differentiating a cause that starts a trend from one that keeps it going?

- How much and what kind of support do I need to offer to make each cause plausible to my readers? Are any causes so obvious that support is unnecessary? Do I need to demonstrate to readers that all of my causes existed before the phenomenon or trend began?

- How can I anticipate readers' objections to my proposed causes? Should I acknowledge the wisdom of some objections? Concede other objections, as King does? Refute other objections, as Pollack and West do?

- How can I anticipate alternative causes readers might propose? Should I acknowledge one or more of these causes? Concede the plausibility of other causes, as West does? Refute other causes as not worth taking seriously, as Pollack does?

The Ending

- How should I end my essay? Should I try to frame the essay by echoing something from the beginning, as West does?

- Should I summarize my causes or, as King and Pollack do, refocus on the key cause?

- Should I conclude with a conjecture about larger implications?

Outlining

A causal analysis may contain as many as four basic parts:

1. A presentation of the subject
2. Plausible causes, logically sequenced
3. Convincing causes and support for each cause
4. A consideration of readers' questions, objections, and alternative causes

These parts can be organized in various ways. If your readers are not likely to think of any causes other than the ones you are proposing, you may want to begin by describing the subject and indicating its importance or interest. Then state your first proposed cause, supporting it convincingly and accommodating, conceding, or refuting readers' likely questions and objections. Follow the same pattern for any other causes you propose. Your conclusion could then mention—and elucidate—the lack of other explanations for your subject.

Presentation of the subject

First proposed cause with support and consideration of objections, if any

Second proposed cause with support and consideration of objections, if any (etc.)

Conclusion

If you need to account for alternative causes that are likely to occur to readers, you could discuss them first and give your reasons for conceding or rejecting them before offering your own proposed causes. Many writers save their own causes for last, hoping that readers will remember them best.

> Presentation of the subject
>
> Alternative causes and consideration of them
>
> Proposed causes with support and consideration of objections, if any
>
> Conclusion

Another option is to put your own causes first, followed by alternatives. This pattern helps you show the relative likelihood of your causes over the others. You might then end with a restatement of your causes.

> Presentation of the subject
>
> Proposed causes with support and consideration of objections, if any
>
> Alternative causes compared with your causes
>
> Concluding restatement of your proposed causes

For more on outlining, see Chapter 11, pp. 518–21.

There are, of course, many other possible ways to organize a causal analysis, but these outlines should help you start planning your own essay.

Drafting

You may want to review the general advice on drafting in Chapter 1, pp. 16–17.

Start drafting your essay, keeping in mind the goals you set while you were planning and these tips on writing causal analyses:

- Remember that in writing about causes, you are dealing with probabilities rather than certainties; therefore, you must resist the urge to claim that you have the final, conclusive answer and instead simply assert that your explanation is plausible. Qualify your statements, and acknowledge readers' objections and alternative causes.

- Try to enliven your writing and to appeal to your readers' interests and concerns. Causal analysis is potentially rather dry.

- Remember that your outline is just a plan. Writers often make major discoveries and reorganize as they draft. Be flexible. If you find your writing taking an interesting, unexpected turn, follow it to see where it leads. You will have an opportunity to look at it critically later.

- If you run into a problem as you draft, see whether any of the invention activities earlier in this chapter can help you solve it. For instance, if you are having difficulty making the subject seem important or interesting, you might analyze your readers further or look in your invention notes for an attention-getting quotation, anecdote, or statistic.

- If, as you draft, you discover that you need more information, just make a note of what you need to find out and go on to the next point. Later you can interview an expert, survey a group, or do further library or Internet research to get the information you need.

Perhaps the most important advice to remember about drafting is to write quickly without worrying about grammar and spelling. Later you can make corrections.

■ **CRITICAL READING GUIDE**

Now is the time to get a good critical reading of your draft. Writers usually find it helpful to have someone else read and comment on their drafts, and all writers know how much they learn about writing when they read other writers' drafts. Your instructor may arrange such a reading as part of your coursework. If not, you can ask a classmate, friend, or family member to read your draft. You could also seek comments from a tutor at your campus writing center. (If you are unable to have someone else read your draft, turn ahead to the Revising section, where you will find guidelines for reading your own draft critically.)

▶ **If You Are the Writer.** In order to provide focused, helpful comments, your reader must know your essay's intended audience, your purpose, and a problem in the draft that you need help solving. Briefly write out this information at the top of your draft.

- *Readers.* Identify the intended readers of your essay. What do you assume they already know and think about your subject and its causes? Do you expect them to be receptive, skeptical, resistant, antagonistic?
- *Purpose.* What do you hope to accomplish with your readers?
- *Problem.* Ask your reader to help you solve the single most important problem you see in your draft. Describe this problem briefly.

▶ **If You Are the Reader.** Reading a draft critically means reading it more than once, first to get a general impression and then to analyze its basic features. Use the following guidelines to assist you in giving critical comments to others on essays that speculate about the causes of phenomena or trends:

1. *Read for a First Impression.* Read the essay straight through. As you read, try to notice any words or passages that contribute to your first impression, and identify those that make weak contributions as well as strong ones.

   After you have finished reading the draft, write a few sentences describing your overall impression. Does the essay hold your interest? What in it most surprises you? What do you like best? Do you find the causal argument convincing? Next, consider the problem the writer identified. If the problem will be covered by one of the other questions listed here, deal with it there. Otherwise, respond to the writer's concerns now.

2. *Evaluate How Well the Subject Is Presented.* How well does the draft present the phenomenon or trend? Does it give enough information to make readers

See pp. 434–35 to review the basic features.

understand and care about the subject? Does it establish that the subject actually exists? If the subject is a trend, does the writer demonstrate a significant increase or decrease over time? Where might additional details, examples, or statistics help?

3. *Consider Whether the Causes and Support Are Convincing.* Look first at the proposed causes, and list them. Do there seem to be too many? Too few? Do any seem either too obvious (not worth mentioning) or too obscure (remote in time or overly complicated)?

   Next, examine the support for each cause—anecdotes, examples, statistics, reference to authorities, and so on. Which support is most convincing? Which seems unconvincing? Where would more support or a different kind of support strengthen the argument?

   Check for errors in reasoning. Does the argument mistakenly take something for a cause just because it occurred before or at the start of the phenomenon or trend? Are any of the proposed causes of the subject actually effects of it instead?

4. *Assess Whether Readers' Likely Objections and Questions Are Anticipated Adequately.* Look for places where the writer acknowledges readers' possible objections to or questions about the proposed causes. How well are objections handled? Should any of them be taken more seriously? Help the writer see other ways of either accommodating or refuting objections. Do any of the refutations attack or ridicule the persons raising the objections? Try to think of other likely questions or objections the writer has overlooked.

5. *Assess Whether Alternative Causes Are Adequately Anticipated.* If alternative causes are acknowledged by the writer, are they presented fairly? Is it clear why they have been accommodated or rejected? Do the refutations seem convincing? Do any of the refutations attack or ridicule the persons proposing the alternative causes? Try to think of other plausible causes readers might prefer.

6. *Consider Whether the Organization Is Effective.* Given the expected readers, are the causes presented in an effective sequence? Raise specific questions about the sequence; suggest a more logical sequence.

   - Look at the *beginning*. Is it engaging? Imagine at least one other way to open the essay. Look for something later in the essay that could be moved to the beginning—an intriguing anecdote, for instance, or a surprising statistic.
   - Look at the *ending*. Is the ending decisive and memorable? Think of an alternative ending. Could something from earlier in the essay be moved to or restated at the end?
   - Look again at any *visuals* the writer has incorporated. Assess how well the visuals are integrated into the essay. Point to any items that do not provide support for the writer's argument.

7. *Give the Writer Your Final Thoughts.* What is this draft's strongest part? What about it is most memorable? What part is most in need of further work?

▓ REVISING

Now you have the opportunity to revise your essay. Your instructor or other students may have given you advice on how to improve your draft. Or you may have begun to realize that your draft requires not so much revising as rethinking. For example, you may recognize that you have come up with obvious causes only, that your causes do not seem to be related to each other in any logical way that would enable you to sequence them in a chain of reasoning, or that you have been unable to anticipate readers' objections or alternative causes. Consequently, instead of working to improve the various parts of your first draft, you may need to write a new draft that radically reshapes your argument. Many students—and professional writers—find themselves in this situation. Often a writer produces a draft or two and gets advice on them from others and only then begins to see what might be achieved.

If you feel satisfied that your draft achieves what you set out to do, you can focus on refining the various parts of it. Very likely you have thought of ways to improve your draft, and you may even have begun improving it. This section will help you get an overview of your draft and revise it accordingly.

Getting an Overview

Consider your draft as a whole, following these two steps:

1. *Reread.* If at all possible, put the draft aside for a day or two before rereading it. When you go back to it, start by reconsidering your audience and your purpose. Then read the draft straight through, trying to see it as your intended readers will.

2. *Outline.* Make a quick scratch outline of the draft.

For an illustration of scratch outlining, see Chapter 12, pp. 540–41.

Charting a Plan for Revision.   Once you have an overview of your draft, you may want to make a double-column chart like the following one to keep track of specific problems you need to solve. In the left-hand column, list the basic features of essays speculating about causes. As you analyze your draft and study any comments you have received from others, note the problems you want to solve in the right-hand column.

Turn to pp. 434–35 to review the basic features.

Basic Features	*Problems to Solve*
A presentation of the subject	
Plausible causes and convincing support	
A logical sequence of causes	
A consideration of readers' objections and alternative causes	

Analyzing the Basic Features of Your Own Draft.   Turn now to the Critical Reading Guide on the preceding pages and use it to identify problems in your draft. Note the problems on your chart.

Studying Critical Comments.   Review all of the comments you have received from other readers. For each comment, look at the draft to determine what might have led the reader to make that particular point. Try to be objective about any criticism. Ideally, these comments will help you see your draft as others see it. Add to your revision chart any problems readers have identified.

Carrying Out Revisions

Having identified problems in your draft, you now need to come up with solutions and—most important—how to carry them out. Basically, you have three ways of finding solutions:

1. Review your invention and planning notes for other information and ideas.
2. Do additional invention writing or research to provide material you or your readers think is needed.
3. Look back at the readings in this chapter to see how other writers have solved similar problems.

The following suggestions, which are organized according to the basic features on your revision chart, will get you started solving some common problems in essays that speculate about causes.

A Presentation of the Subject

- *Is your subject unclear, or is its existence not clearly established?* Discuss it in greater detail. Consider adding anecdotes, statistics, citations from authorities, or other details. If your subject is a trend, be sure you show evidence of a significant increase or decrease over an extended period.

Plausible Causes

- *Do you propose too many causes?* Clarify the role each one plays: Is it obvious? Hidden? Immediate, remote, or perpetuating? (You need not use these labels.) In addition, you may need to emphasize one or two causes—or delete some that seem too obvious, too obscure, or relatively minor.
- *Do you propose too few causes for a complex subject?* Try to think of other possible causes, especially hidden or remote ones. Conduct further research if necessary.

Convincing Support

- *Is your support skimpy or weak?* Look for more or stronger types of support.
- *Do you make errors in reasoning?* Correct them. For example, if you cannot provide convincing support that a proposed cause not only occurred before the phenomenon or trend began but also contributed to it, you will have to delete

that cause or at least present it more tentatively. If you have confused a cause with an effect, clarify their relationship.

A Logical Sequence of Causes

- **Do your readers find the argument disorganized or hard to follow?** Consider rearranging the causes in order of increasing or decreasing importance, grouping related causes together, or moving the refutations of alternative causes to precede your own causes. Try to forge a logical chain of reasoning from cause to cause. Your plan may be more understandable if you forecast it at the beginning. Provide summaries, transitions, and other cues for readers.

For more on cueing the reader, see Chapter 13.

A Consideration of Readers' Objections and Questions

- **Are any of your refutations of readers' possible objections to your proposed causes unconvincing?** Try to provide stronger evidence. If you cannot do so, you may want to accommodate the objections.

- **Do any refutations attack or ridicule people?** Revise them to focus on the objections or alternative causes, not the people who are proposing them.

- **Do readers raise questions about your argument?** You may need to provide more information about your subject or more support for proposed causes.

- **Do readers make any additional objections to your argument?** Consider whether you can acknowledge their validity and incorporate them into your own argument, or explain why they are wrong.

Responses to Alternative Causes

- **Do any of your refutations of alternative causes seem unconvincing?** Try to provide a stronger counterargument, or consider accommodating the alternative causes.

- **Do any refutations attack or ridicule people?** Revise to focus on specific alternative causes that you believe to be implausible rather than the people who are proposing these causes.

- **Do readers suggest any causes you have not considered?** Decide whether the causes are plausible and should be integrated into your argument. If they seem implausible, decide whether to mention and refute them.

The Beginning and Ending

- **Is the beginning dull?** Try opening with a surprising fact or an engaging anecdote or by emphasizing your subject's puzzling nature.

- **Is the ending weak?** Try to make it more emphatic or more interesting, perhaps by restating your main cause or causes, framing (referring to something mentioned at the beginning), or inviting readers to speculate further.

▦ EDITING AND PROOFREADING

Now is the time to check your revised draft for errors in grammar, punctuation, and mechanics and to consider matters of style. Our research has identified several errors that are especially likely to occur in essays speculating about causes. The following guidelines are designed to help you check and edit your essay for these common errors.

Checking Your Use of Numbers.   Whether they are indicating the scope of a phenomenon or citing the increase or decrease of a trend, writers who are speculating about causes often cite dates, percentages, fractions, and other numbers. Look, for example, at these sentences from Sarah West's essay:

> According to a 1994 survey conducted by the Society for Human Resource Management, the percentage of human resource professionals who have reported that their departments handled at least one sexual harassment complaint rose from 35 percent in 1991 to 65 percent in 1994.

> The jury awarded Weeks $7.1 million in punitive damages, twice what she sought in her lawsuit.

West follows the convention of spelling out numbers ("one") that can be written as one or two words and using a combination of numerals and words for a large number ("$7.1 million"). She could have used numerals for the large number: $7,100,000. She uses numerals for dates and percentages.

Conventions for presenting numbers in writing are easy to follow. The following sentences, taken from student essays that speculate about causes, have each been edited to demonstrate conventional ways of using numbers in academic writing.

Spelling Out Numbers and Fractions of One or Two Words

▶ According to the World Health Organization, as many as *one* ~~1~~ person in every *fifty* ~~50~~ may be infected with HIV.

▶ Maybe *two-thirds* ~~2/3~~ of the smoke from a cigarette is released into the air.

Using Figures for Numbers and Fractions of More than Two Words

▶ That year the Japanese automobile industry produced only *4,837* ~~four thousand eight hundred thirty-seven~~ vehicles, mostly trucks and motorbikes.

▶ This study shows that Americans spend an average of *5¹/₃* ~~five and one-third~~ hours a day watching television.

Writing Percentages and Dates with Figures

▶ Comparing 1980 to 1960, we can see that time spent viewing television

increased ~~twenty-eight~~ *28* percent.

Spelling Out Numbers That Begin a Sentence

▶ *Thirty* ~~30~~ percent of commercial real estate in Washington, D.C. is owned by foreigners.

Checking for *Reason Is Because* Constructions. When you speculate about causes, you need to offer reasons and support for your speculations. Consequently, essays that speculate about causes often contain sentences constructed around a *reason is because* pattern. Since *because* means "for the reason that," such sentences say essentially that "the reason is the reason."

REDUNDANT   The *reason* we lost the war *is because* troop morale was down.

If you find this pattern in your writing, there are two easy ways to edit out the redundancy:

CLEAR   The reason we lost the war is that troop morale was down.
CLEAR   We lost the war because troop morale was down.

▶ Her research suggests that one reason women attend women's colleges is ~~because~~ *that* they want to avoid certain social pressures.

▶ ~~A reason older~~ *Older* Americans watch so much television ~~is~~ because they tend to be sedentary.

A WRITER AT WORK

■ ANALYZING CAUSES

When a writer is planning an essay that speculates about causes, identifying and analyzing possible causes are the most important parts of invention and research. Here we look at an invention table of causes and analyses that Sarah West developed for her essay, "The Rise of Reported Incidents of Workplace Sexual Harassment," which appears in this chapter on pp. 426–30.

West worked on this invention activity in stages, and her table of causes shows how her ideas about her subject evolved. When she began the activity, she assumed her subject would be a recent increase in workplace sexual harassment. Later, she modified her subject to focus on an increase in *reported incidents* of workplace sexual harassment, based on what she learned from doing library and Internet research. As you read through her invention table, notice how the causes and analyses reflect West's developing ideas about her subject. With her initial subject in mind, she entered the first three causes in the table and a partial analysis. Then, after she researched her subject and decided to focus on reported incidents, she added the other four causes and completed the analysis.

```
TABLE OF POSSIBLE CAUSES AND ANALYSES
Causes                        Analyses

1. Women are not       Background cause because sexist attitudes
   taken seriously     go back a long way. Definitely a cause that
   at work by men      sustains the increase in sexual harassment.
                       Obvious cause, I guess. My aunt was sexually
                       harassed at work for a long time by her
                       supervisor. She put up with it, and then
                       the man left for a new job. Obviously men
                       wouldn't harass women in any way if they
                       took them seriously, so it's both a neces-
                       sary and sufficient cause.

2. Men are unable      If they understood, they wouldn't do it,
   to understand       making this a necessary cause. Maybe it's
   what sexual         possible that some women don't mind or even
   harassment feels    encourage it, but most women must hate and
   like                resent it. Not a sufficient cause--men might
                       still refrain from doing it even if they
                       couldn't understand the effect it had. A
                       few men probably are able to understand how
                       sexual harassment makes women feel. Perpetu-
                       ating and background cause because it comes
                       from men's basic attitudes that are not easy
                       to change. Not so obvious a cause as my
                       first one.

3. Men are not wor-    A necessary cause--if men feared the conse-
   ried about being    quences of being caught, they wouldn't
   reported            harass. They feel powerful and safe, proba-
```

bly because their bosses are men, who may play or have played the sexual harassment game themselves. A perpetuating cause, important, but maybe not too surprising to women. Can't see what would be the best order for these three causes. Need to find out what the experts have said about this trend.

4. Increased awareness

An immediate and perpetuating cause as well. Awareness of the 1964 Civil Rights Act and knowledge about the nature of sexual harassment at work has been recent and widespread among women. Researchers I read support this. Nearly all women workers had this information. But most business organizations continued to ignore the implications. And most men.

5. 1991 Civil Rights Act

This important legislation put in place penalties for businesses that did not have sexual harassment policies that protected women and punished men who got out of line. Well-documented and publicized cases cost some businesses a lot of money. An immediate cause that brought about the increase in reported cases of harassment. Both a necessary and sufficient cause because of the penalties. That's what caught everybody's attention. This cause wouldn't be obvious to readers who did not know about the 1991 Act. Use Stanko and Werner.

6. Company policies

Immediate, necessary, and sufficient cause. There were policies, manuals, training sessions for men and women. Probably the most immediate cause because women now had specific procedures to follow to report sexual harassment. Martell and Sullivan document these important changes. Also use "Handling" and "Sexual" and HRM report.

7. Media attention

Neither necessary nor sufficient cause, because media attention would not have encouraged women to report harassment. It

```
Causes                    Analyses

7. Media attention        was really the 1991 Act and the well-
   (continued)            publicized company policies. Could be an
                          effect, but I think it is a cause that sus-
                          tains what started with companies' new poli-
                          cies. Probably an obvious cause to readers,
                          who will recognize all the examples of media
                          attention I will use from my reading. Refer
                          to Nelton.
```

   Once West had analyzed all these possible causes, she could decide how to use them to make the most convincing explanation of her subject. She decided to use all four of the causes she came up with from her research (causes 4–7). She thought her readers would find these causes plausible, and she knew she had enough statistics and examples to support them. Then she decided how to order the causes to produce the most logical argument. In addition, she considered potential objections to her argument and accommodations or refutations of them. She found one journalist who was skeptical that there was an increase in reported incidents of sexual harassment, and she tried her best to refute his argument (paragraph 7). Finally, she found one alternative cause for the increase, and she decided to concede part of it and try to refute the rest (paragraph 8).

The report that the biology student wrote about the possible causes of the AIDS epidemic in sub-Saharan Africa and North America (described on p. 408) was accompanied by several visuals, including a color map, downloaded from the Internet, that depicted areas of lesser and greater numbers of AIDS cases across the continent of Africa along with pie charts that showed the relationship between biological sex and AIDS infection in North America and in two regions in Africa. The student also incorporated several tables that presented statistics and other information that would have otherwise taken up unnecessary space and been difficult to grasp.

Making Use of Visuals

Maps, tables, graphs, charts, and diagrams are used to convey information in a way that is easy to read and comprehend. Readers can glean information from these visuals much more quickly and efficiently than they can from statistics that are contained only in written text. Color can be an important element in graphic design: Selecting colors with which to highlight your visuals can be much like selecting the most appropriate and effective words to convey your written ideas. In both cases, you want your choices to enhance readers' understanding of and interest in the argument you are making. Above all, visuals should be clearly designed and easy to read.

It is important to remember, however, that visual aids cannot do all the work for the writer or for readers. Visuals can only represent information, not interpret it. The writer must comment on the information illustrated in graphic aids, explain why the information they show is important, and suggest what the implications of such information might be. Consequently, when you consider integrating visuals into your work, be prepared to explain them carefully in your text. In addition, think about what types of visuals should be included in the text, where and how visuals will make the most sense to your readers, and what labels will need to accompany the visuals for clarity. These decisions will be influenced by whether you are presenting your work as hard copy, an oral presentation to a group, or a document on the Internet.

Selecting Visuals

Visuals are used for specific purposes, and in many cases you will find that one type suits your purpose more effectively than the others. For example, maps can be an appropriate means of illustrating how multiple geographic areas experience some element similarly and/or differently. Different colors are often used to represent contrasts; one familiar example is the televised weather report, where a range of

For more on different types of visuals, see Chapter 25.

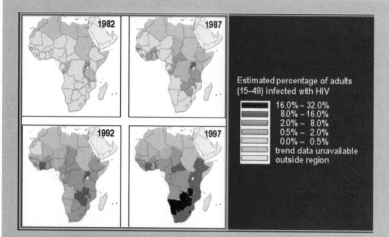

Estimated percentage of adults
(15–49) infected with HIV

16.0% – 32.0%
8.0% – 16.0%
2.0% – 8.0%
0.5% – 2.0%
0.0% – 0.5%
trend data unavailable
outside region

Figure 1. Spread of AIDS over time in Sub-Saharan Africa

temperatures and of precipitation levels are mapped out. The biology student's map (see Figure 1) offers another example.

Pie charts, such as the ones in the student's report (see Figure 2), show the relative percentages of the various parts making up a whole. Finally, diagrams most often illustrate physical relationships or show how things work. For example, the written instructions that come with many products we purchase are often accompanied by diagrams illustrating how to assemble or use the products.

For an example of an instructional process narrative containing diagrams, see Figure 14.3, p. 586.

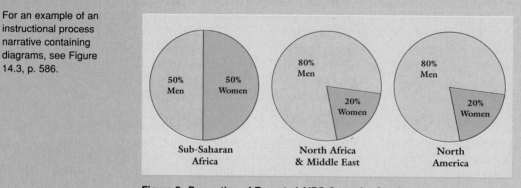

Figure 2. Proportion of Reported AIDS Cases by Gender

THINKING CRITICALLY ABOUT WHAT YOU HAVE LEARNED

Now that you have worked extensively with essays that speculate about causes—reading them, talking about them, writing one of your own—take some time to reflect on what you have learned about causal speculation. What problems did you encounter while you were writing your essay, and how did you solve them? How did reading other causal speculation essays influence your own essay? What ideas do you have about the social or cultural dimensions of this kind of writing?

Reflecting on Your Writing

Write an explanation of a page or so, telling your instructor about a problem you encountered in writing your essay and how you solved it. Before you begin, gather all of your writing—invention and planning notes, drafts, critical comments, revision notes and plans, and final revision. Review these materials as you complete this writing task.

1. ***Identify* one *writing problem you needed to solve as you worked on your essay.*** Do not be concerned with grammar and punctuation; concentrate instead on problems unique to developing an essay that speculates about causes. For example: Did you puzzle over how to present your subject in a way that would interest your readers? Did you have trouble demonstrating that a trend exists? Was it difficult to decide on a logical sequence for presenting causes? Did you worry about the need to identify and address alternative causes?

2. ***Determine how you came to recognize the problem.*** When did you first discover it? What called it to your attention? If someone else pointed out the problem to you, can you now see hints of it in your invention writing? If so, where specifically? When you first recognized the problem, how did you respond?

3. ***Reflect on how you went about solving the problem.*** Did you change the wording of a passage, cut or add causes or refutations, conduct further research, or move paragraphs or sentences around? Did you reread one of the essays in this chapter to see how another writer handled a similar problem, or did you look back at the invention suggestions? If you talked about the problem with another student, a tutor, or your instructor, did talking about it help? How useful was the advice you received?

4. ***Write an explanation of the problem and your solution.*** Be as specific as possible in reconstructing your efforts. Quote from your invention notes or draft essay, others' critical comments, your revision plan, or your revised essay to show the various changes your writing underwent as

you tried to solve the problem. Taking time to explain how you identified a particular problem, how you went about trying to solve it, and what you learned from this experience can help you solve future writing problems more easily.

Reviewing What You Learned from Reading

Write a page or so explaining to your instructor how the readings in this chapter influenced your final essay. Your own essay has undoubtedly been influenced to some extent by one or more of the essays in this chapter as well as by classmates' essays that you have read. These other essays may have helped you decide on an appropriate subject, suggested the need to consider both immediate and background causes, or shown you how to accommodate or refute an important alternative cause. Before you write, take some time to reflect on what you have learned about writing causal speculation from these selections.

1. ***Reread the final revision of your essay; then look back at the selections you read before completing it.*** Do you see any specific influences? For example, if you were impressed with the way one of the readings established the existence of a trend, presented causes in a logical order, used authorities or personal experience and observation to support a cause, or argued convincingly against an alternative cause, look to see where you might have been striving for similar effects in your own writing. Also look for ideas you got from your reading: writing strategies you were inspired to try, specific details you were led to include, effects you sought to achieve.

2. ***Write an explanation of these influences.*** Did one selection have a particularly strong influence on your essay, or were several selections influential in different ways? Quote from the readings and from your final revision to show how your causal speculation essay was influenced by the selections you read. Finally, based on your review of this chapter's readings, point out any further improvement you would now make in your essay.

Considering the Social Dimensions of Causal Speculation

Persuasive writing, as we define it in this text, deals with probabilities and possibilities, not with certainties. Causal speculation is persuasive writing par excellence because it confronts aspects of social life that we do not yet understand and may never fully understand. Without this great social resource, we would feel helpless in the face of threatening social problems. They would seem like random acts of a chaotic universe. Instead, when confronted with the alarming evidence that the teenage suicide rate is high, we can start speculating about why so many teenagers are ending their own lives. We can evaluate competing causes and decide which are the most plausible. Finally, we can take action, feeling reassured that our knowledge is sound, even though it is speculative and likely to change over time. Nevertheless, cautious readers and writers need to be aware of several problems posed by causal speculation.

The Power of Authority.   First, we need to keep in mind that what seems to be the best current explanation for the causes of a trend or phenomenon is not necessarily the only explanation. Speculating about causes tends to give greater voice to certain interests and to minimize or silence others. Some analyses, particularly those of "experts" such as economists, psychologists, and popular authors, are often granted more authority than analyses favored by parents, teachers, community and religious leaders, and other persons most directly affected.

In addition, we need to remember that causal reasoning is always shaped by the analyst's ideology—the set of beliefs, values, and attitudes that determines a person's worldview. For example, Stephen King—a horror writer—has a real interest in establishing the horror movie as a legitimate literary and cinematic form; it is not surprising, then, that he would emphasize psychological benefits as a basis for the popularity of horror movies rather than a more negative factor. Clinical psychologist William S. Pollack is clearly sympathetic to the plight of depressed boys; a less sympathetic analyst might come up with a com-

pletely different explanation for the causes of boys' depression.

Even the way we define a phenomenon or a trend can color our explanation of its causes. For example, following the original acquittal of the police officers accused of beating motorist Rodney King in Los Angeles during the spring of 1992, many people took to the streets, starting fires and looting. While some observers called the disturbance a "riot," others more sympathetically called it an "uprising." These two terms reflect opposite ways of understanding what happened, pointing to entirely different sets of possible causes. A great deal is at stake when society must decide whether the causes were linked to frustration with racism and unequal justice, on the one hand, or to lack of an adequate police "presence" and respect for the law, on the other hand.

1. *Consider how the readings and your own essay are exercises in exerting authority.* We have said that because causal speculation deals with possibilities instead of certainties, writers must be somewhat tentative about their speculations. However, if causal argument is to be convincing, it cannot be too timid. Writers who have studied a subject carefully may feel that they are justified in exerting their authority. Compare the Pollack and West essays. Which seems more assertive? What accounts for your response? What seems to you assertive or unassertive about your own essay? Was it your knowledge or your ideology—your way of looking at the world—that gave you the confidence to be authoritative?

2. *Consider how easy it is to accept a causal explanation.* We have also said that if readers are not alert, they may begin to think that the explanation offered is the only possible one. Is either Pollack's or West's argument so seductive that you find yourself accepting it without question? Explain briefly.

3. *Write a page or so explaining your ideas about authority and ideology in essays speculating about causes.* Connect your ideas to your own essay and to the readings in this chapter.

Causes and Blame. Causal speculations sometimes become exercises in assigning blame. For example, not long ago, a woman's "provocative" attire could be cited in court as a cause (and possible justification) for her being raped. Similarly, women could be blamed for failing to be superwomen, and boys could be blamed for failing to keep a stiff upper lip and pull themselves out of their own depression. In cases like these, causal speculation can become a way for people to avoid confronting social responsibilities and put off working toward solving serious social problems.

1. *Draw some conclusions about individual and social influences on behavior.* Americans are often divided about whether individuals are primarily responsible for their circumstances or whether social, economic, and political conditions best explain people's difficulties and suffering. Where does Pollack position himself on this issue? Explore your own position as well. If you were to write about the causes of depression in boys, which kinds of causes—individual or social—would you emphasize? Why?

2. *Consider how distance between writers and their subjects may lead writers to misunderstand their subjects.* Jill Neimark writes a causal argument about a cultural phenomenon in which she is not personally involved and relies totally on sources, rather than on her own personal experience. She is older than Miss America contestants, well established as a professional writer, and already well educated. How might her causal analysis reflect her own social position? The people most directly affected by social problems seldom get to write causal analyses about their own plight; in our society, analysis is typically left to the experts. Imagine how extended interviews with several Miss Americas might have changed the causal arguments in Neimark's essay.

3. *Write a page or so explaining your ideas on how essays speculating about causes can become exercises in assigning blame.* Connect your ideas to your own essay and to the readings in this chapter.

Interpreting Stories

10

Stories have a special place in most cultures. Elders relate family and cultural history through stories; lessons are taught through moral fables and parables. The bonds of family and community are often strengthened by sharing stories.

Stories have the power to stimulate our feelings and imagination, allowing us to escape our everyday routine and become aware of the wider world around us. They can lead us to look at others with sensitivity and, for a brief time, to see the world through another person's eyes. They can also lead us to see ourselves differently, to gain insight into our innermost feelings and thoughts.

The stories you will read in this chapter may remind you of the essays about remembered events you read and wrote in Chapter 2. Like an autobiographical essay, a story succeeds largely on how well it conveys to readers the significance of an event. As you may remember, essays about remembered events convey significance primarily through vivid descriptive detail showing people in particular places engaged in some kind of dramatic action. Fictional stories work the same way, only the people are called the *characters,* places are called the *setting,* the dramatic action is called the *plot,* and the significance is called the *theme* or *meaning.*

In this chapter, you will be reading and writing essays interpreting a story. The essay interpreting a story is a special kind of academic writing—like the lab report in biology, the ethnography in anthropology, and the brief in law. College students can expect to write interpretive, or analytical essays as they are sometimes called, in English and film studies courses. Although the genre of essays interpreting stories is specialized, you do not have to be an English major to write a successful interpretive essay. Once you have learned the conventions of presenting an interpretive argument, you will be able to use your experience of listening to, viewing, reading, and telling stories to write insightfully about the fictional stories you read.

This activity invites you to practice arguing for your interpretation of a story. Get together with two or three other students to discuss your interpretations of a story you have all read. Your instructor may assign a story for your group or may invite you to choose one from this chapter.

Practice Interpreting a Story: A Collaborative Activity

Part 1. Begin by picking a question for interpretation for your story from the list below. Members of your group may choose the same question or different ones.

Next take a few minutes to make notes of what you will say. Take turns telling the other group members your interpretation and your reasons for it. The others will react, indicating where they agree and disagree with your interpretation.

Questions for Interpretation

For "The Story of an Hour," how do you interpret:

1. the meaning of the final paragraph?
2. what Mrs. Mallard feels was "approaching to possess her" and why she tries "to beat it back" in paragraph 10?
3. Mrs. Mallard's thoughts in paragraph 14?

For "The Use of Force," how do you interpret:

1. the doctor's ambivalence in paragraph 32 about his own actions?
2. the doctor's attitude in paragraph 22 toward the girl and her parents?
3. the girl's behavior?

For "The Hammer Man," how do you interpret:

1. what the speaker sees and how she responds to it in paragraph 13?
2. the way the speaker portrays her family and neighborhood in comparison to the way the folder in the center's office describes her family and neighborhood in paragraph 11?
3. the change in the speaker at the end of the story?

For "Araby," how do you interpret:

1. how the boy sees himself at the end of the story?
2. Mangan's sister in comparison to the way the boy represents her?
3. the changes the boy undergoes in the story?

Part 2. After you have all presented your interpretations and gotten feedback from the group, use the following questions to explore what you learned about interpreting stories:

- What was most challenging for you: choosing a question, responding to it, giving reasons for your interpretation?
- What one thing said by other members of your group, either in response to your interpretation or in presenting their own interpretations, might lead you to change your interpretation or how you argue for it?

AN ANTHOLOGY OF SHORT STORIES

Following are four well-known short stories: "The Story of an Hour" by Kate Chopin, "The Use of Force" by William Carlos Williams, "The Hammer Man" by Toni Cade Bambara, and "Araby" by James Joyce. Your instructor may invite the whole class or small groups to discuss one or more of these stories. You may also be asked to choose one of these stories for your interpretive essay.

Kate Chopin (1851–1904) was born in St. Louis and lived in Louisiana until her husband died in 1882, leaving her with six children. Encouraged by friends, Chopin wrote her first novel, At Fault (1890), when she was nearly forty years old. She wrote many short stories for popular magazines such as Century, Harper's, and Vogue, in which "The Story of an Hour" first appeared in 1894. She published two collections of stories and a second novel, her best known work, The Awakening (1899).

The Story of an Hour

Kate Chopin

1 Knowing that Mrs. Mallard was afflicted with a heart trouble, great care was taken to break to her as gently as possible the news of her husband's death.

2 It was her sister Josephine who told her, in broken sentences; veiled hints that revealed in half concealing. Her husband's friend Richards was there, too, near her. It was he who had been in the newspaper office when intelligence of the railroad disaster was received, with Brently Mallard's name leading the list of "killed." He had only taken the time to assure himself of its truth by a second telegram, and had hastened to forestall any less careful, less tender friend in bearing the sad message.

3 She did not hear the story as many women have heard the same, with a paralyzed inability to accept its significance. She wept at once, with sudden, wild abandonment, in her sister's arms. When the storm of grief had spent itself she went away to her room alone. She would have no one follow her.

4 There stood, facing the open window, a comfortable, roomy armchair. Into this she sank, pressed down by a physical exhaustion that haunted her body and seemed to reach into her soul.

5 She could see in the open square before her house the tops of trees that were all aquiver with the new spring life. The delicious breath of rain was in the air. In the street below a peddler was crying his wares. The notes of a distant song which some one was singing reached her faintly, and countless sparrows were twittering in the eaves.

6 There were patches of blue sky showing here and there through the clouds that had met and piled one above the other in the west facing her window.

7 She sat with her head thrown back upon the cushion of the chair, quite motionless, except when a sob came up into her throat and shook her, as a child who has cried itself to sleep continues to sob in its dreams.

She was young, with a fair, calm face, whose lines bespoke repression and even a 8 certain strength. But now there was a dull stare in her eyes, whose gaze was fixed away off yonder on one of those patches of blue sky. It was not a glance of reflection, but rather indicated a suspension of intelligent thought.

There was something coming to her and she was waiting for it, fearfully. What was 9 it? She did not know; it was too subtle and elusive to name. But she felt it, creeping out of the sky, reaching toward her through the sounds, the scents, the color that filled the air.

Now her bosom rose and fell tumultuously. She was beginning to recognize this 10 thing that was approaching to possess her, and she was striving to beat it back with her will—as powerless as her two white slender hands would have been.

When she abandoned herself a little whispered word escaped her slightly parted 11 lips. She said it over and over under her breath: "free, free, free!" The vacant stare and the look of terror that had followed it went from her eyes. They stayed keen and bright. Her pulses beat fast, and the coursing blood warmed and relaxed every inch of her body.

She did not stop to ask if it were or were not a monstrous joy that held her. A clear 12 and exalted perception enabled her to dismiss the suggestion as trivial.

She knew that she would weep again when she saw the kind, tender hands folded 13 in death; the face that had never looked save with love upon her, fixed and gray and dead. But she saw beyond that bitter moment a long procession of years to come that would belong to her absolutely. And she opened and spread her arms out to them in welcome.

There would be no one to live for her during those coming years; she would live for 14 herself. There would be no powerful will bending hers in that blind persistence with which men and women believe they have a right to impose a private will upon a fellow-creature. A kind intention or a cruel intention made the act seem no less a crime as she looked upon it in that brief moment of illumination.

And yet she had loved him—sometimes. Often she had not. What did it matter! 15 What could love, the unsolved mystery, count for in face of this possession of self-assertion which she suddenly recognized as the strongest impulse of her being!

"Free! Body and soul free!" she kept whispering. 16

Josephine was kneeling before the closed door with her lips to the keyhole, implor- 17 ing for admission. "Louise, open the door! I beg; open the door—you will make yourself ill. What are you doing, Louise? For heaven's sake open the door."

"Go away. I am not making myself ill." No; she was drinking in a very elixir of life 18 through that open window.

Her fancy was running riot along those days ahead of her. Spring days, and sum- 19 mer days, and all sorts of days that would be her own. She breathed a quick prayer that life might be long. It was only yesterday she had thought with a shudder that life might be long.

She arose at length and opened the door to her sister's importunities. There was a 20 feverish triumph in her eyes, and she carried herself unwittingly like a goddess of Victory. She clasped her sister's waist, and together they descended the stairs. Richards stood waiting for them at the bottom.

Some one was opening the front door with a latchkey. It was Brently Mallard who 21 entered, a little travel-stained, composedly carrying his gripsack and umbrella. He had been far from the scene of accident, and did not even know there had been one. He stood amazed at Josephine's piercing cry; at Richards' quick motion to screen him from the view of his wife.

But Richards was too late. 22

When the doctors came they said she had died of heart disease—of joy that kills. 23

William Carlos Williams *(1883–1963) is one of the most important poets of the twentieth century, best known for his long poem* Paterson *(1946–1958). He also wrote essays, plays, novels, and short stories. "The Use of Force" was published initially in* The Doctor Stories *(1933), a collection loosely based on Williams's experiences as a pediatrician.*

The Use of Force

William Carlos Williams

They were new patients to me, all I had was the name, 1 Olson. Please come down as soon as you can, my daughter is very sick.

When I arrived I was met by the mother, a big 2 startled-looking woman, very clean and apologetic, who merely said, Is this the doctor? and let me in. In the back, she added. You must excuse us, doctor, we have her in the kitchen where it is warm. It is very damp here sometimes.

The child was fully dressed and sitting on her father's lap near the kitchen table. He 3 tried to get up, but I motioned for him not to bother, took off my overcoat and started to look things over. I could see that they were all very nervous, eyeing me up and down distrustfully. As often, in such cases, they weren't telling me more than they had to, it was up to me to tell them; that's why they were spending three dollars on me.

The child was fairly eating me up with her cold, steady eyes, and no expression to 4 her face whatever. She did not move and seemed, inwardly, quiet; an unusually attractive little thing, and as strong as a heifer in appearance. But her face was flushed, she was breathing rapidly, and I realized that she had a high fever. She had magnificent blonde hair, in profusion. One of those picture children often reproduced in advertising leaflets and the photogravure sections of the Sunday papers.

She's had a fever for three days, began the father, and we don't know what it comes 5 from. My wife has given her things, you know, like people do, but it don't do no good. And there's been a lot of sickness around. So we tho't you better look her over and tell us what is the matter.

As doctors often do I took a trial shot at it as a point of departure. Has she had a 6 sore throat?

Both parents answered me together, No . . . No, she says her throat don't hurt her. 7

Does your throat hurt you? added the mother to the child. But the little girl's expres- 8 sion didn't change nor did she move her eyes from my face.

Have you looked? 9

I tried, said the mother, but I couldn't see. 10

As it happens we had been having a number of cases of diphtheria in the school to 11 which this child went during that month and we were all, quite apparently, thinking of that, though no one had as yet spoken of the thing.

Well, I said, suppose we take a look at the throat first. I smiled in my best profes- 12 sional manner and asking for the child's first name I said, come on, Mathilda, open your mouth and let's take a look at your throat.

Nothing doing. 13

Aw, come on, I coaxed, just open your mouth wide and let me take a look. Look, I 14 said opening both hands wide, I haven't anything in my hands. Just open up and let me see.

Such a nice man, put in the mother. Look how kind he is to you. Come on, do what 15 he tells you to. He won't hurt you.

At that I ground my teeth in disgust. If only they wouldn't use the word "hurt" I might 16 be able to get somewhere. But I did not allow myself to be hurried or disturbed but speaking quietly and slowly I approached the child again.

As I moved my chair a little nearer suddenly with one catlike movement both her 17 hands clawed instinctively for my eyes and she almost reached them too. In fact she knocked my glasses flying and they fell, though unbroken, several feet away from me on the kitchen floor.

Both the mother and father almost turned themselves inside out in embarrassment 18 and apology. You bad girl, said the mother, taking her and shaking her by one arm. Look what you've done. The nice man . . .

For heaven's sake, I broke in. Don't call me a nice man to her. I'm here to look at 19 her throat on the chance that she might have diphtheria and possibly die of it. But that's nothing to her. Look here, I said to the child, we're going to look at your throat. You're old enough to understand what I'm saying. Will you open it now by yourself or shall we have to open it for you?

Not a move. Even her expression hadn't changed. Her breaths however were com- 20 ing faster and faster. Then the battle began. I had to do it. I had to have a throat culture for her own protection. But first I told the parents that it was entirely up to them. I explained the danger but said that I would not insist on a throat examination so long as they would take the responsibility.

If you don't do what the doctor says you'll have to go to the hospital, the mother 21 admonished her severely.

Oh yeah? I had to smile to myself. After all, I had already fallen in love with the sav- 22 age brat, the parents were contemptible to me. In the ensuing struggle they grew more and more abject, crushed, exhausted while she surely rose to magnificent heights of insane fury of effort bred of her terror of me.

The father tried his best, and he was a big man, but the fact that she was his daugh- 23 ter, his shame at her behavior and his dread of hurting her made him release her just at the critical times when I had almost achieved success, till I wanted to kill him. But his dread also that she might have diphtheria made him tell me to go on, go on though he himself was almost fainting, while the mother moved back and forth behind us raising and lowering her hands in an agony of apprehension.

Put her in front of you on your lap, I ordered, and hold both her wrists. 24

But as soon as he did the child let out a scream. Don't, you're hurting me. Let go of 25
my hands. Let them go I tell you. Then she shrieked terrifyingly, hysterically. Stop it! Stop
it! You're killing me!

Do you think she can stand it, doctor! said the mother. 26

You get out, said the husband to his wife. Do you want her to die of diphtheria? 27

Come on now, hold her, I said. 28

Then I grasped the child's head with my left hand and tried to get the wooden 29
tongue depressor between her teeth. She fought, with clenched teeth, desperately! But
now I also had grown furious—at a child. I tried to hold myself down but I couldn't. I
know how to expose a throat for inspection. And I did my best. When finally I got the
wooden spatula behind the last teeth and just the point of it into the mouth cavity, she
opened up for an instant but before I could see anything she came down again and gripping the wooden blade between her molars she reduced it to splinters before I could get
it out again.

Aren't you ashamed, the mother yelled at her. Aren't you ashamed to act like that in 30
front of the doctor?

Get me a smooth-handled spoon of some sort, I told the mother. We're going 31
through with this. The child's mouth was already bleeding. Her tongue was cut and she
was screaming in wild hysterical shrieks. Perhaps I should have desisted and come
back in an hour or more. No doubt it would have been better. But I have seen at least
two children lying dead in bed of neglect in such cases, and feeling that I must get a
diagnosis now or never I went at it again. But the worst of it was that I too had got
beyond reason. I could have torn the child apart in my own fury and enjoyed it. It was a
pleasure to attack her. My face was burning with it.

The damned little brat must be protected against her own idiocy, one says to one- 32
self at such times. Others must be protected against her. It is a social necessity. And all
these things are true. But a blind fury, a feeling of adult shame, bred of a longing for mus-
cular release are the operatives. One goes on to the end.

In a final unreasoning assault I overpowered the child's neck and jaws. I forced the 33
heavy silver spoon back of her teeth and down her throat till she gagged. And there it
was—both tonsils covered with membrane. She had fought valiantly to keep me from
knowing her secret. She had been hiding that sore throat for three days at least and lying
to her parents in order to escape just such an outcome as this.

Now truly she was furious. She had been on the defensive before but now she at- 34
tacked. Tried to get off her father's lap and fly at me while tears of defeat blinded her eyes.

Toni Cade Bambara (1939–1995) *wrote several short story collections, including* The Sea
Birds Are Still Alive *(1977), and the novels* The Salt Eaters *(1980) and* Raymond's Run
(1990). The following story was originally published in 1966 in Negro Digest *and reprinted in*
Gorilla, My Love *(1972), which won the American Book Award in 1981.*

The Hammer Man

Toni Cade Bambara

I was glad to hear that Manny had fallen off the roof. I had put out the tale that I was down with yellow fever, but nobody paid me no mind, least of all Dirty Red who stomped right in to announce that Manny had fallen off the roof and that I could come out of hiding now. My mother dropped what she was doing, which was the laundry, and got the whole story out of Red. "Bad enough you gots to hang around with boys," she said. "But fight with them too. And you would pick the craziest one at that." 1

Manny was supposed to be crazy. That was his story. To say you were bad put some people off. But to say you were crazy, well, you were officially not to be messed with. So that was his story. On the other hand, after I called him what I called him and said a few choice things about his mother, his face did go through some piercing changes. And I did kind of wonder if maybe he sure was nuts. I didn't wait to find out. I got in the wind. And then he waited for me on my stoop all day and all night, not hardly speaking to the people going in and out. And he was there all day Saturday, with his sister bringing him peanut-butter sandwiches and cream sodas. He must've gone to the bathroom right there cause every time I looked out the kitchen window, there he was. And Sunday, too. I got to thinking the boy was mad. 2

"You got no sense of humor, that's your trouble," I told him. He looked up, but he didn't say nothing. All at once I was real sorry about the whole thing. I should've settled for hitting off the little girls in the school yard or waiting for Frankie to come in so we could raise some kind of hell. This way I had to play sick when my mother was around cause my father had already taken away my BB gun and hid it. 3

I don't know how they got Manny on the roof finally. Maybe the Wakefield kids, the ones who keep the pigeons, called him up. Manny was a sucker for sick animals and things like that. Or maybe Frankie got some nasty girls to go up on the roof with him and got Manny to join him. I don't know. Anyway, the catwalk had lost all its cement and the roof always did kind of slant downward. So Manny fell off the roof. I got over my yellow fever right quick, needless to say, and ventured outside. But by this time I had already told Miss Rose that Crazy Manny was after me. And Miss Rose, being who she was, quite naturally went over to Manny's house and said a few harsh words to his mother, who, being who she was, chased Miss Rose out into the street and they commenced to get with it, snatching bottles out of the garbage cans and breaking them on the johnny pumps and stuff like that. 4

Dirty Red didn't have to tell us about this. Everybody could see and hear all. I never figured the garbage cans for an arsenal, but Miss Rose came up with sticks and table legs and things, and Manny's mother had her share of scissor blades and bicycle chains. They got to rolling in the streets and all you could see was pink drawers and fat legs. It was something else. Miss Rose is nutty but Manny's mother's crazier than Manny. They were at it a couple of times during my sick spell. Everyone would congregate on the window sills or the fire escape, commenting that it was still much too cold for this kind of nonsense. But they watched anyway. And then Manny fell off the roof. And that was that. Miss Rose went back to her dream books and Manny's mother went back to her tumbled-down kitchen of dirty clothes and bundles and bundles of rags and children. 5

My father got in on it too, cause he happened to ask Manny one night why he was sitting on the stoop like that every night. Manny told him right off that he was going to kill me first chance he got. Quite naturally this made my father a little warm, me being his only daughter and planning to become a doctor and take care of him in his old age. So he had a few words with Manny first, and then he got hold of the older brother, Bernard, who was more his size. Bernard didn't see how any of it was his business or my father's business, so my father got mad and jammed Bernard's head into the mailbox. Then my father started getting messages from Bernard's uncle about where to meet him for a showdown and all. My father didn't say a word to my mother all this time; just sat around mumbling and picking up the phone and putting it down, or grabbing my stickball bat and putting it back. He carried on like this for days till I thought I would scream if the yellow fever didn't have me so weak. And then Manny fell off the roof, and my father went back to his beer-drinking buddies.

I was in the school yard, pitching pennies with the little boys from the elementary school, when my friend Violet hits my brand-new Spaudeen over the wall. She came running back to tell me that Manny was coming down the block. I peeked beyond the fence and there he was all right. He had his head all wound up like a mummy and his arm in a sling and his leg in a cast. It looked phony to me, especially that walking cane. I figured Dirty Red had told me a tale just to get me out there so Manny could stomp me, and Manny was playing it up with costume and all till he could get me.

"What happened to him?" Violet's sisters whispered. But I was too busy trying to figure out how this act was supposed to work. Then Manny passed real close to the fence and gave me a look.

"You had enough, Hammer Head," I yelled. "Just bring your crummy self in this yard and I'll pick up where I left off." Violet was knocked out and the other kids went into a huddle. I didn't have to say anything else. And when they all pressed me later, I just said, "You know that hammer he always carries in his fatigues?" And they'd all nod waiting for the rest of a long story. "Well, I took it away from him." And I walked off nonchalantly.

Manny stayed indoors for a long time. I almost forgot about him. New kids moved into the block and I got all caught up with that. And then Miss Rose finally hit the numbers and started ordering a whole lot of stuff through the mail and we would sit on the curb and watch these weird-looking packages being carried in, trying to figure out what simpleminded thing she had thrown her money away on when she might just as well wait for the warm weather and throw a block party for all her godchildren.

After a while a center opened up and my mother said she'd increase my allowance if I went and joined because I'd have to get out of my pants and stay in skirts, on account of that's the way things were at the center. So I joined and got to thinking about everything else but old Hammer Head. It was a rough place to get along in, the center, but my mother said that I needed to be be'd with and she needed to not be with me, so I went. And that time I sneaked into the office, that's when I really got turned on. I looked into one of those not-quite-white folders and saw that I was from a deviant family in a deviant neighborhood. I showed my mother the word in the dictionary, but she didn't pay me no mind. It was my favorite word after that. I ran it in the ground till one day my father got the strap just to show how deviant he could get. So I gave up trying to improve my vocabulary. And I almost gave up my dungarees.

Then one night I'm walking past the Douglas Street park cause I got thrown out of the center for playing pool when I should've been sewing, even though I had already decided that this was going to be my last fling with boy things, and starting tomorrow I was going to fix my hair right and wear skirts all the time just so my mother would stop talking about her gray hairs, and Miss Rose would stop calling me by my brother's name by mistake. So I'm walking past the park and there's ole Manny on the basketball court, perfecting his lay-ups and talking with himself. Being me, I quite naturally walk right up and ask what the hell he's doing playing in the dark, and he looks up and all around like the dark had crept up on him when he wasn't looking. So I knew right away that he'd been out there for a long time with his eyes just going along with the program.   12

"There was two seconds to go and we were one point behind," he said, shaking his head and staring at his sneakers like they was somebody. "And I was in the clear. I'd left the man in the backcourt and there I was, smiling, you dig, cause it was in the bag. They passed the ball and I slid the ball up nice and easy cause there was nothing to worry about. And . . ." He shook his head. "I muffed the goddamn shot. Ball bounced off the rim. . . ." He stared at his hands. "The game of the season. Last game." And then he ignored me altogether, though he wasn't talking to me in the first place. He went back to the lay-ups, always from the same spot with his arms crooked in the same way, over and over. I must've gotten hypnotized cause I probably stood there for at least an hour watching like a fool till I couldn't even see the damn ball, much less the basket. But I stood there anyway for no reason I know of. He never missed. But he cursed himself away. It was torture. And then a squad car pulled up and a short cop with hair like one of the Marx Brothers came out hitching up his pants. He looked real hard at me and then at Manny.   13

"What are you two doing?"   14

"He's doing a lay-up. I'm watching," I said with my smart self.   15

Then the cop just stood there and finally turned to the other one who was just getting out of the car.   16

"Who unlocked the gate?" the big one said.   17

"It's always unlocked," I said. Then we three just stood there like a bunch of penguins watching Manny go at it.   18

"This on the level?" the big guy asked, tilting his hat back with the thumb the way big guys do in hot weather. "Hey you," he said, walking over to Manny. "I'm talking to you." He finally grabbed the ball to get Manny's attention. But that didn't work. Manny just stood there with his arms out waiting for the pass so he could save the game. He wasn't paying no mind to the cop. So, quite naturally, when the cop slapped him upside his head it was a surprise. And when the cop started counting three to go, Manny had already recovered from the slap and was just ticking off the seconds before the buzzer sounded and all was lost.   19

"Gimme the ball, man." Manny's face was all tightened up and ready to pop.   20

"Did you hear what I said, black boy?"   21

Now, when somebody says that word like that, I gets warm. And crazy or no crazy, Manny was my brother at that moment and the cop was the enemy.   22

"You better give him back his ball," I said. "Manny don't take no mess from no cops. 23
He ain't bothering nobody. He's gonna be Mister Basketball when he grows up. Just trying to get a little practice in before the softball season starts."

"Look here, sister, we'll run you in too," Harpo said. 24

"I damn sure can't be your sister seeing how I'm a black girl. Boy, I sure will be glad 25
when you run me in so I can tell everybody about that. You must think you're in the
South, mister."

The big guy screwed his mouth up and let one of them hard-day sighs. "The park's 26
closed, little girl, so why don't you and your boyfriend go on home."

That really got me. The "little girl" was bad enough, but that "boyfriend" was too 27
much. But I kept cool, mostly because Manny looked so pitiful waiting there with his
hands in a time-out and there being no one to stop the clock. But I kept my cool mostly
cause of that hammer in Manny's pocket and no telling how frantic things can get what
with a bigmouth like me, a couple of wise cops, and a crazy boy too.

"The gates are open," I said real quiet-like, "and this here's a free country. So why 28
don't you give him back his ball?"

The big cop did another one of those sighs, his specialty I guess, and then he 29
bounced the ball to Manny who went right into his gliding thing clear up to the back-
board, damn near like he was some kind of very beautiful bird. And then he swooshed
that ball in, even if there was no net, and you couldn't really hear the swoosh. Something happened to the bones in my chest. It was something.

"Crazy kids anyhow," the one with the wig said and turned to go. But the big guy 30
watched Manny for a while and I guess something must've snapped in his head, cause
all of a sudden he was hot for taking Manny to jail or court or somewhere and started
yelling at him and everything, which is a bad thing to do to Manny, I can tell you. And I'm
standing there thinking that none of my teachers, from kindergarten right on up, none of
them knew what they were talking about. I'll be damned if I ever knew one of them rosy-
cheeked cops that smiled and helped you get to school without neither you or your little
raggedy dog getting hit by a truck that had a smile on its face, too. Not that I ever
believed it. I knew Dick and Jane was full of crap from the get-go, especially them cops.
Like this dude, for example, pulling on Manny's clothes like that when obviously he had
just done about the most beautiful thing a man can do and not be a fag. No cop could
swoosh without a net.

"Look out, man," was all Manny said, but it was the way he pushed the cop that 31
started the real yelling and threats. And I thought to myself, Oh God here I am trying to
change my ways, and not talk back in school, and do like my mother wants, but just have
this last fling, and now this—getting shot in the stomach and bleeding to death in Douglas Street park and poor Manny getting pistol-whipped by those bastards and whatnot.
I could see it all, practically crying too. And it just wasn't no kind of thing to happen to a
small child like me with my confirmation picture in the paper next to my weeping parents
and schoolmates. I could feel the blood sticking to my shirt and my eyeballs slipping
away, and then that confirmation picture again; and my mother and her gray hair; and
Miss Rose heading for the precinct with a shotgun; and my father getting old and feeble
with no one to doctor him up and all.

And I wished Manny had fallen off the damn roof and died right then and there and 32 saved me all this aggravation of being killed with him by these cops who surely didn't come out of no fifth-grade reader. But it didn't happen. They just took the ball and Manny followed them real quiet-like right out of the park into the dark, then into the squad car with his head drooping and his arms in a crook. And I went on home cause what the hell am I going to do on a basketball court, and it getting to be nearly midnight?

I didn't see Manny no more after he got into that squad car. But they didn't kill him 33 after all cause Miss Rose heard he was in some kind of big house for people who lose their marbles. And then it was spring finally, and me and Violet was in this very boss fashion show at the center. And Miss Rose bought me my first corsage—yellow roses to match my shoes.

James Joyce (1882–1941), a native of Dublin, Ireland, is considered one of the most influential writers of the early twentieth century. "Araby," one of his most often anthologized stories, first appeared in the collection Dubliners *in 1914. Like his novel* Portrait of the Artist as a Young Man, *published two years later, it relies on scenes from Joyce's own boyhood.*

Araby

James Joyce

North Richmond Street, being blind,[1] was a quiet street 1 except at the hour when the Christian Brothers' School set the boys free. An uninhabited house of two storeys stood at the blind end, detached from its neighbours in a square ground. The other houses of the street, conscious of decent lives within them, gazed at one another with brown imperturbable faces.

The former tenant of our house, a priest, had died in the back drawing-room. Air, 2 musty from having been long enclosed, hung in all the rooms, and the waste room behind the kitchen was littered with old useless papers. Among these I found a few paper-covered books, the pages of which were curled and damp: *The Abbot,* by Walter Scott, *The Devout Communicant* and *The Memoirs of Vidocq.*[2] I liked the last best because its leaves were yellow. The wild garden behind the house contained a central apple-tree and a few straggling bushes under one of which I found the late tenant's rusty bicycle-pump. He had been a very charitable priest; in his will he had left all his money to institutions and the furniture of his house to his sister.

When the short days of winter came dusk fell before we had well eaten our dinners. 3 When we met in the street the houses had grown sombre. The space of sky above us was the colour of ever-changing violet and towards it the lamps of the street lifted their

---

[1] A dead end. The young Joyce in fact lived for a time on North Richmond Street in Dublin.

[2] *The Devout Communicant* is a collection of religious meditations. *The Abbot* is a historical romance set in the court of Mary, Queen of Scots, a Catholic, who was beheaded for plotting to assassinate her Protestant cousin, Queen Elizabeth I. *The Memoirs of Vidocq* is a collection of sexually suggestive stories about a French criminal turned detective.

feeble lanterns. The cold air stung us and we played till our bodies glowed. Our shouts echoed in the silent street. The career of our play brought us through the dark muddy lanes behind the houses where we ran the gauntlet of the rough tribes from the cottages, to the back doors of the dark dripping gardens where odours arose from the ashpits, to the dark odorous stables where a coachman smoothed and combed the horse or shook music from the buckled harness. When we returned to the street light from the kitchen windows had filled the areas. If my uncle was seen turning the corner we hid in the shadow until we had seen him safely housed. Or if Mangan's sister came out on the doorstep to call her brother in to his tea we watched her from our shadow peer up and down the street. We waited to see whether she would remain or go in and, if she remained, we left our shadow and walked up to Mangan's steps resignedly. She was waiting for us, her figure defined by the light from the half-opened door. Her brother always teased her before he obeyed and I stood by the railings looking at her. Her dress swung as she moved her body and the soft rope of her hair tossed from side to side.

Every morning I lay on the floor in the front parlour watching her door. The blind was pulled down to within an inch of the sash so that I could not be seen. When she came out on the doorstep my heart leaped. I ran to the hall, seized my books and followed her. I kept her brown figure always in my eye and, when we came near the point at which our ways diverged, I quickened my pace and passed her. This happened morning after morning. I had never spoken to her, except for a few casual words, and yet her name was like a summons to all my foolish blood. [4]

Her image accompanied me even in places the most hostile to romance. On Saturday evenings when my aunt went marketing I had to go to carry some of the parcels. We walked through the flaring streets, jostled by drunken men and bargaining women, amid the curses of labourers, the shrill litanies of shop-boys who stood on guard by the barrels of pigs' cheeks, the nasal chanting of street-singers, who sang a *come-all-you* about O'Donovan Rossa,[3] or a ballad about the troubles in our native land. These noises converged in a single sensation of life for me: I imagined that I bore my chalice safely through a throng of foes. Her name sprang to my lips at moments in strange prayers and praises which I myself did not understand. My eyes were often full of tears (I could not tell why) and at times a flood from my heart seemed to pour itself out into my bosom. I thought little of the future. I did not know whether I would ever speak to her or not or, if I spoke to her, how I could tell her of my confused adoration. But my body was like a harp and her words and gestures were like fingers running upon the wires. [5]

One evening I went into the back drawing-room in which the priest had died. It was a dark rainy evening and there was no sound in the house. Through one of the broken panes I heard the rain impinge upon the earth, the fine incessant needles of water playing in the sodden beds. Some distant lamp or lighted window gleamed below me. I was thankful that I could see so little. All my senses seemed to desire to veil themselves and, feeling that I was about to slip from them, I pressed the palms of my hands together until they trembled, murmuring: *"O love! O love!"* many times. [6]

---

[3] A contemporary leader of an underground organization opposed to British rule of Ireland.

At last she spoke to me. When she addressed the first words to me I was so con- 7
fused that I did not know what to answer. She asked me was I going to Araby. I forgot
whether I answered yes or no. It would be a splendid bazaar, she said she would love
to go.[4]

"And why can't you?" I asked. 8

While she spoke she turned a silver bracelet round and round her wrist. She could 9
not go, she said, because there would be a retreat that week in her convent. Her brother
and two other boys were fighting for their caps and I was alone at the railings. She held
one of the spikes, bowing her head towards me. The light from the lamp opposite our
door caught the white curve of her neck, lit up her hair that rested there and, falling, lit
up the hand upon the railing. It fell over one side of her dress and caught the white
border of a petticoat, just visible as she stood at ease.

"It's well for you," she said. 10

"If I go," I said, "I will bring you something." 11

What innumerable follies laid waste my waking and sleeping thoughts after that 12
evening! I wished to annihilate the tedious intervening days. I chafed against the work
of school. At night in my bedroom and by day in the classroom her image came between
me and the page I strove to read. The syllables of the word *Araby* were called to me
through the silence in which my soul luxuriated and cast an Eastern enchantment over
me. I asked for leave to go to the bazaar on Saturday night. My aunt was surprised and
hoped it was not some Freemason affair.[5] I answered few questions in class. I watched
my master's face pass from amiability to sternness; he hoped I was not beginning to idle.
I could not call my wandering thoughts together. I had hardly any patience with the serious work of life which, now that it stood between me and my desire, seemed to me
child's play, ugly monotonous child's play.

On Saturday morning I reminded my uncle that I wished to go to the bazaar in the 13
evening. He was fussing at the hallstand, looking for the hatbrush, and answered me
curtly:

"Yes, boy, I know." 14

As he was in the hall I could not go into the front parlour and lie at the window. I left 15
the house in bad humour and walked slowly towards the school. The air was pitilessly
raw and already my heart misgave me.

When I came home to dinner my uncle had not yet been home. Still it was early. I 16
sat staring at the clock for some time and, when its ticking began to irritate me, I left the
room. I mounted the staircase and gained the upper part of the house. The high cold
empty gloomy rooms liberated me and I went from room to room singing. From the front
window I saw my companions playing below in the street. Their cries reached me weakened and indistinct and, leaning my forehead against the cool glass, I looked over at the
dark house where she lived. I may have stood there for an hour, seeing nothing but the

---

[4] Traveling bazaars featured cafés, shopping stalls, and entertainment. Araby was the name
of an English bazaar that visited Dublin when Joyce was a boy.

[5] The Freemasons is a secretive fraternal order with a long history, and to which the Catholic
church has traditionally been opposed.

brown-clad figure cast by my imagination, touched discreetly by the lamplight at the curved neck, at the hand upon the railings and at the border below the dress.

When I came downstairs again I found Mrs. Mercer sitting at the fire. She was an old garrulous woman, a pawnbroker's widow, who collected used stamps for some pious purpose. I had to endure the gossip of the tea-table. The meal was prolonged beyond an hour and still my uncle did not come. Mrs. Mercer stood up to go: she was sorry she couldn't wait any longer, but it was after eight o'clock and she did not like to be out late, as the night air was bad for her. When she had gone I began to walk up and down the room, clenching my fists. My aunt said: 17 .

"I'm afraid you may put off your bazaar for this night of Our Lord."   18

At nine o'clock I heard my uncle's latchkey in the halldoor. I heard him talking to himself and heard the hallstand rocking when it had received the weight of his overcoat. I could interpret these signs. When he was midway through his dinner I asked him to give me the money to go to the bazaar. He had forgotten.   19

"The people are in bed and after their first sleep now," he said.   20

I did not smile. My aunt said to him energetically: 21

"Can't you give him the money and let him go? You've kept him late enough as it is."   22

My uncle said he was very sorry he had forgotten. He said he believed in the old saying: "All work and no play makes Jack a dull boy." He asked me where I was going and, when I had told him a second time he asked me did I know *The Arab's Farewell to His Steed.* When I left the kitchen he was about to recite the opening lines of the piece to my aunt.   23

I held a florin tightly in my hand as I strode down Buckingham Street towards the station. The sight of the streets thronged with buyers and glaring with gas recalled to me the purpose of my journey. I took my seat in a third-class carriage of a deserted train. After an intolerable delay the train moved out of the station slowly. It crept onward among ruinous houses and over the twinkling river. At Westland Row Station a crowd of people pressed to the carriage doors; but the porters moved them back, saying that it was a special train for the bazaar. I remained alone in the bare carriage. In a few minutes the train drew up beside an improvised wooden platform. I passed out on to the road and saw by the lighted dial of a clock that it was ten minutes to ten. In front of me was a large building which displayed the magical name.   24

I could not find any sixpenny entrance and, fearing that the bazaar would be closed, I passed in quickly through a turnstile, handing a shilling to a weary-looking man. I found myself in a big hall girdled at half its height by a gallery. Nearly all the stalls were closed and the greater part of the hall was in darkness. I recognised a silence like that which pervades a church after a service. I walked into the centre of the bazaar timidly. A few people were gathered about the stalls which were still open. Before a curtain, over which the words *Café Chantant*[6] were written in coloured lamps, two men were counting money on a salver. I listened to the fall of the coins.   25

Remembering with difficulty why I had come I went over to one of the stalls and examined porcelain vases and flowered tea-sets. At the door of the stall a young lady   26

---

[6] A music hall.

was talking and laughing with two young gentlemen. I remarked their English accents and listened vaguely to their conversation.

"O, I never said such a thing!"   27

"O, but you did!"   28

"O, but I didn't!"   29

"Didn't she say that?"   30

"Yes. I heard her."   31

"O, there's a . . . fib!"   32

Observing me the young lady came over and asked me did I wish to buy anything.   33
The tone of her voice was not encouraging; she seemed to have spoken to me out of a sense of duty. I looked humbly at the great jars that stood like eastern guards at either side of the dark entrance to the stall and murmured:

"No, thank you."   34

The young lady changed the position of one of the vases and went back to the two   35
young men. They began to talk of the same subject. Once or twice the young lady glanced at me over her shoulder.

I lingered before her stall, though I knew my stay was useless, to make my interest   36
in her wares seem the more real. Then I turned away slowly and walked down the middle of the bazaar. I allowed the two pennies to fall against the sixpence in my pocket. I heard a voice call from one end of the gallery that the light was out. The upper part of the hall was now completely dark.

Gazing up into the darkness I saw myself as a creature driven and derided by van-   37
ity; and my eyes burned with anguish and anger.

READINGS

The following two readings are essays written by students. Sally Crane and David Ratinov argue for different ways of understanding the ending of "Araby," the preceding short story by James Joyce. The section Analyzing Writing Strategies and the Commentary following each reading touch on a few features best illustrated by that essay, capturing its special qualities and strengths.

Sally Crane wrote this interpretive essay about James Joyce's "Araby" for her composition course. As her title suggests, Crane focuses on what the final scene tells about the boy's character. During class discussion, most of the other students said they thought the boy changes at the end of the story. In her essay, Crane argues that he is just as much in the dark at the end of the story as he was at the beginning. (Note: In citing paragraphs, Crane followed her instructor's special directions rather than MLA style.)

Gazing into the Darkness

Sally Crane

Readers of "Araby" often focus on the final scene as the key to the story. They assume the boy experiences some profound insight about himself when he gazes "up into the darkness" (para. 37). I believe, however, that the boy sees nothing and learns nothing—either about himself or others. He's not self-reflective; he's merely self-absorbed.

The evidence supporting this interpretation is the imagery of blindness and the ironic point of view of the narrator. There can seem to be a profound insight at the end of the story only if we empathize with the boy and adopt his point of view. In other words, we must assume that the young boy is narrating his own story. But if the real narrator is the grown man looking back at his early adolescence, then it becomes possible to read the narrative as ironic and to see the boy as confused and blind.

The story opens and closes with images of blindness. The street is "blind" with an "uninhabited house [. . .] at the blind end" (para. 1). As he spies on Mangan's sister, from his own house, the boy intentionally limits what he is able to see by lowering the "blind" until it is only an inch from the window sash (para. 4). At the bazaar in the closing scene, the "light was out," and the upper part of the hall was "completely dark" (para. 36). The boy is left "gazing up into the darkness," seeing nothing but an inner torment that burns his eyes (para. 37).

This pattern of imagery includes images of reading, and reading stands for the boy's inability to understand what is before his eyes. When he tries to read at night, for example, the girl's "image [comes] between [him] and the page," in effect blinding him (para. 12). In fact, he seems blind to everything except this "image" of the "brown-clad figure cast by [his] imagination" (para. 16). The girl's "brown-clad figure" is also associated with the houses on "blind" North Richmond Street, with their "brown imperturbable faces" (para. 1). The houses stare back at the boy, unaffected by his presence and gaze.

The most important face he tries and fails to read belongs to Mangan's sister. His description of her and interpretation of the few words she says to him can be seen as further evidence of his blindness. He sees only what he wants to see, the "image" he has in his mind's eye. This image comes more from what he's read than from anything he's observed. He casts her simultaneously in the traditional female roles of angel and whore:

> While she spoke she turned a silver bracelet round and round her wrist. She could not go, she said, because there would be a retreat that week in her convent. [. . .] She held one of the spikes, bowing her head towards me. The light from the lamp opposite our door caught the white curve of her neck, lit up her hair that rested there and, falling, lit up the hand upon the railing. It fell over one side of her dress and caught the white border of a petticoat, just visible as she stood at ease. (para. 9)

Her angelic qualities are shown in her plans to attend a convent retreat and in her bowed head. Her whorish qualities come through in the way she flirtatiously plays with the bracelet, as if she were inviting him to buy her an expensive piece of jewelry at the bazaar. The "white curve of her neck" and the "white border of a petticoat" combine the symbolic color of purity, associated with the Madonna, with sexual suggestiveness (para. 9). The point is that there is no suggestion here or anywhere else in the story that the boy is capable of seeing Mangan's sister as a real person. She only exists as the object of his adoring gaze. In fact, no one seems to have any reality for him other than himself.

He is totally self-absorbed. But at the same time, he is also blind to himself. He says repeatedly that he doesn't understand his feelings: "Her name sprang to my lips at moments in strange prayers and praises which I myself did not understand. My eyes were often full of tears (I could not tell why)" (para. 5). His adoration of her is both "confused" and confusing to him. He has no self-understanding (para. 5).

The best insight we have into the boy comes from the language he uses. Much of his language seems to mimic the old priest's romantic books: "Her name was like a summons to all my foolish blood" (para. 4); "I imagined that I bore my chalice safely through a throng of foes" (para. 5); "my body was like a harp and her words and gestures were like fingers running upon the wires" (para. 5). Language like this sounds as though it comes out of a popular romance novel, something written by Danielle Steele perhaps. The mixing of romance with soft porn is unmistakable. Perhaps the boy has spent too much time reading the priest's "sexually seductive stories" from *The Memoirs of Vidocq* (para. 2).

I think this language is meant to be ironic, to point to the fact that the narrator is not the young boy himself but the young boy now grown and looking back at how "foolish" he was (para. 4). This interpretation becomes likely when you think of "Araby" as a fictionalized autobiography. In autobiographical stories, remembered feelings and thoughts are combined with the autobiographer's present perspective. The remembered feelings and thoughts in this story could be seen as expressing the boy's point of view, but we read them ironically through the adult narrator's present perspective. The romantic, gushy language the boy uses is laughable. It reveals the boy's blindness toward everyone, including himself. He sees himself as Sir Galahad, the chivalric hero on his own grail quest to Araby. The greatest irony comes at the end when his quest is shown to be merely a shopping trip; and Araby, merely a suburban mall.

Most people interpret the ending as a moment of profound insight, and the language certainly seems to support this interpretation: "Gazing up into the darkness I saw myself as a creature driven and derided by vanity; and my eyes burned with anguish and anger" (para. 37). But here again we see the narrator using inflated language that suggests an ironic stance. So even in the moment of apparent insight, the boy is still playing a heroic role. He hasn't discovered his true self. He's just as self-absorbed and blind in the end as he was at the beginning.

Analyzing Writing Strategies

For more on reasons and support, see Chapter 19, pp. 627–33.

1. To see how interpretive essays develop and **support** their reasons, reread paragraph 5, where Crane argues that the boy cannot see the reality of Mangan's sister, only the two competing images of women he has learned from his religious training and romantic reading. To support this reason, Crane quotes a long pas-

sage from the story. Describe what she does in the rest of the paragraph following the indented quote.

2. One of the **reasons** Crane gives for her interpretation that the boy does not experience "some profound insight about himself" at the end of "Araby" is developed in paragraphs 6–8. Reread these paragraphs and summarize the argument.

Commentary: An Interesting and Clearly Stated Interpretation

Like position papers, evaluations, proposals, and causal speculations, essays interpreting stories make arguments. They state a thesis—asserting an idea about the story's meaning or significance—and try to convince readers that this interpretation is plausible. Like other arguments, the **thesis statement** of an interpretive essay must meet three basic standards: it must be arguable, clear, and appropriately qualified. In addition, the interpretation must be perceived by readers as interesting.

For more on thesis statements, see Chapter 19, pp. 623–26.

Sally Crane's thesis statement identifies itself as arguable by setting up a contrast between her interpretation of the story's ending and that of other readers:

> Readers of "Araby" often [. . .] assume the boy experiences some profound insight about himself when he gazes "up into the darkness." I believe, however, that the boy sees nothing and learns nothing—either about himself or others. He's not self-reflective; he's merely self-absorbed.
>
> The evidence supporting this interpretation is the imagery of blindness and the ironic point of view of the narrator.

Crane summarizes the debate simply: either the boy "experiences some profound insight" at the end or, as Crane herself argues, he "sees nothing and learns nothing."

As we pointed out in the headnote, Crane knew about this debate over the ending from class discussion. Because her essay continues the conversation, she can be confident that the readers of her essay—her instructor and classmates—will find her interpretation interesting, even if they disagree with it. To make her interpretation even more interesting, she uses critical approaches she has learned in English classes. Readers who are not conversant with concepts like *imagery, irony,* and *point of view* may not even understand what Crane is talking about, let alone find it interesting. Your instructor and the Suggestions for Interpreting (pp. 492–93) will help you develop an interpretation that is interesting as well as arguable.

In addition to being arguable and interesting, Crane's thesis statement is clear and appropriately qualified. Readers familiar with the concepts Crane uses are likely to understand her thesis statement, but some readers will probably think it is not appropriately qualified because she makes the broad generalization: "the boy sees nothing and learns nothing." To qualify a thesis statement, writers typically add limiting words like "usually" and "most" in place of absolutes like "nothing" and "all." However, writers who can offer readers convincing support for their generalizations do not hedge. They generalize confidently, letting readers decide for themselves whether the thesis statement is appropriate or needs to be qualified.

Not only does a good thesis statement assert the interpretation, but it also uses key terms to **forecast** the reasons and support that will be offered and to indicate the order in which they will come up in the essay. Crane's first key term, *sees nothing,* introduces the first reason she thinks the boy ultimately "learns nothing"—because throughout the story he cannot understand with any accuracy his own feelings and motivations or anyone else's. In the first sentence of paragraph 2, Crane forecasts that she will support this reason by showing how the story uses "imagery of blindness."

Writers with little experience reading and writing essays interpreting stories may think that stating the thesis at the beginning and forecasting the argument gives too much away. Although stories seldom state their meanings explicitly, essays interpreting stories are expected to do so. Interpretive arguments are most effective when readers have a clear sense of what they are arguing and why.

David Ratinov wrote the following essay about "Araby" for freshman composition. Like Sally Crane, Ratinov is curious about what the boy's final statement might mean. But unlike Crane, Ratinov concludes that the boy does gain insight from seeing the hypocrisy of other characters as well as his own. As you read, notice how Ratinov's interpretation differs from Crane's. (Note: Like Crane, Ratinov cites paragraphs, following his instructor's directions rather than MLA style.)

From Innocence to Insight: "Araby" as an Initiation Story
David Ratinov

"Araby" tells the story of an adolescent boy's initiation into adulthood. The story is narrated by a mature man reflecting upon his adolescence and the events that forced him to face the disillusioning realities of adulthood. The minor characters play a pivotal role in this initiation process. The boy observes the hypocrisy of adults in the priest and Mrs. Mercer; and his vain, self-centered uncle introduces him to another disillusioning aspect of adulthood. The boy's infatuation with the girl ultimately ends in disillusionment, and Joyce uses the specific example of the boy's disillusionment with love as a metaphor for disillusionment with life itself. From the beginning, the boy deludes himself about his relationship with Mangan's sister. At Araby, he realizes the parallel between his own self-delusion and the hypocrisy and vanity of the adult world.

From the beginning, the boy's infatuation with Mangan's sister draws him away from childhood toward adulthood. He breaks his ties with his childhood friends and luxuriates in his isolation. He can think of nothing but his love for her: "From the front window I saw my companions playing below in the street. Their cries reached me weakened and indistinct and, leaning my forehead against the cool glass, I looked over at the dark house where she lived" (para. 16). The friends' cries are weak and indistinct because they are distant emotionally as well as spatially. Like an adult on a quest, he imagines he carries his love as if it were a sacred object, a chalice: "Her image accompanied me even in places the most hostile to romance. [. . .] I imagined that I bore my chalice safely through a throng of foes" (para. 5). Even in the active, distracting marketplace, he is able to retain this image of his pure love. But his love is not pure.

Although he worships Mangan's sister as a religious object, his lust for her is undeniable. He idolizes her as if she were the Virgin Mary: "her figure defined by the light from the half-opened door. [. . .] The light from the lamp opposite our door caught the white curve of her neck, lit up her hair that rested there and, falling, lit up the hand upon the railing" (paras. 3, 9). Yet even this image is sensual with the halo of light accentuating "the white curve of her neck." The language makes obvious that his attraction is physical rather than spiritual: "Her dress swung as she moved her body and the soft rope of her hair tossed from side to side" (para. 3). His desire for her is strong and undeniable: "her name was like a summons to all my foolish blood" (para. 4); "my body was like a harp and her words and gestures were like fingers running upon the wires" (para. 5). But in order to justify his love, to make it socially acceptable, he deludes himself into thinking that his love is pure. He is being hypocritical, although at this point he does not know it.

Hypocrisy is characteristic of the adults in this story. The priest is by far the most obvious offender. What is a man of the cloth doing with books like *The Abbot* (a romantic novel) and *The Memoirs of Vidocq* (a collection of sexually suggestive tales)? These books imply that he led a double life. Moreover, the fact that he had money to give away when he died suggests that he was far from saintly. Similarly, at first glance Mrs. Mercer appears to be religious, but a closer look reveals that she too is materialistic. Her church work—collecting used stamps for some "pious purpose" (presumably to sell for the church)—associates her with money and profit (para. 17). Even her name, Mercer, identifies her as a dealer in merchandise. In addition, her husband is a pawnbroker, a profession that the church frowns upon. Despite being linked to money, she pretends to be pious and respectable. Therefore, like the priest, Mrs. Mercer is hypocritical.

The uncle, as the boy's only living male relative, is a failure as a role model and the epitome of vanity. He is a self-centered old man who cannot handle responsibility: When the boy reminds him on Saturday morning about the bazaar, the uncle brushes him off, devoting all his attention to his own appearance. After being out all afternoon the uncle returns home at 9:00, talking to himself. He rocks the hallstand when hanging up his overcoat. These details suggest that he is drunk. "I could interpret these signs" indicates that this behavior is typical of his uncle (para. 19). The uncle is the only character in the story the boy relies upon, but the uncle fails him. Only after the aunt persuades him does the uncle give the boy the money he promised. From the priest, Mrs. Mercer, and his uncle, the boy learns some fundamental truths about adulthood, but it is only after his visit to Araby that he is able to recognize what he has learned.

Araby to the adolescent represents excitement, a chance to prove the purity of his love and, more abstractly, his hope; however, Araby fulfills none of these expectations. Instead, the boy finds himself in utter disillusionment and despair. Araby is anything but exciting. The trip there is dreary and uneventful, lonely and intolerably slow—not the magical journey he had expected. When he arrives, Araby itself is nearly completely dark and in the process of closing. With his excitement stunted, he can barely remember why he came there (to prove the purity of his love by buying a gift for Mangan's sister).

The young lady selling porcelain and her gentleman friends act as catalysts, caus-   7
ing the boy to recognize the truth of his love for Mangan's sister. Their conversation is
flirtatious—a silly lovers' game that the boy recognizes as resembling his own conversation with Mangan's sister. He concludes that his love for her is no different than the
two gentlemen's love for this "lady" (para. 26). Neither love is pure. He too had only been
playing a game, flirting with a girl and pretending that it was something else and that he
was someone else.

His disillusionment with love is then extended to life in general. Seeing the last rays   8
of hope fading from the top floors of Araby, the boy cries: "I saw myself as a creature
driven and derided by vanity; and my eyes burned with anguish and anger" (para. 37).
At last he makes the connection—by deluding himself, he has been hypocritical and
vain like the adults in his life. Before these realizations he believed that he was driven
by something of value (such as purity of love), but now he realizes that his quest has
been in vain because honesty, truth, and purity are only childish illusions and he can
never return to the innocence of childhood.

Analyzing Writing Strategies

For more on thesis state-
ments, see Chapter 19,
pp. 623–26.

1. Find the thesis statement in Ratinov's essay and underline its key terms. Then
   find and circle where Ratinov uses these key terms in the rest of his essay. Are
   all of the key terms in the essay easy to find, or do any drop out of sight? Also
   determine whether Ratinov's key terms enable him to satisfy the standards of a
   well-written interpretive thesis statement: Is it interesting, arguable, clear, and
   appropriately qualified?

For more on topic sentence
strategies, see Chapter 13,
pp. 560–63.

2. Look closely at each opening sentence in paragraphs 2–8 to see if it functions as
   an effective **topic sentence.** Does it connect the preceding paragraph to the one
   it introduces? What other functions do these opening sentences have?

Commentary: Plausible Reasons and Convincing Support

Ratinov presents three interrelated reasons for his interpretation of the story's ending. His first reason is that the boy deludes himself by imagining his love for Mangan's sister to be noble. Second, he argues that the boy sees the adult characters in
the story as hypocritical and self-centered. Finally, he argues that at the bazaar, the
boy suddenly connects the adults' hypocrisy to his own. His self-delusion ends, thus
completing his initiation into adulthood.

For more on textual evi-
dence, see Chapter 19,
pp. 632–33.

    This chain of reasoning seems plausible. Whether readers accept it as such
depends on how well Ratinov supports the argument. He supports it with **textual
evidence,** primarily quotations of significant passages from the story. He may quote
individual words (paragraph 7), short phrases (paragraph 4), a single sentence (paragraph 8), or strings of sentences (paragraph 2). Unlike Crane who uses a block quo-

tation (paragraph 5), Ratinov's quotes are not long enough to require indentation—more than four lines, according to MLA style. Like Crane, Ratinov uses ellipsis marks enclosed in brackets ([. . .]) to indicate where he has omitted words from his quotation (paragraph 2). Both writers also parenthetically cite the paragraph numbers to indicate where the quotations can be found in the story. By citing paragraphs instead of the author and page number as MLA style dictates, these students are following their instructors' directions. Be sure to follow your instructor's preferred format for citing sources.

For more on MLA quotation style, see Chapter 22, pp. 694–97, and pp. 506–7 in this chapter.

Notice that, like Crane, Ratinov does more than merely quote words from the story. He tells readers what the words mean in the context of the argument he is making. In paragraph 2, for example, Ratinov makes an assertion, which he then supports by quoting two sentences. To make certain that readers understand how the quotation supports his assertion, Ratinov discusses two word choices and their implications.

■ PURPOSE AND AUDIENCE

When you write an essay interpreting a story, you cannot simply tell readers, who may have different interpretations, what you think and expect them to accept your interpretation or even to understand it fully. You need to show how you read the story. Ideally, your readers will see something new in the story after reading your essay. But even if they continue to read the story differently from the way you read it, they may still acknowledge that your interpretation reflects an imaginative, thoughtful reading of the story.

Interpreting a story, then, is not a competition for the "correct" interpretation. Your aim is to develop an interpretation that is insightful and interesting to readers who are already engaged in conversation with other readers about their different ways of reading the story. Readers do not require you to come up with a startling new idea, though they would be pleased if you did. Your readers will be disappointed, however, if your essay is unfocused, if the key terms in your thesis statement are unclear, if you do not give reasons for your interpretation or you do not support them with quotations from the story, or if your essay fails to provide the necessary cues to keep readers on track. Readers will be especially disappointed if they think you are retelling the story rather than developing your own interpretation of the story's meaning or significance.

An Appropriately Presented Subject

The essays interpreting stories in this chapter both focus on a specific subject—one particular story. When an interpretive essay responds to a class discussion or writing assignment, all the writer needs to do is identify the story by name. The readers—the instructor and other students in the class—already know who the author is and when the story was written. Both student writers in this chapter simply refer to "Araby" in the first few words of their opening sentence: "'Araby' tells the story . . ." (Ratinov) and "Readers of 'Araby' . . ." (Crane).

Sometimes, students are asked to choose from a list of stories or to find a story on their own. On such occasions, you may need to give readers a little more information about the story—such as who the author is and the date the story was originally published. To acquaint readers with the story, you also can briefly describe the situation. But avoid retelling the story in detail.

An Interesting and Clearly Stated Interpretation

An interpretation is an idea asserted about the meaning of the story. A good interpretation illuminates the story for readers by adding something interesting to the ongoing conversation in which readers are engaged. The main idea or thesis is usually presented explicitly in a thesis statement near the beginning of the essay and may be summarized again at the conclusion. In addition to being interesting, the thesis statement must be arguable, not a simple statement of fact that anyone who reads the story will know (such as stating that the boy in "Araby" lives in Dublin with his aunt and uncle). Nor should the thesis be obvious, a conclusion that most readers would make (the boy has a crush on Mangan's sister). A good thesis statement should also be clear, not vague or ambiguous, appropriately qualified, not overgeneralized or exaggerated. Crane states her thesis in the second sentence of the opening paragraph: "I believe, however, that the boy sees nothing and learns nothing—either about himself or others." The word *however* refers to the preceding sentence, which summarizes an opposing interpretation expressed by other students in her class.

A good thesis statement forecasts the reasons the writer will use in the essay to develop and support the thesis. Inexperienced writers sometimes are afraid they are ruining the surprise by announcing their thesis and forecasting their argument at the beginning. But readers familiar with this kind of writing have come to expect writers to preview the argument in the opening paragraphs. Explicit forecasting is a convention of literary interpretation similar in purpose to the abstract that precedes many articles in scientific journals. Explicitness does not mean that you have to sacrifice subtlety or complexity in your interpretation. All it means is that you are striving to make your ideas as comprehensible as possible to readers.

Ratinov's opening paragraph provides a good example of explicit forecasting. He explains his main idea,

beginning with his thesis, in the first sentence: "'Araby' tells the story of an adolescent boy's initiation into adulthood." Then, in the five sentences that follow, he previews his argument. Finally, in the last sentence of the opening paragraph, Ratinov provides a succinct summary of his reasons: "At Araby, he realizes the parallel between his own self-delusion and the hypocrisy and vanity of the adult world." Together with *initiation*, the key term in the opening sentence, the last sentence sets out three additional key terms: *self-delusion, hypocrisy,* and *vanity*. These additional key terms signal for readers the steps in Ratinov's argument, specifying what he means when he asserts that the boy's experience can be understood as an initiation story. For key terms to be useful to readers, they must be clear and consistent. Moreover, the reasons that the key terms stand for should be directly connected to the thesis and be well supported.

A Plausible Chain of Reasons with Convincing Support

Writers must argue for their interpretation. They can usually assume their readers will be familiar with the story, but they can never assume readers will understand their interpretation, let alone accept it.

Writers argue for their interpretation not so much to convince readers to adopt it but rather to convince them that it is plausible. An essential strategy writers typically follow is to show readers how they read the story. They do this by supporting their interpretation with textual evidence and explaining what they think these quotations mean in light of the thesis.

The primary source of support for your argument, then, is the story itself, particularly examples gleaned from it. Writers quote, summarize, and paraphrase passages from the story. They do more than just refer readers to a specific passage, however: They also explain the meaning of the passage and its relevance to their thesis. We can see an example of the way writers explain their textual support in the following passage from Ratinov's essay, where he describes what happens when the boy's uncle finally comes home from work, having forgotten that the boy was waiting for him:

> When the boy reminds him on Saturday morning about the bazaar, the uncle brushes him off, devoting all his attention to his own appearance. After being out all afternoon the uncle returns home at 9:00, talking to himself. He rocks the hallstand when hanging up his overcoat. These details suggest that he is drunk. "I could interpret these signs" indicates that this behavior is typical of his uncle. The uncle is the only character in the story the boy relies upon, but the uncle fails him. (paragraph 5)

Notice that Ratinov summarizes the most important details, paraphrasing some of the language, and that he quotes sparingly—only one especially telling phrase. Everything else in this paragraph is Ratinov's commentary. Like Ratinov and Crane, you will want to combine explanatory commentary with quotation, summary, and paraphrase to support and develop your argument.

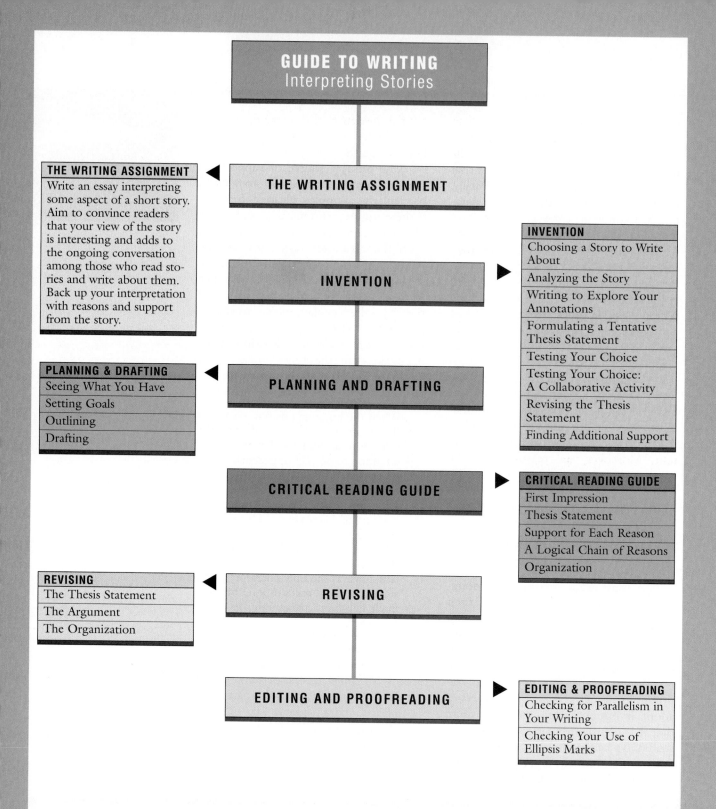

GUIDE TO WRITING
Interpreting Stories

THE WRITING ASSIGNMENT

THE WRITING ASSIGNMENT

Write an essay interpreting some aspect of a short story. Aim to convince readers that your view of the story is interesting and adds to the ongoing conversation among those who read stories and write about them. Back up your interpretation with reasons and support from the story.

INVENTION

INVENTION

Choosing a Story to Write About

Analyzing the Story

Writing to Explore Your Annotations

Formulating a Tentative Thesis Statement

Testing Your Choice

Testing Your Choice: A Collaborative Activity

Revising the Thesis Statement

Finding Additional Support

PLANNING & DRAFTING

Seeing What You Have

Setting Goals

Outlining

Drafting

PLANNING AND DRAFTING

CRITICAL READING GUIDE

CRITICAL READING GUIDE

First Impression

Thesis Statement

Support for Each Reason

A Logical Chain of Reasons

Organization

REVISING

The Thesis Statement

The Argument

The Organization

REVISING

EDITING AND PROOFREADING

EDITING & PROOFREADING

Checking for Parallelism in Your Writing

Checking Your Use of Ellipsis Marks

■ THE WRITING ASSIGNMENT

Write an essay interpreting some aspect of a short story. Aim to convince readers that your view of the story is interesting and adds to the ongoing conversation among those who read stories and write about them. Back up your interpretation with reasons and support from the story.

■ INVENTION

The following activities will help you choose a short story, analyze it, write to explore your annotations, formulate a tentative thesis statement, test your choice, revise your thesis statement, and find additional support in the story for your thesis. To make these activities as useful as possible, spread them out over several days and keep a written record of your invention work.

Choosing a Story to Write About

Choose a story that fascinates, surprises, or puzzles you, one that will be worth spending time on because it excites your imagination. You may have chosen a story already, or your instructor may have assigned you one. If so, go on to the next section, Analyzing the Story.

If you need to choose a story on your own, read several stories before deciding on one to write about. Do not choose a story that seems obvious to you. Your instructor can help you decide whether you have made a good choice.

   Considering Stories Related to Identity and Community.   If you are studying the topic of identity and community, you will see immediately how the stories in this chapter relate to these concerns. Almost any story you choose to write about would allow you to think more about how people develop their individuality and their connections to others. Here are a few widely anthologized stories you might consider writing about:

"The Monkey Garden," by Sandra Cisneros

"The Open Boat," by Stephen Crane

"Fleur," by Louise Erdrich

"A Rose for Emily," by William Faulkner

"My Kinsman, Major Molineux," by Nathaniel Hawthorne

"A Clean, Well-Lighted Place," by Ernest Hemingway

"The Lottery," by Shirley Jackson

"The Metamorphosis," by Franz Kafka

"The Ones Who Walk away from Omelas," by Ursula Le Guin

"A Pair of Tickets," by Amy Tan

"Everyday Use," by Alice Walker

Considering Stories Related to Work and Career. "The Use of Force" (in this chapter) would be useful in writing about the topic of work and career. Here are some additional stories you might consider for exploring this topic:

"Sonny's Blues," by James Baldwin

"The Yellow Wallpaper," by Charlotte Perkins Gilman

"The Birthmark," by Nathaniel Hawthorne

"Reena," by Paule Marshall

"Shiloh," by Bobbie Ann Mason

"Bartleby the Scrivener," by Herman Melville

"Picasso," by Gertrude Stein

"The Catbird Seat," by James Thurber

"A&P," by John Updike

"Why I Live at the P.O.," by Eudora Welty

Analyzing the Story

To help you analyze the story, this section offers suggestions for interpreting that may help you annotate for potentially meaningful details. As you annotate the story, your goal will be to decide on a thesis, an idea about the story's meaning, for which you can develop a reasoned, well-supported argument.

Choosing a Suggestion for Interpreting. *Select one or more suggestions for interpreting that will help you focus on some aspects of the story that seem significant or about which you have questions.* For example:

- If on first reading the story you wondered why a character acts in a particular way, look at the suggestions for interpreting *character.*

- If you were struck by the language used to describe the scene, look at the suggestions for interpreting *setting.*

- If you noticed any kind of pattern in the events in the story, look at the suggestions for interpreting *plot structure.*

- If you had questions about the way the story is narrated, look at the suggestions for interpreting *point of view.*

- If you recognized a familiar motif (for example, a coming-of-age story) or theme (alienation), look at the suggestions for interpreting *literary motif* or *theme.*

You may want to read and annotate the story several times, keeping in mind the different suggestions for interpreting, before you decide on an idea you can use as a working thesis for your draft. Notice also that rereading the story with different suggestions in mind can help you to discover how different aspects of the story work together and can lead you to construct a more fully developed thesis.

Character

To interpret the character psychologically:

- Identify the character's motivations, inner conflicts, and doubts.
- Consider whether the character changes or learns anything in the course of the story.
- Focus on how the character relates to other characters, noting how the character deals with intimacy, commitment, and responsibility.
- Note whether the character seems depressed, manic, abusive, fearful, egotistical, or paranoid. Look for another character who may represent the character's alter ego—the "flip side" of the character's personality.

To interpret the character ethically or morally:

- Decide what you consider to be the character's virtues or vices.
- Consider what influences your judgment of the character—something in the story (such as what the narrator or another character says), something you bring to the story (your views of right and wrong, based on your family upbringing or religious teachings), or something else.
- See whether any of the other characters have different moral values that could be compared and contrasted to the character's values.

To interpret the character from a social perspective:

- Consider how the character fits into and is defined by society—in terms of race, ethnicity, socioeconomic class, sexual orientation, age, or gender.
- Notice who in the story exercises power over whom, what causes the difference in power, what its effects are, and whether the balance of power changes during the story.

Setting

To interpret the setting in relation to the action, mood, or characters:

- Consider how the setting signals what is happening and whether it comments (possibly ironically) on the action.
- Notice how the setting affects the mood—for example, how it heightens suspense or foreboding.

- Look for cause-and-effect connections between the setting and what characters are thinking, doing, or feeling.

To interpret the setting historically or culturally:

- Think of how the historical period or cultural context in which the story is set might affect what happens and does not happen and why.
- Imagine how the meaning might be different if the historical time or cultural situation were different.

To interpret the setting metaphorically or symbolically:

- Assume that the setting is a projection of the thoughts and feelings of the narrator, and then consider what the setting tells you about the narrator's state of mind.
- Assume that the setting symbolizes the social relations among characters in the story, and then consider what the setting tells you about these relationships.
- Assume that the setting stands for something outside the characters' control (such as nature, God, or some aspect of society), and then consider what the setting tells you about the pressures and rules under which the characters function.

Plot Structure

To interpret the plot as realistic (as resembling real-life experience):

- Think of the story as a sequence of stages or steps leading somewhere, mark where each new stage begins, and consider how the sequence could be understood.
- Think of the story as having not only a main plot but also subplots that mirror, undercut, or comment in some way on the main plot.

To interpret the plot as surrealistic (as having symbolic rather than literal meaning):

- Think of the story as a series of images, more like a collage or a dream rather than a realistic portrayal of actual events, and look for ways of understanding the arrangement of these images.

Point of View

To interpret the point of view in terms of what the narrator can see:

- Consider whether the narrator is a character in the story or an all-knowing, disembodied voice who knows what every character thinks, feels, and does.
- Identify any important insights or ideas the narrator has.

- Consider how factors such as the narrator's gender, age, and ethnicity may influence what he or she notices as important.
- Consider what the narrator is not able to see or what the narrator distorts—for example, certain truths about himself or herself, about other characters, or about what happens in the story.

To interpret the point of view in terms of how the narrator represents what he or she sees:

- Characterize the narrator's tone at various points in the story—for example, as satirical, celebratory, angry, bitter, or optimistic.
- Infer what there is about the narrator (or about the situation) that could account for each tone you identify.
- Consider what special agenda or motive may have led the narrator to this particular way of describing characters and scenes or telling the story.
- Imagine how your interpretation might differ if the story were narrated from another character's point of view or by an all-knowing voice.

Literary Motif or Theme

To interpret the story in terms of a traditional story motif (or an ironic reversal of the tradition), consider whether it could be seen as:

- An initiation (or coming-of-age or rite-of-passage) story
- A heroic quest (for love, truth, fame, fortune, salvation of oneself or the community)
- A story about a character's disillusionment or fall from innocence
- A story about family or surrogate families
- A story about storytelling (or some other art) or about becoming a writer or an artist

To interpret the story in terms of a common literary theme, consider whether the following themes are found in the story:

- The American Dream
- Dynamics of Power
- Social Construction of Femininity or Masculinity
- Popular Culture
- Race Relations
- Alienation
- Imagination

For examples of Ratinov's
annotations and invention
writings, see the Writer
at Work section on pp.
507–10.

Annotating with the Suggestions for Interpreting in Mind.   *Annotate details in the story that relate to the focus you have chosen for your interpretation.* To annotate, simply underline, bracket, or highlight words and phrases that seem significant. Circle words to be defined and write their definitions in the margins. Draw lines to connect related words and images. Make marginal notes indicating what you are learning about the story by annotating with the suggestions for interpreting in mind. Write down any further questions you have as you annotate.

Writing to Explore Your Annotations

Write at least a page exploring what you have discovered about the story from analyzing it with the suggestions for interpreting in mind. If you have reread the story several times with different suggestions for interpreting, you may be able to write several pages.

It may help to begin by reviewing the suggestions for interpreting you used and writing your thoughts about each suggestion. For example, if you focused on the suggestions to interpret the character psychologically, you could begin by explaining what you now think are the character's motivations, inner conflicts, and doubts. Then you could go on to discuss how the character changes—what precipitated the change, how it proceeded, how you can tell the character has changed, and why the change is significant.

You may also find it productive to write about patterns of words, figures of speech, characters, or events you found as you were annotating. For instance, when David Ratinov reflected on the annotations he had made using the suggestions for interpreting character, he discovered that several minor characters, in addition to the main character, were hypocritical.

Formulating a Tentative Thesis Statement

Using the suggestions for interpreting, you have annotated the story and explored your annotations. Your aim now is to list ideas you can support with details from the story, explore the connections among these ideas, and draft a tentative thesis statement.

Listing Ideas.   *Write several sentences stating the ideas you have discovered using one or more of the suggestions for interpreting to annotate the story and to explore your annotations.* The only requirement is that you feel confident that you could find specific details and quotations in the story to support each idea. Do not worry about how these ideas relate to one another or even about whether they are contradictory. Simply write down every idea you can think of.

The suggestions for interpreting you used to annotate the story and explore your annotations should lead you, as they led Ratinov, to assert your ideas about the story. For example, writing about several of the characters in "Araby" convinced Ratinov that he could confidently assert the idea that "all the adult characters are hypocrites."

Writing to Develop Connections among Your Ideas. *Write for ten minutes contemplating how the ideas you listed can make a chain of reasons leading to a general conclusion or main idea about the story that would be your thesis.* As you write, you may decide to drop some of the ideas, reformulate others, or add new ideas. Focus your writing on these questions:

- What are the key terms in each idea? (For example, the key term in Ratinov's idea that "all the adult characters are hypocrites" is *hypocrite*.)
- Could any of these ideas be links in a chain of reasons leading to some new, main idea about the story I can make now? (For example, Ratinov links the idea that the boy in "Araby" is *self-deluded* and the idea that adults are *hypocrites* to the boy's discovery that he is a hypocrite too [key terms italicized].)

Drafting the Thesis Statement. *Now that you have asserted some ideas, thought about what their key terms enable you to say about the story, and considered how the terms could work together, write a few sentences stating your main idea or thesis and your reasons or supporting ideas.* Try completing the following sentence for each reason:

> **I think [main idea] about the story because [reason 1, 2, etc.].**

Formulating a thesis statement (even one you know you will revise later) can be a challenge. It may help to review the thesis statements David Ratinov and Sally Crane wrote and to think about how they worded their key terms (italicized):

> "Araby tells the story of an adolescent boy's *initiation* into adulthood [. . .] [by which] he realizes the parallel between his own *self-delusion* and the *hypocrisy* and *vanity* of the adult world. (Ratinov)

> I believe, however, that the boy *sees nothing* and *learns nothing*—either about himself or others. He's not self-reflective; he's merely *self-absorbed*. (Crane)

As you draft your own tentative thesis statement, pay attention to the language you use. It should be clear and unambiguous, emphatic but appropriately qualified. Although you will most probably refine your thesis statement as you draft and revise your essay, trying now to articulate it will help give your planning and drafting direction and impetus.

For more on thesis statements, see Chapter 13, pp. 557–58, and Chapter 19, pp. 623–26.

Testing Your Choice

Now that you have developed a tentative thesis statement, you need to be sure that it says what you want it to say, that your readers will find your interpretation interesting, and that you will be able to find support for it in the story. Review the key terms in your thesis to make sure you can find evidence for each point. Also consider whether your ideas still work together to form a logical chain of reasons. If your ideas still seem workable, you have probably made a good choice. However, if your ideas seem unworkable—that is, if you now think you cannot find examples in the story to support your ideas, or if your ideas seem too obvious or factual—you may need to return to Formulating a Tentative Thesis Statement or even to Analyzing the Story to develop your ideas or find new ones. You even may need to choose a different story and start over. If you are thinking of starting over, discuss the possibility with your instructor before doing so.

**Testing
Your Choice:
A Collaborative
Activity**

At this point, you will find it helpful to get together with two or three other students who have read your story and to get responses to one another's thesis statements. Your partners' feedback will help you determine whether your thesis or main idea is workable and whether you can construct a well-reasoned argument to support it.

> *Writers:* Take turns reading your tentative thesis statement aloud. Then take notes as your partners tell you what your thesis statement leads them to expect from your essay.

> *Listeners:* As the writer speaks, note down what you think are the key terms in the thesis statement. Remember that each of these key terms stands for an idea or a link in the chain of reasons arguing for the overall thesis. So tell the writer what the ideas are that you expect will be developed in the essay. Also indicate if you think the writer will have difficulty supporting any of these ideas, if you do not see how the ideas work together, or if you think any of the ideas are obvious or uninteresting. For example, if you were a member of David Ratinov's group, you might have said that his thesis statement led you to expect his essay to demonstrate three things: (1) the boy is *self-deluded,* (2) the adults are *hypocritical,* and (3) the boy ultimately realizes he has been self-deluded because of his *vanity,* and that this discovery completes his *initiation* into adulthood (key terms are italicized).

Revising the Thesis Statement

Try to improve your thesis statement. Consider whether you want to change your argument to alter the thesis statement or the reasons for it. Clear up any ambiguity or vagueness in your key terms and qualify them more appropriately if necessary. Make explicit why you think your thesis is interesting and arguable by indicating how other readers disagree.

Finding Additional Support

If you do not have enough support for your reasons, reread the story, making additional annotations in passages where you find details you might be able to use. With your key terms in mind, evaluate the support you already have to determine whether it is sufficient to explain and illustrate each reason. Wherever support is lacking, fill it in by doing further annotating. If you cannot find any support for one of your reasons, you need to reconsider whether you should use that reason.

If you find details in the story that contradict any of your reasons, do not ignore the contradiction. Instead, analyze the details to see how you should modify your argument.

■ PLANNING AND DRAFTING

This section will help you review your invention notes, determine specific goals for your essay, make an outline, and get started on your first draft.

Seeing What You Have

Revise your invention writing and annotated text. If some time has elapsed since you last read the story, you may want to reread it now. As you review what you have discovered about the story, consider whether your thesis is arguable and whether you have stated it clearly and directly. Also decide whether you have sufficient support and whether you might have overlooked anything important that could contradict or weaken your argument.

If you cannot find support for all of your reasons, you may not be ready to write a complete draft. You may, however, be ready to begin drafting the parts for which you do have support. Then you can return to the story to search for support for your other reasons. But if your ideas still seem obvious or not likely to be interesting to your readers, you may need to reconsider the direction in which you are going and possibly begin again.

Setting Goals

Before you start drafting, set some goals to guide the decisions you will make as you draft. Consider what you want to say about the story you are interpreting. Here are some questions that will help you set your goals and enable you to get across to your readers exactly what you want to tell them about the story:

Your Purpose and Readers

- Are my readers likely to know this story? If not, how much do I need to tell them about the story so that they can follow my argument? If so, how can I lead them to see my interpretation as interesting, whether or not they agree with it?

- Should I acknowledge readers' possible questions or differing interpretations, as Crane does?

The Interpretation

- How can I explicitly state my thesis and forecast my plan, as Crane and Ratinov do, without sounding stilted or mechanical?
- Which key terms will accurately forecast my reasons?

Reasons and Support

- How can I organize my reasons so that my readers will see how they interrelate or form a chain of reasoning, as Crane and Ratinov do?
- How can I integrate quotations smoothly into my writing?
- How can I connect quotations to my reasons so that readers know why I have chosen these passages to quote?
- How can I make my argument sound authoritative and thoughtful?
- How much textual support must I include for my argument to be convincing?

The Ending

- Should I repeat my key terms, as Crane and Ratinov do?
- Should I reiterate my thesis statement?
- Should I end with a provocative question or with larger implications suggested by my interpretation?

Outlining

For more on scratch outlining, see Chapter 12, pp. 540–41.

At this point, you should try to develop a plan for your draft by composing an informal scratch outline, a simple list of your reasons and support in the order you will introduce them. Make sure that the forecasts in your thesis statement accurately predict the order in which the reasons will appear in the essay. Remember that an outline is meant to be a tentative plan; you may make further discoveries as you draft that will require you to change your plan.

Drafting

You may want to review the general advice on drafting in Chapter 1, pp. 16–17.

Start drafting your essay, keeping in mind the goals you set while you were planning and your purpose for writing—to convince readers that your thesis is plausible. Explain your reasons fully and directly. Do not expect readers to guess at how a supporting quotation illustrates a reason; spell out the connections you want readers to see. Remember that your readers may have different ways of interpreting the passages to which you refer. Indicate exactly why you are citing specific details from the story and how you interpret the writer's choice of words.

If you get stuck while drafting, explore the problem by using some of the writing activities in the Invention section of this chapter. Perhaps the most important advice to remember about drafting is to write quickly without worrying about grammar and spelling. Later you can make corrections.

Now is the time to get a good critical reading of your draft. Most writers find it helpful to have someone else read and comment on their drafts, and all writers know how much they learn about writing when they read other writers' drafts. Your instructor may arrange such a reading as part of your coursework. If not, you can ask a classmate, friend, or family member to read your draft. You could also seek comments from a tutor at your campus writing center. The guidelines in this section can be used by *anyone* reviewing an essay interpreting a story. (If you are unable to have someone else read your draft, turn ahead to the Revising section, where you will find advice for reading your own draft critically.)

▶ **If You Are the Writer.**   In order to provide focused, helpful comments, your reader must know your essay's intended audience, your purpose, and a problem in the draft that you need help solving. The reader must also have read the story you are writing about. Attach a copy of the story to your draft if you think your reader may not already have one, and write out brief answers to the following questions at the top of your draft:

- *Readers.* How do you think your interpretation builds on or contradicts the interpretations your readers are likely to have of the story?

- *Purpose.* What specifically do you want your readers to learn about the story from reading your essay?

- *Problem.* What is the single most important problem you see in your draft?

▶ **If You Are the Reader.**   Use the following guidelines to help you give critical comments to others on essays interpreting stories:

1. *Read for a First Impression.* Read first to grasp the writer's interpretation of the story. As you read, mark in the margin any passages that are particularly convincing as well as any that seem unclear or unsupported. Remember that even if you interpret the story differently, your goal now is to help the writer present his or her interpretation as effectively as possible.

   Write a one-sentence summary of the essay's thesis. Also indicate generally whether you think the writer's interpretation makes sense. Next, consider the problem the writer identified. If the problem will be covered by one of the other questions listed here, deal with it there. Otherwise, respond to the writer's concerns now.

2. *Evaluate the Thesis Statement and How Well It Forecasts the Argument.* Find the thesis statement, and underline its key terms. If you cannot find the thesis statement or cannot identify the key terms, let the writer know. Evaluate the thesis statement on the basis of whether it makes an interesting and arguable assertion (rather than a statement of fact or an obvious point), is clear and precise (neither ambiguous nor vague), and is appropriately qualified (neither overgeneralized nor exaggerated).

Then skim the rest of the essay, underlining each key term as it is brought up. If you cannot find a key term later in the essay but you do see where the reason it stands for is developed and supported, write the key term in the margin to let the writer know that it should be added. If a reason introduced by a key term in the thesis statement is left out of the essay altogether, tell the writer. Also note any important reasons that are developed in the essay but are not announced in the thesis statement.

3. *Indicate Whether Each Reason Is Well Supported.* Look closely at the sections where the reasons are developed. Note whether each reason is supported adequately with textual evidence such as quotations, paraphrases, or summaries. Indicate where support is lacking and let the writer know if you do not understand how a particular quotation relates to the reason it is supposed to support. Point out any passages in the story that the writer could use to bolster this part of the argument or that undermine it.

4. *Evaluate the Argument as a Chain of Reasons.* Summarize briefly for the writer your understanding of how the reasons work together to argue for the thesis. If you do not see how a particular reason fits in, say so. Also note where logical connections linking the chain of reasons could be added, strengthened, or made more explicit.

5. *Suggest How the Organization Could Be Improved.* Consider the overall plan, perhaps by making a scratch outline. Note any places where the argument is hard to follow or where transitions are missing or do not work well.

   • Look again at the *beginning* to see if it adequately forecasts the rest of the essay.
   • Look at the *ending* to see if it is too abrupt, repetitive, or goes off in a new and surprising direction.

6. *Give the Writer Your Final Thoughts.* What is the draft's strongest part? What part is most in need of further work?

■ REVISING

This section will help you get an overview of your draft and revise it accordingly.

Getting an Overview

Consider your draft as a whole, following these two steps:

1. *Reread.* If at all possible, put the draft aside for a day or two. When you do reread, start by reconsidering your purpose. Then read the draft straight through, trying to see it as your intended readers will.

2. *Outline.* Make a scratch outline to get an overview of the essay's development. This outline should identify the key terms and the reasons they stand for as well as the kinds of support you provide for each.

For more on scratch outlining, see Chapter 11, pp. 518–19.

Charting a Plan for Revision. You may want to make a double-column chart like the following one to keep track of any problems you need to solve. In the left-hand column, list the basic features of essays interpreting stories. As you analyze your draft and study any comments you have received from others, note the problems you want to solve in the right-hand column.

Turn to pp. 488–89 to review the basic features.

Basic Features	*Problems to Solve*
An appropriately presented subject	
An interesting and clearly stated interpretation	
A plausible chain of reasons with convincing support	

Analyzing the Basic Features of Your Own Draft. Turn now to the Critical Reading Guide on the preceding pages. Using this guide, identify problems you now see in your draft. Note the problems on your revision chart.

Studying Critical Comments. Review all of the comments you have received from other readers. For each comment, look at the draft to determine what might have led the reader to make that particular point. Try to be objective about any criticism. Ideally, these comments will help you see your draft as others see it. Add to your revision chart any problems readers have identified.

Carrying Out Revisions

Having identified problems in your draft, you now need to figure out solutions and —most important—to carry them out. Basically, you have three ways of finding solutions:

1. Review your invention and planning notes for additional support and ideas.

2. Do further invention writing to answer questions your readers raised or to provide material you or your readers think is needed.

3. Look back at the student essays by Crane and Ratinov to see how other writers have solved similar problems.

The following suggestions, which are organized according to the basic features on your revision chart, will get you started solving some common writing problems in essays interpreting stories. For now, focus on solving the problems identified on your chart. Avoid tinkering with grammar and punctuation; that will come later when you edit.

Your Purpose and Readers

- Will readers recognize which story is the subject of this interpretation? State the title early on in the essay. Consider whether readers need to know the author or date of publication.

- Do readers need to be reminded about what happens in the story? If readers may not remember much about the story, briefly describe it for them, but avoid giving too much plot summary.

The Interpretation

- ***Is your thesis statement hard for readers to find?*** State explicitly at the beginning what your essay will demonstrate, announcing your thesis and forecasting the reasons you will use to argue for it.

- ***Is your thesis statement perceived as unarguable or uninteresting?*** Revise the thesis to make it clear that you are not stating a simple fact about the story or making an obvious point. Relate your interpretation to class discussion, as Crane does.

- ***Are your key terms unclear or not appropriately qualified?*** Revise your key terms to avoid ambiguity and vagueness. If you need to limit or qualify your thesis or reasons, add words like *some* or *usually*.

- ***Are the key terms in the thesis statement not repeated later in the essay?*** Delete any key term from the thesis statement that you do not discuss later in the essay or add language that develops and supports the reason for which this key term stands. If necessary, rewrite the paragraph's topic sentence using the key term.

Reasons and Support

- ***Does the thesis or do any of the reasons used to argue for it seem superficial or thin?*** Try developing your reasons more fully by comparing or contrasting related reasons; classifying your reasons or dividing them into their subparts; or discussing the social, political, and cultural implications of your way of interpreting the story. Consider elaborating on your reasons by rereading the story with another related suggestion for interpreting in mind.

- ***Does support seem lacking?*** Add textual evidence by quoting, paraphrasing, or summarizing key passages. Focus your discussion more closely on the writer's choice of words, explaining what particular word choices mean in relation to your reasons. Consider using other kinds of support, such as information about the story's historical or cultural context.

- ***Does the connection between a reason and its support seem vague?*** Clarify your point by explaining why you think the support you have given illustrates the reason. Do not simply quote from the story. Explain how you interpret each quotation, which words seem significant, and how they demonstrate the point you are making.

- *Are there contradictions or gaps in your argument?* You may need to rewrite sections of your essay to eliminate contradictions or fill in gaps. Before cutting anything, consider whether the contradiction is real or apparent. If it is only apparent, explain more fully and clearly how your reasons relate logically to one another as well as to your thesis. To fill in gaps, you may have to lay out your train of thought more explicitly so that readers can more easily follow your logic.

The Organization

- *Is the essay hard to follow?* Provide more explicit cues: better forecasting, clear topic sentences, logical transitions, brief summaries.

- *Does the opening fail to prepare readers for your argument?* You may need to revise it to forecast your reasons more directly or to give readers a clearer context to help them understand your point.

- *Does the ending seem abrupt?* You may need to tie all the strands of the essay together, reiterate your thesis, or discuss its implications.

▨ EDITING AND PROOFREADING

Now is the time to check your revised draft for problems in grammar, punctuation, and mechanics and to consider matters of style. It may help you to recognize problems if you study your draft in separate passes—first for paragraphs, then for sentences, and finally for words. Our research has identified several problems that occur often in essays interpreting stories: lack of parallel structure (a matter of style) and the misuse of ellipsis marks (a matter of punctuation). The following guidelines will help you check your draft for these common problems.

Checking for Parallelism in Your Writing. When you present similar items together, you must present them in the same grammatical form. All items in a series should be parallel in form—all nouns, all prepositional phrases, all adverb clauses, and so on. Notice, for example, how Sally Crane edited her first-draft sentences to introduce parallel structure:

▶ I believe, however, that the boy sees nothing and ~~is incapable of learning~~ *learns nothing—either*

about himself or others◦ ~~because he is so~~ self-absorbed. *He's not self-reflective; he's merely*

▶ This image comes more from ~~his reading~~ than from ~~his actual observation~~. *what he's read* *anything he's observed.*

▶ The greatest irony comes at the end when his quest is exposed as merely a

shopping trip∕ *and Araby as merely a suburban mall.*

The parallelism makes Crane's sentences easier to read and helps her emphasize some of her points. The parallelism of "sees nothing" and "learns nothing" emphasizes the relationship between these two conditions in a way that the first-draft wording did not; the same is true of "what he's read" and "anything he's observed." In the final sentence, Crane added a parallel phrase as an ironic comment.

Following are several more examples, each edited to show ways of making writing parallel.

▶ To Kafka, loneliness, ~~being isolated~~ *isolation,* and regrets are the price of freedom.

▶ Sarah really cares about her brother and ~~to maintain~~ *values* their relationship.

She lets us know that she was injured by her mother's abuse but avoids saying what she felt after the incident, how others reacted to the incident, and ~~the~~ *what* physical pain she endured.

Checking Your Use of Ellipsis Marks. Ellipsis marks are three spaced periods. They are used to indicate that something has been omitted from quoted text. You will often quote other sources when you interpret a story, and you must be careful to use ellipsis marks to indicate places where you delete material from a quotation. If you are using MLA style, enclose the ellipsis marks in brackets to distinguish them from ellipses the author may have used. Look, for example, at the way Sally Crane uses ellipsis marks in quoting from "Araby."

ORIGINAL TEXT   North Richmond Street, being blind, was a quiet street except at the hour when the Christian Brothers' School set the boys free. An uninhabited house of two storeys stood at the blind end, detached from its neighbours in a square ground.

QUOTED WITH   The street is "blind," with an "uninhabited house [. . .] at the
ELLIPSIS MARKS   blind end."

These ellipsis marks indicate an omission in the middle of the sentence.

If you are using MLA style, follow these few simple rules about using ellipsis marks:

• When you delete text in the middle of a quoted passage, use a period immediately after the closing bracket if what remains forms a complete sentence.

• Use ellipsis marks at the end of a quotation only if the words you are quoting do not form a complete sentence.

• Insert a single space between ellipsis points. Leave a space before the opening bracket and after the closing bracket, but do not leave a space between the opening bracket and the first ellipsis point or between the closing bracket and the last ellipsis point.

- Single words and brief phrases can be quoted without ellipsis marks.

For more on ellipsis marks, see Chapter 22, pp. 694–95.

The following sentences by students have been edited to correct problems with the use of ellipsis marks:

We learn that a former tenant of the boy's house, "⌒a priest, had died in

the back drawing room ⌐[. . .] He had been a very charitable priest; in his will

he had left all his money to institutions and the furniture of his house to his

sister."

The boys lived on "a quiet street⌐ ⌐"

The light shone on "⌐the white border of a petticoat⌐ ⌐"

A WRITER AT WORK

■ USING THE SUGGESTIONS FOR INTERPRETING TO ANALYZE A STORY

In this Writer at Work section, you will see some of the invention work that David Ratinov did for his essay interpreting "Araby," which appears earlier in this chapter (pp. 484–86). Using the Guide to Writing in this book, Ratinov chose the suggestions for interpreting character to guide his analysis of the story. As you will see, he annotated a portion of the story focusing on two characters (Mrs. Mercer and the boy's uncle), wrote to explore his annotations on the passages, and listed ideas for formulating his tentative thesis statement. You will be able to infer from his invention work how his ideas came to form the thesis he developed for his final essay.

Annotating

Ratinov annotated paragraphs 13–24 of "Araby" as he reread them with the suggestions for interpreting character in mind. The annotated passages are reproduced here. Notice the diversity of his annotations. In the text itself, he underlined key words, circled words to be defined, and connected related words and ideas. In the margin, Ratinov defined words, made comments, and posed questions. He also expressed his tentative insights, reactions, and judgments.

2nd mention of uncle fussing—vain? Irritable? rude

On Saturday morning I reminded my uncle that I wished to go to the bazaar in the 13 evening. He was fussing at the hallstand, looking for the hatbrush, and answered me curtly:

"Yes, boy, I know." 14

always unkind to the boy?
uncle's effect on the boy

As he was in the hall I could not go into the front parlour and lie at the window. I left 15 the house in bad humour and walked slowly towards the school. The air was pitilessly raw and already my heart misgave me.

uncle will be late sudden change in mood; big contrast

When I came home to dinner my uncle had not yet been home. Still it was early. I sat 16 staring at the clock for some time and, when its ticking began to irritate me, I left the room.

I mounted the staircase and gained the upper part of the house. The high cold empty

liberated from uncle?

gloomy rooms liberated me and I went from room to room singing. From the front window I saw my companions playing below in the street. Their cries reached me weakened and

isolated from friends

indistinct and, leaning my forehead against the cool glass, I looked over at the dark house where she lived. I may have stood there for an hour, seeing nothing but the brown-clad

romantic, even sensual

figure cast by my imagination, touched discreetly by the lamplight at the curved neck, at the hand upon the railings and at the border below the dress.

merchandise

talkative

When I came downstairs again I found Mrs. Mercer sitting at the fire. She was an old 17 garrulous woman, a pawnbroker's widow, who collected used stamps for some pious pur-

hypocritically religious

pose. I had to endure the gossip of the tea-table. The meal was prolonged beyond an hour

boy doesn't seem to like or trust the adults

and still my uncle did not come. Mrs. Mercer stood up to go: she was sorry she couldn't wait any longer, but it was after eight o'clock and she did not like to be out late, as the night air was bad for her. When she had gone I began to walk up and down the room, clenching my

uncle and Mercer both try to give a false impression

fists. My aunt said:

aunt seems pious too

"I'm afraid you may put off your bazaar for this night of Our Lord." 18

At nine o'clock I heard my uncle's latchkey in the halldoor. I heard him talking to him- 19 self and heard the hallstand rocking when it had received the weight of his overcoat. I could

boy knows uncle is drunk

interpret these signs. When he was midway through his dinner I asked him to give me the money to go to the bazaar. He had forgotten.

boy's fears are justified excuses

"The people are in bed and after their first sleep now," he said. 20

I did not smile. My aunt said to him energetically: 21

aunt to the rescue

"Can't you give him the money and let him go? You've kept him late enough as it is." 22

My uncle said he was very sorry he had forgotten. He said he believed in the old say- 23 *hypocritical what a bore!*
ing: "All work and no play makes Jack a dull boy." He asked me where I was going and, *boy determined to go to bazaar to buy girl a gift*
when I had told him a second time he asked me did I know *The Arab's Farewell to His Steed*.
When I left the kitchen he was about to recite the opening lines of the piece to my aunt.

I held a florin tightly in my hand as I strode down Buckingham Street towards the sta- 24 *boy focused on his task*
tion. The sight of the streets thronged with buyers and glaring with gas recalled to me the
purpose of my journey. I took my seat in a third-class carriage of a deserted train. After an *language shows boy's impatience*
intolerable delay the train moved out of the station slowly. It crept onward among ruinous
houses and over the twinkling river. At Westland Row Station a crowd of people pressed to
the carriage doors; but the porters moved them back, saying that it was a special train for
the bazaar. I remained alone in the bare carriage. In a few minutes the train drew up beside *boy still isolated*
an improvised wooden platform. I passed out on to the road and saw by the lighted dial of
a clock that it was ten minutes to ten. In front of me was a large building which displayed
the magical name.

As you can see, annotating this section of the story with the suggestions for interpreting character in mind led Ratinov to notice how negatively Mrs. Mercer and the uncle are portrayed by Joyce.

Exploratory Writing

Following the instructions in Writing to Explore Your Annotations in this chapter, Ratinov discovered that the two characters are criticized primarily because of their hypocrisy. Here is what he wrote to explore this portion of his annotations:

```
Mrs. Mercer may be a good neighbor to the boy's aunt, but the
boy dislikes her. Joyce plants many clues that she is a hyp-
ocrite. She thinks of herself as a good religious Christian,
but she is pious (an exaggerated Christian, not a believable
one), she collects stamps to sell for charity instead of doing
good works firsthand (my guess), and she gossips. Her husband
got his money in an un-Christian way. Does the boy know all
this or only the narrator much later? I'm sure the boy senses
it. He says he has to endure Mrs. Mercer and her gossiping
with his aunt. Now that I've looked over the evidence for the
uncle's hypocrisy, it seems that his unguardianlike actions
toward the boy--his irresponsibility toward him--are just as
```

```
big a flaw as is his hypocrisy. He seems to be trying to hide
something by drinking and being obsessive about his appear-
ance--a failure to advance at work? He tries to impress people
with a bigger house than he can afford. Says he believes in
things that don't apply to his own actions. I think I can show
that he's a hypocrite like Mrs. Mercer. Because the boy dis-
trusts him, he must sense this hypocrisy.
```

As Ratinov wrote about the hypocrisy of Mrs. Mercer and the uncle, he became increasingly confident that he had not only an interesting idea, but one he could also find support for in the story.

Listing Ideas for the Thesis

Following the advice given in Formulating a Tentative Thesis Statement in this chapter, Ratinov listed ideas he felt confident he could support. In all, he listed five ideas, but notice that the first one came from the exploratory writing he did about Mrs. Mercer and the uncle (shown above):

```
-- All the adult characters are hypocrites.

-- If this is just a story about romance, then all the adult
   characters wouldn't have to be so weak and flawed.

-- Mangan's sister is different from the adults, but through
   her the boy has to face up to what the adult world is all
   about.

-- The adults are initiating the boy into adulthood, but he
   doesn't see it until the end of the story.

-- Growing up means being able to see the world for what it
   actually is, not what you want it to be.
```

From these ideas about hypocrisy, romance, initiation into the adult world, and the connection between growing up and learning to see reality, Ratinov was able to devise the thesis statement he eventually used in his final essay.

Now that you have read and discussed several essays interpreting a story and have written such an essay yourself, take some time to think critically about what you have learned. What problems did you encounter while you were writing your essay, and how did you solve them? How did reading other essays that interpret a story influence your own essay? What ideas do you have about the social and cultural dimensions of literary interpretation?

Reflecting on Your Writing

Write a one-page explanation, telling your instructor about a problem you encountered in writing your essay and how you solved it. Before you begin, gather all of your writing—invention and planning notes, drafts and critical comments, revision plan, and final revision. Review these materials as you complete this writing task.

1. *Identify* one *significant writing problem you encountered while writing the essay.* Do not be concerned with grammar and punctuation; focus instead on a problem specific to writing an interpretation. For example, were you uncertain about which suggestions for interpreting to use for analyzing the story? Did you puzzle over how best to state your thesis and forecast your argument? Did you have trouble deciding which passages from the story to use as support or whether to quote, summarize, or paraphrase them?

2. *Determine how you came to recognize the problem.* When did you first discover it—when you were trying to analyze the story, to find supporting evidence, or to sequence your reasons? If someone else pointed out the problem to you, can you now see signs of it in your invention work? If so, where specifically? When you first recognized the problem, how did you respond?

3. *Reflect on how you went about solving the problem.* Did you consider using a different suggestion for interpreting? Did you reread one of the essays in this chapter to see how another writer handled a similar problem, or did you do additional invention work such as rereading the story to fill in gaps in your original annotations? Did you reword, reorganize, or simply cut something that was problematic? If you talked about the problem with another student, a tutor, or your instructor, how did talking about it help?

4. *Write a brief explanation of the problem and your solution.* Be as specific as possible in reconstructing your efforts. Quote from your invention notes or draft essay, others' critical comments, your revision plan, and your final revision to show the various changes your writing and thinking underwent as you tried to solve the problem. If you are still uncertain about your solution, say so. Taking time to explain how you identified a particular problem, how you went about trying to solve it, and what you learned from this experience can help you solve future writing problems more easily.

Reviewing What You Learned from Reading

Write a page or so explaining to your instructor how the readings in this chapter influenced your final draft. Your own essay interpreting a story may have been influenced to some extent by the essays in this chapter—the two selections on "Araby"—and by classmates' essays that you have read. Before you write, take some time to reflect on what you have learned from these readings.

1. *Reread the final revision of your essay; then look back at the essays you read before completing it.*

Do you see any specific influences? For example, did one of the essays influence the suggestions for interpreting you used or the organization you followed? If you were impressed by the way another writer stated a thesis clearly and emphatically, forecasted reasons, or used quotations as support, look to see where you might have been striving for similar effects in your own essay. Look for ideas you got from your reading: writing strategies you were inspired to try, details you were led to include, effects you sought to achieve.

2. *Write an explanation of these influences.* Did one selection have a particularly strong influence on your essay, or were parts of several selections influential in similar or different ways? Give examples from the readings and from your final revision to show how you built on what you have learned from other writers. Finally, based on your review of the chapter's readings, point out any further improvements you would now make in your essay.

Considering the Social Dimensions of Essays Interpreting Stories

Some genres, like position papers, have a broad general audience, composed of people whose knowledge of current controversial issues varies widely. Other genres, like essays interpreting stories, are highly specialized, read and written by a comparatively small group of people who share certain kinds of knowledge and interests. Students in English courses, whether they major in English or some other field, learn certain ways of reading and writing about stories. For example, they learn that interpretive essays are arguments, requiring arguable assertions, reasons, and supporting evidence.

But to write effectively in this genre, students also must learn what kinds of interpretations are likely to interest their particular readers—people engaged in an ongoing conversation about stories and other works of literature. They need to know some of the specialized vocabulary English majors use as well as the critical approaches to interpreting stories they find

useful. English instructors determine which approaches their students need to become conversant with and they introduce these subjects in lecture and class discussion. They choose stories to read and assign essays to write that will give students opportunities to use these approaches.

The essays written by Crane and Ratinov reflect the kinds of approaches students in English classes are likely to encounter. Both student writers are concerned with the character or character development of the boy in "Araby." They focus on what the boy says to himself at the end, the meaning of which is not obvious but requires interpretation. Their interpretations of the ending differ, but the kinds of interpretations they make fit comfortably within the usual conversation among English majors. Crane writes about the way the story is narrated, arguing that the boy is an unreliable narrator, unable to read others or himself accurately; therefore what he says is ironic, meaning the opposite of what it seems to say. Ratinov writes about a theme common to many stories, the theme of initiation. Crane and Ratinov also discuss images of women, although they emphasize different aspects of the boy's cultural background. Crane emphasizes the chivalric tradition about which the boy reads and Ratinov stresses his religious education. These subjects—irony, initiation, and images of women—are included in the suggestions for interpreting in the Guide to Writing because they represent some of the ways in which English majors understand stories.

1. List some of the subjects you and your classmates discussed in class and wrote about. Where did these subjects come from—class discussion, the suggestions for interpreting in the Guide to Writing, your instructor's questions or lecture, other English classes?

2. Consider whether any subjects were deemed by your instructor or other students as uninteresting or not appropriate for interpreting stories. How did you know they were out of line?

3. Write a page or so about your experience making interpretations in this and other English classes.

CRITICAL THINKING STRATEGIES

A Catalog of
Invention Strategies

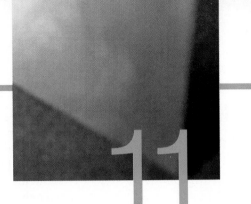

Writers are like scientists: They ask questions, systematically inquiring about how things work, what they are, where they occur, and how more information can be learned about them. Writers are also like artists in that they use what they know and learn to create something new and imaginative.

The invention and inquiry strategies—also known as *heuristics*—described in this chapter are not mysterious or magical. They are available to all writers, and one or more of them may appeal to your common sense and experience. These techniques represent ways creative writers, engineers, scientists, composers—in fact, all of us—solve problems.

Once you have mastered these strategies, you can use them to tackle many of the writing situations you will encounter in college, on the job, and in the community. The best way to learn them is to use them as you write an actual essay. Chapters 2–10 show you when these strategies can be most helpful and how to make the most efficient use of them. The Guides to Writing in those chapters offer easy-to-use adaptations of these general strategies, adaptations designed to satisfy the special requirements of each kind of writing. You will learn how and when to use these strategies and see how to combine them to achieve your goals.

The strategies for invention and inquiry in this chapter are grouped into two categories:

Mapping: A brief visual representation of your thinking or planning

Writing: The composition of phrases or sentences to discover information and ideas and to make connections among them

These invention and inquiry strategies can be powerful tools for thinking about your topic and planning your writing. They will help you explore and research a topic fully before you begin drafting and then help you creatively solve problems as you draft and revise your draft. In this chapter, strategies are arranged alphabetically within each of the two categories.

■ MAPPING

Mapping strategies involve making a visual record of invention and inquiry. Many writers find that mapping helps them think about a topic. In making maps, they usually use key words and phrases to record material they want to remember, questions they need to answer, and new sources of information they want to check. The maps show the ideas, details, and facts they are examining. They also show possible ways whereby materials can be connected and focused. Maps might be informal graphic displays with words and phrases circled and connected by lines to show relationships, or they might be formal sentence outlines. Mapping can be especially useful for collaborative writing situations, to prepare oral presentations, and create visual aids for written or oral reports. Mapping strategies include clustering, listing, and outlining.

Clustering

Clustering is a strategy for revealing possible relationships among facts and ideas. Unlike listing (the next mapping strategy), clustering requires a brief period of initial preparation. You must first come up with a tentative division of the topic into subparts or main ideas. Clustering works as follows:

1. In a word or phrase, write your topic in the center of a piece of paper. Circle it.

2. Also in words or phrases, write down the main parts or central ideas of your topic. Circle these, and connect them with lines to the topic in the center.

3. Next, think of facts, details, examples, or ideas related in any way to these main parts. Cluster these around the main parts.

Clustering can be useful for any kind of writing. You can use it in the early stages of planning an essay to find subtopics and organize information. You may try out and discard several clusters before finding one that is promising. Many writers use clustering to plan brief sections of an essay as they are drafting or revising. (A model of clustering is on the next page.)

Listing

Listing is a familiar activity. We make shopping lists and lists of errands to do or people to call. Listing can also be a great help in planning an essay. It enables you to recall what you already know about a topic and suggests what else you may need to find out. It is an easy way to get started with your invention writing, instead of just worrying about what you will write. A list rides along on its own momentum, the first item leading naturally to the next.

A basic activity for all writers, listing is especially useful to those who have little time for planning—for example, reporters facing deadlines and college students taking essay exams. Listing lets you order your ideas quickly. It can also serve as a first step in discovering possible writing topics.

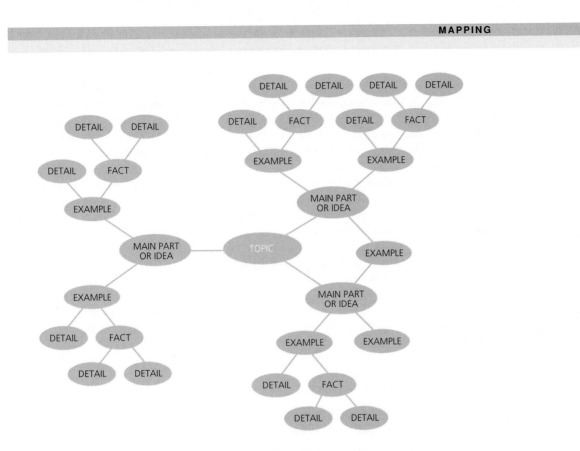

Listing is a solitary form of brainstorming, a popular technique of problem-solving in groups. When you work with a group to generate ideas for a collaborative writing project, you are engaged in true brainstorming. Here is how listing works best for invention work:

1. Give your list a title that indicates your main idea or topic.

2. Write as fast as you can, relying on short phrases.

3. Include anything that seems at all useful. Try not to be judgmental at this point.

4. After you have finished, or even as you write, reflect on the list and organize it in the following way. This step is very important, for it may lead you to further discoveries about your topic.

Put an asterisk next to the most promising items.
Number key items in order of importance.
Put items in related groups.
Cross out items that do not seem promising.
Add new items.

Outlining

Like listing and clustering, *outlining* is both a means of inventing what you want to say in an essay and a way of organizing your ideas and information. As you outline, you nearly always see new possibilities in your subject, discovering new ways of dividing or grouping information and seeing where you need additional information to develop your ideas. Because outlining lets you see at a glance where your essay's strengths and weaknesses lie, outlining can also help you read and revise your essay with a critical eye.

There are two main forms of outlining: informal scratch outlining and formal topic or sentence outlining. (Keep in mind that clustering is also a type of informal outlining.)

The Planning and Drafting sections of the Guides to Writing in Chapters 2–10 illustrate many different scratch outlines.

A *scratch outline* is considered an informal outline because it is little more than a list of the essay's main points. You have no doubt made scratch outlines many times —to plan essays or essay exams, to revise your own writing, and to analyze a difficult reading passage. Here are sample scratch outlines for two different kinds of essays. The first outlines Annie Dillard's essay in Chapter 2, and the second shows one way to organize a position paper (Chapter 6):

Turn to pp. 29–30 to compare this outline to Dillard's essay.

Scratch Outline: Essay about a Remembered Event

1. Gives history of her desire to have a microscope and tells when she got one
2. Describes workplace and supplies
3. Tells of failed efforts to see one-celled animals in hay infusion
4. Tells of failed efforts to see diatoms—one-celled creatures—in diatomaceous earth
5. Summarizes what she saw or failed to see in microscope during the winter
6. Explains that what she wanted to see but failed repeatedly to find was the amoeba (the one-celled animal that lives in the hay infusion and elsewhere)
7. Announces that in late spring she saw the amoeba; tells what led up to her seeing the amoeba; describes the amoeba
8. Tells that as soon as she found the amoeba, she ran upstairs to tell her parents
9. Describes father and mother lounging after dinner
10. Summarizes what her mother said
11. Explains what she understood her mother to mean
12. Reflects on the significance of what she had learned from her mother by telling what happened in the years that followed this event
13. Returns to the time of the event to tell what she did that night—studied the amoeba and gave it pond water
14. Recalls looking forward to seeing many other creatures through the microscope

Scratch Outline: Essay Arguing a Position

Presentation of the issue

Concession of some aspect of an opposing position

Thesis statement

First reason with support

Second reason with support (etc.)

Conclusion

Remember that the items in a scratch outline do not necessarily coincide with paragraphs. Sometimes two or more items may be developed in the same paragraph or one item may be covered in two or more paragraphs.

Topic and *sentence outlines* are considered more formal than scratch outlines because they follow a conventional format of numbered and lettered headings and subheadings:

I. (Main topic)

   A. (Subtopic of I)

   B.

      1. (Subtopic of I.B)

      2.

         a. (Subtopic of I.B.2)

         b.

            (1) (Subtopic of I.B.2.b)

            (2)

   C.

      1. (Subtopic of I.C)

      2.

The difference between a topic and sentence outline is obvious: topic outlines simply name the topics and subtopics, whereas sentence outlines use complete or abbreviated sentences. To illustrate, here are two partial formal outlines of an essay arguing a position, Jessica Statsky's "Children Need to Play, Not Compete," from Chapter 6.

Turn to pp. 255–58 to compare these outlines to Statsky's essay.

Formal Topic Outline

I. Organized sports harmful to children

   A. Harmful physically

      1. Curve ball (Koppett)

      2. Tackle football (Tutko)

B. Harmful psychologically

   1. Fear of being hurt

      a. Little League Online

      b. Mother

      c. Reporter

   2. Competition

      a. Rablovsky

      b. Studies

Formal Sentence Outline

I. Highly organized competitive sports such as Peewee Football and Little League Baseball can be physically and psychologically harmful to children, as well as counterproductive for developing future players.

   A. Physically harmful because sports entice children into physical actions that are bad for growing bodies.

      1. Koppett claims throwing a curve ball may put abnormal strain on developing arm and shoulder muscles.

      2. Tutko argues that tackle football is too traumatic for young kids.

   B. Psychologically harmful to children for a number of reasons.

      1. Fear of being hurt detracts from their enjoyment of the sport.

         a. Little League Online ranks fear of injury seventh among the seven top reasons children quit.

         b. One mother says "kids get so scared. . . . They'll sit on the bench and pretend their leg hurts."

         c. A reporter tells about a child who made himself vomit to get out of playing Peewee Football.

      2. Too much competition poses psychological dangers for children.

         a. Rablovsky reports: "The spirit of play suddenly disappears, and sport becomes joblike."

         b. Studies show that children prefer playing on a losing team to "warming the bench on a winning team."

In contrast to an informal outline in which anything goes, a formal outline must follow many conventions. The roman numerals and capital letters are followed by periods. In topic and sentence outlines, the first word of each item is capitalized, but items in topic outlines do not end with a period as items in sentence outlines do. Every level of a formal outline except the top level (identified by the roman numeral *I*) must include at least two items. Items at the same level of indentation in a topic outline should be grammatically parallel—all beginning with the same part of speech. For example, *I.A.* and *I.B.* are parallel when they both begin with an adverb

(Physically harmful and *Psychologically harmful)* or with a noun *(Harmful physically* and *Harmful psychologically)*; they would not be parallel if one began with an adverb *(Physically harmful)* and the other with a noun *(Harmful psychologically)*.

■ WRITING

Writing is itself a powerful tool for thinking. As you write, you can recall details, remember facts, develop your ideas, find connections in new information you have collected, examine assumptions, and critically question what you know.

Unlike most mapping strategies, *writing strategies* of invention invite you to produce complete sentences. Sentences provide considerable generative power. Because they are complete statements, they take you further than listing or clustering. They enable you to explore ideas and define relationships, bring ideas together or show how they differ, and identify causes and effects. Sentences can also help you develop a logical chain of thought.

Some of these invention and inquiry strategies are systematic, while others are more flexible. Even though they call for complete sentences that are related to one another, they do not require preparation or revision. You can use them to develop oral as well as written presentations.

These writing strategies include cubing, dialoguing, dramatizing, keeping journals, looping, questioning, and quick drafting.

Cubing

Cubing is useful for quickly exploring a writing topic, probing it from six different perspectives. It is known as *cubing* because a cube has six sides. These are the six perspectives in cubing:

Describing. What does your subject look like? What size is it? What is its color? Its shape? Its texture? Name its parts.

Comparing. What is your subject similar to? Different from?

Associating. What does your subject make you think of? What connections does it have to anything else in your experience?

Analyzing. What are the origins of your subject? What are its parts or features? How are its parts related?

Applying. What can you do with your subject? What uses does it have?

Arguing. What arguments can you make for your subject? Against it?

Here are some guidelines to help you use cubing productively.

1. Select a topic, subject, or part of a subject. This can be a person, a scene, an event, an object, a problem, an idea, or an issue. Hold it in focus.

2. Limit your writing to three to five minutes for each perspective. The whole activity should take no more than half an hour.

3. Keep going until you have written about your subject from all six perspectives. Remember that cubing offers the special advantage of enabling you to generate multiple perspectives quickly.

4. As you write from each perspective, begin with what you know about your subject. However, do not limit yourself to your present knowledge. Indicate what else you would like to know about your subject, and suggest where you might find that information.

5. Reread what you have written. Look for bright spots, surprises. Recall the part that was easiest for you to write. Recall the part where you felt a special momentum and pleasure in the writing. Look for an angle or an unexpected insight. These special parts may suggest a focus or topic within a larger subject, or they may provide specific details to include in a draft.

Dialoguing

See pp. 66–67 for an example of dialogue used for invention.

A dialogue is a conversation between two or more people. You can use *dialoguing* to search for topics, find a focus, explore ideas, or consider opposing viewpoints. When you write a dialogue as an invention strategy, you need to make up all parts of the conversation (unless, of course, you are writing collaboratively—on a network, for example). To construct a dialogue by yourself, imagine two particular people talking, hold a conversation yourself with some imagined person, or simply talk out loud to yourself. To construct a dialogue independently or collaboratively, follow these steps:

1. Write a conversation between two speakers. Label the participants *Speaker A* and *Speaker B,* or make up names for them.

2. If you get stuck, you might have one of the speakers ask the other a question.

3. Write brief responses in order to keep the conversation moving fast. Do not spend much time planning or rehearsing responses. Write what first occurs to you, just as in a real conversation, where people take quick turns to prevent any awkward silences.

Dialogues can be especially useful with personal experience and persuasive essays because they help you remember conversations and anticipate objections.

Dramatizing

Dramatizing is an invention activity developed by the philosopher Kenneth Burke as a way of thinking about how people interact and as a way of analyzing stories and films.

Thinking about human behavior in dramatic terms can be very productive for writers. Drama has action, actors, setting, motives, and methods. Since stars and acting go together, you can use a five-pointed star to remember these five points of dramatizing:

Each point on the star provides a different perspective on human behavior. We can think of each point independently and in combination. Let us begin by looking at each point to see how it helps us to analyze people and their interactions.

Action.   An action is anything that happens, has happened, will happen, or could happen. Action includes events that are physical (running a marathon), mental (thinking about a book you have read), and emotional (falling in love). This category also refers to the results of activity (an essay).

Actor.   The actor is involved in the action—either responsible for it or simply affected by it. (The actor does not have to be a person. It can be a force, something that causes an action. For example, if the action is a rise in the price of gasoline, the actor could be increased demand or short supply.) Dramatizing may also include a number of coactors working together or at odds.

Setting.   The setting is the situation or background of the action. We usually think of setting as the place and time of an event, but it may also be the historical background of an event or the childhood of a person.

Motive.   The motive is the purpose or reason for an action—the actor's intention. Actions may have multiple, even conflicting, motives.

Method.   The method explains how an action occurs, including the techniques an actor uses. It refers to whatever makes things happen.

Each of these points suggests a simple invention question:

Action: What?

Actor: Who?

Setting: When and where?

Motive: Why?

Method: How?

This list looks like the questions reporters typically ask. But dramatizing goes further: It enables us to ask a much fuller set of invention questions that we generate by considering relations between and among these five elements. We can think about actors' motives, the effect of the setting on the actors, the relations between actors, and so on.

You can use this invention strategy to learn more about yourself or about other significant people in your life. You can use it, as well, to explore, analyze, or evaluate characters in stories or movies. Moreover, dramatizing is especially useful in analyzing the readers you want to inform or convince.

To use dramatizing, imagine the person you want to understand better in a particular situation. Holding this image in mind, write answers to any questions in the following list that apply. You may draw a blank on some questions, have little to say to some, and find a lot to say to others. Be exploratory and playful with the questions. Write responses quickly, relying on words and phrases, even drawings.

- What is the actor doing?
- How did the actor come to be involved in this situation?
- Why does the actor do what he or she does?
- What else might the actor do?
- What is the actor trying to accomplish?
- How do other actors influence—help or hinder—the main actor?
- What do the actor's actions reveal about him or her?
- What does the actor's language reveal about him or her?
- How does the event's setting influence the actor's actions?
- How does the time of the event influence what the actor does?
- Where does this actor come from?
- How is this actor different now from what he or she used to be?
- What might this actor become?
- How is this actor like or unlike the other actors?

Keeping a Journal

Professional writers often use *journals* to keep notes, and so might you. Starting a writer's journal is quite easy. Buy a special notebook, or open a new file on your computer, and start writing. Here are some possibilities:

- Keep a list of new words and concepts you learn in your courses. You could also write about the progress and direction of your learning in particular courses—the experience of being in the course, your feelings about what is happening and what you are learning.

- Respond to your reading, both assigned and personal. Write about your personal associations as you read, your reflections, reactions, evaluations. Summarize or copy memorable or especially important passages and comment on them. (Copying and commenting have been practiced by students and writers for centuries in special journals called *commonplace books.*)

- Write to prepare for particular class meetings. Write about the main ideas you have learned from assigned readings and about the relationship of these new ideas to other ideas in the course. After class, write to summarize what you have learned. List questions you have about the ideas or information discussed in class. Journal writing of this kind involves reflecting, evaluating, interpreting, synthesizing, summarizing, and questioning.

- Record observations and overheard conversations.

- Write for ten or fifteen minutes every day about whatever is on your mind. Focus these meditations on your new experiences as you try to understand, interpret, and reflect on them.

- Write sketches of people who catch your attention.

- Organize your time. Write about your goals and priorities, or list specific things to accomplish and what you plan to do.

- Keep a log over several days or weeks about a particular event unfolding in the news—a sensational trial, an environmental disaster, a political campaign, a campus controversy, the fortunes of a sports team.

You can use a journal in many ways. All of the writing in your journal has value for learning. You may also be able to use parts of your journal for writing in your other courses.

Looping

Looping is especially useful for the first stages of exploring a topic. As its name suggests, *looping* involves writing quickly to explore some aspect of a topic and then looping back to your original starting point or to a new starting point to explore another aspect. Beginning with almost any starting point, looping enables you to find a center of interest and eventually a thesis for your essay. The steps are simple:

1. Write down your area of interest. You may know only that you have to write about another person or a movie or a cultural trend that has caught your attention. Or you may want to search for a topic in a broad historical period or for one related to a major political event. Although you may wander from this topic as you write, you will want to keep coming back to it. Your purpose is to find a focus for writing.

2. Write nonstop for ten minutes. Start with the first thing that comes to mind. Write rapidly, without looking back to reread or to correct anything. *Do not stop writing. Keep your pencil moving.* Continuous writing is the key to looping. If you get stuck for a moment, rewrite the last sentence. Trust the act of writing to lead you to new insights. Follow diversions and digressions, but keep returning to your topic.

3. After ten minutes, pause to reread what you have written. Decide what is most important—a single insight, a pattern of ideas, an emerging theme, a visual detail, anything at all that stands out. Some writers call this a "center of gravity" or a "hot spot." To complete the first loop, restate this center in a single sentence.

4. Beginning with this sentence, write nonstop for another ten minutes.

5. Summarize in one sentence again to complete the second loop.

6. Keep looping until one of your summary sentences produces a focus or thesis. You may need only two or three loops; you may need more.

Questioning

Asking *questions* about a subject is a way to learn about it and decide what to write. When you first encounter a subject, however, your questions may be scattered. Also, you are not likely to think right away of all the important questions you ought to ask. The advantage of having a basic list of questions for invention, like the ones for cubing and for dramatizing discussed earlier in this chapter, is that it provides a systematic approach to exploring a subject.

The questions that follow come from classical rhetoric (what the Greek philosopher Aristotle called *topics*) and a modern approach to invention called *tagmemics*. Based on the work of linguist Kenneth Pike, tagmemics provides questions about different ways we make sense of the world, the ways we sort and classify experience in order to understand it.

Here are the steps in using questions for invention:

1. In a sentence or two, identify your subject. A subject could be any event, person, problem, project, idea, or issue—in other words, anything you might write about.

2. Start by writing a response to the first question in the following list, and move right through the list. Try to answer each question at least briefly with a word or a phrase. Some questions may invite several sentences or even a page or more of writing. You may draw a blank on a few questions. Skip them. Later, when you have more experience with questions for invention, you can start anywhere in the list.

3. Write your responses quickly, without much planning. Follow digressions or associations. Do not screen anything out. Be playful.

What Is Your Subject?

- What is your subject's name? What other names does it have? What names did it have in the past?

- What aspects of the subject do these different names emphasize?

- Imagine a still photograph or a moving picture of your subject. What would it look like?

- What would you put into a time capsule to stand for your subject?

- What are its causes and results?

- How would it look from different vantage points or perspectives?
- What particular experiences have you had with the subject? What have you learned?

What Parts or Features Does Your Subject Have and How Are They Related?

- Name the parts or features of your subject.
- Describe each one, using the questions in the preceding subject list.
- How is each part or feature related to the others?

How Is Your Subject Similar to and Different from Other Subjects?

- What is your subject similar to? In what ways are these subjects alike?
- What is your subject different from? In what ways are the subjects different?
- What seems to you most unlike your subject? In what ways are the two things unlike each other? Now, just for fun, note how they are alike.

How Much Can Your Subject Change and Still Remain the Same?

- How has your subject changed from what it once was?
- How is it changing now—moment to moment, day to day, year to year?
- How does each change alter your way of thinking about your subject?
- What are some different forms your subject takes?
- What does it become when it is no longer itself?

Where Does Your Subject Fit in the World?

- When and where did your subject originate?
- What would happen if at some future time your subject ceased to exist?
- When and where do you usually experience the subject?
- What is this subject a part of, and what are the other parts?
- What do other people think of your subject?

Quick Drafting

Sometimes you know what you want to say or have little time for invention. In these situations, *quick drafting* may be a good strategy. There are no special rules for quick drafting, but you should rely on it only if you know your subject well, have had experience with the kind of writing you are doing, and will have a chance to revise your draft. Quick drafting can help you discover what you already know about the subject and what you need to find out. It can also help you develop and organize your thoughts.

A Catalog of
Reading Strategies

12

To become a thoughtful, effective writer, you must also become a critical reader. This chapter presents strategies to help you *read with a critical eye*. Reading critically means not just comprehending passively and remembering what you read but also scrutinizing actively and making thoughtful judgments about your reading. When you read a text critically, you need to alternate between understanding and questioning—on the one hand, striving to understand the text on its own terms; on the other hand, taking care to question its ideas and authority. You will benefit greatly from reading what others have written—and reading your own writing—in this way.

The strategies here complement and supplement reading strategies presented in Part One, Chapters 2–10. Critical reading is central to your success with the writing assignments in those chapters. The Connecting to Culture and Experience activity following each reading in Part One helps you think about the selection in light of your own experience and awareness of social issues, while the Analyzing Writing Strategies questions help you understand how the text works and evaluate how well it achieves its purpose with its readers. The Critical Reading Guide in each Part One chapter helps you read other students' drafts as well as your own to find out what is working and what needs improvement.

Reading is, after all, inextricably linked to writing, and the reading strategies in this chapter can help you not only enrich your thinking as a reader, but also participate in conversations as a writer. These strategies include the following:

- *Annotating.* Recording your reactions to, interpretations of, and questions about a text as you read it
- *Taking inventory.* Listing and grouping your annotations and other notes to find meaningful patterns
- *Outlining.* Listing the text's main ideas to reveal how it is organized
- *Paraphrasing.* Restating what you have read to clarify or refer to it
- *Summarizing.* Distilling the main ideas or gist of a text
- *Synthesizing.* Integrating into your own writing ideas and information gleaned from different sources
- *Contextualizing.* Placing a text in its historical and cultural contexts

- *Exploring the significance of figurative language.* Examining how metaphors, similes, and symbols are used in a text to convey meaning and evoke feelings
- *Looking for patterns of opposition.* Analyzing the values and assumptions embodied in the language of a text
- *Reflecting on challenges to your beliefs and values.* Critically examining the bases of your personal responses to a text
- *Evaluating the logic of an argument.* Determining whether a thesis is well reasoned and adequately supported
- *Recognizing emotional manipulation.* Identifying texts that unfairly and inappropriately use emotional appeals based on false or exaggerated claims
- *Judging the writer's credibility.* Considering whether writers represent different points of view fairly and know what they are writing about

These critical reading strategies can help you connect information from different sources and relate it to what you already know; distinguish fact from opinion; uncover and question assumptions; and subject other people's ideas as well as your own to reasoned argument. You can readily learn these strategies and apply them not only to a critical reading of the selections in Part One but also to your other college reading. Although mastering the strategies will not make critical reading easy, it can make your reading much more satisfying and productive and thus help you handle even difficult material with confidence. Critical reading strategies will, in addition, often be useful in your reading outside of school—for instance, these strategies can help you understand, evaluate, and comment upon what political figures, advertisers, and other writers are saying.

■ ANNOTATING

Annotations are the marks—underlines, highlights, and comments—you make directly on the page as you read. *Annotating* can be used to record immediate reactions and questions, outline and summarize main points, and evaluate and relate the reading to other ideas and points of view. Especially useful for studying and preparing to write, annotating is also an essential element of many other critical reading strategies. Your annotations can take many forms, such as the following:

Writing comments, questions, or definitions in the margins

Underlining or circling words, phrases, or sentences

Connecting ideas with lines or arrows

Numbering related points

Bracketing sections of the text

Noting anything that strikes you as interesting, important, or questionable

Most readers annotate in layers, adding further annotations on second and third readings. Annotations can be light or heavy, depending on the reader's purpose and the difficulty of the material. Your purpose for reading also determines how you use your annotations.

The following selection, excerpted from Martin Luther King Jr.'s "Letter from Birmingham Jail," is annotated to illustrate some of the ways you can annotate as you read. Add your own annotations, if you like.

Martin Luther King Jr. (1929–1968) first came to national notice in 1955, when he led a successful boycott against the policy of restricting African American passengers to rear seats on city buses in Montgomery, Alabama, where he was minister of a Baptist church. He subsequently formed a national organization, the Southern Christian Leadership Conference, that brought people of all races from all over the country to the South to fight nonviolently for racial integration. In 1963, King led demonstrations in Birmingham, Alabama, that were met with violence; a bomb was detonated in a black church, killing four young girls. King was arrested for his role in organizing the protests, and while in prison, he wrote the famous "Letter from Birmingham Jail" to answer the criticism of local clergy and to justify to the nation his strategy of civil disobedience, which he called "nonviolent direct action."

King begins his letter by discussing his disappointment with the lack of support he has received from white moderates, such as the group of clergy who published criticism in the local newspaper. As you read the following excerpt from his letter, try to infer from King's written response what the clergy's specific criticisms might have been. Also, notice the tone King uses to answer his critics. Would you characterize the writing as apologetic, conciliatory, accusatory, or in some other way?

¶1. White moderates block progress.

An Annotated Sample from "Letter from Birmingham Jail"
Martin Luther King Jr.

I must confess that over the past few years I have been gravely disappointed with the white moderate. I have almost reached the regrettable conclusion that the Negro's [great stumbling block in his stride toward freedom] is not the White Citizen's Counciler or the Ku Klux Klanner, but the white moderate, who is more

negative vs. positive

devoted to "order" than to justice; who prefers a negative peace which is the absence of tension to a positive peace which is the presence of justice; who constantly says: "I agree with you in the goal you seek, but I cannot agree with your methods of direct action"; who paternalistically believes he can set the timetable for another man's freedom; who lives by a mythical concept of time

order vs. justice

ends vs. means

treating others like children

1

and who constantly advises the Negro to wait for a "more convenient season." Shallow understanding from people of good will is
more frustrating than absolute misunderstanding from people of
ill will. Lukewarm acceptance is much more bewildering than outright rejection.

*¶2. Tension
necessary for
progress.*

I had hoped that the white moderate would understand that   2
law and order exist for the purpose of establishing justice and that
when they fail in this purpose they become the [dangerously
structured dams that block the flow of social progress.] I had
hoped that the white moderate would understand that the present
tension in the South is a necessary phase of the transition from
an [obnoxious negative peace,] in which the Negro passively accepted his unjust plight, to a [substantive and positive peace,] in
which all men will respect the dignity and worth of human personality. Actually, we who engage in nonviolent direct action are

*Tension already
exists anyway.*

not the creators of tension. We merely bring to the surface the
hidden tension that is already alive. We bring it out in the open,
where it can be seen and dealt with. [Like a boil that can never

True?

be cured so long as it is covered up but must be opened with all
its ugliness to the natural medicines of air and light, injustice must
be exposed, with all the tension its exposure creates, to the light
of human conscience and the air of national opinion before it can
be cured.]

*Simile: hidden
tension is "like a
boil"*

In your statement you assert that our actions, even though   3
peaceful, must be condemned because they precipitate violence.
But is this a logical assertion? Isn't this like condemning a robbed
man because his possession of money precipitated the evil act
of robbery? Isn't this like condemning Socrates because his un-

*¶3. Questions
clergymen's logic:
condemning his
actions =
condemning victims,
Socrates, Jesus.*

swerving commitment to truth and his philosophical inquiries
precipitated the act by the misguided populace in which they

made him drink hemlock? Isn't this like condemning (Jesus) because his unique God-consciousness and never-ceasing devotion to God's will precipitated the evil act of crucifixion? We must come to see that, as the federal courts have consistently affirmed, it is wrong to urge an individual to cease his efforts to gain his basic constitutional rights because the question may precipitate violence. [Society must protect the robbed and punish the robber.]

Yes!

I had also hoped that the white moderate would reject the myth concerning time in relation to the struggle for freedom. I have just received a letter from a white brother in Texas. He writes: "All Christians know that the colored people will receive equal rights eventually, but it is possible that you are in too great a religious hurry. It has taken Christianity almost two thousand years to accomplish what it has. The teachings of Christ take time to come to earth." Such an attitude stems from a tragic misconception of time, from the strangely irrational notion that there is something in the very flow of time that will inevitably cure all ills. Actually, time itself is neutral; it can be used either destructively or constructively. More and more I feel that the people of ill will have used time much more effectively than have the people of good will. We will have to repent in this generation not merely for the [hateful words and actions of the bad people] but for the [appalling silence of the good people.] Human progress never rolls in on [wheels of inevitability;] it comes through the tireless efforts of men willing to be co-workers with God, and without this hard work, time itself becomes an ally of the forces of social (stagnation.) [We must use time creatively, in the knowledge that the time is always ripe to do right.] Now is the time to make real the promise of democracy and transform our pending [national

example of a white moderate

Silence is as bad as hateful words and actions.

¶4. Time must be used to do right.

4

metaphor

not moving

elegy*]* into a creative *[*psalm of brotherhood.*]* <u>Now is the time</u> to lift our national policy from the *[*quicksand of racial injustice*]* to the *[*solid rock of human dignity.*]*

metaphors

You speak of our activity in Birmingham as <u>extreme</u>. At first I was rather disappointed that fellow clergymen would see my non-violent efforts as those of an extremist. I began thinking about the fact that <u>I stand in the middle of two opposing forces in the Negro community</u>. One is a *[*force of complacency,*]* made up in part of Negroes who, as a result of long years of oppression, are so drained of self-respect and a sense of "somebodiness" that they have adjusted to segregation; and in part of a few middle-class Negroes, who because of a degree of academic and economic security and because in some ways they profit by segregation, have become insensitive to the problems of the masses. The other *[*force is one of bitterness and hatred,*]* and it comes per-ilously close to advocating violence. It is expressed in the various <u>black nationalist</u> *[*groups that are springing up*]* across the nation, the largest and best-known being <u>Elijah Muhammad's Muslim movement</u>. Nourished by the Negro's frustration over the contin-ued existence of racial discrimination, this movement is made up of people who have lost faith in America, who have absolutely repudiated Christianity, and who have concluded that the white man is an incorrigible "devil."

5   *King accused of being an extremist*

¶5. King in middle of two extremes: complacent & angry.

Malcolm X?

¶6. King offers better choice.

<u>I have tried to stand between these two forces</u>, saying that we need emulate neither the "do-nothingism" of the complacent nor the hatred and despair of the black nationalist. For there is <u>the more excellent way of love and nonviolent protest</u>. I am grate-ful to God that, through the influence of the Negro church, the way of nonviolence became an integral part of our struggle.

6

How did nonviolence become part of King's movement?

¶7. King's movement prevented racial violence. Threat?

<u>If</u> this philosophy had not emerged, by now many streets of the South would, I am convinced, be flowing with blood. And I am

7

Gandhi?

The church?

further convinced that if our white brothers dismiss as "rabble-rousers" and "outside agitators" those of us who employ nonviolent direct action, and if they refuse to support our nonviolent efforts, millions of Negroes will, out of frustration and despair,

If . . . then . . .

seek (solace) and security in black-nationalist ideologies—a development that would inevitably lead to a frightening racial nightmare.

comfort

(Oppressed people cannot remain oppressed forever.) The 8 yearning for freedom eventually manifests itself, and that is what has happened to the American Negro. Something within has reminded him of his birthright of freedom, and something without has reminded him that it can be gained. Consciously or uncon-

worldwide uprising against injustice

sciously, he has been caught up by the (Zeitgeist,) and with his black brothers of Africa and his brown and yellow brothers of Asia, South America and the Caribbean, the United States Negro is moving with a sense of great urgency toward the [promised land of racial justice.] If one recognizes this [vital urge that has engulfed the Negro community,] one should readily understand why public demonstrations are taking place. The Negro has many [pent-up resentments] and latent frustrations, and he must release them. So let him march; let him make prayer pilgrimages to the city hall; let him go on freedom rides—and try to understand why he must do so. If his repressed emotions are not released in nonviolent ways, they will seek expression through violence; this is not a threat but a fact of history. So I have not said to my people: "Get rid of your discontent." Rather, I have

spirit of the times

Not a threat?

¶8. Discontent is normal & healthy but must be channeled.

tried to say that this normal and healthy discontent can be [channeled into the creative outlet of nonviolent direct action.] And now this approach is being termed extremist.

But though I was initially disappointed at being categorized 9 as an extremist, as I continued to think about the matter

I gradually gained a measure of satisfaction from the label. Was not Jesus an extremist for love: "Love your enemies, bless them that curse you, do good to them that hate you, and pray for them which despitefully use you, and persecute you." Was not Amos an

Hebrew prophet

extremist for justice: "Let justice roll down like waters and righteousness like an ever-flowing stream." Was not Paul an extrem

Christ's disciple

ist for the Christian gospel: "I bear in my body the marks of the Lord Jesus." Was not Martin Luther an extremist: "Here I stand; I

Founded Protestantism

cannot do otherwise, so help me God." And John Bunyan: "I will

English preacher

stay in jail to the end of my days before I make a butchery of my conscience." And Abraham Lincoln: "This nation cannot survive half slave and half free." And Thomas Jefferson: "We hold these truths to be self-evident, that all men are created equal. . . ." So the question is not whether we will be extremists, but what kind of extremists we will be. Will we be extremists for hate or for love?

No choice but to be extremists. But what kind?

Will we be extremists for the preservation of injustice or for the extension of justice? In that dramatic scene on Calvary's hill three men were crucified. We must never forget that all three were crucified for the same crime—the crime of extremism. Two were extremists for immorality, and thus fell below their environment. The other, Jesus Christ, was an extremist for love, truth and goodness, and thereby rose above his environment. Perhaps the

¶9. Creative extremists are needed.

South, the nation and the world are in dire need of creative extremists.

Disappointed in the white moderate

I had hoped that the white moderate would see this need. 10 Perhaps I was too optimistic; perhaps I expected too much. I suppose I should have realized that few members of the oppressor race can understand the deep groans and passionate yearnings of the oppressed race, and still fewer have the vision to see that [injustice must be rooted out] by strong, persistent and deter-

¶10. *Some whites have supported King.*

what they did

mined <u>action</u>. I am thankful, however, that some of our white brothers in the South have grasped the meaning of this <u>social revolution</u> and committed themselves to it. They are still all too few in quantity, but they are big in quality. Some—such as Ralph McGill, Lillian Smith, Harry Golden, James McBride Dabbs, Ann Braden and Sarah Patton Boyle—have <u>written</u> about our struggle in eloquent and prophetic terms. Others have <u>marched</u> with us down nameless streets of the South. They have (anguished) in filthy, roach-infested jails, <u>suffering the abuse and brutality</u> of policemen who view them as "dirty nigger-lovers." Unlike so many of their moderate brothers and sisters, they have <u>recognized the urgency of the moment and sensed the need</u> for [powerful "action" antidotes] to combat the [disease of segregation.]

Who are they?

been left unaided

■ CHECKLIST: Annotating

1. Mark the text using notations like these:
   - Circle words to be defined in the margin.
   - Underline key words and phrases.
   - Bracket important sentences and passages.
   - Use lines or arrows to connect ideas or words.

2. Write marginal comments like these:
   - Number and summarize each paragraph.
   - Define unfamiliar words.
   - Note responses and questions.
   - Identify interesting writing strategies.
   - Point out patterns.

3. Layer additional markings on the text and comments in the margins as you reread for different purposes.

■ TAKING INVENTORY

An inventory is simply a list or grouping of items. *Taking inventory* helps you analyze your annotations for different purposes. When you take inventory, you make various kinds of lists to explore patterns of meaning you find in the text. For instance, in reading the annotated passage by Martin Luther King Jr., you might have noticed that many famous people are named or that certain similes and metaphors are used. By listing the names (Socrates, Jesus, Luther, Lincoln, etc.) and then grouping them into categories (people who died for their beliefs, leaders, teachers, and religious figures) you could better understand why the writer refers to these particular people. Obviously, taking inventory of your annotations can be very helpful in writing about a text you are reading.

■ CHECKLIST: Taking Inventory

1. Examine your annotations for patterns or repetitions such as recurring images, stylistic features, repeated words and phrases, repeated examples or illustrations, and reliance on particular writing strategies.

2. List and group the items in the pattern.

3. Decide what the pattern indicates about the reading.

■ OUTLINING

Outlining is an especially helpful critical reading strategy for understanding the content and structure of a reading. *Outlining,* which identifies the text's main ideas, may be part of the annotating process, or it may be done separately. Writing an outline in the margins of the text as you read and annotate makes it easier to find information later. Writing an outline on a separate piece of paper gives you more space to work with and therefore such an outline usually includes more detail.

The key to outlining is distinguishing between the main ideas and the supporting material such as examples, quotations, comparisons, and reasons. The main ideas form the backbone, which holds the various parts and pieces of the text together. Outlining the main ideas helps you uncover this structure.

Making an outline, however, is not simple. The reader must exercise judgment in deciding which are the most important ideas. Because importance is relative, different readers can make different—and equally reasonable—decisions based on what interests them in the reading. Readers also must decide whether to use the writer's words, their own words, or a combination of the two. The words used in an outline reflect the reader's interpretation and emphasis. Reading is never a passive or neutral act; the process of outlining shows how constructive reading can be.

You may make either a formal, multileveled outline with roman (I, II) and arabic (1, 2) numerals together with capital and lowercase letters or an informal scratch outline that lists the main idea of each paragraph. A *formal outline* is harder to make and much more time consuming than a scratch outline. You might choose to make a formal outline of a reading about which you are writing an in-depth analysis or evaluation. For example, here is a formal outline a student wrote for a paper evaluating the logic of the King excerpt. Notice that the student uses roman numerals for the main ideas or claims, capital letters for the reasons, and arabic numerals for supporting evidence and explanation.

Formal Outline

I. The Negro's great stumbling block in his stride toward freedom is . . . the white moderate
   A. Because the white moderate is more devoted to "order" than to justice (paragraph 2)
      1. Law and order should exist to establish justice
      2. Law and order compare to dangerously structured dams that block the flow of social progress
   B. Because the white moderate prefers a negative peace (absence of tension) to a positive peace (justice) (paragraph 2)
      1. The tension already exists
      2. It is not created by nonviolent direct action
      3. Society that does not eliminate injustice compares to a boil that hides its infections. Both can be cured only by exposure (boil simile)
   C. Because even though the white moderate agrees with the goals, he does not support the means to achieve them (paragraph 3)
      1. The argument that the means--nonviolent direct action--are wrong because they precipitate violence is flawed
      2. Analogy of the robbed man condemned because he had money
      3. Comparison with Socrates and Jesus
   D. Because the white moderate paternalistically believes he can set a timetable for another man's freedom (paragraph 4)
      1. Rebuts the white moderate's argument that Christianity will cure man's ills and man must wait patiently for that to happen
      2. Argues that time is neutral and that man must use time creatively for constructive rather than destructive ends
II. Creative extremism is preferable to moderation
   A. Classifies himself as a moderate (paragraphs 5-8)
      1. I stand between two forces: the white moderate's complacency and the Black Muslim's rage
      2. If nonviolent direct action were stopped, more violence, not less, would result

```
        3. "[M]illions of Negroes will, out of frustration
           and despair, seek solace and security in black-
           nationalist ideologies" (paragraph 7)
        4. Repressed emotions will be expressed--if not in non-
           violent ways, then through violence (paragraph 8)
     B. Redefines himself as a "creative extremist" (paragraph
        9)
        1. Extremism for love, truth, and goodness is creative
           extremism
        2. Identifies himself with the creative extremists
           Jesus, Amos, Paul, Martin Luther, John Bunyan, Abra-
           ham Lincoln, and Thomas Jefferson
     C. Not all white people are moderates, many are creative
        extremists (paragraph 10)
        1. Lists names of white writers
        2. Refers to white activists
```

Making a scratch outline takes less time than making a formal outline, but still requires careful reading. A *scratch outline* will not record as much information as a formal outline, but it is sufficient for most critical reading purposes. To make a scratch outline, you first need to locate the topic of each paragraph in the reading. The topic is usually stated in a word or phrase, and it may be repeated or referred to throughout the paragraph. For example, the opening paragraph of the King excerpt (p. 531) makes clear that its topic is the white moderate.

After you have found the topic of the paragraph, figure out what is being said about it. To return to our example: King immediately establishes the white moderate as the topic of the opening paragraph, and at the beginning of the second sentence announces the conclusion he has come to—namely, that the white moderate is "the Negro's great stumbling block in his stride toward freedom." The rest of the paragraph specifies the ways the white moderate blocks progress.

The annotations of the King excerpt include a paragraph-by-paragraph outline (see above). Here is the same outline as it might appear on a separate piece of paper, slightly expanded and reworded:

Paragraph Scratch Outline

```
¶1. White moderates block progress in the struggle for racial
    justice.
¶2. Tension is necessary for progress.
¶3. The clergymen's criticism is not logical.
¶4. King justifies urgent use of time.
¶5. Clergymen accuse King of being extreme, but he claims to
    stand between two extreme forces in the black community.
```

¶6. King offers a better choice.

¶7. King's movement has prevented racial violence by blacks.

¶8. Discontent is normal and healthy but must be channeled creatively rather than destructively.

¶9. Creative extremists are needed.

¶10. Some whites have supported King.

■ CHECKLIST: Outlining

1. Reread each paragraph systematically, identifying the topic and what is being said about it. Do not include examples, specific details, quotations, or other explanatory and supporting material.

2. List the author's main ideas in the margin of the text or on a separate piece of paper.

■ PARAPHRASING

Paraphrasing is restating something you have read using mostly your own words. As a critical reading strategy, paraphrasing can help to clarify the meaning of an obscure or ambiguous passage. It is one of the three ways of integrating other people's ideas and information into your own writing, along with *quoting* (reproducing exactly the language of the source text) and *summarizing* (distilling the main ideas or gist of the source text). You might choose to paraphrase rather than quote when the source's language is not especially arresting or memorable. You might paraphrase short passages but summarize longer ones.

Following are two passages. The first is from paragraph 2 of the excerpt from King's "Letter." The second passage is a paraphrase of the first:

Original

I had hoped that the white moderate would understand that law and order exist for the purpose of establishing justice and that when they fail in this purpose they become the dangerously structured dams that block the flow of social progress. I had hoped that the white moderate would understand that the present tension in the South is a necessary phase of the transition from an obnoxious negative peace, in which the Negro passively accepted his unjust plight, to a substantive and positive peace, in which all men will respect the dignity and worth of human personality.

Paraphrase

King writes that he had hoped for more understanding from white moderates--specifically that they would recognize that law and order are not ends in themselves but means to the greater end of establishing justice. When law and order do not

serve this greater end, they stand in the way of progress.
King expected the white moderate to recognize that the current
tense situation in the South is part of a transition process
that is necessary for progress. The current situation is bad
because although there is peace, it is an "obnoxious" and
"negative" kind of peace based on blacks passively accepting
the injustice of the status quo. A better kind of peace, one
that is "substantive," real and not imaginary, as well as
"positive," requires that all people, regardless of race, be
valued.

When you compare the paraphrase to the original, you can see that the paraphrase contains all the important information and ideas of the original. Notice also that the paraphrase is somewhat longer than the original, refers to the writer by name, and encloses King's original words in quotation marks. Although the paraphrase tries to be neutral, to avoid inserting the reader's opinions or distorting the original writer's ideas, it does inevitably express the reader's interpretation of the original text's meaning. Another reader might paraphrase the same passage differently.

■ CHECKLIST: Paraphrasing

1. Reread the passage to be paraphrased, looking up unfamiliar words in a college dictionary.
2. Translate the passage into your own words, putting quotation marks around any words or phrases you quote from the original.
3. Revise to ensure coherence.

■ SUMMARIZING

Summarizing is one of the most widely used strategies for critical reading because it helps the reader understand and remember what is most important in the reading. Another advantage of summarizing is that it creates a condensed version of the reading's ideas and information, which can be referred to later or inserted into the reader's own writing. Along with quoting and paraphrasing, summarizing enables you to refer to and integrate other writers' ideas into your own writing.

A summary is a relatively brief restatement, primarily in the reader's own words, of the reading's main ideas. Summaries vary in length, depending on the reader's purpose. Some summaries are very brief—a sentence or even a subordinate clause. For example, if you were referring to the excerpt from "Letter from Birmingham Jail" and simply needed to indicate how it relates to your other sources, your summary might focus on only one aspect of the reading. It might look something like this: "There have always been advocates of extremism in politics. Martin Luther King Jr., in 'Letter from Birmingham Jail,' for instance, defends nonviolent civil disobedience as an extreme but necessary means of bringing about racial justice." If, on the other hand, you were surveying the important texts of the civil rights movement, you might write a longer, more detailed summary that not only identifies the reading's main ideas but also shows how the ideas relate to one another.

Many writers find it useful to outline the reading as a preliminary to writing a summary. A paragraph-by-paragraph scratch outline (like the one on pp. 540–41) lists the reading's main ideas in the sequence in which they appear in the original. But summarizing requires more than merely stringing together the entries in an outline. It fills in the logical connections between the author's ideas. Notice also in the following example that the reader repeats selected words and phrases and refers to the author by name, indicating, with verbs like *expresses, acknowledges,* and *explains,* the writer's purpose and strategy at each point in the argument.

Summary

King expresses his disappointment with white moderates who, by opposing his program of nonviolent direct action, have become a barrier to progress toward racial justice. He acknowledges that his program has raised tension in the South, but he explains that tension is necessary to bring about change. Furthermore, he argues that tension already exists. But because it has been unexpressed, it is unhealthy and potentially dangerous.

He defends his actions against the clergy's criticisms, particularly their argument that he is in too much of a hurry. Responding to charges of extremism, King claims that he has actually prevented racial violence by channeling the natural frustrations of oppressed blacks into nonviolent protest. He asserts that extremism is precisely what is needed now--but it must be creative, rather than destructive, extremism. He concludes by again expressing disappointment with white moderates for not joining his effort as some other whites have.

■ CHECKLIST: Summarizing

1. Make a scratch outline of the reading.

2. Write a paragraph or more that presents the author's main ideas largely in your own words. Use the outline as a guide, but reread parts of the original text as necessary.

3. To make the summary coherent, fill in connections between ideas.

■ SYNTHESIZING

Synthesizing involves presenting ideas and information gleaned from different sources. As a critical reading strategy, synthesizing can help you see how different sources relate to one another—for example, offering supporting details or opposing arguments.

When you synthesize material from different sources, you construct a conversation among your sources, a conversation in which you also participate. Synthesizing contributes most to critical thinking when writers use sources not only to support their ideas, but to challenge and extend them as well.

In the following example, the reader uses a variety of sources related to the King passage (pp. 531–37). The synthesis brings the sources together around a central idea. Notice how quotation, paraphrase, and summary are all used to present King's and the other sources' ideas.

Synthesis

When King defends his campaign of nonviolent direct action against the clergymen's criticism that "our actions, even though peaceful, must be condemned because they precipitate violence" (King excerpt, paragraph 3), he is using what Vinit Haksar calls Mohandas Gandhi's "safety-valve argument" ("Civil Disobedience and Non-Cooperation" 117). According to Haksar, Gandhi gave a "non-threatening warning of worse things to come" if his demands were not met. King similarly makes clear that advocates of actions more extreme than those he advocates are waiting in the wings: "The other force is one of bitterness and hatred, and it comes perilously close to advocating violence" (King excerpt, paragraph 5). King identifies this force with Elijah Muhammad, and although he does not name him, King's contemporary readers would have known that he was referring also to Malcolm X who, according to Herbert J. Storing, "urged that Negroes take seriously the idea of revolution" ("The Case against Civil Disobedience" 90). In fact, Malcolm X accused King of being a modern-day Uncle Tom, trying "to keep us under control, to keep us passive and peaceful and nonviolent" (Malcolm X Speaks 12).

■ CHECKLIST: Synthesizing

1. Find and read a variety of sources on your topic, annotating the passages that give you ideas about the topic.

2. Look for patterns among your sources, possibly supporting or refuting your ideas or those of other sources.

3. Write a paragraph or more synthesizing your sources, using quotation, para-phrase, and summary to present what they say on the topic.

■ CONTEXTUALIZING

All texts were written sometime in the past and therefore may embody historical and cultural assumptions, values, and attitudes different from your own. To read critically, you need to become aware of these differences. *Contextualizing* is a critical reading strategy that enables you to make inferences about a reading's historical and cultural context and to examine the differences between its context and your own.

The excerpt from King's "Letter from Birmingham Jail" is a good example of a text that benefits from being read contextually. If you knew little about the history of slavery and segregation in the United States, Martin Luther King Jr., or the civil rights movement, it would be very difficult to understand the passion for justice and impatience with delay expressed in this passage from King's writings. To understand the historical and cultural context in which King organized his demonstrations and wrote his "Letter from Birmingham Jail," you could do some library or Internet research. A little research would enable you to appreciate the intense emotions that swept the nation at the time. You would see that the threat of violence was all too real. Comparing the situation at the time King wrote the "Letter" in 1963 to situations with which you are familiar would help you understand some of your own atti-tudes toward King and the civil rights movement.

Here is what one reader wrote to contextualize King's writing:

Notes from a Contextualized Reading

1. I am not old enough to remember what it was like in the early 1960s when Dr. King was leading marches and sit-ins, but I have seen television documentaries showing demonstra-tors being attacked by dogs, doused by fire hoses, beaten and dragged by helmeted police. Such images give me a sense of the violence, fear, and hatred that King was responding to.

    The tension King writes about comes across in his writing. He uses his anger and frustration creatively to inspire his critics. He also threatens them, although he denies it. I saw a film on Malcolm X, so I could see that King was giving white people a choice between his own nonviolent way and Malcolm's more confrontational way.

2. Things have certainly changed since the sixties. Legal segregation has ended, but there are still racists like the detective in the O. J. Simpson trial. African Americans like General Colin Powell are highly respected and

```
powerful. The civil rights movement is over. So when I'm
reading King today, I feel like I'm reading history. But
then again, every once in a while there are reports of
police brutality because of race (think of Rodney King)
and of what we now call hate crimes.
```

■ CHECKLIST: Contextualizing

1. Describe the historical and cultural situation as it is represented in the reading and in other sources with which you are familiar. Your knowledge may come from other reading, television or film, school, or elsewhere. (If you know nothing about the historical and cultural context, you could do some library or Internet research.)

2. Compare the historical and cultural situation in which the text was written to your own historical and cultural situation. Consider how your understanding and judgment of the reading is affected by your own context.

■ EXPLORING THE SIGNIFICANCE OF FIGURATIVE LANGUAGE

Figurative language—metaphor, simile, and symbolism—enhances literal meaning by embodying abstract ideas in vivid images and by evoking feelings and associations.

Metaphor implicitly compares two different things by identifying them with each other. For instance, when King calls the white moderate "the Negro's great stumbling block in his stride toward freedom" (paragraph 1), he does not mean that the white moderate literally trips the Negro who is attempting to walk toward freedom. The sentence makes sense only if understood figuratively: The white moderate trips up the Negro by frustrating every effort to achieve justice.

Simile, a more explicit form of comparison, uses the word *like* or *as* to signal the relationship of two seemingly unrelated things. King uses simile when he says that injustice is "like a boil that can never be cured so long as it is covered up" (paragraph 2). This simile makes several points of comparison between injustice and a boil. It suggests that injustice is a disease of society as a boil is a disease of the body and that injustice, like a boil, must be exposed or it will fester and infect the entire body.

Symbolism compares two things by making one stand for the other. King uses the white moderate as a symbol for supposed liberals and would-be supporters of civil rights who are actually frustrating the cause.

How these figures of speech are used in a text reveals something of the writer's feelings about the subject. Exploring possible meanings in a text's figurative language involves (1) annotating and then listing the metaphors, similes, and symbols you find in a reading; (2) grouping the figures of speech that appear to express related feelings or attitudes, and labeling each group; and (3) writing to explore the meaning of the patterns you have found.

The following example shows the process of exploring figures of speech in the King excerpt.

Listing Figures of Speech

```
order is a dangerously structured dam
social progress should flow
stumbling block in the stride toward freedom
injustice is like a boil that can never be cured
the light of human conscience and air of national opinion
quicksand of racial injustice
```

Grouping Figures of Speech

```
Sickness: Segregation is a disease; action is healthy, the
     only antidote; injustice is like a boil . . .
Underground: Tension is hidden; resentments are pent up,
     repressed; injustice must be rooted out . . .
Blockage: The dam, stumbling block; human progress never rolls
     in on wheels of inevitability; social progress should
     flow . . .
```

Writing to Explore Meaning

```
     The patterns labeled underground and blockage suggest a
feeling of frustration. Inertia is a problem; movement forward
toward progress or upward toward the promised land is stalled.
The strong need to break through the resistance may represent
King's feelings both about his attempt to lead purposeful,
effective demonstrations and his effort to write a convincing
argument.
     The simile of injustice being "like a boil" links the
two patterns of underground and sickness, suggesting something
bad, a disease, is inside the people or the society. The cure
is to expose or to root out the blocked hatred and injustice
as well as to release the tension or emotion that has long
been repressed. This implies that repression itself is the
evil, not simply what is repressed. Therefore, writing and
speaking out through political action may have curative power
for individuals and society alike.
```

■ CHECKLIST: Exploring the Significance of Figurative Language

   1. Annotate and then list all the figures of speech you find in the reading—
      metaphors, similes, and symbols.

2. Group the figures of speech that appear to express related feelings and attitudes, and label each group.

3. Write one or two paragraphs exploring the meaning of these patterns. What do they tell you about the text?

■ LOOKING FOR PATTERNS OF OPPOSITION

All texts carry within themselves voices of opposition. These voices may echo the views and values of critical readers the writer anticipates or predecessors to whom the writer is responding in some way; they may even reflect the writer's own conflicting values. Careful readers look closely for such a dialogue of opposing voices within the text.

When we think of oppositions, we ordinarily think of polarities: *yes* and *no, up* and *down, black* and *white, new* and *old*. Some oppositions, however, may be more subtle. The excerpt from King's "Letter from Birmingham Jail" is rich in such oppositions: *moderate* versus *extremist, order* versus *justice, direct action* versus *passive acceptance, expression* versus *repression*. These oppositions are not accidental; they form a significant pattern that gives a critical reader important information about the essay.

A careful reading will show that King always values one of the two terms in an opposition over the other. In the passage, for example, *extremist* is valued over *moderate* (paragraph 9). This preference for extremism is surprising. The critical reader should ask why, when white extremists like the Ku Klux Klan have committed so many outrages against African Americans, King would prefer extremism. If King is trying to convince his readers to accept his point of view, why would he represent himself as an extremist? Moreover, why would a clergyman advocate extremism instead of moderation?

Studying the *patterns of opposition* enables you to answer these questions. You will see that King sets up this opposition to force his readers to examine their own values and realize that they are in fact misplaced. Instead of working toward justice, he says, those who support law and order maintain the unjust status quo. By getting his readers to think of white moderates as blocking rather than facilitating peaceful change, King brings them to align themselves with him and perhaps even embrace his strategy of nonviolent resistance.

Looking for patterns of opposition involves annotating words or phrases in the reading that indicate oppositions, listing the opposing terms in pairs, deciding which term in each pair is preferred by the writer, and reflecting on the meaning of the patterns. Here is a partial list of oppositions from the King excerpt, with the preferred terms marked by an asterisk:

Listing Patterns of Opposition

```
moderate                    *extremist

order                       *justice

negative peace              *positive peace
```

absence of justice	*presence of justice
goals	*methods
*direct action	passive acceptance
*exposed tension	hidden tension

■ CHECKLIST: Looking for Patterns of Opposition

1. Annotate the selection for words or phrases indicating oppositions.

2. List the pairs of oppositions. (You may have to paraphrase or even supply the opposite word or phrase if it is not stated directly in the text.)

3. For each pair of oppositions, put an asterisk next to the term that the writer seems to value or prefer over the other.

4. Study the patterns of opposition. How do they contribute to your understanding of the essay? What do they tell you about what the author wants you to believe?

■ REFLECTING ON CHALLENGES TO YOUR BELIEFS AND VALUES

To read critically, you need to scrutinize your own assumptions and attitudes as well as those expressed in the text you are reading. If you are like most readers, however, you will find that your assumptions and attitudes are so ingrained that you are not fully aware of them. A good strategy for getting at these underlying beliefs and values is to identify and reflect on the ways the text challenges you, how it makes you feel—disturbed, threatened, ashamed, combative, or some other way.

For example, here is what one student wrote about the King passage:

Reflections

In paragraph 1, Dr. King criticizes people who are "more devoted to 'order' than to justice." This criticism upsets me because today I think I would choose order over justice. When I analyze my feelings and try to figure out where they come from, I realize that what I feel most is fear. I am terrified by the violence in society today. I'm afraid of sociopaths who don't respect the rule of law, much less the value of human life.

I know Dr. King was writing in a time when the law itself was unjust, when order was apparently used to keep people from protesting and changing the law. But things are different now. Today, justice seems to serve criminals more than it serves law-abiding citizens. That's why I'm for order over justice.

■ CHECKLIST: Reflecting on Challenges to Your Beliefs and Values

1. Identify challenges by marking the text where you feel your beliefs and values are being opposed, citicized, or unfairly characterized.

2. Write a few paragraphs reflecting on why you feel challenged. Do not defend your feelings; instead, analyze them to see where they come from.

■ EVALUATING THE LOGIC OF AN ARGUMENT

An argument includes a thesis backed by reasons and support. The *thesis* asserts an idea, a position on a controversial issue, or a solution to a problem that the writer wants readers to accept. The *reasons* tell readers why they should accept the thesis and the *support* (such as examples, statistics, authorities, and textual evidence) gives readers grounds for accepting it. For an argument to be considered logically acceptable, it must meet the three conditions of what we call the ABC test:

The ABC Test

For more on argument, see Chapter 19. For an example of the ABC test, see Christine Romano's essay in Chapter 8, pp. 373–76.

A. The reasons and support must be *appropriate* to the thesis.

B. The reasons and support must be *believable*.

C. The reasons and support must be *consistent* with one another as well as *complete*.

Testing for Appropriateness

As a critical reader, you must decide whether the argument's reasons and support are appropriate and clearly related to the thesis. To test for appropriateness, ask these questions: How does each reason or piece of support relate to the thesis? Is the connection between reasons and support and the thesis clear and compelling? Or is the argument irrelevant or only vaguely related to the thesis?

For more on analogy, see Chapter 18, pp. 621–22. For more on invoking authorities, see Chapter 19, pp. 629–31.

Readers most often question the appropriateness of reasons and support when the writer argues by analogy or by invoking authority. For example, in paragraph 2, King argues that when law and order fail to establish justice, "they become the dangerously structured dams that block the flow of social progress." The analogy asserts the following logical relationship: Law and order are to progress toward justice what a dam is to water. If you do not accept this analogy, the argument fails the test of appropriateness.

King uses both analogy and authority in the following passage: "Isn't this like condemning Socrates because his unswerving commitment to truth and his philosophical inquiries precipitated the act by the misguided populace in which they made him drink hemlock?" (paragraph 3). Not only must you judge the appropriateness of the analogy comparing the Greek populace's condemnation of Socrates to the white moderates' condemnation of King, but you must also judge whether it is appropriate to accept Socrates as an authority on this subject. Since Socrates is generally respected for his teaching on justice, his words and actions are likely to be considered appropriate to King's situation in Birmingham.

Testing for Believability

Believability is a measure of your willingness to accept as true the reasons and support the writer gives in defense of a thesis.

To test for believability, ask: On what basis am I being asked to believe this reason or support is true? If it cannot be proved true or false, how much weight does it carry?

In judging facts, examples, statistics, and authorities, consider the following points.

Facts are statements that can be proved objectively to be true. The believability of facts depends on their *accuracy* (they should not distort or misrepresent reality), their *completeness* (they should not omit important details), and the *trustworthiness* of their sources (sources should be qualified and unbiased). King, for instance, asserts as fact that the African American will not wait much longer for racial justice (paragraph 8). His critics might question the factuality of this assertion by asking, is it true of all African Americans? How much longer will they wait? How does King know what African Americans will and will not do?

Examples and *anecdotes* are particular instances that may or may not make you believe a general statement. The believability of examples depends on their *representativeness* (whether they are truly typical and thus generalizable) and their *specificity* (whether particular details make them seem true to life). Even if a vivid example or gripping anecdote does not convince readers, it usually strengthens argumentative writing by clarifying the meaning and dramatizing the point. In paragraph 5 of the King excerpt, for example, King supports his generalization that some African American nationalist extremists are motivated by bitterness and hatred by citing the specific example of Elijah Muhammad's Black Muslim movement. Conversely, in paragraph 9, he refers to Jesus, Paul, Luther, and others as examples of extremists motivated by love and Christianity. These examples support his assertion that extremism is not in itself wrong and that any judgment of extremism must be based on its motivation and cause.

Statistics are numerical data, including correlations. The believability of statistics depends on the *comparability* of the data (the price of apples in 1985 cannot be compared to the price of apples in 2000 unless the figures are adjusted to account for inflation), the *precision* of the methods employed to gather and analyze data (representative samples should be used and variables accounted for), and the *trustworthiness* of the sources (sources should be qualified, unbiased, and—except in historical contexts—as recent as possible).

Authorities are people to whom the writer attributes expertise on a given subject. Not only must such authorities be appropriate, as mentioned earlier, but they must be believable as well. The believability of authorities depends on their *credibility,* on whether the reader accepts them as experts on the topic at hand. King cites authorities repeatedly throughout his essay. He refers to religious leaders (Jesus and Luther) as well as to American political leaders (Lincoln and Jefferson). These figures are certain to have a high degree of credibility among King's readers.

Testing for Consistency and Completeness

For more on counter-arguing, see Chapter 19, pp. 634–37.

In looking for consistency, you should be concerned that all the parts of the argument work together and that none of the reasons or support contradict any of the other reasons or support. In addition, the reasons and support, taken together, should be sufficient to convince readers to accept the thesis or at least take it seriously. To test for consistency and completeness, ask: Are any of the reasons and support contradictory? Do they provide sufficient grounds for accepting the thesis? Does the writer fail to counterargue (to acknowledge, accommodate, or refute any opposing arguments or important objections)?

A critical reader might regard as contradictory King's characterizing himself first as a moderate between the forces of complacency and violence and later as an extremist opposed to the forces of violence. King attempts to reconcile this apparent contradiction by explicitly redefining extremism in paragraph 9. Similarly, the fact that King fails to examine and refute every legal recourse available to his cause might allow a critical reader to question the sufficiency of his argument.

> ■ CHECKLIST: Evaluating the Logic of an Argument
>
> Use the ABC test:
>
> A. *Test for appropriateness* by checking that the reasons and support are clearly and directly related to the thesis.
>
> B. *Test for believability* by deciding whether you can accept the reasons and support as true.
>
> C. *Test for consistency and completeness* by ascertaining whether there are any contradictions in the argument and whether any important objections or opposing arguments have been ignored.

■ RECOGNIZING EMOTIONAL MANIPULATION

Many different kinds of essays appeal to readers' emotions. Tobias Wolff's remembered event essay (in Chapter 2) may be terrifying to some readers, David Noonan's profile of brain surgery (in Chapter 4) may be shocking, and Richard Estrada's position paper (in Chapter 6) may be annoying to some readers because of his accommodating tone.

Writers often try to arouse emotions in readers to excite their interest, make them care, or move them to take action. There is nothing wrong with appealing to readers' emotions. What is wrong is manipulating readers with false or exaggerated appeals. As a critical reader, you should be suspicious of writing that is overly or falsely sentimental, that cites alarming statistics and frightening anecdotes, that demonizes others and identifies itself with revered authorities, or that uses symbols (flag-waving) or emotionally loaded words (such as *racist*).

King, for example, uses the emotionally loaded word *paternalistically* to refer to the white moderate's belief that "he can set the timetable for another man's freedom" (paragraph 1). In the same paragraph, King uses symbolism to get an emotional reaction from readers when he compares the white moderate to the "Ku Klux Klanner." To get readers to accept his ideas, he also relies on authorities whose names evoke the greatest respect, such as Jesus and Lincoln. But some readers might object that comparing King's crusade to that of Jesus and other leaders of religious and political groups is pretentious and manipulative. A critical reader might also consider King's discussion of African American extremists in paragraph 7 to be a veiled threat designed to frighten readers into agreement.

■ CHECKLIST: Recognizing Emotional Manipulation

1. Annotate places in the text where you sense emotional appeals are being used.

2. Assess whether any of the emotional appeals are unfairly manipulative.

■ JUDGING THE WRITER'S CREDIBILITY

Writers often try to persuade readers to respect and believe them. Because readers may not know them personally or even by reputation, writers must present an image of themselves in their writing that will gain their readers' confidence. This image cannot be made directly but must be made indirectly, through the arguments, language, and system of values and beliefs expressed or implied in the writing. Writers establish credibility in their writing in three ways:

By showing their knowledge of the subject

By building common ground with readers

By responding fairly to objections and opposing arguments

Testing for Knowledge

Writers demonstrate their knowledge through the facts and statistics they marshal, the sources they rely on for information, and the scope and depth of their understanding. As a critical reader, you may not be sufficiently expert on the subject yourself to know whether the facts are accurate, the sources are reliable, and the understanding is sufficient. You may need to do some research to see what others say about the subject. You can also check credentials—the writer's educational and professional qualifications, the respectability of the publication in which the selection first appeared, and reviews of the writer's work—to determine whether the writer is a respected authority in the field. For example, King brings with him the authority that comes from being a member of the clergy and a respected leader of the Southern Christian Leadership Conference.

Testing for Common Ground

One way writers can establish common ground with their readers is by basing their reasoning on shared values, beliefs, and attitudes. They use language that includes their readers *(we)* rather than excludes them *(they)*. They qualify their assertions to keep them from being too extreme. Above all, they acknowledge differences of opinion and try to make room in their argument to accommodate reasonable differences. As a critical reader, you want to notice such appeals.

King creates common ground with readers by using the inclusive pronoun *we,* suggesting shared concerns between himself and his audience. Notice, however, his use of masculine pronouns and other references ("the Negro . . . he," "our brothers"). Although King addressed his letter to male clergy, he intended it to be published in the local newspaper, where it would be read by an audience of both men and women. By using language that excludes women, a common practice at the time the selection was written, King misses the opportunity to build common ground with half of his readers.

Testing for Fairness

Writers reveal their character by how they handle opposing arguments and objections to their argument. As a critical reader, you want to pay particular attention to how writers treat possible differences of opinion. Be suspicious of those who ignore differences and pretend that everyone agrees with their viewpoints. When objections or opposing views are represented, consider whether they have been distorted in any way; if they are refuted, be sure they are challenged fairly—with sound reasoning and solid support.

One way to gauge the author's credibility is to identify the tone of the argument, for it conveys the writer's attitude toward the subject and toward the reader. Examine the text carefully for indications of tone: Is the text angry? Sarcastic? Evenhanded? Shrill? Condescending? Bullying? Do you feel as if the writer is treating the subject—and you, as a reader—with fairness? King's tone might be characterized in different passages as patient (he doesn't lose his temper), respectful (he refers to white moderates as "people of good will"), or pompous (comparing himself to Jesus and Socrates).

■ CHECKLIST: Judging the Writer's Credibility

1. Annotate for the writer's knowledge of the subject, how well common ground is established, and whether the writer deals fairly with objections and opposing arguments.

2. Decide what in the essay you find credible and what you question.

Part Three

WRITING STRATEGIES

Cueing the Reader

Readers need guidance. To guide readers through a piece of writing, a writer can provide five basic kinds of cues or signals:

1. Thesis and forecasting statements, to orient readers to ideas and organization
2. Paragraphing, to group related ideas and details
3. Cohesive devices, to connect ideas to one another and bring about coherence and clarity
4. Connectives, to signal relationships or shifts in meaning
5. Headings and subheadings, to group related paragraphs and help readers locate specific information quickly

This chapter illustrates how each of these cueing strategies works.

◼ ORIENTING STATEMENTS

To help readers find their way, especially in difficult and lengthy texts, you can provide two kinds of orienting information: a thesis statement, which declares the main point, and a forecasting statement, which previews subordinate points, showing the order in which they will be discussed in the essay.

Thesis Statements

To help readers understand what is being said about a subject, writers often provide a thesis statement early in the essay. The *thesis statement* operates as a cue by letting readers know which is the most important general idea among the writer's many ideas and observations. Here are three thesis statements from essays in Part One:

> O.K., let's cut out all this nonsense about romantic love. Let's bring some scientific precision to the party. Let's put love under a microscope.
> When rigorous people with Ph.D.s after their names do that, what they see is not some silly, senseless thing. No, their probe reveals that love rests firmly on the foundations of evolution, biology, and chemistry.
>
> —ANASTASIA TOUFEXIS, Chapter 5

It seems to me that what Native Americans are saying is that what would be intolerable for Jews, blacks, Latinos and others is no less offensive to them. Theirs is a request not only for dignified treatment, but for fair treatment as well. For America to ignore the complaints of a numerically small segment of the population because it is small is neither dignified nor fair.

—RICHARD ESTRADA, Chapter 6

. . . I could not shake the idea that sooner or later I would get the rifle out again. All my images of myself as I wished to be were images of myself armed. Because I did not know who I was, any image of myself, no matter how grotesque, had power over me. This much I understand now. But the man can give no help to the boy, not in this matter nor in those that follow. The boy moves always out of reach.

—TOBIAS WOLFF, Chapter 2

Most thesis statements, like Toufexis's, can be expressed in a single sentence; others may require two or more sentences, like Estrada's and Wolff's. Wolff's thesis explicitly states the point of a remembered event, but many autobiographical essays imply the thesis rather than state it directly.

Readers naturally look for something that will tell them the point of an essay, a focus for the many diverse details and ideas they encounter as they read. The lack of an explicit thesis statement can make this task more difficult. Therefore, careful writers keep readers' needs and expectations in mind when deciding how to state the thesis as clearly and directly as possible.

Another important decision is where to place the thesis statement. Most readers expect to find some information early on that will give them a context for reading the essay, particularly if they are reading about a new and difficult subject. Therefore, a thesis statement, like that of Toufexis, placed at the beginning of an essay enables readers to anticipate the content of the essay and more easily understand the relationships among its various ideas and details.

Occasionally, however, particularly in fairly short, informal essays and in some autobiographical and argumentative essays, a writer may save a direct statement of the thesis until the conclusion, which is where Estrada and Wolff put theirs. Ending with the thesis has the effect of bringing together the various strands of information or supporting details introduced over the course of the essay and making clear the essay's main idea.

■ Exercise 13.1

In the essay by Jessica Statsky in Chapter 6, underline the thesis statement, the last sentence in paragraph 1. Notice the key terms in this thesis, the words that seem to be essential to presenting Statsky's ideas: "overzealous parents and coaches," "impose adult standards," "children's sports," "activities . . . neither satisfying nor beneficial." Then skim the essay, stopping to read the sentence at the beginning of each paragraph. Also read the last paragraph.

Consider whether the idea in every paragraph's first sentence is anticipated by the thesis key terms. Consider also the connection between the ideas in the last paragraph and the thesis key terms. What can you conclude about how a thesis might assert the point of an essay, anticipate the ideas that follow, and help readers relate the ideas to each other?

Forecasting Statements

Some thesis statements include a *forecast*, which overviews the way a thesis will be developed. For example, note the role of the forecasting statement in this opening paragraph from an essay by William Langer on the bubonic plague:

> In the three years from 1348 through 1350 the pandemic of plague known as the Black Death, or, as the Germans called it, the Great Dying, killed at least a fourth of the population of Europe. It was undoubtedly the worst disaster that has ever befallen mankind. Today we can have no real conception of the terror under which people lived in the shadow of the plague. For more than two centuries plague has not been a serious threat to mankind in the large, although it is still a grisly presence in parts of the Far East and Africa. Scholars continue to study the Great Dying, however, as a historical example of human behavior under the stress of universal catastrophe. <u>In these days when the threat of plague has been replaced by the threat of mass human extermination by even more rapid means, there has been a sharp renewal of interest in the history of the 14th-century calamity. With new perspective, students are investigating its manifold effects: demographic, economic, psychological, moral and religious.</u>
>
> —WILLIAM LANGER, "The Black Death"

This introductory paragraph informs us that Langer's article is about the effects of the Black Death. His thesis (underlined) states that there is renewed interest in studying the social effects of the bubonic plague and that these new studies focus on five particular categories of effects. As a reader would expect, Langer then goes on to divide his essay into explanations of the research into these five effects, taking them up in the order in which they appear in the forecasting statement.

■ Exercise 13.2

Turn to Christine Romano's essay in Chapter 8 and underline the forecasting statement in paragraph 2. (After the first sentence, which states Romano's thesis, the remaining sentences offer a forecast of Romano's main points and the order in which she will take them up.) Then skim the essay, pausing to read the first sentence in each paragraph. Notice whether Romano takes up every point she mentions in the forecasting statement and whether she sticks to the order she promises readers. What can you conclude about how a forecasting statement assists readers?

■ PARAGRAPHING

Paragraph cues as obvious as indentation keep readers on track. You can also arrange material in a paragraph to help readers see what is important or significant. For example, you can begin with a topic sentence, help readers see the relationship between the previous paragraph and the present one with an explicit transition, and place the most important information toward the end. This section illustrates these cues and others.

For additional visual cues for readers, see "Headings and Subheadings" on pp. 570–71.

Paragraph Cues

The indentation that signals the beginning of a new paragraph is a relatively modern printing convention. Old manuscripts show that paragraph divisions were not always marked. To make reading easier, scribes and printers began to use the symbol ¶ to mark paragraph breaks. Later, indenting became common practice, but even that relatively modern custom has changed in some forms of writing today. Instead of indenting, most business writers now distinguish one paragraph from another by leaving a line of space above and below each paragraph. Writing on the Internet is also usually paragraphed in this way.

Paragraphing helps readers by signaling when a sequence of related sentences begins and ends. Such paragraph signals tell them when they can stop holding meaning-making in suspension. Writers must constantly consider the need for this kind of closure so that readers can more easily follow the development of ideas.

Paragraphing also helps readers judge what is most important in what they are reading. Writers typically emphasize important information by placing it at the two points where readers are most attentive—the beginning and the end of a paragraph. Many writers put information to orient readers at the beginning of a paragraph and save the most important information for last.

You can give special emphasis to information by placing it in a paragraph of its own.

■ Exercise 13.3

Turn to Patrick O'Malley's essay in Chapter 7 and read paragraphs 4–6 with the following questions in mind: Does all the material in each paragraph seem to be related? Do you feel a sense of closure at the end of each paragraph? Does the last sentence offer the most important or significant or weighty information in the paragraph?

Topic Sentence Strategies

A *topic sentence* lets readers know the focus of a paragraph in simple and direct terms. It is a cueing strategy for the paragraph, much as a thesis or forecasting statement is for the whole essay. Because paragraphing usually signals a shift in focus, readers expect some kind of reorientation in the opening sentence. They need to know whether the new paragraph will introduce another aspect of the topic or develop one already introduced.

Announcing the Topic.   Some topic sentences simply announce the topic. Here are some examples taken from Barry Lopez's book *Arctic Dreams:*

A polar bear walks in a way all its own.

What is so consistently striking about the way Eskimos used parts of an animal is the breadth of their understanding about what would work.

The Mediterranean view of the Arctic, down to the time of the Elizabethan mariners, was shaped by two somewhat contradictory thoughts.

These topic sentences do more than merely identify the topic; they also indicate how the topic will be developed in subsequent sentences—by describing how bears walk, giving examples of animal parts Eskimos used and explaining what they understood about how each part could be useful, or contrasting two preconceptions about the Arctic.

The following paragraph shows how one of Lopez's topic sentences (underlined) is developed:

> What is so consistently striking about the way Eskimos used parts of an animal is the breadth of their understanding about what would work. Knowing that muskox horn is more flexible than caribou antler, they preferred it for making the side prongs of a fish spear. For a waterproof bag in which to carry sinews for clothing repair, they chose salmon skin. They selected the strong, translucent intestine of a bearded seal to make a window for a snowhouse—it would fold up for easy traveling and it would not frost over in cold weather. To make small snares for sea ducks, they needed a springy material that would not rot in salt water—baleen fibers. The down feather of a common eider, tethered at the end of a stick in the snow at an angle, would reveal the exhalation of a quietly surfacing seal. Polar bear bone was used anywhere a stout, sharp point was required, because it is the hardest bone.
>
> —Barry Lopez, *Arctic Dreams*

■ Exercise 13.4

Turn to David Ratinov's essay in Chapter 10. Underline the topic sentence (the first sentence) in paragraphs 3–5. Consider how these sentences help you anticipate the paragraph's topic and method of development.

Making a Transition. Not all topic sentences simply point to what will follow. Some also refer to earlier sentences. Such sentences work both as topic sentences, stating the main point of the paragraph, and as transitions, linking that paragraph to the previous one. Here are a few topic sentences from "Quilts and Women's Culture," by Elaine Hedges, that use specific transitions (underlined) to tie the sentence to a previous statement:

> Within its broad traditionalism and anonymity, however, variations and distinctions developed.
>
> Regionally, too, distinctions were introduced into quilt making through the interesting process of renaming.
>
> With equal inventiveness women renamed traditional patterns to accommodate to the local landscape.
>
> Finally, out of such regional and other variations come individual, signed achievements.
>
> Quilts, then, were an outlet for creative energy, a source and emblem of sisterhood and solidarity, and a graphic response to historical and political change.

Sometimes the first sentence of a paragraph serves as a transition, and a subsequent sentence states the topic. The underlined sentences in the following example illustrate this strategy:

. . . What a convenience, what a relief it will be, they say, never to worry about how to dress for a job interview, a romantic tryst, or a funeral!

Convenient, perhaps, but not exactly a relief. Such a utopia would give most of us the same kind of chill we feel when a stadium full of Communist-bloc athletes in identical sports outfits, shouting slogans in unison, appears on TV. Most people do not want to be told what to wear any more than they want to be told what to say. In Belfast recently four hundred Irish Republican prisoners "refused to wear any clothes at all, draping themselves day and night in blankets," rather than put on prison uniforms. Even the offer of civilian-style dress did not satisfy them; they insisted on wearing their own clothes brought from home, or nothing. Fashion is free speech, and one of the privileges, if not always one of the pleasures, of a free world.

—ALISON LURIE, *The Language of Clothes*

Occasionally, whole paragraphs serve as transitions, linking one sequence of paragraphs with those that follow. This transition paragraph summarizes what went before (evidence of contrast) and sets up what will follow (evidence of similarity):

Yet it was not all contrast, after all. Different as they were—in background, in personality, in underlying aspiration—these two great soldiers had much in common. Under everything else, they were marvelous fighters. Furthermore, their fighting qualities were really very much alike.

—BRUCE CATTON, "Grant and Lee: A Study in Contrasts"

■ Exercise 13.5

Turn to the Stephen King essay in Chapter 9 and read paragraphs 8–12. As you read, underline the part of the first sentence in paragraphs 9–12 that refers to the previous paragraph, creating a transition from one to the next. Notice the different ways King creates these transitions. Consider whether they are all equally effective.

Positioning the Topic Sentence. Although topic sentences may occur anywhere in a paragraph, stating the topic in the first sentence has the advantage of giving readers a sense of how the paragraph is likely to be developed. The beginning of the paragraph is therefore the most common position for a topic sentence.

A topic sentence that does not open a paragraph is most likely to appear at the end. When a topic sentence concludes a paragraph, it usually summarizes or generalizes preceding information. In the following example, the topic is not stated explicitly until the last sentence.

Even black Americans sometimes need to be reminded about the deceptiveness of television. Blacks retain their fascination with black characters on TV: Many of us buy *Jet* magazine primarily to read its weekly television feature, which lists every black character (major or minor) to be seen on the screen that week. Yet our fixation with the presence of black characters on TV has blinded us to an important fact that *Cosby*, which began in 1984, and its offshoots over the years demonstrate convincingly: There is very little connection between the social status of black Americans and the fabricated images of black people that Americans consume each day. The representation of blacks on TV is a very poor index to our social advancement or political progress.

—HENRY LOUIS GATES JR., "TV's Black World Turns—but Stays Unreal"

When a topic sentence is used in a narrative, it often appears as the last sentence as a way to evaluate or reflect on events:

I hadn't known she could play the piano. She wasn't playing very well, I guess, because she stopped occasionally and had to start over again. She concentrated intensely on the music, and the others in the room sat absolutely silently. My mother was facing me but didn't seem to see me. She seemed to be staring beyond me toward something that wasn't there. All the happy excitement died in me at that moment. Looking at my mother, so isolated from us all, I saw her for the first time as a person utterly alone.

—RUSSELL BAKER, *Growing Up*

It is possible for a single topic sentence to introduce two or more paragraphs. Subsequent paragraphs in such a sequence have no separate topic sentences of their own. Here is a two-paragraph sequence in which the topic sentence opens the first paragraph:

Anthropologists Daniel Maltz and Ruth Borker point out that boys and girls socialize differently. Little girls tend to play in small groups or, even more common, in pairs. Their social life usually centers around a best friend, and friendships are made, maintained, and broken by talk—especially "secrets." If a little girl tells her friend's secret to another little girl, she may find herself with a new best friend. The secrets themselves may or may not be important, but the fact of telling them is all-important. It's hard for newcomers to get into these tight groups, but anyone who is admitted is treated as an equal. Girls like to play cooperatively; if they can't cooperate, the group breaks up.

Little boys tend to play in larger groups, often outdoors, and they spend more time doing things than talking. It's easy for boys to get into the group, but not everyone is accepted as an equal. Once in the group, boys must jockey for their status in it. One of the most important ways they do this is through talk: verbal display such as telling stories and jokes, challenging and sidetracking the verbal displays of other boys, and withstanding other boys' challenges in order to maintain their own story —and status. Their talk is often competitive talk about who is best at what.

—DEBORAH TANNEN, *That's Not What I Meant!*

■ Exercise 13.6

Consider the variety and effectiveness of the topic sentences in your most recent essay. Begin by underlining the topic sentence in each paragraph after the first one. The topic sentence may not be the first sentence in a paragraph, though often it will be.

Then double-underline the part of the topic sentence that provides an explicit transition from one paragraph to the next. You may find a transition that is separate from the topic sentence. You may not always find a topic sentence.

Reflect on your topic sentences, and evaluate how well they serve to orient your readers to the sequence of topics or ideas in your essay.

■ COHESIVE DEVICES

Cohesive devices guide readers, helping them follow your train of thought by connecting key words and phrases throughout a passage. Among such devices are pronoun reference, word repetition, synonyms, repetition of sentence structure, and collocation.

Pronoun Reference

One common cohesive device is pronoun reference. As noun substitutes, pronouns refer to nouns that either precede or follow them and thus serve to connect phrases or sentences. The nouns that come before the pronouns are called *antecedents*. In the following paragraph, the pronouns *(it or its)* form a chain of connection with their antecedent, *George Washington Bridge*.

> In New York from dawn to dusk to dawn, day after day, you can hear the steady rumble of tires against the concrete span of the George Washington Bridge. The bridge is never completely still. It trembles with traffic. It moves in the wind. Its great veins of steel swell when hot and contract when cold; its span often is ten feet closer to the Hudson River in summer than in winter.
>
> —Gay Talese, "New York"

This example has only one pronoun-antecedent chain, and the antecedent comes first, so all the pronouns refer back to it. When there are multiple pronoun-antecedent chains with references forward as well as back, writers have to make sure that readers will not mistake one pronoun's antecedent for another's.

Word Repetition

To avoid confusion, writers often repeat words and phrases. This device is especially helpful if a pronoun might confuse readers:

> The first step is to realize that in our society we have permitted the kinds of vulnerability that characterize the victims of violent crime and have ignored, where we could, the hostility and alienation that enter into the making of violent criminals. No rational person condones violent crime, and I have no patience with sentimental attitudes toward violent criminals. But it is time that we open our eyes to the conditions that foster violence and that ensure the existence of easily recognizable victims.
>
> —Margaret Mead, "A Life for a Life: What That Means Today"

In the next example, several overlapping chains of word repetition prevent confusion and help the reader follow the ideas:

> Natural selection is the central concept of Darwinian theory—the fittest survive and spread their favored traits through populations. Natural selection is defined by Spencer's phrase "survival of the fittest," but what does this famous bit of jargon really mean? Who are the fittest? And how is "fitness" defined? We often read that fitness involves no more than "differential reproductive success"—the production of more surviving offspring than other competing members of the population. Whoa!

cries Bethell, as many others have before him. This formulation defines <u>fitness</u> in terms of <u>survival</u> only. The crucial phrase of natural selection means no more than "the <u>survival</u> of those who <u>survive</u>"—a vacuous <u>tautology</u>. (A <u>tautology</u> is a phrase —like "my father is a man"—containing no information in the predicate ["a man"] not inherent in the subject ["my father"]. <u>Tautologies</u> are fine as definitions, but not as testable scientific statements—there can be nothing to test in a statement true by definition.)

–Stephen Jay Gould, Ever Since Darwin

Notice that Gould uses repetition to keep readers focused on the key concepts of "natural selection," "survival of the fittest," and "tautology." These key terms may vary in form—*fittest* becomes *fitness*, and *survival* changes to *surviving* and *survive* —but they serve as links in the chain of meaning.

Synonyms

In addition to word repetition, you can use *synonyms,* words with identical or very similar meanings, to connect important ideas. In the following example, the author develops a careful chain of synonyms and word repetitions:

> Over time, <u>small bits of knowledge</u> about a <u>region</u> accumulate among <u>local residents</u> in the form of <u>stories</u>. These are <u>remembered</u> in the <u>community</u>; even what is unusual does not become lost and therefore irrelevant. These <u>narratives</u> comprise for a <u>native</u> an <u>intricate, long-term view</u> of a <u>particular landscape</u>. . . . Outside the <u>region</u> this <u>complex</u> but easily shared <u>"reality"</u> is hard to get across without <u>reducing it to generalities</u>, to misleading or imprecise abstraction.

–Barry Lopez, Arctic Dreams

Note the variety of synonym sequences:

"particular landscape," "region"

"local residents," "community," "native"

"stories," "narratives"

"accumulate," "remembered," "does not become lost," "comprise"

"intricate, long-term view," "complex . . . reality," "without reducing it to generalities"

The result is a coherent paragraph that constantly reinforces the author's point.

Sentence Structure Repetition

Writers occasionally repeat the same sentence structure to emphasize the connections among their ideas, as in this example:

> But the life forms are as much part of the structure of the Earth as any inanimate portion is. It is all an inseparable part of a whole. <u>If</u> any animal is isolated totally from other forms of life, <u>then</u> death by starvation will surely follow. <u>If</u> isolated from water, death by dehydration will follow even faster. <u>If</u> isolated from air, whether free or

dissolved in water, death by asphyxiation will follow still faster. If isolated from the Sun, animals will survive for a time, but plants would die, and if all plants died, all animals would starve.

—ISAAC ASIMOV, "The Case against Man"

From the third sentence to the last, Asimov repeats the "If this . . . then that" sentence structure to show that the sentences or clauses are logically related; every one expresses a consequence of isolation.

Collocation

Words collocate when they occur together in expected ways around a particular topic. For example, in a paragraph on a high school graduation, a reader might expect to encounter such words as *valedictorian, diploma, commencement, honors, cap and gown,* and *senior class.* Collocations occur quite naturally to a writer, and they usually form a recognizable network of meaning for readers. The paragraph that follows uses five collocation chains:

housewife, cooking, neighbor, home

clocks, calculated cooking times, progression, precise

obstinacy, vagaries, problem

sun, clear days, cloudy ones, sundial, cast its light, angle, seasons, sun, weather

cooking, fire, matches, hot coals, smoldering, ashes, go out, bed-warming pan

The seventeenth-century housewife not only had to make do without thermometers, she also had to make do without clocks, which were scarce and dear throughout the sixteen hundreds. She calculated cooking times by the progression of the sun; her cooking must have been more precise on clear days than on cloudy ones. Marks were sometimes painted on the floor, providing her with a rough sundial, but she still had to make allowance for the obstinacy of the sun in refusing to cast its light at the same angle as the seasons changed; but she was used to allowing for the vagaries of sun and weather. She also had a problem starting her fire in the morning; there were no matches. If she had allowed the hot coals smoldering under the ashes to go out, she had to borrow some from a neighbor, carrying them home with care, perhaps in a bed-warming pan.

—WAVERLY ROOT AND RICHARD DE ROUCHEMENT, *Eating in America*

■ Exercise 13.7

Now that you know more about pronoun reference, word repetition, synonyms, sentence structure repetition, and collocation, turn to David Noonan's essay in Chapter 4 and identify the cohesive devices you find in paragraphs 1–5. Underline each cohesive device you can find; there will be many devices. You might also try to connect with lines the various pronoun, related-word, and synonym chains you find. You could also try listing the separate collocation chains. Consider how these cohesive devices help you read and make sense of the passage.

■ Exercise 13.8

Choose one of your recent essays, and select any three contiguous paragraphs. Identify the cohesive devices you find in these three paragraphs. Underline every cohesive device you can find; there will be many devices. Try to connect with lines the various pronoun, related-word, and synonym chains you find. Also try listing the separate collocation chains.

You will be surprised and pleased at how extensively you rely on cohesive ties. Indeed, you could not produce readable text without cohesive ties. Consider these questions relevant to your development as a writer: Are all of your pronoun references clear? Are you straining for synonyms when repeated words would do? Do you ever repeat sentence structures to emphasize connections? Do you trust yourself to put collocation to work?

■ CONNECTIVES

A *connective* serves as a bridge, connecting one paragraph, sentence, clause, or word with another. It not only signals a connection but also identifies the kind of connection by indicating to readers how the item preceding the connective relates to the one that follows it. Connectives help readers anticipate how the next paragraph or sentence will affect the meaning of what they have just read. There are three basic groups of connectives, based on the relationships they indicate: logical, temporal, and spatial.

Logical Relationships

Connectives help readers follow the logic of an argument. How such connectives work is illustrated in this tightly and passionately reasoned paragraph by James Baldwin:

> The black man insists, by whatever means he finds at his disposal, that the white man cease to regard him as an exotic rarity and recognize him as a human being. This is a very charged and difficult moment, for there is a great deal of will power involved in the white man's naïveté. Most people are not naturally malicious, and the white man prefers to keep the black man at a certain human remove because it is easier for him thus to preserve his simplicity and to avoid being called to account for crimes committed by his forefathers, or his neighbors. He is inescapably aware, nevertheless, that he is in a better position in the world than black men are, nor can he quite put to death the suspicion that he is hated by black men therefore. He does not wish to be hated, neither does he wish to change places, and at this point in his uneasiness he can scarcely avoid having recourse to those legends which white men have created about black men, the most unusual effect of which is that the white man finds himself enmeshed, so to speak, in his own language which describes hell, as well as the attributes which lead one to hell, as being black as night.
>
> —JAMES BALDWIN, "Stranger in the Village"

Connectives Showing Logical Relationships

- *To introduce another item in a series:* first, second; in the second place; for one thing . . . , for another; next; then; furthermore; moreover; in addition; finally; last; also; similarly; besides; and; as well as

- *To introduce an illustration or other specification:* in particular; specifically; for instance; for example; that is; namely

- *To introduce a result or a cause:* consequently; as a result; hence; accordingly; thus; so; therefore; then; because; since; for

- *To introduce a restatement:* that is; in other words; in simpler terms; to put it differently

- *To introduce a conclusion or summary:* in conclusion; finally; all in all; evidently; clearly; actually; to sum up; altogether; of course

- *To introduce an opposing point:* but; however; yet; nevertheless; on the contrary; on the other hand; in contrast; still; neither; nor

- *To introduce a concession to an opposing view:* certainly; naturally; of course; it is true; to be sure; granted

- *To resume the original line of reasoning after a concession:* nonetheless; all the same; even though; still; nevertheless

Temporal Relationships

In addition to showing logical connections, connectives may indicate temporal relationships—a sequence or progression in time—as this example illustrates:

> That night, we drank tea and then vodka with lemon peel steeped in it. The four of us talked in Russian and English about mutual friends and American railroads and the Rolling Stones. Seryozha loves the Stones, and his face grew wistful as we spoke about their recent album, "Some Girls." He played a tape of "Let It Bleed" over and over, until we could translate some difficult phrases for him; after that, he came out with the phrases at intervals during the evening, in a pretty decent imitation of Jagger's Cockney snarl. He was an adroit and oddly formal host, inconspicuously filling our teacups and politely urging us to eat bread and cheese and chocolate. While he talked to us, he teased Anya, calling her "Piglet," and she shook back her bangs and glowered at him. It was clear that theirs was a fiery relationship. After a while, we talked about ourselves. Anya told us about painting and printmaking and about how hard it was to buy supplies in Moscow. There had been something angry in her dark face since the beginning of the evening; I thought at first that it meant she didn't like Americans; but now I realized that it was a constant, barely suppressed rage at her own situation.
>
> —ANDREA LEE, *Russian Journal*

Connectives Showing Temporal Relationships

- *To indicate frequency:* frequently; hourly; often; occasionally; now and then; day after day; every so often; again and again

- *To indicate duration:* during; briefly; for a long time; minute by minute; while

- *To indicate a particular time:* now; then; at that time; in those days; last Sunday; next Christmas; in 1999; at the beginning of August; at six o'clock; first thing in the morning; two months ago; when

- *To indicate the beginning:* at first; in the beginning; since; before then

- *To indicate the middle:* in the meantime; meanwhile; as it was happening; at that moment; at the same time; simultaneously; next; then

- *To indicate the end and beyond:* eventually; finally; at last; in the end; subsequently; later; afterward

Spatial Relationships

Spatial connectives orient readers to the objects in a scene, as illustrated in these paragraphs:

> On Georgia 155, I crossed Troublesome Creek, then went through groves of pecan trees aligned one with the next like fenceposts. The pastures grew a green almost blue, and syrupy water the color of a dusty sunset filled the ponds. Around the farmhouses, from wires strung high above the ground, swayed gourds hollowed out for purple martins.
>
> The land rose again on the other side of the Chattahoochee River, and Highway 34 went to the ridgetops where long views over the hills opened in all directions. Here was the tail of the Appalachian backbone, its gradual descent to the Gulf. Near the Alabama stateline stood a couple of LAST CHANCE! bars. . . .
>
> —WILLIAM LEAST HEAT MOON, *Blue Highways*

Connectives Showing Spatial Relationships

- *To indicate closeness:* close to; near; next to; alongside; adjacent to; facing

- *To indicate distance:* in the distance; far; beyond; away; there

- *To indicate direction:* up/down; sideways; along; across; to the right/left; in front of/behind; above/below; inside/outside; toward/away from

■ Exercise 13.9

Turn to Amy Wu's essay in Chapter 3. Relying on the lists of connectives just given, underline the *logical* and *temporal* connectives in paragraphs 1–5. Consider how the connectives relate the ideas and events from sentence to sentence. Do you see the need for further connectives to make the relationships clear?

■ Exercise 13.10

Select a recent essay of your own. Choose at least three paragraphs and, relying on the lists of connectives given in the text, underline the logical, temporal, and spatial connectives. Depending on the kind of writing you were doing, you may find few, if any, connectives in one category or another. For example, an essay speculating about causes may not include any spatial connectives; writing about a remembered event might not contain connectives showing logical relationships.

Consider how your connectives relate the ideas from sentence to sentence. Comparing your connectives to those in the lists, do you find that you are making full use of the repertoire of connectives? Do you find gaps between any of your sentences that a well-chosen connective would close?

■ HEADINGS AND SUBHEADINGS

Headings, brief phrases set off from the text in various ways, can provide visible cues to readers about the content and organization of a text. Headings can be distinguished from text in numerous ways, including the selective use of capital letters, bold or italic type, or different sizes of type. To be most helpful to readers, headings should be phrased similarly and follow a predictable system. In this chapter, the headings in the section "Paragraphing," beginning on p. 559, provide a good example of a system of headings that can readily be outlined:

PARAGRAPHING

Paragraph Cues

Topic Sentence Strategies

    Announcing the Topic.

    Making a Transition.

    Positioning the Topic Sentence.

To learn more about distinguishing headings from surrounding text and about setting up systems of headings, see "Typography," pp. 767–70 in Chapter 25: Designing Documents.

Notice that in this example the system has three levels. In the first level, all the letters are capitalized, and the heading stands out most visibly among the others. (It is one of five such capitalized headings in this chapter.) In the second level, the first letter in each word (except for articles and prepositions) is capitalized and the others are lowercased; like the heading in the first level, this second-level heading is aligned with the left margin. The first of these second-level headings has no subheadings beneath it, while the second has three. These subheadings comprise the third level in the system. They are run in as part of the paragraph they introduce, as you can see if you pause now to turn the pages of this section.

All of these headings are set apart from the surrounding text by the special use of capital letters or spacing or both. At each level, they follow a parallel grammatical structure: nouns at the first level, which you can confirm by skimming the chapter in order to look at the other four first-level heads; nouns at the second level ("cues" and "strategies"); and "-ing" nouns at the third level. For papers written in MLA style, note the particular requirement that sentences immediately following headings be able to stand alone grammatically.

For more on MLA style, see Chapter 22.

Headings may not be necessary in the short essays you will be composing for your freshman composition course. Short essays offer readers thesis statements, forecasting statements, well-positioned topic sentences, and transition sentences so that they have all the cues they may need. Headings are rare in some genres, like essays about remembered events and people (Chapters 2 and 3) and essays profiling people and places (Chapter 4). Headings appear more frequently in genres such as position papers, reviews, public policy proposals, and speculations about social problems (Chapters 5–9).

Frequency and Placement of Headings

Before dividing their essays into sections with headings and subheadings, writers need to make sure their discussion is detailed enough to support at least one heading at each level. The frequency and placement of headings depend entirely on the content and how it is divided and organized. Keep in mind that headings do not reduce the need for other cues to keep readers on track.

"The New Terrorism," pp. 201–4 in Chapter 5, uses two headings to cue readers. Both are grammatically parallel (noun phrases):

Attack for Attack's Sake

The Favourite Target

If you take time to read or skim this essay, you will recognize that the first heading subsumes material concerned with defining and illustrating a concept—the new terrorism. The noun phrase "attack for attack's sake" in the heading captures the new terrorism's main feature—the perpetrators' motive to inflict the greatest possible amount of pain, death, terror, and confusion. The second heading covers a much briefer section arguing that the new terrorists' main target "will always be the American heartland." Although the headings encompass unequal amounts of material, they divide the content logically. The writer might have decided to include subheadings under the first heading identifying the main features of the new terrorism, but the essay is relatively brief and the text offers ample cues to guide readers.

■ Exercise 13.11

Turn to William Pollack's essay in Chapter 9 and survey the system of headings. If you have not read the essay, read or skim it now. If you have not worked on this assignment, read Basic Features: Speculating about Causes at the end of the Readings section in order to familiarize yourself with the genre—speculating about causes. Consider how the headings help readers anticipate what is coming and how the argument is organized. Analyze whether the headings substitute for or complement a strong system of other cues for keeping readers on track. Decide whether the headings guide readers through the particular stages of the genre. Finally, try to answer these questions: Do any of the headings suggest subheadings? Might fewer or more headings be helpful to readers? Are the headings grammatically parallel?

For more practice evaluating the effectiveness of headings, review "Dead-End Jobs: A Way Out," in Chapter 7, pp. 307–12.

■ Exercise 13.12

Select one of your essays that might benefit from headings. Develop a system of headings and insert them where appropriate. Be prepared to justify your headings in light of the discussion about headings in this section.

Narrating

14

Narrating is a basic writing strategy for representing action and events. As the term's Latin root, *gnarus* ("knowing"), implies, narrating also serves to help people make sense of events in their own lives as well as events they observe or read about. From earliest childhood, narrating helps us reflect on things that have happened, explain what is happening, and imagine what could happen.

Narrating is one of the most versatile writing strategies, serving many different purposes. It can be used to report on events, present information, illustrate abstract ideas, support arguments, explain procedures, and entertain with stories. This chapter begins by describing and illustrating five basic narrating strategies and concludes by looking at two types of process narrative—explanatory and instructional.

■ NARRATING STRATEGIES

Whether the purpose is to make clear exactly what happened or to dramatize events so that readers can imagine what the experience was like, writers use an array of narrating strategies. Strategies such as calendar and clock time, temporal transitions, active verbs and verb tense, specific narrative action, and dialogue give narrative its dynamic quality, the sense of events unfolding in time. They also help readers track the order in which the events occurred and understand how they relate to one another.

Calendar and Clock Time

Presenting a clear sequence of action is essential to narrative. One of the simplest ways of constructing a clear time sequence is to place events on a timeline with years or precise dates and times clearly marked. Look, for example, at the chronology in Figure 14.1, which presents a series of events in the history of genetics. Chronologies like this one often appear in books and magazines as sidebars accompanying written narratives. A chronology is not itself a narrative, but it shares with narrative two basic elements: Events are presented in chronological order, and each event is marked (in this case, by year) so that readers can understand clearly when events occurred in relation to one another.

1866 Austrian botanist and monk Gregor Mendel proposes basic laws of heredity based on cross-breeding experiments with pea plants. His findings, published in a local natural-history journal, are largely ignored for more than 30 years.

1882 While examining salamander larvae under a microscope, German embryologist Walther Fleming spots tiny threads within the cells' nuclei that appear to be dividing. The threads will later turn out to be chromosomes.

1883 Francis Galton, a cousin of Charles Darwin's and an advocate of improving the human race by means of selective breeding, coins the word eugenics.

1910 U.S. biologist Thomas Hunt Morgan's experiments with fruit flies reveal that some genetically determined traits are sex linked. His work also confirms that the genes determining these traits reside on chromosomes.

1926 U.S. biologist Hermann Muller discovers that X rays can cause genetic mutations in fruit flies.

1932 Publication of Aldous Huxley's novel *Brave New World*, which presents a dystopian view of genetic engineering.

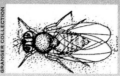

Figure 14.1 Chronology of Events in the History of Genetics
From *Time,* January 11, 1999, pp. 46–47.

Look now at a brief but fully developed narrative reconstructing the discovery of the bacterial cause of stomach ulcers. This narrative was written by Martin J. Blaser for *Scientific American,* a journal read primarily by nonspecialists interested in science. As you read, notice the same narrating strategies you saw in the chronology in Figure 14.1: sequencing events in chronological order and marking the passage of time by specifying when each event occurred (each time marker is underlined):

In 1979 J. Robin Warren, a pathologist at the Royal Perth Hospital in Australia, made a puzzling observation. As he examined tissue specimens from patients who had undergone stomach biopsies, he noticed that several samples had large numbers of curved and spiral-shaped bacteria. Ordinarily, stomach acid would destroy such organisms before they could settle in the stomach. But those Warren saw lay underneath the organ's thick mucus layer—a lining that coats the stomach's tissues and protects them from acid. Warren also noted that the bacteria were present only in tissue samples that were inflamed. Wondering whether the microbes might somehow be related to the irritation, he looked to the literature for clues and learned that German pathologists had witnessed similar organisms a century earlier. Because they could not grow the bacteria in culture, though, their findings had been ignored and then forgotten.

Warren, aided by an enthusiastic young trainee named Barry J. Marshall, also had difficulty growing the unknown bacteria in culture. He began his efforts in 1981. By April 1982 the two men had attempted to culture samples from 30-odd patients— all without success. Then the Easter holidays arrived. The hospital laboratory staff accidentally held some of the culture plates for five days instead of the usual two. On the fifth day, colonies emerged. The workers christened them *Campylobacter pyloridis* because they resembled pathogenic bacteria of the *Campylobacter* genus found in the intestinal tract. Early in 1983 Warren and Marshall published their first report, and within months scientists around the world had isolated the bacteria.

—MARTIN J. BLASER, "The Bacteria behind Ulcers"

1944 Working with pneumococcus bacteria, Oswald Avery, Colin MacLeod and Maclyn McCarty prove that DNA, not protein, is the hereditary material in most living organisms.

1950 British physician Douglas Bevis describes how amniocentesis can be used to test fetuses for Rh-factor incompatibility. The prenatal test will later be used to screen for a battery of genetic disorders.

1953 American biochemist James Watson and British biophysicist Francis Crick announce their discovery of the double-helix structure of DNA, the molecule that carries the genetic code.

1964 Stanford geneticist Charles Yanofsky and colleagues prove that the sequence of nucleotides in DNA corresponds exactly to the sequence of amino acids in proteins.

1969 A Harvard Medical School team isolates the first gene: a snippet of bacterial DNA that plays a role in the metabolism of sugar.

1970 University of Wisconsin researchers synthesize a gene from scratch.

1973 American biochemists Stanley Cohen and Herbert Boyer insert a gene from an African clawed toad into bacterial DNA, where it begins to work. Their experiment marks the beginning of genetic engineering.

Blaser cites specific years, months, days, and a holiday. These calendar markers convey the sense of time passing and indicate precisely when each event occurred and in what order. Calendar time also enables Blaser to emphasize the length of time it took to make the discovery (four years) and to draw attention to the fortunate accident that provided the dramatic turning point.

In addition to calendar time (years, months, days), writers sometimes also refer to clock time (hours, minutes, seconds). Here is a brief narrative from an essay profiling the emergency room at Bellevue Hospital in New York City:

> <u>9:05 P.M.</u> An ambulance backs into the receiving bay, its red and yellow lights flashing in and out of the lobby. <u>A split second later</u>, the glass doors burst open as a nurse and an attendant roll a mobile stretcher into the lobby. When the nurse screams, "Emergency!" the lobby explodes with activity as the way is cleared to the trauma room. Doctors appear from nowhere and transfer the bloodied body of a black man to the treatment table. <u>Within seconds</u> his clothes are stripped away.
>
> —GEORGE SIMPSON, "The War Room at Bellevue"

In this example, we can see that references to clock time (underlined) not only help readers follow the sequence of actions but also contribute dramatic intensity by stressing the speed with which the actions were taken.

■ Exercise 14.1

Turn to the remembered event essay "Handed My Own Life," by Annie Dillard, in Chapter 2, and underline the references to calendar time in paragraphs 5 and 7. How do you think these calendar time markers function in the narrative? What do they tell you about Dillard and her project?

Temporal Transitions

For a more extensive list of connectives showing temporal relationships, see Chapter 13.

Whereas calendar and clock time tend to be used sparingly, writers regularly use temporal transitions such as *when, at that moment, before,* and *while.* Temporal transitions establish a clear sequence of actions in time. They are used to narrate both onetime and recurring events.

Onetime Events.   Writers and readers rely on temporal transitions to show readers how events relate to one another, indicating which event came first, which event followed, and which events happened at the same time. To see how temporal transitions work, let us look at the concluding paragraphs of a remembered event essay in which Russell Baker recounts what happened after his final flight test, his last chance to become a pilot. The "he" Baker refers to is the flight check pilot, T. L. (nicknamed "Total Loss") Smith.

> Back at the flight line, when I'd cut the ignition, he climbed out and tramped back toward the ready room while I waited to sign the plane in. When I got there he was standing at a distance talking to my regular instructor. His talk was being illustrated with hand movements, as pilots' conversations always were, hands executing little loops and rolls in the air. After he did the falling-leaf motion with his hands, he pointed a finger at my instructor's chest, said something I couldn't hear, and trudged off. My instructor, who had flown only with the pre-hangover Baker, was slack-jawed when he approached me.
>
> "Smith just said you gave him the best check flight he's ever had in his life," he said. "What the hell did you do to him up there?"
>
> "I guess I just suddenly learned to fly," I said.
>
> –Russell Baker, "Smooth and Easy"

In this brief narrative, we see how temporal transitions (underlined) show what Baker and Smith were each doing right after the test. For example, look closely at the two transitions in the first sentence. The word *when* presents actions in chronological order (first Baker stopped the plane, and then Smith got out). *While* performs a different function, showing that the next two actions occurred at the same time (Baker signed in as the instructor returned to the ready room). There is nothing complicated or unusual about this set of actions, but it would be hard to represent them in writing without temporal transitions.

Recurring Events.   Temporal transitions also enable writers to show what typically happened over a longer period of time. In the following narrative by Monica Sone about her daily life in an internment camp for Japanese Americans during World War II, we can see how transitions (underlined) help the writer represent actions she routinely performed.

> First I typed on pink, green, blue and white work sheets the hours put in by the 10,000 evacuees, then sorted and alphabetized these sheets, and stacked them away in shoe boxes. My job was excruciatingly dull, but under no circumstances did I want to leave it. The Administration Building was the only place which had modern

plumbing and running hot and cold water; <u>in the first few months and every morn-</u>
<u>ing, after</u> I had typed for a decent hour, I slipped into the rest room and took a com-
plete sponge bath with scalding hot water. <u>During the remainder of the day,</u> I slipped
back into the rest room <u>at inconspicuous intervals,</u> took off my head scarf and wres-
tled with my scorched hair. I stood upside down over the basin of hot water, soaking
my hair, combing, stretching and pulling at it.

—MONICA SONE, "Camp Harmony"

With the time marker *first,* Sone launches her narrative of the actions she typically
took while working, such as typing and alphabetizing. In the third sentence, she
introduces another set of routine actions she took surreptitiously "in the first few
months and every morning."

■ Exercise 14.2

Turn to the remembered event essay "On Being a Real Westerner," by Tobias Wolff,
in Chapter 2. Underline the temporal transitions in paragraph 9, where Wolff relates
a onetime event, and paragraph 5, where he presents recurring events. Notice the
number of transitions he uses and how each one functions. What can you conclude
about Wolff's use of temporal transitions from your analysis of these two paragraphs?
How well do these transitions create a sense of time passing? How effectively do they
help you follow the sequence of actions?

■ Exercise 14.3

Turn to "Love: The Right Chemistry," by Anastasia Toufexis, in Chapter 5. Read paragraph 3, underlining the temporal transitions Toufexis uses to present the sequence
of evolutionary changes that may have contributed to the development of romantic
love. How important are these transitions in helping you follow her narrative?

Verb Tense Markers

In addition to time markers like calendar time and temporal transitions, writers use
verb tense to represent action in writing and to help readers understand when each
action occurred in relation to the other actions. Let us look at some of the ways writers use verb tense to narrate onetime and recurring events.

Onetime Events.   Writers typically use the past tense to represent events that began
and ended some time in the past. Here is a brief passage from a remembered person
essay by Amy Wu. In addition to the temporal transitions *once* and *when* in the opening sentence, which let readers know that this particular event occurred many years
earlier, the writer also uses simple past-tense verbs (underlined):

Amy Wu's essay is reprinted
in Chapter 3.

Once, when I <u>was</u> 5 or 6, I <u>interrupted</u> my mother during a dinner with her friends
and <u>told</u> her that I <u>disliked</u> the meal. My mother's eyes <u>transformed</u> from serene
pools of blackness into stormy balls of fire. "Quiet!" she <u>hissed</u>, "do you not know
that silent waters run deep?"

—AMY WU, "A Different Kind of Mother"

Verbs like *interrupted* and *hissed* show readers Wu's and her mother's actions. The simple past tense of these verbs signals to readers that the series of actions occurred in a straightforward sequence: The young Wu interrupted her mother, and then her mother got angry.

In the next example, by Chang-Rae Lee, we see how verb tense can be used to show more complicated relationships between past actions. Notice that Lee employs two different past tenses: the simple past *(amassed* and *moved)* and the past perfect *(had hoped)*:

> When Uncle Chul <u>amassed</u> the war chest he <u>needed</u> to open the wholesale business he <u>had hoped</u> for, he <u>moved</u> away from New York.
>
> —CHANG-RAE LEE, "Uncle Chul Gets Rich"

You do not have to know the names of these verb tenses to know that the hopes came before the money was amassed. In fact, most readers of English can understand complicated combinations of tenses without knowing their names.

Let us look at another verb tense combination used frequently in narrative: the simple past *(overheard)* and the past progressive *(was leaving)*.

> When Dinah Washington <u>was leaving</u> with some friends, I <u>overheard</u> someone say she <u>was</u> on her way to the Savoy Ballroom where Lionel Hampton <u>was appearing</u> that night—she <u>was</u> then Hamp's vocalist.
>
> —MALCOLM X, *The Autobiography of Malcolm X*

This combination of tenses plus the temporal transition *when* shows that the two actions occurred at the same time in the past. The first action ("Dinah Washington was leaving") continued during the period that the second action ("I overheard") occurred.

Occasionally, writers use the present instead of the past tense to narrate onetime events. Process narratives and profiles typically use the present tense to give the story a sense of "you are there" immediacy. Here is an excerpt from an essay profiling brain surgeons that uses present-tense verbs (underlined) to make readers feel as if they were watching the surgeons in action:

For Noonan's complete essay, see Chapter 4.

> "Drill the hell out of it," Steinberger <u>says</u> to Solomon. The scalp has been retracted and the skull exposed. Solomon <u>presses</u> the large stainless-steel power drill against the bone and <u>hits</u> the trigger. The bit <u>turns</u> slowly, biting into the white skull. Shavings <u>drop</u> from the hole onto the drape and then to the floor. The drill <u>stops</u> automatically when it is through the bone.
>
> —DAVID NOONAN, "Inside the Brain"

Recurring Events. Verb tense, usually combined with temporal transitions, can also help writers narrate events that occurred routinely. In the following passage, for example, Willie Morris uses the helping verb *would* along with the temporal transitions *many times* and *often* to show recurring actions.

> Many times, walking home from work, I <u>would see</u> some unknowing soul venture across that intersection against the light and then freeze in horror when he saw the cars ripping out of the tunnel toward him. . . . Suddenly, the human reflex <u>would take</u>

over, and the pedestrian would jackknife first one way, then another, arms flaying the empty air, and often the car would literally skim the man, brushing by him so close it would touch his coat or his tie. . . . On one occasion, feeling sorry for the person who had brushed against the speeding car, I hurried across the intersection after him to cheer him up a little. Catching up with him down by 32nd I said, "That was good legwork, sir. Excellent moves for a big man!" but the man looked at me with an empty expression in his eyes, and then moved away mechanically and trancelike, heading for the nearest bar.

–WILLIE MORRIS, *North toward Home*

Notice also that Morris shifts to the simple past tense when he moves from recurring actions to an action that occurred only once. He signals this shift with the temporal transition *on one occasion*.

■ Exercise 14.4

Turn to the remembered event essay "Calling Home," by Jean Brandt, in Chapter 2. Read paragraph 3, and underline the verbs, beginning with *got, took, knew,* and *didn't want* in the first sentence. Brandt uses verb tense to reconstruct her actions and reflect on their effectiveness. Notice also how verb tense helps you follow the sequence of actions Brandt took.

Specific Narrative Action

The narrating strategy we call *specific narrative action* uses active verbs and modifying phrases and clauses to present action vividly. Specific narrative action is especially suited to representing the intense, fast-moving, physical actions of sports events. The following example by George Plimpton shows how well specific narrative actions (underlined) work to show what happened during a practice scrimmage. Plimpton participated in the Detroit Lions football training camp in order to write a book profiling professional football. This is what he experienced:

Since in the two preceding plays the concentration of the play had been elsewhere, I had felt alone with the flanker. Now, the whole heave of the play was toward me, flooding the zone not only with confused motion but noise—the quick stomp of feet, the creak of football gear, the strained grunts of effort, the faint *ah-ah-ah* of piston-stroke regularity, and the stiff calls of instruction, like exhalations. "Inside, inside! Take him inside!" someone shouted, tearing by me, his cleats thumping in the grass. A call—a parrot squawk—may have erupted from me. My feet splayed in hopeless confusion as Barr came directly toward me, feinting in one direction, and then stopping suddenly, drawing me toward him for the possibility of a buttonhook pass, and as I leaned almost off balance toward him, he turned and came on again, downfield, moving past me at high speed, leaving me poised on one leg, reaching for him, trying to grab at him despite the illegality, anything to keep him from getting by. But he was gone, and by the time I had turned to set out after him, he had ten yards on me, drawing away fast with his sprinter's run, his legs pinwheeling, the row of cleats flicking up a faint wake of dust behind.

–GEORGE PLIMPTON, *Paper Lion*

In this brief narrative, Plimpton uses active verbs *(erupted, leaned)*. But most of the action is expressed through modifying phrases and clauses. Here are some examples of the two most common kinds of modifiers writers employ to present specific narrative action:

> ***Participial phrases:*** *tearing by me, stopping suddenly, moving past me at high speed*

> ***Absolute phrases:*** *his cleats thumping in the grass, his legs pinwheeling, the row of cleats flicking up a faint wake of dust behind*

As with verb tense, most English speakers know how to construct these phrases and clauses without knowing their grammatical names. By piling up specific narrative actions, Plimpton reconstructs for readers the texture and excitement of his experience on the football field. Combined with vivid sensory description *(the creak of football gear, the strained grunts of effort, the faint* ah-ah-ah *of piston-stroke regularity)*, these specific narrative actions re-create the sights and sounds of people in motion.

■ Exercise 14.5

Turn to paragraph 18 of the remembered person essay by Maya Angelou in Chapter 3. Underline any specific narrative actions you find in this brief paragraph. Then reflect on what they contribute to Angelou's narrative.

■ Exercise 14.6

Make a videotape of several brief—two- or three-minute—televised segments of a fast-moving sports competition such as a football or basketball game. Then, review the tape and choose one segment to narrate using specific narrative actions to describe in detail what you see.

    If you cannot videotape a televised game, go to a place where there is action taking place (for example, where people are playing touch football, where a dog is catching a Frisbee, where a skateboarder or inline skater is practicing a trick). As you watch the action, take detailed notes of what you see. Then, based on your notes, write a few sentences using specific narrative actions to describe the action you witnessed firsthand.

Dialogue

Dialogue is most often used in narratives that dramatize events. In addition to showing people interacting, dialogue can give readers insight into character and relationships. Dialogue may be quoted to make it resemble the give-and-take of actual conversation, or it may be summarized to give readers the gist of what was said. Quoted or summarized, dialogue reconstructs choice bits of conversation rather than trying to present an accurate and complete record.

    The following example from Gary Soto's *Living up the Street* shows how a narrative can combine quoted and summarized dialogue. In this passage, Soto recalls his first experience as a migrant worker in California's San Joaquin Valley.

So it went. Two pans equaled one tray—or six cents. By lunchtime I had a trail of thirty-seven trays behind me while Mother had sixty or more. We met about halfway from our last trays, and I sat down with a grunt, knees wet from kneeling on dropped grapes. I washed my hands with the water from the jug, drying them on the inside of my shirt sleeve before I opened the paper bag for the first sandwich, which I gave to Mother. I dipped my hand in again to unwrap a sandwich without looking at it. I took a first bite and chewed it slowly for the tang of mustard. Eating in silence I looked straight ahead at the vines, and only when we were finished with cookies did we talk.

"Are you tired?" she asked.

"No, but I got a sliver from the frame," I told her. I showed her the web of skin between my thumb and index finger. She wrinkled her forehead but said it was nothing.

"How many trays did you do?"

I looked straight ahead, not answering at first. I recounted in my mind the whole morning of bend, cut, pour again and again, before answering a feeble "thirty-seven." No elaboration, no detail. Without looking at me she told me how she had done field work in Texas and Michigan as a child. But I had a difficult time listening to her stories. I played with my grape knife, stabbing it into the ground, but stopped when Mother reminded me that I had better not lose it. I left the knife sticking up like a small, leafless plant. She then talked about school, the junior high I would be going to that fall, and then about Rick and Debra, how sorry they would be that they hadn't come out to pick grapes because they'd have no new clothes for the school year. She stopped talking when she peeked at her watch, a bandless one she kept in her pocket. She got up with an "Ay, Dios," and told me that we'd work until three, leaving me cutting figures in the sand with my knife and dreading the return to work.

—GARY SOTO, "One Last Time"

Quoted dialogue is easy to recognize, of course, because of the quotation marks. Notice that Soto uses signal phrases—*she asked* and *I told her*—in the first two quotations, but he leaves out the signal phrase in the third, possibly because it is clear from the context who is speaking. The fourth bit of quoted dialogue consists of only one word, *thirty-seven,* but is preceded by a fairly long narrative telling what he did and thought before speaking.

Summarized dialogue can be harder to identify. In this case, however, Soto embeds signal phrases *(she told me* and *she then talked)* in his narrative. He summarizes what his mother talked about without going into detail or quoting words she might have used. Summarizing leaves out information the writer decides readers do not need. In this passage about a remembered event, Soto has apparently chosen to focus on his own feelings and thoughts rather than his mother's.

For more on deciding when to quote, see Chapter 22.

■ Exercise 14.7

In Chapter 3, read paragraphs 17–28 of Gerald Haslam's essay about his great-grandmother, "Grandma." As you read, note any places where Haslam summarizes dialogue instead of quoting it. Look also at the signal phrases he uses and how well they work to help readers identify who is speaking. What does the dialogue tell you about the grandmother and the young Haslam's relationship with her?

■ Exercise 14.8

If you wrote a remembered event essay in Chapter 2 or wrote a bit of narrative in some other essay, reread your essay, looking for one example of each of the following narrating strategies: calendar or clock time, temporal transitions, active verbs and verb tense markers, specific narrative action, and dialogue. Do not worry if you cannot find examples of all of the strategies. Pick one strategy you did use, and comment on what it contributes to your narrative.

■ NARRATING A PROCESS

Process narratives explain how something was done or instruct readers on how it could or should be done. Whether the purpose is explanatory or instructional, process narratives must convey clearly each necessary action and the exact order in which the actions occur. We will look at examples of both types of process narrative.

Explanatory Process Narratives

Explanatory process narratives often relate particular experiences or elucidate processes followed by machines or organizations. Let us begin with an excerpt from a remembered event essay by Mary Mebane. She uses process narrative to let readers know what happened the first time she worked on an assembly line putting tobacco leaves on the conveyor belt.

> The job seemed easy enough as I picked up bundle after bundle of tobacco and put it on the belt, careful to turn the knot end toward me so that it would be placed right to go under the cutting machine. Gradually, as we worked up our tobacco, I had to bend more, for as we emptied the hogshead we had to stoop over to pick up the tobacco, then straighten up and put it on the belt just right. Then I discovered the hard part of the job: the belt kept moving at the same speed all the time and if the leaves were not placed on the belt at the same tempo there would be a big gap where your bundle should have been. So that meant that when you got down lower, you had to bend down, get the tobacco, straighten up fast, make sure it was placed knot end toward you, place it on the belt, and bend down again. Soon you were bending down, up; down, up; down, up. All along the line, heads were bobbing—down, up; down, up—until you finished the barrel. Then you could rest until the men brought you another one.
>
> —MARY MEBANE, "Summer Job"

In this passage, Mebane uses the basic narrating strategies of temporal transitions (*gradually, then, soon*) and simple past-tense verbs to place the actions in time. In addition, specific narrative actions (*bend down, get the tobacco, straighten up fast*) become a series of staccato movements (*down, up; down, up; down, up*) that emphasize the speed and machinelike actions she had to take to keep up with the conveyor belt.

The next example shows how a laser printer functions.

To create a page, the computer sends signals to the printer, which shines a laser at a mirror system that scans across a charged drum. Whenever the beam strikes the drum, it removes the charge. The drum then rotates through a toner chamber filled with thermoplastic particles. The toner particles stick to the negatively charged areas of the drum in the pattern of characters, lines, or other elements the computer has transmitted and the laser beam mapped.

Once the drum is coated with toner in the appropriate locations, a piece of paper is pulled across a so-called transfer corona wire, which imparts a positive electrical charge. The paper then passes across the toner-coated drum. The positive charge on the paper attracts the toner in the same position it occupied on the drum. The final phase of the process involves fusing the toner to the paper with a set of high-temperature rollers.

–RICHARD GOLUB AND ERIC BRUS, *Almanac of Science and Technology*

Like Mebane's process narrative, this one sequences the actions chronologically from beginning ("the computer sends signals to the printer") to end ("fusing the toner to the paper"). Temporal transitions *(then, once, then, final),* present-tense verbs, and specific narrative actions *(sends, scans, shines, strikes)* convey the passage of time and place the actions clearly in this chronological sequence.

The major difference between this narrative and Mebane's is who is doing the action. Mebane performs the actions *(I picked up, I had to bend)* in her narrative; in this one, the actions are performed by different actors, all of them inanimate *(computer, drum, toner, paper)*. Because the actors change from sentence to sentence, readers could easily become confused. Therefore, the writer must construct a clearly marked chain, introducing the actor's name in one sentence and repeating the name or using a synonym in the next sentence (underlined):

To create a page, the computer sends signals to the printer, which shines a <u>laser</u> at a mirror system that scans across a charged <u>drum</u>. Whenever the beam <u>strikes</u> the <u>drum</u>, it removes the charge. The <u>drum</u> then rotates through a <u>toner</u> chamber filled with thermoplastic <u>particles</u>. The <u>toner particles</u> . . .

Our last explanatory process narrative is a graphic sidebar, of the type commonly used in magazines and books. This one comes from a *Newsweek* magazine feature on Matthew Scott, only the third person to receive a hand transplant. Figure 14.2 shows the process narrative titled, "A Second Hand, A Second Chance."

Notice that this process narrative integrates writing with graphics. The procedure is divided into three distinct steps, with each step clearly numbered and labeled *(1. Skin and bones)*. In each step, the graphics are referred to with letters—*Curved incisions (diagram A)*. The graphics themselves incorporate labels—*Donor's hand, Incision, Tourniquet released*. The writer uses some basic narrating strategies to present the actions and make clear the sequence in which they were taken: temporal transitions *(now, while, after)*, present-tense verbs, and specific narrative actions, mostly in the form of active verbs *(secure, stitch, watches)*. Much is left out, of course. Readers could not duplicate the procedure based on this narrative, but it does give *Newsweek* readers a clear sense of what was done during the fifteen hours of surgery.

A Second Hand, A Second Chance

It took a 17-member surgical team about 15 hours to complete Matthew Scott's hand transplant, the first in the United States. The operation is extremely complex. Unlike a solid organ transplant—a kidney, for example—a hand reattachment involves multiple tissues: skin, muscle, tendon, bone, nerves and blood vessels. At right, the procedure:

1 Skin and bones: Doctors give Scott general anesthesia. The flow of blood to his lower arm is restricted with a special tourniquet. Curved incisions (diagram A) are made in the forearm and (donor) wrist. Scott's radius and ulna bones are found and lined up with the donor hand's bones. Metal plates secure the bones together (B).

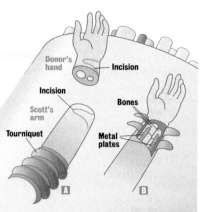

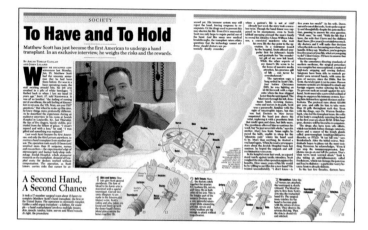

Figure 14.2 Presentation of an Explanatory Process
The two-page layout reproduced here shows how "A Second Hand, A Second Chance" was designed as a sidebar accompanying a longer article, "To Have and to Hold." From *Newsweek,* February 8, 1999, pp. 50–51.

■ Exercise 14.9

In Chapter 4, read paragraphs 5–8 of David Noonan's profile of brain surgery, "Inside the Brain." In these paragraphs, Noonan narrates the process followed by the surgeons to open the skull. As you read, look for and mark the narrating strategies from this chapter that Noonan uses. Then reflect on how well you think the narrative presents the actions and their sequence.

Instructional Process Narratives

For guidelines on designing your own documents, see Chapter 25.

Unlike explanatory process narratives, instructional process narratives must include all of the information a reader would need to perform the procedure presented. Depending on the reader's experience, the writer might need to define technical

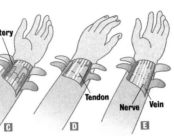

2 Soft tissue: Now, the doctors stitch together the arteries (C), tendons (D), nerves and veins (E) on both sides of the arm. This is the longest part of the surgery. Doctors use a very powerful microscope while connecting arteries, nerves and veins; tendons are big enough to attach without magnification.

Artery

Tendon

Nerve   Vein

C   D   E

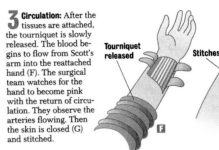

3 Circulation: After the tissues are attached, the tourniquet is slowly released. The blood begins to flow from Scott's arm into the reattached hand (F). The surgical team watches for the hand to become pink with the return of circulation. They observe the arteries flowing. Then the skin is closed (G) and stitched.

Tourniquet released

Stitches

F   G

terms, list tools that should be used, give background information, and account for alternatives or possible problems.

Figure 14.3 presents a rather detailed instructional process narrative from the Sunset *Home Repair Handbook* that gives readers directions for replacing a broken plug.

The instructions begin with general advice on when to replace a plug, followed by a classification of three common types of plugs that also are illustrated in the accompanying graphic. Notice that even though the graphic is not referred to explicitly in the text, readers are unlikely to be confused because the graphic is right next to the relevant paragraph and is clearly titled "Types of plugs."

Paragraphs 4 and 5 briefly explain the procedure for replacing two- and three-prong plugs. These procedures are spelled out in greater detail in the accompanying graphics titled "Replacing a plug with terminal screws" and "Replacing three special types of plugs." The first of these graphics includes four steps that are clearly numbered, illustrated, and narrated. Each step presents several actions to be taken, and its graphic shows what the plug should look like when these actions have been completed. We can identify the actions by looking at the verbs. Step 1 in "Replacing a plug with terminal screws," for example, instructs readers to take four separate actions, each signaled by the verb (italicized): "*Unscrew* and *remove* the new plug's insulating barrier. Using a utility knife, *split* the end of the cord to *separate* the wires; *push* the cord through the plug body." These are active verbs, and the sentences are in the form of clear and efficient commands.

The anonymous authors do not assume that readers know very much, especially on important safety matters. Paragraph 3, for example, presents a note explaining the National Electrical Code ("NEC") for old-style plugs. Also, readers are referred twice (in paragraph 4 and in step 3 of "Replacing a plug with terminal screws") to the explanation of how to strip wires safely, which appears on page 159 of the book.

Any plug with a cracked shell or loose, damaged, or badly bent contacts should be replaced. Also replace plugs that transmit power erratically or get warm when used. If a plug arcs when it's pushed into or pulled out of a receptacle, examine the wires; if they're not firmly attached to the terminal screws, tighten the connections.

The two kinds of common plugs are terminal-screw and self-connecting. In plugs with terminal screws, the wires are attached to screws inside the plug body. Self-connecting plugs clamp onto wires, making an automatic connection. These plugs, as well as two-prong plugs with terminal screws, are commonly used for lamps and small appliances. Three-prong grounding plugs are used for larger appliances and power tools. Detachable cords for small appliances have female plugs with terminal screws.

NOTE: Many old-style plugs with terminal screws have a removable insulating disc covering the terminals and wires. The NEC now requires "dead-front" plugs; such plugs have a rigid insulating barrier.

To replace a plug, cut off the old one plus at least an inch of the cord. For

Types of plugs

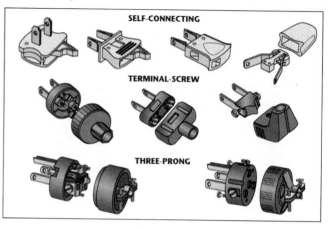

plugs that have terminal screws, split the cord insulation to separate the wires; then strip the insulation from the ends *(page 159)*.

When replacing a two-prong plug, connect the identified conductor to the silver-colored screw. For a three-prong grounding plug, attach the wires to the terminal screws as follows: white neutral wire to silver screw, black hot wire to brass screw, and green grounding wire to green terminal screw.

Replacing a plug with terminal screws

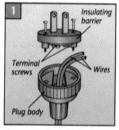 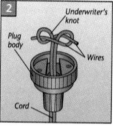 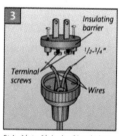 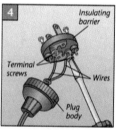

Unscrew and remove the new plug's insulating barrier. Using a utility knife, split the end of the cord to separate the wires; push the cord through the plug body.

Make two loops with the wires, pass the loose ends of the wires through the loops, and pull to form an Underwriter's knot (to prevent strain on connections).

Strip ½ to ¾ inch of insulation off the wire ends, being careful not to nick the wires *(page 159)*. Unscrew the terminal screws to allow space for the wires.

Form loops on wires and wrap them clockwise three-quarters of the way around screws. Tighten the screws, trim excess wire, and reattach the barrier to the body.

Replacing three special types of plugs

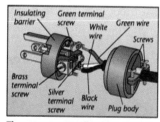 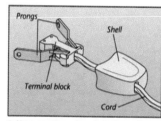 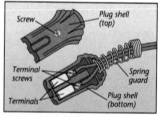

Three-prong grounding plug. Unscrew the insulating barrier; push stripped wires through the plug body into the correct terminal slots. Tighten the terminal screws and reassemble the plug.

Self-connecting plug. Push the cord (don't strip it) through the shell and into the terminal block; squeeze the prongs together to grip the cord and slide into the shell.

Female appliance plug. Unscrew the plug shell; feed the cord through the spring guard. Strip the wire ends *(page 159)*, wrap them clockwise around the terminal screws, and tighten; reassemble the plug.

Figure 14.3 Replacing Plugs
From *Home Repair Handbook* (Menlo Park, Calif.: Sunset, 1999), pp. 156–57.

■ Exercise 14.10

Write a one- to two-page instructional process narrative that tells readers how to make a peanut butter and jelly sandwich or perform some other equally simple procedure such as logging on to the Internet, shortening a pair of pants, separating egg whites from yolks, potting a plant, or filling a fountain pen. Address your narrative to readers who have never done the procedure before or to those who may know something about the procedure but would be interested in how you go about doing it.

Describing

15

Describing comes from the Latin *describere,* meaning "to sketch" or "to copy in writing." Written descriptions create images that help readers imagine what is being described. Readers often use the word *vivid* to characterize description that creates an intense, distinctive image, one that seems to bring the words on the page to life. Good description can also be evocative, calling up memories or suggesting feelings associated with the subject being described. Writers can use description for many purposes: to give readers an impression of a person or place, to illustrate abstract ideas, to make information memorable, or to support an argument. This chapter presents the three basic descriptive techniques of naming, detailing, and comparing; surveys the words writers of English typically use to evoke sense impressions that help to make description vivid; and examines how writers use description to create a dominant impression.

■ NAMING

Naming calls readers' attention to observable features of the subject being described. To describe a room, for example, you might name objects you see as you look around, such as a bed, pillows, blankets, dresser, clothes, books, CD player, and CDs. These objects suggest what kind of room it is and begin to give readers an impression of what it is like to be in this particular room.

Look closely at the following passage describing a weasel that the writer, Annie Dillard, encountered in the woods. As you read, notice the underlined words (such as *face* and *chin*) that Dillard uses to name the weasel's most distinctive or memorable features:

> He was ten inches long, thin as a curve, a muscled ribbon, brown as fruitwood, soft-furred, alert. His <u>face</u> was fierce, small and pointed as a lizard's; he would have made a good arrowhead. There was just a dot of <u>chin</u>, maybe two brown hairs' worth, and then the pure white <u>fur</u> began that spread down his <u>underside</u>. He had two black <u>eyes</u> I didn't see, any more than you see a window.
>
> —ANNIE DILLARD, *Teaching a Stone to Talk*

With these names, readers can begin to put together a mental image of the animal Dillard is describing. She does not name one feature alone but gives readers names for different parts of the weasel. She also uses simple, everyday nouns to name the weasel's features. They are not technical words (like *maxilla* or *mandible,* words scientists might use to refer to its upper and lower jaw), but words like *chin* that all readers of English are likely to know. Words like *chin* are also concrete nouns that refer to specific, observable parts of a weasel's face. The piling up of names, combined with the simplicity and concreteness of the nouns, helps readers begin to imagine what the weasel looked like to Dillard.

Dillard's naming focuses on what she saw. Although writers most commonly name what they see, sight is not the only sense contributing to vivid descriptions. Here is a passage that illustrates some of the nouns writers can use to name smells *(stink)*, sounds *(plunk)*, tastes *(sweetness)*, and touch *(rawness)*:

> When the sun fell across the great white pile of the new Telephone Company building, you could smell the stucco burning as you passed; then some liquid <u>sweetness</u> that came to me from deep in the rings of the freshly cut lumber stacked in the yards, and the fresh plaster and paint on the brand-new storefronts. <u>Rawness</u>, sunshiny rawness down the end streets of the city, as I thought of them then — the hot ash-laden <u>stink</u> of the refuse dumps in my nostrils and the only sound at noon the resonant metal <u>plunk</u> of a tin can I kicked ahead of me as I went my way.
>
> —ALFRED KAZIN, *A Walker in the City*

■ Exercise 15.1

Go to a place where you can sit for a while and observe the scene. It might be a landscape or a cityscape, indoors or outdoors, crowded or solitary. It could be a familiar or a new place. For five minutes, list everything in the scene that you can name using nouns. (A simple way to test if a word is a noun is to see if you can put the word *the, a,* or *an* in front of the word.) Remember, you can name objects you see *(dog, hydrant)* as well as impressions such as smells or sounds you experience at the place *(stench, hiss).*

Then write a page or so that describes the scene for someone who is not there with you. You could choose to write for readers who have been to the place but have not seen what you are seeing there now, or you could write for readers who have never been to this particular place to let them know what to expect when they get there.

■ Exercise 15.2

Turn to "Father," by Jan Gray, in Chapter 3. Read paragraph 12, and underline the names Gray uses to describe her bedroom following her father's punishment of her for not getting home in time to clean her bedroom. Begin underlining with the words *heart, knob, door,* and *bedroom* in the opening sentence. How do you think the amount of naming Gray does, together with the words she chooses, contributes to the description's vividness — measured by your ability to imagine what her bedroom looked like?

■ DETAILING

Naming identifies the notable features of the subject being described; detailing makes the features more specific or particularized. Naming answers the questions "What is it?" and "What are its parts or features?"; detailing answers questions like these:

What size is it?

How many are there?

What is it made of?

Where is it located?

What is its condition?

How is it used?

Where does it come from?

What is its effect?

What is its value?

To add details to names, add modifiers—adjectives and adverbs, phrases and clauses. Modifiers make nouns more specific by supplying additional information. Notice how many modifying details (enclosed in brackets) about number, size, shape, color, texture, and value Dillard provides in her description of the weasel.

> He was [ten inches long], [thin] as a curve, a [muscled] ribbon, [brown] as fruit-wood, [soft-furred], [alert]. His face was [fierce], [small] and [pointed] as a lizard's; he would have made a good arrowhead. There was just a dot of chin, maybe [two brown hairs'] worth, and then the [pure white] fur began that spread down his underside. He had [two black] eyes I didn't see, any more than you see a window.
> —ANNIE DILLARD, *Teaching a Stone to Talk*

Dillard's details provide information that particularizes the weasel. In other words, readers recognize that she is describing a specific weasel, one she encountered, not what a weasel is supposed to look like. Her weasel has certain qualities that make it an individual, such as its length *(ten inches long)* and color *(brown* and *pure white)*. Just as objective physical details like these help readers picture the weasel, other details convey subjective information about Dillard's thoughts and feelings during the encounter. For example, when Dillard writes that the weasel's "face was fierce," she is making a judgment and expressing her feelings. She uses details like this to make readers see the weasel as a wild animal, not a soft and cuddly pet.

In describing people, writers often combine physical details with details characterizing aspects of the individual's personality. These characterizations or evaluations let readers know something about the writer's feelings and thoughts about the person, as the following examples illustrate:

> My father, a [fat], [funny] man with [beautiful] eyes and a [subversive] wit . . .
> —ALICE WALKER, "Beauty: When the Other Dancer Is the Self"

I was afraid of her [higharched bony] nose, her eyebrows [lifted in half-circles] above her [hooded], [brilliant] eyes, and of the [Kentucky] R's in her speech, and the [long] steps she took in her [hightop] shoes. I did nothing but fear her [bearing-down] authority. . . .

—EUDORA WELTY, "Miss Duling"

Walker begins with a physical detail *(fat)* but then chooses details that express her evaluation *(funny, beautiful)* as well as her analysis of the type of humor her father uses *(subversive)*. Similarly, Welty combines physical description *(higharched bony nose)* with subjective judgment *(bearing-down authority)* to enable readers to understand why she feared her former schoolteacher.

Sometimes writers use physical details to symbolize a person's character or the writer's feelings toward that person. We can see, for example, in the following passage describing a first meeting with the swimming coach that author Brad Benioff perceives Rick as overwhelmingly powerful and threatening:

Rick was [not a friendly looking] man. He wore only swim trunks, and his [short], [powerful] legs rose up to meet a [bulging] torso. His [big] belly was [solid]. His shoulders, as if to offset his front-heaviness, were [thrown back], creating a [deep] crease of [excess] muscle from his sides around the small of his back, a crease like a huge frown. His arms were [crossed], [two medieval] maces placed carefully on their racks, ready to be swung at any moment. His [round] cheeks and chin were [darkened] by traces of [black] whiskers. His hair was [sparse]. [Huge], [black], [mirrored] sunglasses replaced his eyes. Below his [prominent] nose was a [thin], [sinister] mustache. I couldn't believe this [menacing-looking] man was the [legendary jovial] Rick.

—BRAD BENIOFF, "Rick"

■ Exercise 15.3

Return to the description you wrote in Exercise 15.1. Put brackets around the details you used to help describe the scene. Add any other details you think of now—details that indicate size, quantity, makeup, location, condition, use, source, effect, value, or any other quality that would make the description more specific and particularized for readers. Then reread your description. What do you think the detailing contributes to the description you wrote?

■ Exercise 15.4

Look again at paragraph 12 of Jan Gray's essay in Chapter 3. In Exercise 15.2, you underlined the names Gray used. Now put brackets around the details. You might begin, for example, with the modifiers *racing* and *front*. How do you think detailing contributes to Gray's description? How do these details help you imagine what Gray's bedroom looked like to her at that particular moment?

■ Exercise 15.5

Turn again to Jan Gray's essay in Chapter 3, this time to the opening paragraph. Read and put brackets around the words that detail the description of Gray's father.

If you have not read the entire essay, read it now, and consider how Gray uses her father's skin condition to symbolize her feelings about him. What do you think her father's skin condition represents to her? What does Gray's description of her father suggest to you about their relationship and her feelings toward him?

◼ COMPARING

In addition to naming and detailing, writers sometimes use comparing to make their description more vivid for readers. Look again at Annie Dillard's description of a weasel, paying attention this time to the comparisons enclosed in parentheses:

> He was ten inches long, thin (as a curve), (a muscled ribbon), (brown as fruitwood), soft-furred, alert. His face was fierce, (small and pointed as a lizard's); (he would have made a good arrowhead). There was just a dot of chin, maybe two brown hairs' worth, and then the pure white fur began that spread down his underside. He had two black (eyes I didn't see, any more than you see a window).
>
> —ANNIE DILLARD, *Teaching a Stone to Talk*

Dillard uses two kinds of comparison in this description: simile and metaphor. Simile and metaphor point out similarities in things that are essentially dissimilar. A *simile* expresses the similarity directly by using the words *like* or *as* to announce the comparison. Dillard uses a simile when she writes that the weasel was "thin as a curve." A *metaphor,* by contrast, is an implicit comparison in which one thing is described as though it were the other. Dillard uses a metaphor when she calls the weasel "a muscled ribbon."

Similes and metaphors can add to the vividness of a description by giving readers additional information to help them picture the subject. For example, Dillard uses the word *thin* to detail the weasel's body shape. But *thin* is a relative term, leading readers to wonder, how thin? Dillard tries to anticipate this question by giving readers two images for comparison: a curve and a ribbon. Both of these comparisons help readers construct a fuller mental image of the weasel.

Comparing can also help convey to readers what the writer feels about the subject. Here is an example of comparing from Brad Benioff's description of Coach Rick that is suggestive of the writer's feelings: "His arms were crossed, two medieval maces placed carefully on their racks, ready to be swung at any moment." Sometimes the similes or metaphors writers use are suggestive but hard to pin down. What do you think Dillard means, for example, by comparing the weasel's eyes to a window: "He had two black eyes I didn't see, any more than you see a window"?

◼ Exercise 15.6

Return to the description you wrote in Exercise 15.1 and may have added to in Exercise 15.3. Reread it, and mark any comparing you used. Try to add one or two more similes or metaphors to your description. How do you think your use of comparing may help readers imagine the subject or get a sense of what you feel about it?

■ Exercise 15.7

Look again at Jan Gray's essay in Chapter 3. Gray concludes paragraph 12 with a metaphor when she uses the word *waltz* to describe the way her father comes into her life every few months. Discuss with one or two classmates the comparison implied in the word *waltz*. What do you think it contributes, if anything, to Gray's description?

Look also at the comparison she uses in the sentence that opens paragraph 13: "I was slowly *piecing my room together* . . . " What does this comparison contribute to the image you have of Gray's bedroom and her feelings about her father?

■ USING SENSORY DESCRIPTION

When writers describe animals, people, or scenes, they usually rely on the sense of sight more than the other senses. Our vocabulary for reporting what we see is larger and more varied than our vocabulary for reporting other sense impressions. Quite a few nouns and verbs designate sounds; a smaller number of nouns, but few verbs, describe smells; and very few nouns or verbs convey touch and taste. It also seems easier to use naming to describe what we see. Nonvisual sense perceptions seem to be less readily divided into distinguishing features. For example, we have many names to describe the visible features of a car but few to describe the sounds a car makes. Nevertheless, writers can detail the qualities and attributes of nonvisual sensations—the loudness or tinniness or rumble of an engine, for instance. They can also use comparing to help readers imagine what something sounds, feels, smells, or tastes like.

The Sense of Sight

When people describe what they see, they identify the objects in their field of vision. Here are two brief examples of visual description. The first selection, by Amy Tan, depicts her mother's kitchen; the second passage, by Tracy Kidder, describes Mrs. Zajac, a grade school teacher.

> On Christmas Eve I saw that my mother had outdone herself in creating a strange menu. She was pulling black veins out of the backs of fleshy prawns. The kitchen was littered with appalling mounds of raw food: A slimy rock cod with bulging eyes that pleaded not to be thrown into a pan of hot oil. Tofu, which looked like stacked wedges of rubbery white sponges. A bowl soaking dried fungus back to life. A plate of squid, their backs crisscrossed with knife markings so they resembled bicycle tires.
> —AMY TAN, "Fish Cheeks"

> She was thirty-four. She wore a white skirt and yellow sweater and a thin gold necklace, which she held in her fingers, as if holding her own reins, while waiting for children to answer. Her hair was black with a hint of Irish red. It was cut short to the tops of her ears, and swept back like a pair of folded wings. She had a delicate cleft chin, and she was short—the children's chairs would have fit her. . . . Her hands kept very busy. They sliced the air and made karate chops to mark off boundaries. They

extended straight out like a traffic cop's, halting illegal maneuvers yet to be perpetrated. When they rested momentarily on her hips, her hands looked as if they were in holsters.

—TRACY KIDDER, *Among Schoolchildren*

■ Exercise 15.8

Write a few sentences describing a teacher, friend, or family member. Do not rely on memory for this exercise; describe someone who is before you as you write so that you can describe in detail what you see. Later, when you are alone, reread what you have written, and make any changes you think will help make this visual description more vivid for your readers.

The Sense of Hearing

In reporting auditory impressions, writers seldom name the objects from which the sounds come without also naming the sounds themselves: the murmur of a voice, the rustle of the wind, the squeak of a hinge, the sputter of an engine. *Onomatopoeia* is the term for names of sounds that echo the sounds themselves: *squeak, murmur, hiss, boom, plink, tinkle, twang, jangle, rasp, chirr.* Sometimes writers make up words like *sweesh* and *cara-wong* to imitate sounds they wish to describe. Qualitative words like *powerful* and *rich* as well as relative terms like *loud* and *low* often specify sounds further. For detailing sounds, writers sometimes use the technique called *synesthesia,* applying words commonly used to describe one sense to another, such as describing sounds as *sharp* and *soft.*

To write about the sounds along Manhattan's Canal Street, Ian Frazier uses many of these describing and naming techniques. He also uses comparison when he refers metaphorically to the horns getting "tired and out of breath."

> The traffic on Canal Street never stops. It is a high-energy current jumping constantly between the poles of Brooklyn and New Jersey. It hates to have its flow pinched in the density of Manhattan, hates to stop at intersections. Along Canal Street, it moans and screams. Worn break shoes of semitrucks go "Ooohhhh nooohhhh" at stoplights, and the sound echoes in the canyons of warehouses and Chinatown tenements. People lean on their horns from one end of Canal Street to the other. They'll honk nonstop for ten minutes at a time, until the horns get tired and out of breath. They'll try different combinations: shave-and-a-hair-cut, long-long-long, short-short-short-long. Some people have musical car horns; a person purchasing a musical car horn seems to be limited to a choice of four tunes—"La Cucaracha," "Theme from *The Godfather*," "Dixie," and "Hava Nagila."
>
> —IAN FRAZIER, "Canal Street"

■ Exercise 15.9

Turn to paragraph 6 of Tobias Wolff's essay in Chapter 2, and find the place where Wolff uses onomatopoeia to describe sound. Then look at paragraph 9, where Wolff describes the sound created by firing the rifle. What do you think these descriptions of sound contribute to this particular essay, which takes place mostly in the silence of Wolff's home?

■ Exercise 15.10

Find a noisy spot—a restaurant, a football game, a nursery school, a laundry room —where you can perch for about half an hour. Listen attentively to the sounds of the place, and make notes about what you hear. Then write a page or so describing the place through its sounds.

The Sense of Smell

The English language has a meager stock of words to express the olfactory sense. In addition to the word *smell,* fewer than a dozen commonly used nouns name this sensation: *odor, scent, vapor, fume, aroma, fragrance, perfume, bouquet, stench, stink.* Although there are other, rarer words like *fetor* and *effluvium,* few writers use them, probably for fear that their readers will not know them. Few verbs describe receiving or sending odors—*smell, sniff, waft*—but a fair number of detailing adjectives are available: *redolent, pungent, aromatic, perfumed, stinking, musty, rancid, putrid, rank, fetid, malodorous, foul, acrid, sweet,* and *cloying.*

Here is an example of how reporter Amanda Coyne uses smell to describe "convict moms" with their children in the prison visiting room:

> Occasionally, a mother will pick up her present and bring it to her nose when one of the bearers of the single flower—her child—asks if she likes it. . . . But most of what is being smelled today is the children themselves. While the other adults are plunking coins into the vending machines, the mothers take deep whiffs from the backs of their children's necks, or kiss and smell the backs of their knees, or take off their shoes and tickle their feet and then pull them close to their noses. They hold them tight and take in their own second scent—the scent assuring them that these are still their children and that they still belong to them.
> –AMANDA COYNE, "The Long Good-Bye: Mother's Day in Federal Prison"

In addition to using *smell* as a verb, Coyne describes the repeated action of bringing the object being smelled to the nose, an act that not only signifies the process of smelling but also underscores the intimacy of the act. To further emphasize intimacy, Coyne connects smelling with other intimate acts of kissing, tickling, pulling close, and holding tight.

Because she is not describing her own experience of smell, Coyne does not try to find words to evoke the effect the odor has. In the next passage, however, Frank Conroy uses comparing in addition to naming and detailing to describe how the smell of flowers affected him:

> The perfume of the flowers rushed into my brain. A lush aroma, thick with sweetness, thick as blood, and spiced with the clear acid of tropical greenery.
> –FRANK CONROY, *Stop-Time*

Naming the objects from which smells come can also be very suggestive.

> The odor of these houses was different, full of fragrances, sweet and nauseating. On 105th Street the smells were of fried lard, of beans and car fumes, of factory smoke and home-made brew out of backyard stills. There were chicken smells and goat

smells in grassless yards filled with engine parts and wire and wood planks, cracked and sprinkled with rusty nails. These were the familiar aromas: the funky earth, animal and mechanical smells which were absent from the homes my mother cleaned.

–LUIS J. RODRIGUEZ, *Always Running: Gang Days in L.A.*

■ Exercise 15.11

Turn to "Uncle Willie," by Maya Angelou, in Chapter 3, and read paragraph 2. Underline the words describing the sense of smell. How do you think this bit of sensory description helps readers imagine the scene?

■ Exercise 15.12

Choose a place with noticeable, distinctive smells where you can stay for ten or fifteen minutes. You may choose an eating place (a cafeteria, a doughnut shop), a place where something is being manufactured (a sawmill, a bakery), or some other place that has strong, identifiable odors (a fishing dock, a garden, a locker room). While you are there, take notes on what you smell, and then write a page or so describing the place primarily through its smells.

The Sense of Touch

Few nouns and verbs name tactile sensations besides words like *touch, feel, tickle, brush, scratch, sting, itch,* and *tingle.* Probably as a consequence, writers describing the sense of touch tend not to name the sensation directly or even to report the act of feeling. Nevertheless, a large stock of words describe temperature *(hot, warm, mild, tepid, cold, arctic),* moisture content *(wet, dry, sticky, oily, greasy, moist, crisp),* texture *(gritty, silky, smooth, crinkled, coarse, soft, leathery),* and weight *(heavy, light, ponderous, buoyant, feathery).* Read the following passages with an eye for descriptions of touch.

A small slab of roughly finished concrete offered a place to stand opposite a square of tar from which a splintered tee protruded.

–WILLIAM RINTOUL, "Breaking One Hundred"

The earth was moldy, a dense clay. No sun had fallen here for over two centuries. I climbed over the brick retaining wall and crawled toward the sound of the kitten. As I neared, as it sensed my presence was too large to be its mother, it went silent and scrabbled away from the reach of my hand. I brushed fur, though, and that slight warmth filled me with what must have been a mad calm because when the creature squeezed into a bearing wall of piled stones, I inched forward on my stomach.

–LOUISE ERDRICH, "Beneath the House"

Here is an example of a writer recalling a childish fantasy of aggression toward her younger sister. Notice the tactile description she uses.

She was baby-soft. I thought that I could put my thumb on her nose and push it bonelessly in, indent her face. I could poke dimples into her cheeks. I could work her face around like dough.

–MAXINE HONG KINGSTON, "The Quiet Girl"

■ Exercise 15.13

Do something with your hands, and then write a sentence or two describing the experience of touch. For example, you might pet a dog, dig a hole and put a plant into the earth, make a pizza, sculpt with clay, bathe a baby, scrub a floor, or massage a friend's back. As you write, notice the words you consider using to describe temperature, moisture content, texture, weight, or any other tactile quality.

■ Exercise 15.14

Turn again to "Uncle Willie," by Maya Angelou, in Chapter 3, and reread paragraph 2, this time looking at the way the writer describes her fear of touching the hot stove. Underline any language that describes the sense of touch. How do you think this sensory description helps readers imagine the scene?

The Sense of Taste

Other than *taste, savor,* and *flavor,* few words name gustatory sensations directly. Certain words do distinguish among types of tastes—*sweet (saccharine, sugary, cloying); sour (acidic, tart); bitter (acrid, biting); salty (briny, brackish)*—and several other words describe specific tastes *(piquant, spicy, pungent, peppery, savory, toothsome).*

In the following passage, M. F. K. Fisher describes the surprisingly "delicious" taste of tar:

> Tar with some dust in it was perhaps even more delicious than dirty chips from the iceman's wagon, largely because if we worked up enough body heat and had the right amount of spit we could keep it melted so that it acted almost like chewing gum, which was forbidden to us as vulgar and bad for the teeth and in general to be shunned. Tar was better than anything ever put out by Wrigley and Beechnut, anyway. It had a high, bright taste. It tasted the way it smelled, but better.
> —M. F. K. FISHER, "Prejudice, Hate, and the First World War"

Fisher identifies the taste of tar as "high" and "bright"—two words that are not typically associated with taste but might be suggestive to readers. Another way she tries to evoke the sense of taste is by comparing tar that acted like chewing gum to actual Wrigley and Beechnut chewing gum. More surprisingly, she compares the taste of tar to its smell.

Ernest Hemingway, in a more conventional passage, tries to describe taste primarily by naming the foods he consumed and giving details that indicate the intensity and quality of the tastes:

> As I ate the oysters with their strong taste of the sea and their faint metallic taste that the cold wine washed away, leaving only the sea taste and the succulent texture, and as I drank their cold liquid from each shell and washed it down with the crispy taste of the wine, I lost the empty feeling and began to be happy and to make plans.
> —ERNEST HEMINGWAY, *A Moveable Feast*

Notice that Hemingway combines taste and touch *(succulent texture* and *crispy taste).* Writer often use words like *juicy, chewy,* and *chunky* to evoke both the taste and the feel of food in the mouth.

■ Exercise 15.15

In the manner of Hemingway, take notes as you eat a particular food or an entire meal. Then write a few sentences describing the tastes you experienced.

■ Exercise 15.16

Turn to "Soup" in Chapter 4. Read paragraph 3, underlining any language that describes or suggests the sense of taste. How do you think this bit of sensory description helps you imagine what the place was like for the writer?

■ CREATING A DOMINANT IMPRESSION

The most effective description creates a dominant impression, a mood or an atmosphere that reinforces the writer's purpose. Writers often attempt to create a dominant impression—for example, when they describe a place in order to set a scene and make readers aware of its atmosphere. Naming, detailing, comparing, and sensory language —all the choices about what to include and what to call things—come together to create this effect, as the following passage by Mary McCarthy illustrates. Notice that McCarthy directly states the idea she is trying to convey in the last sentence of the paragraph.

> Whenever we children came to stay at my grandmother's house, we were put to sleep in the sewing room, a bleak, shabby, utilitarian rectangle, more office than bedroom, more attic than office, that played to the hierarchy of chambers the role of a poor relation. It was a room seldom entered by the other members of the family, seldom swept by the maid, a room without pride; the old sewing machine, some cast-off chairs, a shadeless lamp, rolls of wrapping paper, piles of pins, and remnants of material united with the iron folding cots put out for our use and the bare floor boards to give an impression of intense and ruthless temporality. Thin, white spreads, of the kind used in hospitals and charity institutions, and naked blinds at the windows reminded us of our orphaned condition and of the ephemeral character of our visit; there was nothing here to encourage us to consider this our home.
> –MARY McCARTHY, *Memories of a Catholic Girlhood*

Everything in the room made McCarthy and her brothers feel unwanted, discarded, orphaned. The room itself is described in terms applicable to the children. (Like them, it "played to the hierarchy of chambers the role of a poor relation.") The objects she names, together with their distinguishing details—"cast-off chairs," "shadeless lamp," "iron folding cots," "bare floor boards," "naked blinds"—contribute to this overall impression, thus enabling McCarthy to convey her purpose to her readers.

Sometimes writers comment directly in a description. McCarthy, for instance, states that the sewing room gave "an impression of intense and ruthless temporality," everything serving to remind the children that they were orphans and did not live there. Often, however, writers want description to speak for itself. They *show* rather than tell, letting the descriptive language evoke the impression by itself. Such is the case in the following description by George Orwell of a room for hire:

Hanging from the ceiling there was a heavy glass chandelier on which the dust was so thick that it was like fur. And covering most of one wall there was a huge hideous piece of junk, something between a sideboard and a hall-stand, with lots of carving and little drawers and strips of looking-glass, and there was a once-gaudy carpet ringed by the slop-pails of years, and two gilt chairs with burst seats, and one of those old-fashioned armchairs which you slide off when you try to sit on them. The room had been turned into a bedroom by thrusting four squalid beds in among the wreckage.

—GEORGE ORWELL, *The Road to Wigan Pier*

■ Exercise 15.17

Return to Jan Gray's essay in Chapter 3, and read paragraphs 3 and 4 describing her father's abandoned apartment. What seems to you to be the dominant impression of this description? What do you think contributes most to this impression?

Defining

16

Defining is an essential strategy for all writing. Autobiographers, for example, must occasionally define objects, conditions, events, and activities for readers likely to be unfamiliar with particular terms. In the following example from Chapter 3, the definition is underlined.

> My father's hands are grotesque. He suffers from psoriasis, <u>a chronic skin disease</u> that covers his massive, thick hands with scaly, reddish patches that periodically flake off, sending tiny pieces of dead skin sailing to the ground.
>
> — JAN GRAY, "Father"

When writers share information or explain how to do something, they must often define important terms for readers who are unfamiliar with the subject. This example comes from Chapter 4.

> After the scalp and the skull, the next layer protecting the brain is the dura. <u>A thin, tough, leathery membrane that encases the brain</u>, the dura (derived from the Latin for *hard*) is dark pink, almost red.
>
> — DAVID NOONAN, "Inside the Brain"

To convince readers of a position or an evaluation or to move them to act on a proposal, a writer must often define concepts important to an argument. This example comes from Chapter 5.

> Already, there has been one instance of new terrorists using weapons of mass destruction — <u>the generic term for biological, chemical and nuclear arms.</u>
>
> — "The New Terrorism"

As these examples illustrate, there are many kinds of definitions and many forms that they can take. Some published essays and reports are concerned primarily with the definition of a little-understood or problematic concept or thing. Usually, however, definition is only a part of an essay. A long piece of writing, like a term paper, textbook, or research report, may include many kinds of brief and extended definitions, all of them integrated with other writing strategies.

This chapter illustrates various types of sentence definitions, the most common in writing. When writers use sentence definitions, they rely on various sentence patterns to provide concise definitions. The chapter also provides illustrations of multisentence extended definitions, including definition by word history, or etymology, and by stipulation.

■ SENTENCE DEFINITIONS

Every field of study, every institution, and every activity has its own unique concepts and terms. Coming to a new area for the first time, a participant or a reader is often baffled by the many unfamiliar names for objects and activities. In college, introductory courses in all the academic disciplines often seem like courses in definitions of new terms. In the same way, newcomers to a sport like sailing or rock climbing often need to learn much specialized terminology. In such cases, writers of textbooks and manuals rely on brief sentence definitions, involving a variety of sentence strategies.

Here are some sentence strategies from several widely used introductory college textbooks. These examples illustrate various sentence strategies an author may use to name and define terms for readers.

The most obvious sentence strategies simply announce a definition. (In each of the following examples, the word being defined is in italics, and the definition is underlined.)

A *karyotype* is a graphic representation of a set of chromosomes.

Then, within the first week, the cells begin to *differentiate*—to specialize in structure and function.

B lymphocytes form in the bone marrow and release antibodies that fight bacterial infections.

Geologists refer to the processes of mountain building as *orogenesis* (from the Greek *oro,* "mountain," and *genesis,* "birth").

Posthypnotic suggestions (suggestions to be carried out after the hypnosis session has ended) have helped alleviate headaches, asthma, warts, and stress-related skin disorders.

All of these sentence strategies declare in a straightforward way that the writer is defining a term. Other strategies, signaled by certain sentence structures like clauses and appositives, are less direct but still quite apparent.

During the *oral stage,* which lasts throughout the first 18 months, the infant's sensual pleasures focus on sucking, biting, and chewing.

Hemophilia is called the bleeder's disease because the affected person's blood does not clot.

These sentence definitions—all of which appear in subordinate clauses—add details, express time and cause, or indicate conditions or tentativeness. In all these examples, however, the clauses play a specific defining role in the sections of the text where they appear.

Another common defining strategy is the appositive phrase. Here one word or phrase defines another word or phrase in a brief inserted phrase called an *appositive*. Sometimes the appositive contains the definition; other times it contains the word to be defined.

> *Taxonomy,* the science of classifying groups (taxa) of organisms in formal groups, is hierarchical.

> The actual exchange of gases takes place in small air sacs, the *alveoli,* which are clustered in branches like grapes around the ends of the smallest bronchioles.

■ Exercise 16.1

Look up any three of the following words or phrases in a dictionary. Define each one in a sentence. Try to use a different sentence pattern, like the ones just illustrated, for each of your definitions.

bull market	ecumenism	samba
carcinogen	edema	seasonal affective disorder
caricature	harangue	sonnet
clinometer	hyperhydrosis	testosterone
ectomorph	mnemonic	zero-based budgeting

■ Exercise 16.2

Turn to the essay by David Noonan in Chapter 4, and analyze the sentence definitions in paragraphs 2, 9, 13, and 18. Notice the different kinds of sentence patterns Noonan relies on. (You need not be able to analyze the sentences grammatically in order to examine their patterns.) Keeping in mind that Noonan hopes merely to introduce readers to the technology of brain surgery, not train them to discuss it with experts or do surgery themselves, how helpful do you find these sentence definitions? How do they support Noonan's purpose?

■ EXTENDED DEFINITIONS

At times a writer may need to go further than a brief sentence definition and provide readers with a fuller definition extending over several sentences. Here, for example, is how Janice Castro defines a new kind of worker in the U.S. economy, the "contingent" worker.

> Every day, 1.5 million temps are dispatched from agencies like Kelly Services and Manpower—nearly three times as many as 10 years ago. But they are only the most visible part of America's enormous new temporary work force. An additional 34 million people start their day as other types of "contingent" workers. Some are part-timers with some benefits. Others work by the hour, the day or the duration of a project, receiving only a paycheck without benefits of any kind. The rules of their employment vary widely and so do the attempts to label them. They are called short-timers, per-diem workers, leased employees, extra workers, supplementals,

contractors—or in IBM's ironic computer-generated parlance, "the peripherals." They are what you might expect: secretaries, security guards, salesclerks, assembly-line workers, analysts and CAD/CAM designers. But these days they are also what you'd never expect: doctors, high school principals, lawyers, bank officers, X-ray technicians, biochemists, engineers, managers—even chief executives.

—Janice Castro, "Contingent Workers"

Castro begins by comparing contingent workers to the more familiar temporary workers ("temps") managed by temporary employment agencies. Then she gives examples of contingent workers' working arrangements and lists many names by which these workers are known. Finally, she identifies the various categories of contingent workers. These strategies—comparisons, examples, synonyms, and classification—are often found in extended definitions and in fact in all kinds of explanatory writing. Castro never concisely defines the word *contingent* in the phrase "contingent worker" because she assumes that readers can infer that it means roughly the opposite of permanent, continuing worker.

In this next example, Marie Winn offers an extended definition of television addiction. Like Janice Castro, Winn begins with a comparison. These two experienced writers know that comparison or contrast is often the most effective way to present an unfamiliar term or concept to readers. The key is to know your readers well enough to find a term nearly all of them will know to compare to the unfamiliar term.

People often refer to being "hooked on TV." Does this, too, fall into the lighthearted category of cookie eating and other pleasures that people pursue with unusual intensity, or is there a kind of televison viewing that falls into the more serious category of destructive addiction? . . .

Let us consider television viewing in the light of the conditions that define serious addictions.

Not unlike drugs or alcohol, the television experience allows the participant to blot out the real world and enter into a pleasurable and passive mental state. The worries and anxieties of reality are as effectively deferred by becoming absorbed in a television program as by going on a "trip" induced by drugs or alcohol. And just as alcoholics are only inchoately aware of their addiction, feeling that they control their drinking more than they really do ("I can cut it out any time I want—I just like to have three or four drinks before dinner"), people similarly overestimate their control over television watching. Even as they put off other activities to spend hour after hour watching television, they feel they could easily resume living in a different, less passive style. But somehow or other while the television set is present in their homes, the click doesn't sound. With television pleasures available, those other experiences seem less attractive, more difficult somehow. . . .

The self-confessed television addict often feels he "ought" to do other things—but the fact that he doesn't read and doesn't plant his garden or sew or crochet or play games or have conversations means that those activities are no longer as desirable as television viewing. In a way a heavy viewer's life is as imbalanced by his television "habit" as a drug addict's or an alcoholic's. He is living in a holding pattern, as it were, passing up the activities that lead to growth or development or a sense of accomplishment. This is one reason people talk about their television viewing so ruefully, so apologetically. They are aware that it is an unproductive experience, that almost any other endeavor is more worthwhile by any human measure.

Finally, it is the adverse effect of television viewing on the lives of so many people that defines it as a serious addiction. The television habit distorts the sense of time. It renders other experiences vague and curiously unreal while taking on a greater reality for itself. It weakens relationships by reducing and sometimes eliminating normal opportunities for talking, for communicating.

And yet television does not satisfy, else why would the viewer continue to watch hour after hour, day after day? "The measure of health," writes Lawrence Kubie, "is flexibility . . . and especially the freedom to cease when sated." But the television viewer can never be sated with his television experiences—they do not provide the true nourishment that satiation requires—and thus he finds that he cannot stop watching.

—MARIE WINN, "TV Addiction"

Besides comparing television addiction to drug or alcohol addiction, Winn describes the effects of television addiction and speculates about why addicts find it so hard to break the addiction.

Extended definitions may also include *negative definitions*—explanations of what the thing being defined is *not:*

It's important to be clear about the reverse definition, as well: what dinosaurs are not. Dinosaurs are not lizards, and vice versa. Lizards are scaly reptiles of an ancient bloodline. The oldest lizards antedate the earliest dinosaurs by a full thirty million years. A few large lizards, such as the man-eating Komodo dragon, have been called "relics of the dinosaur age," but this phrase is historically incorrect. No lizard ever evolved the birdlike characteristics peculiar to each and every dinosaur. A big lizard never resembled a small dinosaur except for a few inconsequential details of the teeth. Lizards never walked with the erect, long-striding gait that distinguishes the dinosaurlike ground birds today or the birdlike dinosaurs of the Mesozoic.

—ROBERT T. BAKKER, *The Dinosaur Heresies*

■ Exercise 16.3

Choose one term that names some concept or feature of central importance in an activity or a subject you know well. For example, if you sail, you know terms like *tacking* and *coming about*. If you are studying biology, you have probably encountered terms like *morphogenesis* and *ecosystem*. Choose a word with a well-established definition. Write an extended definition of several sentences for this important term. Write for readers your own age who will be encountering the term for the first time when they read your definition.

■ Exercise 16.4

Return to "Inside the Brain," David Noonan's essay in Chapter 4, and analyze the extended definition of *sterile field* in paragraph 6. How does Noonan define this term? What purpose does the definition serve in the context of the whole selection?

■ HISTORICAL DEFINITIONS

Occasionally, a writer will trace the history of a word, from its first use to its adoption into other languages to its shifting meanings over the centuries. Such a strategy can be a rich addition to an essay, bringing surprising depth and resonance to the definition of a concept. A historical definition may begin with the roots of a word but extends well beyond the word's origins to trace its history over a long period of time. Such a history should always serve a writer's larger purpose, as the example here shows.

In this example, from a special issue of *Time* magazine on the future uses of cyberspace and its potential impact on the economy, Philip Elmer-DeWitt provides a historical definition of the term *cyberspace*.

> It started, as the big ideas in technology often do, with a science-fiction writer. William Gibson, a young expatriate American living in Canada, was wandering past the video arcades on Vancouver's Granville Street in the early 1980s when something about the way the players were hunched over their glowing screens struck him as odd. "I could see in the physical intensity of their postures how *rapt* the kids were," he says. "It was like a feedback loop, with photons coming off the screens into the kids' eyes, neurons moving through their bodies and electrons moving through the video game. These kids clearly *believed* in the space the games projected."
>
> That image haunted Gibson. He didn't know much about video games or computers — he wrote his breakthrough novel *Neuromancer* (1984) on an ancient manual typewriter — but he knew people who did. And as near as he could tell, everybody who worked much with the machines eventually came to accept, almost as an article of faith, the reality of that imaginary realm. "They develop a belief that there's some kind of *actual space* behind the screen," he says. "Some place that you can't see but you know is there."
>
> Gibson called that place "cyberspace," and used it as the setting for his early novels and short stories. In his fiction, cyberspace is a computer-generated landscape that characters enter by "jacking in" — sometimes by plugging electrodes directly into sockets implanted in the brain. What they see when they get there is a three-dimensional representation of all the information stored in "every computer in the human system" — great warehouses and skyscrapers of data. He describes it in a key passage in *Neuromancer* as a place of "unthinkable complexity," with "lines of light ranged in the nonspace of the mind, clusters and constellations of data. Like city lights, receding. . . ."
>
> In the years since, there have been other names given to that shadowy space where our computer data reside: the Net, the Web, the Cloud, the Matrix, the Metaverse, the Datasphere, the Electronic Frontier, the information superhighway. But Gibson's coinage may prove the most enduring. By 1989 it had been borrowed by the online community to describe not some science-fiction fantasy but today's increasingly interconnected computer systems — especially the millions of computers jacked into the Internet.
>
> —Philip Elmer-DeWitt, "Welcome to Cyberspace"

Elmer-DeWitt begins with a story about how William Gibson created the name *cyberspace* for a strange phenomenon he observed — young people's intense concentration while playing video games. *Cybernetics* was already a familiar term used to describe computer-controlled processes like robots in factories. Gibson borrowed the *cyber* portion and combined it with *space* to reflect his imagined realm, the "place that you can't see but you know is there." Elmer-DeWitt also offers details about how Gibson imagined humans would gain access to cyberspace and how it was constructed. Finally, bringing the historical definition into the present, Elmer-DeWitt lists competing terms that have failed to supplant *cyberspace* as the term most people now use to identify the realm of computer data and electronic communication.

■ Exercise 16.5

Any good dictionary tells the origins of words. Historical, or etymological, dictionaries, however, give much more information, enough to trace changes in use of a word over long periods of time. The preeminent historical dictionary of our language is the *Oxford English Dictionary.* Less imposing is *A Dictionary of American English,* and more accessible still is *A Dictionary of Americanisms.* Look up the historical definition of any one of the following words in *A Dictionary of Americanisms,* and write several sentences on its roots and development.

basketball	bushwhack	gerrymander	rubberneck
bazooka	canyon	jazz	sashay
bedrock	carpetbag	lobbying	Scot-free
blizzard	dugout	pep	two-bit
bogus	eye-opener	picayune	
bonanza	filibuster	podunk	

■ STIPULATIVE DEFINITIONS

To stipulate means to seek or assert agreement on something. In a stipulative definition, the writer declares a certain meaning, generally not one found in the dictionary. Stipulative definitions have a variety of important functions, two of which are illustrated here.

In her autobiography, Annie Dillard defines *football* as she understood it as a nine-year-old.

> Some boys taught me to play football. This was fine sport. You thought up a new strategy for every play and whispered it to the others. You went out for a pass, fooling everyone. Best, you got to throw yourself mightily at someone's running legs. Either you brought him down or you hit the ground flat out on your chin, with your arms empty before you. It was all or nothing. If you hesitated in fear, you would miss and get hurt: you would take a hard fall while the kid got away, or you would get kicked in the face while the kid got away. But if you flung yourself wholeheartedly at the back of his knees—if you gathered and joined body and soul and pointed them diving fearlessly—then you likely wouldn't get hurt, and you'd stop the ball. Your fate, and your team's score, depended on your concentration and courage. Nothing girls did could compare with it.
>
> —ANNIE DILLARD, *An American Childhood*

There are recognizable elements of grown-up football in Dillard's definition. Her focus is less on rules and strategy, however, than on the "concentration and courage" required to make a successful tackle and, of course, on the sheer thrill of doing it. She stipulates this definition because it suits her purposes in telling a remembered incident about how she and her fellow football players were chased by a man whose car they had bombed with snowballs.

This next example illustrates how a newspaper columnist can create a stipulative definition of the term *environmentalism* in order to argue for a more realistic approach to protecting the environment.

> Ozone depletion and the greenhouse effect are human disasters. They happen to occur in the environment. But they are urgent because they directly threaten man. A sane environmentalism, the only kind of environmentalism that will win universal public support, begins by unashamedly declaring that nature is here to serve man. A sane environmentalism is entirely anthropocentric: it enjoins man to preserve nature, but on the grounds of self-preservation.
>
> A sane environmentalism does not sentimentalize the earth. It does not ask people to sacrifice in the name of other creatures. After all, it is hard enough to ask people to sacrifice in the name of other humans. (Think of the chronic public resistance to foreign aid and welfare.) Ask hardworking voters to sacrifice in the name of the snail darter, and, if they are feeling polite, they will give you a shrug.
>
> —CHARLES KRAUTHAMMER, "Saving Nature, but Only for Man"

■ Exercise 16.6

In his Chapter 7 proposal about birth control in the schools, Adam Paul Weisman offers a stipulative definition of the role schools play in students' lives (paragraph 11). Read the essay, paying particular attention to this definition. What function does it serve in the essay as a whole?

■ Exercise 16.7

Write several sentences of a stipulative definition for one of the following.

1. Define in your own way game shows, soap operas, police dramas, horror movies, or some other form of entertainment. Try for a stipulative definition of what your subject is generally like. In effect, you will be saying to your readers—other students in your class who are familiar with these entertainments—"Let's for now define it this way."

2. Define in your own way some hard-to-define concept, such as "loyalty," "love," "bravery," "shyness," or "male chauvinism."

3. Think of a new development or phenomenon in contemporary romance, music, television, leisure, fashion, or eating habits, or in your line of work. Invent a name for it, and write a stipulative definition for it.

Classifying

17

Classifying is an essential writing strategy for thinking about and organizing ideas, information, and experience. The process of classifying involves either grouping or dividing. Writers group related items (such as *apples, oranges, bananas, strawberries, cantaloupes,* and *cherries*) and label the general class of items they grouped together (*fruit*). Or they begin classifying with a general class (such as *fruit*) and then divide it into subclasses of particular types (*apples, oranges,* etc.).

This chapter shows how you can organize and illustrate a classification you have read about or constructed yourself.

■ ORGANIZING CLASSIFICATION

Classifying in writing serves primarily as a means of organization, of creating a framework for the presentation of information, whether in a few paragraphs of an essay or in an entire book. This section surveys several examples of classifying, ranging from a simple two-level classification to a complex multilevel system.

The simplest classification divides a general topic into two subtopics. Here is an example by Edward J. Loughram from a proposal to keep at-risk teenagers out of jail and help them lead productive lives. Before he can present his proposed solution, Loughram has to get readers to see that all juvenile offenders are not the same. He does this by explaining that although statistics show that the number of juvenile offenders is rising, they do not take into account the fact that there are two distinct groups (underlined) of young people getting into trouble. He classifies juvenile offenders into these two categories to argue that the problem of delinquency can be solved, at least in part, by interrupting the criminal paths of the second group.

> Two primary factors explain the growing numbers of juvenile offenders. First, there is indeed a rise in serious crime among young people, fueled by the steady stream of drugs and weapons into their hands. These <u>dangerous offenders</u> are committed—legitimately—to juvenile-correction agencies for long-term custody or treatment.
>
> But a second, larger group is also contributing to the increase. It consists of 11-, 12-, and 13-year-old first-time offenders who have failed at home, failed in school, and fallen through the cracks of state and community social-service agencies. These

are <u>not serious offenders</u>, or even typical delinquents. But they are coming into the correctional system because we have ignored the warning signs among them.

             —EDWARD J. LOUGHRAM, "Prevention of Delinquency"

Loughram's is a simple classification with only two categories. Each category is discussed in its own paragraph and labeled clearly. The labels—*dangerous offenders* and *not serious offenders*—make explicit that the basis for Loughram's classification is the seriousness of the crimes.

From Loughram's essay, we see how a writer can use a simple two-category classification to advance an argument. The next example, excerpted from a concept explanation essay by Janice Castro, presents a somewhat more complicated classification system:

> Every day, 1.5 million temps are dispatched from agencies like Kelly Services and Manpower—nearly three times as many as 10 years ago. But they are only the most visible part of America's enormous new temporary work force. An additional 34 million people start their day as other types of "contingent" workers. Some are part-timers with some benefits. Others work by the hour, the day or the duration of a project, receiving only a paycheck without benefits of any kind. The rules of their employment vary widely and so do the attempts to label them. They are called short-timers, per-diem workers, leased employees, extra workers, supplementals, contractors—or in IBM's ironic computer-generated parlance, "the peripherals." They are what you might expect: secretaries, security guards, salesclerks, assembly-line workers, analysts and CAD/CAM designers. But these days they are also what you'd never expect: doctors, high school principals, lawyers, bank officers, X-ray technicians, biochemists, engineers, managers—even chief executives. . . .
>
>   Already the temping phenomenon is producing two vastly different classes of untethered workers: the mercenary work force at the top of the skills ladder, who thrive; and the rest, many of whom, unable to attract fat contract fees, must struggle to survive.
>
>   —JANICE CASTRO, "Contingent Workers"

Castro explains that "contingent" is only one of many labels used to identify this general class of part-time and temporary workers. In the second paragraph, she divides contingent workers into what she calls "two vastly different classes." Although Castro does not label these two types of contingent workers clearly, we can see that her basis for differentiating between these two groups is the amount of money they are paid. Members of one group "thrive," while those of the other "must struggle to survive." Therefore, we can label these groups *well-paid* and *low-paid*. Readers sometimes have to supply labels to clarify for themselves the categories in a classification.

So far, Castro's is a simple two-part classification system like Loughram's. It has two levels: the general class of contingent workers and two subclasses of well-paid and low-paid contingent workers. Castro, however, adds a third level to her classification by listing several types of jobs that fall under her two subclasses. Here is a tree diagram that graphically displays Castro's three-level classification:

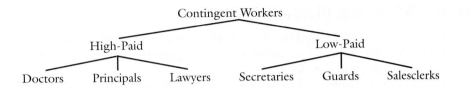

Later in the essay, Castro identifies another class of workers who are not contingent workers but are "a permanent cadre of 'core workers.'" To add this class of core workers to the tree diagram, we should also add a new general class at the top that includes all of the subclasses below it. We could label this most general class "corporate workers." Here is what the expanded tree diagram would look like:

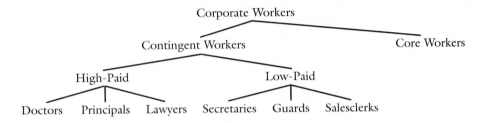

What the tree diagrams show at a glance is that in a classification system, some categories are on the same level, or *coordinate*. Some are on a higher level, *superordinate*. And some are on a lower level, *subordinate*. The highest level represents the most general category, and each lower level identifies increasingly specific types. If Castro took her classification to the most specific level, she would name individuals as examples of workers in each type of job. Whether you construct your own classification system or use someone else's, you want to make sure that each item is placed in an appropriate category on the proper level.

■ Exercise 17.1

Turn to the concept explanation in Chapter 5, "Cannibalism: It Still Exists," and make a tree diagram of the classification in paragraphs 5–12. What do you think is Linh Kieu Ngo's basis for classification? Does each item seem to be placed in an appropriate category and on the proper level?

■ Exercise 17.2

Review the essays you have written so far for this class or for another class, looking for an essay in which you used classifying. What was the purpose of your essay and your basis for classifying? Construct a tree diagram of your classification to see whether each item can be placed in an appropriate category and on the proper level.

■ ILLUSTRATING CLASSIFICATION

We used tree diagrams to illustrate the categories and levels of Castro's classification of workers. Writers, however, sometimes integrate graphics into their own writing to make their classification easy for readers to see at a glance.

Here is an example from *Newsweek* magazine in which Sharon Begley and Martha Brant explain the problem of drug abuse by Olympic athletes. In this passage, the authors classify the performance-enhancing drugs athletes use into five categories (underlined) and present three kinds of information about each drug: what the drug does, how detectable it is, and what the health risks are. This organizational plan is graphically illustrated by the chart that accompanies the written text.

> If doping is, as [the head of IOC's Medical Commission Prince Alexandre] de Merode noticed, suddenly "an important problem," it is partly because the newest doping agents pose the risk of serious health problems, and even death. But the larger reason is that it is ridiculously easy to dope and not get caught. Doping and detection are like an arms race. First, trainers discover a performance-enhancing drug. Then, sports officials develop a test for it. Trainers retaliate by inventing a way to elude the detectors. So far, doping has stayed a lap ahead. "Undetectable drugs are 90 percent of estimated doping cases," says Hein Verbruggen, head of international cycling.
>
> Czech tennis pro Petr Korda tested positive for the steroid nandrolone after the Wimbledon quarterfinals last May, for instance. (Protesting that he did not know how the chemicals got into his system, he avoided the one-year suspension the International Tennis Association is supposed to impose.) But American pro Jim Courier charged that steroids are far from the worst abuse in tennis. "EPO is the problem," Courier told *Newsweek*. "I have pretty strong suspicions that guys are using it on the tour. I see guys who are out there week in and week out without taking rests. EPO can help you when it's the fifth set and you've been playing for four-and-a-half hours." Although the endurance-building effects of EPO last for about two weeks, its use can't be detected in urine at all or in blood for more than a day or so after the athlete stops taking it.
>
> EPO is only one weapon in a pharmaceutical arsenal of performance-enhancing substances flowing through sports. Stimulants like amphetamines, ephedrine and caffeine were the first substances to land on the IOC's list of banned agents, and they're still popular. They provide a quick pop of energy, and so are a favorite of sprinters, cyclists and swimmers. They are an ingredient of many asthma medications. Exercise-induced asthma has inexplicably stricken many Olympians, including 60 percent of the U.S. team in 1994, and medical use of stimulant inhalants is allowed. Are stimulants detectable? Sure, if your trainer's IQ matches his hat size. They clear the urine in hours, so all an athlete has to do is not take them too close to her event. If you've been using too soon before your race, there are always "masking agents." Probenecid, for one, inhibits substances from reaching the urine. And urine tests are all the IOC requires: blood tests, which can detect more substances, are deemed too invasive.
>
> Anabolic steroids, almost all of them derivatives of the hormone testosterone, are the mothers of all doping agents. They build muscles. By most estimates, an athlete can improve strength at least 5 percent by taking steroids either orally or through

DRUG	WHAT DOES IT DO?	MASKING/ DETECTION	RISKS
Human growth hormone (hGH)	Stimulates the intracellular breakdown of body fat, allowing more to be used for energy.	This is a natural hormone, so added amounts don't show up in blood or urine tests.	Muscle and bone disfigurement— jutting forehead, elongated jaw. Also: heart and metabolic problems.
Erythropoietin (EPO)	Increases the number of red blood cells without having to "dope" using one's own blood.	It's extremely difficult to detect because the extra blood cells are the athlete's own.	Extra cells can make blood the consistency of yogurt. This can lead to a clot, heart attack or stroke.
Testosterone	Used to build muscles. It lets the body recover quickly from strenuous exercise.	Rules allow up to five times the natural body level, giving athletes latitude.	Unnatural levels can cause heart disease, liver cancer and impotence.
Steroids/androstenedione	Anabolic steroids are incarnations of testosterone; androstenedione is a precursor molecule.	Water-based steroids (most common) are undetectable in urine after several weeks.	Synthetic testosterone carries the same risks as naturally occurring testosterone.
Stimulants	The first category that the IOC tested for. They delay the symptoms of fatigue.	Stimulants such as amphetamines can be detected; diuretics can dilute them in urine.	Fatigue is the body saying "stop"— overriding that message can be dangerous.

injection during high-intensity training. Drug-detection machines, such as the high-resolution mass spectrometer used at the Atlanta Games in 1996, can be tuned to detect any synthetic steroid; the Atlanta lab tested for 100 different types. But the Dr. Feelgoods of sport can tinker with the molecular structure of common steroids, so they slip through. "There are 72 banned steroids," says one American coach who says he developed drug regimes for athletes in Atlanta, "but the testosterone molecule is changeable in millions of ways. All you have to do is make a steroid not on the list." Or, simply by going cold turkey a few weeks before competition, an athlete can get the muscle-bulking effects without getting caught. If that seems too chancy, athletes can use a diuretic. These drugs, which are also banned, dilute the urine. That makes illicit substances virtually undetectable.

More and more athletes are turning to the source of all steroids: <u>testosterone</u> itself. Natural levels vary, so sports federations and the IOC try to detect doping indirectly. They measure the relative amounts of testosterone and another natural steroid called epitestosterone. In most people, testosterone levels are no more than twice epi levels. But to allow for individual variation, the IOC set the prohibited level at anything over 6 to 1. That means an athlete can dope himself up to, say, five times his normal testosterone levels, and get away with it. How much of an edge would that provide? A male athlete with a typical testosterone/epitestosterone ratio of 1.3 to 1 could boost that to 6 to 1, stay within the IOC limit and improve his performance at least 10 percent. Women, with a natural ratio of 2.5 to 1, could do even better, since they have less testosterone to begin with and so are more sensitive to added amounts. Testosterone can give women beards, deep voices and tough skin. It can make men's breasts swell and testicles shrivel.

The doping agents of choice today are substances that cannot be detected in urine: EPO and <u>human growth hormone</u>. Even though the performance-enhancing effects of hGH are unproved, many athletes believe it boosts energy. (Athletes dubbed the Atlanta Olympics "The Growth Hormone Games.") hGH can also cause grotesque skeletal deformations by stimulating abnormal bone growth. EPO, by increasing the production of red blood cells up to tenfold, can turn blood the consistency of yogurt, making it too thick to flow freely. The misuse of EPO has apparently killed at least 18 Dutch and Belgian cyclists since 1987.

—SHARON BEGLEY AND MARTHA BRANT, "The Real Scandal"

If you compare the chart to the written text, you will see that in some instances the chart simply repeats information that appears in the text, but more often the chart complements or adds to the text. For example, in the last paragraph of the text and in the "Risks" column of the chart, erythropoietin (EPO) is said to turn "blood the consistency of yogurt." The chart then adds to the text by explaining why thickening of the blood is dangerous: "This can lead to a clot, heart attack or stroke."

Although most readers would expect the chart to present the drugs in the order they appear in the essay, that is not the case here. In the essay, the drugs are discussed in this order: EPO, stimulants, steroids, testosterone, and human growth hormone (hGH). But in the chart, the order is hGH, EPO, testosterone, steroids, and stimulants. Except for EPO, the order in the chart reverses the order in the text. If you include a chart with your classification, be sure that your chart corresponds to the written text.

For more information on designing documents with graphics, see Chapter 25.

■ MAINTAINING CLARITY AND COHERENCE

The next example illustrates how writers can help readers follow a classification system even when the subject is new and difficult. The passage comes from a book on physics by Gary Zukav. He uses classifying to explain the concept of mass. Simply defined, mass in physics is a measure of the matter in an object. How mass is calculated is the basis for Zukav's classification of two types of mass: gravitational and inertial.

As you read, notice the cues (underlined) the writer uses to help readers understand the classification.

<u>There are two kinds of mass</u>, which means that there are two ways of talking about it. <u>The first is gravitational mass.</u> The gravitational mass of an object, roughly speak-

ing, is the weight of the object as measured on a balance scale. Something that weighs three times more than another object has three times more mass. Gravitational mass is the measure of how much force the gravity of the earth exerts on an object. Newton's laws describe the effects of this force, which vary with the distance of the mass from the earth. . . .

The second type of mass is inertial mass. Inertial mass is the measure of the resistance of an object to acceleration (or deceleration, which is negative acceleration). For example, it takes three times more force to move three railroad cars from a standstill to twenty miles per hour (positive acceleration) than it takes to move one railroad car from a standstill to twenty miles per hour. . . . Similarly, once they are moving, it takes three times more force to stop three cars than it takes to stop the single car. This is because the inertial mass of the three railroad cars is three times more than the inertial mass of the single railroad car.

— GARY ZUKAV, *The Dancing Wu Li Masters: An Overview of the New Physics*

From this passage, we can see some of the cues writers use to make a classification clear and coherent. Zukav begins by forecasting the classification he will develop *(There are two kinds of mass)*. He then introduces each category in its own paragraph, announced with the transition *(first* and *second)* and presented in the same sentence pattern *(The first is . . .* and *The second type of mass is . . .)*. Careful cueing like this can help make a classification clear to readers.

■ Exercise 17.3

Look back at the paragraphs from Linh Kieu Ngo's essay on cannibalism that you used to make a tree diagram in Exercise 17.1 or at the example by Begley and Brant earlier in this chapter, to examine the strategies these authors use to make their classifications clear and coherent. Notice how each category is introduced and the transitions used to help readers keep track of the categories. What conclusions can you draw about how writers maintain clarity and coherence from your analysis?

■ Exercise 17.4

Look back at the classification you examined in Exercise 17.2 to see how well you were able to maintain clarity and coherence in your classification. What changes would you make, if any, to improve clarity and coherence?

General strategies for coherence are discussed in Chapter 13.

Comparing and Contrasting

18

Comparing and contrasting make writing more memorable. Consequently, whenever you analyze and evaluate two or more things, it is useful to compare them. You might compare two people you know well, two motorcycles you are considering buying for a cross-country tour, three Stephen King novels, four tomato plants being grown under different laboratory conditions, or two theories about the relationship between inflation and wages. But as soon as you begin to compare two things, you usually begin to contrast them as well, for rarely are two things alike in all respects. The contrasts, or differences, between the two motorcycles are likely to be more enlightening than the similarities, many of which may be so obvious as to need no analysis. Comparison, then, brings similar things together for examination, to see how they are alike. Contrast is a form of comparison that emphasizes differences.

The use of comparison and contrast is more than a writing strategy, of course. It is a way of thinking and learning. According to research on learning, we acquire new concepts most readily if we can see how they are similar to or different from concepts we already know.

Professional writers say that comparison and contrast is a basic strategy they would not want to be without. In some writing situations (like the ones we mentioned), it has no substitute. Indeed, some writing is essentially extended comparison. But for all kinds of writing situations, writers regularly alternate comparison and contrast with other writing strategies when they present information.

Chances are that you will confront many test questions and essay assignments asking you to compare and contrast—two poems, three presidents, four procedures. This strategy is popular in all academic disciplines, for it is one of the best ways to challenge students intellectually.

■ TWO WAYS OF COMPARING AND CONTRASTING

There are two ways to organize comparison and contrast in writing: in chunks and in sequence. In chunking, each object of the comparison is presented separately; in sequencing, the items are compared point by point. For example, a chunked comparison of two motorcycles would first detail all pertinent features of the Pirsig Z-1700 XL and then consider all features of the Kawazuki 1750XL, whereas a sequenced comparison would analyze the Pirsig and the Kawazuki feature by feature. In a chunked comparison, the discussion is organized around each separate item being compared. In a sequenced comparison, it is organized around characteristics of the items being compared.

In the following example of chunked comparison, Jane Tompkins contrasts popular nineteenth-century "sentimental" novels with the "Western" novels that provided a reaction against them:

> The female, domestic, "sentimental" religion of the best-selling women writers—Harriet Beecher Stowe, Susan Warner, Maria Cummins, and dozens of others—whose novels spoke to the deepest beliefs and highest ideals of middle-class America, is the real antagonist of the Western.
>
> You can see this simply by comparing the main features of the Western with the sentimental novel. In these books . . . a woman is always the main character, usually a young orphan girl, with several other main characters being women too. Most of the action takes place in private spaces, at home, indoors, in kitchens, parlors, and upstairs chambers. And most of it concerns the interior struggles of the heroine to live up to an ideal of Christian virtue—usually involving uncomplaining submission to difficult and painful circumstances, learning to quell rebellious instincts, and dedicating her life to the service of God through serving others. In these struggles, women give one another a great deal of emotional and material support, and they have close relationships verging on what today we would identify as homosocial and homoerotic. There's a great deal of Bible reading, praying, hymn singing, and drinking of tea. Emotions other than anger are expressed very freely and openly. Often there are long, drawn-out death scenes in which a saintly woman dies a natural death at home. . . .
>
> The elements of the typical Western plot arrange themselves in stark opposition to this pattern, not just vaguely and generally but point for point. First of all, in Westerns (which are generally written by men), the main character is always a full-grown adult male, and almost all of the other characters are men. The action takes place either outdoors—on the prairie, on the main street—or in public places—the saloon, the sheriff's office, the barber shop, the livery stable. The action concerns physical struggles between the hero and a rival or rivals, and culminates in a fight to the death with guns. In the course of these struggles the hero frequently forms a bond with another man—sometimes his rival, more often a comrade—a bond that is more important than any relation he has with a woman and is frequently tinged with homoeroticism. There is very little free expression of the emotions. The hero is a man of few words who expresses himself through physical action—usually fighting. And when death occurs it is never at home in bed but always sudden death, usually murder.
>
> —JANE TOMPKINS, *West of Everything: The Inner Life of Westerns*

The two items being compared—sentimental novels and Westerns—are discussed separately, first one and then the other. Tompkins signals the shift from the first discussion to the contrasting one by a transitional sentence that begins a new paragraph. Each point of contrast is presented in the same order.

Schematically, a chunked comparison looks simple enough. As the preceding example shows, it is easy to block off such a discussion in a text and then provide a clean transition between the various parts. And yet it can in fact be more complicated for a writer to plan than a sequenced comparison. Sequenced comparison may be closer to the way people perceive and think about similarities or differences in things. For example, you may have realized all at once that two navy blazers are different, but you would identify the specific differences—buttons, tailoring, fabric—one at a time. A sequenced comparison would point to the differences in just this way, one at a time, whereas a chunked comparison would present all the features of one blazer and then do the same for the second. A writer using the chunked strategy, then, must organize all the points of comparison before starting to write and then be sure that the points of comparison are presented in the same order in the discussion of each item being compared. With sequencing, however, the writer can take up each point of comparison as it comes to mind.

■ Exercise 18.1

Identify the specific items contrasted in the example comparing sentimental novels and Westerns. Number in sequence each contrast, and underline both parts of the contrast. To get started, in the paragraph about sentimental novels, underline "a woman is always the main character, usually a young orphan girl," and number it "1" in the margin. In the paragraph about Westerns, underline "the main character is always a full-grown adult male," and number this "1" also to complete your identification of both parts of the comparison. Then look for contrast 2 and underline and number the contrasted items, and so on.

Look over your work and consider the pattern of these contrasts. Were they easy to identify? If so, what made them easy to identify? Was any contrast left incomplete? In general, how successful and informative do you find this set of contrasts?

In the next example, from a natural history of the earth, David Attenborough uses sequencing to contrast bird wings and airplane wings:

Bird wings have a much more complex job to do than the wings of an aeroplane, for in addition to supporting the bird they must act as its engine, rowing it through the air. Even so the wing outline of a bird conforms to the same aerodynamic principles as those eventually discovered by man when designing his aeroplanes, and if you know how different kinds of aircraft perform, you can predict the flight capabilities of similarly shaped birds.

Short stubby wings enable a tanager and other forest-living birds to swerve and dodge at speed through the undergrowth just as they helped the fighter planes of the Second World War to make tight turns and aerobatic manoeuvres in a dog-fight. More modern fighters achieve greater speeds by sweeping back their wings while in flight, just as peregrines do when they go into a 130 kph dive, stooping to a kill. Championship gliders have long thin wings so that, having gained height in a thermal up-current, they can soar gently down for hours and an albatross, the largest of flying birds, with a similar wing shape and a span of 3 metres, can patrol the ocean for hours in the same way without a single wing beat. Vultures and hawks circle at very slow speeds supported by a thermal and they have the broad rectangular wings that very slow flying aircraft have. Man has not been able to adapt wings to provide hovering flight. He has only achieved that with the whirling horizontal

blades of a helicopter or the downward-pointing engines of a vertical landing jet.
Hummingbirds have paralleled even this. They tilt their bodies so that they are almost
upright and then beat their wings as fast as 80 times a second producing a similar
down-draught of air. So the hummingbird can hover and even fly backwards.

—DAVID ATTENBOROUGH, Life on Earth

In this example, note the limited, focused basis for the comparison: the shape of
wings. Attenborough specifies this basis in the second sentence of the passage (underlined). Though birds and planes both fly, they have almost nothing else in common.
They are so obviously different that it would even seem silly to compare them in writing. But Attenborough finds a valid—and fascinating—basis for comparison and
develops it in a way that both informs and entertains his readers. A successful comparison always has these qualities: a valid basis for comparison, a limited focus, and
information that will catch a reader's attention.

■ **Exercise 18.2**

Identify the specific items compared in the preceding selection comparing bird wings
and aircraft wings. Underline both items, and number the pair in the margin. To get
started, underline *tanager* and *fighter planes* in the first sentence of the second paragraph. In the margin, number this pair "1." Then identify pair 2 and so on.

Consider the pattern and ordering of the comparisons you have identified. Were
the pairs of items easy to identify? If so, what made them easy to identify? Some comparisons begin by naming a bird, some by identifying a category of aircraft. Did this
lack of predictability present problems for you? Do you see any possible justification
for the writer's having given up the predictability of always beginning each comparison with either a bird or an aircraft? In general, how successful and informative did
you find this comparison of birds' wings and aircrafts' wings?

■ **Exercise 18.3**

Write a page or so comparing or contrasting any one of the following subjects. Be
careful to limit the basis for your comparison, and underline the sentence that states
that basis. Use chunking or sequencing to organize the comparison.

Two ways of achieving the same goal (for example, travel by bus or subway or using
flattery or persuasion to get what you want)

A good and bad job interview

Your relationship with two friends or relatives

Two or more forms of music, dance, film, or computer software

Two religions

Two methods of doing some task at home or on the job

■ **Exercise 18.4**

Read closely the specified comparisons in the following essays from Part One. How
is each comparison organized? (It may or may not be neatly chunked or sequenced.)

Why do you think the writer organizes the comparison in that way? What is the role of the comparison in the whole essay? How effective is it?

"Love: The Right Chemistry," paragraph 14 (Chapter 5)

"The New Terrorism," paragraphs 9–11 (Chapter 5)

"The Rise of Reported Incidents of Workplace Sexual Harassment," paragraph 3 (Chapter 9)

■ ANALOGY

An *analogy* is a special form of comparison in which one part of the comparison is used simply to explain the other. See how John McPhee uses two different analogies —the twelve-month calendar and the distance along two widespread arms—to explain the duration of geologic time.

> In like manner, geologists will sometimes use the calendar year as a unit to represent the time scale, and in such terms the Precambrian runs from New Year's Day until well after Halloween. Dinosaurs appear in the middle of December and are gone the day after Christmas. The last ice sheet melts on December 31st at one minute before midnight, and the Roman Empire lasts five seconds. With your arms spread wide . . . to represent all time on earth, look at one hand with its line of life. The Cambrian begins in the wrist, and the Permian Extinction is at the outer end of the palm. All of the Cenozoic is in a fingerprint, and in a single stroke with a medium-grained nail file you could eradicate human history. Geologists live with the geologic scale. Individually, they may or may not be alarmed by the rate of exploitation of the things they discover, but, like the environmentalists, they use these repetitive analogies to place the human record in perspective—to see the Age of Reflection, the last few thousand years, as a small bright sparkle at the end of time.
>
> –JOHN McPHEE, *Basin and Range*

Analogies are not limited to abstract, scientific concepts. Writers often offer analogies to make nontechnical descriptions or explanations more vivid and entertaining. For example, William Bennett, director of National Drug Control Policy for the Bush administration, has likened government efforts to reduce illegal drug use to war. At the point where this analogy appears in one of Bennett's published essays, Bennett is arguing against people who advocate making drugs legal and available to users to buy like cigarettes. He refers to these advocates as "legalizers."

> I find no merit in the legalizers' case. The simple fact is that drug use is wrong. And the moral argument, in the end, is the most compelling argument. A citizen in a drug-induced haze, whether on his back-yard deck or on a mattress in a ghetto crack house, is not what the founding fathers meant by the "pursuit of happiness." Despite the legalizers' argument that drug use is a matter of "personal freedom," our nation's notion of liberty is rooted in the ideal of a self-reliant citizenry. Helpless wrecks in treatment centers, men chained by their noses to cocaine—these people are slaves.
>
> Imagine if, in the darkest days of 1940, Winston Churchill had rallied the West by saying, "This war looks hopeless, and besides, it will cost too much. Hitler can't

be *that* bad. Let's surrender and see what happens." That is essentially what we hear from the legalizers.

This war *can* be won. I am heartened by indications that education and public revulsion are having an effect on drug use. The National Institute on Drug Abuse's latest survey of current users shows a 37 percent *decrease* in drug consumption since 1985. Cocaine is down 50 percent; marijuana use among young people is at its lowest rate since 1972. In my travels I've been encouraged by signs that Americans are fighting back.

I am under no illusion that such developments, however hopeful, mean the war is over. We need to involve more citizens in the fight, increase pressure on drug criminals and build on anti-drug programs that have proved to work. This will not be easy. But the moral and social costs of surrender are simply too great to contemplate.

–WILLIAM BENNETT, "Should Drugs Be Legalized?"

Analogies are tricky. They may at first seem useful, but actually it is a rare analogy that is consistently useful at all the major points of comparison. Some are downright misleading. For example, in the preceding analogy, comparing efforts to reduce drug use to the Allies' successful struggle to defeat Hitler and his armies certainly heightens the significance of antidrug efforts. Yet neither side in the drug war shells or bombs the other. In fact, nearly all of the shooting and killing seems to occur among dealers protecting their profitable turf.

Thus most writers exercise caution with analogy. Nevertheless, you will run across analogies regularly; indeed, it would be hard to find a book without at least one. For abstract information and in certain writing situations, analogy is often the writing strategy of choice.

■ Exercise 18.5

Write a one-paragraph analogy that explains a principle or process to a reader who is unfamiliar with it. Choose a principle or process that you know well. You might select a basic principle from the natural or social sciences, like morphogenesis, Federalism, or ethnocentrism; or you could consider a bodily movement, like running; a physiological process, like digestion; or a process from your job, like assembling a product. Look for something very familiar to compare it with that will help the reader understand the principle or process without a technical explanation.

Arguing

19

Arguing involves reasoning as well as making assertions. When you write an essay in which you assert a point of view, you are obliged to come up with reasons for your point of view and to find ways to support your reasons. In addition to arguing for your point of view, you must think carefully about what your readers know and believe in order to argue against — to *counterargue* — opposing points of view. If you ignore what your readers may be thinking, you will be unlikely to convince them to take your argument seriously.

This chapter presents the basic strategies for making assertions and reasoning about a writing situation. We focus on asserting a thesis, backing it up with reasons and support, and anticipating readers' questions and objections.

■ ASSERTING A THESIS

Central to any argument is the thesis — the point of view the writer wants readers to consider. The thesis statement may appear at the beginning of the essay or at the end, but wherever it is placed, its job is simple: to announce as clearly and straightforwardly as possible the main point the writer is trying to make in the essay.

There are five different kinds of argumentative essays in Part One of this book. Each of these essays requires a special kind of assertion and reasoning. Here we first define each type of assertion and suggest a question it is designed to answer. Then we illustrate each assertion and question with a thesis from a reading in Chapters 6–10:

- *Assertion of opinion.* What is your position on a controversial issue? (Chapter 6, "Arguing a Position")

  When overzealous parents and coaches impose adult standards on children's sports, the result can be activities that are neither satisfying nor beneficial to children.

  — JESSICA STATSKY, "Children Need to Play, Not Compete"

- *Assertion of policy.* What is your understanding of a problem, and what do you think should be done to solve it? (Chapter 7, "Proposing a Solution")

  Although this last-minute anxiety about midterm and final exams is only too familiar to most college students, many professors may not realize how such

Chapters 6–10 contain essays that argue for each of these kinds of assertions, along with guidelines for constructing an argument to support such an assertion.

623

major, infrequent, high-stakes exams work against the best interests of students both psychologically and intellectually. . . . If professors gave additional brief exams at frequent intervals, students would be spurred to study more regularly, learn more, worry less, and perform better.

— PATRICK O'MALLEY, "More Testing, More Learning"

- *Assertion of evaluation.* What is your judgment of a subject? (Chapter 8, "Justifying an Evaluation")

The movie is a disappointment. A big one.

— DAVID ANSEN, "*Star Wars:* The Phantom Movie"

- *Assertion of cause.* What do you think made a subject the way it is? (Chapter 9, "Speculating about Causes")

The mythic horror movie, like the sick joke, has a dirty job to do. It deliberately appeals to all that is worst in us. It is morbidity unchained, our most base instincts let free, our nastiest fantasies realized . . . and it all happens, fittingly enough, in the dark.

— STEPHEN KING, "Why We Crave Horror Movies"

- *Assertion of interpretation.* What does a story mean, or what is significant about it? (Chapter 10, "Interpreting Stories")

"Araby" tells the story of an adolescent boy's initiation into adulthood. . . . From the beginning, the boy deludes himself about his relationship with Mangan's sister. At Araby, he realizes the parallel between his own self-delusion and the hypocrisy and vanity of the adult world.

— DAVID RATINOV, "From Innocence to Insight: 'Araby' as an Initiation Story"

As these different thesis statements indicate, the kind of thesis you assert depends on the occasion for which you are writing and the question you are trying to answer for your readers. Whatever the writing situation, to be effective, every thesis must satisfy the same three standards: it must be *arguable, clear,* and *appropriately qualified.*

Arguable Assertions

Reasoned argument seems called for when informed people disagree over an issue or remain divided over how best to solve a problem, as is so often the case in social and political life. Hence the thesis statement in a reasoned argument asserts possibilities or probabilities, not certainties. Argument becomes useful in situations in which there are uncertainties, situations in which established knowledge and facts cannot provide the answers.

Therefore, a statement of fact could not be an arguable thesis statement because facts are easy to verify—whether by checking an authoritative reference book, asking an authority, or observing the fact with your own eyes. For example, these statements assert facts:

Jem will be thirty years old on May 6, 2002.

I am less than five feet tall.

Eucalyptus trees were originally imported into California from Australia.

Each of these assertions can be easily verified. To find out Jem's age, you can ask him or look at his driver's license, among other things. To determine a person's height, you can use a tape measure. To discover where California got its eucalyptus trees, you can refer to a source in the library. There is no point in arguing over such statements (though you might question the authority of a particular source or the accuracy of someone's measurement). If a writer were to assert something as fact and attempt to support the assertion with authorities or statistics, the essay would be considered not an argument but a report of information.

Like facts, expressions of personal feelings are not arguable assertions. Whereas facts are unarguable because they can be definitively proved true or false, feelings are unarguable because they are purely subjective. Personal feelings can be explained, but it would be unreasonable to attempt to convince others to change their views or take action solely on the basis of your personal feelings.

You can declare, for example, that you love Ben & Jerry's Chunky Monkey ice cream or that you detest eight o'clock classes, but you cannot offer an argument to support such assertions. All you can do is explain why you feel as you do. Even though many people agree with you about eight o'clock classes, it would be pointless to try to convince others to share your feelings. If, however, you were to restate the assertion as "Eight o'clock classes are counterproductive," you could then construct an argument that does not depend solely on your subjective feelings, memories, or preferences. Your argument could be based on reasons and support that apply to others as well as to yourself. For example, you might argue that students' ability to learn is at an especially low ebb immediately after breakfast and provide scientific support, in addition, perhaps, to personal experience and interviews with your friends.

Clear and Precise Wording

The way a thesis is worded is as important as its arguability. The wording of a thesis, especially its key terms, must be clear and precise.

Consider the following assertion: "Democracy is a way of life." The meaning of this claim is uncertain, partly because the word *democracy* is abstract and partly because the phrase *way of life* is inexact. Abstract ideas like democracy, freedom, and patriotism are by their very nature hard to grasp, and they become even less clear with overuse. Too often, such words take on connotations that may obscure the meaning you want to emphasize. *Way of life* is fuzzy: What does it mean? Moreover, can a form of government be a way of life? It depends on what is meant by *way of life*. Does it refer to daily life, to a general philosophy or attitude toward life, or to something else?

Thus a thesis is vague if its meaning is unclear; it is ambiguous if it has more than one possible meaning. For example, the statement "My English instructor is mad" can be understood in two ways: The teacher is either angry or insane. Obviously, these are two very different assertions. You would not want readers to think you mean one when you actually mean the other.

Whenever you write argument, you should pay special attention to the way you phrase your thesis and take care to avoid vague and ambiguous language.

Appropriate Qualification

In addition to being arguable and clear, an argument thesis must suit your writing situation. If you are confident that your case is so strong that readers will accept your argument without question, state your thesis emphatically and unconditionally. If, however, you expect readers to challenge your assumptions or conclusions, you must qualify your statement. Qualifying a thesis makes it more likely that readers will take it seriously. Expressions like *probably, very likely, apparently,* and *it seems* all serve to qualify a thesis.

■ Exercise 19.1

Write an assertion of opinion that states your position on one of the following controversial issues:

Should English be the official language of the United States and the only language used in local, state, and federal government agencies in oral and written communications?

Should teenagers be required to get their parents' permission to obtain birth control information and contraceptives?

Should high schools or colleges require students to perform community service as a condition for graduation?

Should girls and boys be treated differently by their families or schools?

Should businesses remain loyal to their communities, or should they move wherever labor costs, taxes, or other conditions are more favorable?

These issues are complicated and have been debated for a long time. Constructing a persuasive argument would obviously require careful deliberation and research. For this exercise, however, all you need to do is construct a thesis on the issue you have chosen, a thesis that is arguable, clear, and appropriately qualified.

■ Exercise 19.2

Find the thesis in one of the argument essays in Chapters 6–10. Then decide whether the thesis meets the three requirements: that it be arguable, clear, and appropriately qualified.

■ Exercise 19.3

If you have written or are currently working on one of the argument assignments in Chapters 6–10, consider whether your essay thesis meets the three requirements: that it be arguable, clear, and appropriately qualified. If you believe it does not meet the requirements, revise it appropriately.

■ GIVING REASONS AND SUPPORT

Whether you are arguing a position, proposing a solution, justifying an evaluation, speculating about causes, or interpreting a story, you need to give reasons and support for your thesis.

Reasons can be thought of as the main points arguing for a thesis. Often they answer the question "Why do you think so?" For example, if you assert among friends that you value a certain movie highly, one of your friends might ask, "Why do you like it so much?" And you might answer, "*Because* it has challenging ideas, unusual camera work, and memorable acting." Similarly, you might oppose restrictions on students' use of offensive language at your college *because* they would make students reluctant to enter into frank debates on important issues, offensive speech is hard to define, and restrictions violate the free-speech clause of the First Amendment. These *because* phrases are your reasons. You may have one or many reasons, depending on your subject and your writing situation.

For your argument to succeed with your readers, you must not only give reasons but also provide support. The main kinds of support writers use are examples, statistics, authorities, anecdotes, and textual evidence. Following is a discussion and illustration of each kind, along with standards for judging the reliability of that particular type of support.

Examples

Examples may be used as support in all types of arguments. They are an effective way to demonstrate that your reasons should be taken seriously. For examples to be believable and convincing, they must be representative (typical of all the relevant examples you might have chosen), consistent with the experience of your readers (familiar and not extreme), and adequate in number (numerous enough to be convincing and yet selective and not likely to overwhelm readers).

The following illustration comes from a book on illiteracy in America by Jonathan Kozol, a prominent educator and writer. In these paragraphs, Kozol presents several examples to support a part of his argument that the human costs of illiteracy are high.

Illiterates cannot read the menu in a restaurant.

They cannot read the cost of items on the menu in the *window* of the restaurant before they enter.

Illiterates cannot read the letters that their children bring home from their teachers. They cannot study school department circulars that tell them of the courses that their children must be taking if they hope to pass the SAT exams. They cannot help with homework. They cannot write a letter to the teacher. They are afraid to visit in the classroom. They do not want to humiliate their child or themselves.

Illiterates cannot read instructions on a bottle of prescription medicine. They cannot find out when a medicine is past the year of safe consumption; nor can they read of allergenic risks, warnings to diabetics, or the potential sedative effect of certain kinds of nonprescription pills. They cannot observe preventive health care admonitions. They cannot read about "the seven warnings signs of cancer" or the indications of blood-sugar fluctuations or the risks of eating certain foods that aggravate the likelihood of cardiac arrest.

—JONATHAN KOZOL, *Illiterate America*

These examples probably seem to most readers to be representative of all the examples Kozol collected in his many interviews with people who could neither read nor write. Though all of his readers are literate and have never experienced the frustrations of adult illiterates, Kozol assumes they can recognize that the experiences are a familiar part of illiterates' lives. Most readers will believe the experiences to be neither atypical nor extreme.

■ Exercise 19.4

Identify the examples in paragraphs 9 and 11 in Jessica Statsky's essay in Chapter 6 and paragraphs 16–18 in Amitai Etzioni's essay in Chapter 8. If you have not read the essays, pause to skim them so that you can evaluate these examples within the context of the entire essay. How well do the examples individually and as a set meet the standards of representativeness, consistency with experience of readers, and adequacy in number? You will not have all the information you need to evaluate the examples— you rarely do unless you are an expert on the subject—but make the best judgment you can based on the information available to you in the headnotes and the essays.

Statistics

In many kinds of arguments about economic, educational, or social issues, statistics may be essential. When you use statistics in your own arguments, you will want to ensure that they are up to date (they should be current, the best presently available facts on the subject), relevant (they should be appropriate for your argument), and accurate (they should not distort or misrepresent the subject). In addition, take care to select statistics from reliable sources and to use statistics from the sources in which they originally appeared if at all possible. For example, you would want to get medical statistics from a reputable and authoritative professional periodical like the *New England Journal of Medicine* rather than from a supermarket tabloid or an unaffiliated Web site. If you are uncertain about the most authoritative sources, ask a reference librarian or a professor who knows about your topic.

The following selection comes from an argument speculating about the decline of civic life in the United States. Civic life includes all of the clubs, organizations, and activities people choose to participate in. The author, a Harvard University professor, believes that since the early 1960s, Americans have participated less and less in civic life because they have been spending more and more time watching television. In these paragraphs, he uses statistics to support this possible causal relationship.

The culprit is television.

First, the timing fits. The long civic generation was the last cohort of Americans to grow up without television, for television flashed into American society like lightning in the 1950s. In 1950 barely 10 percent of American homes had television sets, but by 1959, 90 percent did, probably the fastest diffusion of a major technological innovation ever recorded. The reverberations from this lightning bolt continued for decades, as viewing hours grew by 17–20 percent during the 1960s and by an additional 7–8 percent during the 1970s. In the early years, TV watching was concentrated among the less educated sectors of the population, but during the 1970s the viewing time of the more educated sectors of the population began to converge upward. Television viewing increases with age, particularly upon retirement, but each generation since the introduction of television has begun its life cycle at a higher starting point. By 1995 viewing per TV household was more than 50 percent higher than it had been in the 1950s.

Most studies estimate that the average American now watches roughly four hours per day (excluding periods in which television is merely playing in the background). Even a more conservative estimate of three hours means that television absorbs 40 percent of the average American's free time, an increase of about one-third since 1965. Moreover, multiple sets have proliferated: By the late 1980s three-quarters of all U.S. homes had more than one set, and these numbers too are rising steadily, allowing ever more private viewing. . . . This massive change in the way Americans spend their days and nights occurred precisely during the years of generational civic disengagement.

– ROBERT D. PUTNAM, "The Strange Disappearance of Civic America"

These statistics come primarily from the U.S. Bureau of the Census, a nationwide count of the number of Americans and a survey, in part, of their buying habits, levels of education, and leisure activities. The Census reports are widely considered to be accurate and trustworthy. They qualify as original sources of statistics.

■ Exercise 19.5

In Chapter 6, identify the statistics in paragraphs 7–9 of Alan Leshner's essay and paragraphs 5 and 6 of Jessica Statsky's. Underline the statistics you find. If you have not read the essays, pause to skim them so that you can evaluate each writer's use of statistics within the context of the whole essay. How well do the statistics meet the standard of up-to-dateness, relevance, accuracy, and reliance on the original source? (If you find that you do not have all the information you need, base your judgments on whatever information is available to you.) Does the writer indicate where the statistics come from? What do the statistics contribute to the argument?

Chapter 21 provides help finding statistical data in the library.

Authorities

To support an argument, writers often cite experts on the subject who agree with their point of view. Quoting, paraphrasing, or even just referring to a respected authority can add to a writer's credibility. Authorities must be selected as carefully as facts and statistics. One qualification for authorities to support arguments is suggested by the way we refer to them: They must be authoritative—that is, trustworthy and reputable. They must also be specially qualified to contribute to the subject you are writing about. For example, a well-known expert on the American presidency might be a poor choice to support an argument on whether adolescents who commit serious crimes should be tried in the courts as adults. Finally, qualified authorities must have training at respected institutions or have unique real-world experiences, and they must have a record of research and publications recognized by other authorities.

The following example comes from a *New York Times* article about some parents' and experts' heightened concern over boys' behavior. The author believes that the concern is exaggerated and potentially dangerous to boys, and she wants to understand why it is increasing. In the full argument, she is particularly concerned about the number of boys who are being given Ritalin, a popular drug for treating attention-deficit disorder.

> Today, the world is no longer safe for boys. A boy being a shade too boyish risks finding himself under the scrutiny of parents, teachers, guidance counselors, child therapists—all of them on watch for the early glimmerings of a medical syndrome, a bona fide behavioral disorder. Does the boy disregard authority, make snide comments in class, push other kids around and play hooky? Maybe he has a conduct disorder. Is he fidgety, impulsive, disruptive, easily bored? Perhaps he is suffering from attention-deficit hyperactivity disorder, or ADHD, the disease of the hour and the most frequently diagnosed behavioral disorder of childhood. Does he prefer computer games and goofing off to homework? He might have dyslexia or another learning disorder.
>
> "There is now an attempt to pathologize what was once considered the normal range of behavior of boys," said Melvin Konner of the departments of anthropology and psychiatry at Emory University in Atlanta. "Today, Tom Sawyer and Huckleberry Finn surely would have been diagnosed with both conduct disorder and ADHD." And both, perhaps, would have been put on Ritalin, the drug of choice for treating attention-deficit disorder.
>
> —NATALIE ANGIER, "Intolerance of Boyish Behavior"

Notice the way the writer establishes the professional qualifications of the authority she quotes. She places him at a major research university (Emory University) and indicates by his department affiliations (anthropology and psychiatry) that he has special training to comment on how a culture treats its young men. Readers can infer from these two facts that he has almost certainly earned a doctorate in anthropology or psychiatry and that he has probably published research studies. This carefully selected quotation supports the writer's argument that there is a problem and that readers should care about it.

For examples of two formal citation styles often used in college essays, see Chapter 22.

In this example, the writer relies on *informal* citation within her essay to introduce the authority she quotes. In newspapers, magazines, and some books, writers rely on informal citation, mentioning the title or author in the essay itself. In other books and in research reports, writers rely on a *formal* style of citation that allows them to refer briefly in an essay to a detailed list of works cited appearing at the end of the essay. This list provides the author, title, date, and publisher of every source of information referred to in the essay. To evaluate the qualifications of an authority in an argument relying on a list of works cited, you may have to rely solely on the information provided in the list.

■ Exercise 19.6

Turn to Chapter 7. Analyze the way authorities are used in paragraphs 6 and 10 of Adam Paul Weisman's essay. (See paragraph 5 for further information about the authority quoted in paragraph 6, and see paragraph 4 for information about one of the authorities quoted in paragraph 10.) Then analyze how authorities are used in paragraphs 4 and 5 of Patrick O'Malley's essay.

Begin by underlining the authorities' contributions to these paragraphs, whether through quotation, summary, or paraphrase. On the basis of the evidence you have available, decide to what extent each source is authoritative on the subject: qualified to contribute to the subject, trained appropriately, and recognized widely. How does the writer establish each authority's credentials? Then decide what each authority contributes to the argument as a whole. (If you have not read the essays, take time to read or skim them.)

Anecdotes

Anecdotes are brief stories about events or experiences, recounted in an engaging way. If they are relevant to the argument, well told, and true to life, they can provide very convincing support. To be relevant, an anecdote must strike readers as more than an entertaining diversion; it must seem to make an irreplaceable contribution to an argument. If it is well told, the narrative or story is easy to follow and the people and scenes are described memorably, even vividly. There are many concrete details that help readers imagine what happened. A true-to-life anecdote is one that seems to represent a possible life experience of a real person. It has to be believable, even if the experience is foreign to readers' experiences.

See Chapter 14, "Narrating," and Chapter 2, "Remembering Events," for more information about narrating anecdotes.

The following anecdote appeared in an argument taking a position on a familiar issue: gun ownership and control. The writer, an essayist, poet, and environmental writer who is also a rancher in South Dakota, always carries a pistol and believes that other people may have an urgent personal need to carry one and should have the right to do so. To support her argument, she tells several anecdotes, including this one:

> I was driving the half-mile to the highway mailbox one day when I saw a vehicle parked about midway down the road. Several men were standing in the ditch, relieving themselves. I have no objection to emergency urination, but I noticed they'd dumped several dozen beer cans in the road. Besides being ugly, cans can slash a cow's feet or stomach.
>
> The men noticed me before they finished and made quite a performance out of zipping their trousers while walking toward me. All four of them gathered around my small foreign car, and one of them demanded what the hell I wanted.
>
> "This is private land. I'd appreciate it if you'd pick up the beer cans."
>
> "What beer cans?" said the belligerent one, putting both hands on the car door and leaning in my window. His face was inches from mine, and the beer fumes were strong. The others laughed. One tried the passenger door, locked; another put his foot on the hood and rocked the car. They circled, lightly thumping the roof, discussing my good fortune in meeting them and the benefits they were likely to bestow upon me. I felt very small and very trapped and they knew it.

"The ones you just threw out," I said politely.

"I don't see no beer cans. Why don't you get out here and show them to me, honey?" said the belligerent one, reaching for the handle inside my door.

"Right over there," I said, still being polite, "—there, and over there." I pointed with the pistol, which I'd slipped under my thigh. Within one minute the cans and the men were back in the car and headed down the road.

I believe this incident illustrates several important principles. The men were trespassing and knew it; their judgment may have been impaired by alcohol. Their response to the polite request of a woman alone was to use their size, numbers, and sex to inspire fear. The pistol was a response in the same language. Politeness didn't work; I couldn't match them in size or number. Out of the car, I'd have been more vulnerable. The pistol just changed the balance of power.

–LINDA M. HASSELSTROM, "Why One Peaceful Woman Carries a Pistol"

Most readers would readily agree that this anecdote is well told. It has many concrete, memorable details. As in any good story, something happens—there is action, suspense, climax, resolution. There is even dialogue. It is about a believable, possible experience. Most important, as support for an argument, it is relevant to the writer's point, as she makes clear in the final paragraph.

■ Exercise 19.7

Analyze the way an anecdote is used in paragraphs 8 and 9 of Richard Estrada's essay in Chapter 6. Consider whether the story is well told and true to life. Decide whether it seems to be relevant to the whole argument. Does the writer make the relevance clear? Do you find the anecdote convincing?

Textual Evidence

When you argue claims of value (Chapter 8) and interpretation (Chapter 10), textual evidence will be very important. In your other college courses, if you are asked to evaluate a controversial book, you must quote, paraphrase, or summarize passages so that readers can understand why you think the author's argument is or is not credible. If you are interpreting a novel for one of your classes, you must include numerous excerpts to show just how you arrived at your conclusion. In both situations, you are integrating bits of the text you are evaluating or interpreting into your own text and building your argument on these bits.

For these bits of textual evidence to be considered effective support for an argument of evaluation or interpretation, they must be carefully selected to be relevant to the argument's thesis and reasons. You must help readers see the connection between each piece of evidence and the reason it supports. Textual evidence must also be highly selective, that is, chosen from among all the available evidence to provide the support needed without overwhelming the reader with too much evidence or weakening the argument with marginally relevant evidence. Textual evidence usually has more impact if it is balanced between quotation and paraphrase from the text. For these selective, balanced choices of evidence to be comprehensible and convincing to readers, the evidence must be smoothly integrated into the sentences of the argument. Finally, the relevance of textual evidence is rarely obvious: the writer must ordinarily explain the link between the evidence and the writer's intended point.

The following example comes from a student essay in which the writer argues that the main character (referred to as "the boy") in the short story "Araby" by James Joyce is so self-absorbed that he learns nothing about himself or other people. These paragraphs offer reasons why the writer believes readers should take her argument seriously. She attempts to support her reasons with textual evidence from the story.

You can read "Araby" in Chapter 10, pp. 476–80.

> The story opens and closes with images of blindness. The street is "blind" with an "uninhabited house [. . .] at the blind end." As he spies on Mangan's sister, from his own house, the boy intentionally limits what he is able to see by lowering the "blind" until it is only an inch from the window sash. At the bazaar in the closing scene, the "light was out," and the upper part of the hall was "completely dark." The boy is left "gazing up into the darkness," seeing nothing but an inner torment that burns his eyes.
>
> This pattern of imagery includes images of reading, and reading stands for the boy's inability to understand what is before his eyes. When he tries to read at night, for example, the girl's "image [comes] between [him] and the page," in effect blinding him. In fact, he seems blind to everything except this "image" of the "brown-clad figure cast by [his] imagination." The girl's "brown-clad figure" is also associated with the houses on "blind" North Richmond Street, with their "brown imperturbable faces." The houses stare back at the boy, unaffected by his presence and gaze.
>
> —SALLY CRANE, "Gazing into Darkness"

Notice first how the writer quotes selected words and phrases about blindness to support her reasoning that the boy learns nothing because he is blinded. There are ten quotations in these two paragraphs, all of them relevant and perhaps not so many as to overwhelm the reader. The writer relies not only on quotes but also on paraphrases of information in the story. The second and third sentences in paragraph 1 are largely paraphrases. The quotations in particular are integrated smoothly into the sentences so that readers' momentum is not blocked. Most important, the writer does not assume that the evidence speaks for itself; she comments and interprets throughout. For example, in the first paragraph, all the sentences except the fourth one offer some comment or explanation.

For more information on paraphrasing, see pp. 541–42 in Chapter 12.

■ Exercise 19.8

Analyze the use of evidence in paragraphs 2 and 3 of David Ratinov's essay in Chapter 10. If you have not read this essay, pause to skim or read it so that you can evaluate the effectiveness of the evidence in these paragraphs in the context of Ratinov's full argument. The quotes are easy to identify. The paraphrases you could identify with confidence only by reading the story, but you can probably identify some of them without doing so. Then try to identify the phrases or sentences that comment on or explain the evidence. Finally, consider whether Ratinov's evidence in these two paragraphs seems relevant to his thesis and reasons, appropriately selective, well balanced between quotes and paraphrases, integrated smoothly into the sentences he creates, and explained helpfully.

■ COUNTERARGUING

Asserting a thesis and backing it with reasons and support are essential to a successful argument. Thoughtful writers go further, however, by counterarguing—anticipating and responding to their readers' objections, challenges, and questions. To anticipate readers' concerns, try to imagine other people's points of view, what they might know about the subject, and how they might feel about it. Try also to imagine how readers would respond to your argument as it unfolds step by step. What will they be thinking and feeling? What objections would they raise? What questions would they ask?

To counterargue, writers rely on three basic strategies: acknowledging, accommodating or conceding, and refuting. Writers show they are aware of readers' objections and questions (acknowledge), modify their position to accept readers' concerns they think are legitimate (accommodate), or explicitly show why readers' objections are invalid or why their concerns are irrelevant (refute). Writers may use one or more of these three strategies in the same essay. According to research by rhetoricians and communications specialists, readers find arguments more convincing when writers have anticipated their concerns in these ways. Acknowledging readers' concerns and either accommodating or refuting them wins readers' respect, attention, and sometimes even agreement.

Acknowledging Readers' Concerns

When you acknowledge readers' questions or objections, you show that you take their point of view seriously even if you do not agree with it. In the following example, Peter Marin directly acknowledges his readers' possible concerns. These are the opening paragraphs in an article arguing that some of America's homeless have chosen that way of life. Marin knows that readers may immediately doubt this surprising assertion. It seems inconceivable that people would choose to sleep on sidewalks and eat out of garbage cans. He acknowledges three different doubts his readers may have.

> The homeless, it seems, can be roughly divided into two groups: those who have had marginality and homelessness forced upon them and want nothing more than to escape them, and a smaller number who have at least in part chosen marginality, and now accept, or, in a few cases, embrace it.
>
> I understand how dangerous it can be to introduce the idea of choice into a discussion of homelessness. It can all too easily be used for all the wrong reasons by all the wrong people to justify indifference or brutality toward the homeless, or to argue that they are getting only what they deserve.
>
> And I understand, too, how complicated the notion can become: Many of the veterans on the street, or battered women, or abused and runaway children, have chosen this life only as the lesser of evils, and because, in this society, there is often no place else to go.
>
> And finally, I understand how much that happens on the street can combine to create an apparent acceptance of homelessness that is nothing more than the absolute absence of hope.

Nonetheless we must learn to accept that there may indeed be people on the street who have seen so much of our world, or have seen it so clearly, that to live in it becomes impossible.

—PETER MARIN, "Go Ask Alice"

You might think that acknowledging readers' objections in this way—addressing readers directly, listing their possible objections, and discussing each one—would weaken an argument. It might even seem reckless to suggest objections that not all readers would think of. On the contrary, however, readers who expect writers to explore an issue thoroughly respond positively to this strategy because it makes the writer seem thoughtful and reasonable, more concerned with seeking the truth than winning an argument. By researching your subject and your readers, you will be able to use this strategy confidently in your own argumentative essays. And you will learn to look for it in arguments you read and use it to make judgments about the writer's credibility.

■ Exercise 19.9

Richard Estrada acknowledges readers' concerns in paragraphs 6 and 7 of his essay in Chapter 6, and Sarah West does so in paragraphs 7 and 8 of her essay in Chapter 9. How, specifically, do these authors attempt to acknowledge their readers' concerns? What do you find most and least successful in the two acknowledgments? How do the writers' acknowledgments affect your judgment of the writers' credibility?

Accommodating Readers' Concerns

To argue effectively, you must often take special care to acknowledge your readers' objections, questions, and alternative positions, causes, or solutions. Occasionally, however, you may have to go even further. Instead of merely acknowledging your readers' concerns, you may decide to accept some of them and incorporate them into your own argument. This strategy can be very disarming to readers. It is sometimes referred to as *concession,* for it seems to concede that opposing views have merit.

The following example comes from an essay enthusiastically endorsing email. After supporting his own reasons for this positive endorsement, the writer accommodates his readers' likely reservations by conceding that email poses certain problems.

To be sure, egalitarianism has its limits. The ease and economy of sending email, especially to multiple recipients, makes us all vulnerable to any bore, loony, or commercial or political salesman who can get our email address. It's still a lot less intrusive than the telephone, since you can read and answer or ignore email at your own convenience. But as normal people's email starts mounting into the hundreds daily, which is bound to happen, filtering mechanisms and conventions of etiquette that are still in their primitive stage will be desperately needed.

Another supposed disadvantage of email is that it discourages face-to-face communication. At Microsoft, where people routinely send email back and forth all day to the person in the next office, this is certainly true. Some people believe this tendency has more to do with the underdeveloped social skills of computer geeks than with Microsoft's role in developing the technology email relies on. I wouldn't presume to comment on that. Whether you think email replacing live conversation is a good or bad thing depends, I guess, on how much of a misanthrope you are. I like it.

—MICHAEL KINSLEY, "Email Culture"

Notice that Kinsley's accommodation or concession is not grudging. He readily concedes that email brings users a lot of unwanted messages and may discourage conversation in the workplace.

■ Exercise 19.10

How does Patrick O'Malley attempt to accommodate readers in paragraphs 7 and 8 of his Chapter 7 essay arguing for more frequent exams? What seems successful or unsuccessful in his argument? What do his efforts at accommodation contribute to the essay?

Refuting Readers' Objections

Your readers' objections and views cannot always be accommodated. Sometimes they must be refuted. When you refute likely objections, you assert that they are wrong and argue against them. Refutation does not have to be delivered arrogantly or dismissively, however. Writers can refute their readers' objections in a spirit of shared inquiry in solving problems, establishing probable causes, deciding the value of something, or understanding different points of view in a controversy. Differences are inevitable. Reasoned argument provides a peaceful and constructive way for informed, well-intentioned people who disagree strongly to air their differences.

In the following example, an economist refutes one explanation for the increasing numbers of women in the workforce. First, he acknowledges a "frequently mentioned" explanation. Then he concedes a point ("there is little doubt") before beginning his refutation of the causal connection ("but it is not clear"):

One frequently mentioned but inadequately evaluated explanation for the surge of women into paid employment is the spread of time-saving household innovations such as clothes washers and dryers, frozen foods, and dishwashers. There is little doubt that it is easier to combine paid employment with home responsibilities now than it was fifty years ago, but it is not clear whether these time-saving innovations were the cause of the rise in female labor force participation or whether they were largely a response to meet a demand created by working women. Confusion about this point is most evident in comments that suggest that the rapid growth of supermarkets and fast-food outlets is a cause of women going to work. Similar time-saving organizations were tried at least sixty years ago, but with less success because the value of time was much lower then. The absence of supermarkets and fast-food eating places in low-income countries today also shows that their rapid growth in the United States is primarily a result of the rising value of time and the growth of women in the work force, not the reverse.

—VICTOR FUCHS, "Why Married Mothers Work"

As this selection illustrates, writers cannot simply dismiss readers' concerns with a wave of the hand. Fuchs refutes one proposed cause by arguing that it is actually an effect or result of the trend. The last two sentences support his refutation.

As this example illustrates, effective refutation requires a restrained tone and careful argument. Although, reading this, you may not accept the refutation, you can agree that it is well reasoned and supported. You do not feel attacked personally because the writer disagrees with you.

■ Exercise 19.11

Analyze and evaluate the use of refutation in Adam Paul Weisman's essay in Chapter 7 (paragraphs 10–14) and Alan Leshner's essay in Chapter 6 (paragraphs 6–11). How does each writer signal or announce the refutation? How does he support the refutation? What is the tone of the refutation, and how effective do you think the tone would be in convincing readers to take the writer's argument seriously?

■ LOGICAL FALLACIES

Fallacies are errors or flaws in reasoning. Although essentially unsound, fallacious arguments seem superficially plausible and often have great persuasive power. Fallacies are not necessarily deliberate efforts to deceive readers. Writers may introduce a fallacy accidentally by not examining their own reasons or underlying assumptions critically, by failing to establish solid support, or by using unclear or ambiguous words. Here is a summary of the most common logical fallacies (listed alphabetically):

- *Begging the question.* Arguing that a claim is true by repeating the claim in different words. Sometimes called *circular reasoning.*

- *Confusing chronology with causality.* Assuming that because one thing preceded another, the former caused the latter. Also called *post hoc, ergo propter hoc* (Latin for "after this, therefore because of this").

- *Either-or reasoning.* Assuming that there are only two sides to a question and representing yours as the only correct one.

- *Equivocating.* Misleading or hedging with ambiguous word choices.

- *Failing to accept the burden of proof.* Asserting a claim without presenting a reasoned argument to support it.

- *False analogy.* Assuming that because one thing resembles another, conclusions drawn from one also apply to the other.

- *Hasty generalization.* Offering only weak or limited evidence to support a conclusion.

- *Overreliance on authority.* Assuming that something is true simply because an expert says so and ignoring evidence to the contrary.

- *Oversimplifying.* Giving easy answers to complicated questions, often by appealing to emotions rather than logic.

- *Personal attack.* Demeaning the proponents of a claim instead of refuting their argument. Also called *ad hominem* (Latin for "against the man") *attack.*

- *Red herring.* Attempting to misdirect the discussion by raising an essentially unrelated point.

- *Slanting.* Selecting or emphasizing the evidence that supports your claim and suppressing or playing down other evidence.

- *Slippery slope.* Pretending that one thing inevitably leads to another.

- *Sob story.* Manipulating readers' emotions in order to lead them to draw unjustified conclusions.

- *Straw man.* Directing the argument against a claim that nobody actually holds or that everyone agrees is very weak.

Part Four

RESEARCH
STRATEGIES

Field Research

In universities, government agencies, and the business world, field research can be as important as library research or experimental research. If you major in education, communication, or one of the social sciences, you will probably be asked to do writing based on your own observations, interviews, and questionnaire results. You will also read large amounts of information based on these methods of learning about individuals, groups, and institutions. You also might use observations or interviews to help you select or gain background for a service-learning project.

For more on service learning, see Chapter 28.

Observations and interviews are essential for writing profiles (Chapter 4). Interviewing could be helpful, as well, in documenting a trend or phenomenon and exploring its causes (Chapter 9)—for example, you might consult an expert or conduct a survey to establish the presence of a trend. In proposing a solution to a problem (Chapter 7), you might want to interview people involved; or, if many people are affected, you might find it useful to prepare a questionnaire. In writing to explain an academic concept (Chapter 5), you might want to interview a faculty member who is a specialist on the subject. As you consider how you might use such research most appropriately, ask your instructor whether your institution will require you to obtain approval for your field research.

■ OBSERVATIONS

This section offers guidelines for planning an observational visit, taking notes on your observations, writing them up, and preparing for follow-up visits. Some kinds of writing are based on observations from single visits—travel writing, social workers' case reports, insurance investigators' accident reports—but most observational writing is based on several visits. An anthropologist or a sociologist studying an unfamiliar group or activity might observe it for months, filling several notebooks with notes. If you are profiling a place (Chapter 4), you almost certainly will want to make more than one observational visit, some of them perhaps combined with interviews.

Second and third visits to observe further are important because as you learn more about a place from initial observations, interviews, or reading, you will discover new ways to look at it. Gradually, you will have more and more questions that can be answered only by follow-up visits. You also may want to combine observations with other field research, especially if you are preparing an ethnographic study of the culture of a group or organization.

Planning the Visit

To ensure that your observational visits are productive, you must plan them carefully.

Getting Access.   If the place you propose to visit is public, you will probably have easy access to it. If everything you need to see is within view of anyone passing by or using the place, you can make your observations without any special arrangements. Indeed, you may not even be noticed. However, most observational visits require special access. Hence, you will need to arrange your visit, calling ahead or stopping by to introduce yourself, state your purpose, and get acquainted. Find out the times you may visit, and be certain you can gain access easily.

Announcing Your Intentions.   State your intentions directly and fully. Say who you are, where you are from, and what you hope to do. You may be surprised at how receptive people can be to a college student on assignment for a class or a service-learning project. Not every place you wish to visit will welcome you, however. In addition, private businesses as well as public institutions place a variety of constraints on outside visitors. But generally, if people know your intentions, they may be able to tell you about aspects of a place or an activity you would not have thought to observe.

Taking Your Tools.   Take a notebook with a firm back so that you will have a steady writing surface. Remember also to take a pen. Some observers dictate their observations into a tape recorder and transcribe their notes later. You might want to experiment with this method. We recommend, though, that you record your first observations in writing. Your instructor or other students in your class may want to see your notes, and transcribing a recording can take a lot of time.

Observing and Taking Notes

Here are some basic guidelines for observing and taking notes.

Observing.   Some activities invite the observer to watch from multiple vantage points, whereas others may limit the observer to a single perspective. Take advantage of every perspective available to you. Come in close, take a middle position, and stand back. Study the scene from a stationary position, and then try to move around it. The more varied your perspectives, the more details you are likely to observe.

Your purposes in observing are twofold: to describe the activity or place and to analyze it. You will want to look closely at the activity or place itself, but you will also want to think about what makes it special, what seems to you to be significant about it.

Try initially to be an innocent observer: Pretend that you have never seen anything like this activity or place before. Then consider your own and your readers' likely preconceptions. Ask yourself what details are surprising and what reinforces expectations.

Taking Notes.   You will undoubtedly find your own style of notetaking, but here are a few pointers.

- Write on only one side of the page. Later, when you organize your notes, you may want to cut up the pages and file notes under different headings.
- Take notes in words, phrases, or sentences. Draw diagrams or sketches, if they will help you see and understand the place or activity or recall details of it later on.
- Use abbreviations as much as you like, but use them consistently and clearly.
- Note any ideas or questions that occur to you.
- If you are expecting to see a certain behavior, try not to let this expectation influence what you actually do see.
- Use quotation marks around any overheard remarks or conversations you record.

Perhaps the most important advice about notetaking during an observational visit is to record as many details as possible about the place or activity and to write down your impressions as they come to mind. Do not focus on taking notes in a systematic way. Be flexible. Later you will have the chance to reorganize your notes and fill in gaps. At the same time, however, you want to be sure to include details about the setting, the people, and your reactions.

The Setting.   Describe the setting: Name or list objects you see there, and then record details of some of them—their color, shape, size, texture, function, relation to similar or dissimilar objects. Although your notes will probably contain mainly visual details, you might also want to record details about sounds and smells. Be sure to include some notes about the shape, dimensions, and layout of the place as a whole. How big is it? How is it organized?

The People.   Note the number of people you observe, their activities, their movements and behavior. Describe their appearance or dress. Record parts of overheard conversations. Indicate whether you see more men than women, more members of one nationality or ethnic group than of another, more older than younger people. Most important, note anything surprising, interesting, or unusual about the people and how they interact with each other.

Your Personal Reactions.   Write down your impressions, questions, ideas, or insights as they occur to you.

Reflecting on Your Observations

Immediately after your observational visit (within a few minutes, if possible), find a quiet place to reflect on what you saw, review your notes, and fill in any gaps with additional details or ideas. Give yourself at least a half-hour to add to your notes and to write a few sentences about the significance of the place or activity. Ask yourself the following questions:

- What did I learn from my observational visit?
- How did what I observed fit my own or my readers' likely preconceptions of the place or activity?
- What dominant impression do my notes seem to convey?
- What, if anything, seemed contradictory or out of place?

Writing Up Your Notes

Clustering is described in Chapter 11, pp. 516–17. Inventory-taking is described in Chapter 12, pp. 537–38.

Your instructor may ask you to write up your notes on the observational visit, as Brian Cable did after visiting the Goodbody mortuary for his profile essay. If so, review your notes, looking for a meaningful pattern in the details you have noted down. You might find clustering or taking inventory useful for discovering patterns in your notes.

See Chapter 15 for a full discussion of describing strategies.

Assume that your readers have never been to the place, and decide on the dominant impression of the place you want your readers to get from reading your writing. Choose details that will convey this impression. Then draft a brief description of the place. Your purpose is to select details from your notes that will convey to readers a vivid impression of the place.

■ Exercise 20.1

Arrange to meet with a small group (3 or 4 students) for an observational visit somewhere on campus, such as the student center, campus gym, cafeteria or restaurant, or any other place where some activity is going on. Take notes by assigning each person in your group a specific task; one person can take notes on the appearance of the people, for example; another can take notes on their activities; another on their conversations; and another on what the place looks and smells like. Take about twenty to thirty minutes, and then report to each other on your observations. This will give you some good practice on what you will need to do when you observe on your own, and you will get to see some of the difficulties associated with observing people and places.

Preparing for Follow-Up Visits

Rather than repeat yourself in follow-up visits, try to build on what you have already discovered. You should probably do some interviewing and reading before another observational visit so that you will have a greater understanding of the subject when you observe it again. You might want to present your notes from your first visit to your instructor or to a small group from your class so that you could use their responses as well, especially if you are working on a specific assignment such as a profile. It is also important to develop a plan for your follow-up visits: questions to be answered, hypotheses to be tested, types of information you would like to discover.

■ INTERVIEWS

Like making observations, interviewing tends to involve four basic steps: (1) planning and setting up the interview, (2) taking interview notes, (3) reflecting on the interview, and (4) writing up your notes.

Planning and Setting Up the Interview

The initial steps in interviewing involve choosing an interview subject and then arranging and planning for the interview.

Choosing an Interview Subject.   First, decide whom to interview. If you are writing about some activity in which several people are involved, choose subjects representing a variety of perspectives—a range of roles, for example. For a profile of a single person, most or all of your interviews would be with that person. But for a service-learning project, for instance, you might interview several members of an organization in order to gain a more complete picture of its mission or activities. You should be flexible because you may be unable to speak with the person you initially targeted and may wind up interviewing someone else—the person's assistant, perhaps. Do not assume that this interview subject will be of little use to you. With the right questions, you might even learn more from the assistant than you would from the person you had originally expected to see.

Arranging an Interview.   You may be nervous about calling up a busy person and asking for some of his or her time. Indeed, you may get turned down. But if so, it is possible that you will be referred to someone who will see you, someone whose job it is to talk to the public.

Do not feel that just because you are a student, you do not have the right to ask for people's time. You will be surprised at how delighted people are to be asked about themselves, particularly if you reach them when they are not feeling harried. Most people love to talk—about anything! And since you are a student on assignment, some people may feel that they are performing a public service by talking with you.

When introducing yourself to arrange the interview, give a short and simple description of your project. If you talk too much, you could prejudice or limit the interviewee's response. At the same time, it is a good idea to exhibit some sincere enthusiasm for your project. If you lack enthusiasm, the person may see little reason to talk with you.

Keep in mind that the person you want to interview will be donating valuable time to you. Be certain that you call ahead to arrange a specific time for the interview. Arrive on time. Dress appropriately. Bring all the materials you need. Express your thanks when the interview is over. Finally, try to represent your institution well, whether your interview is for a single course assignment or part of a larger service-learning project.

Planning for the Interview.   The best interview is generally the well-planned interview. It will help if you have made an observational visit and done some background reading beforehand. In preparation for the interview, you should do two things in particular: consider your objectives and prepare some questions.

Think about your main objectives.

- Do you want an orientation to the place or your topic (the "big picture") from this interview?
- Do you want this interview to lead you to interviews with other key people?
- Do you want mainly facts or opinions?
- Do you need to clarify something you have heard in another interview, observed, or read?
- Do you want to learn more about the person, the place, or the activity through the interview—or all of these?

The key to good interviewing is flexibility. You may be looking for facts, but your interview subject may not have any to offer. In that case, you should be able to shift gears and go after whatever your subject is in a position to discuss. Be aware that the person you are interviewing represents only one point of view. You may need to speak with several people to get a more complete picture. Talking with more than one person may also help you discover contradictions or problems that could contribute to the significance you decide to emphasize.

Composing Questions.   Take care in composing the questions you prepare in advance; they can be the key to a successful interview. Any question that places unfair limits on respondents is a bad question. Avoid forced-choice questions and leading questions.

Forced-choice questions impose your terms on respondents. Let us assume you are interviewing a counselor at a campus rape crisis center and want to know what he or she thinks is the motivation for rape. You could ask this question: "Do you think rape is an expression of sexual passion or of aggression?" But the counselor might think neither sexual passion nor aggression satisfactorily explains the motivation for rape. A better way to phrase the question would be as follows: "People often fall into two camps on the issue of rape. Some think it is an expression of sexual passion, while others argue it is really not sexual but aggressive. Do you think it is either of these? If not, what is your opinion?" Phrasing the question in this way allows you to get a reaction to what others have said at the same time that it gives the interviewee freedom to set the terms for his or her response.

Leading questions assume too much. An example of this kind of question is this: "Do you think the number of rapes has increased because women are perceived as competitors in a highly competitive economy?" This question assumes that there is an increase in the occurrence of rape, that women are perceived (apparently by rapists) as economic competitors, and that the state of the economy is somehow related to acts of rape. A better way of asking the question might be to make the assumptions more explicit by dividing the question into its parts: "Do you think the number of rapes has increased? What could have caused this increase? I've heard some people argue that the economy has something to do with it. Do you think so? Do you think rapists perceive women as competitors for jobs? Could the current economic situation have made this competition more severe?"

Good questions come in many different forms. One way of considering them is to divide them into two basic types: open and closed. *Open questions* give the respondent range and flexibility. They also generate anecdotes, personal revelations, and expressions of attitudes. *Closed questions* usually request specific information.

Suppose you are interviewing a small-business owner, for example. You might begin with a specific (closed) question about when the business was established and then follow up with an open-ended question such as, "Could you take a few minutes to tell me something about your early days in the business? I'd be interested to hear how it got started, what your hopes were, and what problems you had to face." Consider asking directly for an anecdote ("What happened when your employees threatened to strike?"), encouraging reflection ("What do you think has helped you most? What has hampered you?"), or soliciting advice ("What advice would you give to someone trying to start a new business today?"). Here are some examples of open and closed questions:

Open Questions

- What do you think about *(name a person or an event)*?
- Describe your reaction when *(name an event)* happened.
- Tell me about a time you were *(name an emotion)*.

Closed Questions

- How do you *(name a process)*?
- What does *(name a word or phrase)* mean?
- What does *(name a person, object, or place)* look like?
- How was it made?

The best questions encourage the subject to talk freely but to the point. If an answer strays too far from the point, you may need to ask a follow-up question to refocus the talk. Another tack you might want to try is to rephrase the subject's answer, to say something like "Let me see if I have this right" or "Am I correct in saying that you feel . . . ?" Often, a person will take the opportunity to amplify the original response by adding just the anecdote or quotable comment you have been looking for.

Bringing Your Tools.   As for an observational visit, when you interview someone, you will need a notebook with a firm back so you can write in it easily without the benefit of a table or desk. You might find it useful to divide several pages into two columns by drawing a line about one-third of the width of the page from the left margin. Use the left-hand column to note details about the scene, the person, the mood

For an example of notes of this sort, see Chapter 4, pp. 173–75.

of the interview, and other impressions. Head this column *Details and Impressions*. At the top of the right-hand column, write several questions. You may not use them, but they will jog your memory. This column should be titled *Information*. In it, you will record what you learn from answers to your questions.

Taking Notes during the Interview

Because you are not taking a verbatim transcript of the interview (if you want a literal account, use a tape recorder or shorthand), your goals are to gather information and to record a few quotable bits of information, comments, and anecdotes. In addition, because the people you interview may be unused to giving interviews and so will need to know you are paying attention, it is probably a good idea to do more listening than notetaking. You may not have much confidence in your memory, but if you pay close attention, you are likely to recall a good deal of the conversation afterward. Take some notes during the interview: a few quotations; key words and phrases; details of the scene, the person, and the mood of the interview. Remember that how something is said is as important as what is said. Look for material that will give texture to your writing—gesture, verbal inflection, facial expression, body language, physical appearance, dress, hair, or anything that makes the person an individual.

Reflecting on the Interview

As soon as you finish the interview, find a quiet place to reflect on it and review your notes. This reflection is essential because so much happens in an interview that you cannot record at the time. Spend at least a half-hour adding to your notes and thinking about what you learned.

At the end of this time, write a few sentences about your main impressions from the interview. Ask yourself these questions:

- What did I learn?
- What seemed contradictory or surprising about the interview?
- How did what was said fit my own or my readers' likely expectations about the person, activity, or place?
- How can I summarize my impressions?

Writing Up Your Notes

Your instructor may ask you to write up your interview notes. If so, review them for useful details and ideas. Decide what main impression you want to give of this person. Choose details that will contribute to this impression. Select quotations and paraphrases of information you learned from the person.

You might also review notes from any related observations or other interviews, especially if you plan to combine these materials in a profile, ethnographic study, or other project.

■ QUESTIONNAIRES

Questionnaires let you survey the opinions and knowledge of large numbers of people. You could carry out many face-to-face or phone interviews to get the same information, but questionnaires have the advantages of economy, efficiency, and anonymity. Some questionnaires, such as the ones you filled out when entering college, just collect demographic information: your name, age, sex, hometown, religious preference, intended major. Others, such as the Gallup and Harris polls, collect opinions on a wide range of issues. Before elections, we are bombarded with the results of such polls. Still other kinds of questionnaires, such as those used in academic research, are designed to help answer important questions about personal and societal problems.

This section briefly outlines procedures you can follow to carry out an informal questionnaire survey of people's opinions or knowledge and then write up the results. There are many good texts on designing questionnaires. A sample questionnaire appears in this section (Figure 20.1).

Focusing Your Study

A questionnaire survey usually has a limited focus. You might need to interview a few people in order to find this focus. Or you may already have a limited focus in mind. If you are developing a questionnaire as part of a service-learning project, discuss your focus with your supervisor or other staff members.

As an example, let us assume that you go to your campus student health clinic and have to wait over an hour to see a doctor. Sitting in the waiting room with many other students, you decide that this long wait is a problem that would be an ideal topic for a writing assignment you have been asked to do for your writing class, an essay proposing a solution to a problem (Chapter 7).

You do not have to explore the entire operation of the clinic to study this problem. You are not interested in how nurses and doctors are hired or in how efficient the clinic's system of ordering supplies is, for example. Your primary interest is in how long students usually wait for appointments, what times are most convenient for students to schedule appointments, how the clinic accommodates students when demand is high, and whether the long wait discourages many students from getting the treatment they need. With this limited focus, you can collect valuable information using a fairly brief questionnaire. To be certain about your focus, however, you should talk informally with several students to find out whether they also think there is a problem with appointment scheduling at the clinic. You might want to talk with staff members, too, explaining your plans and asking for their views on the problem.

Whatever your interest, be sure to limit the scope of your survey. Try to focus on one or two important questions. With a limited focus, your questionnaire can be brief, and people will be more willing to fill it out. In addition, a survey based on a limited amount of information will be easier to organize and report on.

Writing Questions

The same two basic types of questions used for interviews, closed and open, are also useful in questionnaires. Figure 20.1 illustrates how these types of questions may be employed in the context of a questionnaire about the student health clinic problem. Notice that the questionnaire uses several forms of *closed questions* (in items 1–6): checklists, two-way questions, multiple-choice questions, and ranking scales. You will probably use more than one form of closed question in a questionnaire in order to collect different kinds of information. The sample questionnaire also uses several *open questions* (items 7–10) that ask for brief written answers. You may want to combine closed and open questions in your questionnaire because both offer advantages: Closed questions will give you definite answers, while open questions can elicit information you may not have anticipated as well as provide lively quotations for your essay.

Whatever types of questions you develop, try to phrase them in a fair and unbiased manner so that your results will be reliable and credible. As soon as you have a collection of possible questions, try them out on a few typical respondents. You need to know which questions are unclear, which seem to duplicate others, and which provide the most interesting responses. These tryouts will enable you to assess which questions will give you the information you need. Readers can also help you come up with additional questions.

Figure 20.1 Sample Questionnaire: Scheduling at the Student Health Clinic

This is a survey about the scheduling of appointments at the campus Student Health Clinic. Your participation will help determine how long students have to wait in order to use clinic services and how these services might be more conveniently scheduled. The survey should take only 3 to 4 minutes to complete. All responses are confidential. Thank you for your participation.

Two-way question —— 1. Have you ever made an appointment at the clinic?   (circle one)

Yes   No

2. How frequently have you had to wait more than 10 minutes at the clinic for a scheduled appointment?   (circle one)

Always   Usually   Occasionally   Never

Multiple-choice questions — 3. Have you ever had to wait more than 30 minutes at the clinic for a scheduled appointment?   (circle one)

Yes   No   Uncertain

4. From your experience so far with the clinic, how would you rank its system for scheduling appointments?   (circle one)

0	1	2	3	4	5

Ranking scale —— no experience   inadequate   poor   adequate   good   outstanding

5. Given your present work and class schedule, when are you able to visit the clinic? (Check all applicable responses.)

_____ 8–10 A.M.	_____ 1–3 P.M.	— Checklist
_____ 10–12 A.M.	_____ 3–5 P.M.	
_____ Noon hour		

6. Given your present work and class schedule, which times during the day (Monday through Friday) would be the most and least convenient for you to schedule appointments at the clinic? (Rank the four choices from *1* for most convenient time, to *4* for least convenient time.)

| _____ Morning | _____ Dinnertime (5–7 P.M.) | — Ranking scale |
| _____ Afternoon (before 5 P.M.) | _____ Evening (7–10 P.M.) | |

7. How would you evaluate your most recent appointment at the clinic?

8. Based on your experiences with scheduling at the clinic, what advice would you give to other students about making appointments?

9. What do you believe would most improve the scheduling of appointments at the clinic? — Open questions

10. If you have additional comments about scheduling at the clinic, please write them on the back of this page.

Designing the Questionnaire

Begin your questionnaire with a brief, clear introduction stating the purpose of your survey and explaining how you intend to use the results. Give advice on answering the questions, and estimate the amount of time needed to complete the questionnaire (see Figure 20.1 for an example). You may opt to give this information orally if you are going to personally hand out the questionnaire to groups of people and have them fill it out immediately. However, even in this case, your respondents will appreciate a written introduction that clarifies what you expect and helps keep them on track.

Select your most promising questions, and decide how to order them. Any logical order is appropriate. You might want to arrange the questions from least to most complicated or from general to specific. You may find it appropriate to group the questions by subject matter or format. Certain questions may lead to others. You might want to place open questions at the end (see Figure 20.1 for an example).

Design your questionnaire so that it looks attractive and readable. Make it look easy to complete. Do not crowd questions together to save paper. Provide plenty of space for readers to answer questions, especially open questions, and encourage them to use the back of the page if they need more space.

Testing the Questionnaire

Make a few copies of your first-draft questionnaire, and ask at least three readers to complete it. Time them as they respond, or ask them to keep track of how long they take to complete it. Discuss with them any confusion or problems they experience. Review their responses with them to be certain that each question is eliciting the information you want it to elicit. From what you learn, reconsider your questionnaire and make any necessary revisions to your questions and design or format.

Administering the Questionnaire

Decide who you want to fill out your questionnaire and how you can arrange for them to do so. The more respondents you have, the better, but constraints of time and expense will almost certainly limit the number. You can mail or email questionnaires, distribute them to dormitories, or send them to campus or workplace mailboxes, but the return will be low. Half the people receiving questionnaires in the mail usually fail to return them. If you do mail the questionnaire, be sure to mention the deadline for returning it. Give directions for its return, and include a stamped, self-addressed envelope, if necessary. Instead of mailing the questionnaire, you might want to arrange to distribute it yourself to groups of people in class or around campus, at dormitory meetings, or at work.

Note that if you want to do a formal questionnaire study, you will need a scientifically representative group of readers (a random or stratified random sample). Even for an informal study, you should try to get a reasonably representative group. For example, to study satisfaction with appointment scheduling at the clinic, you would want to include students who have been to the clinic as well as those who have avoided it. You might even want to include a concentration of seniors rather than first-year students because, after four years, seniors would have made more visits to the clinic. If many students commute, you would want to be sure to have commuters among your respondents. Your essay will be more convincing if you demonstrate that your respondents represent the group whose opinions or knowledge you claim to be studying. As few as twenty-five respondents could be adequate for an informal study.

Writing Up the Results

Once you have the completed questionnaires, what do you do with them?

Summarizing the Results. Begin by tallying the results from the closed questions. Take an unused questionnaire, and tally the responses next to each choice. Suppose that you had administered the student health clinic questionnaire to twenty-five students. Here is how the tally might look for the checklist in question 5 of Figure 20.1.

5. Given your present work and class schedule, when are you able to visit the clinic? (Check all applicable responses.)

_____ 8–10 A.M. 𝍌𝍌𝍌𝍌𝍌𝍌 III *(18)*   _____ 1–3 P.M. III *(3)*

_____ 10–12 A.M. 𝍌𝍌 II *(7)*   _____ 3–5 P.M. 𝍌𝍌 IIII *(9)*

_____ Noon hour 𝍌𝍌𝍌𝍌 III *(13)*

Each tally mark represents one response to that item. The totals add up to more than twenty-five because respondents were asked to check all the times when they could make appointments.

Next, consider the open questions. Read all respondents' answers to each question separately to see the kinds and variety of responses they gave. Then decide whether you want to code any of the open questions so that you can summarize results from them quantitatively, as you would with closed questions. For example, you might want to classify the types of advice given as responses to question 8 in the clinic questionnaire: "Based on your experiences with scheduling at the clinic, what advice would you give to other students about making appointments?" You could then report the numbers of respondents (of your twenty-five) who gave each type of advice. For an opinion question (for example, "How would you evaluate your most recent appointment at the clinic?"), you might simply code the answers as positive, neutral, or negative and then tally the results accordingly for each kind of response. However, the responses to most open questions are used as a source of quotations for your report or essay.

You can give the results from the closed questions as percentages, either within the text itself or in one or more tables. You can find table formats in texts you may be using or even in magazines or newspapers. Conventional table formats for the social sciences are illustrated in the *Publication Manual of the American Psychological Association,* 4th edition (Washington, DC: American Psychological Association, 1994).

Because readers' interests can be engaged more easily with quotations than with percentages, plan to use open responses in your essay. You can quote responses to the open questions within your text, perhaps weaving them into your discussion like quoted material from published sources. Or you can organize several responses into lists and then comment on them.

You can use computer spreadsheet programs to tabulate the results from closed questions and even print out tables or graphs that you can insert into your essay. For

For strategies for integrating quoted material, see Chapter 22, pp. 695–97.

a small, informal survey, however, such programs will probably not save you much time.

Organizing the Write-up.   In organizing your results, you might want to consider a plan that is commonly followed in the social sciences.

> *Reporting Your Survey*
>
> Statement of the problem
>> Context for your study
>>
>> Your question
>>
>> Need for your survey
>>
>> Brief preview of your survey and plan for your report
>
> Review of other related surveys (if you know of any)
>
> Procedures
>> Questionnaire design
>>
>> Selection of participants
>>
>> Administration of the questionnaire
>>
>> Summary of the results
>
> Results: Presentation of what you learned, with limited commentary or interpretation
>
> Summary and discussion
>> Brief summary of your results
>>
>> Brief discussion of their significance (commenting, interpreting, exploring implications, and comparing to other related surveys)

Library and Internet Research

Research requires patience, careful planning, good advice, and even luck. The rewards are many, however. Each new research project leads you to unexplored regions of the library or of cyberspace. You may find yourself in a rare book room reading a manuscript written hundreds of years ago or involved in a lively discussion on the Internet with people hundreds of miles away. One moment you may be keyboarding commands, and the next, you may be threading a microfilm reader, viewing a videodisk, or squinting at the fine print in an index. You may breeze through an encyclopedia entry introducing you to a new subject or struggle with a just-published report of a highly technical research study on the same subject.

This chapter is designed to help you learn how to use the resources available in your college library and on the Internet. It gives advice on how to learn about the library and the Internet, develop efficient search strategies, keep track of your research, locate appropriate sources, and read them with a critical eye. Chapter 22 provides guidelines for using and acknowledging these sources in an essay. It also presents a sample research paper, on home schooling, written in response to an assignment to write an essay speculating about the causes of a trend.

■ ORIENTING YOURSELF TO THE LIBRARY

To conduct research in most college libraries, you will need to become familiar with a wide variety of resources. Online public access catalogs (often called OPACs) provide information on books. Periodical indexes and abstracts, used to locate magazine and journal articles, are available in databases, in print volumes, on CD-ROMs, through the library catalog, or through the World Wide Web. The materials you look up may be in print, on microfilm (reels) or microfiche (cards), or in electronic text files accessible through an electronic periodical index or library Web site.

Taking a Tour

Make a point of getting acquainted with your campus library. Your instructor may arrange a library orientation tour for your composition class. If not, you can join one of the regular orientation tours scheduled by the librarians or design your own tour (for suggestions, see Table 21.1). Because nearly all college libraries are more complex and offer more services than typical high school or public libraries, you will need to learn how your campus library's catalog and reference room are organized, how you can access computer catalogs and databases, whom to ask for help if you are confused, and where you can find books, periodicals, and other materials.

Pick up copies of any available pamphlets and guidelines. Nearly every college library offers a Web page and handouts describing its resources and services. Also

Table 21.1 Designing Your Self-Guided Library Tour

Here is a list of important locations or departments to look for in your college library.

Library Location	Services Provided
Loan Desk	Obtain library cards, check out materials, place holds and recalls, pay fees or fines.
Reference Desk	Obtain help from reference librarians to locate and use library resources.
Information Desk	Ask general and directional questions.
Reserves Desk	Gain access to books and journal articles that are on reserve for specific classes.
Interlibrary Loan Department	Request materials not available on site.
Public Access Computers	Gain access to the library catalog, electronic periodical indexes and abstracts, the campus network, and the Internet.
Current Periodicals	Locate unbound current issues of newspapers, journals, and magazines.
Directories of Books and Journals	Use directories to find the location of books and journals shelved by call numbers.
Reference Collection	Find reference materials such as encyclopedias, dictionaries, handbooks, atlases, bibliographies, statistics, and periodical indexes and abstracts.
Government Publications Department	Locate publications from federal, state, and local government agencies.
Multimedia Resources	Locate nonprint materials such as videos, CD-ROMs and audiotapes.
Microforms	Locate materials on microfilm (reels) and microfiche (cards).
Special Collections	Refer to rare and valuable materials not readily available in most library collections; in larger libraries only.
Archives	Find archival materials, collections of papers from important individuals and organizations that provide source material for original research; in larger libraries only.
Maps and Atlases	Locate maps and atlases in a special location because of their size and format.
Copy Service	Use self-service and special-function copiers.
Reading Rooms	Read in quiet, comfortable areas.
Study Rooms	Study in rooms reserved for individuals or small groups.

look for a floor map of materials and facilities. See whether your library offers any research guidelines, special workshops, or presentations on strategies for locating resources.

Consulting a Librarian

Think of college librarians as instructors whose job is to help you understand the library and get your hands on sources you need to complete your research projects. Librarians at the information or reference desk are there to provide reference services, and most have years of experience answering the very questions you are likely to ask. You should not hesitate to approach them with any questions you have about locating sources. Remember, however, that they can be most helpful when you can explain your research assignment clearly.

Knowing Your Research Task

Before you go to the library to start an assigned research project, learn as much as you can about the assignment. Should you need to ask a librarian for advice, it is best to have the assignment in writing. Ask your instructor to clarify any confusing terms and to define the purpose and scope of the project. Find out how you can narrow or focus the project once you begin the research. Asking a question or two in advance can prevent hours—or even days—of misdirected work. You should try to get to the library as soon as you understand the assignment. If many of your classmates will be working on similar projects, there may be competition for a limited number of books and other resources.

Using Self-Help Options

Library resources and the research environment are constantly changing, and all researchers, including students, need to learn to be self-sufficient in their information quest. Look for and use online help, tutorials, and other self-help guides when using information resources, particularly electronic resources.

■ A LIBRARY SEARCH STRATEGY

For your library research to be manageable and productive, you will want to work carefully and systematically. Although specific search strategies may vary to fit the needs of individual research tasks, the general process presented in Figure 21.1 should help you get started, keep track of all your research, use library materials to get an overview of your subject, locate the sources you need, and read those sources with a critical eye. It is important to remember that research is a recursive, repetitive process, not a linear one. You will be constantly refining and revising your research strategy as you find out more about your topic.

Know your research task

- Keep a research journal
- Keep a working bibliography
- Take notes

Get an overview of your topic

- Look in encyclopedias and subject dictionaries
- Review textbooks
- Explore Internet sites
- Check factual information, correct spelling of terms, dates, etc.
- Construct a list of keywords and phrases
- Develop a preliminary topic statement

Use subject guides to identify possible sources of information on specific topics

Conduct a preliminary search for sources, using keywords and subject headings

- Check the online catalog for books
- Check periodical indexes for references to articles
- Check Internet sites

Evaluate and refine your search by asking yourself

- Is this what I expected to find?
- Am I finding too much?
- Am I finding enough?
- Do I need to modify my keywords?
- Do I need to recheck background sources?
- Do I need to modify my topic statement?

Refine your search based on the answers

Locate sources

- Books
- Magazine and journal articles
- Newspapers
- Internet sites
- Government and statistical sources
- Other sources appropriate to your topic

Read your sources with a critical eye

- For information
- For relevance
- For accuracy
- For comprehensiveness
- For bias
- For currency

Continue to evaluate and refine your search strategy based on the research results

Figure 21.1 Overview of an Information Search Strategy

■ KEEPING TRACK OF YOUR RESEARCH

As you research your topic, you will want to keep a careful record of all the sources you locate by setting up a working bibliography. You will also want to take notes on your sources in some systematic way.

Keeping a Working Bibliography

A *working bibliography* is a preliminary, ongoing record of books, articles, Web sites —all the sources of information you discover as you research your subject. In addition, you can use your working bibliography to keep track of any encyclopedias, bibliographies, and indexes you consult, even though you do not identify these general sources in an essay.

Each entry in a working bibliography is called a *bibliographic citation*. The information you record in each bibliographic citation will help you locate the material you need in the source and refer to it, or *cite* it, in the bibliography—the list of references or works cited you provide at the end of an essay. Recording this information for each source as you locate it, rather than reconstructing it later, will save you hours of work. In addition to the bibliographic information, note the library location where you will be able to find the material and the source where you located the reference, just in case you have to track it down again. (See Figures 21.2 and 21.3 for examples of how to organize bibliographic and other information for a working bibliography.)

As you locate books in the library, record this information in your working bibliography for each book you look up.

Author: _____

Title: _____

Place of publication: _____

Publisher: _____

Date of publication: _____

Library where book is located: _____

Call number: _____

Special location (such as in reference or government publications dept.): _____

Is the book available or checked out?: _____

Figure 21.2 Information for Working Bibliography—Books

As you locate articles in the library, record this information in your working bibliography for each article you look up.

Author of article: _____

Title of article: _____

Title of journal: _____

Volume number: _____ Issue number: _____

Date of issue: _____ Inclusive page numbers: _____

Library and special location: _____

Figure 21.3 Information for Working Bibliography—Periodical Articles

Confirm with your instructor which documentation style is required for your assignment so that you can make all the sources you list in your working bibliography conform to that style of documentation. Chapter 22 presents two common documentation styles, one adopted by the Modern Language Association (MLA) and widely used in the humanities, and the other advocated by the American Psychological Association (APA) and used in the social sciences. Individual disciplines often have their own preferred styles of documentation.

Practiced researchers keep their working bibliography on index cards, in a notebook, or in a computer file. They may keep bibliographic information separate from notes they take on the sources. Many researchers find index cards most convenient because the cards are easy to arrange in the alphabetical order required for the list of works cited or references. Others find cards too easy to lose and prefer instead to keep everything—working bibliography, notes, and drafts—in one notebook. Researchers who use computers set up working bibliographies in word processing programs or bibliographic management programs that can format information according to one of the preset documentation styles (such as MLA or APA) or a customized style created by the user. These programs can also create in-text citations and insert them into the essay text, as well as format the final list of works cited. Some of these documentation programs can interact with electronic indexes and other databases, downloading source information from the database into a bibliographic file and then correctly formatting the information.

Whether you use index cards, a notebook, or a computer file for your working bibliography, the important thing is to make your entries accurate and complete. If the call number for a book is incomplete or inaccurate, for example, you will not be able to find the book in the stacks. If the volume number for a periodical is incorrect, you may not be able to locate the article. If the author's name is misspelled, you may have trouble finding the book in the library catalog.

Taking Notes

After you have located some possible sources, you will want to begin taking notes. If you can obtain a photocopy of the relevant parts, you may want to annotate right on the page. Otherwise, you should paraphrase, summarize, and outline useful information as separate notes. In addition, you will want to write down quotations you might want to use in your essay.

Outlining, paraphrasing, and summarizing are discussed in Chapter 12, and quoting is discussed in Chapter 22.

You may already have a method of notetaking you prefer. Some researchers like to use index cards for notes as well as for their working bibliography. They use 3- by 5-inch cards for their bibliography and larger ones (4- by 6-inch or 5- by 7-inch) for notes. Some use cards of different colors to organize their notes, whereas other people prefer to keep their notes in a notebook, and still others enter their notes into a computer file. Whatever method you use, be sure to keep accurate notes.

Care in notetaking is of paramount importance to minimize the risks of copying facts incorrectly and of misquoting. Another common error in notetaking is copying an author's words without enclosing them in quotation marks. This error could lead easily to plagiarism, the unacknowledged and therefore improper use of another's words or ideas. Double-check all your notes, and be as accurate as you can.

For tips on avoiding plagiarism, see Chapter 22, p. 701.

You might consider photocopying materials from sources that look especially promising. All libraries house photocopy machines or offer a copying service. However, because photocopying can be costly, you will want to be selective. Photocopying can facilitate your work, allowing you to reread and analyze important sources as well as to highlight material you may wish to quote, summarize, or paraphrase. Be sure to photocopy title pages or other publication information for each source you copy, or write this information on the photocopied text, especially if you are copying excerpts from several sources. Bring paper clips or a stapler with you to the library to help keep your photocopies organized.

■ GETTING STARTED

"But where do I start?" That common question is easily answered. You first need an overview of your topic. If you are researching a concept or an issue in a course you are taking, a bibliography in your textbook or your course materials provides the obvious starting point. Your instructor can advise you about other sources that provide overviews of your topic. If your topic is just breaking in the news, you will want to consult current newspapers, magazines, or Internet sites. For all other topics—and for background information—encyclopedias and disciplinary (subject) guides are often the place to start. They introduce you to diverse aspects of a subject, from which you might find a focus for your research.

Consulting Encyclopedias

General encyclopedias, such as the *Encyclopaedia Britannica* and the *Encyclopedia Americana,* give basic information about many topics; however, general encyclopedias alone are not adequate resources for college research. Specialized encyclopedias cover topics in the depth appropriate for college writing. In addition to providing an overview of a topic, a specialized encyclopedia often includes an explanation of issues related to the topic, definitions of specialized terminology, and selective bibliographies of additional sources.

As starting points, specialized encyclopedias have two distinct advantages: (1) They provide a comprehensive introduction to key terms related to your topic, terms that are especially useful in identifying the subject headings used to locate material in catalogs and indexes, and (2) they provide a comprehensive presentation of a subject, enabling you to see many possibilities for focusing your research on one aspect of it.

The following list identifies some specialized encyclopedias in the major academic disciplines:

ART	*Dictionary of Art.* 34 vols. 1996.
BIOLOGY	*Concise Encyclopedia Biology.* 1995.
CHEMISTRY	*Concise Encyclopedia Chemistry.* 1993.
COMPUTERS	*Encyclopedia of Computer Science and Technology.* 15 vols. 1975–.
ECONOMICS	*Fortune Encyclopedia of Economics.* 1993.
EDUCATION	*Encyclopedia of Educational Research.* 1992.
ENVIRONMENT	*Encyclopedia of the Environment.* 1994.
FOREIGN RELATIONS	*Encyclopedia of U.S. Foreign Relations.* 1997. *Encyclopedia of the Third World.* 1992.
HISTORY	*Encyclopedia USA.* 20 vols. 1983–. *New Cambridge Modern History.* 14 vols. 1957–1980, 1990–.
LAW	*The American Law Dictionary.* 1991.
LITERATURE	*Encyclopedia of World Literature in the 20th Century.* 5 vols. 1981–1993. *Encyclopedia of Literature and Criticism.* 1990.
MUSIC	*New Grove Dictionary of Music and Musicians.* 20 vols. 1980.
PHILOSOPHY	*Encyclopedia of Philosophy.* 4 vols. 1973.
PSYCHOLOGY	*Encyclopedia of Psychology.* 2nd edition. 1994.
RELIGION	*Encyclopedia of Religion.* 16 vols. 1987.
SCIENCE	*McGraw-Hill Encyclopedia of Science and Technology.* 20 vols. 1992.
SOCIAL SCIENCES	*International Encyclopedia of the Social Sciences.* 19 vols. 1968–.
WOMEN'S STUDIES	*Women's Studies Encyclopedia.* 3 vols. 1989–1991.

You can locate any of these in the library by doing a title search in the online catalog and looking for the encyclopedia's call number. Find other specialized encyclopedias by looking in the catalog under the subject heading for the discipline, such as "psychology," and adding the subheading "encyclopedia" or "dictionary."

Three particular reference sources can help you identify other specialized encyclopedias covering your topic:

ARBA Guide to Subject Encyclopedias and Dictionaries (1986). Lists specialized encyclopedias by broad subject categories, with descriptions of coverage, focus, and any special features.

First Stop: The Master Index to Subject Encyclopedias (1989). Lists specialized encyclopedias by broad subject categories and provides information about articles within them. By looking under the key terms that describe a topic, you can search for related articles in any of over four hundred specialized encyclopedias.

Kister's Best Encyclopedias (1994). Surveys and evaluates more than 1,000 encyclopedias, both print and electronic. It includes a title and topic index that you can use to find references to encyclopedias on special topics.

Consulting Disciplinary Guides

Once you have a general overview of your topic, you can consult one of the research guides within the discipline. The following guides can help you identify the major handbooks, encyclopedias, bibliographies, journals, periodical indexes, and computer databases in the various disciplines. You need not read any of these extensive works straight through, but you will find them to be valuable references. The *Guide to Reference Books,* edited by Robert Balay, will help you find disciplinary guides for subjects not listed here.

ANTHROPOLOGY	*Introduction to Library Research in Anthropology,* 2nd edition. 1998. By John M. Weeks.
ART	*Visual Arts Research: A Handbook.* 1986. By Elizabeth B. Pollard.
EDUCATION	*Education: A Guide to Reference and Information Sources.* 1989. By Lois Buttlar.
FILM	*On the Screen: A Film, Television, and Video Research Guide.* 1986. By Kim N. Fisher.
GENERAL	*Guide to Reference Books,* 11th edition. 1996. Edited by Robert Balay.
HISTORY	*A Student's Guide to History,* 6th edition. 1994. By Jules R. Benjamin.
HUMANITIES	*The Humanities: A Selective Guide to Information Sources,* 4th edition. 1994. By Ron Blazek and Elizabeth S. Aversa.

LITERATURE	*Reference Works in British and American Literature.* 2 vols. 1998. By James K. Bracken. *Literary Research Guide: An Annotated Listing of Reference Sources in English Literary Studies.* 1998. By James L. Harner.
MUSIC	*Music: A Guide to the Reference Literature.* 1987. By William S. Brockman.
PHILOSOPHY	*Philosophy: A Guide to the Reference Literature,* 2nd edition. 1997. By Hans E. Bynagle.
POLITICAL SCIENCE	*Information Sources of Political Science,* 4th edition. 1986. By Frederick L. Holler.
PSYCHOLOGY	*Library Use: A Handbook for Psychology,* 2nd edition. 1992.
SCIENCE AND TECHNOLOGY	*Scientific and Technical Information Sources,* 2nd edition. 1987. By Ching-chih Chen.
SOCIAL SCIENCES	*The Social Sciences: A Cross-Disciplinary Guide to Selected Sources.* 1996. By Nancy L. Herron.
SOCIOLOGY	*Sociology: A Guide to Reference and Information Sources,* 2nd edition. 1997. By Stephen H. Aby.
WOMEN'S STUDIES	*Introduction to Library Research in Women's Studies.* 1985. By Susan E. Searing.

Consulting Bibliographies

Like encyclopedias and disciplinary guides, bibliographies give an overview of what has been published on the subject. A bibliography is simply a list of publications on a given subject. Its scope may be broad or narrow. Some bibliographers try to be exhaustive, including every title they can find, but most are selective. To discover how selections were made, check the bibliography's preface or introduction. Occasionally, bibliographies are annotated with brief summaries and evaluations of the entries. Bibliographies may be found in a variety of places: in encyclopedias, in the library catalog, and in research guides. All specialized encyclopedias and disciplinary guides have bibliographies. Research articles include bibliographies to document their sources of information.

Even if you attend a large research university, your library is unlikely to hold every book or journal article a bibliography might direct you to. The library catalog and serial record (a list of periodicals the library holds) will tell you whether the book or journal is available on-site or whether you will have to get it through interlibrary loan.

■ IDENTIFYING KEYWORDS AND SUBJECT HEADINGS

To extend your research beyond encyclopedias, you need to find appropriate keywords and subject headings. *Subject headings* are specific words and phrases used in libraries to categorize the contents of books and periodicals. As you read about your subject in an encyclopedia or other reference book, you should keep a list of *keywords* or phrases that describe your topic. Make sure you spell your keywords correctly. Computers are very unforgiving of spelling errors.

One way to begin your search for subject headings is to consult the *Library of Congress Subject Headings* (LCSH), which can usually be found near the library catalog. This reference book lists the standard subject headings used in library catalogs. Here is an example from the LCSH:

Home schooling *(May Subd Geog)* ◄————————————— Place names may follow heading
    Here are entered works on the provision of compulsory education in the home by parents as an alternative to traditional public or private schooling. General works on the provision of education in the home by educational personnel are entered under Domestic Education.

Used for —————————► UF   Education, Home
                          Home-based education
                          Home education   NT = Narrower term
                          Home instruction   SA = See also
                          Home teaching by parents
                          Homeschooling
                          Instruction, Home
                          Schooling, Home
Broader Term ————————► BT   Education
Related Term ————————► RT   Education—United States
                          Education—Parent participation

Subject headings provide you with keywords to use as you look through catalogs and indexes. For example, this sample entry proved particularly useful because when the student found nothing listed in the library catalog under "Home schooling," she tried the other headings until "Education—Parent participation" and "Education—United States" yielded information on three books. Note, too, that this entry explains the types of books that would be found under these headings and those that would be found elsewhere.

Another way to locate subject headings when you are using the library's computer catalog is to select the keyword search option and type in the words or phrases that you think describe your topic. As you review the results of your search, look for the titles that most closely match the topics that you are looking for. When you call up the detailed displays for these titles, look for the section labeled SUBJECT or SUBJECT HEADING. (In the example that follows, this section is abbreviated as "Subj-lcsh.") In many computerized catalogs and indexes, these subject headings are links. You can click on them to look for other materials on the same subject. Make a note of all the subject headings that describe your topic in your working bibliography. Then you can use them the next time you start looking for information on your topic. Here is an example of an online catalog reference to a book on home schooling:

For an example of an online catalog reference to a periodical, see p. 679.

The "imprint" line provides publication information.

The "description" is sometimes called the "physical description."

Subject headings

Title:	Pathways to privatization in education / by Joseph Murphy . . . [et al.]
Imprint:	Greenwich, Conn.: Ablex Pub. Corp., c1998

LOCATION	CALL NO	STATUS
MAIN	LB2806.36 .P38 1998	NOT CHCKD OUT

Description:	xiii, 244 p.; 24 cm
Series:	Contemporary studies in social and policy issues in education
Subj-lcsh	**Privatization in education — United States**
	Educational vouchers — United States
	Home schooling — United States
Add author:	Murphy, Joseph, 1949–
Note(s):	Includes bibliographical references (p. 209–236) and index
ISBN:	1567503632 (cloth)
	1567503640 (pbk.)

Determining the Most Promising Sources

As you follow a subject heading into the library catalog and indexes, you will discover many seemingly relevant books and articles. How do you decide which ones to track down and examine? With little to go on but author, title, date, and publisher or periodical name, you may feel at a loss, but these details actually provide useful clues. Look again, for example, at the online catalog reference to a book on home schooling (see above). The title, *Pathways to Privatization in Education,* is the first clue to the subject coverage of the book. Note that the publication date, 1998, is recent. From the subject headings, you can see that this book focuses on various aspects of the privatization of education, which includes home schooling, and that the geographic focus of the book is the United States. Finally, from the notes, you can see that the book includes an extensive bibliography that could lead you to other sources.

For a discussion of periodical indexes, see p. 672.

Now look at the following entry from *Education Index,* a periodical index:

Home schooling
    Do children have to go to school? [Great Britain] C. Henson. *Child Educ (Engl)* v73 p68 Mr '96
    Homegrown learning [Twin Ridges Elementary School District combines homeschooling with regular classroom instruction] D. Hill. il *Teach Mag* v7 p40-5 Ap '96
    Should we open extracurriculars to home-schoolers? J. Watford; B. Dickinson. il *Am Teach* v80 p4 Mr '96

This entry lists articles that address different aspects of home schooling, briefly describing some of the articles. You can see that the first article deals with the issue from a British point of view, which might provide an interesting cross-cultural perspective for your essay. The title of the third article seems to indicate an argument on the issue; that it appears in a magazine for teachers might give you a sense of that profession's attitudes toward home schooling.

In addition, each entry contains the information that you will need to locate it in a library. Going back to the first article, here is what each piece of information means.

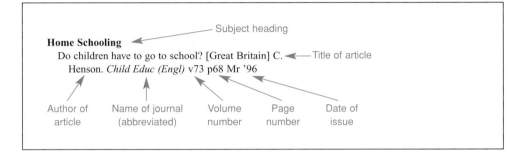

When you look in catalogs and indexes, consider the following points to help you to decide whether you should track down a particular source:

- *Relevance to your topic.* Do the title, subtitle, description, subject headings, and abstract help you determine just how directly the particular source addresses your topic?

- *Publication date.* How recent is the source? For current controversies, emerging trends, and continuing technical or medical developments, you must consult the most recent material. For historical or biographical topics, you will want to start with present-day perspectives but keep in mind that older sources also offer authoritative perspectives.

- *Description.* Does the length indicate a brief or an extended treatment of the topic? Does the work include illustrations that may elaborate on concepts discussed in the text? Does the work include a bibliography that could lead you to other works or an index that could give you an overview of what is discussed in the text? Does the abstract indicate the focus of the work?

From among the sources that look promising, select publications that seem by their titles to address different aspects of your topic or to approach it from different perspectives. Try to avoid selecting sources by the same author, from the same publisher, or in the same journal. Common sense will lead you to an appropriate decision about diversity in source materials.

■ SEARCHING LIBRARY ONLINE CATALOGS AND DATABASES

Through public access computers, most college libraries now offer access to their online catalog and databases. The library catalog is a database listing of books available on-site. Separate databases list the library's other holdings (such as periodicals, government documents, and some specialized CD-ROM products), provide access to periodical and newspaper indexes, and allow you to search the holdings of other libraries. Check your campus library's home page on one of the computers for a list of the resources that are available through its computer system.

Using Different Search Techniques

Many of the tools that are used to locate library sources are electronic, and you will be able to use these tools effectively if you have some idea how they work. Computerized library catalogs and databases consist of hundreds or thousands of records, each representing an individual item. The record is made up of different fields describing the item and allowing users to retrieve it from the database. Here is a record for a book from a library's online catalog with the searchable fields in bold:

Author:	Gordon, William MacGuire, 1935–
Title:	The law of home schooling / William M. Gordon, Charles J. Russo, Albert S. Miles. Topeka, Kan.: National Organization on Legal Problems of Education, c1994.
Location:	Main
Call No:	JLL 74-383 no. 52
Description:	74 p.; 23 cm.
Series:	NOLPE monograph series no. 52.
Notes:	Includes bibliographical references and index.
Subjects:	Home schooling—Law and legislation—United States. Educational law and legislation—United States. Education—Parent participation—United States.
Other entries:	Russo, Charles J.

Basic search strategies include author, title, and subject searches. When you request an *author search,* the computer looks for a match between the name you type and the names listed in the author field of all the records in the online catalog or other database. When you request a *title search,* the computer looks for a match in the title field. Computers are very literal. They only try to match the *exact* terms you enter, and most do not recognize variant or incorrect spellings. That is an incentive to become a good speller and a good typist. In addition, you can be flexible where the computer cannot; for instance, if you were researching the topic of home schooling, you could do a *subject search* not only for "home schooling" but also for "home-schooling." Table 21.2 describes some search capabilities commonly offered by library catalogs and databases.

Table 21.2 Common Search Capabilities Offered by Library Catalogs and Databases

Type of Search	How the Computer Conducts the Search	Things to Know
Author Search (exact) • Individual (*Guterson, David*) • Organization (*U.S. Dept. of Education*)	Looks in the author field for the words entered	• Author searches generally are exact-match searches, so authors' names are entered *last name, first name* (for example, "Shakespeare, William"). If you enter "William Shakespeare," the computer will generate a list of authors whose last names are William. • Organizations can be considered authors. Enter the name of the organization in natural word order. • An exact-match author search is useful for finding books and articles by a particular author.
Title Search (exact) • Book title • Magazine or journal title • Article title	Looks in the title field for words in the exact order you enter them	An exact-match title search is useful for identifying the location of known items, such as when you are looking for a particular journal or book.
Subject Search (exact)	Looks in the subject heading or descriptor field for words in the exact order you enter them	An exact-match subject search is useful when you are sure about the subject heading.
Keyword Search	Looks in the title, note, subject, abstract, and text fields for the words entered	A keyword search is the broadest kind you can use. It is useful during early exploration of a subject.
Title Word Search • Book title • Magazine or journal title • Article title	Looks in the title field of the record for the words entered and ignores word order	Since this is not an exact-match search, entering "home and schooling" will retrieve the same records as entering "schooling and home."
Subject Word Search	Looks in the subject heading or descriptor field of the record for the words entered and ignores word order	Since this is not an exact-match search, entering "education privatization" will retrieve the same records as "privatization education."

Using Boolean Operators

The real power of using an online catalog or other database is demonstrated when you need to look up books or articles using more than one keyword or phrase. For example, suppose you want information about home schooling, but you are only interested in articles about home schooling in California. Rather than looking through an index listing all the articles on home schooling and picking out those that mention California, you can ask the computer to do the work for you by linking your two keywords with the Boolean operator AND. Online searching operates according to *Boolean logic* (developed by and named after George Boole, a nineteenth-century mathematician). To understand Boolean logic, picture two sets of articles: the first contains all the articles in the database about home schooling and the second contains all the articles in the database about California. A third set is formed by all the articles that belong in both sets because they are about both home schooling AND California. There are three Boolean operators: AND, OR, and NOT. Figure 21.4 provides an illustration of how each Boolean operator works.

AND

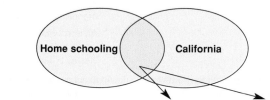

Returns references that contain both the terms **home schooling** AND **California**

- Narrows the search
- Combines unrelated terms
- Is the default used by most online catalogs and databases

OR

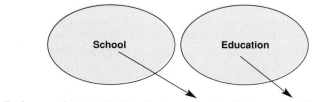

Returns all references that contain either the term **school** OR the term **education,** but not both

- Broadens the search (**"OR is more"**)
- Is useful with synonyms and variant spellings: ("home schooling" and "homeschooling")

NOT

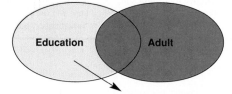

Returns references that include the term **education** but NOT the term **adult**

- Narrows the search
- May eliminate relevant material

Figure 21.4 The Boolean Operators: AND, OR, and NOT

Using Truncation

Another useful search strategy employs what is called *truncation*. With this technique, you can drop the ending of a word and replace it with a truncation symbol. For example, by entering the term "home school#" you would retrieve all the records that had terms such as "home school, home schooling, home schools, home schooled, or home schoolers." Truncation is useful when you want to retrieve both the plural and singular forms of a word or any word for which you are not sure of the ending. Truncation symbols vary with the catalog or database. The question mark (?), asterisk (*), and pound sign (#) are frequently used.

Table 21.3 offers some suggestions for expanding or narrowing your electronic search.

Table 21.3 Electronic Search Tips

If You Find Too Many Sources on Your Topic:	If You Find Insufficient Information on Your Topic:
• Use a subject heading search instead of a keyword search.	• Use a keyword or title search instead of a subject heading search.
• Add a concept word to your search.	• Eliminate unimportant words or secondary concepts from your search terms.
• Use a more precise vocabulary to describe your topic.	• Try truncated forms of your keyword.
	• Use different words to describe your topic.
	• Check the spelling of each term you type.

■ LOCATING SOURCES

The following are guidelines for finding books, periodical articles, newspaper articles, government documents and statistical information, and other types of sources.

Finding Books

The primary source for books is the library's computerized or online catalog. Besides flexibly searching keywords and subject headings, the catalog may tell you whether a book is currently available or checked out. It also allows you to print out source information rather than having to copy it by hand. However, it will require correct spelling and may contain only material received and cataloged after a certain date.

Whether you search a library catalog by author, title, subject, or keyword, each record you find will provide the following standard information. You will need this information to cite the book in your working bibliography and to locate it in the library.

1. *Call number:* This number, which usually appears on a separate line in the online catalog record, is your key to finding the book in the library. Most college

Finding Books

1. Determine keywords or subject headings.
2. Enter terms in the online catalog.
3. Evaluate results.
4. Refine results if necessary.
5. Locate the books.

libraries use the Library of Congress call-number system, whereas the Dewey system is used by most public libraries and some small college libraries. It is important to note the Library of Congress system uses both letters and numbers in the call number, and both are needed to locate a book. Call numbers serve two purposes: They provide an exact location for every book in the library and, because they are assigned according to subject classifications, they group books on the same topic together so that you know where browsing the stacks might be useful. Call numbers also give information about special collections of books kept in other library locations such as the reference room or government publications department. If the online catalog covers more than one library, the name of the library that has the book will also be included.

Examples of records in online catalogs are shown on pp. 666 and 668.

2. *Author:* The author's name appears last name first, followed by birth and death dates. For books with multiple authors, the record includes an author entry under each author's name.

3. *Title:* The title appears exactly as it does on the title page of the book, except that only the first word and proper nouns and adjectives are capitalized.

4. *Publication information:* The place of publication (usually just the city), the publisher, and the year of publication are listed. If the book was published simultaneously in the United States and abroad, both places of publication and both publishers are indicated.

5. *Physical description:* This section provides information about the book's page length and size. A roman numeral indicates the number of pages devoted to front matter (such as a preface, table of contents, and acknowledgments).

6. *Notes:* Any special features such as a bibliography or an index are listed here.

For more on the *Library of Congress Subject Headings* (LCSH), see p. 665.

7. *Subject headings:* Assigned by the Library of Congress, these headings indicate how the book is listed in the subject catalog. They also provide useful links for finding other books on the same subject.

Finding Periodical Articles

Finding Periodical Articles

1. Select an appropriate periodical index or database.
2. Select a search option.
3. Display and evaluate the results of the search.
4. Refine your search strategy if necessary.
5. Interpret results in order to locate the articles.
6. Print, email or download results for later use.

The most up-to-date information on a subject is usually found not in books but in articles published in periodicals. A *periodical* is a publication such as a magazine, newspaper, or journal that is published on an ongoing basis at regular intervals (for instance, daily, weekly, monthly, or annually) and that has different content in each issue. Many periodicals now publish online versions of their print publications. In addition, "webzines" and electronic journals are periodicals published exclusively on the Web. Examples of periodicals include *Sports Illustrated* (magazine), the *New York Times* (newspaper), *Tulsa Studies in Women's Literature* (scholarly journal), *Kairos* (online journal for teachers), and *Slate* (online magazine or "webzine").

Articles in periodicals are usually not listed in the library catalog; to find them, you must use library reference works called *periodical indexes.* Some periodical indexes include *abstracts* or short summaries of articles. Indexes may be available in printed form, in microform, on CD-ROM, through the library's online catalog, or through the campus network. Many indexes and abstracts, including those listed later in this section, are available as computer databases. Regardless of format, periodical indexes all serve the same basic function of leading the user to articles on a specific topic. If you understand how to use one, you will be able to use others.

Distinguishing Scholarly Journals and Popular Magazines

Although they are both called periodicals, *journals* and *magazines* have important differences. Journals publish articles written by experts in a particular field of study, frequently professors or researchers in academic institutions. Journals are usually very specialized in their subject focus, research oriented, and extensively reviewed by specialists prior to publication. They are intended to be read by experts and students conducting research. Magazines, in contrast, usually publish general-interest articles written by journalists. The articles are written to entertain and educate the general public, and they tend to appeal to a much broader audience than journal articles.

Table 21.4 How to Distinguish a Scholarly Journal from a Popular Magazine

Scholarly Journal	Popular Magazine
• The front or back cover lists the contents of the issue.	• The cover features a color picture.
• The title of the publication contains the word *Journal*.	• The title may be catchy as well as descriptive.
• You see the journal only at the library.	• You see the magazine for sale at the grocery store, in an airport, or at a bookstore.
• It does not include advertisements or advertises products such as textbooks, professional books, or scholarly conferences.	• It has lots of colorful advertisements in it.
• The authors of articles have *Ph.D.* or academic affiliations after their names.	• The authors of articles are journalists or reporters.
• Many articles have more than one author.	• Most articles have a single author but may quote experts.
• A short summary (abstract) of an article may appear on the first page.	• A headline or engaging description may precede the article.
• Most articles are fairly long, 5 to 20 pages.	• Most of the articles are fairly short, 1 to 5 pages.
• The articles may include charts, tables, figures, and quotations from other scholarly sources.	• The articles have color pictures and sidebar boxes.
• The articles have a bibliography (list of references to other books and articles) at the end.	• The articles do not include a bibliography.
• You probably would not read it at the beach.	• You might bring it to the beach to read.

Journals contain a great deal of what is called *primary literature,* reporting the results of original research. For example, a scientist might publish an article in a medical journal about the results of a new treatment protocol for breast cancer. *Secondary literature,* published in magazines, is intended to inform the general public about new and interesting developments in scientific and other areas of research. If a reporter from *Newsweek* wrote an article about the scientist's cancer research, this article would be classified as secondary literature. Table 21.4 on p. 673 summarizes some of the important differences between scholarly journals and popular magazines.

Selecting an Appropriate Periodical Index or Abstract

Periodical indexes and abstracts are of two types: general and specialized. Both provide you with information that will help you locate articles on a topic.

General Indexes.   These indexes are a good place to start your research because they cover a broad range of subjects. Most have separate author and subject listings as well as a list of book reviews. General indexes usually list articles from popular magazines, although some of them may include references to basic scholarly journals. Here is a list of the most common general indexes:

> *The Readers' Guide to Periodical Literature* (1900–; online and CD-ROM, 1983–); updated quarterly. Covers about two hundred popular periodicals and may help you launch your search for sources on general and current topics. Even for general topics, however, you should not rely on it exclusively. Nearly all college libraries house far more than two hundred periodicals, and university research libraries house twenty thousand or more. The *Readers' Guide* does not even attempt to cover the research journals that play such an important role in college writing. Here is an example of an entry for "home education":

> > **HOME EDUCATION**
> > Home-school kids in public-school activities. D. Brockett. *The Education Digest* v61 p67–9 N '95
> > Pros and cons of home schooling. il *Parents* v70 p18 N '95
> > Why homeschooling is important for America [address, August 11, 1995] S. L. Blumenfeld. *Vital Speeches of the Day* v61 p763–6 O 1 '95

> *Magazine Index.* On microfilm (1988–), online (1973–), and on CD-ROM as part of InfoTrac (1973–; see below). Indexes over four hundred magazines.

> *InfoTrac.* On CD-ROM or online. Time coverage will vary by subscription. Includes three indexes: (1) the *General Periodicals Index,* which covers over twelve hundred general-interest publications, incorporating the *Magazine Index* and including the *New York Times* and the *Wall Street Journal;* (2) the *Academic Index,* which covers four hundred scholarly and general-interest publications,

including the *New York Times;* and (3) the *National Newspaper Index,* which covers the *Christian Science Monitor, Los Angeles Times, New York Times, Wall Street Journal,* and *Washington Post.* Some entries also include abstracts of articles. This sample InfoTrac entry is from the *General Periodicals Index:*

AUTHOR(s):	Hawkins, Dana
TITLE(s):	Homeschool battles: clashes grow as some in the movement seek access to public schools. illustration photograph
Summary:	An estimated 500,000 students in the US study at home, and there is an increasing tension in some communities as some of the 'homeschoolers' attempt to use the public schools on a limited basis. The parents of one homeschooler in Oklahoma have sued the school district to gain access.
	U.S. News & World Report p57(2) Feb 12 1996 v120 n6
DESCRIPTORS:	Home schooling_Cases Public schools_Cases Education_Parent participation

more follows -- press <RETURN>   (Q to quit)

Access: The Supplementary Index to Periodicals (1979–). Indexes magazines not covered by the *Readers' Guide,* such as regional and particular-interest magazines (the environment, women's issues, etc.).

Alternative Press Index (1970–). Indexes alternative and radical publications.

Humanities Index (1974–; online and CD-ROM, 1984–). Covers 330 periodicals in archaeology, history, classics, literature, performing arts, philosophy, and religion.

Social Sciences Index (1974–; online and CD-ROM, 1983–). Covers four hundred periodicals in economics, geography, law, political science, psychology, public administration, and sociology. The complete text of certain articles is available on the CD-ROM.

Public Affairs Information Service Bulletin (PAIS) (1915–; online and CD-ROM, 1972–). Covers articles and other publications by public and private agencies on economic and social conditions, international relations, and public administration. Subject listings only.

Specialized Indexes and Abstracts.   Specialized indexes list or summarize articles devoted to technical or scholarly research. As you learn more about your topic, you will turn to specialized indexes and abstracts to find references to scholarly articles. The following example from *Sociological Abstracts,* which indexes and summarizes articles from a wide range of periodicals that publish sociological research, is typical of entries found in specialized indexes:

91X2727

Mayberry, Maralee & Knowles, J. Gary (Dept Sociology U Nevada, Las Vegas 89154), **Family Unity Objectives of Parents Who Teach Their Children: Ideological and Pedagogical Orientations to Home Schooling,** UM *The Urban Review,* 1989, 21, 4, Dec, 209–225.

¶ The objectives of parents who teach their children at home are examined, using results from 2 qualitative studies: (1) a study conducted in Ore in 1987/88, consisting of interview & questionnaire data (N = 15 & 800 families, respectively); & (2) an ongoing ethnographic study being conducted in Utah (N = 8 families). Analysis suggests that while families have complex motives for teaching their children at home, most respondents felt that establishing a home school would allow them to maintain or further develop unity within the family. It is concluded that a family's decision to home school is often made in an attempt to resist the effects on the family unit of urbanization & modernization. Policy implications are discussed. 36 References. Adapted from the source document. (Copyright 1991, Sociological Abstracts, Inc., all rights reserved.)

When you compare this entry with the previous citations from the *Readers' Guide* (p. 674) and InfoTrac's *General Periodicals Index* (p. 675), you will see differences in the following features:

- Format of the citations
- The authors' qualifications
- The titles of the articles
- The titles of the publications where the articles appear
- The length of the articles
- The amount of information given about the content of the articles

Here is a list of specialized periodical indexes that cover various disciplines:

ABI/INFORM (1971–) Online.

Accountant's Index (1944–).

America: History and Life (1954–; CD-ROM, 1964–).

American Statistics Index (1973–).

Applied Science and Technology Index (1958–). Online, CD-ROM.

Art Index (1929–; CD-ROM, 1984–).

Biological and Agricultural Index (1964–). CD-ROM.

Education Index (1929–). Online, CD-ROM.

Engineering Index (1920–).

Historical Abstracts (1955–; CD-ROM, 1982–).

Index Medicus (1961–). Online, CD-ROM (called MEDLINE).

MLA International Bibliography of Books and Articles in the Modern Languages and Literature (1921–). Online, CD-ROM.

Music Index. (1949–; CD-ROM, 1981–1989).

Philosopher's Index (1957–). Online.

Psychological Abstracts (1927–). Online (called PsycINFO), CD-ROM (called PsycLIT).

Physics Abstracts (1898–). Online (called INSPEC).

Science Abstracts (1898–).

Sociological Abstracts (1952–). Online, CD-ROM (called Sociofile).

Most periodical indexes and abstracts use their own system of subject headings. *Sociological Abstracts,* for example, has a separate volume for subject headings. Check the opening pages of the index or abstract you are using, or, for online and CD-ROM material, refer to the system documentation to see how it classifies subjects. Then look for periodicals under your most useful subject heading or the heading that seems most similar to it. If you are using the online version of a periodical index, look at information such as the descriptors, thesaurus terms, or subject heading field. Besides telling you what subject headings have been assigned to each reference, the subject headings may function as links to lists of related materials.

Computer Databases.   Most libraries subscribe to online database networks and may own CD-ROM machines that are accessible through the library's computer terminals. Most research databases—like those in the preceding lists—are electronic indexes listing thousands of books and articles.

When you use an online database, check the first screen, which should let you know what information you are accessing. Although you can search a database by author or title, most likely you will use keywords, or descriptors, that describe the subject. Make your descriptors as precise as possible so that your database search results in a manageable list of sources relevant to your topic. Most databases include a thesaurus of keywords or descriptors and a set of guidelines for using Boolean operators or other combining terms in your search. In addition, many databases include a browse function. When you enter a descriptor, the system automatically lists the terms that are close to it alphabetically. If you enter a very general descriptor, the system provides that general term along with subtopics. Use these subtopics to narrow your search further before you ask the system to retrieve records.

Once you have typed in your descriptors, the computer searches the database and lists every reference to them it finds. If your search is extensive, you can usually print the results or download the records to your own disk. Because online databases contain so much information, you may want to consult with a librarian to develop an efficient search strategy. Also keep in mind that most electronic indexes cover only the last ten to fifteen years; you may need to consult older printed versions of indexes as well.

In addition to the database versions of the indexes listed earlier, many libraries subscribe to computer services in particular subject areas that provide abstracts or the full text of articles, either in the database (so you can see them onscreen) or by mail or fax for a fee. The use of computers for scholarly research is becoming more widespread, with new technology being developed all the time, so be sure to check with a librarian about what is available at your library. Some common computer services include the following:

ERIC (Educational Resources Information Center) (CD-ROM, 1969–; online 1966–). Indexes, abstracts, and provides some full texts of articles from 750 education journals.

Business Periodicals Ondisc (1988–) and *ABI/INFORM* (1988–). Provide full-text articles from business periodicals. If your library has a laser printer attached to a terminal, you can print out articles, including illustrations.

PsycBooks (1987–). A CD-ROM database that indexes books and book chapters in psychology.

Carl/Uncover (1988–). <http://www.carl.org/carl.html>. An online document delivery service that lists over three million articles from twelve thousand journals. For a fee, you can receive the full text of the article by fax, usually within a few hours.

Interlibrary networks. Known by different names in different regions, these networks allow you to search in the catalogs of colleges and universities in your area and across the country. In many cases, you can request a book by interlibrary loan. It may take several weeks for you to receive the material. You can also request a copy of an article from a journal to which your own library does not subscribe. Most libraries do not loan their journals but will copy and forward articles for a fee.

Periodicals Representing Particular Viewpoints. Some specialized periodical indexes tend to represent particular viewpoints and may help you identify different positions on an issue.

Index to Black Periodicals (1984–). An author and subject index to general and scholarly articles about African Americans.

Left Index (1982–). An author and subject index to over eighty periodicals with a Marxist, radical, or left perspective. Listings primarily cover topics in the social sciences and humanities.

Chicano Index (1967–). An index to general and scholarly articles about Mexican Americans. Articles are arranged by subject with author and title indexes. (Before 1989, the title was *Chicano Periodical Index.*)

Another useful source for identifying positions is *Editorials on File,* described on p. 680.

Locating Periodicals in the Library. When you identify a promising magazine or journal article in a periodical index, you must go to the library's serial record, online catalog, or periodicals database to learn whether the library subscribes to the periodical and, if so, where you can find the issue you need. Although every library arranges its periodicals differently, recent issues of periodicals are usually arranged alphabetically by title on open shelves. Older issues may be bound like books (shelved by call numbers or alphabetically by title) or filmed and available in microform. Ask a librarian at the reference desk to find out how the periodicals in your library are arranged.

Suppose you want to look up the article on home schooling indexed in *Sociological Abstracts* (see p. 677). Here is a typical record for the *Urban Review* from a library's online catalog or periodicals database. Notice that the title search refers to the title of the journal, *Urban Review,* not the title of the article from the journal.

In this instance, you would learn that the library does subscribe to the *Urban Review* and that you could locate the 1989 article in one of the bound volumes in the library's collection. Remember that no library can subscribe to every periodical, so always copy down references to more articles than you need to look up. This will save you from frustration later when you find out that the library you are using does not subscribe to all the journals you need.

Using Collections of Electronic Journals.   Many large libraries subscribe to services that provide electronic access to the text of journals, usually to recent issues. These services tend to be expensive, so they may not be available in smaller college libraries. Ask the reference librarian if any of them are available to you. Table 21.5 lists some services that provide the full text of journals.

Finding Newspaper Articles

Newspapers provide useful information for many research topics in such areas as foreign affairs, economic issues, public opinion, and social trends. Libraries usually miniaturize newspapers and store them on microfilm (reels) or microfiche (cards) that must be placed in viewing machines to be read. Newspaper indexes such as the *Los Angeles Times Index, New York Times Index,* and *London Times Index* help you locate specific articles on your topic. College libraries usually have indexes to local newspapers as well.

Your library may also subscribe to newspaper article and digest services, such as the following:

Table 21.5 Some Collections of Electronic Journals

Service	Subject Areas	Source	Time Coverage
IDEAL Online Library <http://www.idealibrary.com/index.html>	Science, technology, mathematics, and social sciences	250 journals published by Academic Press, Churchill Livingstone, and W. B. Saunders	1997–present
LEXIS-NEXIS Academic Universe <http://www.lexis-nexis.com/lncc/academic>	Legal, news, government information, and statistics	Various academic journals and other sources	Varies by source
JSTOR <http://www.jstor.org>	Humanities and social sciences	117 academic journals	Provides electronic access to older issues
Project Muse <http://muse.jhu.edu>	Humanities, social sciences, and mathematics	Over forty journals from Johns Hopkins University Press	1996–present
Science Direct <http://www.sciencedirect.com>	Science, technology, medicine, and social sciences	More than a thousand Elsevier Press journals	1997–present

National Newspaper Index. On microfilm (1989–); online (1979–) and on CD-ROM as part of InfoTrac (see p. 674). Indexes the *Christian Science Monitor, Los Angeles Times, New York Times, Wall Street Journal,* and *Washington Post.*

NewsBank (1970–). On microfiche and CD-ROM. Full-text articles from five hundred U.S. newspapers. A good source of information on local and regional issues and trends.

Newspaper Abstracts (1988–; CD-ROM, 1991–). Indexes and gives brief abstracts of articles from nineteen major regional, national, and international newspapers.

Facts on File (weekly; CD-ROM, 1980–). A digest of U.S. and international news events arranged by subject, such as foreign affairs, arts, education, religion, and sports.

Editorials on File (twice monthly). A digest of editorials from 150 U.S. and Canadian newspapers. Each entry includes a brief description of an editorial subject followed by fifteen to twenty editorials on the subject, reprinted from different newspapers.

Editorial Research Reports (1924–). Reports on current and controversial topics, including brief histories, statistics, editorials, journal articles, endnotes, and supplementary reading lists.

African Recorder (1970–). Articles on African issues from African newspapers.

Asian Recorder (1971–). Articles on Asian issues from Asian newspapers.

Canadian News Facts (1972–). On CD-ROM. A digest of current articles from Canadian newspapers such as the *Montreal Star, Toronto Star,* and *Vancouver Sun.* Some articles are available as full text on the CD-ROM.

Foreign Broadcast Information Service (FBIS) (1980–). A digest of foreign broadcast scripts, newspaper articles, and government statements from Asia, Europe, Latin America, Africa, Russia, and the Middle East.

Keesing's Contemporary Archives (weekly). A digest of events in all countries, compiled from British reporting services. Includes speeches and statistics. Index includes chronological, geographic, and topical sections.

Finding Government and Statistical Information

Federal, state, and local governments are making more of their publications and services available through the World Wide Web. Ask a reference librarian for assistance in locating government sources on the Web. In addition, consider consulting the following sources for information on political subjects and national trends. Although these publications are not always listed in library catalogs or databases, they can usually be found in the reference area or the government documents department of college libraries. If these works are not listed in your library's online catalog, ask for assistance in locating them.

Sources for Researching Political Subjects. Two publications that report developments in the federal government can be rich sources of information on political issues. Types of material they cover include congressional hearings and debates, presidential proclamations and speeches, Supreme Court decisions and dissenting opinions, and compilations of statistics.

Congressional Quarterly Almanac (annual). A summary of legislation that provides an overview of government policies and trends, including analysis as well as election results, records of roll-call votes, and the text of significant speeches and debates.

Congressional Quarterly Weekly Report. A news service that includes up-to-date summaries of committee actions, votes, and executive branch activities as well as overviews of current policy discussions and other activities of the federal government.

Sources for Researching Trends. Research can help you identify trends to write about and, most important, provide the statistical evidence you need to demonstrate the existence of a trend. The following resources can be especially helpful:

For guidance on developing an argument that speculates about the causes of a trend, see Chapter 9.

Statistical Abstract of the United States (annual). Issued by the Bureau of the Census, this volume provides a variety of social, economic, and political statistics, often covering several years. It includes tables, graphs, and charts and gives references to additional sources of information. Selected information is available on the Web at <http://www.census.gov/statab/www>.

American Statistics Index (1974–; annual with monthly supplements). This index attempts to cover all federal government publications containing statistical information of research significance and includes brief descriptions of references.

Statistical Reference Index (1980–). Claiming to be "a selective guide to American statistical publications from sources other than the U.S. government," this index includes economic, social, and political statistical sources.

World Almanac and Book of Facts (annual). This publication presents information on a variety of subjects drawn from many sources. It includes such things as a chronology of the year, climatological data, and lists of inventions and awards.

The Gallup Poll: Public Opinion (1935–). This chronological listing of the results of public opinion polls includes information on social, economic, and political trends.

In addition to researching the trend itself, you may want to research others' speculations about its causes. If so, the reports of federal government activities described in the preceding section may be helpful.

Finding Other Library Sources

Libraries hold a vast amount of useful materials other than books, periodicals, and government documents. Some of the following library sources and services may be appropriate for your research.

- *Vertical files:* Pamphlets and brochures from government and private agencies
- *Special collections:* Manuscripts, rare books, and materials of local interest
- *Audio collections:* Records, audiotapes, music CDs, readings, and speeches
- *Video collections:* Slides, filmstrips, and videotapes
- *Art collections:* Drawings, paintings, and engravings
- *Interlibrary loans:* Many libraries can arrange to borrow books from other libraries or have copies of journal articles sent from other libraries as part of an interlibrary loan program. Ask your librarian how long it will take to get the material you need (usually several weeks) and how to use the loan service (some libraries allow you to send an electronic request to the local interlibrary loan office).
- *Computer resources:* Many libraries house interactive computer programs that combine text, video, and audio resources in history, literature, business, and other disciplines.

■ USING THE INTERNET FOR RESEARCH

The *Internet* is a vast global computer network that enables users to store and share information and resources quickly and easily. The World Wide Web is a network of Web sites, each with its own electronic address (called a URL, or uniform resource locator). You may be able to gain access to the Internet through your library or through a commercial Internet service provider (ISP). To search the Web, you also need a *Web browser* such as Netscape or Internet Explorer. By now, most of you are familiar with searching the Internet. This section will provide some basic background information about the Net and introduce you to some tools and strategies that will help you use the Internet more efficiently to find information on a topic.

Library catalogs, electronic periodical indexes and abstracts, full-text electronic journal databases, and many government sites are all a part of the Internet. In addition, many other types of resources on the Web can help you with your research topic.

As you use the Internet for conducting research, be sure to keep the following concerns and guidelines in mind.

- *The Internet has no central system of organization.* On the Internet, a vast amount of information is stored on many different networks, on different servers, and in different formats, each with its own system of organization. The Internet has no central catalog, reference librarian, or standard classification system for the vast resources available there.

- *Personal and commercial Internet sources can be less reliable than Internet sources to which your library or campus subscribes or than print sources.* Because it is relatively easy for anyone with a Web page to "publish" on the Internet, judging the reliability of online information is a special concern. Depending on your topic, purpose, and audience, the sources you find on the Internet may not be as credible or authoritative as library sources, and for some topics most of what you find may be written by amateurs. In most cases, you will need to balance or supplement personal or commercial Internet sources with subscription resources from your library or campus and print sources. When in doubt about the reliability of an online source for a particular assignment, check with your instructor. (See Reading Sources with a Critical Eye later in this chapter for more specific suggestions.)

- *Personal or commercial Internet sources may not be as stable as Internet sources to which the library or campus subscribes.* If you are looking for information on a topic, it is possible that a Web site that existed last week is no longer available today.

- *Internet sources must be documented.* The requirements for documenting source material found on the Internet and source materials found in more traditional sources are the same, though the formats are slightly different. You will need to follow appropriate conventions for quoting, paraphrasing, and documenting the online sources you cite, just as you do for print sources.

Citing Internet sources using MLA style is discussed in Chapter 22, pp. 711–15; APA style is discussed on pp. 722–24.

- *Keep a working bibliography.* A working bibliography for Internet research serves the same purpose as one for library research. It is an ongoing record of all the sources you discover as you research your subject. (See Figure 21.5 for an example.) The working bibliography becomes the draft for the list of works cited at the end of your essay, even if you do not include all these sources in your final list. The working bibliography will also help you keep track of the addresses (URLs) for the Web sites you visit.

As you locate useful Web sites, record this information in your working bibliography for each site you look up:

Author: _____

Title: _____

Site address: _____

Email address of webmaster: _____

Date of publication: _____

Date of latest update: _____

Linkage data: _____

Keywords: _____

Figure 21.5 Information for Working Bibliography—Internet Sources

■ NAVIGATING THE WEB

A *Web browser* is a software program that allows you to display and navigate Web pages on your computer. Web browsers have evolved from basic text-driven browsers such as Lynx into graphical, point-and-click interfaces such as Netscape Navigator and Microsoft Internet Explorer, which support not only text and hypertext links but also sound, images, animation, and video.

Finding Home Pages

A particular Web site usually consists of a home page and pages to which it is linked. A home page is the page you most often find first when you access a Web site; it typically provides a title heading, a brief introduction or overview; and a brief table of contents consisting of links to the information available at that site. In this way, it functions like the opening pages of a book. Figure 21.6 shows the home page for the National Home Education Network (NHEN). The bottom of a home page usually

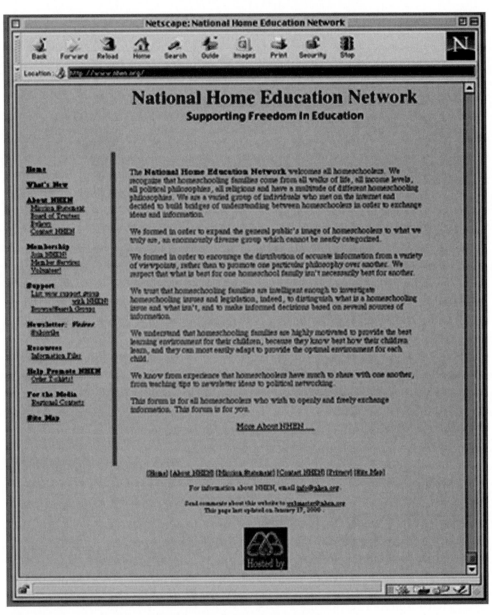

Figure 21.6 Home Page for the National Home Education Network

includes the name of the person or group responsible for the site and an email address to which you can send requests for further information. Companies, educational institutions, government agencies, organizations, clubs, or individuals can sponsor Web sites.

Using Links

On a World Wide Web page (and in other electronic documents, such as email), links to other information are often indicated by underlined text (sometimes with words in bold type or highlighted in another way). For example, the National Home Education Network home page provides a link to the NHEN newsletter, *Voices.* Links can also appear as boxes, buttons, icons, or other graphic images that, when clicked, link to further information. On a color monitor, they are indicated by a different color, and change color once they have been visited. In addition to providing connections to other documents, the links on a home page can perform many other functions — for example, they may open a form to be filled out by the reader, start a video, play music, generate sound, or provide a template for sending an email message to the person responsible for maintaining the Web site.

Understanding URLs

Each Web home page has its own address or uniform resource locator (URL). The URL allows people anywhere in the world to locate a particular Web page. The URL for the National Home Education Network follows the typical pattern: <http:// www.nhen.org>.

- The first part of a URL for a Web page usually consists of the abbreviation *http://* (meaning "hypertext transfer protocol"); it tells the sending and receiving computers how to transfer the information being sent.

- The second part of the URL includes the standard *www.,* to establish that the location being accessed is on the World Wide Web, as well as the Internet address of the institution, government agency, corporation, or organization (and the country, if outside of the United States) where the document is located. The following three-letter suffix tells the domain of the site, that is, who owns the computer storing the information. *nhen.org* is the address of the National Home Education Network site. The suffix *.org* indicates that it is a site maintained by an organization.

  > .com = commercial site
  > .edu = educational institution site
  > .gov = government site
  > .org = organization site
  > .mil = military site
  > .net = Internet service site

- After a slash, the third part of the URL (which may be quite lengthy) gives the address of the directory and file where the page is found as well as the name of the specific page itself (as in *newsletter/index.html* for the NHEN newsletter, *Voices.*

Creating Bookmarks

When you find a Web page that you may want to visit again, it is a good idea to create a bookmark for that page. For example, in the Netscape program you create a bookmark by choosing Add Bookmark from the Bookmarks menu. The title of the Web page and its URL will be stored in the bookmarks list of the computer you are using. If you are using a computer in a lab, not your own computer at home, you will need to download your bookmarks on to a disk if you want to save them. If you want to return to a site and are unfamiliar with using bookmarks, it is a good idea to write down the URL.

Accessing a Web Site

You may directly access a particular Web site in several ways:

- By typing the URL directly into the location box and then pressing Return or Enter on your keyboard
- By selecting Open Location from the file menu and typing the URL into the dialogue box
- By pasting or copying the URL into the location box from some other source, such as the computer's scrapbook or clipboard
- By selecting the URL from the bookmark menu, if you have previously saved a bookmark for that page

The method you use to access a URL may depend on your Web browser.

■ USING SEARCH ENGINES

Because the World Wide Web does not have a central directory that will point you to specific resources, *search engines* are important resources for searching the Web for information on your topic. Search engines will help you look for information, but in order to use them effectively, you should understand their features, strengths, and limitations. Just as there are many periodical indexes available to help you find articles on your topic, there are many search engines available to help you look for information on the Internet. Table 21.6 lists some popular search engines. However, no *single* search engine searches *every* Web site. In fact, according to an article by Steve Lawrence and C. Lee Giles that appeared in the July 8, 1999, issue of *Nature:*

- No one search engine covers more than 16 percent of the Web.
- Search engine overlap "remains relatively low." (This means that different search engines point you to different Web sites even when you enter the same information.)
- Used together, eleven major search engines (AltaVista, EuroSeek, Excite, Google, HotBot, Infoseek, Lycos, MSN Search, Northern Light, Snap, WebCrawler, and Yahoo!) produce 42-percent coverage of the Web.
- "Popularity" of a Web page (that is, a page with many links, which results in the page being accessed many times) is growing in use as a ranking factor in results lists.

Table 21.6 Commonly Used Search Engines and Meta-Search Engines

Name	URL
Search Engines	
AltaVista	<http://www.altavista.com>
EuroSeek	<http://www.euroseek.net>
Excite	<http://www.excite.com>
Google	<http://www.google.com>
HotBot	<http://www.hotbot.com>
Infoseek	<http://infoseek.go.com>
Lycos	<http://www.lycos.com>
MSN Search	<http://search.msn.com>
Northern Light	<http://www.northernlight.com>
Snap	<http://www.snap.com>
WebCrawler	<http://webcrawler.com>
Yahoo!	<http://www.yahoo.com>
Meta-Search Engines (search multiple search engines and directories)	
All-in-One Search Page	<http://www.allonesearch.com>
Dogpile	<http://www.dogpile.com>
MetaCrawler	<http://www.metacrawler.com>
ProFusion	<http://www.profusion.com>
SavvySearch	<http://www.savvysearch.com>
WebTaxi SuperSearch	<http://www.webtaxi.com/taxi/sswebtop.htm>

Always click on the link called "Help," "Hints," or "Tips" on a search engine's Web page to find out more about the recognized commands and advanced search techniques for that specific search engine. Table 21.7 lists some common search engine commands that yield powerful results. These work in most search engines. Double-check the help section if you do not get the results you expect.

Finally, the success of a Web search depends on the keywords you choose; most initial searches yield more sources than any person could look at in a lifetime. Try to narrow your search by using some of the keyword and search techniques described in this chapter (see pp. 664–67 and 667–71). Remember that many different words often describe the same topic. If your topic is ecology, for example, you may find information under the keywords *ecosystem, environment, pollution,* and *endangered species,* as well as a number of other related keywords, depending on the focus of your research. When you find a source that seems promising, be sure to create a bookmark for the Web page so that you can return to it easily later on.

Table 21.7 Common Search-Engine Commands

+	A plus sign **requires** all the terms to be in any records retrieved or at least pages not having all the terms will appear toward the end of the list. Operation is similar to an AND Boolean operator (see p. 669).
-	A minus sign **excludes** pages that have the identified term or at least the pages retrieved will appear toward the end of the list. Operation is similar to a NOT Boolean operator (see p. 669).
" "	Quotation marks around a set of words cause them to be searched together as a phrase; for example, "home schooling."
*	A **truncation** symbol includes related word variations (see p. 671).
a A	If you want the word you are looking for only if it is capitalized (in a proper noun like *California*, for example), capitalize the word when you enter it into the search engine. This will exclude pages that have only noncapitalized instances of the word.

■ READING SOURCES WITH A CRITICAL EYE

From the beginning of your search, you should evaluate potential sources to determine which ones to use in your essay. Obviously, you must decide which sources provide information relevant to the topic. But you must also read sources with a critical eye to decide how credible or trustworthy they are. Just because a book or essay appears in print or online does not necessarily mean that an author's information or opinions are reliable.

Selecting Relevant Sources

Begin your evaluation of sources by narrowing your working bibliography to the most relevant works. Consider them in terms of scope, date of publication, and viewpoint.

Scope and Approach. To decide how relevant a particular source is to your topic, you need to examine the source in depth. Do not depend on title alone, for it may be misleading. If the source is a book, check its table of contents and index to see how many pages are devoted to the precise subject you are exploring. In most cases, you will want an in-depth, not a superficial, treatment of the subject. Read the preface or introduction to a book or the abstract or opening paragraphs of an article and any biographical information given about the author to determine the author's basic approach to the subject or special way of looking at it. As you attend to these elements, consider the following questions:

- Does the source provide a general or specialized view? General sources are helpful early in your research, but then you need the authority or up-to-date coverage of specialized sources. Extremely specialized works, however, may be too technical.
- Is the source long enough to provide adequate detail?
- Is the source written for general readers? Specialists? Advocates? Critics?

- Is the author an expert on the topic? Does the author's way of looking at the topic support or challenge your own views? (The fact that an author's viewpoint challenges your own does not mean that you should reject the author as a source, as you will see from the discussion on multiple viewpoints.)
- Is the information in the source substantiated elsewhere? Does its approach seem to be comparable to, or a significant challenge to, the approaches of other credible sources?

Date of Publication.   Although you should always consult the most up-to-date sources available on your subject, older sources often establish the principles, theories, and data on which later work is based and may provide a useful perspective for evaluating it. If older works are considered authoritative, you may want to become familiar with them. To determine which sources are authoritative, note the ones that are cited most often in encyclopedia articles, bibliographies, and recent works on the subject. If your source is on the Web, consider whether it has been regularly updated.

Viewpoint.   Your sources should represent a variety of viewpoints on the subject. Just as you would not depend on a single author for all of your information, so you do not want to use authors who all belong to the same school of thought. For suggestions on determining authors' viewpoints, see the following Identifying Bias section.

Using sources that represent different viewpoints is especially important when developing an argument for one of the essay assignments in Chapters 6–10. During the invention work in those chapters, you may want to research what others have said about your subject to see what positions have been staked out and what arguments have been made. You will then be able to define the issue more carefully, collect arguments supporting your position, and anticipate arguments opposing it.

Identifying Bias

One of the most important aspects of evaluating a source is identifying any bias in its treatment of the subject. Although the word *bias* may sound accusatory, it simply refers to the fact that most writing is not neutral or objective and does not try or claim to be. Authors come to their subjects with particular viewpoints. In using sources, you must consider carefully how these viewpoints are reflected in the writing and how they affect the way authors present their arguments.

Although the text of the source will give you the most precise indication of the author's viewpoint, you can often get a good idea by looking at the preface or introduction or at the sources the author cites. When you examine a reference, you can often determine the general point of view it represents by considering the following elements.

Title.   Does the title or subtitle indicate the text's bias? Watch for loaded words or confrontational phrasing.

Author. What is the author's professional title or affiliation? What is the author's perspective? Is the author in favor of something or at odds with it? What has persuaded the author to take this stance? How might the author's professional affiliation affect his or her perspective? What is the author's tone? Information on the author may also be available in the book or article itself, the Web page, or in biographical sources available in the library.

Presentation of Argument. Almost every written work asserts a point of view or makes an argument for something the author considers important. To determine this position and the reason behind it, look for the main point. What evidence does the author provide as support for this point? Is the evidence from authoritative sources? Is the evidence persuasive? Does the author accommodate or refute opposing arguments?

For more detail on these argumentative strategies, see Chapter 19.

Publication Information. Is the book published by a commercial publisher, a corporation, a government agency, or an interest group? Is the Web site sponsored by a business, a professional group, an educational institution, or a government agency? What is that organization's position on the topic? Is the author funded by or affiliated with the organization?

Editorial Slant. What kind of periodical or online source published the article — popular, academic, alternative? If the article is available on a Web site, is the site maintained by a commercial or academic organization? Does the site provide links to other Web resources? For periodicals, knowing some background about the publisher or periodical can help to determine bias because all periodicals have their own editorial slants. In cases where the publication title does not indicate bias, reference sources may help you determine this information. Two of the most common are the following:

Gale Directory of Publications and Broadcast Media (1990–, updated yearly). A useful source for descriptive information on newspapers and magazines. Entries often include an indication of intended audience and political or other bias. For example, the *San Diego Union* is described as a "newspaper with a Republican orientation."

Magazines for Libraries (1997). A listing of over 6,500 periodicals arranged by academic discipline. For each discipline, there is a list of basic indexes, abstracts, and periodicals. Each individual listing for a periodical includes its publisher, the date it was founded, the places it is indexed, its intended audience, and an evaluation of its content and editorial focus. Here is an example of one such listing:

> 2605. *Growing Without Schooling.* [ISSN: 0745-5305]
> 1977. bi-m. $25. Susannah Sheffer. Holt Assocs., 2269
> Massachusetts Ave., Cambridge, MA 02140. Illus.,
> index, adv. Sample. Circ: 5,000.
> *Bk. rev:* 0–4, 400–600 words, signed. *Aud:* Ga, Sa.

GWS is a journal by and for home schoolers. Parents and students share their views as to why they chose home schooling and what they like about it. While lesson plans or activities are not included, home schoolers could get ideas for interesting activities from articles chronicling their experiences ("Helping Flood Victims," "Legislative Intern"). "News and Reports" offers home schoolers information on legal issues while the "Declassified Ads" suggest resources geared toward home schoolers. This is an important title for public libraries and should be available to students and faculty in teacher preparation programs.

Using and Acknowledging Sources

22

In addition to your own firsthand observation and analysis, your writing in college will be expected to use and acknowledge secondary sources—readings, interviews, Web sites, computer bulletin boards, lectures, and other print and nonprint materials.

When you cite material from another source, you need to acknowledge the source, usually by citing the author and page or date (depending on the documentation system) in your text and including a list of works cited or references at the end of your paper. It is necessary to acknowledge sources correctly and accurately in order to avoid *plagiarism*. Plagiarism is the act of using the words and ideas of others as if they were your own. By citing sources correctly, you give credit to the originator of the words and ideas you are using, give your readers the information they need to consult those sources directly, and build your own credibility.

This chapter provides guidelines for using sources effectively and acknowledging them accurately. It includes model citations for both the Modern Language Association (MLA) and American Psychological Association (APA) documentation styles and presents a sample research paper that follows the MLA format.

◼ USING SOURCES

Writers commonly use sources by quoting directly, by paraphrasing, and by summarizing. This section provides guidelines for deciding when to use each of these three methods and how to do so effectively.

Deciding Whether to Quote, Paraphrase, or Summarize

As a general rule, quote only in these situations: (1) when the wording of the source is particularly memorable or vivid or expresses a point so well that you cannot improve it without destroying the meaning, (2) when the words of reliable and respected authorities would lend support to your position, (3) when you wish to highlight the author's opinions, (4) when you wish to cite an author whose opinions challenge or vary greatly from those of other experts, or (5) when you are going to discuss the source's choice of words. Paraphrase passages whose details you wish to note completely but whose language is not particularly striking. Summarize any long passages whose main points you wish to record selectively as background or general support for a point you are making.

Quoting

Quotations should duplicate the source exactly. If the source has an error, copy it and add the notation *sic* (Latin for "thus") in brackets immediately after the error to indicate that it is not your error but your source's:

> According to a recent newspaper article, "Plagirism [sic] is a problem among journalists and scholars as well as students" (Berensen 62).

However, you can change quotations (1) to emphasize particular words by underlining or italicizing them, (2) to omit irrelevant information or to make the quotation conform grammatically to your sentence by using ellipsis marks, and (3) to make the quotation conform grammatically or to insert information by using brackets.

Underlining or Italicizing for Emphasis.   You may underline or italicize any words in the quotation that you want to emphasize, and add the words *emphasis added* (in regular type, not italicized or underlined) in brackets immediately after the words you want to emphasize.

> In his introduction, Studs Terkel (1972) claims that his book is about a search for "daily meaning as well as daily bread, for recognition as well as cash, for astonishment rather than torpor [emphasis added]; in short, for a sort of life rather than a Monday through Friday sort of dying" (p. xi).

Using Ellipsis Marks for Omissions.   Ellipsis marks — three spaced periods (. . .) — signal that something has been left out of a quotation. When you omit words from within a quotation, you must use ellipsis marks in place of the missing words. If you are following the MLA style, place brackets around ellipses you have inserted to distinguish them from any ellipsis marks the author may have used. When the omission occurs within the sentence, include a space before the first bracket and after the closing bracket. There should also be spaces between the three ellipsis marks, but not between the opening bracket and the first ellipsis point or between the closing bracket and the last ellipsis point.

> Hermione Roddice is described in Lawrence's *Women in Love* as a "woman of the new school, full of intellectuality and [. . .] nerve-worn with consciousness" (17).

When the omission falls at the end of a sentence, place a sentence period *directly after* the closing bracket.

> But Grimaldi's recent commentary on Aristotle contends that for Aristotle rhetoric, like dialectic, had "no limited and unique subject matter upon which it must be exercised [. . .]. Instead, rhetoric as an art transcends all specific disciplines and may be brought into play in them" (6).

A period plus ellipsis marks can indicate the omission of the rest of the sentence as well as whole sentences, paragraphs, or even pages.

When a parenthetical reference follows the ellipsis marks at the end of a sentence, place the three spaced periods after the quotation, and place the sentence period after the final parenthesis:

> But Grimaldi's recent commentary on Aristotle contends that for Aristotle rhetoric, like dialectic, had "no limited and unique subject matter upon which it must be exercised [. . .]" (6).

Of course, a writer may decide to leave certain words out of a quotation because they are not relevant to the point being made or because they add information readers will not need in the context in which the quotation is being used. When you quote only single words or phrases, you do not need to use ellipsis marks because it will be obvious that you have left out some of the original.

> More specifically, Wharton's imagery of suffusing brightness transforms Undine before her glass into "some fabled creature whose home was in a beam of light" (21).

Using Brackets for Insertions or Changes.   Use brackets around an insertion or a change needed to make a quotation conform grammatically to your sentence, such as a change in the tense of a verb, in the capitalization of the first letter of the first word of a quotation, or in a pronoun. In this example from an essay on James Joyce's "Araby," reprinted in Chapter 10, the writer adapts Joyce's phrases "we played till our bodies glowed" and "shook music from the buckled harness" to fit the tense of her sentences:

> In the dark, cold streets during the "short days of winter," the boys must generate their own heat by "[playing] till [their] bodies glowed." Music is "[shaken] from the buckled harness" as if it were unnatural, and the singers in the market chant nasally of "the troubles in our native land" (30).

You may also use brackets to add or substitute explanatory material in a quotation:

> Guterson notes that among Native Americans in Florida, "education was in the home; learning by doing was reinforced by the myths and legends which repeated the basic value system of their [the Seminoles'] way of life" (159).

Several kinds of changes necessary to make a quotation conform grammatically to another sentence may be made without any signal to readers: (1) A period at the end of a quotation may be changed to a comma if you are using the quotation within your own sentence, and (2) double quotation marks enclosing a quotation may be changed to single quotation marks when the quotation is enclosed within a longer quotation.

Integrating Quotations

Depending on its length, a quotation may be incorporated into your text by enclosing it in quotation marks or set off from your text in a block without quotation marks. In either case, be sure to blend the quotation into your essay rather than dropping it in without appropriate integration.

In-Text Quotations.   Incorporate brief quotations (no more than four typed lines of prose or three lines of poetry) into your text. You may place the quotation virtually anywhere in your sentence:

At the Beginning

"To live a life is not to cross a field," Sutherland quotes Pasternak at the beginning of her narrative (11).

In the Middle

Woolf begins and ends by speaking of the need of the woman writer to have "money and a room of her own" (4)—an idea that certainly spoke to Plath's condition.

At the End

In *The Second Sex,* Simone de Beauvoir describes such an experience as one in which the girl "becomes as object, and she sees herself as object" (378).

Divided by Your Own Words

"Science usually prefers the literal to the nonliteral term," Kinneavy writes, "—that is, figures of speech are often out of place in science" (177).

When you quote poetry within your text, use a slash (/) with spaces before and after to signal the end of each line of verse:

Alluding to St. Augustine's distinction between the City of God and the Earthly City, Lowell writes that "much against my will / I left the City of God where it belongs" (4–5).

Block Quotations.   In the MLA style, put in block form prose quotations of five or more typed lines and poetry quotations of four or more lines. In the APA style, use block form for quotations of forty words or more. If you are using the MLA style, indent the quotation an inch (ten character spaces) from the left margin, as shown in the following example. If you are using the APA style, indent the block quotation five to seven spaces, keeping your indents consistent throughout your paper.

In a block quotation, double-space between lines just as you do in your text. *Do not* enclose the passage within quotation marks. Use a colon to introduce a block quotation, unless the context calls for another punctuation mark or none at all. When quoting a single paragraph or part of one in the MLA style, do not indent the first line of the quotation more than the rest. In quoting two or more paragraphs, indent the first line of each paragraph an extra quarter inch (three spaces). If you are using the APA style, the first line of subsequent paragraphs in the block quotation indents an additional five to seven spaces from the block quotation indent.

```
In "A Literary Legacy from Dunbar to Baraka," Margaret Walker
says of Paul Lawrence Dunbar's dialect poems:
         He realized that the white world in the United
              States tolerated his literary genius only because of
```

his "jingles in a broken tongue," and they found the old "darky" tales and speech amusing and within the vein of folklore into which they wished to classify all Negro life. This troubled Dunbar because he realized that white America was denigrating him as a writer and as a man. (70)

Punctuating Introductory Statements

Statements that introduce quotations take a range of punctuation marks and lead-in words. Let us look at some examples of ways writers typically introduce quotations.

Introducing a Statement with a Colon

A colon usually follows an independent clause placed before the quotation.

As George Williams notes, protection of white privilege is critical to patterns of discrimination: "Whenever a number of persons within a society have enjoyed for a considerable period of time certain opportunities for getting wealth, for exercising power and authority, and for successfully claiming prestige and social deference, there is a strong tendency for these people to feel that these benefits are theirs 'by right'" (727).

Introducing a Statement with a Comma

A comma usually follows an introduction that incorporates the quotation in its sentence structure.

Similarly, Duncan Turner asserts, "As matters now stand, it is unwise to talk about communication without some understanding of Burke" (259).

Introducing a Statement Using that

No punctuation is generally needed with *that*, and no capital letter is used to begin the quotation.

Noting this failure, Alice Miller asserts that "the reason for her despair was not her suffering but the impossibility of communicating her suffering to another person" (255).

Introducing a Statement Using as . . . said

Using *as* to introduce a quotation places the time of the statement in the past tense, not the present. Without *as*, generally use the present tense to describe authors speaking through their writing. Use the past tense for historical events.

The token women writers authenticated the male canon without disrupting it, for as Ruth Bleier has said, "The last thing society desires of its women has been intellectuality and independence" (73).

Punctuating within Quotations

Although punctuation within a quotation should reproduce the original, some adaptations may be necessary. Use single quotation marks for quotations within the quotation:

Original from Guterson (16–17)

E. D. Hirsch also recognizes the connection between family and learning, suggesting in his discussion of family background and academic achievement "that the significant part of our children's education has been going on outside rather than inside the schools."

Quoted Version

Guterson claims that E. D. Hirsch "also recognizes the connection between family and learning, suggesting in his discussion of family background and academic achievement 'that the significant part of our children's education has been going on outside rather than inside the schools'" (16–17).

If the quotation ends with a question mark or an exclamation point, retain the original punctuation:

"Did you think I loved you?" Edith later asks Dombey (566).

If a quotation ending with a question mark or an exclamation point concludes your sentence, retain the question mark or exclamation point, and put the parenthetical reference and sentence period outside the quotation marks:

Edith later asks Dombey, "Did you think I loved you?" (566).

Avoiding Grammatical Tangles

When you incorporate quotations into your writing, and especially when you omit words from quotations, you run the risk of creating ungrammatical sentences. Three common errors you should try to avoid are verb incompatibility, ungrammatical omissions, and sentence fragments.

Verb Incompatibility. When this error occurs, the verb form in the introductory statement is grammatically incompatible with the verb form in the quotation. When your quotation has a verb form that does not fit in with your text, it is usually possible to use just part of the quotation, thus avoiding verb incompatibility.

> ► The narrator suggests his bitter disappointment when "~~I saw myself~~ *he describes seeing himself* as a creature driven and derided by vanity" (35).

As this sentence illustrates, use the present tense when you refer to events in a literary work.

Ungrammatical Omission.   Sometimes omitting text from a quotation leaves you with an ungrammatical sentence. Two ways of correcting the grammar are (1) adapting the quotation (with brackets) so that its parts fit together grammatically and (2) using only one part of the quotation.

▶ From the moment of the boy's arrival in Araby, the bazaar is presented as a

commercial enterprise: "I could not find any sixpenny entrance and [. . .]

hand[ed]
~~handing~~ a shilling to a weary-looking man" (34).
^

▶ From the moment of the boy's arrival in Araby, the bazaar is presented as a

He
commercial enterprise: "I could not find any sixpenny entrance and [. . .]

so had to pay a shilling to get in (34).
^
~~handing a shilling to a weary-looking man" (34).~~
^

Sentence Fragment.   Sometimes when a quotation is a complete sentence, writers neglect the sentence that introduces the quote—for example, by forgetting to include a verb. It is important to make sure that the quotation is introduced by a complete sentence.

leads
▶ The girl's interest in the bazaar ~~leading~~ the narrator to make what amounts
^
to a sacred oath: "If I go [. . .] I will bring you something" (32).

Paraphrasing and Summarizing

In addition to quoting sources, writers have the option of paraphrasing or summarizing what others have written. In a *paraphrase,* the writer restates primarily in his or her own words all the relevant information from a passage, without any additional comments or elaborations. A paraphrase is useful for recording details of the passage when the order of the details is important but the source's wording is not. Because all the details of the passage are included, a paraphrase is often about the same length as the original passage.

In a *summary,* the writer boils down a long passage—several pages or even a whole chapter or book—to its main ideas. Unlike a paraphrase, a summary conveys the gist of a source, using just enough information to record the points the summarizer chooses to emphasize. In choosing what to include in a summary, be sure not to distort the author's meaning. Whereas a paraphrase may be as long as or even longer than the original, a summary is generally much shorter than the original passage.

To avoid plagiarizing inadvertently, you must use *your own words and sentence structures* when paraphrasing or summarizing. If you include an author's original expressions, enclose them in quotation marks. In the examples below, notice that the names for the two groups—"discovery theorists" and "assimilationist theorists"—are in quotation marks. Even when a paraphrase or a summary is restated in your own words, you still need to include a citation in your text that identifies the original source of the ideas. If you are uncertain about a particular paraphrase or summary, ask your instructor for help while you are still drafting your paper.

Here is a passage from a book on home schooling and an example of a paraphrase:

Original Passage

Bruner and the discovery theorists have also illuminated conditions that apparently pave the way for learning. It is significant that these conditions are unique to each learner, so unique, in fact, that in many cases classrooms can't provide them. Bruner also contends that the more one discovers information in a great variety of circumstances, the more likely one is to develop the inner categories required to organize that information. Yet life at school, which is for the most part generic and predictable, daily keeps many children from the great variety of circumstances they need to learn well.

–David Guterson, *Family Matters: Why Homeschooling Makes Sense,* p. 172

Paraphrase

According to Guterson (172), the "discovery theorists," particularly Bruner, have identified the conditions that allow learning to take place. Because these conditions are specific to each individual, many children are not able to learn in the classroom. According to Bruner, when people can explore information in different situations, they learn to classify and order what they discover. The general routine of the school day, however, does not provide children with the diverse activities and situations that would allow them to learn these skills.

Here is an example of a summary of the longer section that contains the original passage:

In looking at different theories of learning that discuss individual-based programs (such as home schooling) versus the public school system, Guterson describes the disagreements among "cognitivist" theorists. One group, the "discovery theorists," believes that individual children learn by creating their own ways of sorting the information they take in from their experiences. Schools should help students develop better ways of organizing new material, not just present them with material that is already categorized, as traditional schools do. "Assimilationist theorists," by contrast, believe that children learn by linking what they don't know to information they already know. These theorists claim that traditional schools help students learn when they present information in ways that allow children to fit the new material into categories they have already developed (171–75).

Introducing Cited Material

Notice in the preceding examples that the source is acknowledged by name. Even when you use your own words to present someone else's information, you must acknowledge that you borrowed the information. The only types of information that do not require acknowledgment are common knowledge (John F. Kennedy was assassinated in Dallas), familiar sayings ("Haste makes waste"), and well-known quotations ("To be or not to be. That is the question").

The documentation guidelines later in this chapter present various ways of citing the sources you quote, paraphrase, and summarize; the important thing is that your readers can tell where words or ideas that are not your own begin and end. You can accomplish this most readily by separating your words from those of the source with *signal phrases* such as "According to Smith," "Peters claims," and "As Olmos asserts." When you cite a source for the first time, you may use the author's full name; after that, use just the last name.

Avoiding Plagiarism

Writers—students and professionals alike—occasionally fail to acknowledge sources properly. The word *plagiarism,* which derives from the Latin word for "kidnapping," refers to the unacknowledged use of another's words, ideas, or information. Students sometimes get into trouble because they mistakenly assume that plagiarizing occurs only when another writer's exact words are used without acknowledgment. In fact, plagiarism applies to such diverse forms of expression as musical compositions and visual images as well as ideas and statistics. So keep in mind that you must indicate the source of any information or ideas you use in your essay, whether you have paraphrased, summarized, or quoted directly from the source.

Some people plagiarize simply because they do not know the conventions for using and acknowledging sources. This chapter makes clear how to incorporate sources into your writing and how to acknowledge your use of those sources. Others plagiarize because they keep sloppy notes and thus fail to distinguish between their own and their sources' ideas. Either they neglect to enclose their sources' words in quotation marks, or they fail to indicate when they are paraphrasing or summarizing a source's ideas and information. If you keep a working bibliography and careful notes, you will not make this serious mistake.

For more on keeping a working bibliography, see Chapter 21, pp. 659–60.

Another reason some people plagiarize is that they doubt their ability to write the essay by themselves. They feel intimidated by the writing task or the deadline or their own and others' expectations. If you experience this same anxiety about your work, speak to your instructor. Do not run the risk of failing a course or being expelled because of plagiarism. If you are confused about what is and what is not plagiarism, be sure to ask your instructor.

■ ACKNOWLEDGING SOURCES

Although there is no universally accepted system for acknowledging sources, there is agreement on both the need for documentation and the details that should be included. Writers should acknowledge sources for three reasons: to give credit to those sources, to enable readers to consult those sources for further information, and to give credibility and authority to the work they produce.

Most documentation styles combine in-text citations keyed to a separate list of works cited or references. The information required in the in-text citations and the order and content of the works-cited entries vary across the disciplines, but two styles predominate: the author-page system, used in the humanities and advocated by the Modern Language Association (MLA), and the author-year system, used in the natural and social sciences and advocated by the American Psychological Association (APA). Check with your instructor about which of these styles to use or whether you should use some other style. A list of common documentation style manuals is provided in Table 22.1.

This section presents the basic features of the MLA and APA documentation styles. In Part One of this book, you can find examples of student essays that follow the MLA style (Linh Kieu Ngo, Chapter 5; Jessica Statsky, Chapter 6; Kristine Potter, Chapter 8; Sarah West, Chapter 9) and that use the APA style (Patrick O'Malley, Chapter 7). For more information about these documentation styles, consult the *MLA Handbook for Writers of Research Papers,* Fifth Edition (1999), or the *Publication Manual of the American Psychological Association,* Fourth Edition (1994).

Table 22.1 Some Commonly Used Documentation Style Manuals

Subject	*Style Manual*	*Online Source*
General	*The Chicago Manual of Style.* 14th ed. 1993.	http://www.bedfordstmartins.com/online/cite7.html
	A Manual for Writers of Term Papers, Theses, and Dissertations. 6th ed. 1996.	—
Online Sources	*Online! A Reference Guide to Using Internet Sources.* 2000.	http://www.bedfordstmartins.com/online/index.html
	Columbia Guide to Online Style. 1998.	http://www.columbia.edu/cu/cup/cgos/idx_basic.html
	Electronic Styles: A Handbook for Citing Electronic Information. 1996.	
Biological Sciences	*Scientific Style and Format: The CBE Manual for Authors, Editors, and Publishers.* 6th ed. 1994.	http://www.bedfordstmartins.com/online/cite8.html
Chemistry	*The ACS Style Guide.* 2nd ed. 1997.	—
Government Documents	*The Complete Guide to Citing Government Documents.* Rev. ed. 1993.	http://www.lib.memphis.edu/gpo/citeweb.htm
Humanities	*MLA Handbook for Writers of Research Papers.* 5th ed. 1999.	http://www.mla.org/style/handbook.htm http://www.bedfordstmartins.com/online/cite5.html
	MLA Style Manual and Guide to Scholarly Publishing. 2nd ed. 1998.	http://www.bedfordstmartins.com/online/cite5.html http://www.uvm.edu/~ncrane/estyles http://www.mla.org/style/manual.htm
Psychology/Social Sciences	*Publication Manual of the American Psychological Association.* 4th ed. 1994.	http://www.apa.org/journals/webref.html http://www.bedfordstmartins.com/online/cite6.html http://www.uvm.edu/~ncrane/estyles

The MLA System of Documentation

Citations in Text

AUTHOR INDICATED IN PARENTHESES

The MLA author-page system requires that in-text citations include the author's last name and the page number of the passage being cited. There is no punctuation between author and page.

> Dr. James is described as a "not-too-skeletal Ichabod Crane" (Simon 68).

Note that the parenthetical citation comes before the final period. With block quotations, however, the citation comes after the final period, preceded by a space (see p. 697 for an example).

AUTHOR INDICATED IN A SIGNAL PHRASE

If the author's name is mentioned in your text, supply the page reference in parentheses following the quoted material as closely as possible without disrupting the flow of the sentence.

> Simon describes Dr. James as a "not-too-skeletal Ichabod Crane" (68).

A WORK WITH MORE THAN ONE AUTHOR

To cite a source by two or three authors, include all the authors' last names; for works with more than three authors, use all the authors' names or just the first author's name followed by *et al.*, meaning "and others," in regular type (not italicized or underlined).

> Dyal, Corning, and Willows identify several types of students, including the "Authority-Rebel" (4).

> The Authority-Rebel "tends to see himself as superior to other students in the class" (Dyal, Corning, and Willows 4).

> The drug AZT has been shown to reduce the risk of transmission from HIV-positive mothers to their infants by as much as two-thirds (Van de Perre et al. 4–5).

TWO OR MORE WORKS BY THE SAME AUTHOR

Include the author's last name, a shortened version of the title, and the page number(s).

> When old paint becomes transparent, it sometimes shows the artist's original plans: "a tree will show through a woman's dress" (Hellman, Pentimento 1).

A WORK WITH AN UNKNOWN AUTHOR

Use a shortened version of the title. Begin the shortened version with the word by which the title is alphabetized in the works-cited list.

An international pollution treaty still to be ratified would prohibit all plastic garbage from being dumped at sea ("Awash" 26).

TWO OR MORE AUTHORS WITH THE SAME LAST NAME CITED IN YOUR ESSAY

In addition to the last name, include each author's first initial in the citation. If the first initials are also the same, spell out the authors' first names.

Chaplin's Modern Times provides a good example of montage used to make an editorial statement (E. Roberts 246).

A CORPORATE OR GOVERNMENT AUTHOR

When you use a parenthetical citation, give the full name of a corporate author if it is brief or a shortened version if it is long. When you name the author in your text such as in a signal phrase, give the full name even if it is long.

A tuition increase has been proposed for community and technical colleges to offset budget deficits from Initiative 601 (Washington State Board 4).

According to the Washington State Board for Community and Technical Colleges, a tuition increase . . . from Initiative 601 (4).

A MULTIVOLUME WORK

When you use two or more volumes, include the volume number and the page number(s) for each volume of the work, separated by a colon and one space.

According to Forster, modernist writers valued experimentation and gradually sought to blur the line between poetry and prose (3: 150).

If you cite only one volume of a multivolume work in your paper, give the volume number in the works-cited entry (see p. 708) and include only the page number(s) in the parenthetical citation.

A LITERARY WORK

For a novel or other prose work available in various editions, provide the page numbers from the edition used as well as other information that will help readers locate the quotation in a different edition, such as the part or chapter number.

In Hard Times, Tom reveals his utter narcissism by blaming Louisa for his own failure: "You have regularly given me up. You never cared for me" (Dickens 262; bk. 3, ch. 9).

For a play in verse, such as a Shakespearean play, indicate the act, scene, and line numbers instead of the page numbers.

At the beginning, Regan's fawning rhetoric hides her true attitude toward Lear: "I profess / myself an enemy to all other joys [. . .] / And find that I am alone felicitate / In your dear highness' love" (King Lear I.i.74–75, 77–78).

Note the brackets placed around the ellipsis marks, which the MLA recommends to distinguish them from ellipses the author may have used. In the MLA style, act and scene numbers may instead be given in arabic numerals: (King Lear 1.1.74–75, 77–78).

See p. 694 for more on using ellipsis marks in quotations.

For a poem, indicate the line numbers and stanzas or sections (if they are numbered), instead of the page numbers. If the source gives only line numbers, use the term *lines* in the first citation and give only the numbers in subsequent citations.

> In "Song of Myself," Whitman finds poetic details in busy urban settings, as when he describes "the blab of the pave, tires of carts [. . .] the driver with his interrogating thumb" (8.153–54).

A RELIGIOUS WORK

For the Bible, indicate the book, chapter, and verse instead of the page numbers. Abbreviate books with names of five or more letters in your parenthetical citation, but spell out full names of books in your text.

> She ignored the admonition "Pride goes before destruction, and a haughty spirit before a fall" (New Oxford Annotated Bible, Prov. 16.18).

A WORK IN AN ANTHOLOGY

Use the name of the author of the work, not the editor of the anthology, but use the page number(s) from the anthology.

> In "Six Days: Some Rememberings," Grace Paley recalls that when she was in jail for protesting the Vietnam War, her pen and paper were taken away and she felt "a terrible pain in the area of my heart—a nausea" (191).

A SECONDARY SOURCE

Include the secondary source in your list of works cited. In your parenthetical citation, use the abbreviation *qtd. in* (in regular type, not italicized or underlined) to acknowledge that the original was quoted in a secondary source.

> E. M. Forster says "the collapse of all civilization, so realistic for us, sounded in Matthew Arnold's ears like a distant and harmonious cataract" (qtd. in Trilling 11).

AN ENTIRE WORK

Include the reference in the text without any page numbers or parentheses.

> In The Structure of Scientific Revolutions, Thomas Kuhn discusses how scientists change their thinking.

A WORK WITHOUT PAGE NUMBERS

If a work has no page numbers or is only one page long, you may omit the page number. If a work uses paragraph numbers instead, use the abbreviation *par(s)*.

The average speed on Montana's interstate highways, for example, has risen by only 2 miles per hour since the repeal of the federal speed limit, with most drivers topping out at 75 (Schmid).

Whitman considered African American speech "a source of a native grand opera" in the words of Ellison (par. 13).

TWO OR MORE WORKS CITED IN THE SAME PARENTHESES

When two or more different sources are used in the same passage of your essay, it may be necessary to cite them in the same parentheses. Separate the citations with a semicolon. Include any specific pages, or omit pages to refer to the whole work.

A few studies have considered differences between oral and written discourse production (Scardamalia, Bereiter, and Goelman; Gould).

MATERIAL FROM THE INTERNET

Give enough information in the citation to enable readers to locate an Internet source in the list of works cited. If the author is not named, give the document title. Include page, section, paragraph, or screen numbers, if available.

In handling livestock, "many people attempt to restrain animals with sheer force instead of using behavioral principles" (Grandin).

List of Works Cited

Providing full information for the citations in the text, the list of works cited identifies all the sources the writer uses. Entries are alphabetized according to the first author's last name or by the title if the author is unknown. Every source cited in the text must refer to an entry in the works-cited list. Conversely, every entry in the works-cited list must correspond to at least one in-text citation.

In the MLA style, multiple works by the same author (or same group of authors) are alphabetized by title. The author's name is given for the first entry only; in subsequent entries, three hyphens and a period are used.

```
Vidal, Gore. Empire. New York: Random, 1987.

---. Lincoln. New York: Random, 1984.
```

The information presented in a works-cited list follows this order: author, title, publication source, year, and (for an article) page range. The MLA style requires a "hanging indent," which means that the first line of a works-cited entry is not indented but subsequent lines of the entry are. The MLA specifies an indent of half an inch or five character spaces.

Books

Here is an example of a basic MLA-style entry for a book:

double-space

author, last name first   *title (and subtitle, if any), underlined*

Campbell, Richard. Media and Culture: An Introduction to Mass

➤➤   Communication. New York: St. Martin's, 1998. ◄

indent one-half inch   *publisher's city and name,*
or 5 typewriter spaces   *year of publication*

A BOOK BY A SINGLE AUTHOR

Guterson, David. Family Matters: Why Homeschooling Makes
     Sense. San Diego: Harcourt, 1992.

A BOOK BY AN AGENCY OR A CORPORATION

Association for Research in Nervous and Mental Disease. The
     Circulation of the Brain and Spinal Cord: A Symposium on
     Blood Supply. New York: Hafner, 1966.

A BOOK BY MORE THAN ONE AUTHOR

Gottfredson, Stephen G., and Sean McConville. America's
     Correctional Crisis. Westport: Greenwood, 1987.

Dyal, James A., William C. Corning, and Dale M. Willows.
     Readings in Psychology: The Search for Alternatives. 3rd
     ed. New York: McGraw, 1975.

A WORK BY MORE THAN THREE AUTHORS

The MLA lists all the authors' names *or* the name of the first author followed by
et al. (in regular type, not italicized or underlined).

Nielsen, Niels C., Jr., et al. Religions of the World. 3rd ed.
     New York: St. Martin's, 1992.

A BOOK BY AN UNKNOWN AUTHOR

Use the title in place of the author.

Rand McNally Commercial Atlas. Skokie: Rand, 1993.

A BOOK WITH AN AUTHOR AND AN EDITOR

If you refer to the author's text, begin the entry with the author's name.

Arnold, Matthew. Culture and Anarchy. Ed. J. Dover Wilson.
     Cambridge: Cambridge UP, 1966.

If you cite the editor in your paper, begin the entry with the editor's name.

> Wilson, J. Dover, ed. <u>Culture and Anarchy</u>. By Matthew Arnold. 1869. Cambridge: Cambridge UP, 1966.

AN EDITED COLLECTION

> Carter, Kathryn, and Carole Spitzack, eds. <u>Doing Research on Women's Communication</u>. Norwood: Ablex, 1989.

A WORK IN AN ANTHOLOGY OR A COLLECTION

> Fairbairn-Dunlop, Peggy. "Women and Agriculture in Western Samoa." <u>Different Places, Different Voices</u>. Ed. Janet H. Momsen and Vivian Kinnaird. London: Routledge, 1993. 211-26.

TWO OR MORE WORKS FROM THE SAME ANTHOLOGY

To avoid repetition, you may create an entry for the collection and cite the collection's editors to cross-reference individual works to the entry.

> Atwan, Robert, and Jamaica Kincaid, eds. <u>The Best American Essays, 1995</u>. New York: Houghton, 1995.

> Paley, Grace. "Six Days: Some Rememberings." Atwan and Kincaid 187-92.

ONE VOLUME OF A MULTIVOLUME WORK

If only one volume from a multivolume set is used, indicate the volume number after the title.

> Freud, Sigmund. <u>The Complete Psychological Works of Sigmund Freud</u>. Vol. 8. Trans. James Strachey. London: Hogarth, 1962.

TWO OR MORE VOLUMES OF A MULTIVOLUME WORK

> Sandburg, Carl. <u>Abraham Lincoln</u>. 6 vols. New York: Scribner's, 1939.

A BOOK THAT IS PART OF A SERIES

Include the series title in regular type (not underlined or in quotation marks), followed by the series number and a period. If the word *Series* is part of the name, include *Ser.* before the number. Common abbreviations may be used for selected words in the series title.

Kirsch, Gesa, and Duane H. Roen. <u>A Sense of Audience in
Written Communication</u>. Written Communication Annual:
An Int. Survey of Research and Theory 5. Newbury Park:
Sage, 1990.

A REPUBLISHED BOOK

Provide the original year of publication after the title of the book, followed by normal publication information for the edition you are using.

Takaki, Ronald. <u>Strangers from a Different Shore: A History of
Asian Americans</u>. 1989. New York: Penguin, 1990.

A LATER EDITION OF A BOOK

Rottenberg, Annette T. <u>The Structure of Argument</u>. 2nd ed.
Boston: Bedford, 1997.

A BOOK WITH A TITLE IN ITS TITLE

Do not underline a title normally underlined when it appears within the title of a book.

Kinney, Arthur F. Go Down Moses: <u>The Miscegenation of Time</u>.
New York: Twayne, 1996.

Brooker, Jewel Spears, and Joseph Bentley. <u>Reading</u> The Waste
Land: <u>Modernism and the Limits of Interpretation</u>.
Amherst: U of Mass P, 1990.

Use quotation marks around a work normally enclosed in quotation marks when it appears within the title of a book.

Miller, Edwin Haviland. <u>Walt Whitman's "Song of Myself": A
Mosaic of Interpretation</u>. Iowa City: U of Iowa P, 1989.

A TRANSLATION

If you refer to the work itself, begin the entry with the author's name.

Tolstoy, Leo. <u>War and Peace</u>. Trans. Constance Garnett. London:
Pan, 1972.

If you cite the translator in your text, begin the entry with the translator's name.

Garnett, Constance, trans. <u>War and Peace</u>. By Leo Tolstoy.
1869. London: Pan, 1972.

A DICTIONARY ENTRY OR AN ARTICLE IN A REFERENCE BOOK

"Tempera." The American Heritage College Dictionary. 3rd ed.
      1993.

Suber, Howard. "Motion Picture." The Encyclopedia Americana.
      1991 ed.

AN INTRODUCTION, PREFACE, FOREWORD, OR AFTERWORD

Holt, John. Introduction. Better than School. By Nancy
      Wallace. Burnett: Larson, 1983. 9-14.

Articles

Here is an example of a basic MLA-style entry for an article in a journal:

author, last name first — *article title, in quotation marks* — *periodical title, underlined*

Ficaro, Barbara. "Canterbury's First Dean." Sixteenth Century
      Journal 18 (1987): 343-46.

double-space; indent one-half inch or 5 typewriter spaces — *volume number* — *date, in parentheses, followed by colon* — *page numbers*

AN ARTICLE FROM A DAILY NEWSPAPER

Wilford, John Noble. "Corn in the New World: A Relative Late-
      comer." New York Times 7 Mar. 1995, late ed.: C1+.

AN ARTICLE FROM A WEEKLY OR BIWEEKLY MAGAZINE

Bai, Matt. "Ventura's First Round." Newsweek 15 Feb. 1999:
      30-32.

AN ARTICLE FROM A MONTHLY OR BIMONTHLY MAGAZINE

Rohn, Alfie. "Home Schooling." Atlantic Monthly Apr. 1988:
      20-25.

AN ARTICLE IN A SCHOLARLY JOURNAL WITH CONTINUOUS ANNUAL PAGINATION

The volume number follows the title of the journal.

Natale, Jo Anna. "Understanding Home Schooling." Education
      Digest 9 (1993): 58-61.

AN ARTICLE IN A SCHOLARLY JOURNAL THAT PAGINATES EACH ISSUE SEPARATELY

The issue number appears after the volume number. A period separates the two
numbers.

Epstein, Alexandra. "Teen Parents: What They Need to Know."
High/Scope Resource 1.2 (1982): 6.

AN ANONYMOUS ARTICLE

"Awash in Garbage." New York Times 15 Aug. 1987, sec. 1: 26.

AN EDITORIAL

"Stepping Backward." Editorial. Los Angeles Times 4 July 1989:
B6.

A LETTER TO THE EDITOR

Rissman, Edward M. Letter. Los Angeles Times 29 June 1989: B5.

A REVIEW

Anders, Jaroslaw. "Dogma and Democracy." Rev. of The Church
and the Left, by Adam Minchik. New Republic 17 May 1993:
42-48.

If the review does not include an author's name, start the entry with the title of the review and alphabetize by that title. If the review is untitled, begin with the words *Rev. of* and alphabetize under the title of the work being reviewed.

AN UNSIGNED ARTICLE

Begin with the article title, alphabetizing the entry according to the first word after any initial *A, An,* or *The.*

"The Odds of March." Time. 15 Apr. 1985: 20+.

Electronic Sources

The range of information available through the worldwide network of computers known as the Internet is astonishing. Setting guidelines for regulating and using this information is an ongoing process. Most of the following guidelines for citing Internet sources are derived from the *MLA Handbook for Writers of Research Papers,* Fifth Edition (1999), and the MLA Web site. Models for citing a few other kinds of Internet sources not covered by the MLA guidelines are based on Andrew Harnack and Eugene Kleppinger, *Online! A Reference Guide to Using Internet Sources* (New York: Bedford/St. Martin's, 2000). These models will help you incorporate electronic sources of information and data into your own essays.

For more information on using the Internet for research, see Chapter 21, pp. 683–84.

For more information on citing Internet sources in the MLA style, go to <http://www.mla.org/style/sources.htm>.

In-text reference   When citing an Internet source in the body of your text, use the author's name or the document title if the author's name is not given. Do not use the URL (uniform resource locator) for your reference.

List of works cited   For most sources accessed on the Internet, you should provide the following information:

- Name of author or compiler (if available)
- Title of document (underlined)
- Date of electronic publication or latest update (if available)
- Name of sponsoring institution, if any
- Date of access
- URL (in angle brackets)

PROFESSIONAL OR PERSONAL WEB SITE

Meldrum, Ron. <u>Genealogy and History of the Meldrum Family</u>.
    1 Jan. 1996. 18 Jan. 2000 <http://www.royalriver.net/
    meldrum>.

If the author's name is not known, begin the citation with the title, underlined.

<u>American Horticultural Society</u>. 18 Jan. 2000. AHS. 24 Jan.
    2000 <http://www.ahs.org>.

For an untitled professional or personal Web site, put a description such as *Home page* (in regular type, not underlined), followed by a period, in the position a title would normally be cited.

Polhemus-Annibell, Wendy. Home page. Jan. 2000. 24 Jan. 2000
    <http://wpannibell.homepage.com>.

A BOOK OR POEM AVAILABLE ONLINE

Blind, Mathilde. <u>Dramas in Miniature</u>. London: Chatto & Windus,
    1891. <u>Victorian Women Writers Project</u>. Ed. Perry Willett.
    3 Oct. 1997. Indiana U. 13 Oct. 1997 <http://www.
    indiana.edu/~letrs/vwwp/blind/dramas.html>.

Mosko, Marc. "Muir Woods." Home page. 1996. 13 Oct. 1997
    <http://www.tear.com/poems/mosko/muirwoods.html>.

AN FTP (FILE TRANSFER PROTOCOL), TELNET, OR GOPHER SITE

Substitute *ftp*, *telnet*, or *gopher* for *http* at the beginning of the URL.

Greig, Alastair. <u>Home Magazines and Modernist Dreams:
    Designing the 1950s House</u>. 21 Nov. 1995. 11 July 1996
    <ftp://coombs.anu.edu.au/coombs papers/coombs archives/
    urban-research-program/working-papers/wp-047-1995.txt>.

If you use command, address, and path elements instead of a URL, do not use closing punctuation or angle brackets with the prefixes *ftp, telnet,* or *gopher.*

AN ONLINE SCHOLARLY PROJECT OR REFERENCE DATABASE

For a complete online scholarly project or reference database, provide the title, underlined, and the name of the editor, if given. Then give the electronic publication information—the version number (if any), the date of electronic publication or latest update, and the name of the sponsoring organization—followed by the date of access and the URL (in angle brackets).

```
The Ovid Project. Ed. Hope Greenberg. 13 Mar. 1996. U of
     Vermont. 13 Oct. 1997 <http://www.uvm.edu/hag/ovid/
     index.html>.
```

For an article within a scholarly project or reference database, begin with the author's name, if known, and the title of the work, enclosed in quotation marks. Follow with the information about the database or project.

```
Lee, Vernon. "Limbo." Victorian Women Writers Project. Ed.
     Perry Willett. Aug. 1998. Indiana U. 17 Feb. 2000
     <http://www.indiana.edu/~letrs/vwwp/lee/limbo.html>.
```

MATERIAL FROM A DATABASE ON CD-ROM

```
Braus, Patricia. "Sex and the Single Spender." American
     Demographics 15.11 (1993): 28-34. ABI/INFORM. CD-ROM.
     UMI-ProQuest. 1993.
```

If no print version is available, include the author, title, and date (if provided) along with information about the electronic source.

MATERIAL PUBLISHED ON A CD-ROM, MAGNETIC TAPE, OR DISKETTE

```
Picasso: The Man, His Works, the Legend. CD-ROM. Danbury:
     Grolier Interactive, 1996.
```

A WORK FROM AN ONLINE SUBSCRIPTION SERVICE

To cite an article from an online service to which you subscribe personally such as America Online, begin with the author's name, if known, and the title of the work, enclosed in quotation marks. Give the title of the online service provided, underlined, along with the date of publication, the provider's name, the date of access, and the word *Keyword,* followed by the keyword used.

```
Weeks, W. William. "Beyond the Ark." Nature Conservancy. Mar.-
     Apr. 1999. America Online. 2 Apr. 1999. Keyword: Ecology.
```

For a work from an online service to which a library subscribes, first list the information about the work (author, title, publication data). Then give the name of the subscription service, the name of the library, the date of access, and the URL of the service (in angle brackets) if available.

> "Breaking the Dieting Habit: Drug Therapy for Eating Disorders." Psychology Today Mar. 1995: 12+. Electric Lib. Ohio State U Main Lib., Columbus, OH. 31 Mar. 1999 <http://www.elibrary.com>.

AN ARTICLE FROM AN ONLINE JOURNAL

MLA includes the volume number and issue number, if given, after the title of the journal. The number of pages, paragraphs, or other sections appears after the colon, if the source gives them. The date of access and the electronic address appear at the end.

> Robbins, Bruce. "Celeb-Reliance: Intellectuals, Celebrity, and Upward Mobility." Postmodern Culture 9.2 (1999): 22 pars. 19 Jan. 2000 <http://jefferson.village.virginia.edu/pmc/text-only/issue.199/9.2robbins.txt>.

A NEWSGROUP (USENET) POSTING

Include the author's name (if you know it), the title or subject line of the posting, and the identifying phrase *Online posting*. Follow the posting date with the access date. Enclose the newsgroup's name, preceded by the word *news:* and no space, in angle brackets.

> Conrad, Ed. "Proof of Life after Death." Online posting. 8 July 1996. 9 July 1996 <news:sci.archeology>.

A LISTSERV POSTING

Include the list's name after the posting date. For a listserv that archives postings at a Web site or listserv address, provide the URL, enclosed in angle brackets.

> Martin, Francesca Alys. "Wait--Did Somebody Say 'Buffy'?" Online posting. 8 Mar. 2000. Cultstud-l. 8 Mar. 2000. <http://lists.accomp.usf.edu/cgi-bin/lyris.pl?visit=cultstud-l&id=111011221>.

For a listserv with no Web site, provide the list moderator's email address in place of a URL.

AN EMAIL MESSAGE

The subject line of the posting is enclosed in quotation marks before its date. Identify the type of message and the person who received it.

Somer, Tina. "Medea." Email to the author. 9 Mar. 1996.

SYNCHRONOUS COMMUNICATION

For a posting in a forum such as a MOO, MUD, or IRC, provide the name(s) of any specific speaker(s) you are citing; specify the event, and supply its date, the name of the forum, the date of access, and the URL, beginning with *telnet*. (If an archived version of the posting is available, cite the *http* address instead.)

Patuto, Jeremy, Simon Fennel, and James Goss. Online discussion of "The Mytilene Debate." 9 May 1996. MiamiMOO. 28 Mar. 1998 <telnet://moo.cas.edu/cgi-bin/moo?look+4085>.

COMPUTER SOFTWARE

SPSS/PC+ Studentware Plus. Diskette. Chicago: SPSS, 1991.

Other Sources

A LECTURE OR PUBLIC ADDRESS

Timothy, Kristen. "The Changing Roles of Women's Community Organizations in Sustainable Development and in the United Nations." UN Assn. of the US. Seattle. 7 May 1997.

A GOVERNMENT DOCUMENT

If the author is known, the author's name may either come first or be placed after the title, introduced with the word *By*.

United States. Dept. of Health and Human Services. Clinical Classifications for Health Policy Research, Version 2: Hospital Inpatient Statistics. Rockville: AHCPR Publications Clearinghouse, 1996.

A PAMPHLET

Harborview Injury Prevention and Research Center. A Decade of Injury Control. Seattle: Harborview Medical Center, 1995.

PUBLISHED PROCEEDINGS OF A CONFERENCE

If the name of the conference is part of the title of the publication, it need not be repeated. Use the format for a work in an anthology (see p. 708) to cite an individual presentation.

> Duffett, John, ed. <u>Against the Crime of Silence</u>. Proc. of the
>   Intl. War Crimes Tribunal, Nov. 1967, Stockholm. New
>   York: Clarion-Simon, 1970.

A PUBLISHED DOCTORAL DISSERTATION

If the dissertation was published by University Microfilms International, add *Ann Arbor: UMI,* and the year. List the UMI number at the end of the entry.

> Botts, Roderic C. <u>Influences in the Teaching of English, 1917-</u>
>   <u>1935: An Illusion of Progress</u>. Diss. Northeastern U,
>   1970. Ann Arbor: UMI, 1971. 71-1799.

AN UNPUBLISHED DOCTORAL DISSERTATION

> Bullock, Barbara. "Basic Needs Fulfillment among Less Devel-
>   oped Countries: Social Progress over Two Decades of
>   Growth." Diss. Vanderbilt U, 1986.

A LETTER

> Hannah, Barry. Letter to the author. 10 May 1990.

A MAP OR CHART

> <u>Mineral King, California</u>. Map. Berkeley: Wilderness P, 1979.

A CARTOON

Provide the cartoon's title (if given) in quotes directly following the artist's name.

> Wilson, Gahan. Cartoon. <u>New Yorker</u> 14 July 1997: 74.

AN ADVERTISEMENT

> Reliance National Employment Practices Liability.
>   Advertisement. <u>Wired</u> May 1997: 196.

A WORK OF ART OR MUSICAL COMPOSITION

> De Goya, Francisco. <u>The Sleep of Reason Produces Monsters</u>.
>   Norton Simon Museum, Pasadena.

```
Beethoven, Ludwig van. Violin Concerto in D Major, op. 61.

Gershwin, George. Porgy and Bess.
```

If a photograph is not part of a collection, identify the subject, the name of the person who photographed it, and when it was photographed.

```
Washington Square Park, New York. Personal photograph by
     author. 24 June 1995.
```

A PERFORMANCE

```
Hamlet. By William Shakespeare. Dir. Jonathan Kent. Perf.
     Ralph Fiennes. Belasco Theatre, New York. 20 June 1995.
```

A TELEVISION PROGRAM

```
"The Universe Within." Nova. Narr. Stacy Keach. Writ. Beth
     Hoppe and Bill Lattanzi. Dir. Goro Koide. PBS. WNET, New
     York. 7 Mar. 1995.
```

A FILM OR VIDEOTAPE

```
Boyz N the Hood. Writ. and Dir. John Singleton. Perf. Ice
     Cube, Cuba Gooding Jr., and Larry Fishburne. Columbia,
     1991.

Casablanca. Dir. Michael Curtiz. Perf. Humphrey Bogart. 1942.
     Videocassette. MGM-UA Home Video, 1992.
```

A MUSIC RECORDING

Indicate the medium ahead of the name of the manufacturer for an audiocassette, audiotape, or LP; it is not necessary to indicate the medium for a compact disk.

```
Beethoven, Ludwig van. Violin Concerto in D Major, op. 61.
     U.S.S.R. State Orchestra. Cond. Alexander Gauk. David
     Oistrikh, violinist. Audiocassette. Allegro, 1980.

Springsteen, Bruce. "Dancing in the Dark." Born in the U.S.A.
     Columbia, 1984.
```

AN INTERVIEW

```
Lowell, Robert. "Robert Lowell." Interview with Frederick Sei-
     del. Paris Review 25 (1975): 56-95.

Franklin, Ann. Personal interview. 3 Sept. 1999.
```

The APA System of Documentation

Citations in Text

AUTHOR INDICATED IN PARENTHESES

The APA author-year system calls for the last name of the author and the year of publication of the original work in the citation. If the cited material is a quotation, you also need to include the page number(s) of the original. If the cited material is not a quotation, the page reference is optional. Use commas to separate author, year, and page in a parenthetical citation. The page number is preceded by *p.* for a single page or *pp.* for a range.

Dr. James is described as a "not-too-skeletal Ichabod Crane" (Simon, 1982, p. 68).

AUTHOR INDICATED IN SIGNAL PHRASE

If the author's name is mentioned in your text, cite the year in parentheses directly following the author's name, and place the page reference in parentheses before the final sentence period.

Simon (1982) describes Dr. James as a "not-too-skeletal Ichabod Crane" (p. 68).

SOURCE WITH MORE THAN TWO AUTHORS

To cite works with three to five authors, use all the authors' last names the first time the reference occurs and the last name of the first author followed by *et al.* subsequently. If a source has more than six authors, use only the last name of the first author and *et al.* (in regular type, not italicized or underlined) at first and subsequent references.

First Citation in Text

Dyal, Corning, and Willows (1975) identify several types of students, including the "Authority-Rebel" (p. 4).

Subsequent Citations

The Authority-Rebel "tends to see himself as superior to other students in the class" (Dyal et al., 1975, p. 4).

TWO OR MORE WORKS BY THE SAME AUTHOR

To cite one of two or more works by the same author or group of authors, use the author's last name plus the year (and the page, if you are citing a quotation). When more than one work being cited was published by an author in the same year, the works are alphabetized by title and then assigned lowercase letters after the date (1973a, 1973b).

When old paint becomes transparent, it sometimes shows the artist's original plans: "a tree will show through a woman's dress" (Hellman, 1973b, p. 1).

UNKNOWN AUTHOR

To cite a work listed only by its title, the APA uses a shortened version of the title.

An international pollution treaty still to be ratified would prohibit all plastic garbage from being dumped at sea ("Awash," 1987).

SECONDARY SOURCE

To quote material taken not from the original source but from a secondary source that quotes the original, give the secondary source in the reference list, and in your essay acknowledge that the original was quoted in a secondary source.

E. M. Forster says "the collapse of all civilization, so realistic for us, sounded in Matthew Arnold's ears like a distant and harmonious cataract" (as cited in Trilling, 1955, p. 11).

List of References

The APA follows this order in the presentation of information for each source listed: author, publication year, title, and publication source; for an article, the page range is given as well.

When the list of references includes several works by the same author, the APA provides the following rules for arranging these entries in the list:

- Same-name single-author entries precede multiple-author entries:

```
Aaron, P. (1990).

Aaron, P., & Zorn, C. R. (1985).
```

- Entries with the same first author and a different second author are alphabetized under the first author according to the second author's last name:

```
Aaron, P., & Charleston, W. (1987).

Aaron, P., & Zorn, C. R. (1991).
```

- Entries by the same authors are arranged by year of publication, in chronological order:

```
Aaron, P., & Charleston, W. (1987).

Aaron, P., & Charleston, W. (1993).
```

- Entries by the same authors with the same publication year should be arranged alphabetically by title (according to the first word after *A, An,* or *The*), and lowercase letters (*a, b, c,* and so on) are appended to the year in parentheses:

```
Aaron, P. (1990a). Basic . . .

Aaron, P. (1990b). Elements . . .
```

The APA recommends that only the first line of each entry be indented five to seven spaces for papers intended for publication, but that student writers may choose instead to use a hanging indent of five to seven spaces. Ask your instructor which format is preferred. The following examples demonstrate a hanging indent of five spaces.

Books

A BOOK BY A SINGLE AUTHOR

```
Guterson, D. (1992). Family matters: Why homeschooling makes
     sense. San Diego: Harcourt Brace.
```

A BOOK BY AN AGENCY OR A CORPORATION

```
Association for Research in Nervous and Mental Disease.
     (1966). The circulation of the brain and spinal cord: A
     symposium on blood supply. New York: Hafner.
```

A BOOK BY MORE THAN ONE AUTHOR

The APA cites all authors' names regardless of the number.

```
Gottfredson, S. G., & McConville, S. (1987). America's
     correctional crisis. Westport, CT: Greenwood.

Dyal, J. A., Corning, W. C., & Willows, D. M. (1975). Readings
     in psychology: The search for alternatives (3rd ed.). New
     York: McGraw-Hill.
```

A BOOK BY AN UNKNOWN AUTHOR

Use the title in place of the author.

```
Rand McNally commercial atlas. (1993). Skokie, IL: Rand
     McNally.
```

When an author is designated as "Anonymous," identify the work as "Anonymous" in the text, and alphabetize it as "Anonymous" in the reference list.

A BOOK WITH AN AUTHOR AND AN EDITOR

```
Arnold, M. (1966). Culture and anarchy (J. D. Wilson, Ed.).
     Cambridge: Cambridge University Press. (Original work
     published 1869)
```

AN EDITED COLLECTION

Carter, K., & Spitzack, C. (Eds.). (1989). Doing research on women's communication. Norwood, NJ: Ablex.

A WORK IN AN ANTHOLOGY OR A COLLECTION

Fairbairn-Dunlop, P. (1993). Women and agriculture in western Samoa. In J. H. Momsen & V. Kinnaird (Eds.), Different places, different voices (pp. 211-226). London: Routledge.

A TRANSLATION

Tolstoy, L. (1972). War and peace (C. Garnett, Trans.). London: Pan Books. (Original work published 1869)

AN ARTICLE IN A REFERENCE BOOK

Suber, H. (1991). Motion picture. In Encyclopedia Americana (Vol. 19, pp. 505-539). Danbury, CT: Grolier.

AN INTRODUCTION, PREFACE, FOREWORD, OR AFTERWORD

Holt, J. (1983). Introduction. In N. Wallace, Better than school (pp. 9-14). Burnett, NY: Larson.

Articles

AN ARTICLE FROM A DAILY NEWSPAPER

Wilford, J. N. (1995, March 7). Corn in the New World: A relative latecomer. The New York Times, pp. C1, C5.

AN ARTICLE FROM A WEEKLY OR BIWEEKLY MAGAZINE

Bai, M. (1999, February 15). Ventura's first round. Newsweek, 133, 30-32.

AN ARTICLE FROM A MONTHLY OR BIMONTHLY MAGAZINE

Rohn, A. (1988, April). Home schooling. Atlantic Monthly, 261, 20-25.

AN ARTICLE IN A SCHOLARLY JOURNAL WITH CONTINUOUS ANNUAL PAGINATION

The volume number follows the title of the journal.

Natale, J. A. (1993). Understanding home schooling. Education Digest, 9, 58-61.

AN ARTICLE IN A SCHOLARLY JOURNAL THAT PAGINATES EACH ISSUE SEPARATELY

The issue number appears in parentheses after the volume number.

> Epstein, A. (1982). Teen parents: What they need to know. High/Scope Resource, 1(2), 6.

AN ANONYMOUS ARTICLE

> Awash in garbage. (1987, August 15). The New York Times, p. A26.

A REVIEW

> Anders, J. (1993, May 17). Dogma and democracy [Review of the book The church and the left]. The New Republic, 208, 42-48.

If the review is untitled, use the bracketed information as the title, retaining the brackets.

Electronic Sources

For more information on using the Internet for research, see Chapter 21, pp. 683–84.

The APA guidelines for citing online resources are currently being discussed and evaluated. It is generally agreed that citation information must allow readers to access and retrieve the information cited. For the time being, if your source is available both in print and online, the APA prefers that you cite the print version.

Some of the following guidelines are derived from the *Publication Manual of the American Psychological Association,* Fourth Edition (1994), and the APA Web site. Models for citing other kinds of Internet sources not covered by the APA guidelines are based on Andrew Harnack and Eugene Kleppinger, *Online! A Reference Guide to Using Internet Sources* (New York: Bedford/St. Martin's, 2000). These models will help you incorporate electronic sources of information into your own essays.

For answers to frequently asked questions on citing Internet sources in the APA style, go to <http://www.apa.org/journals/webref.html>.

In-text reference   When citing an Internet source in the body of your text, follow the guidelines for citing print sources (see p. 718). Instead of page numbers, however, the APA allows you to use paragraph numbers for electronic text. If paragraph numbers are not available, give a division used within the document (such as a chapter number or heading) instead.

List of references   For most sources accessed on the Internet, you should provide the following information:

- Name of author or compiler (if available)
- Publication date (in parentheses; if unavailable, use the abbreviation *n.d.*)
- Title of document
- URL or path followed to locate the site
- Date of access (in parentheses)

A PROFESSIONAL OR PERSONAL WEB SITE

When you cite an entire Web site, the APA does not require an entry in the list of references. You may instead give the name of the site in your text and its Web address in parentheses. If you wish to include an entry in the references list, however, follow these formats:

American Horticultural Society. (2000, January 18). Retrieved January 24, 2000 from the World Wide Web: http://ahs.org

Meldrum, Ron. (1996, January 1). Home page. Genealogy and History of the Meldrum Family. Retrieved January 24, 2000 from the World Wide Web: http://www.royalriver.net /meldrum

If a personal Web site is untitled, give a description such as *Home page,* followed by a period.

AN FTP (FILE TRANSFER PROTOCOL), TELNET, OR GOPHER SITE

Greig, Alastair. (1995, November 21). Home Magazines and Modernist Dreams: Designing the 1950s House. Retrieved July 11, 1996 from the World Wide Web: ftp://coombs .anu.edu.au/coombs papers/coombs archives/urban-research -program/workingpapers/wp-047-1995.txt

Goody, J. (1993, Spring). History and anthropology: Convergence and divergence. Bulletin of the Institute of Ethnology, 75(2). Academica Sinica, 75. Retrieved June 2, 1999: gopher://gopher.sinica.edu.tw/00/ioe/engbull /75b.txt

MATERIAL FROM A DATABASE ON CD-ROM

Braus, P. (1993). Sex and the single spender. American Demographics, 15(11), 28-34. Retrieved from ABI/INFORM database (UMI-ProQuest, CD-ROM, 1993 release)

A WORK FROM AN ONLINE SUBSCRIPTION SERVICE

Weeks, W. W. (1999, March/April). Beyond the ark. Nature Conservancy. Retrieved April 2, 1999 from America Online: Keyword: Ecology

Breaking the dieting habit: Drug therapy for eating disorders. (1995, March). Psychology Today, 12+. Retrieved March 31, 1999 from Electric Library database on the World Wide Web: http://www.elibrary.com

AN ARTICLE FROM AN ONLINE JOURNAL

```
Robbins, B. (1999). Celeb-reliance: Intellectuals, celebrity,
    and upward mobility. [22 paragraphs]. Postmodern Culture,
    9(2). Retrieved January 19, 2000 from the World Wide Web:
    http://jefferson.village.virginia.edu/pmc/text-only/issue
    .199/9.2robbins.txt
```

A NEWSGROUP (USENET) POSTING

Include the author's name (if known) and the date of the posting, in parentheses. The subject line of the posting is given as plain text, followed by the retrieval date and the newsgroup name. If you do not know the author's name, begin the citation with the author's email address, and alphabetize the posting by the first letter of this email address in your list of references.

```
Conrad, E. (1996, July 8). Proof of life after death.
    Retrieved July 9, 1996 from the newsgroup: sci.archeology
```

A LISTSERV POSTING

Provide the author's name, the date of the posting, the subject line, and the retrieval date, followed by the listserv address or, if available, the URL for the list's archives.

```
Sherman, M. (1995, February 15). Writing process and self-
    discipline. Retrieved February 16, 1995 from the list-
    serv: eng13764@ebbs.english.vt.edu

Carbone, N. (1996, January 26). NN 960126: Follow-up to Don's
    comments about citing URLs. Retrieved February 17, 1996
    from the listserv: http://www.ttu.edu/lists/acw-1
```

AN EMAIL MESSAGE

In the APA style, it is not necessary to list personal correspondence, including email, in your reference list. Simply cite the person's name in your text, and in parentheses give the notation *personal communication* (in regular type, not underlined or italicized) and the date.

COMPUTER SOFTWARE

If an individual has proprietary rights to the software, cite that person's name as you would for a print text. Otherwise, cite as you would an anonymous print text.

```
SPSS/PC+ Studentware Plus [Computer software]. (1991).
    Chicago: SPSS.
```

Other Sources

A GOVERNMENT DOCUMENT

U.S. Department of Health and Human Services. (1996). Clinical
classifications for health policy research, version 2:
Hospital inpatient statistics (AHCPR Publication No.
HCUP-3). Rockville, MD: Author.

AN UNPUBLISHED DOCTORAL DISSERATION

Bullock, B. (1986). Basic needs fulfillment among less developed countries: Social progress over two decades of
growth. Unpublished doctoral dissertation, Vanderbilt
University, Nashville, TN.

A TELEVISION PROGRAM

Hoppe, B., & Lattanzi, B. (1995). The universe within
(G. Koide, Director). In P. Apsell (Producer), Nova.
Boston: WGBH.

A FILM OR VIDEOTAPE

Singleton, J. (Writer and Director). (1991). Boyz n the hood
[Film]. New York: Columbia.

A MUSIC RECORDING

If the recording date differs from the copyright date, the APA requires that it should
appear in parentheses after the name of the label. If it is necessary to include a number for the recording, use parentheses for the medium; otherwise, use brackets.

Beethoven, L. van. (1806). Violin concerto in D major, op. 61
[Recorded by USSR State Orchestra]. (Cassette Recording
No. ACS 8044). New York: Allegro. (1980)

Springsteen, B. (1984). Dancing in the dark. On Born in the
U.S.A. [CD]. New York: Columbia.

AN INTERVIEW

When using the APA style, do not list personal interviews in your references list. Simply cite the person's name (last name and initials) in your text, and in parentheses give
the notation *personal communication* (in regular type, not italicized or underlined)
followed by a comma and the date of the interview. For published interviews, use the
appropriate format for an article.

■ SOME SAMPLE RESEARCH PAPERS

As a writer, you will want or need to use sources on many occasions. You may be assigned to write a research paper, complete with formal documentation of outside sources. Several of the writing assignments in this book present opportunities to do library or field research—in other words, to turn to outside sources. Among the readings in Part One, the essays listed here cite and document sources. (The documentation style each follows is given in parentheses.)

"Cannibalism: It Still Exists," by Linh Kieu Ngo, Chapter 5, pp. 206–10 (MLA)

"Children Need to Play, Not Compete," by Jessica Statsky, Chapter 6, pp. 255–58 (MLA)

"More Testing, More Learning," by Patrick O'Malley, Chapter 7, pp. 314–18 (APA)

"Asthma on the Web," by Kristine Potter, Chapter 8, pp. 363–70 (MLA)

"The Rise of Reported Incidents of Workplace Sexual Harassment," by Sarah West, Chapter 9, pp. 426–30 (MLA)

■ AN ANNOTATED RESEARCH PAPER

Here is a student research paper speculating about the causes of a trend—the increase in home schooling. The author cites statistics, quotes authorities, and paraphrases and summarizes background information and support for her argument. She uses the MLA documentation style.

½"
Dinh 1

Cristina Dinh — *Double-space*

Professor Cooper

English XXX — *Double-space*

5 November 1999

Educating Kids at Home — *Title centered*

Every morning, Mary Jane, who is nine, doesn't
have to worry about gulping down her cereal so she
can be on time for school. School for Mary Jane is
literally right at her doorstep.

In this era of growing concerns about the — *Paragraphs indented five spaces*
quality of public education, increasing numbers of
parents across the United States are choosing to
educate their children at home. These parents
believe they can do a better job teaching their
children than their local schools can. Home
schooling, as this practice is known, has become a
national trend over the past twenty years. Patricia — *Author named in text; parenthetical page reference falls at end of subsequent sentence*
Lines, a senior research associate at the U.S.
Department of Education, estimates that in 1970 the
nationwide number of home-schooled children was
15,000. By the 1990-91 school year, she estimates
that the number rose to between 250,000 and 350,000
(5). From 1986 to 1989, the number of home-schooled
children in Oregon almost doubled, from 2,671 to
4,578 (Graves B8). Home-school advocates believe
that the numbers may even be greater; many home
schoolers don't give official notice of what they
are doing because they are still afraid of
government interference.

What is home schooling, and who are the
parents choosing to teach their children at home?
David Guterson, a high-school teacher whose own — *Author named and identified to introduce quotation*
children are home schooled, defines home schooling
as "the attempt to gain an education outside of
institutions" (5). Home-schooled children spend the
majority of the conventional school day learning in
or near their homes rather than in traditional
schools; parents or guardians are the prime
educators. Cindy Connolly notes that parents teach

Dinh 2

their children the same subjects--math, science, music, history, and language arts--that are taught in public schools but vary the way they teach these subjects. Some home-schooling parents create structured plans for their children, while others prefer looser environments (E2). While home schoolers are a diverse group--libertarians, conservatives, Christian fundamentalists--most say they home school for one of two reasons: they are concerned about the way children are taught in public schools or they are concerned about exposing their children to secular education that may contradict their religious beliefs (Guterson 5-6).

Author named in parenthetical citation; no punctuation between name and page numbers

The first group generally believes that children need individual attention and the opportunity to learn at their own pace in order to learn well. This group says that one teacher in a classroom of twenty to thirty children (the size of typical public-school classes) cannot give this kind of attention. These parents believe they can give their children greater enrichment and more specialized instruction than public schools can provide. At home, parents can work one-on-one with each child and be flexible about time, allowing their children to pursue their interests at earlier ages. Many of these parents, like home-schooler Peter Bergson, believe that

Quotation of more than four lines typed as a block and indented ten spaces

Brackets indicate addition to quotation

> home schooling provides more of an opportunity to continue the natural learning process that's in evidence in all children. [In school,] you change the learning process from self-directed to other-directed, from the child asking questions to the teacher asking questions. You shut down areas of potential interest. (qtd. in Kohn 22)

Parenthetical citation of secondary source falls after period

The second, and larger, group, those who home school their children for religious reasons, accounts for about 90 percent of all home

Dinh 3

schoolers, according to the Home School Legal Defense Association and the National Association of State Boards of Education (Kohn 22). This group is made up predominantly of Christian fundamentalists but also includes Buddhists, Jews, and black Muslims.

What causes underlie the increasing number of parents in both groups choosing to home school their children? One cause for this trend can be traced back to the 1960s, when many people began criticizing traditional schools. Various types of "alternative schools" were created, and some parents began teaching their children at home (Friedlander 20). As the public educational system has continued to have problems, parents have seen academic and social standards get lower. They mention several reasons for their disappointment with public schools and for their decision to home school. A lack of funding, for example, leaves children without new textbooks. One day a mother found out her sons were reading books that they read from the year before (Monday C11). Many schools also cannot afford to buy laboratory equipment and other teaching materials. At my own high school, the chemistry teacher told me that most of the lab equipment we used came from a research firm he worked for. In a 1988 Gallup poll, lack of proper financial support ranked third on the list of the problems in public schools; poor curriculum and poor standards ranked fifth on the list (Gallup and Elam 34).

Work by two authors cited

Parents also cite overcrowding as a reason for taking their kids out of school. Faced with a large group of children, a teacher can't satisfy the needs of all the students. Thus, a teacher ends up gearing lessons to the students in the middle level, so children at both ends miss out. Gifted children and those with learning disabilities particularly suffer in this situation. At home, parents of these children say they can tailor the

Dinh 4

material and the pace for each child. Studies show that home-schooling methods seem to work well in preparing children academically. For example, in 1989, 74 percent of Oregon's home-schooled kids scored above the fiftieth percentile, and 22 percent above the ninetieth percentile, on *Source of statistics cited* ————— standardized tests (Graves B9).

In addition, home-schooling parents claim that their children are more well rounded than those in school. Because they don't have to sit in classrooms all day, home-schooled kids can pursue their own projects, often combining crafts or technical skills with academic subjects. Home schoolers participate in outside activities such as 4-H competitions, field trips with other children, parties, gym activities, Christian pageants, and Boy Scouts or Girl Scouts (Shenk D6). Some school districts even invite home-schooled children to participate in sports and to use libraries and computer facilities (Guterson 186). A school district near Seattle trains home-schooling families in computer skills, giving them access to the resources of the Internet (Hawkins 58).

Many home-schooling parents believe that these activities provide the social opportunities kids need without exposing their children to the peer pressure they would have to deal with in school. Occasionally, peer values can be good; often, however, students in today's schools face many negative peer pressures. For example, many kids think that drinking and using drugs are cool. When I was in high school, my friends would tell me a few drinks wouldn't hurt or affect driving. If I had listened to them, I wouldn't be alive today. Four of my friends were killed under the influence of alcohol. In 1975, according to the National Institute on Drug Abuse, 45 percent of high school seniors answered "yes" when asked if they had "ever used" marijuana; in 1981, the number rose to 60

Dinh 5

percent, a 13 percent increase over six years (Hawley K3). In 1986, 1987, and 1988 Gallup polls, use of drugs ranked first among the problems in public schools, and the number of students who use drugs was increasing (Gallup and Elam 34).

Another reason many parents decide to home school their kids is that they are concerned for their children's safety. In addition to fears that peer pressure might push their children into using drugs, many parents fear drug-related violence in and near public schools. There are stories practically every week about drug-related violence in schools--even in elementary schools. Home-schooling parents say they want to protect their children from dangerous environments. As Sam Allis notes about home-schooling parents, "There are no drugs in their bathrooms or switchblades in the hallways" (86).

The major cause of the growing home-schooling trend is Christian fundamentalist dissatisfaction with "godless" public schools. Maralee Mayberry, a professor of sociology at the University of Nevada, states in a 1987 survey that 65 percent of Oregon parents who choose home schooling do so because they feel that public schools lack Christian values (Graves B9). Kohn notes that <u>Growing without Schooling</u>, a secular home-schooling newsletter started by education critic John Holt, has 5,000 subscribers, whereas <u>The Parent Educator and Family Report</u>, a newsletter put out by Raymond Moore, a Christian home-school advocate and researcher, has 300,000 subscribers (22). Luanne Shackelford and Susan White, two Christian home-schooling mothers, claim that because schools expose children to "[p]eer pressure, perverts, secular textbooks, values clarification, TV, pornography, rock music, bad movies [. . .] [h]ome schooling seems to be the best plan to achieve our goal [to raise good Christians]" (160). Moore claims that children in

Paraphrase of original source with author and page number of secondary source cited at end of sentence

Brackets used to indicate change in capitalization

Ellipsis marks, enclosed in brackets, used to indicate words left out of quotation

Dinh 6

Quotation cited in a secondary source

public schools are more likely to "turn away from their home values and rely on their peers for values" (qtd. in Kilgore 24). Moore believes that home-schooled kids are less vulnerable to peer pressure because they gain a positive sense of self-worth fostered by their parents.

Single quotation marks indicate a quotation within a quotation

Page-number citation placed close to quotation, before comma but after quotation marks

In addition, those who cite the lack of "Christian values" are concerned about the textbooks used in public schools. For example, Kohn notes that Moore talks of parents who are "'sick and tired of the teaching of evolution in the schools as a cut-and-dried fact,' along with other evidence of so-called secular humanism" (21), such as textbooks that contain material that contradicts Christian beliefs. Moreover, parents worry that schools decay their children's moral values. In particular, some Christian fundamentalist parents object to sex education in schools, saying that it encourages children to become sexually active early, challenging values taught at home. They see the family as the core and believe that the best place to instill family values is within the family. These Christian home-schooling parents want to provide their children not only with academic knowledge but also with a moral grounding consistent with their religious beliefs.

Internet source cited with author's name; page numbers unavailable

Other home-schooling parents object to a perceived government-mandated value system that they believe attempts to override the values, not necessarily religious in nature, of individual families. Home schooling, for these parents, is a way of resisting what John Gatto describes as unwarranted intrusion by the federal government into personal concerns.

Armed with their convictions, home-schooling parents, such as those who belong to the Christian Home School Legal Defense Association, have fought in court and lobbied for legislation that allows them the option of home schooling. In the 1970s,

Dinh 7

most states had compulsory attendance laws that
made it difficult, if not illegal, to keep school-
age children home from school. By 1993, thirty-two
states permitted home schooling, ten allowed it
with certain restrictions, and eight insisted that
the home school be a legal private school (Guterson
91). Because of their efforts, Mary Jane can start
her school day without leaving the house.

Works-cited list begins on a new page, one inch top margin

Title centered

Double-space throughout

Entries in alphabetical order by authors' last names

Entry begins flush with left margin

Subsequent lines indent five spaces

Angle brackets enclose the URL

Period after author, after title, and at end of entry

Dinh 8

1"

Works Cited

Allis, Sam. "Schooling Kids at Home." Time 22 Oct. 1990: 84-85.

Connolly, Cindy. "Teen-agers See Advantages to Attending School at Home." Omaha World Herald 18 Sept. 1990: 32. NewsBank: Education 1990: fiche 106, grids E1-E3.

Friedlander, Tom. "A Decade of Home Schooling." The Home School Reader. Ed. Mark and Helen Hegener. Tonasket: Home Education, 1988.

Gallup, Alec M., and Stanley M. Elam. "The 20th Annual Gallup Poll: Of the Public toward the Public Schools." Phi Delta Kappan Sept. 1988: 34.

Gatto, John Taylor. "The Nine Assumptions of Modern Schooling." The Education Liberator. 30 May 1996. 19 Oct. 1999 <http://www.sepschool.org>.

Graves, Bill. "Home School: Enrollment Increases in Oregon, Nation." Oregonian 4 Nov. 1990: D1. NewsBank: Education 1990: fiche 135, grids B8-B9.

Guterson, David. Family Matters: Why Homeschooling Makes Sense. San Diego: Harcourt, 1992.

Hawkins, Dana. "Homeschool Battles: Clashes Grow as Some in the Movement Seek Access to Public Schools." U.S. News & World Report 12 Feb. 1996: 57-58.

Hawley, Richard A. "Schoolchildren and Drugs: The Fancy That Has Not Passed." Phi Delta Kappan May 1987: K1-K3.

Kilgore, Peter. "Profile of Families Who Home School in Maine." 1987. 1-47. ERIC ED 295 280.

Kohn, Alfie. "Home schooling." Atlantic Apr. 1988: 20-25.

Lines, Patricia. Estimating the Home School Education Population. Washington: U.S. Dept. of Education, 1991.

Dinh 9

Monday, Susan McAtee. "In-House Education." <u>San Antonio Light</u> 18 Mar. 1990: <u>NewsBank: Education</u> 1990: fiche 27, grids C11, C13.

Shackelford, Luanne, and Susan White. <u>A Survivor's Guide to Home Schooling</u>. Westchester: Crossway, 1988.

Shenk, Dan. "Parents Find Home-Schooling Has Special Rewards." <u>Elkhart Truth</u> 20 Mar. 1988: <u>NewsBank: Education</u> 1988: fiche 41, grid D6.

Part Five

WRITING FOR ASSESSMENT

Essay Examinations

23

Essay exams are inescapable. Even though the machine-scorable multiple-choice test has sharply reduced the number of essay exams administered in schools and colleges, essay exams will continue to play a significant role in the education of liberal arts students. Many instructors—especially in the humanities and social sciences—still believe that an exam that requires you to write is the best way to find out what you have learned and, more important, how you can use what you have learned. Instructors who give essay exams want to be sure you can sort through the large body of information covered in a course, identify what is important or significant, and explain your decision. They want to see whether you understand the concepts that provide the basis for a course and whether you can use those concepts to interpret specific materials, to make connections on your own, to see relationships, to draw comparisons and find contrasts, and to synthesize diverse information in support of an original assertion. They may even be interested in your ability to justify your own evaluations based on appropriate standards of judgment and to argue your own opinions with convincing reasons and supporting evidence. Remember that your instructors want to encourage you to think more critically and analytically about a subject; they feel, therefore, that a written exam provides the best demonstration that you are doing so.

As a college student, then, you will face a variety of essay exams, from short-answer identifications that require only a few sentences to take-home exams that may involve hours of planning and writing. You will find that the writing activities and strategies discussed in Parts One and Three of this book—particularly narrating, describing, defining, comparing and contrasting, and arguing—as well as the critical thinking strategies in Part Two will help you to do well on these exams. This chapter provides some more specific guidelines for you to follow in preparing for and writing essay exams and analyzes a group of typical exam questions to help determine which strategies will be most useful.

But you can also learn a great deal from your experiences with essay exams in the past, the embarrassment and frustration of doing poorly on one and the great pleasure and pride of doing well. Do you recall the best exam you ever wrote? Do you remember how you wrote it and why you were able to do so well? How can you be certain to approach such writing tasks confidently and to complete them successfully? Keep these questions in mind as you consider the following guidelines.

■ PREPARING FOR AN EXAM

First of all, essay exams require a comprehensive understanding of large amounts of information. Because exam questions can reach so widely into the course materials— and in such unpredictable ways—the best way to ensure that you will do well on them is to keep up with readings and assignments from the very start of the course. Do the reading, go to lectures, take careful notes, participate in discussion sessions, organize small study groups with classmates to explore and review course materials throughout the semester. Trying to cram weeks of information into a single night of study will never allow you to do your best.

Then, as an exam approaches, find out what you can about the form it will take. No question is more irritating to instructors than the pestering inquiry "Do we need to know this for the exam?" but it is generally legitimate to ask whether the questions will require short or long answers, how many questions there will be, whether you may choose which questions to answer, and what kinds of thinking and writing will be required of you. Some instructors may hand out study guides for exams or even lists of potential questions. However, you will often be on your own in determining how best to go about studying.

Try to avoid simply memorizing information aimlessly. As you study, you should be clarifying the important issues of the course and using these issues to focus your understanding of specific facts and particular readings. If the course is a historical survey, distinguish the primary periods and try to see relations among the periods and the works or events that define them. If the course is thematically unified, determine how the particular materials you have been reading relate to those themes. If the course is a broad introduction to a general topic, concentrate on the central concerns of each study unit and see what connections you can discover among the various units. Try to place all you have learned into perspective, into a meaningful context. How do the pieces fit together? What fundamental ideas have the readings, the lectures, and the discussions seemed to emphasize? How can those ideas help you digest the information the course has covered?

One good way to prepare yourself for an exam is by making up questions you think the instructor might ask and then planning answers to them with classmates. Returning to your notes and to assigned readings with specific questions in mind can help enormously in your process of understanding. The important thing to remember is that an essay exam tests more than your memory of specific information; it requires you to use specific information to demonstrate a comprehensive grasp of the topics covered in the course.

■ READING THE EXAM CAREFULLY

Before you answer a single question, read the entire exam so that you can apportion your time realistically. Pay particular attention to how many points you may earn in different parts of the exam; notice any directions that suggest how long an answer should be or how much space it should take up. As you are doing so, you may wish to make tentative choices of the questions you will answer and decide on the order in which you will answer them. If you have immediate ideas about how you would organize any of your answers, you might also jot down partial scratch outlines. But before you start to complete any answers, write down the actual clock time you expect to be working on each question or set of questions. Careful time management is crucial to your success on essay exams; giving some time to each question is always better than using up your time on only a few and never getting to others.

You will next need to analyze each question carefully before beginning to write your answer. Decide what you are being asked to do. If your immediate impulse is to cast about for ideas indiscriminately, it can be easy at this point to become flustered, to lose concentration, even to go blank. But if you first look closely at what the question is directing you to do and try to understand the sort of writing that will be required, you can begin to recognize the structure your answer will need to take. This tentative structure will help you focus your attention on the particular information that will be pertinent to your answer. Consider this question from a sociology final:

> Drawing from lectures on the contradictory aspects of American values, discussions of the "bureaucratic personality," and the type of behavior associated with social mobility, discuss the problems of bettering oneself in a relatively "open," complex, industrial society such as the United States.

Such a question can cause momentary panic, but you can nearly always define the writing task you face. Look first at the words that give you directions: *draw from* and *discuss*. The term *discuss* is fairly vague, of course, but here it probably invites you to list and explain the problems of bettering oneself. The categories of these problems are already identified in the opening phrases: contradictory values, bureaucratic personality, certain behavior. Therefore, you would plan to begin with an assertion (or thesis) that included the key words in the final clause (bettering oneself in an open, complex, industrial society) and then take up each category of problem—and perhaps other problems you can think of—in separate paragraphs.

This question essentially calls for recall, organization, and clear presentation of facts from lectures and readings. Though it looks confusing at first, once you sort it out, you will find that it contains the key terms for the answer's thesis, as well as the main points of development. In the next section are some further examples of the kinds of questions often found on essay exams. Pay particular attention to how the directions and the key words in each case can help you define the writing task involved.

■ SOME TYPICAL ESSAY EXAM QUESTIONS

Following are nine categories of exam questions, divided according to the sort of writing task involved and illustrated by examples. You will notice that although the wording of the examples in a category may differ, the essential directions are very much the same.

All of the examples are unedited and were written by instructors in six different departments in the humanities and social sciences at two different universities. Drawn from short quizzes, midterms, and final exams for a variety of first- and second-year courses, these questions demonstrate the range of writing you may be expected to do on exams.

Define or Identify

See Chapter 16 for more on defining.

Some questions require you to write a few sentences defining or identifying material from readings or lectures. Such questions almost always allow you only a few minutes to complete your answer.

You may be asked for a brief overview of a large topic, as in Question 23.1. This question, from a twenty-minute quiz in a literature course, was worth as much as 15 of the 100 points possible on the quiz.

Question 23.1

Name and describe the three stages of African literature.

Answering this question would simply involve following the specific directions. A student would probably *name* the periods in historical order and then *describe* each period in a separate sentence or two.

Other questions, like Question 23.2, supply a list of specific items to identify. This example comes from a final exam in a communication course, and the answer to each part was worth as much as 4 points on a 120-point exam.

Question 23.2

Define and state some important facts concerning each of the following:

A. demographics

B. instrumental model

C. RCA

D. telephone booth of the air

E. penny press

With no more than three or four minutes for each part, students taking this exam would offer a concise definition (probably in a sentence), then briefly expand the definition with facts relevant to the main topics in the course.

Sometimes the list of items to be identified can be quite complicated, including quotations, concepts, and specialized terms; it may also be worth a significant number of points. The next example contains the first five items in a list of fifteen that opened a literature final. Each item was worth 3 points, for a total of 45 out of a possible 130 points.

Question 23.3

Identify each of the following items:

1. projection
2. "In this vast landscape he had loved so much, he was alone."
3. Balducci
4. *pied noir*
5. the Massif Central

Although the directions do not say so specifically, it is crucial here not only to identify each item but also to explain its significance in terms of the overall subject. In composing a definition or an identification, always ask yourself a simple question: Why is this item important enough to be on the exam?

Recall Details of a Specific Source

Sometimes instructors will ask for a straightforward summary or paraphrase of a specific source—for example, a report on a book or a film. To answer such questions, the student must recount details directly from the source and is not encouraged to interpret or evaluate. In the following example from a sociology exam, students were allowed about ten minutes and required to complete the answer on one lined page provided with the exam.

For more on summarizing and paraphrasing, see Chapter 12, pp. 541–43.

Question 23.4

In his article "Is There a Culture of Poverty?" Oscar Lewis addresses a popular question in the social sciences: What is the "culture of poverty"? How is it able to come into being, according to Lewis? That is, under what conditions does it exist? When does he say a person is no longer a part of the culture of poverty? What does Lewis say is the future of the culture of poverty?

The phrasing here invites a fairly clear-cut structure. Each of the five specific questions can be turned into an assertion and supported with illustrations from Lewis's article. For example, the first two questions could become assertions like these: "Lewis defines the culture of poverty as _____," and "According to Lewis, the culture of poverty comes into being through _____." The important thing in this case is to summarize accurately what the writer said and not waste time evaluating or criticizing his ideas.

Explain the Importance or Significance

Another kind of essay exam question asks students to explain the importance of something covered in the course. Such questions require specific examples as the basis for a more general discussion of what has been studied. This type of question often involves interpreting a literary or cinematic work by concentrating on a particular aspect of it, as in Question 23.5. This question was worth 10 out of 100 points and was to be answered in seventy-five to one hundred words.

Question 23.5

In the last scene of *The Paths of Glory,* the owner of a café brings a young German woman onto a small stage in his café to sing for the French troops, while Colonel Dax looks on from outside the café. Briefly explain the significance of this scene in relation to the movie as a whole.

In answering this question, a student's first task would be to reconsider the whole movie, looking for ways in which this one brief scene illuminates or explains larger issues or themes. Then, in a paragraph or two, the student would summarize these themes and point out how each element of the specific scene fits into the overall context.

You may also be asked to interpret specific information to show that you understand the fundamental concepts of a course. The following example from a communication midterm was worth a possible 10 of 100 points and was allotted twenty minutes of exam time.

Question 23.6

Chukovsky gives many examples of cute expressions and statements uttered by small children. Give an example or two of the kinds of statements that he finds interesting. Then state their implications for understanding the nature of language in particular and communication more generally.

Here the student must start by choosing examples of children's utterances from Chukovsky's book. These examples would then provide the basis for demonstrating the student's grasp of the larger subject.

Questions like these are usually more challenging than definition and summary questions because you must decide for yourself the significance, importance, or implications of the information. You must also consider how best to organize your answer so that the general ideas you need to communicate are clearly developed.

Apply Concepts

See Chapter 5 for more on explaining a concept.

Very often, courses in the humanities and the social sciences emphasize significant themes, ideologies, or concepts. A common essay exam question asks students to apply the concepts to works studied in the course. Rather than providing specific information to be interpreted more generally, such questions present you with a general idea and require you to illustrate it with specific examples from your reading.

On a literature final, an instructor posed this writing task. It was worth 50 points out of 100, and students had about an hour to complete it.

Question 23.7

Many American writers have portrayed their characters or their poetic speaker as being engaged in a quest. The quest may be explicit or implicit, it may be external or psychological, and it may end in failure or success. Analyze the quest motif in the work of four of the following writers: Edwards, Franklin, Hawthorne, Thoreau, Douglass, Whitman, Dickinson, James, Twain.

On another literature final, the following question was worth 45 of 130 points. Students had about forty-five minutes to answer it.

Question 23.8

Several works studied in this course depict scapegoat figures. Select two written works and two films, and discuss how their authors or directors present and analyze the social conflicts that lead to the creation of scapegoats.

Question 23.7 instructs students to *analyze,* and Question 23.8 instructs them to *discuss;* yet the answers for both questions would be structured very similarly. An introductory paragraph would define the concept—the *quest* or a *scapegoat*—and refer to the works to be discussed. Then, a paragraph or two would be devoted to the works, developing specific support to illustrate the concept. A concluding paragraph would probably attempt to bring the concept into clearer focus, which is, after all, the point of answering these questions.

Comment on a Quotation

On essay exams, an instructor will often ask students to comment on a quotation they are seeing for the first time. Usually, such quotations will express some surprising or controversial opinion that complements or challenges basic principles or ideas in the course. Sometimes the writer being quoted is identified, sometimes not. In fact, it is not unusual for instructors to write the quotation themselves.

A student choosing to answer the following question from a literature final would have risked half the exam—in points and time—on the outcome.

Question 23.9

Argue for or against this thesis: "In *A Clockwork Orange,* both the heightened, poetic language and the almost academic concern with moral and political theories deprive the story of most of its relevance to real life."

The directions here clearly ask for an argument. A student would need to set up a thesis indicating that the novel either is or is not relevant to real life and then point out how its language and its theoretical concerns can be viewed in light of this thesis.

The next example comes from a midterm exam in a history course. Students had forty minutes to write their answers, which could earn as much as 70 points on a 100-point exam.

Question 23.10

"Some historians believe that economic hardship and oppression breed social revolt; but the experience of the United States and Mexico between 1900 and 1920 suggests that people may rebel also during times of prosperity."

Comment on this statement. Why did large numbers of Americans and Mexicans wish to change conditions in their countries during the years from 1900 to 1920? How successful were their efforts? Who benefited from the changes that took place?

Although here students are instructed to "comment," the three questions make clear that a successful answer will require an argument: a clear *thesis* stating a position on the views expressed in the quotation, specific *reasons* for that thesis, and *support* for the thesis from readings and lectures. In general, such questions do not require a "right" answer: Whether you agree or disagree with the quotation is not as important as whether you can argue your case reasonably and convincingly, demonstrating a firm grasp of the subject matter.

See Chapter 19 for more on these components of an argument.

Compare and Contrast

Instructors are particularly fond of essay exam questions that require a comparison and contrast of two or three principles, ideas, works, activities, or phenomena. To answer this kind of question, you need to explore fully the relations between things of importance in the course, analyze each thing separately, and then search out specific points of likeness or difference. Students must thus show a thorough knowledge of the things being compared, as well as a clear understanding of the basic issues on which comparisons and contrasts can be made.

Often, as in Question 23.11, the basis of comparison will be limited to a particular focus; here, for example, students are asked to compare two works in terms of their views of colonialism.

Question 23.11

Compare and analyze the views of colonialism presented in Memmi's *Colonizer and the Colonized* and Pontecorvo's *Battle of Algiers*. What are the significant differences between these two views?

Sometimes instructors will simply identify what is to be compared, leaving students the task of choosing the basis of the comparison, as in the next three examples from communication, history, and literature exams, respectively.

Question 23.12

In what way is the stage of electronic media fundamentally different from all the major stages that preceded it?

Question 23.13

What was the role of the United States in Cuban affairs from 1898 until 1959? How did its role there compare with its role in the rest of Spanish America during the same period?

Question 23.14

Write an essay on one of the following topics:

1. Squire Western and Mr. Knightley
2. Dr. Primrose and Mr. Elton

Whether the point of comparison is stated in the question or left for you to define for yourself, it is important to limit your answer to the aspects of similarity or difference that are most relevant to the general concepts or themes covered in the course.

See Chapter 18 for more on comparing and contrasting.

Synthesize Information from Various Sources

In a course with several assigned readings, an instructor may give students an essay exam question that requires them to pull together (synthesize) information from several or even all the readings.

For more on synthesizing, see Chapter 12, pp. 544–45.

The following example was one of four required questions on a final exam in a course in Latin American studies. Students had about thirty minutes to complete their answer.

Question 23.15

On the basis of the articles read on El Salvador, Nicaragua, Peru, Chile, Argentina, and Mexico, what would you say are the major problems confronting Latin America today? Discuss the major types of problems with references to particular countries as examples.

This question asks students to do a lot in thirty minutes. They must first decide which major problems to discuss, which countries to include in each discussion, and how to use material from many readings to develop their answers. To compose a coherent essay, a student will need a carefully developed forecasting statement.

For more on forecasting statements, see Chapter 13, p. 559.

Analyze Causes

See Chapter 9 for more on analyzing causes.

In humanities and social science courses, much of what students study concerns the causes of trends, actions, and events. Hence, it is not surprising to find questions about causes on essay exams. In such cases, the instructor expects students to analyze causes from readings and lectures. These examples come from midterm and final exams in literature, sociology, cultural studies, and communication courses, respectively.

Question 23.16

Why do Maurice and Jean not succumb to the intolerable conditions of the prison camp (the Camp of Hell) as most of the others do?

Question 23.17

Given that we occupy several positions in the course of our lives and given that each position has a specific role attached to it, what kinds of problems or dilemmas arise from those multiple roles, and how are they handled?

Question 23.18

Explain briefly the relationship between the institution of slavery and the emergence of the blues as a new African American musical expression.

Question 23.19

Analyze the way in which an uncritical promotion of the new information technology (computers, satellites, etc.) may support, unintentionally, the maintenance of the status quo.

Although these questions are presented in several ways ("what kinds of problems," "explain the relationship," "analyze the way"), they all require a list of causes in the answer. The causes would be organized under a thesis statement, and each cause would be argued and supported by referring to lectures or readings.

Criticize or Evaluate

See Chapter 8 for more on evaluation.

Occasionally, instructors will include essay exam questions that invite students to evaluate a concept or a work. Nearly always, they want more than opinion: They expect a reasoned, documented judgment based on appropriate standards of judgment. Not only do such questions test students' ability to recall and synthesize pertinent information, but they also allow instructors to find out whether students understand and can apply criteria taught in the course.

On a final exam in a literature course, a student might have chosen one of the following questions about novels read in the course. Each would have been worth half the total points, with about an hour to answer it.

Question 23.20

Evaluate *A Passage to India* from a postcolonial critical standpoint.

Question 23.21

A Clockwork Orange and *The Comfort of Strangers* both attempt to examine the nature of modern decadence. Which does so more successfully?

To answer either of these questions, a student would obviously have to be very familiar with the novels under discussion and would have to establish standards for evaluating works of literature. The student would initially have to make a judgment favoring one novel over the other (though not necessarily casting one novel as "terrible" and the other as "perfect"). The student would then give reasons for this judgment, with supporting quotations from the novels, and probably use the writing strategies of comparison and contrast to develop the argument.

This next question was worth 10 of 85 points on a communication course midterm. Students were asked to answer "in two paragraphs."

See Chapter 18 for more on comparing and contrasting.

Question 23.22

Eisenstein and Mukerji both argue that movable print was important to the rise of Protestantism. Cole extends this argument to say that print set off a chain of events that was important to the history of the United States. Summarize this argument, and criticize any part of it if you choose.

Here students are asked to criticize or evaluate an argument in several course readings. The instructor wants to know what students think of this argument and even though this is not stated, why they judge it as they do. Answering this unwritten "why" part of the question is the challenge: Students must come up with reasons and support appropriate to evaluating the argument.

■ PLANNING YOUR ANSWER

The amount of planning you do for a question will depend on how much time it is allotted and how many points it is worth. For short-answer definitions and identifications, a few seconds of thought will probably be sufficient. (Be careful not to puzzle too long over individual items like these. Skip over any you cannot recognize fairly quickly; often, answering other questions will help jog your memory.) For answers that require a paragraph or two, you may want to jot down several ideas and examples to focus your thoughts and give you a basis for organizing your information.

For longer answers, though, you will need to develop a much more definite strategy of organization. You have time for only one draft, so allow a reasonable period —as much as a quarter of the time allotted the question—for making notes, determining a thesis, and developing an outline. Jotting down pertinent ideas is a good way to begin; then you can plan your organization with a scratch outline (just a listing of points or facts) or a cluster.

For questions with several parts (different requests or directions, a sequence of questions), make a list of the parts so that you do not miss or minimize one part. For questions presented as questions (rather than directives), you might want to rephrase each question as a writing topic. These topics will often suggest how you should outline the answer.

You may have to try two or three outlines or clusters before you hit on a workable plan. But be realistic as you outline—you want a plan you can develop within the limited time allotted for your answer. Hence, your outline will have to be selective—it will contain not everything you know on the topic but rather what you know that can be developed clearly within the time available.

For information on clustering and outlining, see Chapter 11, pp. 516–21.

■ WRITING YOUR ANSWER

As with planning, your strategy for writing depends on the length of your answer. For short identifications and definitions, it is usually best to start with a general identifying statement and then move on to describe specific applications or explanations. Two sentences will almost always suffice, but make sure you write complete sentences.

For longer answers, begin by stating your forecasting statement or thesis clearly and explicitly. An essay exam is not an occasion for indirectness: You want to strive for focus, simplicity, and clarity. In stating your point and developing your answer, use key terms from the question; it may look as though you are avoiding the question unless you use key terms (the same key terms) throughout your essay. If the question does not supply any key terms, you will find that you have provided your own by stating your main point. Use these key terms throughout the answer.

If you have devised a promising outline for your answer, you will be able to forecast your overall plan and its subpoints in your opening sentences. Forecasting shows readers how your essay is organized and has the practical advantage of making your answer easier to read. You might also want to use briefer paragraphs than you ordinarily do and signal clear relations between paragraphs with transition phrases or sentences.

See Chapter 13 for more on forecasting and transitions.

As you begin writing your answer, freely strike out words or even sentences you want to change by drawing through them neatly with a single line. Do not stop to erase, and try not to be messy. Instructors do not expect flawless writing, but they are put off by unnecessary messiness.

As you continue to write, you will certainly think of new subpoints and new ideas or facts to include later in the essay answer. Stop briefly to make a note of these on your original outline. If you find that you want to add a sentence or two to sections you have already completed, write them in the margin or at the top of the page, with a neat arrow pointing to where they fit in your answer.

Do not pad your answer with irrelevancies and repetitions just to fill up space. You may have had one instructor who did not seem to pay much attention to what you wrote, but most instructors read exams carefully and are not impressed by the length of an answer alone. Within the time available, write a comprehensive, specific answer without padding.

Watch the clock carefully to ensure that you do not spend too much time on one answer. You must be realistic about the time constraints of an essay exam, especially if you know the material well and are prepared to write a lot. If you write one dazzling answer on an exam with three required questions, you earn only 33 points, not enough to pass at most colleges. Being required to answer more than one question may seem unfair, but keep in mind that instructors plan exams to be reasonably comprehensive. They want you to write about the course materials in two or three or more ways, not just one way.

If you run out of time when you are writing an answer, jot down the remaining main ideas from your outline, just to show that you know the material and with more time could have continued your exposition.

Write legibly and proofread what you write. Remember that your instructor will likely be reading a large pile of exams. Careless scrawls, misspellings, omitted words, and missing punctuation (especially missing periods needed to mark the ends of sentences) will only make that reading difficult, even exasperating. A few minutes of careful proofreading can improve your grade.

◼ MODEL ANSWERS TO SOME TYPICAL ESSAY EXAM QUESTIONS

Here we analyze several successful answers and give you an opportunity to analyze one for yourself. These analyses, along with the information we have provided elsewhere in this chapter, should greatly improve your chances of writing successful exam answers.

Short Answers

A literature midterm opened with ten items to identify, each worth 3 points. Students had about two minutes for each item. Here are three of Brenda Gossett's answers, each one earning her the full 3 points.

> Rauffenstein: He was the German general who was in charge of the castle where Boeldieu, Marical, and Rosenthal were finally sent in The Grand Illusion. He, along with Boeldieu, represented the aristocracy, which was slowly fading out at that time.
>
> Iges Peninsula: This peninsula is created by the Meuse River in France. It is there that the Camp of Hell was created in The Debacle. The Camp of Hell is where the French army was interned after the Germans defeated them in the Franco-Prussian War.
>
> Pache: He was the "religious peasant" in the novel The Debacle. It was he who inevitably became a scapegoat when he

```
was murdered by Loubet, La Poulle, and Chouteau because he
wouldn't share his bread with them.
```

The instructor said only "identify the following" but clearly wanted students both to identify the item and to indicate its significance to the work in which it appeared. Gossett does both and gets full credit. She mentions particular works, characters, and events. Although she is rushed, she answers in complete sentences. She does not misspell any words or leave out any commas or periods. Her answers are complete and correct.

Paragraph-Length Answers

One question on a weekly literature quiz was worth 20 points of the total of 100. With only a few minutes to answer the question, students were instructed to "answer in a few sentences." Here is the question and Camille Prestera's answer:

> In *Things Fall Apart,* how did Okonkwo's relationship with his father affect his attitude toward his son?

```
Okonkwo despised his father, who was lazy, cowardly, and in
debt. Okonkwo tried to be everything his father wasn't. He
was hardworking, wealthy, and a great warrior and wrestler.
Okonkwo treated his son harshly because he was afraid he saw
the same weakness in Nwoye that he despised in his father. The
result of this harsh treatment was that Nwoye left home.
```

Prestera begins by describing Okonkwo and his father, contrasting the two sharply. Then she explains Okonkwo's relationship with his son Nwoye. Her answer is coherent and straightforward.

Long Answers

Many final exams include at least one question requiring an essay-length answer. John Pixley had an hour to plan and write this essay for a final exam in a literature course in response to Question 23.7:

> Many American writers have portrayed their characters or their poetic speaker as being engaged in a quest. The quest may be explicit or implicit, it may be external or psychological, and it may end in failure or success. Analyze the quest motif in the work of four of the following writers: Edwards, Franklin, Hawthorne, Thoreau, Douglass, Whitman, Dickinson, James, Twain.

John Pixley's Answer

```
     Americans pride themselves on being ambitious and on       1
being able to strive for goals and to tap their potential.
Some say that this is what the "American Dream" is all about.
```

It is important for one to do and be all that one is capable of. This entails a quest or search for identity, experience, and happiness. Hence, the idea of the quest is a vital one in the United States, and it can be seen as a theme throughout American literature.

Key term, quest, *is mentioned in introduction and thesis.*

In eighteenth-century colonial America, Jonathan Edwards dealt with this theme in his autobiographical and personal writings. Unlike his fiery and hard-nosed sermons, these autobiographical writings present a sensitive, vulnerable man trying to find himself and his proper, satisfying place in the world. He is concerned with his spiritual growth, in being free to find and explore religious experience and happiness. For example, in Personal Narrative, he very carefully traces the stages of religious beliefs. He tells about periods of abandoned ecstasy, doubts, and rational revelations. He also notes that his best insights and growth came at times when he was alone in the wilderness, in nature. Edwards's efforts to find himself in relation to the world can also be seen in his "Observations of the Natural World," in which he relates various meticulously observed and described natural phenomena to religious precepts and occurrences. Here, he is trying to give the world and life, of which he is a part, some sense of meaning and purpose.

2 *First writer is identified immediately.*

Edwards's work and the details of his quest are presented.

Although he was a contemporary of Edwards, Benjamin Franklin, who was very involved in the founding of the United States as a nation, had a different conception of the quest. He sees the quest as being one for practical accomplishment, success, and wealth. In his Autobiography, he stresses that happiness involves working hard to accomplish things, getting along with others, and establishing a good reputation. Unlike Edwards's, his quest is external and bound up with society. He is concerned with his morals and behavior, but, as seen in part 2 of the Autobiography, he deals with them in an objective, pragmatic, even statistical way, rather than in sensitive pondering. It is also evident in this work that Franklin, unlike Edwards, believes so much in himself and his quest that he is able to laugh at himself. His concern with society can be seen in Poor Richard's Almanac, in which he gives practical advice on how to find success and happiness in the world, how to "be healthy, wealthy, and wise."

3 *Transition sentence identifies second writer. Key term* (quest) *is repeated.*

Contrast with Edwards adds coherence to essay.

Another key term from the question, external, *is used.*

Franklin's particular kind of quest is described.

Still another version of the quest can be seen in the mid-nineteenth-century poetry of Walt Whitman. The quest that he portrays blends elements of those of Edwards and Franklin.

4 *Transition sentence identifies third writer. Key term is repeated.*

Comparison of Whitman to Edwards and Franklin sustains coherence of essay.

In "Song of Myself," which is clearly autobiographical, the speaker emphasizes the importance of finding, knowing, and enjoying oneself as part of nature and the human community. He says that one should come to realize that one is lovable, just as are all other people and all of nature and life. This is a quest for sensitivity and awareness, as Edwards advocates, and

Whitman's quest is defined.

for great self-confidence, as Franklin advocates. Along with Edwards, Whitman sees that peaceful isolation in nature is important; but he also sees the importance of interacting with people, as Franklin does. Being optimistic and feeling good--both in the literal and figurative sense--are the objects of this quest. Unfortunately, personal disappointment and national crisis (i.e., the Civil War) shattered Whitman's sense of confidence, and he lost the impetus of this quest in his own life.

Transition: Key term is repeated, and fourth writer is identified.

This theme of the quest can be seen in prose fiction as   5
well as in poetry and autobiography. One interesting example is "The Beast in the Jungle," a short story written by Henry James around 1903. It is interesting in that not only does the principal character, John Marcher, fail in his lifelong quest, but his failure comes about in a most subtle and frustrating

Quest of James character is described.

way. Marcher believes that something momentous is going to happen in his future. He talks about his belief to only one person, a woman named May. May decides to befriend him for life and watch with him for the momentous occurrence to come about, for "the beast in the jungle" to "pounce." As time passes, May seems to know what this occurrence is and eventually even says that it has happened; but John is still in the dark. It is only long after May's death that the beast pounces on him in his recognition that the "beast" was his failure to truly love May, the one woman of his life, even though she gave him all the encouragement that she possibly, decently could. Marcher never defined the terms of his quest until it was too late. By just waiting and watching, he failed to find feeling and passion. This tragic realization, as someone like Whitman would view it, brings about John Marcher's ruin.

Conclusion repeats key term.

As seen in these few examples, the theme of the quest is   6
a significant one in American literature. Also obvious is the fact that there are a variety of approaches to, methods used in, and outcomes of the quest. This is an appropriate theme for American literature seeing how much Americans cherish the right of "the pursuit of happiness."

Pixley's answer is strong for two reasons: He has the information he needs, and he has organized it carefully and presented it coherently.

■ Exercise 23.1

The following essay was written by Don Hepler. He answered the same essay exam question as his classmate John Pixley. Analyze Hepler's essay to discover whether it meets the criteria of a good essay exam answer. Review the criteria mentioned earlier in this chapter in Writing Your Answer and in the annotated commentary of John Pixley's answer. Try to identify the features of Hepler's essay that contribute to or work against its success.

Don Hepler's Answer

The quest motif is certainly important in American literature. By considering Franklin, Thoreau, Douglass, and Twain, we can see that the quest may be explicit or implicit, external or psychological, a failure or a success. Tracing the quest motif through these four authors seems to show a developing concern in American literature with transcending materialism to address deeper issues. It also reveals a drift toward ambiguity and pessimism.

Benjamin Franklin's quest, as revealed by his Autobiography, is for material comfort and outward success. His quest may be considered an explicit one because he announces clearly what he is trying to do: perfect a systematic approach for living long and happily. The whole Autobiography is a road map intended for other people to use as a guide; Franklin apparently meant rather literally for people to imitate his methods. He wrote with the assumption that his success was reproducible. He is possibly the most optimistic author in American literature because he enjoys life, knows exactly why he enjoys life, and believes that anyone else willing to follow his formula may enjoy life as well.

By Franklin's standards, his quest is clearly a success. But his Autobiography portrays only an external, not a psychological, success. This is not to suggest that Franklin was a psychological, failure. Indeed, we have every reason to believe the contrary. But the fact remains that Franklin wrote only about external success; he never indicated how he really felt emotionally. Possibly it was part of Franklin's overriding optimism to assume that material comfort leads naturally to emotional fulfillment.

Henry David Thoreau presents a more multifaceted quest.   4
His Walden is, on the simplest level, the chronicle of
Thoreau's physical journey out of town and into the woods. But
the moving itself is not the focus of Walden. It is really
more of a metaphor for some kind of spiritual quest going on
within Thoreau's mind. Most of the action in Walden is mental,
as Thoreau contemplates and philosophizes, always using the
lake, the woods, and his own daily actions as symbols of
higher, more eternal truths. This spiritual quest is a success
in that Thoreau is able to appreciate the beauty of nature and
to see through much of the sham and false assumptions of town
life and blind materialism.

Thoreau does not leave us with nearly as explicit a   5
"blueprint" for success as Franklin does. Even Franklin's
plan is limited to people of high intelligence, personal
discipline, and sound character; Franklin sometimes seems to
forget that many human beings are in fact weak and evil and
so would stand little chance of success similar to his own.
But at least Franklin's quest could be duplicated by another
Franklin. Thoreau's quest is more problematic, for even as
great a mystic and naturalist as Thoreau himself could not
remain in the woods indefinitely. This points toward the idea
that the real quest is all internal and psychological; Thoreau
seems to have gone to the woods to develop a spiritual
strength that he could keep and take elsewhere on subsequent
dealings with the "real world."

The quest of Frederick Douglass was explicit in that he   6
needed physically to get north and escape slavery, but it
was also implicit because he sought to discover and redefine
himself through his quest, as Thoreau did. Douglass's motives
were more sharply focused than either Franklin's or Thoreau's;
his very humanness was at stake, as well as his physical
well-being and possibly even his life. But Douglass also makes
it clear that the most horrible part of slavery was the mental
anguish of having no hope of freedom. His learning to read,
and his maintenance of this skill, seems to have been as
important as the maintenance of his material comforts, of
which he had very few. In a sense, Douglass's quest is the
most psychological and abstract so far because it is for
the very essence of freedom and humanity, both of which
were mostly taken for granted by Franklin and Thoreau. Also,
Douglass's quest is the most pessimistic of the three;

Douglass concludes that physical violence is the only way out,
as he finds with the Covey incident.

   Finally, Mark Twain's Huckleberry Finn is an example   7
of the full range of meaning that the quest motif may assume.
Geographically, Huck's quest is very large. But again, there
is a quest defined implicitly as well as one defined
explicitly, as Huck (without consciously realizing it)
searches for morality, truth, and freedom. Twain's use of the
quest is ambiguous, even more so than the previous writers',
because while he suggests success superficially (i.e., the
"happily ever after" scene in the last chapter), he really
hints at some sort of ultimate hopelessness inherent in society. Not even Douglass questions the good or evil of American
society as deeply as Twain does; for Douglass, everything will
be fine when slavery is abolished; but for Twain, the only
solution is to "light out for the territories" altogether--and
when Twain wrote, he knew that the territories were no more.

   Twain's implicit sense of spiritual failure stands in   8
marked contrast to Franklin's buoyant confidence in material
success. The guiding image of the quest, however, is central
to American values and, consequently, a theme that these
writers and others have adapted to suit their own vision.

Exercise 23.2

Analyze the following essay exam questions in order to decide what kind of writing task they present. What is being asked of the student as a participant in the course and as a writer? Given the time constraints of the exam, what plan would you propose for writing the answer? Following each question is the number of points it is worth and the amount of time allotted to answer it.

1. Cortazar is a producer of fantastic literature. Discuss first what fantastic literature is. Then choose any four stories by Cortazar as examples, and discuss the fantastic elements in these stories. Refer to the structure, techniques, and narrative styles that he uses in these four stories. If you like, you may refer to more than four, of course. (Points: 30 of 100. Time: 40 of 150 minutes.)

2. During the course of the twentieth century, the United States has experienced three significant periods of social reform—the progressive era, the age of the Great Depression, and the decade of the 1960s. What were the sources of reform in each period? What were the most significant reform achievements of each period as well as the largest failings? (Points: 35 of 100. Time: 75 of 180 minutes.)

3. Since literature is both an artistic and ideological product, writers comment on their material context through their writing.
   a. What is Rulfo's perspective of his Mexican reality, and how is it portrayed through his stories?

    b. What particular themes does he deal with, especially in these stories: "The Burning Plain," "Luvina," "They Gave Us the Land," "Paso del Norte," and "Tell Them Not to Kill Me"?

    c. What literary techniques and structures does he use to convey his perspective? Refer to a specific story as an example.

(Points: 30 of 100. Time: 20 of 50 minutes.)

4. Why is there a special reason to be concerned about the influence of television watching on kids? In your answer, include a statement of the following:

    a. Your own understanding of the *general communication principles* involved for any television watcher.

    b. What is special about television and kids.

    c. How advertisers and producers use this information. (You should draw from the relevant readings as well as lectures.)

(Points: 20 of 90. Time: 25 of 90 minutes.)

5. Analyze the autobiographical tradition in American literature, focusing on differences and similarities among authors and, if appropriate, changes over time. Discuss four authors in all. In addition to the conscious autobiographers—Edwards, Franklin, Thoreau, Douglass—you may choose one or two figures from among the following fictional or poetic quasi-autobiographers: Hawthorne, Whitman, Dickinson, Twain. (Points: 50 of 120. Time: 60 of 180 minutes.)

6. How does the system of (media) sponsorship work, and what, if any, ideological control do sponsors exert? Be specific and illustrative. (Points: 33 of 100. Time: 60 of 180 minutes.)

7. Several of the works studied in this course analyze the tension between myth and reality. Select two written works and two films, and analyze how their authors or directors present the conflict between myth and reality and how they resolve it, if they resolve it. (Points: 45 of 130. Time: 60 of 180 minutes.)

8. *Man's Hope* is a novel about the Spanish Civil War written while the war was still going on. *La Guerre Est Finie* is a film about Spanish revolutionaries depicting their activities nearly thirty years after the civil war. Discuss how the temporal relationship of each of these works to the civil war is reflected in the character of the works themselves and in the differences between them. (Points: 58 of 100. Time: 30 of 50 minutes.)

9. Write an essay on one of these topics: The role of the narrator in *Tom Jones* and *Pride and Prejudice* or the characters of Uncle Toby and Miss Bates. (Points: 33 of 100. Time: 60 of 180 minutes.)

Writing Portfolios

A writing portfolio displays your work. Portfolios for college composition courses usually include a selection of your writing for the course and an essay reflecting on your learning in the course. The contents of a portfolio will, of course, vary from writer to writer and from instructor to instructor. This chapter provides some advice for assembling a writing portfolio using the resources in *The St. Martin's Guide to Writing*.

■ THE PURPOSES OF A WRITING PORTFOLIO

Portfolios are widely used for many purposes, most generally to display an individual's accomplishments. Artists present portfolios of their work to gallery owners and patrons. Designers and architects present portfolios of their most successful and imaginative work to show potential clients what they can do. Some colleges request applicants to submit portfolios of high school writing; outstanding portfolios sometimes qualify students for college credit or placement in advanced courses. Graduating seniors may be asked to submit a portfolio of their best work for evaluation, sometimes leading to special recognition or rewards. Instructors applying for new positions or advancement may compile a portfolio to demonstrate excellence or innovation in their teaching. No matter what the specific purpose or occasion, a portfolio can present a rich opportunity to show what you can do.

Creating a portfolio for a composition course enables you to present your best, most representative, or most extensively revised writing and, to some extent, collaborate with your instructor in assessing your work. Your instructor will assign the final grade, but how you select the materials included in your portfolio and describe them in your introductory essay may have some influence on your instructor's judgment. Most importantly, selecting your work and composing a reflective essay gives you an opportunity to think critically about your learning in the course. Thinking critically, as we explain in Chapter 1, is a kind of metacognition that helps learners consolidate, reinforce, and therefore better remember and apply what they have learned. Putting together your portfolio, you reflect on what you have learned about the basic features of different genres, the writing strategies that help your writing achieve its purpose

For more on the process of thinking critically, see pp. 12–13.

for your particular readers, the composing strategies that enable you to manage complex and challenging writing assignments, and the reading and researching strategies that contribute to your success in college. In addition, reviewing your work can increase your satisfaction with your courses as you become more aware of the specific ways in which your knowledge is growing. Finally, it can give you insights into your own intellectual development, help you recognize your strengths and weaknesses, and discover your interests.

Whether or not you are asked to turn in a writing portfolio, you might want to consider keeping one as a valuable personal record of an important period in your intellectual development. You might even wish to update the portfolio each term, adding interesting work from all your courses or perhaps from all the courses in your major.

■ ASSEMBLING A PORTFOLIO FOR YOUR COMPOSITION COURSE

Some instructors give students free rein in deciding what to include in their portfolio, but most instructors specify what the portfolio should include. They usually ask students to select a certain number of the essays assigned in the course. They may specify that certain types of essays be included, such as one based on personal experience or observation and another based on library and Internet research, along with other materials like in-class writing or responses to readings. Many instructors also ask students to include materials that reflect their writing process for at least one of the essays (such as invention work, drafts, and critical responses). In addition to a selection of course materials, instructors usually require a reflective essay or letter that introduces the portfolio and evaluates the writer's own work.

Instructors who require portfolios often do not assign grades to individual drafts or revisions, but wait until the end of the term to grade the entire portfolio. In such cases, instructors may ask students to submit a midterm portfolio for an in-progress course evaluation. A midterm portfolio usually includes plans for revising further one or more of the assigned essays.

There are many possible ways of assembling portfolios, and you will need to determine exactly what your instructor expects your portfolio to include. Here are some of the variables:

- Of the essays assigned in the course, how many should be included in the portfolio?
- How many of the essays assigned throughout the course may be revised further for the portfolio?
- What process work should be included?
- What other material written or collected for the course should be included (such as exercises, notes from collaborative activities, analyses of readings, downloaded Web pages)?

- What material from other courses, workplace projects, or service-learning projects may be included?

- Should the portfolio be introduced by a reflective essay or letter? If so, how long should it be? Are there any special requirements for this essay?

- How should the portfolio be organized? Should there be a table of contents? How should each entry be labeled and each page be numbered?

- Will the essays be graded when they are turned in, at midterm, or only at the end of the term when the final portfolio is submitted?

For more on service learning, see Chapter 28.

The following sections review specific resources in *The St. Martin's Guide to Writing* that can help you select work to include in your portfolio, reflect on what you have learned, and organize your portfolio.

Selecting Work

Your instructor will very likely specify a list of what to include in your portfolio. Whatever materials you include, you have some important decisions to make, and these decisions reveal a lot about you as a writer. Here are some suggestions to help you make selections:

- If you are asked to select only your best essays, you might begin by rereading your essays to see how well each one develops the basic features of its genre. Also review any critical responses you received from your instructor, classmates, writing center tutors, or other critical readers.

- If you are asked to make further revisions to one or more of your essays, you might begin by rereading the latest revision of each essay, using the Critical Reading Guide for that genre, or getting a critical response to each essay from your instructor, a classmate, or a writing center tutor. It may also help to review any critical responses you received on earlier drafts and the revision chart you made earlier to see what else you could do to improve the essay. Be sure to edit and proofread your essays carefully.

- If you are asked to select essays based on personal experience, you might choose from the remembering events and remembering people essays you wrote for Chapters 2 and 3. If you are asked for essays based on firsthand observation and analysis, look at what you wrote for the profile (Chapter 4), the story interpretation (Chapter 10), or the concept explanation (Chapter 5). If you are asked to include argument essays, review the writing you did for Chapters 6–9.

- If you are asked to select essays incorporating library or Internet research, look at the essays you wrote for Chapters 5–9.

- If you are asked to select essays with a range of different purposes and audiences, you might begin by reviewing the Purpose and Audience sections of the Part

One chapters you used. Then reread your invention notes defining the particular purpose and audience for each essay you wrote.

- If you are asked to include examples of your writing process work, look in your process materials for your most imaginative invention work, for a first draft and one or more revisions showing significant rethinking or reorganization, for your critical reading response to another student's draft showing perceptive criticism and helpful suggestions, or for sentences you edited and the chart of your common errors.

- If you are asked to include a complete process for one essay, you might choose process materials that show the quality as well as quantity of work you have done. To reflect the quality of your work, look for examples of thoughtful invention and substantive revision you can point out in your reflective essay.

- If you are asked to select essays that show the progress you have made in the course, you may want to choose essays that underwent radical change through the term.

Reflecting on Your Work and Your Learning

Many instructors require a written statement in the form of an essay or letter introducing the portfolio. Some ask for a simple description of the work presented in your portfolio; others prefer an evaluation of your work; still others may want you to connect your learning in this course to other courses and to work you hope to do in the future. Keeping the following considerations in mind will help you write a thoughtful, well-organized statement to your instructor about what you have learned:

- *Introduce and describe your work.* Because you will need to refer to several works or parts of a work, name each item in your portfolio in a consistent way. In describing an essay, give its title, genre (using the title of the chapter in *The St. Martin's Guide*), purpose, audience, and topic.

- *Justify your choices.* When you justify what you see as your "best" work, you think critically about the standards you are using to evaluate good writing in each genre. *The St. Martin's Guide* sets forth clear criteria for each kind of writing in the Basic Features and Critical Reading sections in Chapters 2–10. Review these sections as you judge the success of your essay, and refer to them as you explain your choice.

If you need help writing an evaluation, review Chapter 8.

- *Illustrate your growth as a writer with specific examples.* You may have selected work to show how you have grown as a writer, but you should not assume your readers will read the portfolio as you do without some guidance. You need to show them where they can find evidence that supports your statements by citing relevant examples from the work included in your portfolio. Summarize or quote your examples and be sure to tell readers what you think the examples illustrate. Also refer to them in a way that will help readers locate them with ease—perhaps by page and paragraph number (see the next section for some suggestions for organizing your portfolio).

- Use *The St. Martin's Guide* to help you reflect on your learning. Your instructor may ask you to consider what you learned in writing and revising a particular essay as well as what you learned about the process of writing that essay. In either case, it will help you to anchor your reflections in the specific work you have done using this book. Consider what you have learned analyzing and discussing the readings, inventing and researching, participating in group inquiry, planning and drafting, getting and giving critical comments, and revising and editing. Look again at the Thinking Critically about What You Have Learned sections in Chapters 2–10. There you will find questions that will help you reflect on how you solved problems when revising an essay, how reading influenced your writing, and how your writing can be situated and understood in a larger social context. You may well be able to use material you have already written for these sections in your portfolio reflective essay.

Organizing the Portfolio

Some instructors prescribe the portfolio's design and organization, while others allow students to be creative. Portfolios may be presented in an inexpensive manila folder, a looseleaf, or on a Web site. Follow your instructor's specific guidelines. Here are some possibilities for organizing your portfolio:

- *Include a cover or front page.* The design of the front page may be left up to you. But be sure to indicate the class section number, the instructor's name, your own name, and the date.

- *Include a table of contents.* Portfolios, like books, need a table of contents so that readers can see at a glance what is included and where it is located. The table of contents should appear at the beginning of the portfolio, identify all of the parts of the portfolio, and specify the page on which each part begins. You may decide to renumber all of the pages in the portfolio consecutively even though some of the material already has page numbers. If you add new page numbers, consider using a different color, putting the new page numbers in a new place, or using a letter- or word-number sequence (such as *Event-1, Position-1,* etc.). Whatever you decide, be consistent.

- *Include a reflective essay or letter.* Most instructors want the reflective essay to be the first item in the portfolio following the table of contents. In this position, the reflective essay introduces the material in the portfolio. Your instructor may use your reflective essay as a guide, reading the sections of the portfolio you specifically refer to in your essay before skimming the rest of the material.

- *Label each item.* If your instructor does not specify how you should label your work, you need to develop a clear system on your own. You may need to explain your system briefly in a note on the table of contents or in your reflective essay where you refer to particular items in your portfolio. For example, you could use *The St. Martin's Guide* chapter number to identify each essay assignment. To indicate process materials, consider using the chapter number and title and the relevant heading from that chapter's Guide to Writing section (such as Chapter 2: Exploring Your Present Perspective). To identify different drafts, you could write on the top left margin of every page the chapter number, essay title, and draft number. For drafts that received a critical reading, you might want to add the notation "Read by *S*." You should also date all of your work.

- *Sequence the material.* If your instructor does not indicate how you should order the work included in your portfolio, you will have to decide yourself. The sequence of materials should be consistent with the way you introduce your work in the reflective essay. If your instructor asks you to present two or more examples of your best work, you may want to begin with the essay you consider your very best. If your instructor asks you to show the progress you have made in the course, you could begin with your weakest essay and either show how you improved it or how later essays were stronger. If your instructor asks you to demonstrate growth, you might organize your work by the particular areas that improved. For example, you could show that you learned to revise substantively by presenting earlier and later revisions of an essay from early in the course and following them with a pair of revisions from a subsequent and more extensively reworked essay. Or to show that you learned to edit or altogether avoid certain sentence errors, you could give examples of a particular error being corrected in a revision and the same error being avoided in a later first draft.

Part Six

Six

WRITING AND SPEAKING TO WIDER AUDIENCES

Designing Documents

This chapter introduces basic components of document design, discusses some of the more common formats of paper and electronic documents you may be called upon to create in your college courses or in the workplace, and offers guidelines for designing documents that many students, instructors, and business writers have found effective.

When you are required to use a particular document format such as the MLA or APA style for an academic writing assignment, you will not have to make many choices about design elements; the MLA and APA specify rules for spacing, margins, heading formats, and so on, and your instructor will expect you to follow the established style. For writing assignments that do not require you to follow a particular academic format, you will have more flexibility.

For more on MLA or APA style, see Chapter 22.

■ ELEMENTS OF DOCUMENT DESIGN

Paper and electronic documents differ in important ways, but both employ basic principles of design, using typography, visuals, and white space to enhance readability. These principles have been developed over the centuries as increasing numbers of people have gained access to reading material, and designers today can benefit not only from this accumulated knowledge but also from studies that have examined how the eye moves over the page, how readers actually read documents, and how reading takes place within different contexts.

Typography

Typography is the designer's term for the letters and symbols that make up the print on the page. You are already using important aspects of typography when you use capital letters, italics, boldface, or different sizes of type to signal a new sentence, identify the title of a book, or distinguish a heading from body text.

Word processing programs and personal computers now enable you to use dozens of different typefaces (fonts), bold and italic versions of these fonts, and a range of font sizes. Fortunately, you can rely on some simple design principles to make good typographic choices for your documents.

Choose Fonts That Are Easy to Read.   A *font family* consists of the font in different sizes as well as in its boldface and italic forms. Not all fonts are suitable for extended pieces of writing.

Considering Font Style.   Sentences and paragraphs printed in fonts that imitate *calligraphy* or handwriting are not only difficult to read but also informal in appearance. For most academic and business writing, you will probably want to choose a traditional font, such as Courier or Times New Roman, which is easy to read and does not call attention to itself. This book is set in Galliard.

Considering Font Size.   To ensure that your documents can be read easily, you also need to choose an appropriate font size (traditionally measured in units called *points*). For most types of academic writing, a 12-point font is the standard size used for the main (body) text. However, for Web pages, you should consider using a larger font to compensate for the added difficulty of reading from a computer monitor. For overhead transparencies and computer-projected displays, you should use an even larger font size (such as 32-point) to ensure that the text can be read from a distance.

Combining Font Styles and Sizes.   Although computers now make an abundance of font styles and sizes available to writers, you should avoid confusing readers with too many typographical features. Limit the fonts in a document to one or two font families. A common practice is to choose one font family for all titles and headings and another for the body text.

Use Boldface, Italics, and Font Size to Distinguish between Headings and Body Text.   Titles and headings are often distinguished from body text by boldface, italics, or font size. These elements of typography are helpful in calling attention to certain parts or sections of a piece of writing, showing the hierarchy of its headings and subheadings as well as offering readers visual cues to its overall organization. However, you should always check with your instructor about the conventions for using (or not using) these elements in the particular discipline you are studying.

Distinguishing between Headings and Subheadings.   Headings for major sections (level-one headings) must be visually distinct from headings that subdivide the major sections (level-two headings) and from headings that appear within the subdivisions (level-three headings). The most important headings should have more impact than any subheadings. The typography should reflect this hierarchy of the headings. Here is one possible system for distinguishing among three levels of headings:

LEVEL-ONE HEADING

Level-Two Heading

Level-Three Heading

Notice that the level-one and level-two headings are given the greatest prominence by the use of boldface, and that they are distinguished from one another by the use of all capital letters for the major headings versus upper- and lowercase letters for the subheadings. The third-level heading, italicized but not boldfaced, is less prominent than the other two headings but can still be readily distinguished from body text. Whatever system you use to distinguish headings and subheadings, be sure to apply it consistently throughout the document.

For more on selecting appropriate headings and subheadings, see Chapter 13, pp. 570–71.

Positioning Headings Consistently. In addition to keeping track of the font size and style of headings, you need to position headings in the same way throughout a piece of writing. You will want to consider the spacing above and below headings and determine whether the headings should be aligned with the left margin, indented a fixed amount of space, or centered on the page.

Note: When you are required to observe the MLA or APA style of document design, you should maintain the regular double-spacing of body text, center level-one headings (but do not add extra space above or below them), type headings in the same font and size used for the body text (do not use boldface or italics), and capitalize the important words in headings. While the MLA offers no specific guidelines for styling multiple levels of headings, the APA has specific formats for up to five levels of headings. For more information on the APA style for headings and subheadings, consult the *Publication Manual of the American Psychological Association* (4th edition, 1994) or the APA Web site at <http://www.apa.org/apa-style>.

Using Type Size to Differentiate Headings from Text. In documents that do not need to observe the MLA or APA style, you may wish to use font size to help make headings visually distinct from the body of the text. If you do so, avoid using up unnecessary space. To accompany 12-point body text, for instance, 14-point headings will suffice. The default settings for heading and body text styles on most word processing and desktop publishing programs are effective.

Consider Using Numbered and Bulleted Lists. Lists are often an effective way to present information in a logical and visually coherent way. Use a *numbered list* (1, 2, 3) to present the steps in a sequential process or to set forth items that readers will need to refer to easily (for instance, see Figure 12, p. 783). Use a *bulleted list* (marking each new item with a "bullet"—that is, a dash, circle, or box) to highlight key points when the order of the items is not significant (for instance, see p. 780).

For examples of numbered and bulleted lists, see pp. 780 and 783.

Add Colors Sparingly and Systematically, If at All. Color printers, photocopiers, and online technology facilitate the use of color typography, but this technology does not necessarily make text easier to read. In most academic writing, the first and only color you should use is black. If you think using an additional color will increase your readers' understanding of what you have to say, experiment with a color that contrasts well with the black type and white background to see whether the mix of colors provides you with the flexibility you need. In addition, consider whether all members of

Although you should avoid using color in most academic writing, in other writing situations color can help readers follow the organization of your document. For an example, notice the use of color to differentiate headings in one of the Guides to Writing in Chapters 2–10 of this book.

your potential audience will have access to a full-color version of the document. Check with your instructor if you are not sure whether it would be appropriate for you to use more than one color in your writing for the class.

Visuals

Charts, graphs, tables, diagrams, drawings, maps, and photographs add visual interest and are often more effective at conveying information than prose alone. Be certain, however, that each visual has a valid role to play in the document; if the visual is merely a decoration, leave it out.

You can create visuals on a computer, using the drawing tools of a word processing program, the charting tools of a spreadsheet program, or software specifically designed for creating visuals. You can also download visuals from the World Wide Web or photocopy or scan visuals from print materials.

Choose the Appropriate Visual.   Select the type of visual that best suits your purpose. The following list identifies various types of visuals, explains what they are best used for, and provides examples.

- *Tables.*   A table is used to display numerical data and similar types of information. It usually includes several related items as well as variables for each item. For example, Table 1 shows changes in the number and percentage of U.S. households in three income ranges during a period of twenty-four years.

- *Bar graphs.*   A bar graph compares the values of two or more items, such as how many licensed practical nurses and how many registered nurses serve a given population (see Figure 1).

- *Line graphs.*   A line graph shows change over time, such as births per thousand Americans between 1820 and 2000 (see Figure 2).

Table 1
Changes in the Number (in millions) and Percentage of U.S. Households in Three Income Ranges, 1970–1994[a]

	Less than $25,000		$25,000 to $74,999		$75,000 or more	
Year	Number	Percent	Number	Percent	Number	Percent
1970	25.3	39.1%	35.0	54.1%	4.4	6.8%
1975	29.4	40.3	38.0	52.1	5.5	7.5
1980	32.5	39.4	42.1	51.1	7.8	9.5
1985	34.4	38.9	43.9	49.6	10.2	11.5
1990	35.3	37.4	46.5	49.3	12.5	13.3
1994	39.0	39.4	46.5	47.0	13.5	13.6

[a] Income is reported in 1994 CPI-U-XI adjusted U.S. dollars.

Source: U.S. Census Bureau.

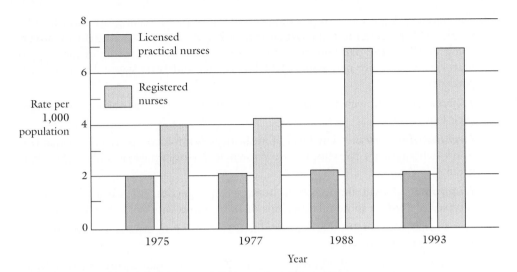

Figure 1. Active Michigan Nurses per 1,000 Population, Selected Years
Source: Michigan Department of the State Registrar and Division of Health Statistics,
Michigan Department of Community Health.

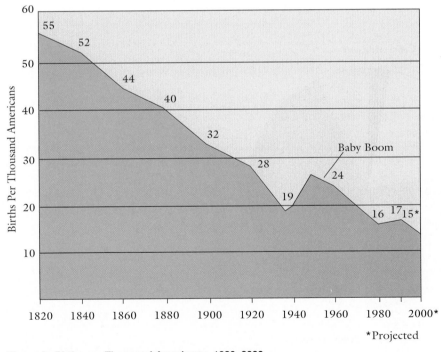

Figure 2. Births per Thousand Americans, 1820–2000
Source: Data from *Historical Statistics of the United States, Colonial Times to 1970* (1975);
Statistical Abstract of the United States, 1998.

- *Pie charts.* A pie chart shows the percentage of parts making up a whole. The whole (100 percent) in the chart shown in Figure 3 is the total spent on advertising in 1998; the parts are the amounts spent by various media in the United States, such as daily newspapers (22.1 percent) and broadcast television (19.9 percent).

- *Flowcharts.* A flowchart shows the stages in a process and their relationships. (See Figure 4.)

- *Organization charts.* The lines of authority within a company or an organization—who reports to whom—are shown in an organization chart. (See Figure 5.)

For another example of a diagram, see Chapter 14, p. 586.

- *Diagrams.* A diagram depicts an item or its properties, often using symbols. It is typically used to show relationships or how things function. (See Figure 6.)

- *Drawings.* A drawing shows a simplified version or an artist's interpretation of an object. (See Figure 7.)

- *Photographs.* Although photographic images are generally assumed to duplicate what the eye sees, a photograph may, in fact, be manipulated in a variety of ways for special effects. Photographs that have been altered should be so identified. (See Figure 8.)

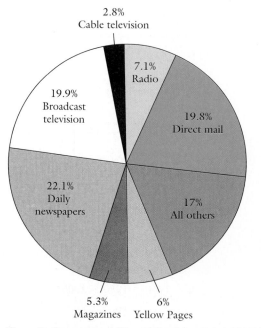

Figure 3. Newspapers' Slice of the Advertising Pie (1998)
Together, broadcast and cable television edge out newspapers as the leading advertising medium in the United States. *Source:* McCann Erickson Inc., Newspaper Association of America.

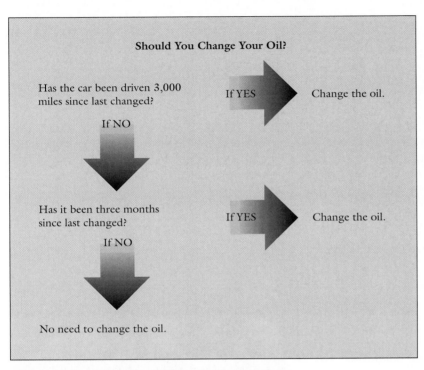

Figure 4. Flowchart Showing Oil-Changing Decision Process

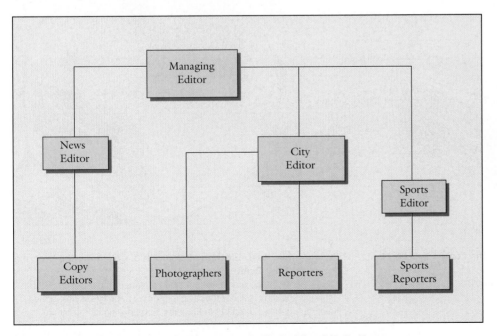

Figure 5. Organization Chart for the Newsroom of a Typical Small Daily Newspaper

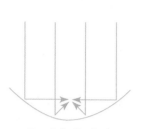
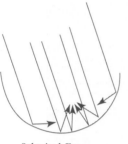
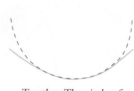

Parabolic: Perfectly focuses parallel rays, but from one direction only; must be aimed.

Spherical: Focuses imperfectly, but equally well from any direction; does not need to be aimed.

Together: The circle of curvature nearly coincides with the parabola near the vertex.

Figure 6. Diagram of a Liquid Reflector Telescope
Source: Mare Frantz, Indiana University, Purdue University, Indianapolis.

Figure 7. Drawing of a Cell from the Leaf of a Corn Plant, Identifying Various Cellular Structures
Compare with the photograph in Figure 8.

Labels: Cell wall, Cell membrane, Nuclear envelope, Nucleus, Nucleolus, Mitochondrion, Starch grain, Chloroplast, Vacuole

Figure 8. Electron Micrograph of Cells from the Leaf of a Corn Plant
Note the measurement scale provided at the bottom right; it is a reminder that this image has been greatly magnified so that the parts of the cell can be distinguished by the human eye.

0.5 µm

- *Maps.* A map may show geographical areas, lay out the spatial relationships of objects, or make a historical or political point. (See Figure 9.)

- *Screen shots.* A screen shot duplicates the appearance of a computer screen and is often used to reproduce a Web page in a print document. (See Figure 16 on p. 791 for an example.)

Create Titles, Label the Parts, and Cite Your Sources. Number your visuals of the same type in sequential order and give each one a title or caption. Refer to tables as *Table 1, Table 2,* and so on, and to other types of visuals as *Figure 1, Figure 2,* and so on. Make sure each title reflects both the subject of the visual (for example, income levels) and its purpose (to compare and illustrate changes in those income levels): *Figure 1. Percentage of U.S. Households in Three Income Ranges, 1990–2000.* Notice that MLA style requires that the title for a table be placed above the table and the title for a figure be placed below the figure.

To help readers understand a visual, clearly label all of its parts. In a table, for instance, give each column a heading; likewise, label each section of a pie chart with the percentage and the item it represents.

Finally, cite the source of the visual or the source of the information it contains. When you borrow a visual from another document or create a visual from borrowed information, you must cite your source in a note (see Table 1 and Figure 1 for examples of source notes).

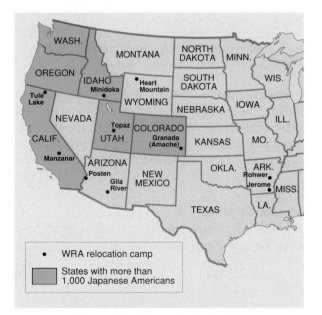

Figure 9. Western Relocation Authority Centers
During World War II, ethnic prejudice was strong, and although they posed no threat to national security, Japanese Americans were forced to go to "Western Relocation Authority" camps. As the map indicates, people were often taken a great distance from their homes.

Note: If you use a borrowed visual in an essay intended for publication, such as on a Web page or in the campus newspaper, you must obtain written permission from the copyright holder (usually the author, publisher, or organization holds the copyright). Write a letter asking permission to use the visual. Identify yourself and the visual you want to use, where you found the image, how you intend to use it, and where it will be published. Ask whether you need to use a particular credit line. Remember to enclose a photocopy of the visual with your permission request.

Integrate the Visual into the Text.   Visuals should facilitate, not disrupt, the reading of the body text. To achieve this goal, you first need to introduce and discuss the visual in your text and then insert the visual in an appropriate location.

Introducing the Visual.   Ideally, you should introduce each visual by referring to it in your text, immediately *before* the visual appears. An effective textual reference answers the following questions:

- What is the number of the visual?
- Where is the visual located?
- What kind of information does it contain?
- What important point does the visual make or support?

Here is an example of an effective introduction for the line graph shown earlier (Figure 2):

> Note the sharp increase in births during the late 1940s (see Figure 2 on p. 771). Now recognized as the beginning of a significant demographic phenomenon, the "baby boom" coincided with U.S. soldiers' return home following World War II.

Placing the Visual in an Appropriate Location.   MLA style requires and APA style recommends that you place a visual in the body of your text as soon after the discussion as possible, particularly when the reader will need to consult the visual. In APA style, visuals can also be gathered at the end of an essay if they contain supplemental information that may or may not be of interest to the reader or if the visuals take up multiple pages.

For more on overhead transparencies and computer-projected displays, see Chapter 26, pp. 795–96.

Design the Visual with Its Final Use in Mind.   If you plan to incorporate a computer-generated visual into an overhead transparency or a computer-projected display, try to envision what you see on the computer screen as it would appear enlarged on a screen. Similarly, if you are designing the visual for use on a Web page, consider how the visual will appear when it is displayed on a computer screen (see p. 791 for an example).

Use Common Sense When Creating Visuals on a Computer.   If you use a computer program to create visuals, keep this advice in mind:

- *Make the decisions that your computer cannot make for you.*   A computer can automatically turn spreadsheet data into a pie chart or bar graph, but only you can decide which visual—or what use of color, if any—is most appropriate.

- *Avoid "chart junk."*   Many computer programs provide an array of specific effects that can be used to alter visuals, including three-dimensional renderings, textured backgrounds, and shadowed text. Such special effects often detract from the message of the visual.

- *Use clip art sparingly.*   Clip art consists of icons, symbols, and other simple, copyright-free drawings that identify recurring topics. Because clip art simplifies ideas, it is of limited use in conveying the complex information contained in most academic writing.

White Space

Another basic element of document design, white space, is simply the open space surrounding the text on a printed page or computer screen. You use white space typographically in your documents when you separate a heading from the body text, when you set the margins on the page, and even when you double-space between lines of text. In all of these cases, white space makes your document easier to read. When used generously, white space facilitates reading by keeping the pages of a document uncluttered and by helping the eye find and follow the text. Of course, "white" space can be any color that contrasts clearly with the text on the page.

Use "Chunking" to Break Up Dense Text.   "Chunking," the breaking up of text into smaller units, also facilitates reading. Paragraphing is a form of chunking that divides your text up into units of closely related information. In most academic essays and reports, the text is double-spaced and paragraphs are distinguished by indenting the first line five character spaces.

For more on paragraphing, see Chapter 13, pp. 559–63.

In single-spaced text, you may want to facilitate easier reading by adding extra space between paragraphs, rather than indenting the first lines of paragraphs. This format is referred to as *block style* and is often used in memos, letters, and electronic documents. When creating electronic documents, especially Web pages, you might consider chunking your material into separate "pages" or screens, with links connecting the chunks.

For more on Web page design, see pp. 789–91.

Use Adequate Margins to Frame the Text on the Page.   Adequate margins are an important component of white space and general readability. If your margins are too small, the page may seem cluttered. For academic essays, use one-inch margins on all sides unless your instructor (or the style manual you are following) advises differently. In general, you should turn off your word processor's justification and automatic hyphenation functions so that the width of the right margin will vary slightly (a format known as *ragged right*) but word spacing will be more uniform. (Note, however, that justification and end-of-line hyphenation are acceptable options for students following the APA style.)

When your margins are too wide, readers may question their purpose. Some instructors, however, ask students to leave large margins to accommodate marginal comments. Multiple columns are an option you might consider, particularly if you are using type that is smaller than the conventional 10- or 12-point size, since smaller fonts require shorter lines for readability. However, multiple columns can be difficult to format.

For rules on formatting long quotations in the MLA and APA styles, see Chapter 22, pp. 696–97.

Consider Using White Space to Emphasize Selected Text Elements. To call attention to special text elements such as quotations, lists, and examples, you could put extra space above and below. But be sure to check the relevant style manual for spacing conventions.

For special-purpose documents such as a circular announcing an event, you may wish to experiment with colored papers as a background. If the background is dark, however, make sure the black type remains legible.

■ DESIGNING PAGE LAYOUT

The arrangement of text, visuals, and white space on a page—called the *page layout* —has a major impact on the readability of a document and may influence the reader's attitude about the document. A well-designed page is inviting to read and easy to scan.

Frequently, many of your major page layout decisions will be predetermined by the kind of document you are preparing. Letters and memos, for example, have evolved through the years to meet the needs of readers. Because your readers will bring certain long-held expectations to these kinds of documents, altering an established format can cause confusion. Similarly, most aspects of the page design of an academic research paper are prescribed by the style manual used in the field of study, such as that of the MLA (humanities), APA (social sciences), or CBE (sciences). These styles have specific rules for margins, line spacing, headers, footers, bibliographies, and so on. Your instructor may have special format requirements as well. Always be sure to check whether there are special format requirements for your academic writing assignments.

Considering the Context in Which Your Document Will Be Read

When considering page design, you will want to analyze the context in which your document will be read. For instance, if you are writing an essay for a college course, your instructor will read it carefully. Your design decisions should make sustained reading as easy a process as possible; therefore, you will want to present a neat, clearly printed paper. Fonts that are too small to read easily or print that is too light to see clearly will make the reader's job unnecessarily difficult. Use double-spaced text and one-inch margins to leave your instructor room to write comments on the paper.

When you write for wider audiences, however, you cannot expect all readers to read your writing closely. Some readers may skim through an essay looking for key points or for information that is important specifically to them. For these readers, headings, bullets, and chunking are important design elements that help them "see" the main points of your writing as well as find the information that is of most interest to them. If readers are following written instructions to perform a task, they probably will be moving back and forth between reading and doing the task. In this context, you will need to design the document in a way that will make it easy for readers to find their place on the page as they move back and forth between text and task. Large fonts, informative headings, numbered lists, and substantial amounts of white space help readers find their place on the page with ease.

Analyzing the Context in Which Your Document Will Be Read

To analyze the context in which a document is read or used, ask yourself the following questions:

- *Where will my document be read?* Will the document be read in a well-lighted, spacious, quiet room? Or will it be read on a laptop computer screen on a noisy, lurching city bus?

- *Do my readers have specific expectations for this kind of document?* Am I writing a memo, letter, or report that my readers expect will follow certain design conventions?

- *How will the information be used?* Are my readers reading to learn, to be entertained, or to complete a task? Are they most likely to skim the document or to read it carefully?

■ SAMPLE DOCUMENTS

Earlier in this chapter you saw examples of various types of visuals; in this section you will take a look at various types of documents that you may be asked to prepare. Each sample document is accompanied by a discussion of appropriate design conventions. As you examine the documents, try also to analyze the way that typography, visuals, and white space are used to guide the reader's eye across the page. What design features make the documents easy to read? What features make finding specific information within the documents easy? What features make the document easy to use?

In addition to examining the sample documents with these questions in mind, look at the sample research paper in Chapter 22, pp. 727–33.

Memos

Memos, such as the one shown in Figure 10, are "internal" correspondence, often through email, between employees of the same organization (in contrast to business letters, which are sent to people outside the organization). The following conventions for writing a memo are well established and, in most cases, should not be altered. In addition, check to see whether your organization has specific guidelines for its memos (such as the use of preprinted letterhead or memo forms).

- *Heading.*   A memo should carry the major heading *Memorandum* or *Memo*. If you are using letterhead stationery, position the heading just below the letterhead. The heading may be centered on the page or positioned at the left margin (depending on your organization's guidelines). In either case, the heading should be distinguished in some way from the rest of the body text, such as by using a larger font size, boldfacing the type, or capitalizing all letters.

- *Content headings.*   Just below the heading and separated by at least one line of space are the content headings: *To, From, Subject,* and *Date.* Place the content headings at the left margin and in the same size font as the body text.

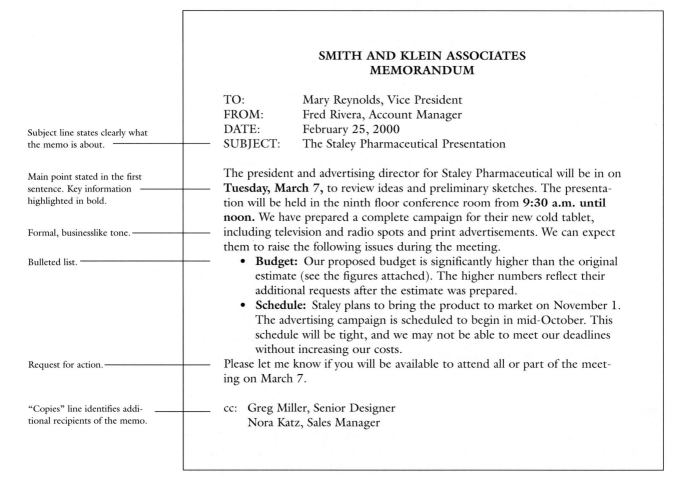

**SMITH AND KLEIN ASSOCIATES
MEMORANDUM**

Subject line states clearly what the memo is about. ——————

TO: Mary Reynolds, Vice President
FROM: Fred Rivera, Account Manager
DATE: February 25, 2000
SUBJECT: The Staley Pharmaceutical Presentation

Main point stated in the first sentence. Key information highlighted in bold. ——————

Formal, businesslike tone. ——————

Bulleted list. ——————

The president and advertising director for Staley Pharmaceutical will be in on **Tuesday, March 7,** to review ideas and preliminary sketches. The presentation will be held in the ninth floor conference room from **9:30 a.m. until noon.** We have prepared a complete campaign for their new cold tablet, including television and radio spots and print advertisements. We can expect them to raise the following issues during the meeting.

- **Budget:** Our proposed budget is significantly higher than the original estimate (see the figures attached). The higher numbers reflect their additional requests after the estimate was prepared.
- **Schedule:** Staley plans to bring the product to market on November 1. The advertising campaign is scheduled to begin in mid-October. This schedule will be tight, and we may not be able to meet our deadlines without increasing our costs.

Request for action. ——————

Please let me know if you will be available to attend all or part of the meeting on March 7.

"Copies" line identifies additional recipients of the memo. ——————

cc: Greg Miller, Senior Designer
     Nora Katz, Sales Manager

Figure 10. A Sample Memo

- *Body text.* The main text of a memo is usually presented in block style: single-spaced with an extra line of space between paragraphs. (Do not indent the first line of paragraphs in block style.) If you need to call attention to specific information, consider presenting it in a numbered or bulleted list, or highlight the information visually by using boldface or extra white space above and below it. In a memo announcing a meeting, for example, you might boldface the date, time, and place of the meeting so the reader can quickly find the information, or you might set off the date, time, and place on separate lines.

Letters

The business letter (exemplified in Figure 11) is the document most often used for correspondence between representatives of one organization and representatives of another (though email messages are increasingly being used in place of business letters). Like most other workplace documents, a business letter is written to obtain information about a company's products, to register a complaint, to respond to a complaint, or to introduce other documents (such as a proposal) that accompany the letter. As with the memo, the design conventions for letters are long established, although letters have more variations. Check to see whether there are specific business letter guidelines for your organization.

The heading of a business letter consists of the contact information for both the sender and receiver of the letter. Block style is the most commonly used format for business letters.

Be sure to state the purpose of your letter in the first few lines and to provide supporting information in the paragraphs that follow. Always maintain a courteous and professional tone throughout a business letter. Avoid using such stilted clichés as *enclosed herewith* and *as per your letter of Wednesday last,* but do include enough information to identify clearly any documents you refer to in the letter.

Email

Email, or electronic mail, is sent over a computer network from one user of the network to one or more other users. Increasingly, students and instructors rely on email to exchange information about assignments and schedules as well as to follow up on class discussions (see Figure 12). Email messages are usually concise, direct, relatively informal, formatted like paper memos, and limited to a single subject. Effective emails include a clear subject line.

Begin an email message by stating the main point; give additional information in subsequent paragraphs. If your email program enables you to do so, consider using headings to organize your material and bulleted or numbered lists to make your points stand out.

In many organizations, email messages are replacing handwritten or typed memos. When you send a memo electronically, make sure the headings automatically provided by the email program convey the same essential information as the content headings in a traditional memo. If you are part of a large or complex organization,

A letterhead providing informa-tion the recipient will need to communicate with the sender.

Full-block format: Each new line starts at the left margin.

Letter is single-spaced, with double-spacing between para-graphs and other major parts.

The author refers to earlier correspondence to state pur-pose of the letter, a common and effective way to begin a business letter.

Elaboration, support, and detail.

Signature.

Author's and typist's initials if typist is not author.

MetroType
409 South 8th Street
Pawkett, KY 45397
Phone: 502.555.1234   Fax: 502.555.4321   Email: type@micran.net

January 24, 2000

Mr. Carl Boyer
Boyer Advertising Co.
1714 North 20th Street, Suite 16
Pawkett, KY 45397

Dear Mr. Boyer:

Thank you for your letter of January 18, 2000. You asked whether MetroType could provide one of your clients with mail-merged letters after first converting your client's files from WordPerfect to Microsoft Word. We certainly can. As I mentioned on the phone earlier today, creat-ing mail-merge documents is one of our key services, and we frequently convert word processing files for customers who are moving from one program to another.

Much of the file conversion is done automatically; however, we have noticed that some parts of a file (such as accented characters and graphics) aren't always converted accurately. For this reason, we will compare a printout of your client's original files to a printout of the converted files and then make whatever corrections are necessary. For an additional fee, we can also proofread the final documents. If your client is interested in having us proofread the documents, I would be happy to furnish you with a quote.

If you have any other questions, please call me at (502) 555-1234. In the meantime, I'll look forward to hearing from you again.

Sincerely yours,

Trudy L. Philips

Trudy L. Philips
Owner/Director
TLP/dmp

Figure 11. A Sample Business Letter

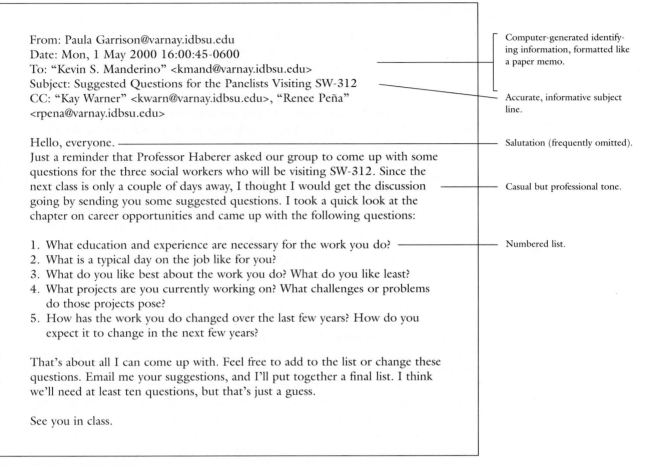

From: Paula Garrison@varnay.idbsu.edu
Date: Mon, 1 May 2000 16:00:45-0600
To: "Kevin S. Manderino" <kmand@varnay.idbsu.edu>
Subject: Suggested Questions for the Panelists Visiting SW-312
CC: "Kay Warner" <kwarn@varnay.idbsu.edu>, "Renee Peña"
<rpena@varnay.idbsu.edu>

Hello, everyone.
Just a reminder that Professor Haberer asked our group to come up with some
questions for the three social workers who will be visiting SW-312. Since the
next class is only a couple of days away, I thought I would get the discussion
going by sending you some suggested questions. I took a quick look at the
chapter on career opportunities and came up with the following questions:

1. What education and experience are necessary for the work you do?
2. What is a typical day on the job like for you?
3. What do you like best about the work you do? What do you like least?
4. What projects are you currently working on? What challenges or problems
   do those projects pose?
5. How has the work you do changed over the last few years? How do you
   expect it to change in the next few years?

That's about all I can come up with. Feel free to add to the list or change these
questions. Email me your suggestions, and I'll put together a final list. I think
we'll need at least ten questions, but that's just a guess.

See you in class.

Labels (right margin):
- Computer-generated identifying information, formatted like a paper memo.
- Accurate, informative subject line.
- Salutation (frequently omitted).
- Casual but professional tone.
- Numbered list.

Figure 12. A Sample Email Message

you may want to repeat your name and add such information as your job title, division, and telephone extension in a "signature" at the end of the document.

Email is a broader medium of communication than the business memo. Nevertheless, in anything other than quick emails to friends, you should maintain a professional tone. Avoid sarcasm and humor, which may not come across as you intend, and be sure to proofread and spell-check your message before sending it. Also, because email messages are accessible to many people other than the person to whom you are writing, always be careful about what you write in an email message.

While email messages are among the simplest forms of electronic documents, new software programs allow you to attach files, insert hypertext links, and even insert pictures and graphics into your email documents. As a matter of courtesy, check to be sure that the recipient of your email message has the necessary software to read these more technologically advanced documents before you include them with the message.

For information on Web pages, which are another common type of electronic document, see pp. 789–91.

Résumés

A résumé is used to acquaint a prospective employer with your work experience, education, and accomplishments. All résumés contain such basic information as your name, address, phone number, and email address (if you have one).

The format of résumés varies among disciplines and professions. Some professions require more traditional formatting, while others allow for more flexibility in design. Be sure to research your field and the potential employers to see if a particular résumé format is preferred. Also see whether putting your résumé on a Web page might be advisable.

Résumés may also vary in terms of what is emphasized—educational or work experience, for example. A recent college graduate and a professional with years of experience would not benefit from using the same résumé format. Tailor your résumé to the job for which you are applying. If you have little work experience, focus your résumé on your grade point average, the courses you have taken, the projects you have completed, and the applicable skills and abilities you have acquired in college. (For an example of such a résumé, see Figure 13 on the next page.) If you have extensive, relevant, and continuous work experience, consider a chronological résumé, listing the jobs you have held (beginning with the most recent job) and describing the duties, responsibilities, and accomplishments associated with each one. If you have shifted directions during your adult life, consider organizing your résumé in a way that emphasizes the strengths and skills you have acquired and used in different settings—for instance, your experience speaking in front of groups, handling money, or working with machinery.

The résumé is a good example of why the context in which a document is read is so important. An employer may receive dozens of résumés for one position. Your résumé may not be read closely in a first screening. Consequently, your résumé should highlight your important qualifications visually so that the reader can quickly find the pertinent information by scanning the page.

Do not include such personal information as your height, weight, and age. Do mention personal interests or hobbies if they are relevant to the position. Finally, proofread your résumé carefully; it must be error-free. Your résumé is the first impression you make on a potential employer. Do everything you can to make a good first impression.

Job-Application Letters

A job-application letter (sometimes called a *cover letter*) is sent with a résumé when you apply for a job. One purpose of the job-application letter is to tell your reader why you have enclosed your résumé. However, its primary purpose is to persuade your reader that you are a qualified candidate for employment. For college students and recent graduates, most job-application letters (such as the one shown in Figure 14) consist of four paragraphs.

1. The *first paragraph* identifies which position you are applying for and how you became aware of its availability. Or, if you are not applying for a particular position, the first paragraph expresses your desire to work for that particular organization.

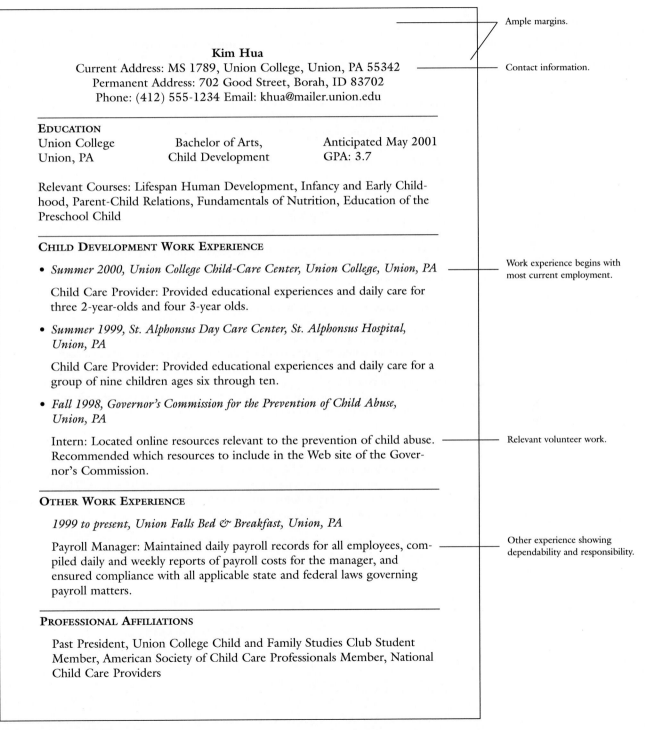

Kim Hua
Current Address: MS 1789, Union College, Union, PA 55342 — Contact information.
Permanent Address: 702 Good Street, Borah, ID 83702
Phone: (412) 555-1234 Email: khua@mailer.union.edu

Ample margins.

EDUCATION

Union College	Bachelor of Arts,	Anticipated May 2001
Union, PA	Child Development	GPA: 3.7

Relevant Courses: Lifespan Human Development, Infancy and Early Childhood, Parent-Child Relations, Fundamentals of Nutrition, Education of the Preschool Child

CHILD DEVELOPMENT WORK EXPERIENCE

- *Summer 2000, Union College Child-Care Center, Union College, Union, PA* — Work experience begins with most current employment.

  Child Care Provider: Provided educational experiences and daily care for three 2-year-olds and four 3-year olds.

- *Summer 1999, St. Alphonsus Day Care Center, St. Alphonsus Hospital, Union, PA*

  Child Care Provider: Provided educational experiences and daily care for a group of nine children ages six through ten.

- *Fall 1998, Governor's Commission for the Prevention of Child Abuse, Union, PA*

  Intern: Located online resources relevant to the prevention of child abuse. — Relevant volunteer work. Recommended which resources to include in the Web site of the Governor's Commission.

OTHER WORK EXPERIENCE

1999 to present, Union Falls Bed & Breakfast, Union, PA

Payroll Manager: Maintained daily payroll records for all employees, compiled daily and weekly reports of payroll costs for the manager, and ensured compliance with all applicable state and federal laws governing payroll matters. — Other experience showing dependability and responsibility.

PROFESSIONAL AFFILIATIONS

Past President, Union College Child and Family Studies Club Student Member, American Society of Child Care Professionals Member, National Child Care Providers

Figure 13. A Sample Résumé

Modified-block format: Your address, the date, and the signature block begin at the center of the page.

308 Fairmont Street
Warren, CA 07812
June 9, 2000

Ms. Ronda Green
Software Engineer
Santa Clara Technology
P.O. Box 679
Santa Clara, CA 09145

Dear Ms. Green:

Purpose of the letter.

I am responding to your February 11 post in the Usenet newsgroup comp .software.testing announcing that Santa Clara Technology is accepting résumés for an entry-level engineer position in the Quality Assurance Department. I think that my experience in quality assurance and my educational background qualify me for this position.

Education paragraph.

As my résumé states, I graduated this past May from the University of Southern California (USC) with a Bachelor of Science degree in Interdisciplinary Studies. The Interdisciplinary Studies program at USC allows students to develop a degree plan spanning at least two disciplines. My degree plan included courses in computer science, marketing, and technical communication. In addition to university courses, I have completed courses in team dynamics, project management, and C and C++ programming offered by the training department at PrintCom, a manufacturer of high-end laser printers.

Work-experience paragraph.

Throughout last summer, I worked as an intern in the quality-assurance department of PrintCom. I assisted quality-assurance engineers in testing printer drivers, installers, and utilities. In addition, I maintained a database containing the results of these tests and summarized the results in weekly reports. This experience gave me valuable knowledge of the principles of quality assurance and of the techniques used in testing software.

Concluding paragraph.

I would appreciate the opportunity to discuss further the education, skills, and abilities I could bring to Santa Clara Technology. You can reach me any workday after 3 p.m. (PST) at (907) 555-1234 or by email at sstur17@axl.com.

Sincerely yours,

Shelley Sturman

Shelley Sturman

Enclosure: résumé

Figure 14. A Sample Job-Application Letter

2. The *second paragraph* briefly describes your education, focusing on specific achievements, projects, and relevant course work.

3. The *third paragraph* briefly describes your work experience, focusing on relevant responsibilities and accomplishments. (The second and third paragraphs should not merely restate what is in your résumé; rather, they should help persuade your reader that you are qualified for the job.)

4. The *fourth paragraph* expresses your willingness to provide additional information and to be interviewed at the employer's convenience.

Lab Reports

A lab report generally consists of the following five sections:

1. The *Introduction* provides background information: the hypothesis of the experiment, the question to be answered, how the question arose.

2. The *Methods* section describes how you conducted the research or performed the experiment.

3. The *Results* section describes what happened as a result of your research or experiment.

4. The *Discussion* section consists of your reasoning about your results.

5. The *References* section cites the sources you used in conducting the research, performing the experiment, or writing the lab report.

The content and format of a lab report may vary from discipline to discipline or from course to course. Before writing a lab report, be certain that you understand your instructor's requirements. The sample in Figure 15 shows excerpts from a lab report written by two students in a soils science course. It uses the documentation format advocated by the Council of Biology Editors (CBE).

```
Bulk Density and Total Pore Space

                             Joe Aquino and Sheila Norris
                                             Soils 101
                                         Lab Section 1
                                     February 21, 1999


                    Introduction
        Soil is an arrangement of solids and voids. The
    voids, called pore spaces, are important for root
    growth, water movement, water storage, and gas exchange
    between the soil and atmosphere. A medium-textured soil
```

Background information that the reader will need to understand the experiment.

Figure 15. A Sample Lab Report   *(continued)*

good for plant growth will have a pore-space content of about 0.50 (half solids, half pore space). The total pore space is the space between sand, silt, and clay particles (micropore space) plus the space between soil aggregates (macropore space).[1]

[The Introduction continues with a discussion of the formulas used to calculate bulk density, particle density, and porosity.]

Detailed explanation of the methods used.

Methods

To determine the bulk density[2] and total pore space of two soil samples, we hammered cans into the wall of a soil pit (Hagerstown silt loam). We collected samples from the Ap horizon and a Bt horizon. We then placed a block of wood over the cans so that the hammer did not smash them. After hammering the cans into the soil, we dug the cans, now full of soil, out of the horizons; we trimmed off any excess soil. The samples were dried in an oven at 105°C for two days and weighed. We then determined the volume of the cans by measuring the height and radius, as follows:

$$\text{volume} = \frac{1}{4}r^2h$$

We used the formulas noted in the Introduction to determine bulk density and porosity of the samples. Particle density was assumed to be 2.65 g/cm^3. The textural class of each horizon was determined by feel; that is, we squeezed and kneaded each sample and assigned it to a particular textural class.

Results

We found both soils to have relatively light bulk densities and large porosities, but the Bt horizon had greater porosity than the Ap. Furthermore, we determined that the Ap horizon was a silt loam, whereas the Bt was a clay (see Table 1).

Presents the results of the experiment, with a table showing quantitative data.

Table 1 Textural class, bulk density, and porosity of two Hagerstown soil horizons

Textural Class	Ap Silt Loam	Bt Clay
Bulk density (g/cm^3)	1.20	1.08
Porosity	0.55	0.59

[The Results section continues with sample calculations.]

Discussion

Both soils had bulk densities and porosities in the range we would have expected from the discussions in the lab manual and textbook. The Ap horizon is a medium-textured soil and is considered a good topsoil for plant growth, so a porosity around 0.5 is consistent with those facts. The Bt horizon is a fine-textured horizon (containing a large amount of clay), and the bulk density is in the predicted range.

Explains what was significant about the results of the research.

[The Discussion section continues with further discussion of the results.]

[The References section begins on a new page.]

References

1. Brady NC, Weil RR. The nature and properties of soils. 11th ed. New York: Prentice-Hall; 1996. 291 p.
2. Blake GR, Hartge KH. Bulk density. In: Klute A, editor. Methods of soil analysis. Part 1. 2nd ed. Agronomy 1986;9:363-376.

The references are in the format recommended by the Council of Biology Editors (CBE).

Electronic Documents: Web Pages

Electronic documents range from simple email messages to complex, interactive World Wide Web pages. While electronic documents often offer the potential for expanded use of color and visuals (including animation and video), the general principles of design used for paper documents can be applied to electronic documents with only minor modification. Here again you will want to analyze the context in which the document will be read. Will your reader be reading from a computer screen or printing the document on paper for reading? If the reading takes place on a computer screen, how big is the screen and how good is the resolution? Reading from a computer screen is more difficult, so you will want to avoid small fonts and confusing backgrounds that distract from the text.

The elements of print document design remain the same for Web pages and other electronic documents, with one important addition, *hypertext links* (also known as *hot links* or simply *links*). *Hypertext* is a system of codes that enables authors to link text or graphics on a particular section of the electronic document to additional text or graphics, to Web pages, or to short clips of video, animation, or sound. Readers navigate a hypertext in a nonlinear fashion, starting almost anywhere they like and

For a discussion of email and a sample document, see pp. 781–83.

For more on Web site design, see Kristine Potter's essay in Chapter 8.

branching off whenever a hypertext link piques their curiosity. Hypertext can make it easy for readers to access different sections of an electronic document. If an electronic document is long, for example, you can display an outline of its major headings and subheadings. These headings can then link to the text that accompanies them. The two most common types of electronic documents that you are likely to encounter as a writer are email and Web pages.

A World Wide Web page is an electronic document stored on a *Web server,* a computer running special software and connected to the network of computers that makes up the World Wide Web. A Web server displays Web pages at the command of computer users accessing the server using a software program called a *Web browser.* Early on, most Web pages consisted of simple text on a gray background, and Web page authors needed to know HTML (hypertext markup language) programming to create a page. Today, increasingly sophisticated Web browsers allow for visual images, sounds, and other forms of interactive multimedia. Numerous software programs, called *HTML editors,* also provide those not familiar with HTML programming with an easy way to create Web pages, and most new word processing programs allow a document to be converted into HTML with the simple click of a button. Figure 16 shows a sample Web page.

A unique aspect of a Web page is its global audience. When you publish a Web page, you are writing to the world—or at least to people around the world who have access to the Web. Among other things, having a global audience means that you are writing to culturally diverse readers, many of whom may be unfamiliar with things you take for granted. For instance, if you refer to football on your Web page, many South American readers might first think of the sport Americans call soccer. Likewise, a visual that you find mildly humorous might strike readers from other cultures as blasphemous, insulting, or obscene. Therefore, in order to design an effective Web page, consider carefully who will be reading it and what you want it to convey to your global audience.

As you design a Web page, beware of letting fancy graphics and multimedia applications distract from your message. Yes, you can add a textured background to the screen that will make it look like marble or cloth, but will that background make reading the text easier? Will a sound file improve your communication, or are you adding sound simply because you can? Consider the following guidelines when designing a Web page:

- *Make sure your text is easy to read.* Many Web pages are difficult to read because of their textured and colored backgrounds. Keep the background of a Web page light in tone so that your text can be read with ease. Colored fonts can also be difficult to read. Always avoid vibrant colors for long blocks of text.

- *Keep your Web pages short.* Readers find it difficult to read a Web page that requires extensive scrolling on the screen. Break up long text blocks into separate Web pages that require no more than one or two screens of scrolling. Use hypertext links to connect the text blocks and to help readers navigate among the pages.

- *Limit the file size of your Web pages.* A Web page that is filled with visuals and sound files can be an annoyance to readers because the page may take several

Title providing clear identification of the site. ———

Links to help readers who are seeking specific information.

Highly readable links to the main pages of the Web site, with spot illustrations that help readers visualize the type of information they can access via the links.

Subtle background colors do not interfere with type.

Buttons linking to the main pages of the site provide another way for readers to access the information represented visually above.

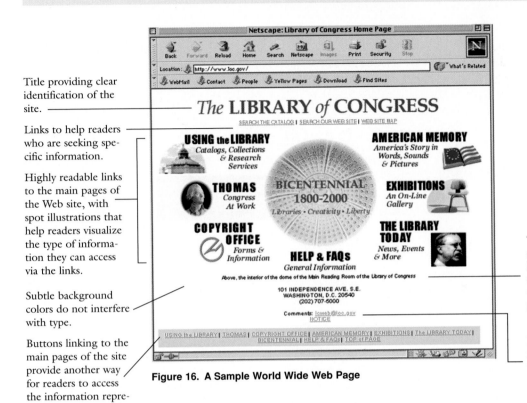

This caption identifies the significance of the largest illustration and helps visitors to the Web site associate it with the Library's physical location in Washington, D.C.

Email link to the person responsible for maintaining the Web site.

Figure 16. A Sample World Wide Web Page

minutes to load into a Web browser. Limiting your use of visuals and sound files so that your pages load quickly will help ensure that your document is read. This advice is especially important for the opening page of a Web site (also called a *home page*). You will encourage readers' interest in your Web site by making sure they do not have to wait too long to load the page and read your document.

- *Use hypertext links effectively.* Make sure that all of your links work correctly and that all pages of a Web site include a link back to your home page so readers can access it easily. You can make your text easier to read by judiciously limiting the number of links you embed in text. In addition to embedded text links, consider including a list of important links at one side of your document for readers' convenience.

- *Use the elements of document design.* Remember what you have learned in this chapter about typography, visuals, and white space when you go about creating Web pages. Most principles of good paper document design apply to Web page design as well.

Oral Presentations

26

At some point in your academic career, you will probably be asked to give an oral presentation. In fact, you may give many oral presentations before you graduate, and you almost certainly will give oral presentations on the job. This chapter contains practical suggestions for preparing and giving effective oral presentations.

Be Ready

Many people are terrified at the thought of public speaking, particularly people who have little experience with it. Even experienced public speakers can become jittery before giving an oral presentation. The key to defeating nervousness and anxiety is to research and prepare. If you have researched your subject thoroughly and have planned your presentation in detail, then you should be able to relax. If you find that you are still anxious, take a few slow, deep breaths before starting your presentation. It is also helpful not to think of your presentation as a performance. Remember that you are communicating a message. Think of your presentation as simply talking to an audience.

Understand the Kind of Oral Presentation You Have Been Asked to Give

The list that follows identifies the four basic types of oral presentations.

- *Impromptu presentation.* An impromptu oral presentation is given without preparation. In a history class, for example, your instructor may call on you to explain briefly a concept you are studying, such as "manifest destiny." As best you can, you would recall what you have read and summarize the information. While impromptu presentations are given without preparation, they do require knowledge of the subject matter.

- *Extemporaneous presentation.* In an extemporaneous presentation, you prepare beforehand and speak from notes or an outline. For example, in a management class, you might prepare a report on a business that you recently visited. In most academic and business situations, extemporaneous talks are preferred because they are informal yet well organized. Extemporaneous presentation often includes outlining your major points on a board or as a transparency for an overhead projector.

- *Scripted presentation.* Reading from a script is one way to ensure that you say exactly what you want to say—and that you take no more than the time you have been allotted. Because you read to your audience, a scripted presentation can be stiff and boring unless it is carefully planned and rehearsed. Scripted presentations also need to be written so that the audience can easily follow the presentation by just hearing it. Sentences often need to be shorter than in a document that is read. You will also need to provide more transitions and cues than in documents that are read. (See Use Cues to Orient Listeners on the next page.) A simple guideline to remember is that if your writing is difficult for you to read aloud, it will be difficult to hear as well.

- *Memorized presentation.* This type of oral presentation is written and committed to memory beforehand. For instance, at a sales meeting, you might evaluate a new product in relation to its competition. However, most people prefer scripted talks because of the difficulty of memorizing a lengthy oral presentation.

Assess Your Audience and Purpose

To give effective oral presentations you need to assess your audience and your purpose. Even for an impromptu presentation, you should take a few moments to think about whom you are speaking to and why. To assess your audience, ask the same questions you would ask about readers: Why are the members of my audience here? What do they already know about my subject? How do they feel about my topic? What objections might they have to my argument?

Define your purpose by completing the following statement: "In this oral presentation, I want to. . . ." For instance, you may want to speculate on the causes of the recent trend of companies' hiring numerous part-time and temporary contingent workers or argue your position on the ethics of this new hiring policy.

Determine How Much Information You Can Present in the Allotted Time

Your presentation should be exactly as long as the time allotted. Using substantially less time will make your presentation seem incomplete or superficial; using substantially more time may alienate your audience. Plan your presentation to allocate sufficient time for an introduction, concluding remarks, and follow-up questions (if a question-and-answer session is to be part of the presentation). If you are giving a scripted presentation, each double-spaced page of text will probably take two minutes to deliver. Time yourself to be sure.

Use Cues to Orient Listeners

Listening is one of the most difficult ways to comprehend information, in part because listeners cannot look back at previous information or scan forward, as readers can. To help your audience follow your oral presentation, use the same cues you would use to orient readers—but use them more frequently and overtly. Here are three basic cues that are especially helpful for listeners.

- *Thesis and forecasting statements.* Begin your presentation with thesis and forecasting statements that announce to audience members what you intend to communicate (your thesis) and the order in which you will present your material (your forecast). For instance, if you will present an argument about deregulation in the telecommunications industry, you can begin by asserting your position and preview the reasons you will offer to support your position.

- *Transitions.* Provide transitions when you move from one point to the next to help your audience follow the twists and turns of your presentation. For example, when you have finished discussing your first reason, state explicitly that you are now turning to your second reason.

- *Summaries.* End your oral presentation with a summary of the main points you have made. Also look for opportunities to use summaries throughout the presentation, particularly when you have spent a long time discussing something complicated. A brief summary that indicates the point you are making and its relation to your overall thesis can help listeners understand how the parts of your argument fit together to support your thesis.

- *Visuals.* Visual presentation of these cues will reinforce them. Your thesis, forecasting statements, transitions, and summaries can all be presented visually.

For further discussion and illustration of orienting cues, see Chapter 13.

Prepare Effective and Appropriate Visuals

For presentations that you plan ahead of time, you can use a variety of visuals—from simple lists and graphs to sophisticated computer demonstrations—to help both you and your audience. For instance, an overhead transparency or other projected image listing the major points of your presentation will help you make a forecasting statement that your listeners will pay attention to and remember. You can even leave the visual on display as you talk, referring to it to make a transition or adding to it as you answer questions.

Various technologies are available for displaying visuals. Writing on a board or flip chart has several advantages: low cost, high visibility, and the ability to compose or alter on the spot. To present a long passage or detailed graphic, photocopied handouts are preferable, although they can be distracting.

Overhead transparencies are a popular way to display visuals during a presentation. An overhead transparency consists of text, graphics, or both printed on a sheet of 8½- by 11-inch film (see Figure 26.1 for an example). When illuminated by an overhead projector, the material is enlarged and projected on a screen. Overhead

Simple design. ————

Bulleted list defines main ——
points.

Large, easy-to-read font.

Ample space around text ——
and graphics.

Illustration clarifies text
and adds visual interest. ——

Figure 26.1 Sample Overhead Transparency

transparencies can help your audience follow and remember your presentation. If you use them, think of them as integral to your presentation, not just decorative. They should be concise, easy to read, and uncluttered. You may use an overhead transparency to list the main points of your presentation, to signal transitions from one topic to another, and to summarize information you have presented.

Easy-to-use computer presentation software such as Microsoft PowerPoint is becoming increasingly widespread and extends the capabilities of the overhead transparency to include animation.

For more on designing documents, see Chapter 25.

As you prepare visuals, keep in mind that they must be legible to everyone in your audience, including people seated in the back of the room. Use a large, easy-to-read font and generous amounts of space around text.

Verify That You Will Have the Correct Equipment and Supplies

Well before your presentation is scheduled to begin, verify that the presentation room contains all of the equipment and supplies you will need. For example, if you plan to use an overhead projector, make sure it is in the room, placed correctly, and working well. Anticipating your needs (bring a marker) as well as potential problems (bring a spare bulb) will make your presentation go smoothly and help reduce your anxiety.

Rehearse Your Presentation

Rehearsing will help you to become more familiar with your material, to fit the material into the allotted time, and to feel more confident about speaking in public. If possible, rehearse in the same room in which you will give the presentation, using the same equipment. Also try to rehearse before an audience of colleagues or friends who can give you constructive criticism. Rehearsing a script or memorized presentation will enable you to plan your delivery. For a scripted talk, mark cues very selectively on your printed text to remind yourself when to pause or emphasize a word or phrase.

Deliver the Oral Presentation Professionally

Before your presentation, try to relax: Take a few deep breaths, drink some water, or step outside for some fresh air. If someone is to introduce you, give that person information about yourself and your presentation. Otherwise, begin by introducing yourself and your title or topic.

These guidelines will help you make a professional impression:

- As you speak, try to make eye contact with the people in the room.
- Use your hands to gesture as you would in a conversation; your hands should neither be clamped rigidly at your sides nor doing something distracting such as playing with your jewelry.
- If you are behind a lectern, avoid slouching, leaning on it, or gripping it tightly throughout the presentation.
- If you are using visuals, be careful not to block the audience's view of them. After introducing a new visual, resume making eye contact with audience members; talk to the audience, not the visual.
- Try to avoid distracting vocal mannerisms, such as repeatedly saying "uh," "like," or "you know."
- Speak loudly enough so that all members of the audience can hear you, and speak clearly and distinctly. Nervousness may cause you to speak too rapidly, so watch your pace.
- Do not speak in a monotone. Instead, let the pitch of your voice rise and fall naturally, especially when giving a scripted presentation.
- Dress appropriately for your audience and the formality of the situation in which you are speaking. The focus should be on your message, not on how you are dressed.

End Your Presentation Graciously

If no question-and-answer session is scheduled to follow your presentation, end the presentation by thanking your audience for giving you the opportunity to speak. If appropriate, offer to answer any questions in a private conversation or in a follow-up correspondence.

If a question-and-answer session follows your presentation, politely invite questions by saying something like, "If you have any questions, I would be happy to try to answer them now."

Working with Others

27

Although writing usually requires a solitary, individual effort, there are many occasions when writers may seek advice and feedback from friends, colleagues, or mentors on what we regard as their own *individual writing projects*. For instance, they may ask the advice of a librarian about researching their subject in the library or on the Internet, try out their argument on a co-worker or fellow student, seek help to improve a draft, or get someone to check for grammar errors. There are also some occasions when writers work together in small groups or teams to research, plan, and compose written reports—what we call *joint writing projects*.

Working with others is often referred to as *collaboration,* a term that we use throughout this chapter to mean working cooperatively with others to make writing better. Because collaborating with others on individual projects and especially on joint writing projects can be challenging and sometimes difficult, the following advice will help you anticipate the difficulties so that you can realize the full potential of collaboration.

■ WORKING WITH OTHERS ON YOUR INDIVIDUAL WRITING PROJECTS

From the very beginning of your work on an assignment in this book, you are collaborating with others in order to write the best essay you possibly can. Your instructor is a collaborator, as are other students in your class. For instance, their comments about the readings will help you understand more about the genres you will be writing, and their responses to your invention work and to drafts of your essays will give you many ideas. Of course, you yourself collaborate with other students when you give them your insights on the readings and on their writing.

In every assignment chapter there are four special activities that enable you to collaborate with other students in a purposeful way. In Chapter 6, "Arguing a Position," for example, these are the activities:

> ***Practice Arguing a Position: A Collaborative Activity.*** In this activity toward the beginning of the chapter, you work with two or three other students to try out a brief argument and discover how much you already know about this genre.

Connecting to Culture and Experience. This activity, following each of the readings, invites you to examine with other students some of the important ideas and underlying assumptions of the reading. In small group discussion, you can explore your responses and develop your understanding.

Testing Your Choice: A Collaborative Activity. Partway through the invention work, at a point where you need to assess realistically whether you have made a wise topic choice, this activity guides you in presenting your topic to a few other students and getting their response and advice. From discovering what you have to say about your topic in this first public tryout and from reflecting on what other students have to say, you can decide whether you have chosen a topic you can write about convincingly.

Critical Reading Guide. Once you have a draft of your essay, anyone using the Critical Reading Guide can give you a comprehensive evaluation of your draft, and you can do likewise for others with their drafts. Because in Chapter 6 the Critical Reading Guide reflects the particular requirements of a successful essay arguing a position on a controversial issue, anyone using it to evaluate your draft will be able to give you focused, relevant advice. When you use the guide to evaluate another student's draft, you will be learning how to evaluate position essays, including your own.

In these four formal activities, you collaborate with others to develop your individual writing projects by discovering what you may know about a project before you get very far into it, assessing your progress after a period of initial work, and evaluating your first attempts to draft a complete essay. There are many other occasions for fruitful collaboration in the assignment chapters. You may use the activities informally with another student, or your instructor may ask you to do them in class or on your own time. For instance, in Chapter 6 you might work with other students to complete the Analyzing Writing Strategies tasks that follow every reading. You and another student might exchange revisions of your essays to help each other with final editing and proofreading. Or you might meet or exchange email messages with two or three other students to work on the challenging task, Considering the Social Dimensions of Position Papers, that concludes the chapter. These activities may seem easier or more enjoyable if you work on them with other students. Most important, however, is that they will very likely be more productive, increasing your understanding of writing that takes positions on issues through the exchange of many more ideas than you might have come up with on your own.

Collaboration on your individual projects need not always be so purposeful and organized. It continues usefully in the most casual, brief encounter on or off campus with a classmate. You might lament the upcoming deadline for a first draft of the essay, telling each other what you still have to accomplish in the little time remaining. You might talk about what happened when you tried one of the book's collaborative activities. You might continue a discussion of a reading that began in class. You might describe the most formidable problem you must solve before you can complete your draft. If you are both doing library research on the same or a similar issue, you might tell each other about useful sources you have discovered.

Following are guidelines for successful collaboration on individual writing projects. These guidelines apply to formal, planned meetings to improve writing itself—from invention work through planning and revising:

- Whenever you read someone else's writing, have the writer inform you about his or her purpose and readers. Collaboration is always more effective when writers focus on helping other writers achieve their purposes for their particular readers. If a writer is explaining a concept to readers who know nothing about it, as might be the case in Chapter 5, "Explaining a Concept," your comments are likely to be unhelpful if you assume the essay is addressed to someone who shares your understanding of the concept.

- Know the genre the writer is working in. If a writer is proposing a solution to a problem and you are evaluating the writing as though it were an essay arguing a position, your advice is likely to be off the mark.

- When you evaluate another writer's work, be sure you know the stage of its development. Is it a set of tentative notes for a first draft? A partial draft? A complete draft? A revision? If it is a draft, you want to focus on helping the writer develop and organize ideas; whereas if it is a revision, you might focus exclusively on cueing and coherence or editing and proofreading.

- When you evaluate someone's writing, be helpful and supportive but also frank and specific. You do a writing partner no favor if you shrink from criticizing and giving advice. If your criticism seems grounded in the purpose, audience, and genre, it will probably not seem arbitrary or personal to your partner.

- Bring as much writing as possible to a scheduled meeting with other writers. The further along your writing is the more you can learn from the collaboration, and your partners will feel that their time has been well spent.

- Try to be receptive to criticism. Later, you can decide whether to change your essay, and how.

■ WORKING WITH OTHERS ON JOINT WRITING PROJECTS

In addition to collaborating with others on your individual writing projects, your instructor may give you the opportunity to write an essay with other students—a joint project in which you collaborate to produce a single essay. For instance, in Chapter 6, "Arguing a Position," you could collaborate to construct a persuasive argument for a position you share with two or three other students on a controversial issue. In Chapter 5, "Explaining a Concept," you could work with a few other students to research and explain a concept, perhaps using graphics or hands-on activities to help others grasp the concept and its implications. In Chapter 7, "Proposing a Solution," you have an opportunity to practice researching and writing proposals, by far the most common type of joint writing project in college, business, and the community.

Look, for example, at the workplace writing example on p. 295. A pharmaceuticals company decided to invest time and money in finding a solution to a problem the company saw as damaging to its business as well as to the community. The company assigned a team of seven division managers and a technical writer, gave them a budget to pay for outside consultants, and asked them to present a written proposal to the state legislature and local school board in six months' time.

The pharmaceuticals team divided the project into a series of research and writing tasks like those outlined in the Guide to Writing in Chapter 7. The team members scheduled due dates for each task and progress reports to identify problems as they arose. They assigned responsibility for each task either to individuals or small groups and identified which tasks might need consultation with outside experts.

When people collaborate on large writing projects like that of the pharmaceutical company, they usually divide up the work. For example, they might divide responsibilities according to the expertise of different group members. Someone who knows the problem firsthand might work on developing ways to explain the problem to those who have not experienced it directly. People who have experience making forecasts and planning budgets or hiring and managing people might be assigned to research and draft those aspects of the proposal. Everyone in the group might read and suggest revisions in the draft, and individuals may be assigned parts to strengthen and clarify. When a final draft seems near, one person might be assigned the job of improving cueing and coherence, while another might be in charge of editing and proofreading, and a third might work on document design.

Writing collaboratively on a joint project certainly has benefits. Collaboration not only draws on the expertise and energy of different people, but can also be synergistic, creating an outcome that is greater than the sum of its parts. One difficulty of collaborative writing projects, however, is that it takes time and effort to learn how to work effectively with others. Writers working on a joint project need to spend a lot of time communicating with one another. They must learn to anticipate conflicts and resolve them constructively. They should be realistic in scheduling and do their assigned tasks responsibly. They have to be flexible in their writing processes and open to different points of view.

Your instructor may decide how large your group should be and may even assign students to particular groups. If you are unhappy being in a particular group, discuss it with your instructor as soon as possible. To help group members work together constructively on joint writing projects, here are some ground rules you will want to discuss and implement:

- Begin by establishing clear and easy means of communicating with one another. Exchange email addresses or establish a listserv, but also exchange phone numbers in case servers go down.

- Expect to spend a lot of time planning the project together and discussing who will do what and when. Discuss how the group should divide responsibilities. To decide how best to collaborate, you will need to plan the project so that you know what needs to be accomplished and in what order. Remember, however, to remain flexible and keep lines of communication open to deal with problems as they arise.

- Set a schedule of regular meetings. The meetings can take place in person, over the Internet, or by telephone. Agree on how to run the meetings. For example, should someone lead each discussion and should the role of discussion leader rotate? Should notes or minutes be taken at each meeting and then reviewed subsequently to make sure that nothing important has been left out or misunderstood? Should each meeting have an agenda and, if so, how and when should it be developed for each subsequent meeting? Should votes be taken or should everything be decided by consensus?

- Try to treat each other with respect and consideration, but do not be surprised by disagreements and personality conflicts. Arguing can stimulate thinking—inspiring creativity as well as encouraging each person to explain ideas clearly and systematically. But arguing can also encourage aggressiveness in some people and withdrawal in others. Recognize that people interact differently in groups and have different ways of contributing. If there is a problem in the way the group interacts, address it immediately, perhaps by calling a special meeting to work out a solution. Try to avoid placing blame. Consider, for example, whether taking turns would assure that everyone contributes to the discussion and no one dominates. Urge everyone to refrain from characterizing other people and instead to speak only about what they themselves think and feel by making "I" rather than "you" statements.

- Keep track of everyone's progress. Consider creating a chart so that all members can see at a glance what they need to do and when. Schedule regular progress reports so that any problems can be identified immediately. If someone is having difficulty completing a particular task, other group members should volunteer to help so that the project is not stalled.

- If the group will make an oral presentation of the written proposal, plan it carefully, giving each person a role. Rehearse the presentation as a group to make sure it satisfies the time limit and other requirements of the assignment.

For more on oral presentations, see Chapter 26.

After setting its ground rules, the pharmaceuticals team divided its work in much the same way as that suggested in the Guide to Writing a proposal in Chapter 7. Here are some highlights of the team's researching and writing process:

- To answer the kinds of questions listed on p. 327 of the Guide to Writing, under Analyzing and Defining the Problem (such as what caused the problem? what is its history? what are its bad effects?), the team assigned a small group to conduct library and Internet research. From this initial research, a specialist in the field of vocational training was interviewed and subsequently hired as a consultant by the team.

- As their attempts to analyze the problem continued, the team members turned to the next task in the Guide to Writing, Identifying Your Readers (p. 328). They assigned several small groups to do field research: to observe and conduct interviews at local high schools, to interview school board members and others in the community, and to interview state legislators who would be involved eventually in judging the proposal.

- They turned next to finding a solution. In researching the problem, they had collected many different ideas on how the problem might be solved as well as criticisms of each possible solution. The whole team reviewed this material and after lengthy discussion agreed on several principles a good solution to this problem would need to have: (1) Students would have to begin vocational training as early as the tenth grade; (2) equipping area high schools and hiring specialized teachers would be too expensive; and (3) on-site training would not only make modern equipment and specialized teachers readily available to students, but would also motivate students and help them learn efficiency and accountability.

- Before figuring out how to implement these principles, the team members tested their ideas by consulting with a variety of people, many of whom they had interviewed earlier. This research helped them anticipate objections to their proposed solution and consider the specific steps necessary to implement their solution. Half of the team focused on drafting arguments to defend the solution, while the other half focused on drafting the implementation section. Leaders of the two groups kept in close communication.

- When they had a coherent argument for their solution and a plan for implementation worked out, the team members met to review the entire draft. They identified some problems and asked the drafting groups to do some revision.

- They showed the revised draft to a wide array of people, including business leaders, school board members, parent groups, representatives of teachers' unions, and interested students. They then categorized the problems and suggestions for revision offered by these critical readers and sent the draft back to the original drafting groups for another revision.

- The final revised draft was reviewed for clarity, coherence, and mechanics before being submitted to the company's board of directors and, after minor revisions, distributed to the state legislature and the local school board. It was also published in local newspapers and business magazines and on the company's Web site.

If you collaborate with other students to develop a proposal, you will not have as many outside resources as the pharmaceuticals company team in this model. The decisions this team made, however, mirror the kinds of decisions you and your fellow students will have to make.

Writing in Your Community

28

Service learning combines classroom education with life experience. Through partnerships with community organizations, colleges and universities can offer students ways to see how the knowledge that they are gaining in school can be put to work beyond the campus. Research and experience show that such programs not only provide valuable service to those who need it, but also help students learn and retain course content. Students also often discover that their skills and knowledge can help others. If your composition class has a service-learning component, you will have an opportunity to learn more about your community, to become an active participant in that community, and to apply your writing skills to your community experience.

In service-learning programs, students are most often placed in off-campus positions with government bureaus such as local parks and recreation departments or nonprofit organizations that offer community support services such as care for the homeless. In these positions students apply what they are studying in class. Here are a few examples:

- Nursing students teach expectant mothers about prenatal and infant care.
- Chemistry students tour local elementary schools demonstrating the fun of science.
- Botany students teach fourth graders about plants native to their region.
- Zoology students help gather samples for a study of local amphibian populations.
- Political science students work with the local government to increase voter turnout.
- English students tutor grade school children who are having trouble learning to read and write.

Whatever form your service-learning experience takes, it can serve as a valuable resource for your writing. While you will probably find much to write about in your service experience, you may also find writing is a part of your service. When writing is part of your service, you move beyond having classmates and instructors as your primary audience, and enter the realm of public discourse.

■ USING YOUR SERVICE EXPERIENCE AS SOURCE MATERIAL

Finding a Topic

College students frequently find topic selection one of the more difficult parts of the writing process. One of the many advantages of service learning is that it can make finding an engaging subject for your writing much easier and more rewarding. The service experience should present numerous issues that might be fruitfully explored through your writing. Simply paying attention to the issues that come to bear on your service experience should help you generate a substantial list of ideas. You might ask yourself some simple questions:

- Who is most affected by the situation, and how are these people affected?
- How long has this situation existed?
- What are the results of this situation?
- What forces shape the situation? Can anything be done to alter these forces?
- How have other organizations successfully handled this issue? How else might the situation be improved?
- What common perceptions do people hold about this situation? What are my own perceptions?
- Are these perceptions inaccurate? How might they be changed?

For example, if your service experience includes working at a clinic that serves low-income families without health insurance, you might write about the long-term effects on children of insufficient medical care. You might also write a proposal to address the problem faced by people who have little or no medical coverage. Or perhaps you are interested in writing an argument advocating universal health care coverage. There are dozens of possible essay topics in any service experience.

Gathering Sources

In traditional college writing settings, research is often limited, by time and availability, to what one can find in the library or on the Internet. A service-learning environment can provide field research sources that would otherwise be difficult to tap. The most significant of these potential sources is the people who run the organization in which you are doing your service. If you have focused your writing on the kinds of issues that are relevant to your service, these people can serve as experts. Many of the people you work with will have years of experience and specialized training, and probably will have researched the subject themselves. Take advantage of your opportunity to tap their knowledge. When approached courteously, people are often more than willing to discuss their thoughts on something important to them.

Depending on the situation, your service site might also be a good place to circulate a questionnaire or conduct a survey to help you gather information about your subject. Of course, your own observations and experiences as you perform your service will prove to be invaluable as well. You might consider keeping a daily journal in which you record your experiences and observations as you perform your service. When you are ready to begin writing you will already have done some early invention work.

The service organization itself might also be a good source of information. Such organizations often both collect and produce literature that is relevant to their mission. Your organization might even maintain its own small library of resource materials that, as a service provider, you could have access to. Frequently such organizations are also part of a network of similar groups who share their expertise through newsletters, trade journals, Web sites, or online discussion groups. Explore these unique resources.

Keep in mind that there are ethical considerations involved. Many service-learning environments, such as those that involve counseling, tutoring, or teaching, can make you privy to information that should be kept confidential, especially if you are working with minors. Be sure that you are open about your information-gathering, and that everyone who you might use as a source knows your intentions. Any questionnaires should include a disclosure stating what you intend to do with the information gathered. Any information gained from interviews should be properly attributed, but you should consider carefully maintaining the anonymity of anyone whom you use for examples in your writing, unless you have your subjects' explicit permission to use their names. Err on the side of caution and consideration, and ask your instructor if you have any questions about how to treat sensitive material.

For suggestions on making observations, conducting interviews, and creating questionnaires, see Chapter 20.

Writing *about* Your Service Experience

Writing in a service-learning program is really no different from other writing situations. You still must identify for yourself the kind of writing you are doing, generate ideas through invention, and refine those ideas into a finished product through a process of drafting and revision. Service learning, however, may put you in a position to write for a nonacademic audience. For example, you might write an editorial for your campus or local newspaper in which you argue for increased support for your service organization or project. You might craft a letter to local government officials or even representatives to the national legislature suggesting a solution to a particular problem. When you do such writing, pay particular attention to your audience and purpose. Ask yourself how you might best appeal to the needs of your audience and how you can present your position in a convincing way. Remember that writing is action, and as such it can be a powerful tool.

The service-learning experience can provide you with subject matter for many of the academic writing activities discussed in Part One of this textbook. While you can no doubt generate your own list of ideas, here are some to consider:

Chapter 2: Remembering Events

- Write about your first day of service. What happened? How did you feel? What did you learn? How did it differ from what you expected to learn?

- Write about a particularly difficult day. Why was it difficult? How did you handle the situation? What would you do differently? What did you learn from the experience?

Chapter 3: Remembering People

- Write about one of the people you are working with. What makes this person special or distinctive? How does he or she act? What have you learned from this person?

- Write about someone you were able to help in some way. What kind of assistance did you give? How did this person respond to your help? How did you feel afterward?

Chapter 4: Writing Profiles

- Write about the place where you are doing your service. What does it look like? How does it make you feel? How does the location reflect or affect what goes on there? What does go on there?

- Write about one of the people you have met doing your service. What is he or she like? How is he or she typical (or atypical) of the people in the same position? What makes this person special or different?

Chapter 5: Explaining a Concept

- Write about a concept with which you were unfamiliar before you did your service. What does the concept mean? How is it important in the context of your service experience? How does what you learned about this concept make you think differently now?

- Write about a concept that you knew but now understand differently because of your service. How has your understanding of the concept changed? What caused that change? How might you explain that change to someone who does not share your experience?

Chapter 6: Arguing a Position

- Write an argument in support of the service organization you are working with. Why should people support it? How can they support it? Why is it a worthwhile endeavor?

- Write an argument about the value of service learning. What have you gained from this experience? Who should participate? What are the advantages of service learning to individuals and the community?

Chapter 7: Proposing a Solution

- Write about a process or procedure within or affecting the organization you are working with that you think needs to be improved. Why does it need to be improved? How might it be improved? What would the effect of the improvements be?

- Write about a policy, law, or practice that you think should be eliminated or revised because it negatively affects the organization you are working with. What would be the benefit of eliminating or revising it? Why was it created or instituted in the first place? What additional steps, if any, would need to be taken in order to remedy the problem?

Chapter 8: Justifying an Evaluation

- Write about how effectively the organization you are working with satisfies its objectives. How do you measure its effectiveness? In what ways does it succeed? In what ways does it fail?

- Write about your school's service-learning program. In what ways is it most successful? In what ways could it be improved?

Chapter 9: Speculating about Causes

- Write about the causes for a problem or situation that you have encountered through your service-learning experience. What brought the problem about? What circumstances perpetuate it?

- Write about why service-learning programs have become common. What function do they serve that traditional education models do not? What demand do they meet? Why are so many colleges and universities involved in such partnerships?

Writing *for* Your Service Organization

Some service-learning situations will put you in a position not just to write *about* your service experience, but also to write *as part of* your service experience. You might be asked to create flyers, brochures, press releases, or Web pages for a community organization. You might help craft presentations or reports. Keep in mind that while these may not be academic writing activities, they are still writing activities, and the strategies presented in this text still apply. You might be asked, for example, to help write a brochure that explains the purpose and function of the organization. In effect, you would be writing a profile of the organization, and you would need to keep in mind the basic features of profiles outlined in Chapter 4.

Such writing situations give you an opportunity to practice recognizing the kinds of writing you are asked to do. While in class you might be asked to select a topic and write an essay in which you argue a position (Chapter 6) or propose a solution (Chapter 7), in your service experience you might simply be asked to create a flyer that explains the importance of a no-kill animal shelter or a brochure that urges people to carpool as a way of cutting down traffic congestion. By identifying what kind of writing activity you are being asked to do, you can identify what basic features your readers will expect to find.

For suggestions on how to make such collaboration run smoothly and successfully, see Chapter 27, pp. 801–4.

Writing in organizations is frequently a collaborative process. Everyone involved in the process is expected to do his or her part. When your written document will be used to represent your organization in any way, respect the expertise of the staff, especially when their assessment of the audience differs from your own. In some situations, your service writing may be heavily edited—or not used at all. Make sure your instructor and service-learning program administrators are aware of any instances in which you and members of the organization are having difficulty reaching a consensus.

Finally, remember that nonacademic writing often requires greater attention to presentation than most kinds of academic writing. One-inch margins and double-spaced text simply are not enough when you are trying to create eye-catching documents such as brochures and press releases. Document design can not only make a piece of writing more visually attractive and thereby stimulate readers' interest, but can also help readers with different needs identify which parts of the document they will find most relevant. Therefore, carefully consider the layout and configuration of your document, and take advantage of the flexibility that even a simple word-processing program can give you.

For more on document design, see Chapter 25.

Acknowledgments

Text Credits

Maya Angelou. "Uncle Willie." From *I Know Why the Caged Bird Sings* by Maya Angelou. Copyright © 1969 and renewed 1997 by Maya Angelou. Reprinted by permission of Random House, Inc.

David Ansen. "Star Wars: The Phantom Movie." From *Newsweek,* May 17, 1999. Copyright © 1999 Newsweek, Inc. All rights reserved. Reprinted by permission.

Toni Cade Bambara. "The Hammer Man." From *Gorilla, My Love* by Toni Cade Bambara. Copyright © 1966 by Toni Cade Bambara. Reprinted by permission of Random House, Inc.

Rick Bragg. "100 Miles Per Hour, Upside Down and Sideways." From *All Over But the Shoutin'* by Rick Bragg. Copyright © 1997 by Rick Bragg. Reprinted by permission of Pantheon, a division of Random House, Inc.

Annie Dillard. "Handled My Own Life." From *An American Childhood* by Annie Dillard. Copyright © 1987 by Annie Dillard. Reprinted by permission of HarperCollins Publishers, Inc.

Richard Estrada. "Sticks and Stones and Sports Team Names." From the *Los Angeles Times,* October 29, 1995. Copyright © 1995 The Washington Post Writers Group. Reprinted with permission.

Amitai Etzioni. "Working at McDonald's." Copyright © 1986 Amitai Etzioni, author of *The Spirit of Community.* Director, George Washington University Center for Communitarian Policy Studies. Reprinted by permission of the author.

Gerald Haslam. "Grandma." Copyright © 1983 by Gerald Haslam. Originally appeared in *New York Arts Review,* January 1983, as "The Horned Toad." It later appeared in *Hawk Flights: Visions of the West* (Seven Buffaloes Press, 1983) and *The Constant Coyote: California Stories,* University of Nevada Press, 1990. Reprinted by permission.

James Joyce. "Araby." From *The Dubliners* by James Joyce. Copyright © 1916 by B. W. Heubsch. Definitive text copyright © 1967 by The Estate of James Joyce. Reprinted by permission of Viking Penguin, a division of Penguin Putnam Inc.

Martin Luther King, Jr. An annotated sample from "Letter from a Birmingham Jail." Copyright © 1963 by Martin Luther King, Jr. Copyright renewed 1991 by The Heirs to The Estate of Martin Luther King, Jr. Reprinted by arrangement with The Heirs to the Estate of Martin Luther King, Jr., c/o Writers House, Inc. as agent for the proprietor.

Stephen King. "Why We Crave Horror Movies." © Stephen King. Reprinted with permission. All rights reserved.

Alan I. Leshner. "Why Shouldn't Society Treat Substance Abusers?" From the *Los Angeles Times,* June 11, 1999, p. 7. Copyright © 1999 by Alan I. Leshner, Ph.D., Director, National Institute on Drug Abuse, National Institutes of Health. Reprinted by permission.

Jill Neimark. "Why We Need Miss America." From *Psychology Today,* September/October 1998: 41–43, 72–73. Copyright © 1998 Sussex Publishers, Inc. Reprinted by Permission.

Mariah Burton Nelson "Adventures in Equality." Excerpt from *The Stronger Women Get, the More Men Love Football: Sexism and the American Culture of Sports* by Mariah Burton Nelson. Copyright © 1994 by Mariah Burton Nelson. Reprinted with permission of Harcourt, Inc.

Katherine S. Newman. "Dead-End Jobs: A Way Out." From *The Brookings Review,* Fall 1995. Copyright © 1995 Katherine S. Newman. Reprinted by permission.

"The New Terrorism." From *The Economist,* August 15, 1998, pp. 17–19. Copyright © 1998 The Economist Newspaper Group, Inc. Reprinted with permission. Further reproduction prohibited. www.economist.com

David Noonan. "Inside the Brain." Excerpt from *Neuro-Life on the Frontlines of Brain Surgery & Neurological Medicine* by David Noonan. Copyright © 1989 by David Noonan. Reprinted with the permission of Simon & Schuster.

Perry Orenstein. "The Daily Grind: Lessons in the Hidden Curriculum." From *School Girls: Young Women, Self-Esteem and the Confidence Gap* by Peggy Orenstein. Copyright © 1994 by Peggy Orenstein and American Association of University Women. Used by permission of Doubleday, a division of Random House, Inc.

William S. Pollack. "Why Boys Become Depressed." From *Real Boys: Rescuing Our Sons From the Myths of Boyhood* by William S. Pollack. Copyright © 1998 by William S. Pollack. Reprinted by permission of Random House, Inc.

Carol Potera. "Internet Addiction." Originally titled "Trapped in the Web" from *Psychology Today,* March/April 1998, vol 31, #2, p. 66. Copyright © 1998 Sussex Publishers, Inc. Reprinted by permission.

Rob Ryder. "10 Is a Crowd, So Change the Game." From *The New York Times,* March 8, 1998. Copyright © 1998 by The New York Times Company. Reprinted by permission.

"Soup." Originally titled "Slave" from The Talk of the Town section in *The New Yorker* magazine, January 23, 1989. Copyright © 1989 by The New Yorker Magazine, Inc. All rights reserved. Reprinted by permission.

Anastasia Toufexis. "Love: The Right Chemistry." From *Time,* February 15, 1993. Originally titled "The Right Chemistry." Copyright © 1993 Time, Inc. Reprinted by permission.

Adam Paul Weisman. "Birth Control in the Schools: Clinical Examination." From *The New Republic,* March 16, 1987. Copyright © 1987 by Adam Paul Weisman. Reprinted by permission of The New Republic.

William Carlos Williams. "The Use of Force." From *The Collected Stories of William Carlos Williams.* Copyright © 1938 by William Carlos Williams. Reprinted by permission of New Directions Corporation.

Tobias Wolff. "On Being a Real Westerner." From *This Boy's Life* by Tobias Wolff. Copyright © 1989 by Tobias Wolff. Used by permission of Grove/Atlantic, Inc.

Amy Wu. "A Different Kind of Mother." Originally published in *The Chinese American Forum,* Volume 9, No. 1, July 1993, pp. 26–27. Copyright © 1993 by Amy Wu. Reprinted by permission of the author.

Picture Credits

24 (left), Frank Siteman/Monkmeyer; (right), Barbara Rios/Photo Researchers; **72,** Photo: Dorothea Lange/Farm Security Administration—Office of War Information Photograph Collection/Library of Congress Prints and Photographs Division; **78** (left), George Shelley/The Stock Market; (right), Edward Lettau/Photo Researchers; **93,** Courtesy of Chinese American Forum, Vol. 9, No. 1. July, 1993; **128** (left), Bill Stormont/The Stock Market; (right), Enrico Azzato/International Stock Photography; **182** (left), Alexander Tsiaras/Science Source/Photo Researchers; (right), Painting: *Portrait of Dora Maar* (detail) by Pablo Picasso, © 2000 Estate of Pablo Picasso/Artists Rights Society (ARS), New York/Photo Giraudon/Art Resource; **188,** © 1993 Time Inc. Reprinted by permission. **203,** © 1998 The Economist Newspaper Group, Inc. Reprinted with permission. Further reproduction prohibited. <www.economist.com>; **233,** Maria Burwell; **236** (left), Russell D. Curtis/Photo Researchers; (right), Farrell Grehan/Photo Researchers; **250,** "Adventures in Equality" cartoon. Copyright © Tim Egan. Reprinted by permission. **287,** "Women in Power: A Score Card" & "Still An All Boy's Club" from *Business Week,* November 22, 1999. Copyright © 1999 Business Week, Inc. Reprinted with permission. **292** (left), Sie SRL/The Stock Market; (right), Julie Nicholls/The Stock Market; **345,** Gabe Palmer/The Stock Market; **350** (left), Everett Collection; (right), Riccardo Marcialis © Photri, Inc./The Stock Market; **355,** Lucasfilm/Photofest; **401 and 402,** Photofest; **406** (left), Warren Faidley/International Stock Photography; (right), Vic Ramos/International Stock Photography; **418,** Photograph courtesy of Miss American Organization, Atlantic City, NJ (all rights reserved); **464** (left), Bill Binzen/The Stock Market; (right), Kenfre, Inc./International Stock Photography; **14-2, 3,** (1866) Corbis-Bettmann; (1910) The Granger Collection; (1944) Hank Morgan-Science Source/Photo Researchers; (1950) Saturn Stills—Science Photo Library/Photo Researchers; (1953) UPI/Corbis-Bettmann; (1973) Ken M. Highfill/Photo Researchers; (chart) © 1999 Time Inc. Reprinted by permission. **14-12, 13,** Diagram by Christoph Blumrich, © 1999 Newsweek, Inc. All Rights Reserved. Reprinted by permission; photo by Jeanne Friebert/SIPA Press. **14-14,** from *Home Repair Handbook,* copyright © 1999. Sunset Publishing Corporation, Menlo Park CA 94025; **17-5, 6,** ©1999 Newsweek, Inc. All rights reserved. Reprinted by permission. **25-8** (Fig. 7), Illustration by Shirley Baty. From *Biology* 5e by Helena Curtis & N. Sue Barnes. Copyright © 1989 by Worth Publishers. Reprinted by permission. **25-8,** (Fig. 8.) Photo courtesy of Michael A. Walsh.

Author and Title Index

Subject Index

Submitting Papers for Publication

To Students and Instructors

We hope that we'll be able to include essays from more colleges and universities in the next edition of *The Guide* and our accompanying anthology, *Sticks and Stones and other student essays.* Please let us see essays written using *The St. Martin's Guide* you'd like us to consider. Send them with this Paper Submission Form and the Agreement Form on the back to *The Guide,* Bedford/St. Martin's, 33 Irving Place, New York, NY 10003.

PAPER SUBMISSION FORM

Instructor's Name _____

School _____

Address _____

Department _____

Student's Name _____

Course _____

Writing activity the paper represents _____

This writing activity appears in chapter(s) _____
of *The St. Martin's Guide to Writing*

Agreement Form

I hereby transfer to Bedford/St. Martin's all rights to my essay,

(tentative title), subject to final editing by the publisher. These rights include copyright and all other rights of publication and reproduction. I guarantee that this essay is wholly my original work, and that I have not granted rights to it to anyone else.

Student's signature X: _____

Please type

Name: _____

Address: _____

_____

_____

Phone: _____

Please indicate the reader or publication source you assumed for your essay:

_____

Write a few sentences about the purpose or purposes of your essay. What did you hope to achieve with your reader?

_____

_____

_____

_____

Bedford/St. Martin's representative: _____